1950
T cc

Political Dynamics

IN THE

Middle East

THE MIDDLE EAST
Economic and Political Problems and Prospects

Studies from a research program of
The Rand Corporation
and
Resources for the Future, Inc.
Sidney S. Alexander, *Program Director*

PUBLISHED

Marion Clawson, Hans H. Landsberg, *and* Lyle T. Alexander
The Agricultural Potential of the Middle East

Sam H. Schurr *and* Paul T. Homan
with Joel Darmstadter, Helmut Frank, John J. Schanz, Jr.,
Thomas R. Stauffer, *and* Henry Steele
Middle Eastern Oil and the Western World: Prospects and Problems

Charles A. Cooper *and* Sidney S. Alexander *(eds.)*
Economic Development and Population Growth in the Middle East

Paul Y. Hammond *and* Sidney S. Alexander *(eds.)*
Political Dynamics in the Middle East

IN PREPARATION

Sidney S. Alexander
The Economics and Politics of the Middle East

Political Dynamics

IN THE

Middle East

EDITED BY

Paul Y. Hammond

Associate Head
Social Science Department
The Rand Corporation
Santa Monica, California

AND

Sidney S. Alexander

Professor of Economics and Management
Massachusetts Institute of Technology
Cambridge, Massachusetts

American Elsevier
Publishing Company, Inc.
NEW YORK

AMERICAN ELSEVIER PUBLISHING COMPANY, INC.
52 Vanderbilt Avenue, New York, N.Y. 10017

ELSEVIER PUBLISHING COMPANY
335 Jan Van Galenstraat, P.O. Box 211
Amsterdam, The Netherlands

International Standard Book Number 0-444-00110-7

Library of Congress Card Number 71-161688

Contents

vii

ix

Chapter 13. Western Europe and the Middle East

Pierre Rondot

Contributors

Halim Barakat
Department of Sociology and Anthropology
American University of Beirut
Beirut, Lebanon

Abraham S. Becker
Economics Department
The Rand Corporation
Santa Monica, California

Leonard Binder
Department of Political Science
University of Chicago
Chicago, Illinois

Peter Câlvocoressi
University of Sussex
Sussex, England

Peter Dodd
Department of Sociology and Anthropology
American University of Beirut
Beirut, Lebanon

Saul Friedlander
The Eliezer Kaplan School of Economics and Social Sciences
The Hebrew University of Jerusalem
Jerusalem, Israel

Charles F. Gallagher
American Universities Field Staff
Rome, Italy

Paul Y. Hammond
Social Science Department
The Rand Corporation
Santa Monica, California

Arnold L. Horelick
Social Science Department
The Rand Corporation
Santa Monica, California

Jacob C. Hurewitz
Department of Political Science
Columbia University
New York, New York

Malcolm H. Kerr
Department of Political Science
University of California
Los Angeles, California

Don Peretz
SWANA (Southwest Asian and North African) Program
State University of New York
Binghamton, New York

William B. Quandt
Social Science Department
The Rand Corporation
Santa Monica, California

Pierre Rondot
Institute of Political Studies of Paris, Lyon, and Grenoble, France
International Institute of Advanced Administrative Studies
Paris, France

Nadav Safran
Department of Political Science
Harvard University
Cambridge, Massachusetts

P. J. Vatikiotis
School of Oriental and African Studies
University of London
London, England

Foreword

The studies in this volume constitute part of a larger research program on the economics and politics of the Middle East, inspired by the desire to identify the economic problems of the area and to explore the role economic development might play in reducing tensions there. It soon became obvious that the issues transcended the narrow boundaries of economics, and a thorough study of the political and social realities was also needed. These studies, as well as others not included here, were accordingly commissioned to that end. To make the job manageable at all, the topics had to be parceled out to experts on many different subjects, with the result that problems which cut across the lines of division escaped unified treatment.

An integrating study was accordingly also included in the program to bring the separate threads together and to supply, to the extent practicable, the missing elements. That study is still in progress. Pending its appearance, an overview of at least one important aspect of the political dynamics of the Middle East may be particularly in order: the relation of the superpowers to the Arab-Israeli conflict. I shall be brief, at the expense of offering many judgments unsupported by argument, though I believe them to be supported by the facts. Greater detail is to be forthcoming; meanwhile it can be found in the various essays of this book as well as in the literature at large. Nor do I speak for these, or other, contributors to the project, with whom I am in friendly disagreement on many points. They speak for themselves.[1] This is the way it looks to me.

The most pressing need in appraising the political problems of the Middle East is to recognize their dependence on U.S.-Soviet relations. This dependence is, incredibly, frequently ignored, or more often lip-service is paid to it, but its implications are not drawn. The whole modern history of the area is largely the outcome of local developments triggered, sustained, and constrained by the actions of external powers, and the influence of external economies, societies, and ideas. The modernization of Egypt was largely conditioned by the Napoleonic invasion and the British occupation, both incidents in the struggle between Britain and France. The preservation of the Ottoman Empire until World War I, and the subsequent division of its Arab territories among the newly constituted successor states, were largely by-products of inter-European rivalry. In the future as well, many of the area's develop-

---

[1]This works both ways. I am not necessarily in agreement with the views of the respective contributors, or of my co-editor. They are responsible scholars, and we may leave their views as well as mine open to scholarly criticism.

ments will depend principally on the relations between external powers, particularly the U.S. and the Soviet Union.

Conflict in the Middle East is proceeding at many levels. At the highest level is the U.S.-Soviet conflict, largely governing the shape, extent, and intensity of the conflicts at lower levels. At the lower, or local, levels there are three main strands of conflict closely interwoven with each other and with the lines of superpower influence. They are the Arab-Israeli conflict, the inter-Arab rivalries, and the internal strains between conservative and revolutionary orientations generated in each country by the ongoing process of modernization. These local tensions provide the points of entry and of leverage for superpower influence. Their importance is amplified from local to global levels through their linkage to superpower relations.

If the reader is inclined to agree that superpower relations are the primary factors determining the course of events in the Middle East, but doubts that the implications of so obvious a fact could have been missed in the literature, or more importantly, in the conduct of diplomacy, he gives evidence of his knowledge of the world as it is, but not of the history and literature of the Middle East. The history and the literature can take care of themselves, however. How the future state of the Middle East depends on superpower relations is what concerns us here.

For the superpowers, Russia and the U.S., the two basic alternatives are either détente or continued jockeying. For Communist China and for France, so long as they are interested, there is only one policy—to fish in troubled waters. For Britain, there is the role of a semidetached peacemaker ultimately committed to support the U.S. as its part of the Great Alliance.

Under U.S.-Soviet détente the local tensions could be expected to work out in local conflicts and transformations, with the turbulence regionally contained. A peaceful settlement of the Arab-Israeli conflict would then be possible. With continued superpower jockeying, which appears to be more probable for the near future at the time of writing, the most salient local conflict, that between Israel and the Arabs, will, at a minimum, continue to involve an arms race plus limited military intervention by the Soviet Union. There may also be some local exercise of arms, or in plain language, warfare, since one way to stay ahead in the arms race is to destroy the other side's armaments, or military emplacements, when they become too threatening.

Right now the United States with the Sixth Fleet in the Mediterranean and a great navy behind it, has clear-cut local military superiority. But it is most reluctant to use it. Ironically, the threat to use it must be all the more frequently and flamboyantly made in order to overcome the positive evidence of the reluctance. Such threats, once they are made, may indeed serve to overcome the reluctance itself, through commitment. The bluff, once made, may cease to be a bluff. Or it may still be taken to be bluff after it has become dead earnest. The unintended must be expected. The situation is, therefore, unstable.

The Soviet Union has a military capability in the Middle East much inferior to that of the U.S., but a much greater willingness to use it within the limits set by the U.S. will to retaliate. It therefore makes no verbal threats, but proceeds in stealth to strengthen its military position, while disavowing that intention, or even denying that it has done what it has done. The obvious counterstrategy for the United States, if it is unwilling either to use its military force against Russia, or peacefully to accord Russia a position of influence in the area on a parity with its own, is to supply Israel with enough arms to match the combination of Arab and Soviet military power committed to the area. This is the shape the arms race can be expected to take in the absence of a détente.

Even short of full-scale war the implications are staggering. The end is hardly predictable, but one possible future stage, if détente is not achieved, would seem to be a large land-based Soviet air capability in the Middle East, protected by Soviet ground forces, largely "advisers" and anti-aircraft personnel, matched principally by a greatly enlarged Israeli air force. Even an enlarged Sixth Fleet, say with three attack carriers instead of two, would then be reduced to a poor third in the local military picture. Its net offensive airpower of the order of 150 planes over and above an equal number necessary for its own defense screen could be overmatched by a few hundred Soviet bombers based on unsinkable land bases that might be established in Egypt, Syria, and Iraq, with a proportional complement of fighters, ground-to-air missiles, and surface-to-surface missiles, both land-based and seaborne.

Could the arms race really go that far? That depends entirely on whether Russia would welcome such a development, for only Russia is problematic in this context. There is little doubt that the other parties would stay in the game, however high Russia raised the bid. For the U.S. is clearly committed to support Israel with enough arms to meet the combined threat from Arab and Soviet forces in the area. Israel is certainly committed to accepting and deploying those arms, and Egypt to trying to get ahead of Israel in the arms race. Russia is in the ironic position that it probably could establish, if it wanted to, an air power in the Middle East that could dominate the Sixth Fleet, but only under condition that its local air power was in turn dominated by Israel's.

If, as I believe it will, the United States matches with arms to Israel any increase in Egyptian military strength including Soviet military forces in Egypt, the Soviets are hardly likely to stay in the game they started early in

1970. They must be banking on some other outcome—possibly a negotiated peace based on the military balance as changed by its latest move[2] or else an inhibition on the U.S. response because of the U.S. desire to keep its friends in the Arab world. The arms race is likely to be highly disadvantageous to the Russians. The superior wealth of the U.S. gives it a real advantage. The influence that Russia gains by the arms race does Russia little good, since it is likely to remain in a militarily inferior local position. The U.S. impotence in Vietnam is not matched in the Middle East—we may not be able to fight effectively against an indigenous underground movement, but we can certainly supply modern arms effectively to a government that can use them efficiently. The roles are reversed in the Middle East and Vietnam—it is Russia that is bogged down in the Middle East unless there is a political settlement. The direct military involvement of the Russians risks ignominious defeat at the hands, not of the U.S., but of Israel. It is hard to believe that the Russians, in their direct involvement, are engaging in anything but a temporary expedient.

The arms race might be frozen, *de facto,* at a stage far short of that just sketched, at any time the U.S. is ready to accord Russia its desired position in the area. But, unless motivated by the benefits of a détente that accorded it parity of influence in the area, Russia can hardly be expected to agree to a real peace in the Middle East, which would eliminate the tension that is a necessary condition for its power and influence there. Nor is it likely that any practically conceivable settlement would qualify as a "real peace."

It is true that the Arab-Israeli tension might be substantially reduced from its present level without achieving so peaceful a state as to undercut Russia's position of influence. That is what Russia may well be after as a short-term objective. By procuring the return of the lost territories it would put the Egyptians, and less significantly the Jordanians and the Syrians, under obligations of gratitude to the Soviets. But gratitude in international affairs carries about as much weight as the Pope's divisions. It is on the expectation of future rather than the memory of past favors that Russia must depend for its continuing influence. A demonstration of Soviet power to achieve the return of the lost territories would be more significant as a hint of possible future favors and a validation of Soviet credibility in the Third World than as a deposit in the insolvent bank of gratitude.

Furthermore, a political settlement would have to involve such compromises between the desirable and the attainable as to put the Russians more in the position of arguing the Egyptians into it than of presenting them with

[2]At time of writing this latest move was to join the Egyptians in installing ground-to-air missiles near the Suez Canal in apparent contravention of the promise to the U.S. at the time of negotiation of the cease-fire of August 7, 1970.

a gift. The attractiveness of the settlement to Russia derives primarily from the resulting stabilization of its position rather than from the gratitude of its clients. It would reduce the risk of an open military conflict with the U.S. As American post-Vietnam weariness becomes more and more evident, that risk is correspondingly reduced, however, so that a political settlement can be expected progressively to lose some of its value to the Soviets. But a secondary interest of the Russians in a political settlement may still be great enough to insure continued Soviet commitment to that objective. Only by a political settlement can Russia realistically hope to be able to pacify, if not satisfy, its clients. In the absence of a political settlement it may continue to offer its clients arms, but not the satisfaction of attaining the ends toward which the arms are directed. So long as the lost territories are not recovered the situation is too unstable even for Russia's appetite for instability. A political settlement, must, of course, include the return of substantially all of the lost territories. Since Israel would continue to exist as a Jewish state, tension could not be expected to be completely relaxed, but it would be reduced to a more manageable level.

The Soviets would also welcome the opening of the Suez Canal, though if it were also opened to the Sixth Fleet, the net naval gains would hardly be substantial except under circumstances in which the U.S. is politically neutralized. The economic advantage of the freighter time saved on the Odessa-Haiphong run must be deemed a second-order consideration, comparable to a less than a penny a gallon effect on British oil product prices from the closure of Suez, and on a much smaller volume of shipments.

A settlement agreeable to Russia would seem to Israel to be at her expense since it would involve Israeli withdrawal from the occupied territories without liquidation of Arab intentions of further cutting back Israel. The accompanying demilitarization arrangements and security guarantees would not be likely to appear sufficiently effective to reassure Israel. But more study of their possibilities (hardly any seems to have been made) is required to ascertain what security for Israel could in fact be attained through such arrangements. The alternative of continued occupation, entailing as it does Russian direct military involvement on the west bank of the Suez Canal, offers less security than the Israelis are wont to attribute to it. On the other hand, a "real peace" would hardly serve Russia's purpose. Continued controlled tension is clearly in Russia's interest given its apparent objective of maintaining its role in the area, an objective more valuable to the Russians than the gratitude of the Arabs or the opening of Suez. Nevertheless, the Soviets many continue to maneuver to obtain all three of these ends.

If we view diplomacy and its limiting form—the making of war—as conducted by rationally calculating minds, the outbreak of war must always involve a mistaken calculation on the part of one or both parties. Certainly a rational leader of Germany would not have invaded Poland in 1939 if he had foreseen the outcome, nor would Japan have attacked Pearl Harbor. Closer to the Middle East, Nasser, in May 1967, would not have done what he did if he were proceeding rationally and was not mistaken about the outcome. It is the mistaken calculations that are important in unstable situations; their possibility contributes powerfully to the instability inherent in such situations.

In the Middle East right now the "mistakes" are legion. Quotation marks are appropriate because calling these policies mistakes imputes to the "decisionmakers" a greater degree of monolithic rationality than they actually possess. Nor are the "decisionmakers" really decisionmakers. They are actors in a tragedy, fulfilling their fate. Hitler followed *his* bent, as did the Japanese militarists theirs. Nasser in 1967 did what he had to do.

If, however, we do regard the countries concerned each as having a single rational mind, it is most impressive how unrealistically they seem to view the current situation in the Middle East. This is notoriously the case so far as the Arab states and the commandos are concerned, but it is not so generally recognized how much of the Israeli position and that of the U.S. and the Soviet Union is, and has been, founded on misconceptions.

Let us take the Israelis first. Instead of posing the options in realistic terms—the choice between the best attainable contractual settlement and the way things are likely to develop in the absence of such a settlement—the Israelis posed it in false terms. They were choosing, they felt, as Friedlander says, between real peace and safety first, with the latter identified with the *status quo*. These are simply not the realistic alternatives. "Real peace," as the Israelis understand the term, would require a complete change of heart of the Arabs, which is certainly not to be expected as part of a package deal in the immediate future. Nor is safety first to be found in the *status quo,* defined as retention of the occupied territories on an indefinitely provisional basis. For it may already be seen, though subsequent to Friedlander's time of writing (1969) that the genuine alternative to a contractual settlement involves direct military participation of the Soviet Union in a war of attrition against Israel.

Posing the problem as a choice between real peace and safety first was a "cop-out," an avoidance of the genuine problems of decision. Since real peace is certainly not attainable there would be no way other than safety first. "No other way" indeed became a slogan in Israel. Any negotiated settlement, it was apparently believed, must be inferior to that safety first policy which, conveniently, required no decision except not to decide. There is no evidence that much attention was paid to any "third way" between real peace and no settlement at all. Such discussion of peace terms as there was, and there was a great deal, concentrated on what territories would have to be retained even if a real peace was to be achieved. As unilateral considerations these were bound to be unrealistic, just as unilateral Arab demands, including dezionization of the Israel State and return of all the refugees, were unrealistic.

The Israeli discussions were unrealistic because they focused on the Arab states rather than on Russia. As Dayan put it in September, 1970, "When I was young I thought the way to prepare for war in the Middle East was to learn Arabic and the geography of the desert. Now it seems that it is more important to study Russian and electronics."[3] Dayan must have been a young man until very recently. Significantly, Dayan, in the speech quoted, failed to state the implications for Israel policy of the changed point of view, nor has anyone else in the government. The general tendency among Israelis, when their mistaken formulation of the alternatives as real peace or the *status quo* was revealed in 1970 by direct Russian military participation in the defense of Egypt, was to call to the attention of the U.S. its job of containing Russian involvement in the area. But the full implications have not yet been incorporated into Israeli thinking, and Eban has not yet withdrawn his oft-stated contention that peace in the area must be sought at the local rather than at the superpower level. It is true that only the local parties can make peace, but until the superpowers make their peace the Arabs and Israelis will not make theirs. The pressure of events, however, may be expected to make this increasingly clear. Since the shakeup in the Israel government consequent on acceptance of the August, 1970 ceasefire, there has been some tendency to view the problem more flexibly—a willingness to explore what benefits might be gained from possible concessions.

It may seem surprising for me to argue that the U.S. has also erred in concentrating on local conditions. It cannot reasonably be claimed that we ignored either the actual or potential presence of the Russians in the Middle East. Indeed we saw their shadow and fought against their presence even when they were not there, thus helping their entry. The primary target of our Middle East policy since the early Fifties has been the limitation of Russian power and influence and the meeting of Russian threats, real or imagined. What we have ignored is not the importance of Russian interest in the area, but its implications. Much of our policy is directed to the local conditions, without really taking into account the position of the Russians. How can this be—it may be asked—the first toddling step of each newborn American proposal is over the threshold of the Soviet Embassy. The U.S. has certainly recognized that any settlement must be acceptable to the

[3]*The Jerusalem Post Weekly,* September 18, 1970, p. 7.

Russians. It has not recognized what that requires. Against the evidence of the innumerable meetings with the Russians on the Middle East, I adduce the evidence of what came out of the meetings—disappointments and deceptions. Clearly the Russians cannot be expected voluntarily to agree to a settlement that expels them from the Middle East unless the alternative is a major blow to them—one that the U.S. is not psychologically prepared to deliver, however well prepared we are militarily.

That the U.S. has so far failed to recognize the nature of its options is, I think, revealed by Quandt's paper. In the long run the U.S. can have low tension in the Middle East only if it is prepared to offer some substitute for tension in affording Russia a position in the area. In the short run, it is true, the U.S. can make continued tension so costly to the Russians that they would be willing to relax it. In fact there is already more tension than the Russians need or want, so that they would welcome a political settlement which would reduce the economic and diplomatic cost to them of maintaining their position in the area. This fact has been misconstrued in U.S. diplomacy, which continues to seek Russian agreement to a settlement that would reduce Russia's influence in the area.[4] The Russians are indeed interested in reducing the cost of their influence, but not the strength of it. A settlement along the lines sought by the U.S. is probably attainable. But if it is attained, it will not be found to have reduced Russia's involvement in the area, as Becker points out. It may, and I think would, nonetheless be desirable in that it would reduce both arms cost and diplomatic strain and would impove the chances of avoiding open U.S.-Soviet military conflict.

The realistic choice for the U.S. is either to limit the Russian position in the area by the credible threat of force, either directly or through Israel by (however imperfect) proxy, or to accept Russia's position and to try to make the best of it.

The threat of direct U.S. force in situations challenging Russian response is undoubtedly foreclosed by the post-Vietnam mood of the U.S. Even a direct military involvement that had low risk of confrontation with the Soviets, as in the Jordan crisis of September, 1970, was found to be more than the U.S. public "had a stomach for," although it was, apparently, held in reserve as an alternative possibly superior to Israeli intervention. In the event, the first line of defense, the Jordanian army plus the shadow of

---

[4]"I would merely say to you that we are interested in reducing Soviet influence in the area. The best possible way to reduce the Soviet influence is to achieve a political settlement that meets legitimate concerns of both sides..." (Joseph Sisco on NBC "Meet the Press," July 12, 1970, reported in *New Middle East,* August 1970, p. 10.) The telltale sign here is that "both sides" means Israel and Arab, and not American and Russian.

Israeli intervention, held, the choice is then credible force via Israel as proxy or a local détente with Russia. So far, the first option is being followed; it is not even certain that the second is offered. So the Communist contention that Israel is an outpost of U.S. imperialism, palpably false for the first twenty years of Israel's existence, is on the verge of becoming true—a self-fulfilling prophecy. For if Russia seeks to establish its imperium in the Middle East through direct military support to Egypt, the simplest reply of the United States is to meet the bid with increased arms aid to Israel.

The policy currently being pursued (in late 1970), trying to negotiate Russia out of its desired position, is based on an illusion nourished by the Soviets' declared willingness to seek a political settlement. There is a strong presumption of that willingness, but not that an attainable settlement would so far reduce the tension as to erode Russia's position in the Middle East. It would be a small but highly crucial step to shift this diplomatic policy to a search for the most congenial way to offer Russia a place in the Middle East. Such a shift might offer a genuine alternative to the arms race, although it may be that no possible Russian position is congenial to the United States. That seems doubtful, however, though I do not envy the diplomat who has to explore the question.

Not all the misconceptions are on the side of Israel and the U.S. The Arabs, particularly Egypt, are welcoming Soviet military aid in the hope that they can use it to force Israel to mend its ways. But the Soviets are not interested in letting things go that far. They are endowing the Arabs with instruments whose effective use they are not inclined to permit. One reason why a political settlement is important for the Russians is that it will exorcise some of the curse of frustration that is laid on their arms gifts to the Arabs. Some observers foresee an ultimate disillusionment of the Arabs with this support that will never attain its end, but it seems to me that the process can go on indefinitely. The Arabs can long sustain against all the evidence the hope of eventual victory; it is all they have. They will need armaments to help sustain that hope even if it remains unrealistic. Should a political settlement be in view, Russian arms aid will undoubtedly contribute to the Arab bargaining position. In the absence of a political settlement, the Russians will have to pay by various concessions for the restraint they will almost certainly have to continue to impose on the use of the arms whose supply is their lever of influence. Clearly, they would prefer the settlement.

Similar considerations underlie Soviet rejections of American proposals to discuss arms limitations on Middle Eastern states. A delicate but crucial distinction must be made between an agreed arms limitation and a *de facto* one. The Russians would almost certainly welcome, for reasons of economy as well as stability, a slow-down of the arms race that would still leave them their position of influence. A political solution would doubtless have such an effect. All things considered, such an outcome would be highly favorable to the Russians. An explicit arms limitation, on the other hand, would tend to destroy Russia's leverage since that leverage depends on the Arab belief that they can obtain more arms through Russia than through the West. Once the Arab states were limited by a superpower agreement to effective military inferiority to Israel, although possibly with greater numbers of planes and tanks, continued dependence on Russia would be pointless. So, while Russia would welcome a *de facto* stabilization of the arms race under conditions that would still preserve its importance to its Arab clients, until a general détente is achieved it is likely to continue to reject an agreed arms limitation that would undercut its influence.

It may be presumed that the Russians are making mistakes right now in the Middle East as they have in the past. Their general strategy of maintaining the tension, but at a controlled level, seems to be consistent with their apparent objectives, however. They did indeed drive the tension higher than they needed in 1967, but the results were not entirely unfavorable to their interests. Their continued probing is likely to reveal operationally what most observers are ready to conclude subjectively, the limited will of the United States to get directly involved in military action against the Russians in the Middle East. Nevertheless, the Russians' own direct military involvement in a situation where they are locally weaker, not only than the United States, but than Israel with U.S. arms support, risks serious embarrassment. It requires an intensified restraint on Egypt to avoid military action, unwelcome both to Israel and to Russia, that would show up the weakness in Russian local military capability. The Russians have indeed made turnabouts whenever their probing has revealed the sticking point of U.S. determination. That is why we give the name, "probing" to their style of diplomacy. But Russian probing, like American shows of force, may lead to undesired commitments, hard to evade. Retreating in the face of U.S. determination is one thing, in the face of Israeli determination, another.

Russian complicity with Nasser in violating the stand-still provisions of the August, 1970 ceasefire was said to indicate that they underrated the value to them of the U.S. desire to achieve a political settlement, not only in the Middle East but in the Cold War at large. But other interpretations are possible. They may have correctly judged the U.S. interest in a Middle East settlement, and in SALT, as so intense as to survive the violations; or perhaps the violations were the price of Nasser's concurrence in the ceasefire. The Israeli suspicion that the U.S. arranged the 1970 ceasefire fully expecting to blink at Egyptian violations of the standstill provision, inserted to overcome Israeli hesitation, imputes to the U.S. too great a degree of

Machiavellianism. The most convincing rationale that can be offered for Russian concurrence in the Egyptian violations is that they felt that a strong military position would be required to attain acceptable terms in the political settlement they are seeking, and interests elsewhere would not be seriously affected.

The Russians may have misjudged the reactions of the U.S. as they misjudged those of Israel in 1967, when they apparently based their policy on a highly accurate intelligence evaluation of the Eshkol government, but a grossly erroneous grasp of the dynamics of Israeli politics that swept Dayan into that government and Israel to war. They are not likely, however, to concentrate on local conditions but will look first to the U.S. reaction to any contemplated policy and then to the local consequences. Neither the local consequences nor the U.S. reactions are so clearly calculable that their ultimate implications can be taken into account. That is what makes the game dangerous.

I have been urged by my Rand colleagues to formulate for each of the leading participants in the Arab-Israeli conflict the policy that would best serve his ends if he acted rationally and perceived the situation clearly. The utility of such an exercise may be questioned. As a predictive device it must fail because the participants are driven by forces other than cold calculation, nor are they likely to perceive the situation as I do. In particular, internal political compulsions will prevent each of the parties from acting in its own best interest. The U.S. is likely to be shackled by an isolationist reaction to Vietnam and a long lag in our recognition of Russia as a global power. Russia is trapped by its current dogma, Israel is unable to resolve its policy because of the internal divisions a decision would reveal, and the Arab governments are strait-jacketed by twenty-five years of "victory-or-death" sloganeering.

As a normative device, however, to help judge what the parties should do, according to their values, not ours, the exercise has more to recommend it, provided we can accurately gauge both the values motivating the participants and the realistic alternatives they face. The principal service to be rendered by the exercise is to delineate the realistic alternatives against the background of the regnant values as best I can perceive them. If others perceive either the values or the alternatives differently, they are, of course, free to draw their own conclusions accordingly. Surely, if a study of the political dynamics of the Middle East is to have practical value, it must bear on the question of the best policy for all concerned in the current imbroglio.

Actually, the task is considerably eased once it is recognized that such an inquiry boils down to finding a mutually agreeable settlement that is better for all concerned than any realistic alternative. The form such a settlement must take if it is to be realized at all can, I believe, be recognized fairly easily, as can the most probable realistic alternative. To characterize that alternative we need engage in no farfetched speculation, but we can take as our starting point the state of the arms race and of the "war of attrition" immediately in prospect. Any further progression would quite obviously be worse for all concerned. For Egypt and Jordan it would mean the abandonment of economic development, more costly arms expenditures, and even more costly occasional exercises in military futility, since there is no realistic prospect of attaining their ends by military means. For Egypt it also implies greater dependence on Russia. For Russia, further progression of the war of attrition implies heavier economic burdens and more serious risk of embarrassment at the least, and at worst, military conflict with the U.S. For Israel also, an intensified war of attrition will be costly in imposing unwanted casualties, diverting its economic progress to arms production, increasing its military and economic dependence on the U.S. and threatening its democratic institutions and ultimately the lives of its people. For the U.S. it means an increased economic burden, impairment of its relations with Russia as well as with the Arab states, and above all, the danger of military involvement.

A more detailed argument in support of the contention that intensification of the arms race and the war of attrition would be worse for all parties hardly seems necessary. There remains only the possibility to be disposed of that in the absence of a peaceful settlement things will get better for at least one of the parties. This expectation has been implicit in Israel's attitude, "if Israel remains strong, the Arabs will eventually come to their senses."[5] The belief that time works in Israel's favor so long as it remains strong fails to take the commitment of the Soviet Union into account. Even without that commitment it is questionable whether time would work in favor of Israel, but with the Russians deeply involved it is fairly certain that things will not get better for Israel, in the absence of a settlement, but are likely to get worse. So long as the territories remain occupied it is incumbent on Egypt to struggle for them, for Russia to support that struggle, and for the commandos to do their part. Only if Russia should tire of the game or be diverted elsewhere, say to a struggle with China or to unrest at home or in Eastern Europe, is there hope for time to work for the Israelis. Even then the situation is likely to resemble the nineteen years before 1967 when the improvement in Middle Eastern affairs was hardly substantial.

The argument that Egypt would be better off to abandon the war of attrition, to forget about Israel, and to turn to its own problems of economic development is an appeal to American and Israeli values, not to Egyptian. Such a shift in the focus of public policy is not likely to be in the interest of

[5]Prime Minister Golda Meir on NBC's "Today" program, 22 Oct. 1970.

survival of any Egyptian regime. Egypt's need for economic development does not accordingly furnish the grounds for hope that, in the absence of a settlement, the Egyptians will abandon the contest. Western observers have often noted that Russia also would do better to concentrate on its internal economic problems instead of pursuing global power, but the Kremlin has not seen it that way. Similar suggestions have been made for the United States.

In the alternative context of a peace settlement in which a higher Egyptian priority, the quest for dignity, has been satisfied, Egypt's welfare needs would indeed furnish the basis of the ultimate acceptability of such a settlement to the Egyptians. Even if an imperfect peace settlement is attained, those needs give hope that time will then work to reduce the tensions. A settlement, even an imperfect one, is the prior condition for time to work in favor of peace.

We may then take as the most favorable realistic alternative to a political settlement the stage of the arms race and the war of attrition that has already been reached. Basically that consists of Egyptian attacks on the Israel forward position, with Russian support against Israeli retaliation, with occasional interruptions by ceasefires. Projected into the future the situation may be expected to get worse in the absence of a peace settlement.

In the formulation of a peace settlement which would offer advantages to all concerned, account must be taken of three important respects in which the current situation differs from the pre-1967 state of affairs: the greater role of the Russians, the apparent willingness of Egypt and Jordan to accept the existence of Israel, and the rise of Palestinian consciousness. All three of these tendencies must be reflected in the peace settlement.

The Russian participation makes a settlement urgent for Israel, as contrasted with a prolonged occupation of the conquered territories. Israeli preference for the *status quo* essentially ignores the fact that the Russians are there. Even if the Russians were not there a settlement would be desirable; but they are there, so a settlement is imperative.

The newly achieved willingness of Egypt and Jordan to accept the existence of Israel promises to make a peace settlement possible. That willingness was manifested in their acceptance of the 1970 ceasefire which already cost Hussein one civil war and subjected Egypt and Jordan to strain with other Arab states.

The rise of Palestinian consciousness offers an opportunity to separate the Palestinian question from the foreign policy of the Arab governments, but requires that the settlement recognize the rights of the Palestinians to compensation, if not repatriation, and to a political framework of their choice, either within Jordan or in a state of their own. It may at least be hoped that such a settlement, offering due regard for Palestinian interests short of a major Palestinian repatriation into Israel, would induce some shift of Palestinian energies toward positive development outside Israel. There is a strong presumption that the great majority of the Palestinians would welcome such a peaceful settlement. Therefore, it would threaten to cut the ground out from under the diehard guerrilla leadership who will for that reason, as well as for basic principles, oppose it. A troublesome problem might remain, but surely less of a problem than when the Palestinians were offered neither compensation, resettlement, nor their own political framework.

As previously noted, there is little question of the shape that a package settlement would have to take if it is to be achieved at all. The local conditions are already embodied, with some necessary ambiguities, in the Security Council Resolution of November 22, 1967. The entire room for maneuver in a final settlement lies within the ample range of indeterminancy of those ambiguities, and in the relationship of the U.S. and Russia to the area, a matter unmentioned in the November, 1967 Resolution.

The following conditions would almost certainly have to be satisfied to make a settlement acceptable to all parties:

> Israel would have to withdraw from all, or almost all, of the occupied territories, to recognized boundaries close to those of May, 1967. Safeguards would have to be established to make those borders secure.

> All countries concerned would have to terminate belligerency explicitly and recognize each other's sovereignty and borders. Safeguards against attacks on each other, either by regular or irregular forces, would have to be established.

> Jerusalem would have to be a unified city, the seat of the capital of Israel, with the Moslem holy places under an Arab flag, and the Arab residents citizens of an Arab state.

> Free passage for all nations through Suez and for Israel through the Strait of Tiran and the Red Sea would have to be assured.

> The Palestinians would have to be offered, individually, a choice between repatriation and resettlement under terms that would induce almost all to accept resettlement. Arrangements would have to made to help the resettlement of those who chose that alternative. The Palestinians would also have to be offered, collectively, their choice of the governmental arrangement under which they are to live, as citizens either of a newly constituted Palestinian state or of Jordan, either unified or federated.

Russia would have to be accorded a role in the Middle East comparable, in some sense, with that of the U.S.

There is some question whether such an outcome can be realized even conceptually, or whether it determines an empty set because it entails practical impossibilities. I cannot claim to have an answer to that question. It is a sad reflection on the approach to peace in the area that little official attention has been paid by the parties concerned to the study of the possible arrangements that might satisfy these conditions. Self-appointed advocates have indeed advanced numerous proposals, but these have not been seriously faced up to by either the local governments or the superpowers. There is a presumption, however, that the necessary arrangements can be devised, not in perfection, but in reasonably practical form, so that, with all its imperfections, a settlement on these lines would still be better for all concerned than the most probable alternative.

In characterizing these arrangements as advantageous to all concerned I am not claiming that, if they were offered as a package right now, they would be immediately accepted. I am claiming that, if the principal parties could eventually come to an agreed settlement this is where they would end up. The only serious exception would be the Palestinian guerrilla leadership which might cling to the demand for a dezionization of Israel which is clearly inconsistent with an agreed settlement to which Israel is a party.

It is the tragedy of the Middle East that it is improbable that such a settlement can be attained—though it is by no means impossible. The principal difficulties are path obstacles in the way of moving toward a settlement, as distinct from the costs and benefits of the settlement itself. No detailed list of these path obstacles is required here. They are written large in the history of the post-1967 negotiations. Because of them a peaceful settlement must be regarded as improbable, even though advantageous for all concerned. The obstacles are of four general kinds, closely interrelated.

First, there are the political costs each government faces in agreeing to a compromise solution, even if it is in the interest of its country to do so. Some of these costs have already been incurred in the acceptance of the 1970 ceasefire which entailed a civil war in Jordan, a split in the Israel government, and strain between the governments of Egypt and Jordan, on the one hand, and the commandos and other Arab governments on the other.

These political difficulties proceed largely from another path obstacle, the highly charged semantics of the conflict. Compromise on any issue may be regarded as betrayal of fundamental principles, even when it is not.

There are also errors of perception—failures to see facts as they are, failures born of deep psychological needs and past conditioning. These affect the governments of the superpowers as well as those of the local states. The chief errors of perception, as I see them, have already been discussed: the U.S. belief that it can negotiate Russia out of its position of influence, the Israeli belief that time will work in its favor if it remains strong, the Arab belief that the U.S. and Russia will force Israel to accommodate to Arab demands, the Russian belief that they will gain some profit from the influence they are acquiring over their Arab clients.

Finally, small short-run advantages may be grasped at the expense of large long-run gains. Indeed a sacrifice of the long run to the short is often regarded as characteristic of the Middle East—the so-called "bazaar mem-tality." Many observers, particularly in the U.S., thought that the Egyptian violation of the standstill provisions of the August, 1970 ceasefire was just one more example of this tendency to sacrifice paramount long-run interests for a minor short-run advantage. It did not turn out that way, even though it might have, so at best this example demonstrates a readiness to risk the sacrifice of the long-run gain for short. Such a readiness is general in the Middle East, and not uncommon elsewhere. So, in spite of the fact that a settlement along the lines sketched would be to the advantage of all parties, it may not be attained because its realization would require taking some short-run risks for the long-run gains, and this may run counter to the mental sets of the parties.

Yet the gains from a settlement, if only it could be posed as a realistic alternative, might be sufficient to overcome the obstacles. For the local parties the gains would be substantial. Israel would gain peace and security, with a good chance that time would work to consolidate the basis of that peace. For the Arab states, and particularly for Egypt, a settlement offers a chance to accept with dignity the continued existence of Israel, and so to free themselves from a heavy burden that threatens their future. In an important sense the interests of the Arabs and Israelis are not diametrically opposed. At the top of their value hierarchies the Arab states place dignity; Israel, peaceful survival. The peaceful survival of Israel under the changed conditions envisaged, need no longer be at the expense of Arab dignity. The challenge to peacemaking in the Middle East is to untie the tangled knot binding these factors to each other, so as to permit their joint satisfaction. With respect to the occupied territories, Israel's interest is in security, while the Arab interest is in sovereignty. Again there is no necessity of conflict. Demilitarization of the territories, if it can be made effective, would preserve Israel's security while returning sovereignty to the Arab states.

On the U.S.-Soviet level, however, the game is being run closer to zero sum: we apparently are trying to minimize Russian influence and maximize ours, while Russia is trying to maximize its influence and minimize ours.

If our interests really were diametrically opposed, there would be nothing left for us but to continue the rivalry and to accept the arms race. But there is good reason to believe that a Soviet-American détente with respect to the Middle East would be advantageous to both parties. If this comes to be recognized, the way to a peaceful settlement is open; if not, the conflict must continue until the distant day when Egypt tires of the treadmill to which it is condemned by the arms race and dissolves the bond with Russia. Or, Russia may some day throw its own air power into the conflict so massively as to foreclose our matching it with aid to Israel and so may pose for us the dilemma of direct involvement or backing down. That is unlikely, but it remains a possibility whose implication is that if we are unwilling to become directly involved Israel must be kept well ahead in the arms race with a surplus of pilots so that, in a crisis, we need supply only planes and not direct support. The United States must face up to its unwillingness to become directly involved. The Russians are likely to probe that unwillingness.

The critical step in achieving peace in the Middle East is to resolve the U.S.-Soviet rivalry in the area. That resolution will require, on the part of the United States, both an offer and a threat. The offer must be a future state of the relationship of the two powers in the area that affords a reasonable place to each. The threat is to match by military aid to Israel any increase of Soviet military support to the Arabs. Both the offer and the threat must be made clearly and distinctly.

The best policy for the U.S. would accordingly seem to be to speak softly and to let Israel carry a big stick. We can afford to offer Russia a genuine role in the area through diplomatic recognition of its position, but not at the expense of Israel's security. Israel can be kept strong enough to preserve its security, but constrained by mutual agreement not to use that strength in a provocative way. Its military activities would thus be confined to the repulsion of attack, if it should come, and would exclude rubbing Egypt's (and hence Russia's) nose in the dirt by gay sallies over Cairo. We should certainly encourage Israel to withdraw from the occupied territories under any conditions that would offer genuine safeguards against such withdrawal endangering Israel's security. These limitations on Israel's actions are consistent only with correspondingly strong military support. If we wish, for "even-handedness," to limit our military support of Israel, we must then also limit our restrictions on Israel's actions. Some level of U.S. arms support is more valuable to Israel than retention of the occupied territories, especially if these are to be effectively demilitarized.

The notion that we can "distance" ourselves from Israel is an illusion so long as we remain committed to its preservation. That commitment must carry with it a responsibility to insure that Israel's policies do not embroil us unnecessarily. We have no monopoly of wisdom, but we do have a stake in the outcome which requires our participation in the process. Double harness may chafe our diplomats, but that is a hazard of the profession.

Russia's best policy would seem to be to seek the most favorable arrangement it can make with the U.S. while continuing to give Egypt such military support as will most enhance its bargaining power. Of course, in making a deal with the U.S. it must not appear to be letting Egypt or Syria down. There is ample room for this in the possible return of occupied territories and in guarantees of territorial integrity. Russia can continue to be Egypt's patron while restraining the war of attrition by offering or securing guarantees of Egyptian territorial integrity that will afford the Egyptian government the opportunity to hail the settlement as an achievement of security against any future Israeli aggression. This requires that, in a settlement, the neutralization of the Sinai Peninsula be couched in terms that include superpower guarantees of that neutrality against the entry of both Israeli and Egyptian armed forces. A Soviet role in that guarantee will help assure Russia's continuing position in the area, at the possible cost of weakening the value of the neutralization to Israel. The latter would still have to depend, in the first instance, on its own military strength to back up the neutralization of the territories, and ultimately, on U.S. arms support. Pending a settlement Russia would find it best to continue to give the most massive military support to Egypt consistent with that support being defensive in nature so as to limit the escalation of U.S. support to Israel. Russia can continue to negotiate with the U.S. in such a manner as to sustain or revive our willingness to limit our support to Israel in the interest of a settlement so long as we are willing to follow that line. But if no settlement is achieved Russia would do well to reduce its direct military involvement, which has such great potential for embarrassment, should Israel react actively to the war of attrition. Up to a certain point, of course, the threat to the Russians, raising the possibility of strong Russian response, renders such an Israeli reaction less probable, but should the war of attrition become less supportable to Israel, the option of direct ground force retaliation is open. Russia is, accordingly, involved in a very delicate situation, all the more threatening in that delicacy of touch has not characterized Russian diplomacy in the past.

The best policies for Israel and Egypt largely depend on the policies of the U.S. and Russia. If the superpowers continue to be diametrically opposed, the local powers are trapped in the arms race. Israel, with its existence at stake, will certainly welcome all the support it can obtain from the United States, and must look to the latter to restrain Russia's involvement. Egypt indeed might eventually tire of its treadmill and gradually turn away from the conflict, but that is likely to take a long time. In the meantime, even a government that recognized the national interest in freeing itself from the frustrating burden of the conflict with Israel will find it difficult to do so.

If, however, the superpowers should agree on a settlement along the lines outlined above, it would clearly be in the interest of the local powers to accept it. Nor would it have to be imposed. It would be a victory for both parties. The tragedy of the Middle East, and for the world as well, lies in the improbability of achievement of the settlement, largely attributable to the failure of the U.S. and Russia to come to a détente.

Sidney S. Alexander

Cambridge, Massachusetts

Preface

This volume on the political and social problems and prospects of the Middle East is part of a broad program of research on the economics and politics of the Middle East that has been supported by a grant from the Ford Foundation and carried forward jointly by The Rand Corporation and Resources for the Future, Inc., under the general direction of Professor Sidney S. Alexander. The aim of the program has been to contribute to the formation of sound policy judgments about the Middle East on the part of all concerned through improved understanding about the economic, demographic, and related political facts of life there.

To this end, one group of studies, published in a companion volume, was directed toward the economic and demographic problems of the area.[1] Those studies, as well as the one in this volume, were primarily the responsibility of The Rand Coporation. Two other volumes in this series, primarily the responsibility of Resources for the Future, Inc., deal with the problems related to Middle East oil and agriculture, respectively.[2] Other studies in the program have been published, or await publication, in monographic form.[3]

In addition, an overview volume is now being prepared under the authorship of Professor Alexander. The interested reader can anticipate some of the argument of that volume by reading Professor Alexander's introduction to the present one.

In the first chapter of this volume, I attempted to identify and weave together the major propositions and issues posed by the chapters that follow. Such a summary effort is bound to do injustice to the summarized material; the shortcomings of Chapter 1 should not be taken as an indication of the quality of succeeding chapters. The interested reader will need to find out for himself what they say. He may also want to ponder what they do not

[1]Charles A. Cooper and Sidney S. Alexander (eds.), *Economic Development and Population Growth in the Middle East,* American Elsevier, New York, 1972.

[2]Sam H. Schurr and Paul T. Homan, *Middle Eastern Oil and the Western World,* American Elsevier, New York, 1971; Marion Clawson, Hans H. Landsberg, and Lyle T. Alexander, *The Agricultural Potential of the Middle East,* American Elsevier, New York, 1971.

[3]Adel Daher, *Current Trends in Arab Intellectual Thought,* RM-5979-FF, The Rand Corporation, December 1969; William E. Hoehn, *Prospects for Desalted Water Costs,* RM-5971-FF, The Rand Corporation, October 1969; and R. E. Huschke, R. R. Rapp, and C. Schutz, *Meteorological Aspects of Middle East Water Supply,* RM-6267-FF, The Rand Corporation, March 1970.

say: what issues they do not cover, or cover inadequately; which important issues might be more easily resolved by better data. He should be aware, however, that the chapters in this volume were written mostly in 1969, and in no case have been revised to reflect events beyond the spring of 1970.

The purpose of this volume is to provide such an understanding of the political facts of life in the Middle East as is necessary for sound political judgments on the part of all concerned. But that is an ideal goal and we have fallen short of it. It will be appropriate for critical reviewers to ask how much closer we reasonably could have been expected to come.

The critical reader should go further to ask himself questions about the uses of learning to cope with the problems of the Middle East—what the humanities and the social sciences can do that they are not now doing, that they now do badly, or at least not very well, to deal with the economic and political problems of the Middle East. In following a practice common in economic studies, the frame of reference included the assumption that a peaceful settlement of the Arab-Israeli conflict was soon to be achieved. The assumption was recognized as unrealistic but nonetheless useful. Models of economic development often assume peace and factor out important political determinants of economic change. In the present volume, war and its prospect are a distinct and appropriate part of the analysis in each study. For better or for worse, our models of national political development and decay, and of regional political systems, are highly contingent upon conflict and violence.

Paul Y. Hammond

Santa Monica, California
January 6, 1971

Introduction

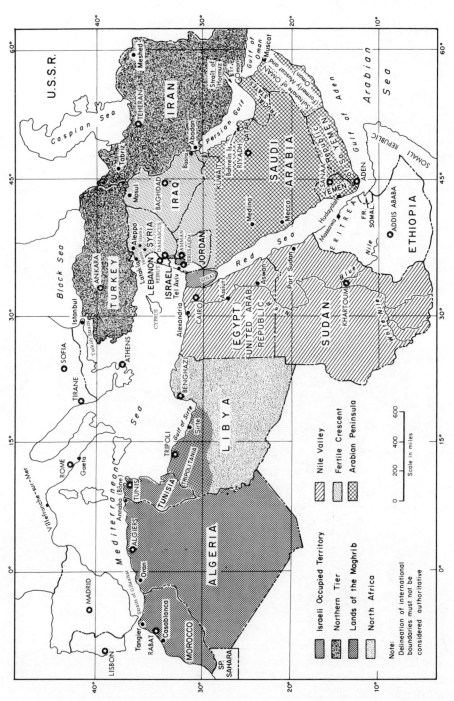

Map I — The region of the Middle East

Israeli Occupied Territory

Northern Tier

Lands of the Maghrib

North Africa

Nile Valley

Fertile Crescent

Arabian Peninsula

Note:
Delineation of international boundaries must not be considered authoritative

Scale in miles
0   200   400   600

PART I

Introduction

The chapters in this volume have been grouped into five parts. Each part will be accompanied by an explanatory and introductory note. Chapter 1 provides the editor's perspective on the Middle East. Chapters 2 and 3 deal respectively with the most persistent of the region's indigenous forces, Arab nationalism, and with the most disconcerting condition in the region, its precarious military balance. Chapter 2 was written by Malcolm Kerr, Professor of Political Science at the University of California, Los Angeles, and author of *The Arab Cold War 1958-1967: A Study of Ideology in Politics* (New York: Oxford University Press, 1967); Chapter 3 by Jacob C. Hurewitz, Professor of Government at Columbia University, New York, and author of *Middle East Politics: The Military Dimension* (Council on Foreign Relations, 1969). Kerr deals with Arab politics as a cross-national linkage based on certain ethnic-cultural ties. Hurewitz considers the military capabilities present in and bearing upon the Middle East, treating them as national government outputs that are competitive and therefore potentially disruptive.

Kerr's task has been to assess the strength and growth potential of Arab nationalism. As a supranational factor he finds it persistently unsettling. At both the international and the regional level he finds Arab politics chaotic and turbulent, without consistent, common purposes. Unlike most other analytic models of comparative politics, which deal mainly with equilibria and secular change at the national level, Kerr stresses the lack of a secular drift in Arab state political behavior. Despite their turbulence, therefore, the behavioral propensities of the Arab states are static: they go on doing the same things in the same ways.

Hurewitz's chapter on the regional military balance presents a disturbing picture of the growth of Russian power in the Middle East: a sizeable— and historic—increase in the Soviet military presence in the Mediterranean, an openhandedness with military assistance since 1967, and since spring 1969, a willingness to promote limited war at the same time the United States is conspicuously trying to reduce its foreign presence.

On the American side he makes note of some of the stresses between North Atlantic Treaty Organization (NATO) forces and the American Sixth Fleet in the Mediterranean. The NATO alliance has since its beginning in 1950 enabled its members to subordinate their military postures to American policies, and all members (with the conspicuous exception of

Gaullist France) have been willing to do so for the substantial benefits that resulted. It was in the Mediterranean that the British and French aspired unsuccessfully to independent naval status in 1956—a fact that has made the national status of the Sixth Fleet a particular point of criticism. The far more significant national status of the strategic air command, also emulated by the British nuclear forces for a time, did not come under similar criticism until the early sixties, and then with much greater restraint.[1] Hurewitz notes that, in a similar vein, the Soviet Union and the United States have both been inclined to let the interests of their clients and protégés in the Middle East suffer at the expense of their military competition in the region.

These two chapters are not a systematic or rigorous study of the Middle East region, its relative political and economic integration, or its trends as a region, any more than is this volume a comprehensive coverage of the region's politics. The Middle East is so far from being a closed political system as to make partitioning it for rigorous analysis inappropriate where, as is the case here, methodology is not the principal interest. Rather, we are more concerned in this section and in the book as a whole with general dimensions of power and behavior and their changes, and with the prospects of conflict and of reconciliation.

---

[1]These points are developed in greater detail in my *The Cold War Years: American Foreign Policy since 1945* (New York: Harcourt, Brace, 1969), pp. 86–90, 150–154, 198–201.

CHAPTER 1

An Introductory Perspective on the Middle East

Paul Y. Hammond

I. Scope and Focus

This is a book about contemporary political and social factors affecting the stability of the Middle East and North Africa from Morocco to Iran. Its intent has been to go beyond current issues to consider underlying conditions within the region and to assess the political implications of the behavior and attitudes of the nations located or involved in it. Reflecting the exigencies of the Arab-Israeli conflict (a major fact of life in the region and the main focus of great-power interest there), the book considers at some length and from several aspects that regional segment from Egypt to Iraq within which the conflict has mainly taken place.

This volume does not attempt to resolve issues of direct controversy in the Arab-Israeli dispute but, rather, to consider some of the larger correlatives of the dispute in the course of examining broader political and social conditions. In order to do that it examines the Middle East region at three political levels: (1) the internal workings of individual states, (2) interstate relations within the region, and (3) the role of outside powers in the region. In addition it examines the Palestine refugee issue as a special case not confined by these dimensions of analysis. The level of interstate relations within the region has been given the least attention.

The chapters that follow have been written in various settings by different authors with diverse backgrounds—some on American university campuses, some in Santa Monica at The Rand Corporation, some in Europe, some in the Middle East. In each case an expert has been commissioned to analyze a selected segment of the contemporary scene. The objective has been a set of studies that could be helpful to policymakers.

The book includes the Maghrib states of Morocco, Algeria, Tunisia, and the Tripolitanean part of Libya mainly because of their link to Arab nationalism; it includes Iran because of her growing role in this same area. It excludes Lebanon as a separate entity, the Palestine commandos because they seemed less important at the time of its undertaking, and Turkey because her main foreign policy objectives are directed outside the region. Its scope and coverage have been influenced by difficulties encountered in commissioning research on certain aspects of Middle Eastern affairs. These difficulties aside, the coverage and focus of the chapters reflect an approach to the region that, while fairly straightforward, deserves some explanation.

The core Middle East area occupies a commanding position geographically between Asia, Europe, and Africa. The shortest distance from Europe to the Indian Ocean lies across it, and the region contains about two-thirds of the discovered oil reserves in the world. It is a historical theater of rivalry between Russia and Western European powers and, more recently, between Russia and the United States.

Because of its oil and geography, the Middle East is an area of political and economic rivalry (though not as yet military conflict) for those powers. Britain and France have historic ties to the region that have diminished to predominantly commercial interests, mainly in oil. They, together with the rest of Western Europe and Japan, depend heavily upon the Middle East for oil. The Soviet Union now uses little Middle East oil but has established and is expanding its military and naval presence in the region.

The geopolitical value of the Middle East has declined with the development of long-range aircraft and of oil tankers too large to ply the Suez Canal. Persian Gulf and Arabian Peninsular oil have become less vital with the rapid expansion of North African oil production. Nonetheless, Europe's (and Japan's) dependence on Middle East oil, the Soviet-American power rivalry in the region, and the flashpoint potential of the Arab-Israeli conflict have kept the central region salient for outside powers, and even to some extent for the North African Arab states that are outside it—Libya, Tunisia, Algeria, and Morocco.

Two competitive centers of political interest are located at either end of the region, one in the western Mediterranean and the other in the Persian Gulf. In the West, France and the United States pursue (not very successfully) arms and economic policies intended to deny the Soviet Union influence in Arab North Africa. In the East, the British withdrawal from the Persian Gulf is activating that area as a region of political and naval rivalry. Iran has begun to assert its growing national strength there.

Certain common interests work to structure and stabilize the politics of the Middle Eastern region. At the very least, no one wants a major Soviet-American confrontation there, since it would very likely risk war and gain nothing. At the same time, Iran, the Arab states, and Turkey have developed diplomatic postures that take account of the presence of both major powers in the region and some of them—probably all the radical Arab states and certainly Israel—would be embarrassed by the precipitate withdrawal of one great power's influence in favor of the other's. The oil-producing states want the oil companies to keep lifting oil and their markets buying it, and this link induces cooperation among producers and consumers and between them. Beyond these common interests, however, conflicts predominate. The main one originating outside the region is bipolar: the Soviet Union and the United States each prefers to have more influence and to see the other have less. American objectives sometimes conflict with NATO interests and with French or British interests. Within the region Israel and her Arab neighbors quarrel, and the Arab states are at odds over leadership and influence among themselves, and some of them with Iran and the Persian Gulf Arab powers. Kerr (Chap. 2, below) explains pan-Arabism as a supranational political identity that has taken its main impetus from the national identity problems of Syrians, Lebanese, Palestinians, and Iraqis, even though the issues of Arab unity and leadership have revolved around Egypt. He emphasizes in this way Egypt's central role in Arab politics, but does not see Egypt as able to rule any other Arab state, and marks other limits to pan-Arab cohesion precisely where one might expect the opposite, in dealing with Israel. Their common effort to contain and diminish Israel has been badly weakened by a parallel effort to avoid lending juridical support to Israel's existence. Also, the Arab states have never been able to agree for long on how to cope with Israel and have used the Israeli issue against one another. Kerr infers from this record of Arab factionalism that the reduction of Arab tensions following the Six-Day War in 1967 was a short-run aftermath of that war.

II. Summary of Findings

Elements of Conflict

Arab Politics

In other respects, however, the war effected deeper changes. It caused a shift in Arab priorities, from Israel's destruction to Israel's containment—a shift that must have been a severe disappointment to the Palestinians. The Palestinian resistance movement emerged much strengthened out of the humiliations and disappointments wrought by the war, and its strength has, in turn, affected the behavior of the Arab states. By this account, then, Arab politics have helped to secure the legitimacy that such states as Iraq, Syria, and Jordan now have; they have helped to provide Egypt with an instrument of regional influence; and they have proved to be an impetus for political radicalization in the Middle East which (even if often overestimated) remains, or has become, a factor to be reckoned with in the region. The achievement of the first two of these aims has been limited by the pursuit of individual national interests in conflict with one another. The Arab commando movement is less constrained by the divergent national purposes of the Arab states.

The Military Picture

Hurewitz (Chap. 3, below) shows that Soviet military power in the Middle East has grown from nothing to a major presence. The Soviet Mediterranean squadron is not a match for the American Sixth Fleet in the Mediterranean, but it can reduce or spoil the latter's utility. The Soviet squadron also makes the reopening of the Suez Canal attractive to the U.S.S.R. An open canal would permit them, with little additional expenditure on their Mediterranean naval force, to establish a naval presence in the Persian Gulf and the Indian Ocean.

Hurewitz acknowledges that the Soviet Union has suffered discouragements as well as successes in the region, and that her clients must face certain disincentives in acquiring arms from Moscow: mainly Russian influence within their governments and base-use privileges for Soviet naval and air forces. Despite massive Soviet arms deliveries, the Arab states have not gained military superiority over Israel—not yet, at least. He also notes that the United States encounters serious disincentives to be present and strong in the Middle East. For one thing, the Sixth Fleet is a source of friction with NATO allies. They participate reluctantly in exercises with it in the Mediterranean because "such exercises underscore their inadequacy," and they resent the fleet's independence of the NATO Mediterranean Command. Hurewitz sees as a further constraint on American action in the Middle East, and a major one, the "protracted and preoccupying war in Vietnam." He claims that it led to a wasting of American connections with the Arab states from 1967 to 1969 as the Johnson Administration attempted to win popular support for its Vietnam policy at the expense of a balanced political posture in the Middle East.

Hurewitz sees military logic as dictating that Israel hold the occupied areas but political logic as posing serious problems: the loss of cultural homogeneity, of egalitarianism, and perhaps even of democracy, of keeping irredentism alive in neighboring Arab states, and of multiplying opportunities for guerrilla warfare.

Pending a détente, he concludes, the United States must keep its regional military superiority, while the Soviet objective will be to whittle it down. If the Russians do that and keep Arabs dependent upon them, they will achieve major Soviet objectives. Soviet aid need not move the balance toward the Arabs. Moscow can also gain by heating up the Arab-Israeli dispute, Hurewitz observes, because heating it up weakens U.S. policy, which in the Nixon Administration has returned to the pre-1968 position of "counterpolarization."

Russia has three choices, according to Hurewitz. It can promote peace, limited war, or full-scale war. Since the spring of 1969 it has been promoting limited war. It need run no graver risks as long as it continues to be as successful as it has been. Hence, the Soviets will try to stabilize the limited war and prevent its escalation.

These regional conditions do not provide a reassuring picture of Middle Eastern politics, nor do politics at the national level of the states indigenous to the region and those most directly involved in the Arab-Israeli conflict.

The Participants

Israel

The behavior of no single state in the Middle East is more important than Israel's. Egypt's behavior would be a match in importance if her behavior were a key to Arab behavior, but that may no longer be the case. Soviet behavior would rank ahead of Israel's if Moscow controlled Egypt, Syria, Jordan, and Lebanon; but it does not. If Israel simply dances on Washington's leadstrings, then American behavior is crucial, but Washington's influence on Tel Aviv hardly amounts to control.

Israel's behavior deserves attention in its own right. No other state in contemporary times survives and prospers in such a hostile neighborhood. In Friedlander's view (Chap. 4, below) the government of Israel would agree with her Arab enemies that her existence has been the main cause of their enmity. Beyond that undisputed reason, however, what effect has Israel's behavior had on the hostility of her neighbors? Do her actions provoke or diminish Arab hostility? How stable is her regime under the heavier security pressures at the end of the 1960s? What effect do these pressures have on the quality of Israeli public life?

Safran (Chap. 5, below) finds from his interpretation of the Israeli system a considerable reserve capacity to endure stress. Israel's is a multiparty political system that forms governments through complex partisan coalitions. The Israeli government, under stress, has managed to avoid or suspend partisan discussions and contests on the basic options and issues raised by the war. Because the national political coalition is built on compromises, however, Israel's government has been unable to take initiatives to respond effectively to challenges and opportunities from the outside, except with military acts.

Pressure will not destroy the coalition government in Israel, and in any case the infra-structure of Israeli politics is stable, Safran argues. The kind of crisis he foresees that would force an election would also oblige the political system to answer major foreign policy questions, and answering them would give the new political leadership a mandate to decide and act.

The breakdown of the present coalition, therefore, would mean new political strength.

One might infer from Safran's interpretation that it is easier for the Israeli political system to support militant than conciliatory foreign policy. But his interpretation does not support a view of either unstable or volatile Israeli behavior. Rather, he finds the major drawback to be rigidity in diplomacy.

United Arab Republic

Nasser was a standard-setter for the entire third world in his dealings with the great powers. The U.A.R.'s "positive neutralism" has doubtless been venturesome and often successful. Its policy toward Israel has also been at times venturesome—but scarcely as successful. Sometimes Nasser's personal involvement with the U.A.R.'s diplomacy led his country's foreign rivals to believe that *he* was their problem and hence, that removing him would solve it. One objective of Israel's deep air incursions into Egypt in 1969 and 1970 was to topple Nasser through military humiliations; the coordinated Anglo-French attack on Egypt in 1956 had a similar objective. How much difference Nasser's political demise would have made in the U.A.R.'s foreign policy behavior we will never know. What difference his death makes is another matter.

Kerr (Chap. 6, below) considers that Nasser's positive neutralism and assertive Arab and third-world leadership was a consequence of his regime's insecure legitimacy. The regime needed the strength that external prestige and accomplishments gave it. He also sees Nasser's foreign policy as rooted in long-standing expectations about Egypt's role in the Middle East, in her geographic centrality and in her human resources, in her revolutionary regime's dependence upon the Egyptian army, and in persistent foreign exchange deficits. The Egyptian army continues to be a vital support for the regime. To keep the army content requires Soviet arms, the possession of which itself has had an effect on the U.A.R.'s foreign policy, particularly in dealing with Israel and, during most of the past decade, Yemen. Further, Soviet and American economic aid until 1969 enabled Cairo to meet its foreign exchange problems, since it was unable or unwilling to do so in any other way. In effect discounting appearances since 1967, Kerr concludes that the Nasser regime really hoped to maintain the superpowers' competitive interest in the U.A.R. However, if the U.A.R.'s oil production were to generate revenues large enough to solve her foreign exchange problems, the government might no longer consider itself dependent upon outside economic aid, although it would probably still depend upon great-power support for military armaments aid and for coping with her foreign debt repayment problems.

Syria, Jordan, and Iraq

Are the Fertile Crescent states too preoccupied with their own problems to be seriously intent upon Israel's liquidation? Obsessed, perhaps, but not preoccupied. Vatikiotis (Chap. 7, below), focusing in great detail on Syria, but examining also the political factionalism in Iraq and Jordan, demonstrates that in all three states all regimes are necessarily concerned mainly with the internal political game, which is itself a variant of traditional politics that includes ethnic and ideological factionalism. That being the case, the external behavior of these states can be taken as the expedient pursuit of limited objectives — objectives limited in that they can be easily overridden by other considerations.

The Refugee Issue

Could the Palestinian refugees be repatriated at reasonable risks to Israeli security and reasonable costs to the Israeli economy? Could they, or some of them be resettled in the Arab states where they now live or elsewhere? Peretz (Chap. 8, below), by tracing the refugee issue historically, demonstrates the reality of its political dimensions, whatever the merits of the moral issues involved or the weight of economic constraints. He rejects the view that resolving the Arab-Israeli conflict would permit a settlement of the refugee issue, or that settling the issue would resolve the conflict. He holds that, short of a peace settlement, each power located or involved in the Middle East could take steps that would ameliorate the refugee problem.

A majority of Barakat and Dodd's Arab refugee respondents (Chap. 9, below) expressed a desire to return to their home communities. These investigators considered the question of resettlement too sensitive to include in their survey, yet concluded that their respondents' desire to return home precluded their willingness to resettle elsewhere. (Peretz holds a contrary view about the potential acceptance of resettlement.) The Arab respondents were pessimistic about the prospects of their being permitted to return to their homes or that there would be a political solution to the Palestine problem. Again, the non-economic factors seem to predominate, and militate against substituting resettlement for repatriation. While this study is not generally encouraging about a solution, it indicates some possibilities for amelioration—in marking limits to the expectations and the ethnic antagonism of the refugees for Jews and depicting some of the social dynamics which have fed and limited both expectations and antagonisms.

The Regional Bystanders

The North African Arab states—Morocco, Tunisia, and Algeria—have generally remained aloof from the Arab-Israeli conflict, and are unlikely to become more involved in it, according to Gallagher (Chap. 11, below). These Maghrib states have normally been passive absorbers of both Middle East and Western European culture. France, having liquidated her status as colonial ruler, is now developing her economic and cultural ties with the Maghrib again, doubtless with the oil potential in the region helping to assuage feelings on both sides. Politically, Morocco and Tunisia have tried to offset French influence, Tunisia by turning to the United States, Morocco by cultivating both Moscow and Washington. Algeria, with a closer tie to France, has balanced French influence with ties to the radical Arab states of the Middle East and, more importantly, to the Soviet Union. However, as the creator of the myth of Arab victory in revolution, the Algerian government was particularly galled by the defeat of Arab arms in 1967.

The magnitude of the public reactions to the Arab defeat, even though they quickly subsided, took the government of Tunisia, and to some extent that of Morocco, by surprise. The Algerian regime simply turned the public reaction into regime support by assuming a militant—and disgusted —posture. The reactions in all three states demonstrated an ambivalent and volatile but not a particularly dangerous feeling among their publics toward the Middle East Arab regimes.

Since the war a modest but noticeable support for the Arab commando movement has developed in the Maghrib that evidently reflects the same outlook. Unless the Arab-Israeli conflict escalates further, or at least in some way achieves and sustains considerably greater visibility than it had during 1969 and the first half of 1970, however, the Maghrib states are unlikely to become more involved in the Middle East. Even if the Arab commando organizations were to assume control of an Arab state such as Jordan, they are unlikely to provide the success with arms that would forestall Maghribi disillusionment and disinterest.

Iran, at the other end of the region, has now achieved a high level of domestic tranquility, impressive successes in domestic economic reform under a traditional government, and some prospect for a stable succession. At the same time, Iran has moved from a close identity with the United States back to a more traditional role of buffer state. Professor Binder (Chap. 10, below), taking note of internal political tensions in Iran that are mainly concentrated in a politically frustrated middle class, and of Iran's growing capability as a government and an economy, anticipates an increasing regional power role asserted by the Shah not only to take the place of British military power in the Persian Gulf after its scheduled withdrawal in 1971, but also to satisfy middle-class aspirations.

The Extraregional Powers

Outside powers have usually considered their position in the Middle East secondary to their interests in Europe or the Far East. This fact explains the absence of a major power conflict there so far. Calvocoressi (Chap. 12, below) considers British pro-Zionist policy, as it was established during World War I, to be evidence of the Middle East's secondary position in British priorities at the time and throughout the period of declining British power in the Middle East after World War II. Being secondary, Britain's Middle East interests have also been limited. Her most persistent objective has been to deny other powers an equal role in the area. Faced with reducing her role in the Middle East, Britain accepted American power as a replacement, but continues to want to deny Soviet power dominance in the region.

The Western European Powers

Perhaps because of West Germany's interests in Libyan oil, Rondot (Chap. 13, below) expects relations between the Federal Republic of Germany (F.R.G.) and the Arab states to improve in the future. In the past 20 years, however, Bonn's interest in the Arab states has plainly taken second place to her diplomatic competition with the German Democratic Republic (G.D.R.) and her special relationship with Israel.

France has come to play a much more active role in the Middle East than any other Western European state. Her participation in the attack against Egypt in 1956 severed her relations with the Arab states and until 1962, when Algeria achieved her independence, France's Arab policy was paralyzed by her Algerian war. Once that conflict was resolved de Gaulle moved France into a neutral position in the region: on the one hand, fostering better relations with the Arab states and, on the other, developing Israel into a major customer of France's arms industry and nurturing Israel's nuclear power facilities (and hence her candidacy as a nuclear military power). De Gaulle's aggressive diplomacy maximized the effect of France's limited power in the Middle East—without, however, raising France to a major-power position there. Much as Britain became an advocate of summit diplomacy in the 1950s in pursuit of a general East-West détente, France became an advocate of four-power negotiations in the mid-1960s to protect her own neutrality in the region. But increasingly she became more severe with Israel and more forthcoming with the Arab states. Israel's pre-emptive action in the Six-Day War ignored French diplomatic warnings, and precipitated a French arms embargo, demonstrating that France was unable to play a role commensurate with her aspirations in the eastern Mediterranean. Since then she has concentrated her diplomacy and trade mainly on the North African states not directly involved in the conflict with Israel.

The arms embargo against Israel defied French public opinion when it was highly pro-Israel, but it did not demonstrate the independence of France's foreign policy from French oil interests. Increasingly, the two have coincided.

De Gaulle left France a strong national political executive office, the French Presidency, that can operate with much more independence of public moods than was possible under the Fourth Republic. But it is likely that present and future governments of the Fifth Republic will be less independent of short-run domestic political trends than was de Gaulle. None of the Western European states can be expected to play an important role in the near future in stabilizing the Middle East because of constraints, visible in the case of France, that are imposed upon them by their oil needs and investments and their fluctuating public moods. But these states, or at least France, should be able to play significant secondary roles as stabilizers, providing they work within the reach of their power. France failed in her undertaking in the early 1960s to be even-handed about the Arab-Israeli conflict, and her arms embargo after the Six-Day War helped to polarize the Middle East in the late 1960s by leaving the Israeli government suddenly dependent on the United States for arms. By 1970 France had assumed a role more commensurate with her power, one in which she played a conflict-moderating role in the region as an alternative to the Soviet Union as a source of arms for Libya and the Maghrib states; and through her commercial ties with these states, as a rival to Soviet and American influence there.

The United States and the Soviet Union

Characterizations of the American role in the Middle East vary from sympathetic descriptions of the United States as an even-handed balancer, to critical descriptions of the United States as puzzlingly ambivalent in its support of Israel, or — still more critical — as supportive of Israel as an outpost of colonialism and imperialism. Critics also have charged that American policy in the Middle East is simply a sideshow of the cold war, and that in the process of promoting its opposition to the Soviet Union the United States has encouraged the polarization of Middle Eastern political forces.

Quandt (Chap. 14, below) finds the U.S. government predisposed, because of its own pragmatism, to favor moderate, practical regimes, including the traditional Arab states, and to be put off by radical regimes, including the radical Arab states. By his account, the polarization of the Middle East is not wholly a product of the cold war. He also finds American popular support for Israel (which is mainly but not entirely ethnically related) conspicuous but not overwhelming—an influence that runs counter to the relatively low-key lobbying efforts of the oil companies. Oil and ethnics, that is to say, are more in opposition to each other than radical Arab accusations of Israel as "the outpost of imperialism" would seem to mean.

It has been common to perceive Soviet behavior in the Middle East as following a grand design of expansion in that region. Horelick (Chap. 15, below) provides a contrary interpretation of Russian behavior: that it has been improvised. In any case, the Soviet role has grown. Becker (also Chap. 15, below), in contemplating future Soviet alternatives in the Middle East, observes that for the Soviet Union to play a minor future role in the region some intervening discontinuity in regional conditions or in Soviet behavior would have to occur—something that might be induced, for example, by a major East European or Chinese challenge, or just possibly a major Soviet domestic disruption.

Becker identifies as major dependent variables of the Soviet future in the Middle East two in particular, risk and control. He speculates about risk as a function of U.S. behavior and of the action of Soviet clients. The Soviet Union's propensity to control its clients he considers to be a function of perceived risks and commitments. Actions of her Arab state clients that appear to cause danger for the Soviet Union induce the Soviets to increase their control over these clients. However, a high degree of Soviet control is not likely in the Middle East, Becker reasons, and Soviet expansion is therefore inhibited by the risks associated with presence and commitment without control. This difficulty Russia shares with the United States. Hence, superpower restraint in the Middle East depends in part upon the willingness of each power to permit indigenous forces to control events and constrain its rival.

III. Potential Change Agents and Their Impact

The preceding paragraphs indicate that the Middle East is a power arena which, at least for the present, no one power can entirely dominate. It follows that, to be prudent, each power, regardless of its size, must adapt its behavior to the expected behavior of the other powers active in the arena. By stating the matter in these terms our analysis depicts system interactions and interrelationships as dependent for stability upon successful estimations of the behavior of other parties. In the remainder of this chapter we will consider selected major factors in the region to see whether, despite the interconnection mentioned above, they are or might be independent and hence capable of being political control points in the region.

Israel's Activism

Israel's diplomacy has been by no means as successful as were her major pre-emptive military operations in 1956 and 1967. The success in 1967 in redrawing Israeli boundaries to conform with perceived security needs was phenomenal, yet external security problems have remained and grown. Internal security problems have grown as well, mainly because of the increased numbers of Arabs and territories under Israeli control—by 1971 an estimated 1.25 million[1] as compared with 2.5 million Israeli citizens. The Israeli government should be able to cope with the increased security problem; yet handling it cannot fail to affect the character of Israel's public life. What changes should we expect? Will they affect Israel's behavior on the international scene? In particular, should we expect Israel to be increasingly belligerent or more conciliatory? Is Israel locked into a tragic pursuit of security?

Israel's diplomatic, economic, and military security posture in 1970 are not what she set out to make them in the mid-1960s, before or during the Six-Day War. She now occupies territories conquered from Egypt, Jordan, and Syria that were taken to solve immediate military security problems and to serve in the short- or mid-term as bargaining assets with the Arabs. Israel is now incorporating some of these territories by means of economic integration and a creeping colonization, with the result that the political feasibility of giving them up diminishes steadily.[2] The prospect that Israel will become what she did not set out to be, an expansive power, or even an imperial state with a sizeable minority of Arabs, is as a consequence not inconsiderable.

If ever a modern state has been subjected to conditions that could produce an imperial ethos, it is Israel. She is surrounded by hostile states that have claimed they want her elimination; her population is a small fraction of her enemies', and her people have had a historical experience of extraordinary if not unique repression that serves to justify considerable internal discipline. In addition, her defense budget is now more than 25 percent of her gross national product (GNP); she conducts an expensive limited war with her neighbors that amounts to a high relative level of military operations. By all accounts, Israel has maintained a strong civil authority; the wonder is that she has not only avoided becoming a garrison state, but has even avoided the serious raising of the question.

One need not look far to find substantial explanations for Israel's

---

[1]Don Peretz, "Israeli Diversity: The Problems of Internal Oppositions" (University of Southern California, 1970), mimeo., p. 25.

[2]Ann Mosely Lesch, *Israel's Occupation of the West Bank: The First Two Years* (RM-6296-ARPA, The Rand Corporation, in press).

resistance to the garrison-state pressures within which she lives. The extraordinary collection of political and technical talent in Israel, the strong commitment to modern democratic values and the high incentive to keep her internal political situation attractive to private and public sources of foreign capital and of diplomatic and military support are some of the most conspicuous ones. Israel has been, moreover, a highly innovative democratic regime, and may be able to continue to be. On the other hand, democratic institutions are not immune to erosion from the perceived imperatives of national security. The behavior of the United States government in denying constitutional rights to the Japanese-American minority on the Pacific Coast during World War II invites comparison.

Israel has been considered *sui generis* in so many respects that one is inclined to expect and hope her to be in this one. The evidence to the contrary, however, cannot be dismissed. There is the propensity of the Israeli government to take military actions in pursuit of short-range security interests without facing their wider political consequences beforehand. For example, the military operations of the Six-Day War were evidently planned in elaborate (if contingent) detail beforehand. But only after these operations had been carried out, the war was over, and the Arab states had failed to accept Israeli conditions for settlement were the implications of living with the territorial status that resulted from these operations faced—and then only piecemeal. Evidently Israel made her war plans with no more regard for political objectives than American military planners displayed during World War II.

Since the war, Israelis have been settled in some of the occupied territories while their government's position remains that most territories are available for bargaining with the Arab states. Retaliation and collective responsibility have been established as principles for dealing with Arabs within the jurisdiction of Israel. Expansion, moreover, has not reduced the immediate need for military violence, but increased it. Defense expenditures have risen, although according to one estimate (Safran's, Chap. 5, below) they will decline within the next two or three years.

To some extent Israel's achievements are her own weakness. Unquestionably in Washington, Paris, and Moscow the efficiency of the Israeli military establishment leads governments to weigh Israeli weapons much more heavily in the balancing scale than Egyptian or Syrian weapons. Militarily, Israel operates like a finely tuned watch, and suffers the instabilities inherent in fine-tuning: Her very high level of performance can more easily slip than the less remarkable levels of performance of her Arab opponents. For example, the effort required to keep law and order in the conquered territories could erode democratic values, producing a shift in Israel's political climate to the right. In that case, probably those segments of Israel's professional and learned élites who were particularly sensitive to the political climate would expatriate, unless the swing to the right was offset by a crisis atmosphere that would increase internal cohesion. Either way, the result might then be a state in which the major political issues would not be aired but would be handled inconspicuously as technical or administrative matters, or at least matters for discreet compromises among politicians. Political leadership might then pass into the hands of the technically competent and politically insensitive. Such a regime would not be particularly attractive in the West, and its Western support would gradually waste away. Israel's survival with the degree of autonomy and outside support that she now has, that is to say, depends upon her being very competent and politically very attractive. Anything less exposes some of her vulnerabilities. The mood evident in the United States since the late 1960s of withdrawal and retrenchment from an extended international position may even sharpen the dilemmas of Israel's internal politics and external security. American proponents of pullback in Southeast Asia have not been conspicuous advocates for pulling back in the Middle East; and in fact have sometimes specifically proposed support for Israel in order to stop Russian expansion in the Middle East,[3] or because of Israel's self-reliance and other virtues, or both. To forestall the erosion of American support, Israel must remain politically attractive enough to induce Americans to make it an exception.

Addressing the question of political decay, Safran argues that a garrison state would not come about through the party system, as it did in Italy in the 1920s and Germany in the 1930s. Indeed, he concludes that heavier pressure brought upon the Israeli political apparatus by a long-term settlement proposal would force the unresolved issues of security and diplomacy into the open political arena where they would be resolved in an election, with the result that the government then formed would have more freedom to maneuver than its predecessors have had.

One can imagine scenarios that would break the internal deadlock of Israel's politics to her advantage. But other contingencies must also be considered. In the spring of 1970, next to the Prime Minister the most conspicuous figure in the Israeli cabinet was Moshe Dayan, whose chief constituency, it may not be unreasonable to say, is the armed forces. Safran's argument offers little reassurance against a possible deterioration of democratic values through persistent bureaucratic aggrandizement, through the military establishment's influence on all or many parties in the coalition because of its claim to public loyalty, trust, and respect.

Possibly the most encouraging aspect of these unpleasant prospects is

[3]See, for example, George W. Ball "Suez is the Front to Watch," *New York Times Magazine* (June 28, 1970), pp. 10-11+.

that they are most likely to occur only if the Arab-Israeli conflict remains intense but not acute—if the Soviet Union and the United States are willing and the disputants are willing to live under sustained tension in the Middle East. So long as that has been the case—at least as long as Israel's diplomacy and national security policy have been immobilized by its coalition government—her opportunity to be a change agent has resulted mainly from taking military initiatives. The Soviet Union's direct military intervention in the Suez front in 1970 severely limited Israel's potential for military initiative, at least temporarily. It remains to be seen what effect the Soviet involvement will have in the longer term.

Egyptian Leadership, Arab Nationalism, and Arab Unity

Before the Soviet intervention, one reputed objective of Israeli military operations, which included deep aerial penetrations into Egypt, was to topple the Nasser government. The diplomacy that followed upon the Soviet intervention cast Nasser as the only Arab nationalist with sufficient political stature to lead Israel's enemies into negotiations. Nasser's (and Egypt's) leadership of Arab nationalism in the region has been a persistent agent of change that invites our attention.

Egypt's administrative chaos should not be mistaken for significant political vulnerability. As governments in less developed countries go, Egypt's under Nasser proved adaptable. If its political response to the military disaster of the Six-Day War is any indication, only formidable and incessant military defeats will break it. Shattering it by the kind of blows that the British and French attempted in 1956, and that Israel struck then and again in 1967, or by the more limited and incessant blows of Israeli air power and artillery since 1967, is not likely. Furthermore, were the Egyptian government to break under external pressures, any likely successor would be at least as militant though perhaps a less effective opponent of its predecessor's destroyers. Israel is unlikely to obtain a more amenable opponent than was Nasser, although it might get a less ingenious one.

Nasser was not toppled by Iraeli military blows; but did he become a servant of Moscow? The U.A.R. is highly dependent on the Soviet Union for arms supplies and, since the spring of 1970, for the effectiveness of its air defense operations. Doubtless this dependence means less freedom of choice for Egypt in military operations. The Soviet involvement also means an increased risk for the Russians that Egypt will draw them into a military campaign that they do not want to occur and especially do not want to be a part of. Such Soviet involvement is not easy to square with the general reluctance of the Russians to become involved where they cannot wholly control and with Moscow's perception of the Nasser regime as opportunistic and non-Communist, unless these internal constraints are weak or unless Moscow is confident that it can control the risks in the Middle East. But the Egyptian government has its own reasons for avoiding utter dependence upon Moscow and its efforts to avoid such dependence can be expected to make it difficult and costly for the Soviet Union to increase its control over Cairo. More than likely, Egypt will remain an important and to some extent an independent actor in the Middle East in the future, as it has in the past, and that fact may be the most important constraint on the Soviet behavior in the Middle East.

The limits of Egypt's own capabilities as a change agent in the Middle East have probably already been marked by her own efforts—to use Arab nationalism as an instrument of her own leadership assertions, to attempt political union with Syria and Iraq, to play one great power against another. But the instrument may be changing, and with it Egypt's potential, or at least the potential of pan-Arabism, as an agent of change.

The Arab commando movements by the spring of 1970 had had an important impact on the Fertile Crescent states. Jordan was the most severely affected by the expanded strength of the Arab commandos, for Hussein had been unable to control their Jordanian-based attacks against Israel, the Israeli border areas becoming a permanent battleground. The Hussein government has had to survive, particularly since 1967, in the midst of several grave uncertainties about its internal political base, and the way in which to balance its position among the Arab states with its support from the United States and Great Britain. The new strength of the Arab commandos has added to these uncertainties, narrowing the range of choice for Hussein. Evidently he is unable to close his borders (or even Amman) to them. If he cannot, then he is unable to settle with Israel unless his authority can be reinforced from outside Jordan.

Of course, if the commando groups themselves were to continue to grow in strength and influence, they would eventually induce a major social and political revolution in Jordan. While that possibility should not be ruled out, it is assumed here to be low because the movement's main appeal is —or appears to be—as a militant minority that does not govern.

In Syria the 1966 Ba'athist coup radicalized the government and the commandos have made little additional difference. It is in Lebanon that they have made the most noticeable difference. Lebanon has been a stable regime delicately balanced between its Muslim and Christian populations, the most moderate of eastern Arab regimes in its relations with Israel. The commando movement has driven Lebanon up against some formidable dilemmas: between, on the one hand, permitting commando operations against Israel and incurring Israeli retaliations that humiliate the Lebanese regime, drive Lebanese refugees out of the border area, and exacerbate the Christian-Muslim conflict implicit in the Lebanese body politic; and on the other, suppressing the commandos, incurring the Muslim majority's wrath, and exposing Lebanon to pressures from the radical Arab regimes. As described, it would be inappropriate to call Lebanon itself a change agent in the Middle East, but hardly to deny that title to the Arab commandos.

What of Arab nationalism as a potential agent of change? The answer becomes much clearer if we do not equate Arab nationalism with a unified group of states, but allow for it to appear in different configurations of concerted effort. One might expect the political rivalries within the Arab bloc—the differences between western and eastern Arab states, between traditional and radical governments, and within most or all Arab regimes between radicals and conservatives—to moderate the will for conflict with Israel by limiting the capacity to pursue it. To some extent that may be true. It is probably also the case that some Arab radicals, despairing of nationalist unity under ordinary conditions, are drawn to militant action as itself the unifier. (Surely that is a precept the Arab commandos have demonstrated.) To go one step further, if Egypt (with Soviet help) were to go it alone against Israel in the Sinai, with some measurable success, doubtless her pre-eminence in the Arab world would be re-established. A cohesive Arab alliance might escalate the conflict with Israel simply because of its capacity to act; but more likely the process of inducing cohesion would moderate the whole enterprise. By the same token, a disintegrating Arab unity could mean a reduced challenge to Israel, not only because of the reduced effectiveness of the common effort, but because it could mean that the Arab states were turning inward. Disintegrating unity might also induce an Arab state to seize the initiative, and the leadership of Arab nationalism, as just noted.

Given these possibilities, can we tell whether the Maghrib states will dissociate themselves from the eastern Arab and increasingly look northward to Europe? At best, they are ambivalent about Israel. Vatikiotis depicts the Fertile Crescent states as mainly driven in their internal politics by parochial, inward-looking perspectives and political games. (An interesting implication of this picture is that Syria's and Iraq's hostility to Israel is not—perhaps more accurately, was not at first—a fundamental one.) Kerr depicts Egypt as more beset by her internal problems than her anxieties about Israel until Israel occupied the Sinai. Syria and Egypt can scarcely neglect their lost territories. They cannot afford to turn inward. Jordan plainly cannot. The constant desperation of Hussein's government means that it cannot avoid a preoccupation with either its external or internal political situation. Iraq's Ba'athists have staked their legitimacy too much on radical Arab nationalism to turn inward.

Even if we assume that the Arab commando organizations will not grow large and powerful enough to rule anywhere but in Jordan, the movement will certainly contribute to important changes in the political dimensions of the Arab world. The main changes are the challenge to the U.A.R.'s leadership, changes in the cohesion of the Arab bloc that are related to that challenge, and the possibility of Jordan's looking to Moscow rather than Washington for arms and assistance.

Arab nationalists, as long as Nasser and Egypt have led Arab nationalism, have had to promote Egyptian interests along with their own objectives. But that situation has changed. The Ba'athist regimes in Iraq and Syria, particularly considering their anti-Israeli militancy, are possible competitors to Nasser's government as leader of radical Arabs. Furthermore, the defeat of Egyptian arms in 1967 set back Egypt's reputation in the Arab world. While it has partially recovered, Egypt's heavy dependence upon Soviet arms and economic assistance has limited the recovery. Tripower negotiations in 1963 between Egypt, Syria, and Iraq failed to produce an agreement on unity because of the Nasser regime's unwillingness to give up its exclusive claim to defining the terms of Arab unity. It may be a long time before Egypt has the special status in the Arab world to stand on that issue again.

The Arab commando movement has also become an important radical force quite distinct from Nasserism. Until the Six-Day War the Arab commando groups, the Fedayeen—principally the Palestine Liberation Organization (PLO), *al-Fatah,* and the Popular Front for the Liberation of Palestine (PFLP) — had been tolerated and to some extent encouraged by the radical Arab states. The groups represented Palestinian operations that could not be kept under the control of the states from which they operated—primarily Syria, Jordan, and the U.A.R.—without embarrassment to these states for their failure to pursue the interests of the Palestinian refugees more energetically. Since the war, the number of Fedayeen has grown dramatically, fed by the radicalizing despair of the defeat, by their successes against Israeli arms, and by the growth of the movement itself, since it gives credence to their claim to be the rallying point for Arab nationalism.

In the short run, and certainly the medium term also, the political potential of the Fedayeen movement is in (1) the radicalizing pressure they are able to bring against Arab regimes, (2) the possibility that they may be able to overturn the weaker Arab regimes, (3) their capacity to induce Israeli retaliation against the population and territory of Arab states contiguous to Israel, and (4) in complicating any negotiation of a settlement with Israel. That is to say, within Arab states they radicalize politics, and between Arab states and Israel they catalyze military violence and confuse the issue of who speaks for the Arabs. How far the Fedayeen groups will be able to go in each of these respects is plainly an important variable in the Middle East political situation.

The Fedayeen groups will probably stop growing in size and influence long before their movement becomes the unifier of the entire Arab nation. Well short of that extreme possibility, however, some important effects can be attributed to their growth and potential growth. By mid-1970 the commandos had thrown into doubt who governs in Jordan and threatened to upset Lebanon's internal political balance. Syria has sponsored its own Fedayeen group (al-Sa'iqâh, "The Thunderbolt"), but launched it at Israel from Jordan and Lebanon. By this means it delayed, but did not avoid, Israeli retaliation. By mid-1970 Israel had attacked military camps near the Syrian capital of Damascus.

The growth potential of the commando movement can be gauged by its potential sources of revenue and manpower, by the likelihood that Arab governments will take effective steps to quell, compete with or otherwise discredit commando operations, and by the growth and survival capabilities of the commando groups themselves.

The commandos are weakened by factional divisions over politics and tactics, and by credibility problems—disparities between claims and performance and, as compared with Israel (though not the Arab regimes), their propensity to be overly manipulative with their propaganda. Their interests are incompatible in the short run with Jordan's and Lebanon's. While less immediately in conflict with other Arab states, the Fedayeen groups are rival claimants for the resources and popular support of these states and are potential catalysts of Israeli violence against them. The Fedayeen are tolerated and to some extent supported by these states, but only within limits. Both radical and moderate Arab states have interests— different interests to be sure—in limiting the growth potential of the commandos. If in pursuing their goals, moreover, the Fedayeen destroy the regime in Jordan and force the disintegration of the regime in Lebanon, moderate Arab governments would appreciably increase their opposition to the Fedayeen. In short, the plausible further developments in the commando movement—pitting themselves against regimes that get in their way and increasing their claims on Arab manpower and funds—imply an increasing opposition to them from the Arab regimes.

The commando groups have not as yet pictured themselves as nascent governments, and the logic of their situation does not carry them in that direction.[4] Running a country—even Jordan—would tie them down, commit their resources, and reduce their pan-Arab appeal. It might also dim their mystique.

[4]See interview with Abu Omar, al-Fatah representative, in New York Times, June 20, 1970.

Another limit than can be expected to work against their expansion is the Soviet Union. Even though the Soviets have provided the commandos with some arms, Moscow's enthusiasm is likely to diminish as they grow stronger because of the additional uncertainties they introduce into Soviet political-risk calculations. Soviet spokesmen may make it quite plain to Arab clients that they cannot expect her support if they cannot hold their own internal situation under control.

Finally, what are the prospects that the commando organizations will not impair their own effectiveness with further growth? Michael Hudson has marshaled some indications of fairly strong group motivation and cohesion.[5] The prospect that the commando groups can control their factional infighting, exploit opportunities to attack Israel, acquire resources, and win more Arab supporters will turn heavily on the quality of their leadership, just as the U.A.R.'s influence has depended upon Nasser's qualities as a political leader. The commando leaders have proved resourceful but effective mainly within a fairly narrow range of activities. It is not yet clear that they can handle larger and more complex organizational tasks (as indeed they recognize in avoiding government administrative tasks). The commando organizations now attract a greater variety of Arabs and therefore have available more diverse skills than before 1967. If the old leadership cadres can diversify their skills from among their new members, they should be able to improve their adaptive potential.

In sum, the stronger the commando groups grow the more resistance they are likely to encounter to their further growth, although there seem to be no distinct upper bounds to their growth. As long as they do not lose in a major showdown with Arab governments, however, they will probably remain catalysts of Arab-Israeli violence, inducing more radically anti-Israeli postures by the weaker Arab regimes. Nasser remained until his death the major figure in the Arab world. The commando organizations and the Ba'athist regimes in Syria and Iraq competed with but not supplant him, making the Arab world more nationalist and less unified.

Besides the pluralization of nationalist leadership, another source of factionalism within the Arab world, more remote but possibly more profound, might be interstate rivalry over oil reserves. Iran has successfully demanded high extraction quotas from the oil companies to increase revenues for her ambitious economic development program. Saudi Arabia, Algeria, and Libya also have started to press for more oil revenues. Conditions necessary if not sufficient to induce serious competition among oil producers may now or soon exist in these and several states within the

[5]Michael Hudson, "Structural and Ideological Development in the Palestinian Guerrilla Movement," Institute of World Affairs, University of Southern California, Los Angeles, California (April, 1970), mimeo.

region: (1) the government's commitment to national economic development, and (2) a significant proportion of public revenues derived from oil. Although Saudi Arabia's commitment to economic development is not as conspicuous as the Iranian Shah's, it is unmistakable; we could expect the Saudi Arabians to join the postulated competition. Algeria and Libya now have national development regimes. Oil production is soaring in Libya. In Algeria it is rising more slowly. But in both countries it has already reached a ratio to total revenues that makes increasing them a conspicuous objective of economic planning. Both countries, like the Shah of Iran, press for revenue increases by promoting their national production (or by dickering over royalties). The U.A.R. probably has the requisite national development regime, and hence, should her oil production grow enough, Cairo might also be competing for oil markets. The same could be said for Iraq and, still more remotely, Syria.

The transfer of oil revenue income from the conservative, oil-rich Arab states to Egypt and Jordan after their defeat in 1967 established a precedent that could serve to raise the pressure for higher oil revenues in general, but also reduce the competition among producers over shares. If they cannot agree on how to distribute revenues or on the production quotas and revenue rates that determine revenues, or cannot do so without inducing substantial stresses among themselves (which is the more likely case), then their competition — whether it is open or kept discreet — will weaken their cohesion.

If prospects develop for dividing the Arab states in any of these ways, one should expect Western European foreign offices to be particularly interested in promoting the split in order to assure Western Europe competitive sources of oil. While many of the oil companies, in addition to the oil-producing Arab states, would want to avoid competing with each other in this way, the stakes for Western Europe are high enough to assure that, if there is any prospect for the postulated competition to develop, the best of Western European diplomatic talent would go into helping it to come about.

Iran as an Active Regional Power

Iran's potential role as an agent of change in the Middle East is linked to the scheduled withdrawal of British power from the Persian Gulf by 1971. Iran's expanding objectives within the region could induce Iraq, at least, and possibly other Arab states to diversify their foreign-relations objectives. By attempting to expand her hegemony in the Gulf, Iran could find herself in increasing conflict with Iraq and the Persian Gulf sheikdoms. An alliance with Israel, more likely tacit than otherwise, would reinforce this conflict. On the other hand, Iranian attempts to moderate and conciliate conflicts and to achieve working relationships with the Persian Gulf sheik-doms, where common interests and hence the motivation to cooperate could be quite substantial, could divide Arab interests. Saudi Arabia, for example, could tolerate such an alliance more easily than could Iraq. If Arab unity diminishes sufficiently, a Saudi Arabian–Iranian alliance could develop against Arab radicalism that would further exacerbate the traditionalist-radical divisions among Arab states.

The U.S.S.R. and the United States

By mid-1970 the Soviet Union had established a naval presence in the Mediterranean that, although not a strong rival to the American Sixth Fleet, had a sizeable spoiling potential for Sixth Fleet capabilities. Soviet land-based air power was also growing in Egypt because Russian pilots and air control technicians had assumed military operations roles in the air defense of the U.A.R. By mid-1970 the credibility of active Soviet military support for Arab arms against Israel as well as the American military position in the Mediterranean had increased substantially above what it had ever been before, raising serious questions about the magnitude of Soviet ambition in the Middle East.

Developments in American foreign policy were moving at the same time in quite a different direction. The public furor over Vietnam had drawn an unprecedented degree of public attention, and therefore linked the efficacy of American power in the Middle East to domestic political responses about Indochina.

Public opinion surveys indicated that public sympathy for Israel jumped significantly during the 1967 war, and although the surveys show a decline since then, presumably the 1967 high indicates a strong propensity to rally round Israel that is scarcely confined to ethnic Jewish voters. The strong disillusionment over foreign commitments induced by the frustrating and tragic experience in Vietnam will probably produce a general reduction of American overseas commitments. Yet a widespread (if élite-centered) public attitude accepts the foreign involvement of the United States as a moral requirement.[6] The turning inward, therefore, is not likely to occur without some strong pangs of conscience.

These pangs have established palliatives. The most conspicuous one in the decade before the United States switched to internationalism in World War II was the concentration on Western Hemisphere obligations, and Latin America as a palliative is not to be ruled out now. But it has serious drawbacks. Probably no palliative offers greater immediate gratification than more backing for Israel. In this light it is significant that in the spring

---

[6]See Alfred O. Hero, *Americans in World Affairs* (Boston: World Peace Foundation, 1959).

of 1970 as serious an advocate of prompt withdrawal from Vietnam as Senator McGovern advocated increased U.S. arms supply to Israel. The outcome would probably be a strengthened American link to Israel and the further polarizing of Middle Eastern politics.

Disentanglement from Vietnam may permit the United States diplomatic gains such as Gaullist France made after liquidating the French entanglement in Vietnam and North Africa. If a conspicuous outcome of an American withdrawal from Vietnam were to be a freeing of resources and capabilities now committed to Vietnam, and if Soviet boldness in the Middle East has been due to that fact, presumably Moscow would become more interested in a Middle East détente. The more likely outcomes, however, are much less attractive: the polarization mentioned above and less credibility to American threats and promises in the Middle East.

The Western European Powers

Western European states most likely will move closer to the Arab side in the Middle East. The economic incentives to do so are enormous. But if they are not overwhelming, one interesting possibility is a posture like that of the United States—visibly sympathetic enough with Israel to inhibit their own political (and to some extent their economic) links with Arab states. In any case, Western Europe's long-term future role in the Middle East, like that of the United States, will have to be congruent with domestic opinion. Reactions to the Six-Day War in Western Europe and the United Kingdom showed what Walter Z. Laqueur has termed "philo-Semitism."[7] The war became a major domestic issue in France and Italy, with government policy running from neutral to pro-Arab while public sympathy ran strongly in favor of Israel. Laqueur claims that even in Warsaw, Budapest, and Prague the pro-Israeli sentiments were strong. Public-opinion surveys mostly bear out these contentions.[8]

The same reaction is unlikely to occur again. But it is probable that public sentiments and economic interests will remain somewhat out of kilter, and possible, therefore, that in the future the Western European powers will fluctuate in their alignment behavior in the Middle East. Given the rise in public sentiment in Europe in favor of Israel after the Six-Day War, and the peripheral interest of these governments in any particular Middle East policies except where access to oil is involved, one might

[7] Walter Z. Laqueur, "Israel, the Arabs, and World Opinion," in the pro-Israeli *Commentary,* Vol. 44, No. 2 (August, 1967) pp. 49-59.

[8] These surveys have been compiled by Hazel Erskine in "The Polls: Western Partisanship in the Middle East," *Public Opinion Quarterly,* XXXIII (Winter, 1969-1970), 627-639.

expect to see Europeans play a destabilizing role in the Middle East that is less sensitive to regional than to domestic conditions.

The Regional Political System

It is much clearer that the Soviet-American rivalry in the Middle East raises the stakes of conflict than that there would be no risk of conflict in its absence. Undisputed, single great-power hegemony would have made the region more stable, but that is no longer a realistic prospect. Neither great power will or must accept the other's hegemony in the region, and few if any states within the region would either. The present division between Soviet and American influence in the region, with its potential for a direct confrontation between the two powers, augments conflicts internal to the region and multiplies their danger; but any great power alignment of comparable clarity is also likely to be volatile and dangerous.

Western Europe's presence is less clearly linked to the region's potential volatility, in part because the United States has been the major challenger of Soviet expansion in the region. In the Middle East, as in Europe itself, French diplomatic mobility—to take the most conspicuous example—depends in part upon American diplomatic immobility.

Dynamic stability depends upon system stabilizers. Where, in this regional system, should we look for stronger stabilizers? Which agents of change—which variables—offer the most promising prospects for improving the region's stability?

In the short run, the United States is more likely than the Soviet Union to induce stability by diversifying its client roster in the Middle East, while both powers are likely to stabilize by limiting their commitments to their clients. Over a somewhat longer term, the Arab state bystanders are likely to improve their capacity to stabilize by granting and withholding support to Israel's neighbors, providing the conflict does not feed the popular basis for their hostility to Israel enough to preclude their holding back. The growing power of Iran will also increase the diversity of the region's power matrix.

None of the states involved, not those located in the Middle East nor those with a political presence there, can permit itself to become preoccupied with the balance of power in the region. All of them have other interests, including formidable domestic imperatives. As long as there are no crises in the region, they are unlikely to pursue their regional goals with anything like unwavering determination. It is more likely that the Soviet Union and the United States will take initiatives in periods of acute danger to themselves than during periods of quiescence in the Middle East. Their clients in the Middle East, recognizing this situation, are likely to use crises to win further commitments from Moscow and Washington. On the other hand, although Israel and her Arab neighbors are more sensitive to the risks involved in less acute conflicts, the fact that they have great power supporters discourages them from accommodation with one another. Crises, then, provide dangers and opportunities, while the prospects of crises provide grounds for not attempting to change the conflicted status quo in the short run.

For changes not associated with crises, one must look to mid- and long-term trends. Oil is providing the region with a very substantial foreign exchange, much of which will be used for economic development; and that, in turn, is likely to cause considerable instability. Yet oil should also diversify interest conflicts in the region and thereby strengthen its power as a stabilizer.

A major condition of stability in the Middle East, as elsewhere, is the behavioral propensities of the national governments that are major actors in the region. The role of national governments in economic development varies conspicuously. Their role in regional political conflict, however, is necessarily major—certainly it is in the Middle East. In the short term, the prospects for significant change in the capabilities of national governments in the Middle East to absorb and control the conflict of the region are not very large; but over the long term they may become a significant dimension in regional stability.

CHAPTER 2

Regional Arab Politics and the Conflict with Israel

Malcolm H. Kerr

I. Inter-Arab Relations

A discussion of inter-Arab politics inevitably begins with the common assumption among the mass of politically conscious Arabs that they constitute a single nation which ought to be united. What makes this idea interesting and important is that it continues to be far removed from any prospect of realization, and yet survives undiminished in the Arabs' minds as a political ideal. It means that every Arab leader needs to bend his words and visible actions toward a nonexistent state of affairs: he must either affirm the existence of a relationship of solidarity and mutual confidence with other Arab governments for whom, in reality, he may feel considerable mistrust, or at least appear to be working toward the establishment of such a relationship when there is no realistic prospect of it. It means that every Arab state's affairs become the legitimate business of every other, that no government's effectiveness in dealing with its own domestic problems can suffice to provide that government with good political credentials, that no government is entirely free (even in the eyes of its own citizens) to follow its own foreign policy based on its own national interest, and that even such limited forms of positive cooperation as do materialize among Arab states are subjected to the accusation that they do not go far enough. All in all, however appealing the vision may be, in practice preoccupation with the idea of unity has become a paralyzing myth in several Arab states, constantly demanding unrealism and inviting frustration. It is an albatross around the necks both of Arab leaders and of those outsiders who seek to develop constructive relations with them.

Ideological Problems

Certainly, in the abstract, the notion that the Arabs should be united, pan-Arabism, is a reasonable and attractive proposition. The standard justifications offered for it by Arab political leaders and intellectuals are eminently straightforward: there is a common language which has served as the vehicle of a very considerable common cultural heritage; a common religion; a long history of shared political community; an unbroken geographical continuity of Arabic-speaking territory from Morocco to the Arabian Peninsula; there have been common experiences of subjection to

European domination in recent generations, and common contemporary concerns for social and economic modernization. All of this, however, could equally well be said of the Latin American Spanish-speaking countries, among whom there is a strong sense of community but very little talk of political unification; and whatever it tells us of the rational plausibility of Arab unity, it tells us little about the emotional force behind the idea.

The idea not only carries emotion, in fact, but more particularly something of the mystique of a sacred symbol or ritual. It connotes devotion, rectitude, honor, and a supernaturally determined destiny. In this respect, it appears to reflect a transfer of some of the psychological elements of religion. Other nationalisms, of course, commonly do the same, but it is just possible, if we are seeking explanations of why Arab nationalism should focus on the elusive goal of unification, that some elements of the Arabs' own particular religious inheritance will offer significant clues.

Historically, Islam is to some extent the particular national religious property of the Arabs, like Hinduism among the Indians or Shinto among the Japanese. If the Arabs are a minority among all Muslims, they are nonetheless the people among whom it first spread, the native speakers of its sacred language, and the inhabitants of its holy places. The theme of social, moral, and political solidarity among believers finds its original example in the virtuous community founded and left behind by the Prophet in the Arab city of Medina; and according to a widely held Arab view, the subsequent corruption of the community was bound up with the progressive alienation of subsequent Muslim empires from their Arab origin and their exposure to the influences of foreign elements: Persians, Turks, Byzantines, and so on.

Furthermore, the modern political emancipation of Arabic-speaking countries, particularly at the eastern end of the Mediterranean, happens to have been accompanied more or less simultaneously by the modern revival, reform, and reinvigoration of the Arabic language and of its prestige as the vehicle of classical culture. In Egypt and the Fertile Crescent states of Syria, Iraq, Jordan, and Lebanon, for example, the language of government since the sixteenth century had been Turkish, and the use of literary Arabic had been largely confined to religious ritual and learning. In the nineteenth and twentieth centuries, simultaneously there was a vast expansion in literacy, a vast expansion of the fields of culture covered by education, a movement of religious reform within educated circles that emphasized the virtues of Islamic classicism, and the political movement of secularism which preached that modern nationhood must be linguistic and cultural in its foundation rather than religious or imperial; that is, that the Arabs were distinct as a natural political community both from the Ottoman Turks and from the Europeans. These simultaneous historical developments and ideological messages naturally gave rise to a certain amount of confusion and contradiction, in which it became equally plausible to be an Arab nationalist in order to escape from the outmoded religious prescriptiveness of the Ottoman Empire, or in order to reassert that prescriptiveness in a new and more vigorous guise now that the Ottoman Empire was failing. But the revival of Arabic, the assertion of Islam's modern social relevance, and the spread of the idea of national self-determination seemed to make for no more than the most superficial separation of religious from political loyalties. No one had shown clearly what it might mean to be an Arab, and what the Arab national heritage might mean, without reference to Islam. The language inevitably dragged religion in its wake, in a way that the Turkish language or the Persian language could not; and with religion came also the idea of the united and virtuous community that the Arabs had once been and ought to be again.

A more mundane, but probably more directly relevant, level of explanation for the appeal of pan-Arabism lies in the absence of local political or communal tradition binding together the domestic society of each Arab state. The present-day states of Syria, Lebanon, Jordan, and Iraq are all lacking in distinctive historical backgrounds as separate entities. For four centuries before World War I, their present area comprised a series of administrative subdivisions of the Ottoman Empire which did not by any means coincide with the present frontiers separating them. Individual cities possessed their own political and social traditions — Damascus, Aleppo, Mosul, Baghdad, Beirut — but not the entities now defined as modern states. Transjordan was an improvisation of the British Colonial Office in 1921, an "empty lot" of desert territory in which the recently established control of the Amir Abdullah of the Hejaz was provisionally recognized. Lebanon was an amalgam of a reasonably cohesive and distinct entity of Christian and Druze mountain-village communities lumped together by the French government in 1920 with the city of Beirut and with Muslim-populated area along the coast and in the interior. The state of Syria is only a rump segment of a much broader area to which the name was commonly applied, and for which independence was claimed by an Arab regime in Damascus for a few months in 1920, until it was evicted by a French army; and for 30 or 40 years afterward, the idea of a "Greater Syria," comprising most or all of the Fertile Crescent area but excluding other Arabic-speaking territories, commanded more enthusiasm among the politically minded intelligentsia than the idea of pan-Arab nationalism. The idea of a Syrian nationalism confined to the post-1920 borders, on the other hand, has never commanded any enthusiasm at all, nor has the idea of Jordanian or Iraqi nationalism, nor Lebanese nationalism except among the Christian and Druze part of the population.

Other portions of the eastern Arab world were more fortunate in having some kind of local identity to cling to; consequently, the mythology of pan-Arabism found less of a void of loyalties to fill in the minds of politically conscious people there. Egypt had its ages-long history of successive civilizations, and its own well-defined geography, to absorb the attentions and sense of identity of its population; to be an Egyptian was to belong, without serious question, to a "real" nation. Something similar could be said, up to a point, of the Arabs of Saudi Arabia. True, until the early 1920s they had been, variously, Hejazis, Nejdis, Hasawis, and so on, but collectively they were too isolated geographically in the Arabian Peninsula from other Arabs to the north and west, too provincial, and in some cases too tribal in social organization to feel the need for wider political attachments than those they already had. Furthermore, the puritanical Wahhabi religious dispensation imposed on them by the Saud family provided a sufficient basis of moral community. Certainly, they saw themselves as "Arabs," indeed as the original Arabs, but they did not need to commune with Syrians or Iraqis or Egyptians to convince themselves of their Arabness, any more than New England Yankees need to associate with immigrant Irishmen or Italians in order to feel American.

Pan-Arabism, then, arose as the reflection of the national identity problem of Syrians, Lebanese, Palestinians, and Iraqis rather than of Egyptians or Arabians, to say nothing of the hopelessly isolated Yemenis. As no local nationalism had grounds on which to develop in the Fertile Crescent states, it was the wider nationalism that attracted loyalty. And because of the close contact between the society of these states and that of Egypt, as well as the considerable political interest that Egyptian governments developed in the Fertile Crescent countries, it was natural in time for a proposition to arise that their Arab national identity bound them and Egyptians together as well.

It might have been plausible for greater attachments to existing state entities to develop, had the internal political process in each of them not been so frequently disrupted by quarrels over forms of government and over the fitness of competing factions to rule. In the 1920s and 1930s this was not so much the ideological question that it came to be afterward with the rise of Socialist, Communist, and other revolutionary doctrines and movements. In Syria and Iraq (as also in Egypt) the dominant issue was, rather, which circle of political notables possessed the personal qualities — or somehow, the access to power — to run the constitutional machinery that had been established under Western tutelage and to deal effectively with the French or British authorities from whom fuller independence was being popularly demanded. In due course the faction emerging on top in each country did so with tarnished credentials. In Iraq the pro-British faction loyal to the monarchy owed its position to the fact that the British army chased their rivals away in 1941; in Egypt both King Farouk and the Wafd Party had compromised fatally with Britain in 1942; in Syria the Nationalist Party regime was charged with hopeless incompetence and corruption and blamed for failure in the Palestine war of 1948. King Abdullah in Transjordan, by contrast, ran an autocratic government without room for factional infighting, but his role in the Palestine war spoiled his good name in Arab nationalist circles, and he was assassinated in 1951 by a Palestinian.

With this kind of background, it was difficult for any local regime in these states to develop a legitimate reputation, and the belief grew that as long as political life was restricted to the provincial level of small states, it would never rise above the uninspiring quality that local bosses could provide. It would, however, perhaps be more to the point to observe that these local regimes had grown up in an era where the only serious political question of interest to the public had been how to secure full independence from foreign rule — the kind of issue that invited rhetoric and philosophizing on the grand scale, and stimulated a utopian and militant political mentality rather than one attuned to the nuts-and-bolts problems of sound administration.

By the 1940s a widespread tendency had developed among politically conscious Arabs in several states to view their political problems primarily in moralistic and ideological terms, so that salvation came to be sought through charismatic revolutionary movements: the Muslim Brotherhood of Hassan al-Banna, the Young Egypt movement of Ahmad Hussein, the Syrian National Social Party of Antun Saadeh, and so on. By the 1950s, the time of the rise of Nasser and of the Ba'ath ("Resurrection") Party centered in Syria, utopian revolutionary politics rejecting the established order of institutions were already common. So were military coups: Iraq had experienced several from 1936 to 1941, and Syria had three in 1949 alone — each one proclaiming an end to corruption and the beginning of the millennium. As army officers came under the influence of utopian ideologies, civilian revolutionaries came to depend on the officers to bring them to power by coup, with the inevitable result, of course, that the civilian role within these movements was diminished. This was clearly the case in Syria in the 1950s and 1960s, in which the Syrian National Social Party, the Nasserite movement, and particularly the Ba'ath Party came under the leadership of obscure military men of the narrowest intellectual horizons. It was also the case in Iraq from 1958 onward, in the factional infighting among Ba'athists, Nasserites, Communists, and other less clearly defined groups.

This pattern of factionalism and military takeover decisively undercut the supposition, which many intellectuals in the Arab world clung to, that the battle lines in inter-Arab politics could be simply drawn between those wanting to give the Arab world a thorough housecleaning and those wanting to maintain an established order of corruption and privilege. It is true that revolution and socialism are real and fundamental issues, which separate Arab governments into two groups between whom only limited arm's-length cooperation is generally possible. However, there is not much prospect that the victory of revolution over conservative oligarchies in all Arab countries would decisively enhance the possibilities of union, for the revolutionary political process has become closely bound up with the opportunism and willfulness of competing military cliques. Furthermore, as I shall argue in the next section (pp. 36-39), the problem of unity cannot be separated from the practical diplomatic interests of diverse Arab states, the most powerful of which — Egypt — possesses distinct national needs and attitudes of her own that do not always accord with those of others.

The Issue of Egyptian Leadership

Since World War II, the vexed issues of Arab unity and Arab leadership have centered around Egypt. Alone among the Arab states, Egypt has consistently conducted herself as a regional "great power," with interests and influence throughout the area and beyond. Other Arab states have tended to be closely involved only with their immediate neighbors. Egypt has pursued alliances or quarrels with states ranging all the way from Morocco to Iran, and with others throughout Africa and Asia. She has a universal "presence" in the Arab world, somewhat like the American presence in Europe or Latin America: people in these countries have grown accustomed to seeing Egyptians on the streets, to reading Egyptian books, to seeing Egyptian movies. As in the case of the United States, what happens in Egypt is of interest to everyone else, but not the reverse: Egyptians tend to view the happenings of other Arab states as somewhat boring and provincial.

Egypt's "great-power" role in the region has been the result of a number of circumstances, both permanent and temporary. Perhaps the strongest single basis for her leadership has been her overwhelming lead in human resources. No one else can begin to match her in numbers of bureaucrats, teachers, businessmen, bankers, military officers, engineers, lawyers, doctors, mechanics, journalists, and so on. There are always surplus Egyptian personnel available for technical jobs to be filled in surrounding countries. For example, thousands of Egyptian teachers at all levels have served in the rest of the Arab world, including every country without exception; Egyptian lawyers have written the civil codes of Syria and Iraq; Egyptian contracting companies have undertaken large-scale public construction projects in Jordan; Egyptian agronomists and irrigation engineers have served in the Sudan. The list could be expanded to great length.

Conversely, every Arab state sends large numbers of visitors, especially university students, to Egypt. Four large state universities—Cairo, Ain Shams, Alexandria, Assiut—with a combined student population of about 140,000 including some 30,000 to 40,000 non-Egyptians, give Egypt an enormous edge in cultural resources and attractions over others.

Furthermore, the Egyptian government for over a century has possessed a more extensive and more fully organized administration than any other state. Although the cumbersomeness of the bureaucracy has for some time been a serious problem in Egypt, its members are by no means incompetent, and the government is in a position to undertake a wide variety of functions that in other states are performed in skimpy fashion, if at all. Thus, during the 1958-1961 union with Syria and during the 1962-1967 intervention in Yemen, the Egyptian government was in a position to dispatch not only military forces but also officials and technicians of all sorts to fill the administrative vacuum in each of those two states. Not that such actions proved to be resounding political successes—indeed, the omnipresence of Egyptians proved widely irritating to Syrians and Yemenis—but they demonstrated Cairo's ability to assert herself on her own initiative well outside Egypt's borders. Likewise, the formidable Egyptian intelligence apparatus, which has become so familiar to the leaders of other Arab states, rests on the same combination of the availability of technically competent personnel and organizational capacity.

The fact that Egypt's total population of over 30 million is three times as large as that of each of the next most populous Arab states (Morocco, Algeria, Sudan) is not crucially important, for the great bulk of Egypt's populace, like that of the others, lives in wretched circumstances and contributes nothing to the power of the regime. The important consideration is the availability of educated personnel, regardless of their proportionality, and an organizational framework within which to mobilize them. An annual average of 25,000 persons received university degrees in recent years, and a thousand Egyptians returned home each year with European, Soviet, and American postgraduate degrees. The vast majority of these graduates find their way into state or state-controlled employment and are bound to constitute an important national resource.

There are other foundations for Egyptian pre-eminence among the Arabs. She is centrally located geographically between the western and eastern Arab world; she sits astride vital waterways; her armed forces, however inept they showed themselves to be against Israel in 1967, have long been larger and better equipped than those of other Arab states. Her geography and her army and air force have caused other Arabs to assume that they must depend primarily on Egypt in any confrontation with Israel. This has meant that Egyptian generals have always commanded those ventures in military cooperation that Egypt has from time to time negotiated with other Arab states, such as the Syrian-Jordanian-Egyptian defense treaty of October 24, 1956; the Syrian-Jordanian-Lebanese-Egyptian agreement of January, 1964, to establish a joint command for protection of projected efforts to divert the Jordan River headwaters; and the Egyptian-Jordanian defense treaty of May 30, 1967. It has also meant that whoever ruled Egypt had a natural popular clientele to cultivate among other Arabs who sensed their dependence on Egypt, and Gamal Abdel Nasser of course exploited this opportunity quite successfully for most of his period in office. By contrast, successive Syrian governments in the 1950s and 1960s have sought to gain influence by cultivating the reputation of anti-Israel militancy, and have largely failed, not because they were not really militant, but because few Arabs could be convinced that what Syria did would make a decisive difference.

All the foregoing considerations on which Egyptian leadership among the Arab states has been based are essentially independent of the added influence of the Egyptian revolution. The attempt to play a leading role dates back several years before the 1952 revolution to the time when Syria, Lebanon, and Transjordan became formally independent (1943-1946), and to the creation of the Arab League in 1944-1945 and the establishment of its headquarters in Cairo under an Egyptian Secretary-General. An informal alliance of the Egyptian and Saudi dynasties against the Hashemite kingdoms of Iraq and Jordan dated back still earlier. In 1949 Cairo played an influential role in forestalling union between Syria and Iraq, and in 1950 it almost brought about the expulsion of Jordan from the Arab League on grounds of the latter's deviant policy toward Israel. Had the 1952 revolution never occurred, or had it fallen into the hands of much more conservative men, one can still imagine the Egyptian government playing a predominant role in inter-Arab affairs.

In actuality, however, the revolution gave Egypt a considerable added regional influence. For one thing, it provided her with a useful image of purpose, progress, and egalitarianism which stirs mass enthusiasms elsewhere and made Nasser a figure whom the leaders of other states had to emulate, court, or fear. For another thing, the revolution made Cairo the natural capital of subversion in other Arab and African countries, providing both a haven for innumerable exiles from them over the years, and funds and advice. Thus the revolution has provided Egypt with leverage both over other governments and over their opponents.

Added to this, and perhaps of the greatest importance, is the personal prestige that Nasser built up throughout the Arab world as a charismatic figure. As the man who removed the British from Egypt after 74 years of occupation, defied the Western powers in obtaining Soviet arms and nationalizing the Suez Canal, hobnobbed around the world with the likes of Nehru, Tito, Chou En-lai, and Khrushchev, and, above all, emerged triumphant from the Suez war of 1956, Nasser came to be regarded in the eyes of the Arab masses as a divinely inspired champion of righteous causes. Even when it remained possible for Nasser's enemies to criticize individual Egyptian policies, it was difficult for them to attack Nasser personally.

Some of Nasser's aura of invincibility faded after the Syrian secession from the United Arab Republic in 1961 and after the Egyptian intervention in Yemen bogged down in the years following; and the catastrophe inflicted upon Egypt in the Six-Day War dealt his reputation an almost fatal blow—more, however, in Egypt itself than elsewhere. Yet it was always remarkable how well Nasser survived these setbacks, and how widespread was the tendency among his adherents to view him as the victim of the treachery or incompetence of other men and to expect confidently that he would rise again for fresh triumphs.

The Objectives of Egyptian Regional Policy

It would not be altogether beside the point to say that Egypt, like any other state, has naturally tended to exercise the influence that her circumstances have made possible. There are, however, more concrete considerations. The first and most important of these is geopolitical. It is natural for Egyptian leaders to see their own influence in the surrounding area as a useful support for Egypt's national security. That they should think in these terms is partly a reflection of Egypt's historic vulnerability: in modern as well as earlier times she has been invaded and occupied on repeated occasions—by France, Britain, the Ottoman Turks, Italy, Germany, again France and Britain, and Israel. The overriding preoccupation of Egyptian foreign policy in the years before and just after the 1952 revolution was to get rid of the British occupation of the Canal Zone; and it was during these years that pre- and post-revolutionary regimes in Cairo sought to fight against the consolidation of British positions in the Fertile Crescent states (the proposed Middle East Defense Organization in 1951, the Baghdad Pact in 1955). The areas surrounding Egypt were seen as potential staging areas for fresh attacks on her, or at least for organizing Egypt's diplomatic isolation within the Middle East. These were not idle fears. The Suez expedition of 1956 could not have been carried out without British control of Cyprus, and the post-Suez Eisenhower doctrine attempt by the United States to put Abdel Nasser in the Middle Eastern doghouse depended upon cooperation from pro-Western regimes in Jordan, Lebanon,

Saudi Arabia, and Iraq. The Egyptian-led political counterattack, which
led to the union with Syria, civil war in Lebanon, and revolution in Iraq
in 1958, ended the Western effort to isolate Egypt.

Since that time, the Egyptian assumption seems to have been that
Egyptian influence in the other Arab states would have a pre-emptive
value: it would keep other foreign influence out, and keep threats to Egypt's
independence at arm's length. More than that, success in establishing
Egyptian hegemony in the Arab world would mean that Egypt would
become a political broker for those having business to do with the other
states of the region. Thus, for example, Britain was induced to turn her
emergency role of protecting Kuwait against Iraq in 1961 over to an
Egyptian-led inter-Arab force; the United States was induced to subsidize
the Egyptian economy with large-scale food shipments from 1959 to 1965;
the Soviet Union was induced to soft-pedal its support for Communist
parties in Iraq, Syria, and Egypt, and to channel its aid to Yemeni, South
Arabian, and Congolese revolutionaries through Egyptian hands. It was,
of course, possible to overplay this game: the Yemen and Congo affairs
undermined the profitable relationship with the United States, which in
turn contributed indirectly to the fiasco of 1967 at the hands of Israel.
It was all very well for Egypt to establish her predominance among the
Arabs, provided this was not done in a manner that would be provocative
to Israel and ignored the fact that the Israeli state in their midst was
stronger militarily than all of them combined.

That Egypt has been a revolutionary state since 1952 has no doubt
strengthened her motive to pursue pre-emptive regional hegemony, for
like other revolutionary states (for example, the United States in its first
few decades, France after 1789, Russia after 1917, China after 1949)
she has imagined, rightly or wrongly, that counterrevolutionary forces were
out to surround and undermine her and that some sort of "Monroe Doctrine" for the area was essential for her survival. Thus she has seen it as
her task to make the Middle East safe for revolution, and particularly for
her own brand.

On the more material side, furthermore, the ambitious economic development program of the Egyptian revolutionary regime, which has plunged
into industrialization and social-overhead investment on a massive scale
simultaneously with large military expenditures, has provided a powerful
incentive to develop political leverage over the oil-producing states. It is
not possible to spell out the reasoning here in simple terms: there is no
evidence that Egyptian leaders have sought a direct takeover of, say, Saudi
Arabia, followed by appropriation of a major part of her oil income for
Egyptian use. That they somehow, however vaguely, have hoped to translate Egyptian influence into some form of greater access to Arab oil capital,

through an inter-Arab development bank, bilateral low-cost loans, or whatever, seems undeniable. The financial transfusion granted to Egypt by Saudi Arabia, Kuwait, and Libya after the 1967 war was no doubt a special case, but it testified in part to the relief felt by the rulers of those states at the prospect that in return for their aid they could look forward to respite from Egyptian-sponsored political difficulties at home. It also gave Egypt a vested interest in maintaining normal oil production in those states, and normal relations with the oil companies.

Probably the Egyptian regime has proceeded in its relations with the oil states, as in some of its other relations, more from instinct and improvisation than from strategy. Generally Egypt's relations with Kuwait have been very cordial, while those with Saudi Arabia have been chronically strained; with Libya, they have been somewhere in between, that is, always correct on the surface, but never marked by any great mutual confidence. What may account best for the perennial tension with Saudi Arabia is not simply the fact that she has a large oil income much of which is squandered by the royal family, but that since 1957 she has repeatedly sought to play a countervailing role to Egypt on the inter-Arab scene as a second Arab "great power," thwarting Egyptian objectives in the process: for example, after Suez in the period of the Eisenhower doctrine, during the Yemen war, and in 1966-1967, in promoting the so-called Islamic Pact. It is of course the oil income that has made it possible for Saudi Arabia to play a leading role; and the combination of her wealth, the backwardness of her society, and the conservatism of her regime has presented a tempting target for revolutionary propaganda. It is also a little too easy to jump to the conclusion that Egypt has sought simply to cash in on the royalties. Certainly she would welcome this, but more immediately she must be concerned that her efforts to maintain predominant influence in other Arab states, as custodian of her Middle Eastern Monroe Doctrine, not be hampered from Riyadh. Seen in this light, Egyptian-Saudi tension has been of the same order as Egyptian-Iraqi tension was during the pre-1958 period of Nuri al-Said and the monarchy.

The Dynamics of Inter-Arab Rivalries

This point leads us into consideration of inter-Arab rivalry on a broader level. Resistance to Egyptian policy has been of two main kinds: first, on the part of those who are more or less content with their minor-power status but wish to preserve their autonomy and seek to ward off Egyptian attempts to manage their affairs; second, on the part of those with leadership ambitions of their own. At different times and in different degrees, the latter category has included Iraq, Syria, Saudi Arabia, and Algeria. In practice, however, these two forms of resistance are not always distinguishable from each other. Nor is either of them ideologically determined: both have arisen from time to time on both the right and the left. But when the resisting regime is conservative, the contest has naturally tended to assume ideological overtones.

Short of asserting their own ambitions for leadership, however, all Arab states have at one time or another found themselves resisting Egypt's pretensions: King Hussein in Jordan, Camille Chamoun in Lebanon, numerous leftist and rightist regimes in Syria, Iraq, and Sudan, Yemen, and so on. Here we are not concerned with rivalry for leadership properly speaking, but simply friction between Egypt's regional inclinations and the instinct of local politicians for power and survival in their own constituency.

It is readily within Egypt's capability and, she tends to believe, in her interest to make her point of view known and her presence felt in all Arab countries: but it is beyond her reach to enforce her will altogether. Her representatives and her local supporters chronically run up against local obstacles. There is something obstinately provincial about the culture, the society, the problems, the personalities of each Arab state that shields it from the guidance of outsiders, including fellow Arabs—unless the latter should happen to bring decisive military force along with them. Egypt has done this to some extent only in Yemen, and even there she had her difficulties.

On the other hand, Nasser's personal prestige since Suez has been great enough in many other capitals to mobilize pan-Arab sentiment and to provide some local politicians with a cause to use against their rivals, or against the government of the day, if they wished to do so. This has been most notably and continuously the case in Lebanon, where the atmosphere and the political system are open to all influences and where the Egyptian connections of certain politicians and publicists (and, for that matter, the French, British, American, Saudi, or additional connections of others) are taken for granted as an integral part of the political landscape. The display of such connections, however, tends on many occasions to produce antagonistic reactions, with little positive gain for any party but with an exacerbation of the already existing problems of instability. For amid all this factionalism in several Arab states, no one possesses a knockout punch. Sudan, Libya, Jordan, Lebanon, Syria, and Iraq all have their Nasserite leaders and followers, as well as those espousing other competing messages: the Egyptian cause is too strong in each case to be driven away once and for all, but has nothing at hand to bring it firmly to power either. If Nasser was in some sense the Bismarck of the Arab world, as some say, he badly missed the power to defeat the Austrians (for example, Syria, 1961, and Yemen, 1962-1967), let alone the French (that is, Israel, 1967). The discussions later on in this study of Egypt's difficulties in Syria during the

1958-1961 union, and in Yemen after 1962, may serve to illustrate the tensions and frustrations arising from the combination of persistence and ultimate impotence of Egypt's role.

We shall now examine in greater detail the pattern of relations between Egypt and three of the Arab states that have contested her leadership at various periods: Iraq, Syria, and Saudi Arabia.

Iraq

Until July, 1958, Egypt's leading challenger for Arab leadership was the Hashemite monarchy of Iraq. Although the Iraqi regime was increasingly unpopular within and without its own territory by the mid-1950s as it gathered a reputation as a repressive oligarchy tied to the apron strings of the British Foreign Office, the oligarchy was sufficiently cohesive, sophisticated, and authoritative, and in its own way patriotic, to carry on a vigorous and effective foreign policy. This policy was based on the premise of Iraqi leadership of the Fertile Crescent area (Syria, Lebanon, Jordan) and championship of Arab interests in Palestine, and within the framework of a partnership with Britain which the Iraqi leaders viewed as wholly constructive and mutually advantageous.

The oligarchy—led by the perennial Prime Minister, Nuri al-Said, and the regent, Prince Abdul Ilah—were in many ways products of a past generation: Nuri and other politicians were renegade officers from the Ottoman army who had served with Prince Faisal of the Hejaz and T. E. Lawrence in the Arab Revolt of 1916-1918, after which Faisal and his descendants had assumed the Iraqi throne with British assistance; British arms were required in 1941 to restore this group to power after an anti-British *coup d'état;* and the cool relations with Saudi Arabia that persisted until 1957 arose from the fact that it was the Saudi family that had chased the Hashemites from the Hejaz in the early 1920.

None of this was particularly edifying to the younger, educated, nationalist-minded generation in any of the Arab states, and by the mid-1950s, when the struggle for Arab hegemony broke wide open between Cairo and Baghdad, it was easy for Nasser and his followers to turn the contest into an ideological affair for the benefit of public opinion. But the most crucial issue between them was the difference in their conceptions of the strategic order in the region. The Egyptians managed to obtain Britain's agreement to evacuate her Suez base in 1954, and saw this as the beginning of the end of Britain's strategic position in the area generally, believing that once Britain was gone other great powers could be kept out as well. The Iraqis countered immediately thereafter by joining the Baghdad Pact, which was to perpetuate the British strategic presence in Iraq under a new guise, on the theory that a continued and familiar, if modified, British role was the best alternative to an uncontrollable scramble in the region between the United States and the Soviet Union. Had Cairo and Baghdad each been content to limit its conceptions to its own territory, perhaps no clash would have occurred. But, the Egyptian view was that the British threat to Egypt's independence was only one step removed if British bases remained in nearby states; and the Iraqi (and British) conception of the Baghdad Pact was that it was an arrangement for general extension and application to Jordan and hopefully also Syria and Lebanon, as well as Iraq. Consequently, the contrasting British treaties with Egypt in 1954 and Iraq in 1955 touched off a new and intense Egyptian-Iraqi rivalry for influence in the lesser states in between: Syria, Lebanon, and Jordan. The United States and the Soviet Union lost little time in involving themselves in this contest.

The Iraqi policy was undercut by Britain's Suez fiasco in 1956 and the union of Egypt and Syria in February 1958, and collapsed altogether with the revolution in Baghdad a few months later. Nasser's policies of regional hegemony and neutralism seemed vindicated, and they persisted for almost another decade until the Six-Day War. But other challengers arose. First the new revolutionary regime in Iraq under Abdul Karim Qasim proved surprisingly uncooperative with Nasser and sought to undermine his position in Syria, and second, in Saudi Arabia. Qasim posed a challenge not only because he failed to join the United Arab Republic but because he relied on local Communist support and sought Soviet backing. This signified that the Arab world could be dominated only by one or another great power, if not Britain, then perhaps the Soviet Union. This was in direct contradiction to Nasser's insistence that his leadership was, if anything, an antidote to Soviet influence.

Qasim's effort to pose a regional alternative to Nasser did not succeed, partly because he was not in fact a Communist, and it was unclear just what he represented; but more particularly because his home front inside Iraq was so disorganized. Since his overthrow in 1963, no Iraqi regime has been able to muster the internal control and confidence of pre-1958 days and thereby mount a consistent and influential Arab policy.

Qasim was succeeded in 1963 by a military-dominated regime of the Ba'ath Party, closely allied to a similar regime that seized power at about the same time in Syria; and for nine months the two of them sought to compete with Egypt as leaders of the pan-Arab left, first by attempting to maneuver Nasser into a federal union on terms that would give them a preponderant voice, and when that negotiation failed, by blaming the failure on him and preparing a union of their own. This enterprise collapsed, however, in November 1963 with the overthrow of the Iraqi Ba'athists by army officers more sympathetic to Nasser, led by President Abdel Salam Aref and (after his death in 1966) his brother Abdel Rahman Aref. The latter, in turn, was ousted in 1968 by the Ba'ath.

The five years of rule by the Aref brothers brought a modicum of stability to Iraq and a general alignment of Iraqi foreign and Arab policy with that of Egypt, but with little positive effect. The regime failed to exercise much influence beyond its borders in its own right—nothing like that of the pre-1958 monarchy, nor even as much as Qasim—and did not contribute much to the strength of its Egyptian ally.

One reason for this lay with the chronic internal difficulties that beset the Arefs: the never-ending Kurdish rebellion which preoccupied the Army and drained the treasury, the quarrels and conspiracies among ambitious officers, the lack of a firm and well-organized base of popular support, and the stagnation of the economy. Another reason was the artificial basis of relations with Egypt. The two governments in 1964 announced plans for eventual union, which caused Iraq to attempt rather implausibly to reorganize its political and economic life as a carbon copy of that of Egypt; but it was clear that this was only a holding operation, for neither Nasser nor the Arefs really desired union. Nasser, remembering his experience in Syria a few years before, could sense the impossibility of trying to control Iraq, with its geographical remoteness, its deep divisions among Kurds and Sunni and Shiite Arabs, its tendency toward violent factionalism, and its pressing need to put its administrative and economic affairs in order. Nor did the Iraqi leaders themselves wish to be controlled from Cairo, much as they found it useful to advertise Nasser's patronage of them in order to strengthen their position within Iraq. Under these circumstances, the attempts on several occasions by fervently pro-Nasser Iraqi officers to seize power in Baghdad and precipitate the union were embarrassing to both governments.

Abdel Rahman Aref sought to acquire a measure of independent Arab leadership after the 1967 war with Israel by adopting an especially militant posture, taking the lead, for example, in cutting off the shipment of oil to leading Western states until the Khartoum Conference (see below, p. 66), and stationing a sizeable military force in Jordan. These measures were not of great consequence, however. Aref's removal in July, 1968, caused little excitement and made little difference, even to the Egyptians. His Ba'athist successors (who belonged to a faction different from the one that had meanwhile emerged in control in Syria) inherited Aref's debilitating domestic problems, and in the atmosphere of the aftermath of the Arab defeat of 1967 found no significant opening for the development of an influential position.

Syria

While Iraq declined in the 1960s from the status of a major rival to Egypt to that of a rather minor power seeking mainly to conserve its own autonomy, Syria underwent an opposite evolution, especially after the Ba'athist seizure of power in 1963.

In 1958 the Syrians, in a great outburst of political desperation and popular enthusiasm, delivered themselves body and soul to Nasser, after finding themselves unable to set their own house in order. With virtually unlimited constitutional powers at his command, Nasser nonetheless found himself quite powerless to bring any lasting reorganization of political life to Syria on his own; and when a Syrian military uprising occurred three and a half years later, there was no way to suppress it.

Nasser's problem during the period of union was essentially insoluble. It was the same problem that he was to face later with other close and dependent allies such as Yemen under Sallal or Iraq under Aref. No one in Syria possessed enough moral authority or cohesive military force to control the country on his own, but no one really was prepared to turn governance over to Egyptians either. The Syrian Ba'athists in 1958—like Presidents Aref and Sallal later on in Iraq and Yemen—sought to use Egyptian prestige to shore up their own position at the expense of other people; in fact, Egyptian favor became a commodity over which they and rival factions competed. The Egyptians were quite capable of coming in with blueprints, administrative cadres, and military staff officers and giving a great deal of heavy-handed guidance, but this inevitably stimulated resentment and mistrust, and set jealous local factions against each other. All in all, the Egyptians in Syria suffered three main disabilities: as they and the Syrians discovered somewhat to their surprise, they were foreigners; they lacked economic resources with which to give the Syrians a real boost; and their military presence was less than overwhelming, so that in the end they could not enforce their will when political persuasion had failed. Yet given the internal disabilities of the Syrians themselves at the time, and given the importance Egypt has attached to preventing others from establishing their own influence in neighboring Arab states, it is hard to see how Nasser could have been expected to refuse the union that the Syrians urged on him in 1958.

The Egyptian government was defeated by these problems in Syria despite the fact that during their three and a half years there, they incurred very little disruption from any outside rival: neither from any of the great powers, nor from Arab or other regional competitors. (The only exceptions were Qasim's propaganda in 1959, and at the end in September, 1961, support for the Damascus coup from Turkey, Saudi Arabia, and Jordan.)

By and large, Syria during the union, like Iraq under the Aref brothers, was an instance of the Egyptian drive for regional hegemony stumbling over intractable local problems.

It is curious that despite this failure on the part of Egypt, her influence and prestige remained great enough in Syria that subsequent Syrian regimes were constantly on the defensive, and saddled with an onus of guilt for the breakup of the union, or at least for failing to restore it. Nasser had been unable to establish the legitimacy of his own rule in Syria, but was none-theless able to deny legitimacy to others. Both the conservative politicians and their military allies who ruled Syria from 1961 to 1963, and the Ba'athists who replaced them from 1963 to 1966, found themselves alter-nating between two poles: joining in anti-Egyptian alignments and castigat-ing Nasser, on the one hand, and emulating his policies and seeking to share in his prestige, on the other. Thus the regime that followed the seces-sion drew close to Nasser's enemies, Saud and Hussein, and bitterly attacked Egypt at Arab League meetings, but paid lip service to "socialism" and dutifully endorsed the Yemeni revolution in the fall of 1962. Thus also the Ba'ath in 1963, having come to power in both Syria and Iraq as we have seen, was extremely wary of Nasser's influence in both countries and took pains to purge the army officer ranks of Nasserites, but at the same time made their pilgrimage to Cairo to negotiate with Nasser for a tripartite federal union that they knew he would try to dominate at their expense. The Syrian Ba'ath politicians fell increasingly under the domination of the ambitious officers surrounding them after 1963, and splits developed among both officers and civilians. A coup in February, 1966, installed a new faction, still calling itself Ba'athist but professing more radical idealogi-cal tendencies and following a somewhat different line of policy toward neighboring states.

The old-line civilian Ba'athists, such as the founders of the party, Michel Aflaq and Salah al-Din Bitar, suffered from certain compulsions and com-plexes about Arab unity. They had made their careers preaching it, and particularly preaching the notion of unity among socialist-minded regimes. When they discovered during the union with Egypt that Nasser's inclina-tion was to use their own formula at their expense, they were put in a dilemma that carried over to the time of their emergence in power in Damascus in 1963. They did not know how to abandon the game of capi-talizing on enthusiasm for revolutionary Arab unity, but it had become a game that Nasser, with his personal prestige and the traditionally influential role of Egypt behind him, was bound to dominate. The only thing the Syrians could do was to try to outdistance Egypt in militancy on nationalist and revolutionary issues: solidarity with Algeria and republican Yemen, hostility to the monarchies of Jordan, Saudi Arabia, and even Morocco, close ties with Moscow and Peking, bellicosity on the Israeli armistice line, and espousal of the idea of a popular war of Palestinian liberation. Nasser's ally Abdel Salam Aref they denounced as a reactionary fraud. (He had, after all, ousted the Ba'ath in Iraq.) But none of these initiatives could make a great deal of difference as long as Nasser kept his inter-Arab fences mended and his own house in reasonable order: for it was he rather than the Syrians who was popularly viewed as the one capable of getting things done. The Syrians, by contrast, were few in number, poor in resources, weak in leadership, and incapable of managing their own affairs successfully. Thus in the 1964-1965 period of Arab summitry, Nasser kept the Syrians neatly boxed in.

The new Syrian regime of 1966 was free of the "unity complex" of its predecessors and felt no embarrassment over the fact that it was not prepared to accept Egyptian leadership. They said little of Arab unity and much of revolution. They intensified the leftist postures of the previous regime, redoubling its castigation of the Arab conservatives and moderates and stepping up border tension with Israel. None of this might have mattered very much had Egypt's relations with the monarchies and with the United States and Britain not worsened, thereby driving Nasser to seek the Syrians' support more or less on their terms. These developments will be discussed at the end of the next section (pp. 61 ff, below).

Saudi Arabia and the Yemen Conflict

Each Arab challenger to Egypt's leadership has brought into play a different set of instruments at its disposal. Iraq under the monarchy possessed some oil wealth and an intelligent and promising plan of economic development, but more particularly a very strong and stable political leadership in the person of Nuri al-Said and his reliance on a long-standing alliance with what was traditionally the most influential outside power in the region. With the disappearance of this leadership, Iraqi pretensions on the Arab front were drastically undercut.

Syria's instruments were twofold: her geographical position as the nucleus of the Fertile Crescent or "Greater Syria" region, and the ideological energy of the Ba'ath Party. These sufficed, however, for no more than abortive challenges to rival Arab states, and enabled the Syrians to play an occasional disruptive role but not one that encouraged the deference or the dependence of others. They lacked resources, they lacked consistency, and they lacked leadership.

Saudi Arabia's obvious political resource has been her oil. Her revenues have enabled her for the past two decades to subsidize the treasuries of other states, to grease the palms of politicians and newspaper editors, and to buy modern armaments. Equally important, the location of American oil interests in her territory has given her considerable leverage in Washington. It has provided her with American patronage and enabled her to purvey a measure of American prestige for her own purposes in the area, somewhat as Nuri al-Said was able to do with British prestige and Nasser with that of the Soviet Union.

In addition to the oil, the Saudis have benefited at times from their steady reputation as religious and political conservatives and from the symbolic importance of their custodianship of the principal Islamic holy places. They are natural antidotes to the radicalism of Cairo or Damascus, for those regimes or individuals in need of protection or encouragement. And finally, as a residual defensive weapon, the Saudis can fall back on the imperviousness of their own provincial society to the progressive political outlook and secular culture of those Arabs from outside the Arabian Peninsula with whom they come in contact.

For Saudi Arabia as for Iraq and Syria, how much can be made of such advantages depends heavily upon the quality of leadership. Indeed, perhaps it is more important for her than for them, in that she suffers far more than they do from the lack of well-educated and experienced technical and managerial personnel to support that leadership. King Abdel Aziz Ibn Saud, until 1953, and King Faisal, since 1965, possessed great political shrewdness and commanding domestic reputations, and hence were able to translate Saudi Arabia's advantages into an independent and influential role in Arab affairs; King Saud, during his rule from 1953 to 1965, was a much weaker figure, and played a correspondingly more defensive role. Yet Saudi Arabia's relations with Egypt in the 1960s seem to suggest fairly narrow lower and upper limits. Given his financial and geographic advantages, even Saud was able to survive Egyptian attacks on him and to counter the Egyptian intervention in Yemen; and conversely, given the traditionalism of his appeal, even Faisal could not conduct much more than a holding operation against Nasser.

This ambiguous situation was well illustrated by the course of the civil war in Yemen and the critical events it led to. Egyptian policy in Yemen was hampered both by on-the-spot difficulties with the Yemenis and by the considerable outside competition from Saudi Arabia. Looking backward, it has been easy to say that the Egyptian plunge into Yemen in support of the 1962 coup against the monarchy there was a costly blunder. The royalist forces—tribesmen in the interior conducting guerrilla-style operations— could not be defeated by whatever modern equipment and level of manpower the Egyptians could pour in. The regime Egypt sought to shore up was a floundering, quarrelsome, exasperating group without a firm political hold on even that part of the countryside the Egyptian army policed for them. The war strained Egypt's relations with several other states (notably the United States), impaired her prestige, and was terribly expensive for a country with serious problems at home that she could ill afford to neglect. When the 1967 defeat by Israel provided a compelling excuse for withdrawal, the Egyptians were glad to get out.

Thus the Egyptian adventure in Yemen, as long as it lasted, was strikingly parallel in many ways to the American adventure in Vietnam. But as in the Vietnam case, the fact that it went so badly does not by any means entitle us to conclude that it was embarked upon in a fit of feeblemindedness or recklessness, nor that the lessons are so clear that no Egyptian government would do anything of the kind again. Despite a good deal of talk (as by Americans in Vietnam) about modernizing the country and protecting it against aggression from its neighbors, the Egyptians were not in Yemen for the sake of the brown eyes of the Yemenis, nor to conduct social experiments, but to assert their strategic interest, conceived in terms of geopolitics and prestige. It was a chance to turn the tables on the forces hostile to the Egyptian revolution and to Egyptian regional influence, at a time—only a year after the Syrian secession from the U.A.R—when the Egyptian regime was isolated and on the defensive. A successful revolution in backward Yemen aided by Egypt would regain the initiative for Cairo; it might stimulate an internal challenge to the Saudi Arabian regime; and perhaps most significantly, it would offer Egypt direct access to the hinterland of Britain's restive South Arabian protectorate, and thus a chance to influence events there. All of this would add up to the strengthening of Egypt's own national security and of her own revolution.

The Saudi regime opposed the Yemeni revolution for precisely the reasons that led Egypt to support it. It was a test of the Saudis' ability to protect their back yard, and more than that, to demonstrate that revolution was not the wave of the future, especially revolution led from Cairo. Their intervention was materially a much more modest affair than that of the Egyptians, consisting primarily of the provision of supplies, funds, and diplomatic support to the royalist-led tribesmen in the hills. All the inevitable resentments of the Yemeni population that built up against the Egyptians as overbearing foreign intruders could only play into the hands of the Saudis. Moreover, the irritations felt in London and Washington as the Yemen war proceeded were increasingly translated into Western diplomatic and military commitments to Riyadh.

In the long run the whole complex of foreign involvements in Yemen came to look rather silly. Certainly the Egyptians had cause to regret their intervention, for not only did the war go badly but the Yemeni Republican politicians proved exceedingly difficult to get on with; Cairo alternately kept the Yemeni President, Field Marshal Sallal, on prolonged "medical" visits to Egypt and detained large numbers of his opponents: eventually

Sallal was ousted altogether. If the Saudis worried about an Egyptian triumph, or the triumph of revolution, in Yemen, surely all the difficulties their enemies ran into with the local population and with each other were enough to allay Saudi fears. Occasional Saudi-Egyptian efforts to negotiate an end to the affair foundered on the failure of local Yemeni factions to cooperate.

Ironically, although it had long been freely predicted that an Egyptian pullout would bring the swift collapse of the republic, when the Egyptians finally did depart in the autumn of 1967, the collapse failed to occur. It was quite an anticlimax. With some Soviet assistance in place of that of Egypt, the Yemeni revolution survived—but with little benefit to Egypt. It had been another demonstration of the ambiguous, inconclusive, over-committed role of the Egyptian revolutionary regime in the other Arab states: a capability, and a felt need, to become heavily involved in events in the region, and to stimulate a good many fears and expectations on the part of Arab antagonists and clients, but in the end an inability to control the events that had been set in motion.

In the light of this background, the Saudi attempt in 1966 to launch a regional counteroffensive against Egyptian leadership was a deplorable overreaction. Throughout 1964 and 1965, the Egyptian government had entered one of its milder phases, with the emphasis on toning down some of its commitments and reaching some stable terms with other Arab states. The succession of Arab summit meetings (January and September, 1964, and September, 1965), the effort to steer clear of a confrontation with Israel over the Jordan River diversion question, the attempt to negotiate an end to the Yemen war, and a concern at home to put growing financial problems under control were all parts of this phase. It was at this juncture, late 1965 and early 1966, that King Faisal of Saudi Arabia embarked on a round of diplomatic visits and consultations pointing toward the establishment of what became known as the Islamic Pact, in which, ostensibly, all Muslim states regardless of their internal political systems would be brought together in a solidarity conference at Mecca and presumably some more permanent arrangement afterward. It was clear, however, that if such radicals as Egypt, Syria, and Algeria participated, they would be heavily outnumbered by conservatives and thus boxed in; while if they stayed out, they might find the conservatives organized against them. The fact that Faisal devoted all of his visible attentions to courting participants of the more conservative variety and induced King Hussein of Jordan to endorse the movement without waiting for any sign of approval or acquiescence from the members of the radical group, seemed to indicate that Faisal's preference was for a wholly conservative membership, devoted to resisting the evils of socialist revolution and Soviet influence. In its effect, the

Islamic Pact amounted to a rerun of the Eisenhower doctrine. For neither the Egyptians nor almost anyone else in the Arab world doubted that Faisal's initiative and Hussein's cooperation carried the approval of London and Washington, despite the denials of the latter.

The entire Arab Left launched the same broadside of denunciation that had been used so effectively against the Baghdad Pact and the Eisenhower doctrine a decade earlier. Faisal's conference never took place, but the effects were nonetheless serious. The period of Arab summitry was ended; the already faltering relations between Cairo and Washington deteriorated still further; and in November, 1966, Nasser, in search of local allies as in 1955-1958, drew close together in a military alliance with the Syrian Ba'athist regime for which he had previously had such scant respect. On paper it was a defense alliance against Israel; in political reality, it was intended as a defense against Saudi Arabia and her supposedly American-supported challenge to Egyptian leadership. But in the end, by a series of mishaps, it did in fact lead Egypt and Syria, and the hapless Jordanians as well, into war with Israel.

For, once Nasser had committed himself to Syria's defense, he was bound to face the consequences of the Syrians' reckless actions along their border with Israel. He ended up in May, 1967, threatening Israel with his army in Sinai, to deter her from launching a punitive attack on Syria, because in his race with King Faisal for inter-Arab leadership he needed Syrian support and he needed to preserve his reputation as the Arab champion against Israel. The taunts he received from Jordan, challenging him to close the Straits of Tiran to Israeli shipping, further put this reputation to the test, and he responded by closing the Straits. Under more relaxed circumstances on the inter-Arab front, such as those in the 1964-1965 summit period, it seems doubtful that either the Syrians or the Jordanians would have been able to force Nasser into such initiatives. Nor would King Hussein have felt the same compulsion, once the chips were down, to throw in his lot with Nasser by signing the fateful alliance of May 30 with him. (Jordan had stood aside, for example, in the 1956 Suez war.) Thus in the struggle for Arab leadership in 1967, power politics without either real military strength or effective great-power support proved a dangerous game for both Nasser and his rivals.

Prospects

What do these events suggest for the future? Regardless of the short-term outcome of the 1967 war, which is discussed toward the end of this chapter, the following general conclusions seem to emerge.

First, with or without further *coups d'état* in various Arab capitals, it is quite unreasonable to expect serious inter-Arab frictions to disappear. There is no reason to expect the long-established Egyptian instinct for playing a dominating role in the region to be abandoned (although it may fluctuate to a degree); but at the same time, given its limited means, it has no prospect of achieving any finally decisive success, and in the meantime, other Arab states, ideologically well disposed or not, will continue to resist Egypt's urge to lead them. How far each regime will go in playing out this familiar pattern of competition will of course depend to some extent on the encouragement or restraint coming from the Soviet Union and the United States. As long as the Soviets retain their stake in Egypt, and the United States its stake in Saudi Arabia, there will no doubt be temptations to view competition between them in ideological and cold-war terms, with each of them seen as the leader of a leftist or rightist bloc. But for one thing, neither superpower can more than temporarily assure the cohesiveness of any "bloc" of its supposed Middle Eastern clients. For another, neither can count on being able to turn on or off the will of its chief Arab ally to score points against the other.

A second general conclusion, however, is that there is a lower limit than may generally be realized to the utility of manipulation of Arab "clients" by the great powers. Given the ultimate impotence of both Egypt and Saudi Arabia—to say nothing of lesser Arab states—in trying to determine events outside their own frontiers, in many situations there would seem to be rather little for Moscow or Washington to hope for, or to fear, from what Cairo and Riyadh may set out to do. Egypt could not defeat the Yemeni royalists; Saudi Arabia could not defeat the Yemeni republicans; Egypt cannot control the Syrians; Saudi Arabia cannot control Jordan. Nor can Russia control Egypt; nor the United States, Saudia Arabia. They can egg them on in unpredictable ventures, or attempt to restrain them, but not always successfully. The Islamic Pact affair and the crisis of May, 1967, both point to the ability of local clients to stir up trouble and the inability of the great powers to limit the consequences.

Third, inter-Arab rivalries have had and are likely to continue to have a debilitating effect on Arab policy toward Israel, to which we now turn.

II. The Arab Position toward Israel

Arab policies toward Israel have consistently suffered from three main disabilities, which have prevented them from either pressing their claims effectively or adjusting the substance of their claims to political realities. One of these disabilities consists of the lack of military and economic means by which to bring direct pressure on Israel herself, coupled with the lack of general political leverage over those great powers upon whose good will Israel is dependent. The second disability is the failure of the

Arabs to draw up any meaningful plan for a solution to the problem, on the basis of which to prepare a negotiating position. The third disability, closely related to the first two, lies in the divisions among the Arabs themselves.

There are several reasons for these weaknesses. An obvious one is that Arab society generally lacks the economic, social, educational and technological bases necessary to mobilize large armies and train them to use advanced modern equipment effectively. This problem is characteristic of most underdeveloped societies, and I shall not dwell upon it here. What will be emphasized here are problems arising from political circumstances particular to the Arab world. The Palestinian Arabs themselves have never been effectively organized politically; the other Arab states have been too divided to fill the gap, and the entire Arab position has long been a major object of inter-Arab mistrust. Furthermore, the interests of the Palestinian Arabs are essentially somewhat different from those of the Arab states.

Military and Political Weakness

The Arabs have dealt with the problem of a Jewish state in Palestine from a position of weakness since the beginning of the issue at the close of World War I. The establishment of the Jewish national home was made possible by the existence of a British Mandate over Palestine, set up at a time when Palestine and surrounding territories were all under British or French military occupation and none was politically independent. Under the Mandate the British government was committed, however reluctantly, to permitting large-scale Jewish immigration, land settlement, and communal institutional development, and to restraining local Arab resistance to this process; armed Arab opposition arose in the late 1930s but was suppressed by British forces, and the leadership provided to the Palestine Arab community by the Arab Higher Committee was broken by the arrest or exile of its members. British policies in Palestine adopted from time to time to placate Arab sentiment (for example, the Passfield White Paper of 1930, and the White Paper of 1939, both projecting a drastic reduction of Jewish immigration and land acquisition) foundered sooner or later as more powerful counterpressures were brought to bear on the British government from other sources. The Arab states that were independent during the 1930s—Yemen, Saudi Arabia, Egypt, and Iraq—were ineffectual in their efforts to influence the course of British policy.

In 1947 the Arabs likewise failed to persuade either the United Nations Special Committee on Palestine or the General Assembly to adopt proposals favorable to themselves, and the partition plan was adopted over their objections. As this plan then collapsed for lack of any effective supervision and as British forces left Palestine, the Arabs failed militarily, not only to prevent the establishment of the Jewish state, but even to contain it within the proposed partition boundaries or within the predominantly Jewish-inhabited areas of the country. In the 1949 armistice negotiations, the Arab states were outmaneuvered on several practical questions (in the midst of the negotiations the Jordanians were intimidated into withdrawing from several areas, leaving villages separated from farmland); in the spring of 1949 Israel won admission to the United Nations without making the firm concession on frontiers and on the readmission of Arab refugees which the Arab states had sought to secure in negotiations at Lausanne; by 1955 the Egyptians and the Syrians had been outmaneuvered by Israel in issues arising from the demilitarized status of the El Auja and Huleh districts, respectively; in 1956 Egypt lost control of the Straits of Tiran; in 1964 the Arabs collectively failed to prevent Israel from making her own use of the disputed Jordan River waters; in 1967 they failed not only to back up their provocative military challenge to Israel, but even to defend themselves minimally against her response. Throughout Israel's first two decades of statehood, the Arabs failed to discourage mass immigration into Israel, massive American private and public financial support for her, and large-scale German reparations. Meanwhile they also failed to prevent Israel's development of normal relations with a majority of U.N. members including many African and Asian states, or to win any Israel concession on the vital issue of the return of refugees.

This partial list of failures is catalogued to underline the fact that the Arabs' intransigent position, before and after 1948, has consistently lacked effective means of military, economic, or diplomatic support. It has consistently been a policy demanding a strong bargaining position, but based in actuality on weakness and frustration. The 1967 defeat showed that many years of massive economic and military support provided to Egypt and Syria from the Soviet Union, and to Jordan from the West, as well as what appeared to be strenuous efforts by some Arab governments to develop the resources and capabilities of their societies, had in fact added up to very little in terms of usable national power. More than this, the Arabs after this passage of time remained altogether isolated from public sympathy in those countries where it might be relevant to their political needs, namely Western Europe and the United States. They could neither help themselves nor persuade others to help them meaningfully. Israel's success on these very fronts underscored the contrast: she had been founded and was maintained with the help of consistent and considerable aid from abroad, and at decisive moments relied successfully on her own initiative in determining and securing her own vital interests.

The Arab Failure to Advance Solutions

In their failure to mount effective military or political action, the Arabs have been decisively hampered by their own uncertainty on strategic fundamentals. They have been unable since the beginning of the conflict to decide clearly and realistically on their long-run objectives, and have therefore failed to develop any effective operational principles consistent with their capabilities.

In the absence of a policy based on calculation, the Arabs have fallen back on conviction. Here the record is clear and consistent, although the depth of it is not always recognized abroad. Arab opinion has been virtually unanimous since the time of the Balfour Declaration in declaring that the Zionist movement constituted an elementary aggression at their expense and was therefore completely unacceptable. The salient fact involved in Israel's establishment, in Arab opinion, was that colonizing intruders displaced an already long-settled population and thereby usurped the latter's right both to a normal livelihood and to national self-determination. That these developments occurred at a historical juncture when decolonization and nationalism were most pervasively in the air throughout much of the world, naturally sharpened the resentful Arab attitude.

These views need not be elaborated or evaluated in this paper. It should simply be emphasized that they carry great conviction in Arab minds, and this conviction does not lessen as one moves up the scale of education and social standing or from right to left along the political spectrum. There has been some tendency among intellectuals, politicians, and other spokesmen in contact with the outside world to take the virtues of the Arab case against Israel for granted as obvious and undeniable, and thus to overestimate the possibilities of propaganda. As a result the propaganda is often simplistic, and it is too readily supposed that it is a viable substitute for more substantive forms of policy.

To be sure, many Arabs in responsible positions are acutely conscious that their case is not self-evident to opinion abroad, that their own confidence in the legitimacy of their grievances against Israel is no sufficient basis for an effective policy, and that they cannot do without some form of cost-benefit strategy that takes account of power realities. Many would claim, in fact, that the fundamental Arab position has been a realistic one. They would argue that as long as the preponderance of power is on Israel's side it is imperative to avoid open warefare with her, but that it is equally important to preserve the integrity of their case against Israel, and to avoid granting her permanent concessions pending the time when Arab superiority in numbers and resources will shift the balance. Hence the present need is to conduct a holding operation by preventing Israel's integration into the

Middle Eastern society of nations, while limiting the damage that Israel can do to them. This phase may last a long time, during which the Arabs run admitted risks of vulnerability to Israeli retribution, but the argument is that Arab society can absorb these risks—even when they eventuate in such disasters as that of 1967. Meanwhile, admittedly this puts the Arabs in the contradictory position of holding Israel to her international responsibilities while seeking to remain relatively free of their own, but they are hardly alone in the history of nations in attempting to derive some benefit from such a double standard.

The difficulty with this analysis is not that it is irrational or unrealistic in itself, but that it is incomplete as the basis for a consistent policy as long as the ultimate objective is left indeterminate. If the objective has some identifiable limit, it becomes easier to exercise the restraint and marshal the international support that can restrict the damage incurred from Israel in the interim. Without such a limit, the objective tends to be thought of by the public, and perhaps by some policymakers as well, in utopian terms, with the result that in moments of crisis (such as May, 1967) it is sentiment rather than reasoned strategy that rises to the surface.

The objective has not been defined partly because the competing Arab states and political movements have been unable to agree on it: to do so would require that their leaders enjoy a more uniform outlook on the world in general, and more confidence in their relations with their publics and with each other than has been the case. Particularly, they would have to be freed of the temptation to practice one-upmanship against each other. Partly also, however, they have not defined their objective because the practical pressure on them to do so has never been overwhelming. Each government could always reasonably hope to sidestep the next crisis by adroit improvisation; war with Israel was always a risk, but never inevitable, as long as the Arabs themselves did not intend to begin one. The argument mentioned earlier, that the costs of military defeats could be absorbed anyway, seems to be a rationalizaton for the Arab incapacity to avoid the risk.

As an astute Anglo-Arab commentator forcefully pointed out shortly after the June war, the Arabs have been unable to decide whether their policy should aim at destroying the Israeli state or only at the limited objective of containing it.[1] Not only the rhetoric, but also concrete policies, have fluctuated between these two ideas under varying circumstances. If Israel's very existence as an independent state is unacceptable, then it is necessary to prepare either to defeat her decisively in battle or to force her eventual disintegration from within by continuing military intimidation,

[1]Cecil Hourani, "The Moment of Truth," *Encounter* (November, 1967), pp. 3-14.

diplomatic isolation, and economic blockade. On the other hand, if the object is to limit Israel's size and power and to extract a major accommodation from her on the Arab refugee question, then some internationally recognizable basis for defining Israel's rights and obligations as a state becomes necessary, and the Arab states must make plain not only what they demand of Israel, but what they are prepared to concede to her. Here, as I shall note later, significant steps were made after 1967, but by then they were insufficient to accomplish the desired purpose.

The idea of destroying Israel has itself been ambiguously projected. What would destruction mean? Massacre? Physical demolition of cities? Presumably not, some occasional rhetoric from the most extreme sources notwithstanding. When pressed on this question by outsiders, Arab spokesmen have almost invariably declared that destruction of Israel simply signifies the de-Zionizing of the state, and the termination of its specifically Jewish character: especially the termination of the organized encouragement of immigration of Jews from abroad, and the second-class status of the Arab citizens. It has never been made clear, however, what institutions and communal or individual rights would replace those now in existence, were the Arab states to be in a position to enforce their will; and the fact that Israeli Jews today are in roughly the same number as all Palestinian Arabs combined (unlike the situation at the time of Israel's birth when the Jews were outnumbered 2 to 1), poses some unanswered questions.

Thus, although the "destruction of Israel" might be conceived of in the bloodless form of demographic and constitutional modifications that would perhaps strike some people and governments abroad as being humanly and politically constructive, there has been no elaboration of such a conception from the Arab side to enable it to become a viable political proposal. It is, however, the common theme of Arab public discussion; public opinion has never received encouragement to think or express itself in more modest terms, and as a result those in authority have no sure way of estimating how the public might respond to any explicit abandonment of the "destruction-of-Israel" idea.

On the other side of the coin, Israel is held by the Arab side to be obligated by a number of international agreements and principles; the United Nations General Assembly's partition resolution of 1947; other Assembly resolutions calling for the right of repatriation for Arab refugees; the 1949 armistice agreements; the inadmissibility of territorial acquisition by conquest; etc. The belief is common that Israel has always sought territorial expansion, and the fact that she has expanded from previously drawn borders (in 1948 and 1967) is felt to be conclusive evidence of such intent, just as the occurrence of Israeli punitive raids on neighboring territory is believed to be evidence of her inherently aggressive nature, and of the assertion that despite what her leaders say, they do not really want peace. On many occasions prior to 1967 Arab authorities such as President Nasser stated to Westerners that peace would be possible if Israel would accept the U.N. resolutions, that the Egyptian blockade of the Suez Canal to Israel shipping was a response to Israel's exclusion of the refugees, and that the record would show that it was Israel who failed to respect the armistice agreements. All these arguments, in purporting to hold Israel to her international agreements and obligations, logically implied an Arab willingness to respect Israel's rights that were the counterpart of those obligations: in the case of the armistice agreements, military security on Israel's side of the line; in the case of the U.N. resolutions, sovereign existence within the partition boundaries. The response of the Egyptian and Jordanian governments to the November 22, 1967, Security Council resolution was in line with this approach of limited objectives: in response to Israeli withdrawal, they were ready to renounce claims of belligerency and respect Israel's sovereign rights within recognized frontiers.

The counterpart of these alternative Arab verbal approaches has been their pattern of action. In line with the "destruction" theme have been the refusal to enter into diplomatic or commercial relations or to negotiate peace terms, the encouragement or countenancing, in some cases, of border sabotage operations by guerrilla groups, and again in some cases, the buildup of very large air and armored forces. In line with the "containment" theme, on the other hand, has been a noticeable and repeated effort to avoid actual confrontation once crisis was in the air, and in some cases, measures taken to prevent border infiltration. The evasion pattern was most clearly evident in the Arab response to Israel's diversion of Jordan River water in 1964-1965, which Arab spokesmen had several times previously declared would constitute an act of war. First Nasser called a summit meeting; there it was agreed that war was impossible and that instead the Arabs should do their own diverting of the headwaters before they reached Israeli hands; then it was agreed that before these operations could begin, arrangements must be made to defend them against Israeli attack. Finally, when little could be done to arrange for such a defense, the Arab diversionary works were abandoned altogether. In the midst of these developments (May, 1965), Nasser told a congress of Palestinians in Cairo that a war for the liberation of Palestine was unthinkable as long as the Arab states were divided. It was clear to discerning observers that this meant an indefinite, if not permanent, delay.

Again, it seems noteworthy that after each of the three major Arab defeats there has been an indication of readiness to accept a return to a guaranteed version of the *status quo ante:* in 1949 at Lausanne, an espousal of the essence of the 1947 partition plan; in 1956-1957, an Egyptian willingness to have U.N. troops protect Israeli shipping in the Straits of Tiran and keep the peace on the Egyptian-Israeli armistice line; after the 1967 war, a willingness to accept practical guarantees for the preservation, and even expansion, of the rights Israel had enjoyed prior to the crisis. On the other hand, the continued refusal in each of these three cases to consider establishing formal peace with Israel pointed to the more militant side of Arab policy, according to which mere containment of Israel was not enough.

In short, the Arab states have shown neither the will to make peace nor the readiness to make war. Being indisposed to do either, they have tended to compromise by cultivating a warlike posture but then attempting to maintain that posture in a state of suspended animation. In 1967 their terrible mistake was to try to reap positive—more than just defensive—gains from such a posture without being prepared to follow through with actual fighting. In other words, they allowed a defensive policy to become a revisionary one. They were not prepared to attack, and almost certainly did not intend to, yet they failed to gain the political benefit of being the defending party, and thus enjoyed none of the Western diplomatic support they needed.

In conclusion, the Arab effort to contain Israel and to defend themselves against her military superiority is seriously undermined by the counterpart effort to keep in doubt the principle of Israel's independent existence. As long as the very question of existence is kept open, there is little room for any serious elaboration of the means by which the international community can be expected to underwrite the containment effort. All that could be secured was a very general, and in practice undependable, commitment from the three Western powers to uphold the territorial integrity of both sides — undependable because Israel's disrespect for Arab security could always be attributed to Arab disrespect for hers. In consequence, Britain and France readily discarded their commitment in 1956 at Suez, and the United States did so (if in more passive fashion) during and after the war of 1967. As long as Israel's right to exist was in question, it would be natural for many outside onlookers to conclude that in fact it was the only question. The more modest but practically speaking more substantial question from the standpoint of Arab interests (What kind of Israel should the Arabs accept, and on what terms?) went unexamined, because the Arabs failed to raise it convincingly, let alone put forward their own answer.

Inter-Arab Divisions

The most coherent single reason for the Arab failure to define their position clearly lies with their own internal divisions. A decision to moderate their objectives in Palestine, and define them in some meaningful and practical form which the Irsaelis and other interested states can recognize and respond to, would require considerably more consensus, collective responsibility, and mutual restraint than the inter-Arab scene has afforded in the past two decades. We have seen in the United States how difficult it is for politicians to carry on intelligent public discussion of the much less sensitive question of relations with Communist China.

Each Arab regime has been so internally insecure and, in the atmosphere provided by the pan-Arab idea, so exposed to criticism by its neighbors that its leaders have tended to shrink from taking unorthodox positions on the ritually symbolic question of Palestine and Israel. It is a problem that has offered innumerable opportunities to embarrass one's rival, should he seem to take an independent position, for the established official position of intransigence neatly symbolizes several important virtues: honor, protection of one's kinsmen, courage, and steadfastness in the face of adversity. It is sometimes remarked that the presence of Israel in the Arab midst is in some sense functional, that if it did not exist the Arabs would have to invent it, and so on. It may be true that it provides a useful psychological symbol, but in terms of any serious political analysis the proposition is a very shallow one. Israel presents the collectivity of Arab states with a problem much too difficult for them to cope with in their present condition of political weakness. Consequently it has served to sharpen their divisions and their insecurities by providing each faction among them with a stick with which to beat the others. That the Arab states "agree on the problem of Israel when they cannot agree on anything else" is demonstrably untrue. On the contrary, although it is undoubtedly a problem about which they share common sentiments and raise common slogans, they have never been able to agree for any sustained period of time on how to deal with it.

Like other Middle Eastern issues, the problem of Israel has aroused concern in the U.A.R. that initiative should not be left to fall into the hands of other Arab states. Because of the sensitivities and dangers associated with this particular issue, cultivation of leadership of the Arab approach to it has been both an opportunity and a precaution. Until 1967 it enhanced Egypt's general prestige by emphasizing her indispensability to the Arabs collectively for their security, thus entitling her to pass judgment on their foreign and military policies. At the same time it provided Egypt with some insurance against the danger that another Arab state would trigger a crisis with Israel in which Egypt's own security would be threatened. But there were inherent contradictions in this double strategy: to enhance her own leadership on the Palestine issue, Egypt continually found it expedient to strike a militant posture, building up her armed forces and issuing defiant declarations, and at the same time seeking to sidestep whatever crises such a posture might stimulate. But as the events of 1967 showed, this brinkmanship could not always work. The crisis was stimulated by Syria's reckless behavior; to maintain leadership in Arab policy, Cairo escalated the tension; and in the end, the conflict proved impossible for her to avoid.

There is a long record of competition among rival Arab states to use the Israeli issue against each other and for their own individual advantages, beginning with their uncoordinated and disastrous intervention in Palestine in May, 1948. There is also a long record of competitive efforts to promote rival organizations and movements among the Palestinians. The most conspicuous of such efforts have been those made through the auspices of the Arab League, in which Egyptian influence has been traditionally predominant. The "All-Palestine government" headquartered at Gaza in September, 1948, was used unsuccessfully as a weapon against the move of King Abdullah of Transjordan to incorporate the rump Arab-held territory of central Palestine (the "West Bank") into his domain: and from 1964 to 1967, the Palestine Liberation Organization (PLO) directed by Ahmad Shukairy developed into a considerable threat to the authority of King Hussein over the Palestinian subjects he had inherited from his grandfather Abdullah. Paradoxically and significantly, the original Egyptian motive in supporting the creation of the PLO appears to have been one of caution: the PLO would serve to pre-empt the stimulus for the Palestinians to organize under more reckless auspices, such as the nascent guerrilla group *al-Fatah* with its Syrian sponsors; and by putting in charge such a man as Shukairy, who was capable of commanding very little respect and would always be dependent on Cairo, one could hope that the PLO would never develop the means of causing much trouble. Certainly there was no Egyptian interest in 1964-1965 in embarrassing King Hussein, with whom a reconciliation was in progress. But in time difficulties between Hussein and Shukairy inevitably did arise, as well as other difficulties between Hussein and Nasser, with the result that the PLO became a weapon against the Jordanian regime instead of a tranquilizer.

That the Arab states used the cause of Palestine against each other, but were unable to agree what else to do with it, was symptomatic of the serious problem they each faced in establishing orderly progress and authority within their own societies. The situation was made possible in the first place, however, because Palestinian Arabs themselves had always lacked effective organization and leadership of their own. Until 1948 they were victims of factionalism among their own prominent families (the Nashashibis and the Husseinis) and of their failure to respond to the limited opportunity that the British Mandate gave them to establish their own communal institutions in a manner analogous to that of the Jews. The leadership briefly provided by the Arab Higher Committee in 1936-1937 was suppressed, along with the rebellion it directed, by British armed force, and it was only ineffectually reconstituted by the time of the 1948 war. From that time on the population was scattered over Israel, Jordan, the Gaza Strip, Lebanon, and Syria, and many of its best educated members drifted off in search of employment in other countries. Just as the Palestinian community found itself dependent on the outside Arab states in 1948 for military support that the latter were incapable of providing, so also, then and afterward, it had to depend on them for political and diplomatic leadership with no better result. And despite their inability to render assistance, the Arab states did succeed in preventing the Palestinians from developing institutions of their own, by means of their insistence on sponsoring and exploiting Palestinian organizations for their own competitive purposes.

Thus Palestinian interests remained in the hands of non-Palestinian Arab regimes whose interests were bound to be somewhat different. For the governments of the Arab states, although Israel was a hated neighbor, it was practical to coexist with her as long as she was confined to her own territory; for the Palestinians, Israel's national existence entailed the denial of theirs. The no-war, no-peace policy of the Arab states was a *de facto* compromise between their own practical interests and those of the Palestinians. It was an expensive compromise, for it drew then into a conflict from which they could not withdraw once they were involved, and which could only damage their own prosperity, security, international diplomacy, and domestic political stability; but until 1967 the price they paid was not prohibitive, and the Palestinians were not in a position to force them into making heavier commitments.

The Impact of the War of 1967 on Inter-Arab Relations

The June war widened and dramatized the gulf between the interests of the Arab states and those of the Palestinians. The consuming need felt by the Egyptian and Jordanian governments to secure Israeli withdrawal from their territories, coupled with the shock of discovering the extent of their own impotence, led them to offer concessions and guarantees to Israel that would have been unthinkable at any previous time since 1949. In explicit and implicit ways, during the two years following the war, they made plain their readiness to renounce the will-o'-the-wisp of Israel's destruction and settle for the limited aim of containing her — provided only that they could be spared the ultimate humiliation of according legitimacy to Israel through formal recognition, something which they would have been unable to justify either to themselves or to critical Arab rivals.

This proposed strategic concession was not sufficient to satisfy the Israeli government, but more than enough to alarm large numbers of Palestinians, especially the younger generation among the refugees. For the Palestinians appeared to count for little in Egypt's and Jordan's plans; the important thing was for the governments to reach their own accommodations.

It was in reaction against this situation, as it had built up for 20 years, that the Palestinian resistance movement dramatically emerged after the June war and declared its insistence on keeping the struggle with Israel open—on escalating it, in fact, and stimulating additional clashes between Israel and Egypt and Jordan so as to forestall a settlement between them. In so doing, they posed an implicit challenge to the authority and the established state interests of both the Cairo and Amman regimes, especially the latter. But for some of the same reasons that the Arab states had previously found it difficult to turn their backs on the unattainable goal of destroying the Israeli state, so Egypt and Jordan could not now readily disavow the Palestinian resistance groups, especially considering the wide popular acclaim for these groups within each of the Arab states.

The longer the stalemate continues between Israel, Jordan, and Egypt, the more likely it will become that the violence practiced by the Palestinian resistance groups across the cease-fire lines, and the retaliations of the Israeli armed forces, will suffice to inhibit concessions from either side. This will presumably depend, however, on whether the resistance movement grows in strength. It is quite possible, and in this writer's view probable, that the movement will decline somewhat or remain at a static level. This could happen for a number of reasons. Their operations in Israeli-held territory have been costly; in time, the popular enthusiasm that has brought them large numbers of volunteers may decline; and most significantly, sharp divisions have arisen among the Fedayeen themselves.[2] Beneath the surface, deep mistrust is believed to prevail between the Fedayeen and the governments of both Jordan and Egypt. In Jordan their provocations of Israel bring reprisals that are damaging to the government, and King

---

[2]In mid-1969 informed estimates of the total numbers of active and trained Fedayeen ranged from 8000 to 10,000, plus several thousand others still in training. These were divided among four main groups and a plethora of minor splinter groups. The largest single group, comprising about half the total, was the Movement for the Liberation of Palestine (*al-Fatah*) led by Yasir Arafat. Others were the Palestine Liberation Forces, the commando arm of the Palestine Liberation Organization; *al-Sa'iqâh*, a Syrian-inspired Ba'athist group; and the Popular Front for the Liberation of Palestine, militantly leftist but split into ideologically antagonistic subgroups. While *al-Fatah* and the PLF have eschewed partisan and doctrinal involvements, preach only the fight for an Arab Palestine, and have been satisfied to leave the governance of Jordan to King Hussein, the others are avowedly hostile to Hussein and refuse to separate the issue of Palestinian liberation from that of socialist revolution. The warring factions of the PFLP declined to take the seats allotted to them in 1968 in the councils of the Palestine Liberation Organization, which Arafat was elected to head.

Hussein is conscious of the fact that they recognize his authority only at their own convenience. In Egypt Nasser must reckon with the Fedayeen as rivals for Arab prestige and leadership, and with the ties many of them have to non-Palestinian partisan movements of which he had already had cause to be suspicious (for example, the Muslim Brotherhood, the Ba'ath, the Arab Nationalist Movement, and the Communists). For their part, the Fedayeen of all stripes can only fear that Jordan or Egypt or both, will sell them out in a deal with Israel. The prospect that the Fedayeen may be drawn increasingly into inter-Arab factional involvements does not augur well for their independent political influence, or for their ability to upset the status quo within Israel and the occupied territories. It does, however, suggest a continuing and debilitating role for them in the inter-Arab political arena, stimulating an atmosphere of general frustration and mutual recrimination and the indefinite continuation of the tension in Arab policy between containment of Israel and revenge. Quite different results might be expected from a significant growth in strength of the Palestinian resistance movement. The most dramatic possibility would then arise: that the Fedayeen might overthrow King Hussein's regime, seize governmental power for themselves, and transform eastern Jordan into a Palestinian frontier-warrior state. Should they do so, they would present some of the other Arab states with much sharper dilemmas than those they have faced before; verbal support and token material assistance for the Palestinian cause would no longer suffice. Clearly it would no longer be within Egypt's power to control the level or timing of the conflict with Israel, for the initiative would pass to the new Palestinian-Jordanian regime. Furthermore, with a territory and regime of their own, the Palestinian militants would be in an unprecedented position to distinguish forcefully between their full-fledged and half-hearted Arab supporters, with the former exposed to all the risks of war with Israel and the latter to their own agonizing reappraisals and political upheavals. Likewise the Palestinians themselves would be faced for the first time with a clear choice of their own—a choice that lack of organized and responsible leadership has denied them ever since the Balfour Declaration—between the prospect of a final showdown with Israel on the battlefield and a negotiated settlement on terms acceptable to Israel. The prospect of the Arab states and the Palestinians being confronted with such stark choices leads some in Israel to hope that the Fedayeen will indeed seize power from King Hussein; and with opposite expectations, that hope is shared by some among the Arabs, although assuredly the latter do not include members of established governments.

It remains to consider the impact of the Six-Day War on relations among the established Arab states. While the problem of Israel before 1967 was a chronic irritant in these relations, the major dynamics of conflict and cooperation stemmed from other concerns. Since 1967, however, the Israeli problem has become the all-important factor, and does not seem likely to recede very much in the next several years. One reason for this we have just discussed: the upsurge of Palestinian nationalism, and with it the possibility that Palestinian militants may develop a lasting influence over the policies of several Arab governments. A second and more direct reason is that Israel emerged from her victory in possession of sizeable pieces of Egyptian, Jordanian, and Syrian territory, leaving these three states (or at least the first two of them) overwhelmingly preoccupied with the task of getting back what they had lost.

In the short run at least, the war had the effect of greatly diminishing inter-Arab tensions and restoring the cooperative atmosphere that had more or less prevailed in the 1964-1965 period of Arab summitry. Whatever mistrust may have persisted beneath the surface, previously hostile regimes now worked closely together. Iraqi forces were stationed in Jordan, and others in Syria; Jordanian-Syrian diplomatic relations, ruptured just before the war, were restored; Nasser and Hussein became comrades in misfortune; Egyptian forces were withdrawn from Yemen; and Egypt (as well as Jordan) became the beneficiary of large budgetary subsidies from Saudi Arabia, Kuwait, and Libya.

The most significant of these reconcilations were ratified at the emergency Arab summit conference at Khartoum, toward the end of the summer of 1967. A number of critical issues were in the air, and resolved along lines of compromise. While both Jordan and Egypt were eager to grasp at whatever diplomatic straws they could in order to secure Israeli withdrawal, other Arab states—ranging from Algeria and Syria to Iraq and Saudi Arabia—advocated maximum intransigence. The result was an agreement on the quest for a "political solution"—that is, a resort to diplomacy and the consideration of compromise formulas for Israeli withdrawal—balanced by the explicit rejection of recognition of Israel, direct negotiations with her, and the signature of a peace treaty. The boycott of the Western oil market, championed by the Iraqis, was dropped as a fruitless and self-damaging measure in deference to the larger and more business-minded oil-producers—Libya, Kuwait, and Saudi Arabia—but in return, these were persuaded to assume responsibility for Jordan's and Egypt's losses of income resulting from the war, at an aggregate rate of £ 135 million a year for the indefinite future.

The Khartoum formulas, and the other aspects of inter-Arab cooperation following the war, concealed a wealth of continuing disagreements and mutual suspicions, which seemed certain to come into the open if the wounds inflicted by Israel continued without remedy for very long. On the other hand, were a compromise settlement with Israel to be arrived at, or were Egypt and Jordan somehow to make some form of stable adjustment to their defeat, and thus dissipate the atmosphere of crisis, some of the old antagonisms could reappear. Thus, for example, the failure of diplomatic initiatives through the United Nations and the great powers would naturally reinforce the more militant view that such initiatives were a waste of time, vindicating the refusal of the Syrians to participate in them, and providing them and others with an opportunity to discredit the Egyptian and Jordanian governments for their faintheartedness. The Saudis, already unenthusiastic in any case about paying Egypt's bills, might well invoke this line as an excuse both to save the money and squeeze Egypt's pocketbook, and to seek credit by championing a more intransigent line in regard to Israel. Such a temptation might be especially great if their royal colleague King Hussein were to fall from power.

For the time being, however, the Khartoum formulas and the arrangement of subsidies have served Faisal and the other oil monarchs well. As long as Egypt remains preoccupied with the Israeli occupation of Sinai and financially dependent on the monarchies, it is hardly in a position to give them trouble. From this standpoint the arrangement has amounted from their point of view to a valuable, if expensive, insurance policy. Yet this is not to say that they will see fit indefinitely to continue paying the premium. (Faisal, for example, is said to have agreed only very grudgingly at Khartoum to grant Nasser more than the most token sum.) How effectively Nasser's successors might be able to retaliate against Faisal or the other oil monarchs, once freed of these golden chains, is a highly speculative question. We have already seen in the instance of the Yemen affair that even at the height of his prestige, Nasser's potential in the Arabian Peninsula was limited. Still, he was often able to put the Saudi monarchy on the defensive. With the chaos prevailing in the People's Republic of Southern Yemen since the British withdrawal from southern Arabia, and the uncertain future of the Persian Gulf principalities, there is no lack of raw material for conflict in which both Saudi Arabia and Egypt, as well as others, might plausibly play influential and competing roles. But in the light of the evidence of previous years, it seems unlikely that the Egyptian role could become a decisive one.

A continuation of the stalemate with Israel could eventually drive Cairo and Amman apart, even without a change of regime in either of them, by leading one or the other to shift its strategy and tactics. The fact that Egypt banks on Soviet support, and Jordan on American, does not enhance the likelihood that they will follow a common course of action indefinitely.

It would be conceivable, if not very promising, for the Egyptians to give up altogether on diplomatic remedies and devote themselves fully to an intensified conflict across the Suez Canal. It would be equally possible, and equally dangerous, for King Hussein to choose some favorable moment for a crackdown on the Palestinian guerrillas, in hopes of then being able to make a major diplomatic approach to Israel with the assistance of the United States. Or conversely, it would even be conceivable for the Egyptian government to obtain acceptable terms from Israel, while Jordan was still unable to do so. But in any case, these or other such clear differences in Egyptian and Jordanian policies or fortunes would provide ample occasion for mutual recrimination between them, together with efforts by each to mobilize support for itself from among the other Arab states.

The longer the stalemate continues, the more likely are Egypt and Jordan to adjust, however unhappily, to the new status quo and allow their interest in limited accommodations with Israel to erode. As the shock of the 1967 defeat wears off, and as they learn to cope with the practical day-to-day consequences of the territorial losses, the old policy of ambiguously pursuing the containment or the ultimate defeat of Israel seems likely to reassert itself. The losses sustained in 1967 would certainly not have seemed worth risking in many Arab eyes before the war had they been clearly foreseen, and for a time after the war they seemed too great to be endured; but then, much the same might have been said of the defeat of 1948, which the Arab states eventually learned to live with well enough to invite its repetition. It is difficult to imagine the particular steps by which the rump state of Jordan might adjust permanently to its post-1967 burden of Palestinian refugees and guerrillas, or Egypt to the loss of the Suez Canal. Yet both states may manage to do so, for there do not seem to be any ultimate pressures against them available to any outside power, while domestically there still remains considerable room for adjustment through political radicalization.

This is not as cheerful a prospect as it may seem. If Jordan and Egypt, together with Syria, do manage to absorb their misfortunes, we should not expect the adjustment to be accompanied by resignation, but by a drastic intensification of the insecure and hostile attitudes that have marked the Arabs' political relationship in recent decades, both among themselves and with outsiders. Thus while there is no present prospect that the conflict-ridden Arab atmosphere will improve greatly, there is a prospect that it may grow much worse.

CHAPTER 3

Changing Military Perspectives in the Middle East

Jacob C. Hurewitz

I. Introduction

Between 1963 and 1969 the U.S.S.R. became a Mediterranean naval power. This novelty has profoundly disturbed the Western powers, who have heretofore exclusively controlled naval affairs in the Mediterranean. It is probably no less disturbing to the strategists in the Kremlin, who have had no precedents to guide them in overcoming the obstacles that the Soviet Union faces in its new role, despite the prospect of ending its intrinsically landlocked condition and the fears of encirclement that condition used to engender.

Ironically, the U.S.S.R. has established a permanent military presence in the Mediterranean and the Middle East by deploying there the weakest of its armed forces.[1] Despite manifest inferiority as a fighting machine alongside the American Sixth Fleet, the fast-growing Soviet Mediterranean Squadron, as Moscow still officially designates it—or the Mediterranean fleet, as it might more aptly be named in view of its size and composition—has repaid handsome dividends in peacetime military diplomacy. Its most serious inadequacy as a fighting force is the lack of air cover. The Red navy generally relies on a land-based air arm, except for a new, modest but expanding, sea-based helicopter force. In peacetime, however, the Soviet air force is still hemmed in by a band of third states lying outside the Russian alliance system and denying it firm overflight privileges. Moreover, on the Mediterranean coast and in the Middle East, the U.S.S.R. has neither

[1]This analysis was completed in February, 1970, before the author learned about the Soviet plan to deploy in Egypt SA-3s with Soviet crews to man them. A weapon system still untested in combat, the SA-3s had not even been used in North Vietnam. Moscow gave advance assurance to the United States that the introduction of Soviet fighting personnel into Egypt to operate such a sophisticated weapon system was essential for the defense of a hard-pressed protégé. The SA-3s, the United States was told, would be emplaced only around Alexandria and Cairo in the delta and around the Aswan Dam in Upper Egypt. In March and April, even before the missile launchers were fully installed in the stated positions, the Kremlin sent to Egypt, without prior notification to the United States, Soviet combat pilots together with MIG-21js, the latest version of the fighter-interceptor to protect the launchers. With the Sovietization of the Egyptian air defense, international and regional military rivalry in the Middle East entered a new phase. The present study may therefore be viewed as an assessment of the developments leading up to the latest major change in the rules of military competition in the postwar Middle East.

facilities for stationing ground troops nor air bases, although it does enjoy tenuous, disguised base rights for naval air reconnaissance in Egypt. These conditions effectively weaken the Soviet Mediterranean fleet.

This contrasts with potential wartime conditions, when the Soviet Union would become a strategic power in the Middle East. Of course, it is already a cultural power there, since its empire embraces several Muslim republics in the Caucasus and Central Asia. In wartime, Soviet ground and air forces would be pre-positioned for more effective combat in the Middle East than would the comparable forces of the United States. Paradoxically, the Soviet Mediterranean fleet would probably not long survive the outbreak of a general war.

Much of the success of Soviet naval diplomacy in the Mediterranean and the Middle East during the last half of the 1960s may be attributed to the overreaction of the United States navy. American naval spokesmen and their supporters in Congress have overstressed the "modernity" of Soviet naval vessels and their enlarging numbers alongside the "aging" ships and the fixed numbers of certain classes (e.g., the Polaris submarines and the attack carriers) of the United States navy, thereby implying that the American ships are at a growing disadvantage. A qualitative comparison would, of course, show the continuing superiority of the United States navy over its Soviet rival. The exaggeration has been partly a function of American naval salesmanship to persuade Congress to give the navy steadily larger appropriations to meet the mounting costs of modernization. However, it also results from the very novelty of Soviet naval diplomacy in a changing international-military environment.

Closely linked to Soviet naval policies in the Mediterranean are Soviet arms transfer policies in the Arab area; both are intended to enhance Soviet prestige and influence at the expense of the United States and the other Western powers.

The Western powers were hardly less alarmed in 1955-1956 when they lost the monopoly of the modern arms market in the Middle East than they are today over the loss of the naval monopoly in the Mediterranean. They then feared an immediate Soviet search for military rights in protégé states and the infiltration of Soviet agents in the guise of military technicians and advisers to plot a Communist seizure of power. These fears have recently come alive again because of mounting evidence that the U.S.S.R. has procured shore-based facilities in Egypt, the state that had epitomized, in the postwar Arab world, the struggle against European imperialism, foreign bases, and infringement of sovereignty.

In the postwar Middle East, the Soviet political strategy was to encourage every measure that would accelerate British and French disimperialism and exclude the United States. By this means, the Soviet Union obviously expected to secure, south of its borders, a reduction and possibly a total withdrawal of Western military capability. However, the very weakness of Britain and France in an area of traditional Western supremacy, but persistent Russian security interest, brought the United States into ever deeper military commitment, first in the "Northern Tier" (the non-Arab Muslim northern part of the Middle East) and then in the Arab states and Israel. Before the Suez crisis of 1956-1957, the United States had preferred to share with Britain and France, under their leadership, collective responsibility for safeguarding common Western interests in the Middle East below the Northern Tier against possible Soviet expansion. When the United States, after 1956, assumed the primary military and diplomatic responsibility for safeguarding Western interests in the Middle East, the Soviet political strategy was redirected to limiting and preferably eliminating the American military presence there. However, the Soviet strategy merely stimulated the growth of American military commitment.

After the overturn of the monarchy in Iraq in 1958, for example, the Baghdad Pact — linking the United States and Great Britain with the non-Arab Northern Tier and Iraq — appeared on the verge of disintegration. Having failed formally to accede to the pact or to its successor, the Central Treaty Organization (CENTO), the United States nevertheless entered into bilateral alliances with the remaining three regional members — Turkey, Iran, and Pakistan. Far more cautious in the Arab-Israeli zone after 1955, rather than setting up alliances, the United States preferred its NATO allies merely to compete with large-scale Soviet arms exports to Egypt, Syria, and Iraq. By the mid-1960s, however, the United States itself had become a major supplier to Jordan and Saudi Arabia, as well as to Israel, although the principal NATO allies still cooperated in reactive arms-balancing in the Arab-Israel zone. More important than alliances or arms vending was the buildup of the Sixth Fleet, which until the mid-1960s gave the United States flexibility in the Mediterranean and the Middle East by nearly liberating it from enslavement to the good will of the coastal states. Not until the late 1960s, when the U.S.S.R. pierced the Western barriers in some strength and finally projected its naval power into the Mediterranean, did the practical possibility arise of a superpower military confrontation in the Middle East.

The Arab-Israeli war (the Six-Day War) of June, 1967, provided the United States and the U.S.S.R. the first opportunity for military intervention on opposing sides — not that either had planned such a course. However, both were indirectly involved, and such involvement might have led to military intervention under the stress of a regional war. On the outbreak of the Six-Day War, however, the Kremlin took the hot-line initiative in arranging mutual military restraint with the White House, under which

both powers kept their naval vessels an agreed distance from the scene
of fighting. The significance of the hot-line exchange for later developments
must be assessed in historical context.

In the Arab-Israeli zone, the Soviet Union began manipulating local
crises ("brinkmanship") soon after it became, in the mid-1950s, an arms
purveyor to selected Arab states. It apparently hoped to discourage the
United States from accepting military obligations in the area. So long
as the Soviet Union was not a Mediterranean power, however, the United
States could use the Sixth Fleet and shore-based facilities to threaten to
intervene (as in Jordan and Syria in 1957) or actually to intervene (as in
Lebanon in 1958) with almost no risk of military confrontation with the
U.S.S.R. The Soviet Union, on its side, backed down in the late 1950s
whenever the United States showed force or a willingness to use force.
Indeed, for more than six years after the American intervention in Lebanon,
the U.S.S.R. ceased to resort to brinkmanship.

Only after 1964, when the United States became progressively distracted
in Vietnam, did the U.S.S.R. resume its provocative probing in the Arab-
Israeli zone, culminating in the crisis that led to the Six-Day War. Undeniably, the Soviet Union did not want a war that its protégés would lose.
Since the Soviet leaders nevertheless did stir up tension in the area by giving
the Egyptians and Syrians false "intelligence" reports, one must conclude
that they expected the United States to prevent Israel from going to war.

The novelty in the Arab-Israeli third round was not the Kremlin's signal
to the White House that the Soviet Union would not intervene, but the
American countersignal that the United States also would not. The Soviet
initiative, immediately after the invasion of Czechoslovakia, for bilateral
negotiations with the United States and quadrilateral negotiations with
Britain and France to "settle" the Arab-Israel dispute reinforced the
expectations of American and Western diplomats and observers that "the
implicit understanding" of June, 1967, might be broadened into a durable,
explicit agreement on avoidance of a superpower military confrontation
in the Middle East. The United States, moreover, has kept the Sixth Fleet
out of the southeastern Mediterranean since June, 1967. In this area, meanwhile, the Soviet navy procured its first land-based facility in the Mediterranean; in 1969 it began staging maneuvers off the Egyptian and Syrian
coasts.

II. The Opposing Navies

Since its confirmation as a Black Sea power in the treaty of Küçük Kaynarca
(1774), Russia has been attempting to anchor itself in the Mediterranean,
failing at every trial except the last. As recently as 1945-1947, Josef Stalin
tried to browbeat Turkey into accepting the U.S.S.R. as a senior partner

in the "defense" of the Turkish Straits, by which he meant to assure his navy free transit between the Black and Mediterranean seas, while denying that right to all other major powers. However, instead of keeping the major Western maritime powers out of the eastern Mediterranean, Stalin's clumsy machinations helped bring the United States into it and cemented an American-Turkish alliance that has enabled American naval units to visit the Black Sea even in the face of rising anti-Americanism in Turkey.

The Soviet Union

By 1967 the U.S.S.R. had apparently established itself in the Mediterranean. It has found—in underway naval refuelings, replenishment, and repair—a peacetime method of circumventing its vulnerability at the Turkish Straits. One reason for the success has been the continuing dramatic expansion of the Soviet navy as part of a large program of maritime development. The policymakers in Moscow have clearly recognized that a massive strategic nuclear arsenal does not by itself make the Soviet Union a global power. At the outset, in 1963, Soviet naval vessels did not have access to Mediterranean ports for other than extremely limited courtesy calls. To establish a permanent naval presence in the Mediterranean, therefore, the U.S.S.R. had to imitate the American practice of underway refueling, replenishment, and repair. For ports, the Soviet navy substituted anchorages in shallow international waters across the Mediterranean from Cyprus to Gibraltar. Following the Six-Day War, the U.S.S.R. acquired limited, secret, and informal naval- and air-base rights in Egypt and was suspected of seeking them also in Algeria; and, once the Suez Canal is reopened, it will probably pursue similar policies in Yemen, the People's Republic of Southern Yemen, and Somalia, where Soviet port personnel are already installed. Of the three ports concerned (Hudaydah, Berbera, and Aden), Aden is the one to watch most closely.

Following Britain's announcement of its intention to withdraw from the Persian Gulf before the end of 1971, Soviet naval vessels began paying courtesy calls at the gulf ports of Iraq and Iran, thus revealing future intentions. The visits were relatively few, since, with the Suez Canal closed, the ships had to come from eastern Siberia or around the Cape of Good Hope. The great distance of the Indian Ocean from major sources of supply would create new logistical problems if the Soviet Union establishes a continuous naval presence east of Suez. But these problems should no longer overwhelm the Soviet navy now that it has anchored itself in the Mediterranean. The greatest delaying factor is not logistics, but the continued closure of the Canal.

The Soviet Mediterranean fleet tends to expand in the summer and contract in the winter, on a steadily rising scale. From a maximum level of 20 vessels in 1966, it grew to 30 just before the Arab-Israeli war the following June and to 45 immediately after the war. In 1968 it ranged between 35 and 52 vessels, including guided-missile cruisers and destroyers, landing craft, submarines, and, for the first time, a helicopter carrier; there were also the customary electronic trawlers and logistical support ships. In the summer of 1969 the Soviet Mediterranean fleet exceeded 60 ships.

The United States

In seeking shore-based facilities, the Soviet Union is reversing an American trend. When the United States created its Sixth Fleet in 1948, it enjoyed easy entry almost everywhere in the Mediterranean for courtesy calls and for bunkering and repair. Major ports, naval bases, and dockyards on the northern Mediterranean coast belonged, after 1949, to NATO allies; on the southern coast, they belonged to British and French dependencies. But, once Britain and France had dismantled their Arab empires, the Sixth Fleet encountered increasing difficulty in visiting the U.S.S.R.'s Arab military protégés, particularly Egypt and Algeria. After June, 1967, the Sixth Fleet became shy about showing the flag even in friendly Arab states such as Libya (which Soviet naval ships visited for the first time in 1969 while it was still a kingdom) and Tunisia, to say nothing of Lebanon.

In the Tripartite Declaration of May, 1950, the United States, Britain, and France warned the Arab states and Israel that any forcible shift of boundaries or armistice lines would not be tolerated. In the Baghdad Pact, the United States and Britain were trying by military partnership with the Northern Tier states and Iraq to continue the total military exclusion of the U.S.S.R. from the region. But the pact only opened the door via Egypt, Syria, and Yemen — and eventually Iraq and Algeria — to Soviet entry as arms salesmen. This role later eased the establishment of a Russian military presence in the Middle East. The pact also broke Western solidarity by excluding and thereby alienating France.

Then, in the fall of 1956, Britain, France, and Israel attempted by force to undo the effects of the Egyptian nationalization of the Suez Canal Company. Instead, their action temporarily shattered Western unity in the Middle East. British and French military leadership there ended suddenly in November 1956, when the United States compelled them to abandon their unfinished Suez campaign. Two months later, the Eisenhower doctrine verbalized the principle of unilateral American guardianship of existing regimes in the region against direct or indirect Soviet encroachment.

Now, American strategists, and not their British and French colleagues, were charged with framing the contingency plans to keep clear for American and Allied forces the Middle East lines of communication by land, sea, and air between Europe and Asia and Africa; and to protect the sources and the routes of oil supply, especially from the Persian Gulf to the European markets. When the bases that secured these lines of communication disappeared in the independent Arab states, the United States and its allies had to develop substitutes.

In 1956 the United States military system in the Middle East comprised a network of shore-based facilities and a steadily enlarging fleet. Before the advent of long-range missiles, the United States nuclear offense was built into the earth-encircling Strategic Air Command (SAC), including Middle East bases close to primary Soviet targets. In 1951 France leased to SAC the rights to five bases in Morocco; after achieving independence, Morocco continued the arrangement until 1963.

In 1948 Britain approved the reactivation for air transport — (and later for the Strategic Air Command) of Wheelus Field, an American World War II facility in Libya. In 1954 sovereign Libya prolonged the lease for 17 years, simultaneously permitting NATO forces to train and refuel there. The lease was terminated by agreement in December, 1969, less than four months after the overthrow of the monarchy, when the United States pledged to remove its forces (4600 officers and men) and equipment by June 30, 1970. Owing to Arab-American differences over Israel, Dhahran Field in Saudi Arabia, built in 1945, never developed into a full-fledged SAC base; however, after the lapse of renewed written agreements, verbal understanding has allowed it to continue in limited service for transit and support.

The most elaborate air and ground facilities available to the United State in the Middle East were erected in Turkey, after its admission to NATO in 1952. Under the NATO arrangement, Turkey allowed the installation of radar screens along its Soviet border, and the construction of air bases that could handle all types of airplanes, including strategic bombers. Starting in 1959, 15 Jupiter Intermediate Range Ballistic Missiles (IRBMs) were fixed to pads in Turkey. For reconnaissance over the U.S.S.R., the United States was also allowed to launch U-2 flights from bases in Turkey and Pakistan. Peshawar, the base in Pakistan phased out in 1969, was equipped with elaborate electronic listening devices for monitoring Soviet and Chinese communications traffic.

III. Shifts in Military Diplomacy

After the hardened-silo emplacement of Intercontinental Ballistic Missiles (ICBMs) in the continental United States, the Mediterranean and the Middle East lost most of their value for American strategic offense. Bombers and seaborne missiles nevertheless continued to be employed. Land-based facilities in the Mediterranean and the Middle East, however, were shifted about. Even before the abandonment of the installations in Morocco, bases were leased in Spain for bombers and Polaris submarines. The headquarters of the Sixth Fleet moved from Villefranche in 1966, when France withdrew from NATO's integrated military system, to Gaeta in Italy. Growing nationalist agitation, however, deterred the United States from acquiring mainland positions. Over the years, it has relied more and more on its Sixth Fleet, which normally operates under national command and which, through the headquarters of the United States Naval Forces in Europe, receives its orders from the non-NATO American Commander-in-Chief in Europe and its fuel and supplies directly from the United States. The fleet serves, in effect, as a roving base, projecting American naval and air power across the Mediterranean and the Middle East.

Even after 1956 the mission of the Sixth Fleet was confined almost entirely to the Mediterranean. The fleet, it is true, deployed a token squadron in the Persian Gulf (a small flagship and two destroyers), operating out of the British-protected principality of Bahrein. Otherwise, responsibility for upholding Western interests east of Suez fell chiefly on the British command with headquarters at Aden. With modest land, sea, and air forces strung along the southern and eastern coasts of the Arabian Peninsula, Aden became Britain's major base in southwest Asia until it was given up in 1967. Early in the following year, Britian announced that it would terminate its responsibilities in the Persian Gulf before the end of 1971.

The Relative Strengths of the Soviet and American Mediterranean Fleets

The Soviet fleet in the Mediterranean is still no match, as a fighting force, for the Sixth Fleet. For one thing, the Sixth Fleet has a mission of diplomacy and strategic *offense,* since the Polaris submarines carry weapons with strategic nuclear warheads and the carriers have a residual strategic capability. The Soviet fleet's mission in the Mediterranean is diplomacy and strategic *defense.* A Soviet nuclear offensive capability in the Mediterranean would be useless, because the vessels would be too remote from primary targets. Soviet submarines with nuclear missiles are deployed more effectively in the Atlantic and Pacific Oceans.

Moreover, two attack carrier task forces give the Sixth Fleet air and naval power that is independent of land-based facilities. The Soviets neither have nor evidently plan to build attack carriers. Even if they were to start such a building program, construction and assimilation into their Mediterranean fleet would take at least a decade. So far, the Russians have produced only helicopter carriers (each displacing less than a third the tonnage of the largest American attack carriers), which in the future might also accommodate VTOLs (vertical takeoff and landing craft). Significantly, the *Moskva,* the first helicopter carrier that was put into service in 1968, began shuttling back and forth between the Black and the Mediterranean seas for successive training exercises. The *Leningrad,* the second Soviet carrier, has not yet (February, 1970) appeared in the Mediterranean. Such carriers do not furnish the Soviet fleet with air power equivalent to that of the Sixth Fleet. This accounts for the Soviet effort to develop land-based aid power in Egypt, and probably elsewhere in the Arab world. However, such concealed land facilities, already useful for reconnaissance, are politically vulnerable.

In the past five years, the Soviet navy has been developing an amphibious capability. An estimated 2000 to 3000 marines (or naval infantry, as the Russians call them), or about one-third of the total force, have been deployed in the Mediterranean. So far as is publicly known, the naval infantry have not engaged in amphibious exercises there. In brief, although the Soviet Mediterranean fleet could carry out a small, unopposed amphibious operation, its landing support capabilities are no more reliable than its air defense or air cover.

The Soviet navy has weapon and delivery systems, the counterparts of which do not appear in the American inventory — cruise, or air-breathing, guided ship-to-surface (ship or shore) missiles of ranges from 15 to 200 or more miles, each fitted with a homing or terminal guidance device. The longer-range cruise missiles are placed on cruisers, destroyers, and submarines (which must surface to launch the weapon). The Russians have also developed patrol boats of the *Osa* and *Komar* class especially to carry short-range cruise missiles. By the end of 1968 the Soviet Union had sold or given to Egypt, Syria, and Algeria 30 or more such vessels, armed with Styx missiles (with ranges of 15 to 20 miles) of the type that sank the Israeli destroyer *Eilat* in October, 1967. American naval observers assume that, in a crisis, the Soviets would commandeer these boats, since the Mediterranean fleet has none. These observers also note that, unless the Soviet fighting ships were immediately sunk in combat, their surface-to-air missiles would check the air capability of the Sixth Fleet; the ship-to-surface missiles would inhibit its free movement; and the growing ASW (antisubmarine warfare) capability would limit the role of American submarines, perhaps even depriving the Polaris submarines of their protective concealment.

But such alleged advantages, which can be tested only in a superpower war, have hardly neutralized the Sixth Fleet. To pare down the American strategic superiority in the Mediterranean and the Middle East, which after all represents a wartime strategic threat to the U.S.S.R., must be a primary objective of Soviet military diplomacy in the region. Since the Soviet Union cannot hope to reach this goal by purely naval means in the proximate future, it must try to do so through military diplomacy. This accounts for the U.S.S.R.'s persistent encouragement of divisions within NATO over Mediterranean and Middle East policies and attempts to destroy or at least weaken the American alliances with Turkey, Iran, and Pakistan. It also explains Soviet efforts to discourage Spain from renewing base rights for American strategic bombers and Polaris submarines. But, above all, it elucidates Soviet stratagems to hem in the Sixth Fleet by discouraging Egypt, and therefore the U.S.S.R.'s other Arab military protégés, from resuming diplomatic relations with the United States.

American Military Diplomacy

The threatened appearance of the Soviet fleet in the Mediterranean and east of Suez has hardly dispelled the uncertainty of Western replacement for the expiring British regime in south Arabia and the Persian Gulf. From the American viewpoint, the timing of the British announcement of with-drawal from the Persian Gulf was unfortunate. A dozen years ago, if the United States had faced the prospect of a permanent, growing, and unchal-lenged Soviet naval presence in this region, the American response would doubtless have been decisive: American naval expansion on both sides of Suez that the U.S.S.R. could not hope to overtake in the foreseeable future (e.g., a new fleet, or at least a third carrier task force), accompanied by a warning that any attempt to use naval power to enhance Soviet prestige and influence in the Middle East would not be tolerated.

The Suez crisis of 1956-1957, for example, broke about a year after the start of Soviet arms aid to Egypt; by the fall of 1956, Syria, Yemen, and Afghanistan also became arms clients of the U.S.S.R. American riposte then was the Eisenhower doctrine, approved by both houses of Congress early in March, 1957,[2] which authorized the President

> to undertake, in the general area of the Middle East, military assistance programs with any nation or group of nations of that area desiring such assistance. Furthermore, the United States regards as vital to the national interest and world peace the preservation of the independence and integrity of the nations of the Middle East. To this end ... the United States is prepared to use armed forces to assist any such nation or group of such nations requesting assistance against armed aggression from any country controlled by international communism.

The application of the doctrine was immediate. In April, 1957, a task force of the Sixth Fleet, including the carrier *Forrestal* and an amphibious contingent of 1800 marines, steamed to the eastern Mediterranean to help King Hussein cling to his throne; for a full decade thereafter, the United States financed the modernization of Hussein's army, enabling him to

[2] Eighty-fifth Congress, First Session, Public Law No. 85-87, March 9, 1957.

become a vigorous ruler. At the height of a Syrian-Turkish crisis the following October, the American government delayed the withdrawal of several ships that had joined the fleet for maneuvers. At the same time, the State Department made a special point of warning Chairman Khrushchev to "be under no illusion that the United States, Turkey's friend and ally, takes lightly its obligations under the North Atlantic Treaty and is not determined to carry out the national policy expressed in the Joint Congressional Resolution on the Middle East [the Eisenhower doctrine]." [3]

What is the record of Soviet action and American response in the late 1960s? The Soviet navy has moved into the Mediterranean for keeps. American policymakers must now determine how that still-evolving condition affects our national interest. So far, they have been reacting to the Soviet challenge with caution. They have not expanded American naval power in the Mediterranean since June, 1967, when it first became obvious that the Russians could maintain a respectable naval force there. The inclination of the American admirals was to enlarge and further diversify the Sixth Fleet; the political decision was to maintain the status quo— neither expand nor contract. This decision reflected the new mood of the American people.

Current dissension over foreign military commitments has caused the United States to hesitate. However, American naval observers are convinced that, once the Suez canal is opened, the Soviet Union will establish at Hudaydah, Berbera, and Aden other informal and secret (or even open) stations like that at Alexandria to enhance Soviet military influence in the Arabian Peninsula. The U.S.S.R. might also acquire such a base at Basra from a friendly but frightened Iraqi regime. Yet, even with naval and air bases at the southern opening of the Red Sea or in the Persian Gulf, the Soviet Union could hardly expect to bar American naval vessels from these waters by establishing an exclusive position comparable to Britain's.

Since its creation in 1948, the Sixth Fleet has moved into the vicinity of erupting crises. As the visible defender of Western interests, it presented itself as a stablizing force. America no longer enjoys that kind of flexibility, since the Soviet fleet may now interpose its ships between a critical shore and American ships, thus forming a strategic barrier with a tactically inferior force. Even in June, 1967, when the Soviet fleet was smaller and less self-assured than it is today, its very presence inhibited the actions of the Sixth Fleet. The combatant units of the Sixth Fleet deployed in the eastern Mediterranean during the Six-Day War were forbidden to approach closer to the theater of battle than 300 miles. (The *Liberty*, an electronic communications ship that the Israelis damaged on June 8, 1967, was not attached to the Sixth Fleet.) The Soviet naval units in the eastern Mediter-

[3] *Department of State Bulletin*, Vol. 37, October 28, 1957, p. 674.

ranean at that time were bound by comparable instructions. However, at a distance of some 300 miles, the Sixth Fleet was only a half-hour away from the warring armies; the Russian fleet was at least a half-day away.

The United States' naval technical superiority is not likely to be equaled by the U.S.S.R. in the coming decade, for the technological gap narrows slowly. The credibility gap, if it should open, may widen swiftly. In recent years, American influence among the Middle East states has measurably declined, less because of the Soviet naval presence than because of the Vietnam conflict, which has tarnished our reputation for invincibility, once universally accepted in the region, particularly after the 1958 American intervention in Lebanon.

Moreover, since it became evident that the United States could win neither a military nor a political victory in Vietnam, American public opinion has become increasingly divided over foreign military policies. In the first two postwar decades, American foreign interests, policies, and commitments expanded. At the start of the third, contraction set in. By 1969 the prevailing attitudes in Congress, reflecting sentiment across the country, favored curtailing foreign aid and commitments, particularly military commitments. Serious observers are questioning the value of force in support of peacetime diplomacy, stressing the danger of foreign military involvements that might lead to new Vietnams.

This mood has affected American military diplomacy in the Middle East, for which Congress is reluctant to permit the navy to accept new obligations. On the contrary, some Senators have considered the desirability of withdrawing one of the two carrier task forces. For American military diplomacy to be credible, America must convince the Middle East states and the Soviet Union that her resolve is fixed, and that she prefers diplomatic settlement but is prepared to use force, if necessary. Such credibility is especially important when America enters into negotiations with the U.S.S.R. to formulate rules for military competition in the future. Because of the American penchant for acquiescing in an informal arrangement for avoiding military confrontation without gaining something concrete in return for harnessing its technical superiority, the United States is in danger of giving more than she gets in the Mediterranean and the Middle East.

The mood to compromise, though induced by the frustrations in Vietnam, is reinforced in the Middle East by spreading anti-Americanism in those Arab states whose governments have become Soviet military protégés and even among America's formal allies in the non-Arab Muslim countries, particularly Pakistan and Turkey. The evidence indicates that the United States is tiring of its unilateral responsibility for military diplomacy and defense of Western interests in the Middle East. A major pressure is the urgency to make the unilateral obligation multilateral.

So long as the NATO coalition held together under American leadership, the unilateral burden did not seem oppressive. Indeed, the unilateral responsibility gave the United States flexibility in crisis management. Moreover, allies cooperated and contributed during crises. For example, during the 1958 Lebanon intervention, Britain simultaneously sent troops into Jordan. This occurred even when many Britons were protesting that the landing of American troops in Lebanon was no less gunboat diplomacy than the 1956 British and French military intervention in Egypt. Moreover, the British did not conceal their dissatisfaction with the American refusal to place under NATO command either the American military facilities in the Middle East (except those in Turkey) or the Sixth Fleet. Even to an unquestionably pro-American study group of the Royal Institute of International Affairs, these refusals "made both fleet and bases appear rather the instruments of military isolationism than of the common alliance, outposts as it were of the 'Fortress America School'." [4] In brief, America's major transatlantic allies in the late 1950s resented American unilateral responsibility because it seemed to force acceptance of American leadership. Allied grievances sharpened in the third postwar decade when the Western coalition was losing its cohesiveness and the United States could no longer invariably count on its support.

Other factors also inhibit the current cooperation of the Western powers in the Mediterranean. None of the allies has even begun to modernize its navy along American lines, since none can afford it. As a result, even the navies of the major Western European countries often participate reluctantly in joint training exercises or any other integrated program with Sixth Fleet, because such exercises underscore their own inadequacy. In any case, the conviction prevails among the NATO members and all Mediterranean states that, in any showdown with the Soviet Union, the United States would bail them out. One primary American problem now is to persuade its allies that the shift in the American mood toward isolationism includes strong opposition to any enlargement of American obligations in the Mediteranean and the Middle East. This would seem to rule out, for the foreseeable future, the further expansion of the Sixth Fleet and the early development of a powerful navy east of Suez to fill the vacuum created by the impending British withdrawal.

Meanwhile, the Sixth Fleet is progressively losing access to the shore. In times past, the fleet visited ports in all Mediterranean countries except Albania and Israel. Following the Six-Day War, however, American naval ships were barred from all Arab states for at least a year; the fleet was still

---

[4] Royal Institute of International Affairs, *British Interests in the Mediterranean and Middle East: A Report by a Chatham House Study Group,* (London: Oxford University Press, 1958), p. 41.

barred from Syria, Egypt, and Algeria throughout 1969; nor did it visit Lebanon in that period.

America shall clearly have to pay in the Middle East for the preoccupying war in Vietnam. There is even danger that the United States in its present mood, in the state of disarray of its grand coalition, and with declining faith in a unilateral peacekeeping role, may seek too abruptly to contract its commitments in the Middle East. Precipitate action could destroy U.S. political leadership and subordinate Western interests and America's regional friends to the needs of Soviet security. The American search for companionship in bearing the risks of peacekeeping in a seething area must be seen in this light.

The American political will to use naval power without hesitation in support of peacetime diplomacy in the Mediterranean and the Middle East has thus undeniably weakened in the last three years. Meanwhile, the political will of the U.S.S.R. has undergone no comparable change, although it may have moderated its objectives. In past crises, including the Six-Day War, the U.S.S.R. spoke loudly but wielded a small stick. America can only speculate on the likely role of the Soviet Mediterranean fleet in future Middle East crises.

Soviet Military Diplomacy

The Soviet military expansion into the Mediterranean and the Middle East started erratically. Clearly, in retrospect, a major restraint was the U.S.S.R.'s difficulty in becoming a Mediterranean naval power. Security planners in the Kremlin did not begin to learn how to float a fleet at that distance until after the second Cuban crisis. Having mastered the logistical principles by June, 1967, the Kremlin began to support a program of naval expansion.

The overall plans are probably not nearly as calculating as many American observers suspect. The program of naval expansion may well be evolving pragmatically, as successive obstacles are overcome and opportunities occur. The assertion, for example, that the procurement of a naval base at Alexandria resulted from a complex Kremlin plot initiated before the Six-Day War simply does not ring true. The Soviet government must have been grossly embarrassed by the outbreak of a war, to which its diplomacy in the spring of 1967 had contributed but which it genuinely would have preferred to avoid. Quite apart from a superpower military confrontation that such a war risked, the Russians could hardly have been elated by their inability to go to the military aid of their protégés until after the negotiation of the cease-fire — a failure well noted in the Arab world. The U.S.S.R. later paid for Egyptian rearmament, at an estimated cost of $500 million by the end of 1968. We do not know the exact terms of the naval base contract. It is undeniable that the U.S.S.R. received the facilities partly as political payment for a scale of rearmament that a defeated Egypt could not otherwise afford, and that the presence of Soviet ships deters Israel. However, it is no less true that few Egyptians know about the base, and that neither the Egyptian nor the Soviet government discusses it openly, except in the case of Egypt to deny its existence. Such developments and behavior spring, not from advance planning, but from diplomatic bungling and opportunism.

We can only guess at the nature of the base at Alexandria. Even if the Soviet fleet enjoys no more than the right to repair ships and maintain warehouse facilities for spare parts rather than weapons, many of these repairs and parts must require security-cleared Soviet guards. Such personnel are also required when ships undergo basic repair, because their weapons and ammunition must be removed. These privileges encroach upon Egyptian sovereignty. The existence of even a modest base, however, is worth all the anchorages in the Mediterranean, since it permits more substantial pre-positioning of naval stores and more elaborate repairs than can be managed at sea. The U.S.S.R. did not procure comparable air-base facilities in Egypt although, in the spring of 1968, Soviet pilots began flying Tu-16s with Egyptian markings on Soviet naval reconnaissance missions. The hidden Soviet-Egyptian arrangements in an emphatically nationalistic country can yield only political difficulty in the long run. But, if the Russians could muddle into the arrangements, they might also be able to muddle through the use of the facilities for some time to come.

The very existence of the facilities, tenuous as they may be, has worried and stirred the imaginations of many American naval observers. They see the experiment at Alexandria already repeated at Latakia (Syria) and Marsa al-Kabir (Algeria). It is improbable that the Soviet navy has any shore facility in either Syria or Algeria. Indeed, Soviet relations with Syria were strained in the spring of 1969 over Syrian flirtations with China, and Colonel Houari Boumedienne is unlikely to abridge Algerian sovereignty by voluntarily offering any foreign power the elaborate naval base recently vacated by France. Still, there was suspicion in 1968-1969 that some Tu-16s tracking vessels of the Sixth Fleet in the central Mediterranean ended their flights in Algeria. In any case, the Egyptian experience is hardly a model for Soviet base procurement: lead a protégé into a disastrous war in which you cannot aid it, then finance the costly rearmament for stealthy access to coastal installations of uncertain durability. This is a game, not of politics, but of chance.

American naval observers also see Russia already in possession or at least in command of the choke points on the only naval passageway from the Mediterranean to the Arabian Sea—Alexandria at the upper end of

the Red Sea and Aden or Hudaydah near the Bab al-Mandab at the lower
end. But this lane has been closed since the blockage of the Suez in June,
1967, and its continued blockage has crippled Soviet development of a
permanent naval presence in Indian, Arabian, and possibly Persian waters.
Thus the urgent need for an open canal pressures the U.S.S.R. to seek an
Arab-Israeli settlement. Once the waterway is functioning again, the Soviet
naval buildup east of Suez will undoubtedly be promptly pursued.

The same observers are also convinced that the Soviet Union deliberately
chose for its bases the naval choke points on the Mediterranean-Red-
Arabian lane. More persuasive is the argument that these points were part
of the British Empire in the Middle East, and Arab hostility to Britain
opened the door to Soviet entry in the People's Republic of Southern Yemen
as in Egypt. If the Soviet navy should procure a base at Aden and keep
the one at Alexandria after the canal is reopened and—an even more
significant condition—if it should gain overwhelming influence over the
Arab governments that own the real estate, the Soviet navy would become
the true heir of the Royal Navy in the Middle East.

The Mediterranean is important for the U.S.S.R. not only for defense
against Western strategic attack, but also as a main route to the Atlantic
and Indian oceans. Therefore, it might be expected to support the traditional American and Western principle of keeping international sea lanes
open to all naval vessels. This position is certain to persist, at least as long
as Britain remains at Gibraltar and the Turkish government controls the
Straits. Without mastery over the Straits, the Soviet Union cannot, in
peacetime, project its naval power into the Mediterranean at will. It is
bound by the 1936 Montreux Convention that requires advance Soviet
notification of intention to send naval vessels through the Straits, while
"submarines must travel by day and on the surface, and must pass through
the Straits singly" (Article 12). Besides, if Turkey is threatened by or
actually engaged in war, it is authorized to stop the movement through the
Straits of all foreign naval vessels. The U.S.S.R. is then most vulnerable at
the Turkish Straits, for without transit through the waterway in an international crisis (as in both world wars), it would have great difficulty in
keeping a fleet in the Mediterranean.

Equally vulnerable is the Soviet supporting air power. Because Soviet
naval air power, except for the helicopters on the small carriers, is land-
based and separated from the Mediterranean by a layer of third states
(none belonging to the Warsaw Pact), the U.S.S.R. has had, in peacetime,
to seek overflight rights from the individual countries. After the Six-Day
War, Yugoslavia cooperated for the crash airlift of military equipment to
Egypt. The route continued open as late as December, 1967, and January,
1968, for the flight of squadrons of Soviet bombers to Egypt. After the

invasion of Czechoslovakia in August, 1968, it may be assumed that Yugoslavia withdrew the privileges. In peacetime, if the Soviet Union wishes to increase its influence over the Mediterranean powers that are not formal allies, it must not violate their air space.

In brief, though Soviet naval power in the Mediterranean has been expanding, it is still technically inferior to American naval power and has vulnerabilities that inhibit the Soviet Union from experimenting with even more adventurous policies. The visible expansion of Soviet naval power in the past two years has nevertheless divulged a possible pattern for the future. The Soviet Union will probably seek bases in several Arab countries along the Mediterranean and Arabian coasts. Since the U.S.S.R. has begun to break out of its traditional peacetime confinement, it may be expected to project its naval power east of Suez whenever opportunities arise.

Manifestly, the Mediterranean fleets of the Soviet Union and the United States labor under restraints that limit the rivalry. Yet, without agreed superpower rules for the competition, the regional disputants are able to play the United States and the Soviet Union off against each other. This should become clear in considering the superpowers' arms transfer policies to the Arab states and Israel, which are primary modes of interplay in the international and regional military balances.

IV. Arms Transfers to the Arab-Israeli Zone

The U.S.S.R. became an arms supplier before it became a naval power in the Middle East. The object of both activities was to gain political influence for strategic ends; in both, the U.S.S.R. modeled itself after the United States. As a naval power, the Soviet Union has never overtaken its rival. As an arms purveyor to the Arab states, it became the pacesetter in the area almost immediately, forcing the United States and its allies to modify their practices. However, the Soviet methods, despite their dramatic short-term consequences, have not necessarily yielded returns of long-range value to the security of the U.S.S.R.

The Arab states cannot produce the sophisticated weapons in their own armed forces' inventories; Israel can produce some and is the only Middle East state that can entertain realistic aspirations for sophisticated weapons autonomy in the 1970s. But even Israel still imports sophisticated hardware and many components for weapons of domestic manufacture. In short, Israel as well as the Arab states depends on external sources of supply. This dependence has entangled the superpowers in the interweaving Arab-Israeli arms races. For a decade and a half, Israel has engaged in spirited arms rivalry with Egypt alone and also with the group of Arab states in the immediate neighborhood.

In addition, an overlapping and geographically wider but purely Arab contest after the Six-Day War threatened in the late 1960s to range the Soviet against the Western protégés. The arms races in the Arab-Israeli zone are the most frenzied in the nonindustrial world. A half-dozen states (Egypt, Iraq, Israel, Jordan, Lebanon, and Syria) have received, since the end of World War II, equipment worth probably close to $9.0 billion; 70 percent of it went to Egypt and Israel. In this zone, Lebanon is the military laggard. In a neighborhood where governments are today lavishing between 15 and 20 percent or more of their GNP on their armed forces, Lebanon has never allotted its Ministry of Defense more than 3.5 percent.

The superpower competition in arms aid to the Arab states and Israel has been a component of the Soviet-American arms race and cold war since the mid-1950s. The technological revolution initiated by electronics, aeronautics, and rocketry threw arms manufacture in the United States and the Soviet Union into a crescendo of innovation. Never before did such costly and sophisticated weapons systems become outmoded so quickly. In the nonindustrial world, the obsolescent arms were highly coveted.

All arms transfers from industrial to nonindustrial states, whether by grant or by sale (for cash, by discount, or on credit), and instruction in the use and care of the military weapons and vehicles represent military aid. From the outset, Egypt and Israel have been hyperactive contestants. The moment either state imported a new weapon system, the other felt threatened and imported a comparable system. The other Arab military modernizers soon followed suit.

The superpowers have tried to sway the external policies of their military protégés by regulating the types, volume, and costs of their arms exports. In the rivalry for prestige and influence, however, the superpowers have been less concerned with the effects of their military aid policies on their protégés than on the Soviet-American military balance in the region, for example, the rights of access to or through Arab territory. The manipulation of the arms transfers enabled the superpowers to enhance their immediate political influence in the individual countries, but it also exacerbated the regional frictions and intensified the irrepressible Arab-Israeli dispute. Moreover, it created special opportunities for the U.S.S.R. and special problems for the United States, since Arab public opinion was conditioned by the policies toward Israel and toward Britain and France's residual imperial positions in the Arab area.

In 1955 the United States sold no equipment directly to Israel or any Arab state but did to those that do not border on Israel: Saudi Arabia, to which it sent a military training mission in 1952 as part of the arrangement for the use of the Dhahran base; and Iraq, which signed a military aid agreement with the United States in April, 1954, in the Baghdad Pact preliminaries (American military equipment trickled into Iraq until the overturn of the monarchy in 1958). Still, the United States was determined that regimes friendly to the West should receive modern weapons.

To permit the purchase of needed equipment, the United States for a decade (1957-1967) gave annual budget-support grants to Jordan nearly equaling the sums expended on its armed forces. Until the mid-1960s Jordan bought most of its arms from Britain. To Israel, the United States in these years gave other forms of economic aid, such as the discount sale of agricultural surplus, saving the government hard currency that could be redirected to weapons purchases—mainly from France until June, 1967, when it suspended sales. Starting in January, 1969, France also stopped the shipment of spare parts for several months. Israel bought other equipment (chiefly naval vessels and gear and tanks) from Britain and received, as reparations, an assortment of weaponry from West Germany. France met most of Lebanon's needs.

At first the United States acted as the supermanager of Western arms sales to pro-Western Arab regimes and to Israel. It tried to inhibit the arms races by planning with its two allied suppliers the volume and types of exports so as to restore uneasy weapons balances that Soviet shipments continually upset. The United States, becoming a selective supplier in the mid-1960s, modified its decade-old policy of encouraging Arab governments and Israel to buy from Western Europe. The United States sought a new mode of flexibility by providing its protégés with classes of equipment that would match in quality the weapons included in the immense shipments from the Soviet Union to Arab states. Moreover, the Pentagon began offering easy credit terms to American clients under a secret revolving fund.

The United States also tried unilaterally to slow the races down by delaying the negotiations and deliveries. For example, as early as September, 1962, it agreed to sell Hawk ground-to-air missiles to Israel, but postponed the signature of the contract until May, 1963, and the first deliveries for nearly two years longer. In 1965 used M-48 tanks were sent considerably faster, but only because Israel insisted on buying them before overhaul, in order to equip them with Israeli parts and weapons. The purchase of A-4 planes by Israel, negotiated for more than a year, was finally arranged in February, 1966, with first deliveries scheduled for December, 1967; delayed by the Six-Day War, A-4s did not begin to reach Israel until February, 1968.

Meanwhile, to escape pro-Israel charges, the United States did not disclose sales of M-48 tanks to Israel until February, 1966, after the Department of Defense could also report sales to Arab states: the Anglo-American agreement on an air-defense package for Saudi Arabia and the sale of M-48s to Jordan. Two months later, the Department of State announced that Jordan would be allowed to buy F-104s, before revealing the following month that Israel would be procuring the A-4s. Thus, from being an arms balancer by remote control in the Arab-Israeli zone, the United States became a direct balancer at the start of the third postwar decade.

Boasting that its military aid had no strings attached, the U.S.S.R. did not insist that the purchasers of Soviet arms join the Communist alliance. Moreover, it did not restrict the shopping list to tactical weapons, as the United States did (until it became a major supplier) in sales to nonaligned Middle East states. Nor did Moscow rigidly fix the amounts; the customer could request military hardware in large quantities. These were sales, as were Western arms that went to nonaligned Middle East states. Unlike the Western powers, however, the U.S.S.R. accepted local rather than hard currency for the later purchase of local primary products and arranged a flexible schedule of deferred payments, including long-term, low-interest credit.

In retrospect, we can see that the Soviet arms export policies were designed to tie the Arab customers to the U.S.S.R. yet leave them formally uncommitted. The U.S.S.R. overwhelmed its protégés with huge amounts of sophisticated hardware at variable bargain prices. It obviously hoped to establish a reputation for generosity and friendship, while satisfying a pent-up demand. Moreover, the initial high volume of exports was designed to flush non-Soviet weapons out of new customer countries. This strategy worked in Egypt, Syria, and Algeria, but not in Iraq.

Soviet arms transfer policies to the Arab states have caused much speculation in the West, some of it exaggerated. The Soviet Union has been suspected of crowding the Arab arsenals with equipment for ready redistribution to other Soviet clients. Algeria and Egypt, for example, ferried arms to the Congo in 1965, and to Nigeria in 1967 and 1968. Or the oversupply may be a form of stockpiling for later Soviet use. Some observers, meanwhile, believe that the U.S.S.R. has sent proportionately too few spare parts, suggesting yet another means of tightening Soviet controls. The same has been said of the restricted training given Arabs in the use and care of Soviet equipment before June, 1967, especially in Egypt (but that could be due less to Soviet than to Arab policy). In 1967-1969, moreover, the number of Soviet military technicians and advisers in Egypt rose sharply, variously estimated between 3000 and 6000.

The U.S.S.R. has been able to convince many Arabs that its arms transfer policies, reinforced by political and propaganda supports, reflect its material endorsement of the Arab case against Israel and of the Arab hostility toward the Western powers. This is demonstrated by the steady enlargement of the Soviet arms market and the corresponding erosion of the

American and Western arms markets in the Arab area. Where the Russians have become the sole arms providers (Egypt, Syria, Yemen, Algeria, the People's Republic of Southern Yemen, and Sudan), or virtually the sole provider (Iraq), the United States can bring to bear almost no influence on the regimes. The only exception at the time of writing (February, 1970) is Yemen. Of all the Arab arms customers of the U.S.S.R., only Morocco (which has made few Soviet purchases in the past year) did not sever diplomatic relations with the United States in June, 1967; none has resumed relations since then. Among the Mediterranean Arab states, only Lebanon, Libya, and Tunisia do not buy military weapons from the Soviet Union; and units of the Sixth Fleet, since the Six-Day War, have visited only two of these states—Libya and Tunisia—as well as Morocco. On the other hand, in the Arab East, Lebanon and Jordan have managed so far to resist popular pressures for arms procurement from the Soviet Union, as have oil-rich Saudi Arabia and Kuwait (and Libya in the Maghrib).

When the Soviet Union inaugurated its military aid diplomacy of polarization in the Arab-Israeli zone, it emphasized the policy of not insisting that its Arab military protégés formally align themselves with the socialist camp. That type of nonalignment has lost much of its meaning in the Arab states. In the mid-1960s all Soviet military protégés except Yemen adopted Socialism. In the name of Arab (as distinct from international) Socialism, they advocated the overthrow of the other Arab regimes, including Socialist Tunisia, all of which favored cooperation with the West. Throughout 1969 the U.S.S.R. still hailed the "liberation" movement of the military republics as progressive, and the defenders of the status quo as instruments of Western imperialism and reaction.

Here, too, the Soviet Union enjoyed psychological advantages with the Arab masses that the United States and its allies could not neutralize. Reactive to the Soviet policies, American military aid programs were a part of the diplomacy of antipolarization, that is assisting both Israel and the Arab states and upholding the status quo, unless it was peaceably modified. Such a proposition could hardly commend itself to Arab nationalists, and was acceptable to Arab regimes only as long as the United States embodied the goal in economic and military aid. When the Sixth Fleet roamed the Mediterranean unchallenged, for instance, Arab regimes friendly to the West found comfort behind its shield. An oil-poor regime such as Jordan's found it indispensable to side with the United States, because survival depended on annual grants. But most of these regimes contrived to keep alive not by popularity but by the presence of the Sixth Fleet and, even more, the U.S.-aided modernization of the armed forces that enabled them to suppress domestic opposition. (The Arab military regimes, armed by the U.S.S.R., of course treated their domestic opponents no less harshly.)

Understandably, after June, 1967, the American position was undermined throughout the Arab world, where the United States generally was held responsible for Israel's military supremacy, its massive victory, and its alleged territorial expansionism. With the termination of budget support to Jordan and the slow arms deliveries to Morocco, the United States found it steadily more difficult to conduct the diplomacy of antipolarization. There are those who argue that the Soviet diplomacy of polarization has been paying off, as attested by the multiplying Arab clients who, viewing military aid not merely as a means of military modernization but also as security aid, are influenced by the Soviet willingness to deliver the latest and the best at concessional prices, to send technicians and receive trainees, to support the clients diplomatically, and to promise continued potent defense help. On the other hand, Soviet influence in the Arab area has its own built-in limitations, which have surfaced since June, 1967.

The Soviet line on military aid was weak because it failed to carry military conviction. The primary purpose of military aid, as viewed by the aided states, was to strengthen them militarily, so they could overwhelm their enemy. But the more military aid the U.S.S.R. pumped into the Arab states, encouraging them in the belief that such arming would alter the military balance in their favor, the more obvious became the military and technological gap between themselves and Israel. Nasser could claim in 1956 that Egypt had really defeated Israel and that only the military action of Britain and France had enabled Israel to appear triumphant in the battlefield. In 1967 that assertion rang hollow to the Arab masses, as the true facts became known.

However emphatic nationalism becomes in its urge to destroy Israel, the fact remains that Israel has been growing more, not less, powerful—and its military aid comes from the West. Moreover, in 1967 the U.S.S.R. failed to assist the Arabs until the fighting was over. And in Egypt the Soviet Union began demanding repayment in privileges for its navy and naval air force. These were hardly signs of disinterested and effective aid. The message may not have reached the Arab masses loud and clear as yet, but it has certainly reached the Egyptian government. It has probably also reached the Ba'athist Alawi regime in Syria, where the Soviet resupply immediately after June, 1967, was fast, but later new delivery slow. In fact, the Syrian courtship of Communist China early in 1969, reflecting dissatisfaction with Soviet military aid, seems to have served as a useful ploy, for Soviet arms shipments were accelerated before the summer's end.

The U.S.S.R.'s loss is not necessarily an American gain even in the lingering cold war in the Middle East. Neither superpower can buy with arms transfers the kind of influence that it seeks. The Soviet Union can hardly be pleased to pay most of the costs for the weapons that it sends to

Egypt, or to carry the full burden of aid, economic as well as military, in the seven Arab states that have become exclusive Soviet arms clients. On the other hand, the mere export of arms in large quantities rekindles the aspirations of Arab nationalists, particularly the Palestine Arabs, to destroy U.S.-supported Israel, or at the very least to enable them to win a political victory that will nullify the effects of the military defeat. At the start of 1970 Israel was still clutching the occupied districts tenaciously, pending a negotiated settlement.

The harm in the Arab-Israeli zone created by the superpower rivalry cannot swiftly be undone. Placing the overfed states on a weapons diet would not be easy, even with superpower cooperation. Other industrial suppliers would be delighted to seize the markets abandoned by the superpowers. Besides, the U.S.S.R. will not easily agree to decrease the shipments to its clients, which would be more adversely affected than Israel by such a reduction. Clearly, the only real solution is to persuade the Arab states and Israel to negotiate a settlement, and to build up mutual confidence that will lessen their need for arms.

V. The Arab-Israeli Conflict Environment

An arms balance is not the same as a military balance. Since the mid-1950s, except for the intervals of rearmament after Israel's two preemptive strikes, the weapons inventory of the Egyptian armed forces has consistently exceeded that of Israel. Yet we can see in retrospect that at no time could Egypt validly claim military superiority over Israel. Clearly, if the antagonists have weapons systems of the same or similar class and generation, the number of arms and men do not count as much as the education, the military professionalism, the skill, the leadership, and the morale of the men who use the arms.

In all these respects, the advantage lies with Israel, as it also does in organization, planning, logistics, and coordination. The Arab armies have in fact been steadily modernized. So, too, has the Israeli Defense Force (IDF). Therefore, unless Soviet advisers have been scrambled in among the officers of the Egyptian and Syrian armies, the Arab armies have probably fallen farther and farther behind the IDF.

The Military Balance

No Arab state, not even Egypt, has developed a military industry that can produce more than a modicum of weapons, ammunition, and spare parts. No Arab army, not even the Egyptian army, adjusts the imported equipment, particularly the vehicles, to local conditions. The materiel captured by Israel in Sinai in 1967 had not been converted into desert-worthy automotive equipment.

Israel, on the other hand, uses its industrial capacity to full advantage in the military competition. Lack of confidence in the reliability of outside sources of military supply was reflected in the ever-widening range of light and medium weapons and spare parts that Israel manufactured, of military vehicles that it assembled, and of heavy equipment that it upgraded and adapted to its special military needs. With each such import, Israel procured both the product and the technology—for once its technicians learned to repair a piece of equipment, its military industry could also manufacture it. So long as the item in question was in high demand and could be produced locally, a domestic copy was likely to appear in Israel's arsenal. Moreover, all locally manufactured items appear in Israel's military industrial catalogue for sale abroad, wherever politically and militarily feasible, to help fund the expanding military industry.

More than that, Israel's industry, wherever militarily significant, upgraded automotive equipment, improved the firing power of tanks by adding guns or substituting large ones, and standardized engines and parts of military vehicles and other complex martial machinery of diverse origins. Regardless of the outward appearance of a tank or the nationality of its manufacturer, the insides were fitted with uniform parts and locally produced guns to simplify maintenance. Because of the wide assortment of tanks—American, British, and French—of various generations, Israel also bought hundreds of tanks in the surplus market, collecting for repairs caterpillars and other heavy parts that Israel did not find economical to manufacture. Aircraft do not lend themselves to such easy cannibalization. But the Israeli air force is still reducing the variety of spares for servicing the imported planes. It is now reportedly experimenting in the use of American engines on French-built bodies, as a step in this direction.

Instead of building a military industry gradually and along rational lines, Egypt tried, a decade ago, to leap into the production of prestigious weapons. Scientists, engineers, and skilled workers were recruited in West Germany among those who had been employed in World War II in the development and production of rockets and aircraft. Other technicians came from Austria, Switzerland, and Spain. Most of the expatriates, eventually numbering about 500, worked in the jet airplane program for designing and manufacturing a trainer and a fighter. Both were intended to reach the supersonic speed of Mach 2 to 2.5 but, in test runs with British engines as late as 1965, the Egyptian planes could not fly faster than Mach 1. European expatriates also tried to develop surface-to-surface missiles with a range of more than 250 miles. They tested prototypes of two one-stage rockets with payloads varying between 500 pounds and a ton and also planned to combine both in a two-stage rocket, but the more complex weapon was never tested, so far as is publicly known. The requisite missile

components, especially for the guidance systems, could neither be manufactured in Egypt nor procured abroad, so these, too, never went into
production.

On the airplane and missile projects, it was estimated that Egypt was
spending at least $50 million in 1965, when the costs were still mounting.
Significantly, these experiments were undertaken with the cooperation of
West Europeans as individuals, which suggests an Egyptian search for some
independence from the Soviet bloc. Even when Egypt severed diplomatic
relations with West Germany in 1965, Nasser did not accept East German
offers to replace West German skilled labor on advantageous terms.

The Egyptian air force has probably been more than replenished in all
major types of aircraft. The MIG-21 is still the primary fighter, while the
Su-7 has replaced the Tu-16 as the primary bomber. Many new pilots have
already returned to Egypt, after eighteen months of training in the Soviet
Union; others will follow. The Egyptians, with Soviet advice, have
attempted to apply the major lessons of 1967. Airfields are now dispersed,
aircraft are housed in hardened hangars, and some planes are allegedly
sheltered in Algeria and Sudan. There are more SA-2s (advanced antiaircraft missiles) and more radar screens than there were in 1967, but
whether the Egyptians and the Russians have worked out an adequate
defense against the low-flying tactics of the Israeli air force remains to be
seen. The Egyptian air force in 1967 had about 500 combat planes; in
mid-1969 the number may have been close to 600.

If so, it was nearly double the size of the Israeli air force, which had
also grown larger in the interval. The ratio between the two in 1969
actually represented a slight improvement for Israel, since on the eve of the
Six-Day War it was 2.5 to 1.0 (On the other hand, though the Egyptian
pilots and ground crews still perform more poorly than the Israelis, they
are certainly better trained today than they were in 1967 and can probably
keep more planes in the air and reduce the turnaround time for sorties.)
Moreover, the interruption of aircraft imports from France notwithstanding,
the Israeli air force has increased its versatility. The United States delivered
the original order of 48 A-4 Skyhawk bombers before the end of 1968,
and in 1969 was reportedly enlarging their number under a fresh contract.
To these were added 50 F-4s by the end of summer, 1970. (However,
Israel did not receive any Mirage Vs from France even after the Pompidou
Administration established itself.) If the F-4s, or Phantoms, are assimilated,
Israel will acquire a multipurpose plane unmatched in any Arab state.
Israel also bought more Hawk ground-to-air missiles as part of its reinforced
air defense in the Sinai Penisula.

Moreover, the test models of the Egyptian rockets and jets disturbed
Israel's security planners, who stepped up their own rival programs. Israel

already manufactured jet trainers under French license, repaired all jets added to its air force, and used the same facilities to service civilian jets of airlines operating in Israel and allegedly, on occasion, even to overhaul military planes of the French air force. However, it contracted to buy fighters and bombers from France and the United States, and the Israeli air force recommended to Dassault most of the changes that went into the creation of the Mirage V, a simplified copy of the Mirage IIIC with fewer electronic gadgets (and therefore cheaper and easier to maintain), yet with larger bomb and fuel capacity. Israel did not itself enter into more elaborate production to satisfy its own military needs until 1969, when it began to make, in partnership with a French- Jewish firm, engines for airplanes that might be offered competitively to the Latin American, Asian, and African markets.

In theory, Israel could have developed missiles of all types domestically. The local editions, however, particularly the desired surface-to-surface missiles, were certain to perform more poorly than the imports. In this respect, Israel and Egypt shared the same difficulties, since many components, especially for the guidance systems, had to be imported. However, instead of merely importing talent from the West, Israel also invested, in the mid-1960s, in the government-supported industrial talent of France, which lagged well behind the superpowers and Britain in missile production. Indeed, Israel sent its own scientists and engineers to France to collaborate in the venture. Since President de Gaulle appeared determined to achieve missile, aircraft, and nuclear independence from the United States, France, at the time, probably welcomed Israeli investment of capital and scientific skill in research and engineering for a mobile medium-range, surface missile. As a carrier of high explosives that would make up in penetrability what it might lose in accuracy, the mobile missile would, seemingly, give Israel a psychological edge in the competition with Egypt. It would also constitute an obvious delivery system for a nuclear bomb.

A missile large enough to accommodate a nuclear warhead would make that option credible to the Arab states. At Dimona in the Negev in 1960, Israel began the construction, with French assistance, of a 24-mW(th) nuclear research reactor that, on completion in 1964, yielded enough plutonium for one bomb per year, with fissile material to spare. The reactor's probable cost of $75 million or more was excessive for a pure research project. Israel did find an economical reactor fuel—uranium extracted from phosphates as a by-product of its fertilizer plant at the Dead Sea. Israel has thus been able to stockpile plutonium, although there is no evidence of its having built a facility to separate the plutonium from the uranium in the fuel rods. Scantier are indications of the actual construction of a bomb, and scantier still of the testing of one.

Unconfirmed rumors have been rife about Israel's attempt to buy parts in the West for building a bomb. But Leonard Beaton believes that, instead of erecting a separation plant, the Israelis have probably constructed a laboratory-level separation capability.[5] If so, he conjectured (April, 1969) that "the Israelis have a substantially larger amount of irradiated fuel rods—perhaps enough for about three bombs—than separated plutonium, which might now be enough for one bomb." Beaton is on the right track when he concludes that Israel has acquired bargaining leverage with the United States by agreeing not to exercise the nuclear option. He suspects that Israel has used this leverage in negotiating the contract for the 50 F-4s. In any case, because of Israel's military superiority, it has a "far greater interest in a nuclear option than in a nuclear force. A buildup of nuclear weapons on both sides would remove Israel's superiority in major conventional war, which is the present basis for her security." If Beaton's reasoning is sound, Israel has assured itself an open option without actually having to produce bombs.

The Economic and Social Context

The force levels in the Arab-Israeli zone must be viewed in the larger context. Israel's insistence on remaining militarily more powerful than its Arab neighbors derives from elementary rules of a military balance. The challenged state can deter or defeat the challenger only through military superiority. Under the British Mandate in Palestine, the Jews were the challengers and the Arabs the challenged, since the Jews refused to accept a status quo—an integrated Palestine—that precluded their sovereignty. After 1949 the roles reversed, for Israel endorsed the new status quo of the armistice. The Arab states, however, vowed to "liberate Arab Palestine" and destroy Israel. After the decisive victory in June, 1967, Israel proclaimed the end of the armistice system and the erasure of the armistice lines, which could only signify a permanent modification of the country's boundaries. The Arab states categorically opposed any territorial changes, thereby retroactively, but only implicitly, endorsing the 1949 armistice lines.

More and more Palestine Arabs, meanwhile, subscribe to the liberation of Palestine; in that doctrine, they are rediscovering their political identity, which was shattered in the war of 1947-1949. Pliant and passive refugees are being transformed into dedicated Fedayeen or guerrillas, crusading to recreate a Palestinian political entity. Despite their seeming inability to unite militarily (there may be at any one time as many as a dozen guerrilla societies), the Fedayeen have nonetheless been contributing to the Arab military effort through sabotage and terrorism against the Jews of Israel,

[5] Leonard Beaton, "Why Israel Does *Not* Need the Bomb," *The New Middle East*, No. 7 (April, 1969), pp 9-11.

Arabs cooperating with Israel, and with Israeli planes and offices in Europe. Through such exploits and the machinery the Fedayeen have fashioned to raise the necessary funds, the resistance movement has been elevated to a crusade, particularly in the Arab East. The greatest weakness of the Palestine Arab cause, however, is neither political doctrine, growing revenue, nor even military action, but the fragility of political organization. In the current reintegrative effort, the Palestine Arabs seem to be mistaking the unity of political sentiment for effective political organization and thus might be repeating the miscalculation that led to political disaster at the Mandate's end.

As politically unrealistic as the position of the Fedayeen may now appear, it is at least frank. By accompanying an implicit rather than an explicit endorsement of the 1949 armistice lines with a categorical rejection of direct negotiation, the Arab states confirm their adamant refusal to accept the reality of Israel and lack candor, thus outraging Israel. On the other hand, the Arabs are no less outraged by the principle of balanced power as interpreted by Israel. They reject, without qualification, the notion that Israel is permanently entitled to military primacy. Egypt is particularly determined to alter the balance in its favor. The Arab states can hardly be expected to acquiesce in an immutable military inferiority to Israel. This largely accounts for the Arab states' heavy emphasis on rearmament since the Six-Day War. It also helps expain why Nasser and his government permitted a Soviet military presence on Egyptian soil, a condition that Arab nationalists can view as only a shade less noxious than Israel's military strength.

But as victor, unencumbered by a U.N. presence except at the cease-fire lines, Israel has enjoyed more options than the Arab states. Israel's military planners feel that the cease-fire positions provide the IDF with the best possible defense along what Israel considers "natural" boundaries: the Suez Canal, the Jordan River, and the Golan Heights. In the Sinai Peninsula, Israel now has the advantages that once belonged to Egypt. Air bases, launching pads for antiaircraft missiles, and radar screens honeycomb the peninsula, for the first time giving Israel elbow room for air defense in depth. With Sinai under occupation, major civilian targets in Israel are at least 150 miles from the closest Egyptian airfields. To protect the air defense system in the peninsula, the IDF has dug itself into formidable fortifications along the east bank of the Canal.

The soldiers in the estimated seven Egyptian divisions on the canal's west bank probably outnumbered Israelis across the waterway by five or more to one in the artillery exchanges that began in the spring of 1969. By the following fall, Egyptian commandos with growing frequency were crossing the Canal at night to ambush early-morning Israeli patrols. If the Egyptians had felt able to take serious cross-Canal action, they doubtless would have done so. Moreover, the Egyptians did not commit air power to the military operations until early in the summer; by the fall, Egyptian pilots were gaining confidence but were still no match for the enemy.

Without air support, the Egyptians cannot realistically hope to retake the Peninsula. The exploratory probes, which may be expected to increase in frequency and range, must have convinced the Egyptians that they are not yet ready by themselves to establish a foothold on the east bank, let alone to recapture the Peninsula as a whole. From Egypt's standpoint, apart from the contribution to the war of attrition (examined below), the artillery duel, the commando raids, and the intermittent air and occasional naval action undoubtedly have had a double purpose: to convey to Washington (and New York) the urgency of the crisis and to harden the Egyptian soldiers to live combat with the enemy. On the Canal's other side, many IDF recruits were also undergoing their "baptism" of fire.

In the fall of 1969 Israel was still resisting mounting Soviet and Arab diplomatic and military pressure to return the occupied districts to the Arab states unconditionally. Until Israel gains firm safeguards for its future security, the military planners in Tel Aviv insist that Israel has every right to use the districts for strategic defense. In the larger area, the IDF may even be able to develop a second-strike capability. The Arab states, meanwhile, cannot be relaxed about the lost lands for fear that Israel will present them with a *fait accompli,* which they feel has perhaps already taken place. They are convinced that the seizure of the Sinai Peninsula, the West Bank, and the Golan Heights attests to Israel's inherent expansionism, that these are but the second installment of a master plan for the conquest of all the Arab territories from the Nile to the Euphrates — thus attributing to the official policy of Israel what a handful of Jewish religious fundamentalists once contended is Israel's right by divine promise.

Under the circumstances, Egypt must feel considerably more secure with Soviet naval vessels at Alexandria and Soviet technicians and advisers down to the company level of the infantry and even to the fire-control centers of the artillery. But above all, the military inferiority compels all Arab states, particularly Egypt, to give top priority to military modernization and expansion. Nasser may have been exaggerating when he "disclosed" in November, 1969, that Egypt had a half-million men under arms and that its military budget in 1969-1970 would exceed $1 billion, but the Egyptian armed forces are undoubtedly expanding.

Israeli military strategy rests on deterring the enemy by massive technical superiority, decreasing its own dependence on external sources of military supply by a steadily expanding military industry, raising the morale of the citizen army, and planning to win any war with the smallest possible num-

ber of casualties by protecting its small population—its greatest vulnerability—and by fighting only on enemy territory. The last objective places
a premium on a first-strike capability, which is also promoted by the desire
to escape international restraints in the event of a future use of open force.

The overall Arab military strategy, as reflected in the action by regulars
and irregulars along and across the cease-fire lines starting in the spring of
1969, calls for a war of attrition both to reduce Israel's already small
population and to prevent hardening of the cease-fire lines. A version of
limited war for small powers, such fighting is designed to bleed the IDF
with cross-Canal and -river exchanges, to force it into a defensive posture,
and to weaken the morale of the civilian population by a sustained high
casualty rate among the soldiers and by sabotaging and terrorizing civilians
on the highways, in the villages, and in the towns. The war of attrition
arises from a general acknowledgment of Israel's military superiority and
Arab numerical preponderance. Too remote at the cease-fire lines from
targets of civilian harassment, the Egyptian army has restricted itself to the
gradual escalation of artillery fire, of military commando raids on the east
bank of the Canal and, starting in the summer of 1969, of air assaults.

On the eastern front, the erratic performance of the regular forces has
disappointed the Egyptians. Gathered in Jordan were Iraqi and Syrian
troops together with token Saudi Arabian and Pakistani units, but the
unified command that the several forces were supposed to form failed to
materialize as late as February, 1970, although Syrian officers seemed to be
commanding the Iraqi troops. The only army to function with some professionalism was the Jordanian army, engaging intermittently in artillery
duels with the IDF. Along the frontier, Jordanian and Iraqi troops also
tried to terrorize the Jewish farmers in the established villages of Israel
proper, and in the new villages on the West Bank. Only rarely, even in the
Golan Heights, did Syrian forces engage in similar action against Jewish
villages. Effective coordination of the four Arab armies and the creation of
a unified eastern command that would shore up the Arab military stance
seem as remote as ever. Each of the four Arab regimes is distracted by
domestic problems: Syria, by declining Alawi popularity; Jordan, by the
growing independence of the Fedayeen; Iraq, by the continuing civic war
with the Kurds; and Saudi Arabia, by the internal repercussions of the
subtle resurgence of doctrinal division between the Soviet and the Western
protégés.

In the circumstances, Egypt has doubly welcomed the multiplying
Fedayeen raids on the eastern front, which take a steady toll of lives and
property and create stubborn problems of internal security in Israel. Syria
has become the principal center for Palestine Arab guerrilla organization

and management. Apart from its own closely supervised group of Fedayeen, Syria before and for some time after the Six-Day War furnished a sanctuary for *al-Fatah,* the guerrilla arm of the Palestine Liberation Organization backed by the Arab League. However, *al-Fatah,* which represents over half the Fedayeen, mounts its guerrilla operations against Israel not from Syria but from Jordan and Lebanon. Indeed, the war of attrition in Damascus has been directed less against Israel than against the two pro-Western Arab regimes. The Syrian government worked closely with *al-Fatah* in wresting freedom of assembly, organization, and operation from King Hussein in 1968 and from the Lebanese government a year later, abridging the sovereignty of both regimes and assuring Israel counteraction. It should be noted that all the military regimes favored greater freedom for the Fedayeen in Jordan and Lebanon, while denying the same rights to the guerrillas in their own states.

The Fedayeen raids together with the growing militancy of the Arab governments are forcing Israel to escalate its military response. The Israeli air force has tried to lure the Arab air forces into combat, for with undoubted superiority it would prefer full-scale air action. Whenever the Israeli casualties mount on the southern front (as the Israelis have designated the cease-fire line along the canal), in addition to the daily artillery exchanges, the IDF stages occasional commando raids on countervalue targets: refineries, powerlines, bridges, and coastal defenses in the Gulf of Suez. The countervalue targets attacked on the northern front (as the Israelis have designated the combat zone along the Jordanian, Syrian, and Lebanese frontiers), largely in response to the Fedayeen, included the commercial airlines in Beirut, destroyed late in 1968, and Jordan's East Ghawr Canal, incapacitated in mid-1969. The IDF has also attacked Fedayeen camps in Jordan, Syria, and Lebanon.

The military threat of the Fedayeen to Israel appears at the moment less than its threat to the Palestine Arabs in the Gaza Strip and on the West Bank. Israel began in June, 1967, to soften the Palestine Arab resistance in the occupied districts by giving them freedom of movement even into Israel itself. However, throughout 1969 the Israel security forces also meted out collective punishment to those who resisted Israeli investigation of guerrilla movements and activities as well as those who harbored the guerrillas. The Israeli security forces clearly have been unable to devise effective measures to check the Fedayeen in a limited-war context. Still, there seems to be less destruction of Jewish morale than of Jewish-Arab relations in Israel. The Arabs contend that these developments will destroy Israel in the end. Indeed they may; in the meantime, the Palestine Arab residents of Israel and of the occupied districts are suffering more than the Israeli Jews.

The American Position

Greater still is the threat to the American position. For years the Soviet
Union has been trying to subvert the pro-Western Arab regimes by enticing
them with generous military aid, by encouraging Soviet military clients to
stage an ideological struggle against them, and most recently by trading on
the Fedayeen. In the name of the liberation of Palestine, the Arab world in
1969 was being radicalized, a process that the Soviet Union has fostered
by indirect manipulation. The immediate victims in this instance were the
American protégés and, of course, American prestige. The diplomacy of
polarization was working as never before, as exemplified by the Lebanese
crisis of October-November, 1969.

Military logic dissuades Israel from loosening its grip on the occupied
territories, at least until there is a formal settlement. The cease-fire lines
give the state maximum military security. Political logic is conflicting. On the
one hand, in the long run, assimilation of the occupied districts would
create many new problems (e.g., the loss of cultural homogeneity,
egalitarianism, and perhaps even democracy, while keeping irredentism
alive in the neighboring Arab states and multiplying opportunities for
guerrilla warfare) that could only weaken the domestic and external
security of the state. On the other hand, while the conquered lands ought
eventually to be returned, they are nevertheless valuable now for diplomatic
bargaining. Military logic among the Arab states calls for intensified military
modernization to achieve parity with Israel. One might infer from the
policies of 1969 that Egypt saw no early prospect of attaining military
parity either alone or jointly with Israel's other immediate neighbors.
Thus it may have decided that, in the foreseeable future, the Arabs alone
could not displace Israel by purely military means.

After the second round, when a similar military condition prevailed,
Egypt arranged Israel's withdrawal from the Sinai Peninsula and the Gaza
Strip by diplomacy. This largely accounts, after the third round, for Egypt's
heavy dependence on superpower diplomacy to retrieve the lost lands.
From the outset, Egypt could count on the Soviet Union, which in its
pursuit of the diplomacy of polarization in the Arab-Israeli zone demanded
that Israel return all occupied districts without reservation before any
settlement with the Arab states might be arranged. But without American
cooperation, the Soviet-Arab strategy could not work; and the Nixon
Administration continued into the early fall of 1969 to support Israel's
contention that the return of the captured lands must be negotiated by the
Arabs and the Israelis. The modification of the United States stand on the
occupied districts, proposed to the Soviet Union in October, 1969, and to
the four powers in December, aroused fears in Israel and hopes in Egypt
that the international community would, once again, convert a military

defeat into a political victory. As seen in Washington, however, the United States demarche was designed to enlist Arab friendship, as a first major step toward revitalizing the American diplomacy of antipolarization, virtually abandoned since mid-1967.

Long before the fall of 1969 the very refusal of the Arab states to recognize Israel and deal with it directly had strengthened Israel's determination to keep its military supremacy. This alone, Israel's security planners were more convinced than ever, could guarantee the survival of the state. The conviction was reconfirmed, as 1969 ended, by a sudden sense of isolation from the four powers, since France was only slightly less hostile toward Israel than was the Soviet Union, and the United States seemed to be joining Britain as a neutral. In the circumstances, Israel was bound to reinforce its military self-reliance.

VI. Conclusions: The Game of Military Politics in the Middle East

The international military balance in the Middle East seemed to be undergoing radical change in 1969, although the outcome was far from clear, even after President Nixon's report on foreign policy in February, 1970. The military capability of the United States in the Middle East still exceeded the U.S.S.R.'s and, with the American technological lead, could continue to do so in the foreseeable future. It was the lack of political will rather than inadequate military capability that tended to offset American superiority in the Middle East, as elsewhere in the world. This raised a basic question: Was the international military balance in the Middle East beginning its mutation from American to Soviet superiority? Or was this only an illusory consequence of indecision, as the United States sorted out its new world role in the light of fateful decisions on Vietnam?

Of course, American military engagement and bargaining opportunity in East Asia and the Middle East differ in many ways. In East Asia, the Soviet Union and Communist China may be expected to scramble for the spoils as the United States withdraws and, if the withdrawal becomes large enough, Japan will certainly take a greater interest in its own defense. In these circumstances, the United States might ally more closely with Japan and trade on Soviet and Chinese difficulties. In the Middle East, the United States has committed no ground forces, and has grown visibly tired of the unilateral obligations of military-political predominance. The only active contender for military-political leadership in the region is the Soviet Union. Communist China can entertain no serious aspirations for a spoiler's role in the Middle East in the early 1970s. Britain's decline in the Mediterranean and the Middle East has still not run its course, while the reawakening French interest in an independent role in the Arab Mediterranean coastal states is still untested.

Stalin would have been amused by the immobilization of American military diplomacy in the Middle East, a condition that the U.S.S.R. has bought cheaply. It merely enticed the United States into bilateral negotiations, not on the issues dividing the superpowers, but on issues dividing the Arab states and Israel. Such negotiations for an Arab-Israeli settlement in an atmosphere of mutual superpower distrust were unrealistic, a fact that the Soviet Union, but not the United States, recognized immediately. The superpowers did not yet have a common purpose and, therefore, could not work toward a common goal. Meanwhile, partly in anticipation of an accord with the U.S.S.R. on the Arab-Israeli dispute, the United States lapsed into military-political inaction in 1969. For the predominant power, such inaction amounted to abdication of leadership, giving the primary challenger greater military-political flexibility in the Middle East.

The paramount United States military interest in the Middle East in 1970 remains unchanged: the safeguarding of American national security as far from the continental United States as possible and the fostering of close cooperation with friendly states that face the same or comparable security threats, so that the combined resources might be used for their mutual benefit.

Since 1957 the United States contribution to joint endeavors in the Middle East has been to shield the cooperating regional and interested extraregional states. In return, the cooperating states permitted the United States access to their territory during crises and, in some instances, continuously with permanent military installations. For these facilities, the United States has had to pay a price than an economy-minded Congress, responding to national skepticism about the validity of the principles of American foreign military-political programs, seems progressively less willing to sustain. One condition of unchallenged predominance was unilateral obligation. Since the United States is now less prepared to carry such military burdens in the Middle East singlehandedly, it is trying to find a workable alternative.

Thus, President Nixon emphasized partnership in his February 1970 foreign policy report and his acknowledgment of extraregional involvement in the Arab-Israeli dispute: "all the more dangerous because the outside powers' interests are greater than their control." The offer of cooperation and the rejection of unilateral American concessions were designed to stop the speculation on the Nixon Administration's determination to hold the military-political line in the Middle East and to negotiate more imaginatively with the Soviet Union. This resolve remained to be tested in Congress, which must allocate supporting funds. In brief, the search for partnership and accommodation in the Middle East would still have to overcome the stubborn realities of American domestic as well as international and regional politics.

Safeguarding American national security in the Middle East, as elsewhere, requires a favorable international military balance, with the United States in the long run offering concessions only to replace the unilateral military obligation by a more generalized system. Pending a Soviet-American détente, it would have been desirable to recreate, together with Britain and France, an exclusively Western system. But neither Western European ally has a strong incentive to resume obligations of which the United States relieved them in such humiliating circumstances in 1956.

A broadened NATO involvement might provide an alternative Western system. However, expansion of NATO's role now appears no more than a theoretical possibility, despite a number of half-measures in 1968-1969. The Mediterranean and the Middle East were, after all, never major NATO responsibilities even at the height of its vigor in the 1950s, although the coalition made it easier for the Mediterranean members to accommodate American naval vessels and for their navies to engage in joint maneuvers with the Sixth Fleet. It seems late in the day for NATO to develop an effective Mediterranean policy, and we shall have all we can do to keep that coalition alive for its diminishing activities in Europe.

Given the disabilities under which the United States must pursue its military policies in the Middle East, a formal détente with the Soviet Union would seem most cogent. The basis for a Soviet-American détente in the Middle East, it is often argued, already exists. Neither superpower wants nuclear proliferation or a military confrontation there. A formal Soviet-American conventional détente in the Arab-Israeli area has two prerequisites: superpower agreement on mutual military policies and on the military terms for an Arab-Israeli general settlement. The Soviet-American exchanges in 1968-1969 on the specifics for an Arab-Israeli political settlement seem premature. The superpower negotiations should have focused first on the stabilization of the international military balance in the region. Moreover, even if the superpowers reach a formal conventional détente in the Arab-Israeli area, we ought not have exaggerated expectations.

Without a firm, formal agreement on superpower military policies on the Arab states and Israel, the Arab-Israeli tensions are unlikely to be calmed in the near future. However, without a détente, neither superpower may be expected to make unilateral military concessions. The reopening of the Suez Canal without advance Soviet political assurances would simply ease Soviet naval expansion east of Suez and multiply American anxieties about expensive competition. The institution of arms-transfer controls, on the other hand, would disadvantage the Soviet Union, since much of its military influence in the Arab states derives from generous and uninterrupted arms aid. The Arab states would undoubtedly believe that the curtailment of arms imports would shackle them permanently in military inferiority to Israel. Unconditional Israeli withdrawal from the occupied districts would merely undermine Israel's security.

A final choice, the resuscitation of the United Nations peacekeeping machinery in the Arab-Israeli dispute, depends for effectiveness on a Soviet-American military détente in the Mediterranean and the Middle East. The reactivation of the U.N. machinery was the thinly veiled purpose of the four-power talks in 1969; but without a superpower détente, a four-power agreement in the Security Council under the sponsorship of the permanent members is simply unattainable. Still, if peacekeeping could be inserted into Security Council resolutions on the Arab-Israeli dispute, problems of conflicting commitment might be eliminated, while the obligations and risks might be spread across the international community. The primary problem then would be to convince Israel that the major organs of the United Nations would handle the issues before them on merit, not partisan preference. Thus, the key to military-political stabilization is a Soviet-American détente in the Mediterranean and the Middle East.

Given the superpower rivalry, the paramount goal of American military policy affecting the Middle East should be the stabilization there of the international and regional balances so as to protect American national security. The Soviet exchanges with the United States (and also with Britain and France) in 1968-1969 may have been partly intended to stabilize the Arab-Israeli regional balance. Yet it is undeniable that there was less military stability in the Arab-Israeli area at the start of 1970 than there was a year earlier.

Since 1945, there have been various choices for stabilizing the international military balance in the Middle East. Total American disengagement would, in effect, deliver the region to the U.S.S.R. The United States would have to stop using the Middle East for residual strategic deterrence, placing the non-communist Mediterranean states in Europe and in the Middle East, including Israel and the friendly Arab states, under Soviet hegemony. Such a policy would boost the efforts of the Soviet Union to become a global power, while the United States moved into reverse by restricting its strategic mobility and by relying increasingly on nuclear weaponry in the continental United States.

Total disengagement from the Middle East became a hypothetical choice under President Nixon's "status quo" doctrine of February, 1970: He merely warned that the United States would regard Soviet attempts in the Middle East "to seek predominance" or "to exploit local conflict for its own advantage or to seek a special position of its own" as matters "of grave concern." Moreover, he reaffirmed the "long-standing obligations and relationships" of the United States with a number of Middle East states. He asserted his Administration's "intention to maintain careful watch on the balance of military forces and to provide arms to friendly states as the need arises," pending a reactivation of the Arab-Israeli cease-fire and an agreement to slow down arms transfers to the Middle East.

In brief, the President and his security advisors seemed to have recognized that it is the better part of military-political and economic wisdom to continue old policies until a basis for change, such as diplomatic agreement, is found. The superpowers in 1970 are playing their latest game of bluff. At the time of writing, it is the first game that the Soviet Union might win in the Middle East, if the United States continues to ignore the signals. If, in the end, the superpowers should fail to negotiate an orderly rearrangement of the military-political responsibility in the Middle East, and if the United States should militarily disengage from there, the dangers of a nuclear war would almost certainly multiply. Without forward positions of conventional defense, the United States would be surrendering an important American cushion against a general nuclear war.

The Arab states and Israel have both violated the armistice and the cease-fire regimes. But as revisionists, the Arab states and the Palestine Arabs were prone to initiate such action, compelling Israel to retaliate. The Arabs clearly started the limited war in April, 1969; the Israelis escalated it. Because this was a limited war, Israel's acquisition of air superiority was slow. It was obvious by the start of 1970, however, that Israel sought the same flexibility for its air force that it had won in the Six-Day War. The air forces of the three eastern Arab states remain too weak to constitute a serious threat. After June, 1967, the Egyptian air force, the only one to give Israel pause, suffered a double disadvantage—the distance from targets in Israel proper and the inferiority of the Soviet-made MIG-21 and the Su-7 alongside the American-made Phantom and Skyhawk. Israel evidently needed seven to eight months to neutralize the Egyptian air defense—anti-aircraft, radar, and SA-2s—in the Canal Zone and to inhibit the Egyptian air force from more than occasional raids across the Canal and rare dog-fights with the Israeli air force.

Israel's major problems are economic and demographic: how to pay for the necessary sophisticated arsenal and provide military manpower without crippling the economy. It cannot afford to take high risks in actual combat unless it has the assured support of a major power for sophisticated weapons replenishment. Uncertainty over such support somewhat reduces the likelihood of an early pre-emptive strike, which would precipitate a full-scale war. At the start of 1970 it appeared that Israel's assertion of air mastery over the Canal Zone, short of pre-emption, has restored the military initiative to Israel.

So long as the United States and the U.S.S.R. are competing in the Arab-Israeli area, there is no prospect of regional agreement, since the super-powers have drawn the regional states into the international rivalry. This prevents the Arab states, the Palestine Arabs, and Israel from finding their own level of regional accommodation.

In trying to manipulate the Arab-Israeli military balance for this purpose, the Soviet Union has had three choices: it can promote peace, limited war, or full-scale war. It obviously views peace as disadvantageous at present, because it would give Israel what it seeks, while barring the Arab states' demand for Israel's unconditional rollback to the armistice lines and denying the Palestine Arabs their aspirations to liberate their homeland. Such a policy would dissolve Soviet influence in the Arab world. On the other hand, full-scale war without superpower intervention would almost certainly result in a resounding Israeli victory that would undermine Soviet influence.

The promotion and support of limited war, the policy that the Soviet Union has pursued since the spring of 1969, has seemingly yielded high returns at nominal initial costs. It has sharpened Arab-Israeli tension, increased Arab dependence on the U.S.S.R., strangled pro-Western regimes in Jordan and Lebanon, reduced American influence in the Arab area, weakened the symbolic impact of the Sixth Fleet in peacetime diplomacy, frozen the fleet out of the southeastern Mediterranean, drained the Israeli economy, and strained Israeli manpower despite the widening Arab-Israeli technological gap—all at a cost of only a few Soviet lives. Therefore, Moscow would like to stabilize the limited war. Meanwhile, to compensate for the lack of real Soviet concern about the Arab casualties or damage to Arab society, Soviet propaganda pours out words of peace and inveighs against Israeli "aggression," aided and abetted by "American imperialism," so as to reinforce world opinion against a full-scale regional war.

Soviet policies suggest that their framers feel that time and geography favor the U.S.S.R. This feeling would seem confirmed by recent regional history. But the benefits are likely to be ephemeral, for the anti-Americanism of today in emphatically nationalist states may turn into anti-Russianism tomorrow.

Moreover, American military influence in the Middle East has not been entirely destroyed, for it remains to be seen how the surviving oil-rich monarchies (Saudi Arabia and Kuwait) will manage their military orientation. After the Six-Day War, by financially assisting Egypt and Syria as well as Jordan, they checked the earlier trend toward the destruction of monarchies. Tunisia and Morocco also benefited from this policy. United States influence on the Arab monarchies even after the overthrow of Libya's King Idris in September, 1969, was demonstrated at the December Arab summit conference at Rabat (Morocco). In resisting demands by Egypt and the other military republics for an increase in the annual subventions to Arab states actively engaged in the limited war, Saudi Arabia and Kuwait seemed to be responding to the renewed American diplomacy of antipolarization.

American military logic calls for ending the limited war by reinstating the cease-fire as a first step toward negotiating a formal settlement. That would help to stabilize regional politics and enable the United States to check or halt the erosion of its position in the Middle East. Failing the restoration of the cease-fire, the United States may be expected to continue supporting Israel to enable it to preserve its military superiority. Even if the Soviet Union refuses to cooperate in ending the limited war, the United States seems hardly likely to encourage Israel to overcome Soviet obstruction by pre-emption, since a full-scale regional war might entrap the superpowers. Nevertheless, Israel's visible escalation of the limited war at the turn of 1970 began to enlarge the Soviet risks.

Soviet diplomacy in the Arab-Israeli area depends heavily on a heating device (ostensibly unqualified support for the Arab cause against Israel) with a built-in cooling system (the United States desire to prevent a full-scale regional war). But United States influence on Israel in matters deeply affecting that state's security is severely circumscribed; thus, if the Soviet diplomatic device gets overheated, the American cooling system may break down again, as it did in 1967.

PART II

The Participants

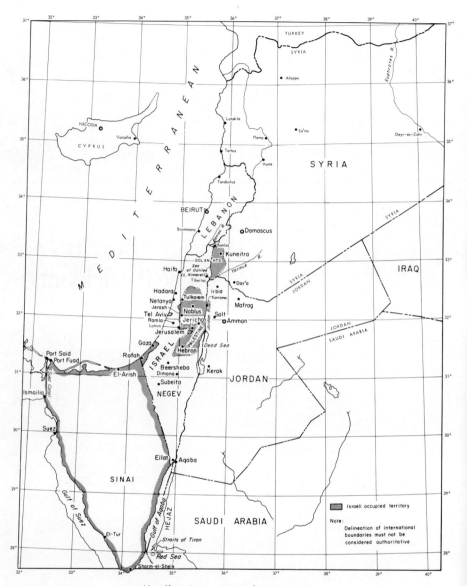

Map II — Areas of Arab/Israeli conflict

PART II

The Participants

Two chapters in this part deal with Israel and two with her Arab neighbors. In Chapter 4 Saul Friedlander describes Israeli perceptions about Arab state protagonists and infers policy choices for Israel from his description. Nadav Safran in the following chapter interprets the Israeli party system, considers its effect upon the conduct of foreign relations, and discusses Israel's future handling of her national security conflict and the effect of that conflict upon the character of Israel's domestic political life. Chapters 6 and 7 concern the Arab states that have been the most in conflict with Israel. Malcolm Kerr deals with the United Arab Republic (U.A.R.), and P. J. Vatikiotis with Jordan, Syria, and Iraq.

Friedlander devotes much attention to the reciprocal perceptions of hostility and threat in the traditional ethnic conflict between Arabs and Jews. He pictures most Jews as having a conscious and unconscious common identity, and attributes to Arabs a common view of Jews as inferior people who have humiliated Arabs in establishing and expanding Israel. He attributes a uniform intransigence to the Arab hatred of the Jew and depicts Israeli perceptions of Arab hostility as nearly unanimous.

Safran explains Israel's external security policy in other terms, as flowing from a coalition in national politics that avoids the articulation and debate of foreign policy issues. He examines Israel's party system for the light it casts on Israel's foreign policy behavior. This is an area of considerable strength in the theory of politics and the result is a powerful explanation. Foreign policy, however, consists of more than the output of partisan politics. In this sector of public policy the government apparatus can be a particularly independent force. The public bureaucracy in Israel is highly permeated by other elements of Israeli society, but is also prominent and prestigious, especially in its military establishment. The demands upon the military for high performance doubtless produce powerful bureaucratic pressures. Safran touches upon these matters, but they are peripheral to his main concern. He considers two events that raise questions about military bureaucratic pressures, the Lavon affair and Eshkol's displacement by Dayan as Minister of Defense. Yet the issues raised by both events, the considerable demands made by the military functions of government under present conditions upon the entire Israeli polity, remain outside the scope of his analysis.

Safran indicates that Israel is proceeding with competence to cope with the economic and political problems of the military seige. He argues that once the necessary investments have been made in order to develop a military-industrial complex, the balance-of-payments problem will be corrected, and the proportion of GNP devoted to military expenditures, which is large, can be reduced. As a democratic state with ambitious domestic welfare programs, however, Israel faces some formidable difficulties in the future. The economic problems created by the high level of military efforts, for instance, while they can be reduced, may still persist. Michael Bruno has raised questions about the efficiency of Israel's capital investments under the duress of a military seige that could affect her future economic growth rate and could reduce the likelihood of reaching satisfactory solutions to the balance-of-payments problem or the high proportion of the GNP devoted to military expenditures.[1]

It is not uncommon in Europe and the United States to perceive of Arab state politics, particularly Egyptian politics, as preoccupied with the conflict with Israel. Kerr's chapter in this part corrects this misperception by sketching the Nasser government's persistent and considerable domestic troubles and showing that they severely limited the government's choices in every direction. The government's authority was linked conspicuously to aspirations for Arab unity, and, although opposition to Israel has served as a rallying point for Arab nationalists, that opposition also imposed its own demands and constraints on the U.A.R. national leadership. Whatever else it has also been, the conflict with Israel has been another complication for the U.A.R.'s leaders.

Vatikiotis presents the politics of the Fertile Crescent states as revolving mainly around factions that are a mixture of quite parochial ethnic and ideological conflicts. Like the U.A.R., the behavior of these states in external affairs is severely constrained by domestic factors. Unlike the U.A.R. none of them has had a chief of state able to keep his political authority free of serious challenge—a Nasser—to preside over the government for nearly twenty years. The play of factional political conflict has, consequently, been a more important component of the political dynamics of Syria, Iraq and Jordan.

When taken together, Kerr's and Vatikiotis' interpretations suggest something more about the role in Arab politics played by the Israeli issue. National political systems in these states utilize only a narrow segment of the population; they may need issues that are generally appealing but not directly salient to organized economic and other interests. Given the limited range of choice of the Arab governments in handling their own domestic problems, and the secondary priority of their foreign policy, the Israeli issue can provide them with some additional room for political maneuver—up to a point where danger mounts and options narrow. Realistic

[1]Michael Bruno, *Economic Development Problems of Israel, 1970-1980* (RM-5975-FF, The Rand Corporation, April, 1970).

foreign policy behavior can be sacrificed up to that point and the crisis potential of the Arab-Israeli conflict neglected in order to cope with pressing domestic matters.

These fine points of Israeli and Arab state behavior are scarcely academic matters. Any effort to cope with the Arab-Israeli conflict by any power in the Middle East turns upon them. The extreme interpretations of behavior in both camps aside, it is on the margin of their present conduct that diplomacy must work. The chapters in this part are not reassuring for what they say and imply about the marginal propensities of Israeli and Arab state behavior, for they do not exclude the possibility of the reciprocal escalation of fear and violence. On the other hand, they also do not exclude the possibility of the diminution of both fear and violence if some changes occur in the regional political environment.

Saul Friedlander is Professor of History and International Relations at the Hebrew University in Jerusalem, and author of *Reflexions sur l'avenir d'Israël* (Reflections on the Future of Israel, 1969. Paris: Editions du Sevil, 1969).

Nadav Safran is Associate Professor of Government at Harvard University, and author of *From War to War: The Arab-Israeli Confrontation, 1948-1967* (New York: Pegasus, 1969).

P. J. Vatikiotis is Professor of Politics at the School of Oriental and African Studies, University of London. He is the author of *Modern History of Egypt* (New York: Praeger, 1969).

CHAPTER 4

Policy Choices before Israel

Saul Friedlander

I. Introduction

Like any decisionmaking group, the men who make the major political decisions in Israel see the situation before them through a prism reflecting both their own immediate or recent experience and the legacy of the past experience of their people, the Jewish people. At the heart of this past collective experience is the unique bond between the Jewish people and their ancestral land, Palestine. If, as Zvi Werblowsky has said, the Jewish people are a group of individuals sharing the same religious beliefs, a people who believe themselves to have a certain specific historical consciousness, then their ties with the Chosen Land are part of their historical consciousness, and of their religious and national identity.[1] Understood in this way, Zionism as a political movement appears to many Jews as the ultimate phase of the messianic aspiration to return to the Holy Land; hence, the "de-Zionization" of Israel so often mentioned recently would be anathema to them. Born of an age-long aspiration, Israel is desired as the homeland of any Jew who wishes to come, whoever he is and wherever he comes from.

For the Zionists, the establishment of a Jewish state became the only possible solution to the Jewish problem—the failure to be assimilated into the modern world. Hence the Jewish nature of the state, the will to maintain a political and social order that guarantees Jewish majority becomes not only a historical right, because of the peculiar link between the Jewish people and the Holy Land, but a historical necessity. It would be impossible to understand some of the fundamental political choices Israel has had to make if these facts were not taken into account.

The Nazi persecution and destruction of one-third of the Jewish population during World War II had an equally fundamental influence on the conscious, and even more on the unconscious, mind of the Jewish community. From 1945 onward there were numerous Jews who identified themselves with these events. During the crisis of 1967, Jewish reactions both in Israel and in the outside world, the Diaspora, showed that the memory of the holocaust of World War II had again come to the surface.

[1]Z. Werblowsky, "Israel et Eretz Israel," *Les Temps Modernes,* No. 253 bis (1967), p. 376.

Since then, consciously or unconsciously, Israel considers herself as a community whose total physical destruction may be intended. Such a feeling will of necessity inspire the utmost caution, even inflexibility, in regard to anything that might seem to weaken the country's security in the slightest degree. The common emotional heritage is engrained deeply enough to overcome any internal dissension in time of crisis.

The society of Israel is a society in rapid transformation, one in which the structures of an essentially agrarian economy are being replaced by those of an advanced industrial society. But all social groups do not participate in this change to the same degree: a cleavage has become apparent between the Israelis from Europe and America and those from Africa and the Middle East. Further, there are internal political tensions brought about by the conflict between generations. But the tensions caused by the generation gap or by the evolution of social structures have practically no influence on national cohesion and the behavior of the community in periods of crisis. It would be misleading to attribute to the internal tensions of Israeli society any important influence on the basic political options before the Jewish nation.

There is another factor that exerts a continuous and decisive influence on the options before Israel: the support given to the Jewish state by the majority of the Jews who have settled outside of Israel. This support, which Israel knows she can reckon on in all circumstances, gives her a guarantee of additional political and above all financial power which considerably strengthens her own resources. For this reason alone, it would be inaccurate to assess Israel's potential according to the criteria usually applied to a country of less than 3 million inhabitants.

II. The Arab-Israeli Conflict

The conflict between Jews and Arabs has lasted for over 50 years. On the eve of the June, 1967, war, the Arab nations thought that the end of Israel had come; after victory, many Israelis thought that this time peace was inevitable. Nearly three years after the end of hostilities most aspects of the situation suggest that the crisis of 1967 was merely another stage in a gradually worsening conflict. Under these circumstances, what are the options facing Israel?

The Political Factors

To understand the choices before Israel, we must first describe the situation in which the country is placed—a situation determined by the attitudes and policies of the surrounding Arab states, by greatpower policies, and by Israels' military strength, as well as by the evolution of the relationship between Israelis and Arabs in the territories which were occupied after the 1967 war and by the refugee problem.

Although this situation is not necessarily viewed in the same manner by all Israelis, the author believes that, apart from a few details, he is presenting the view of the majority of those Israelis who participate in any capacity in the process of making major political, military, and economic decisions.

The Attitudes of the Arabs

Emotional Attitudes. The Arab attitudes which are described here are, in outline, those observed by the majority of Israelis who have influence on the formation of decisions. It may be that, in fact, the hatred of the politically conscious Arabs toward Israel, for instance, is less fierce than is believed in Israel, or that certain conditions (such as the relative degree of coexistence in the occupied territories) attenuate it; but what matters here is not the whole scale of Arab attitudes, but those dominant attitudes that the Israelis recognize or believe that they recognize within the Arab world.[2]

Among these attitudes, Arab humiliation seems to be foremost. Just when the Arab world had tried to reassert its greatness, it was beaten three times by a handful of adversaries and, what is more, by Jews. In the Muslim world the Jew, although a member of a related religion, had come to be considered with contempt in the course of the last centuries. Although Islam has never displayed the excesses of Christian anti-Semitism, the Jew was nonetheless a second-class person, one of a far lower quality than a Muslim. The existence of the state of Israel thus became a constant reminder to the Arabs of their humiliation. Their refusal to recognize the existence of Israel and to negotiate with the Jewish state in spite of these defeats represents to the Israelis a denial of the humiliation and an affirmation that in spite of everything, Arab greatness will assert itself in the long run. To most Israelis it therefore seems that the humiliation the Arabs felt from their defeat at Jewish hands is thus made bearable by their refusal to negotiate or even to recognize the existence of Israel.

A second Arab attitude is supported by a number of rationalizations, the purpose of which is to explain the strength of Israel, not by the Jews' intrinsic qualities, but by the support which the nation obtains from Western imperialist countries. The Israelis believe that this image of Israel as the servant of imperialism is becoming more and more deeply rooted in the Arabs' consciousness. The Arab defeat may seem less difficult to endure when it is no longer seen as inflicted by a tiny Jewish state, but

[2]Many Israelis think that they will be able to transform the fundamental attitudes which we shall describe among the Arab populations that are under their control.

by the entire imperialist West. Such a rationalization of events enables the Arab world to believe in a final victory, as the course of history must sooner or later lead to the downfall of Western imperialism.

Many Israelis believe that behind these Arab attitudes there lies a deeper emotion, the feeling of an injustice that must be avenged, and that the Arabs consider themselves to be the victims of repeated acts of aggression by Jews, not only during the last few years but ever since the beginning of Zionism. Most Israelis also believe that they are hated by the Arabs, that they appear to the Arabs as complete aliens, agents of all the evil forces of the world, cruel and treacherous beings.

Political Attitudes. How do the Israelis characterize the Arab foreign policies which derive from these attitudes?

In Israeli opinion, there can hardly be any question of a unified Arab policy toward Israel, but since the 1950s, the foreign policies of Egypt, that is, the United Arab Republic (U.A.R.), have dominated all the other Arab countries, at least those directly involved in the conflict with Israel. Having secured the removal of the last traces of British control in 1954, Egyptian foreign policy turned to two essential aims: the unification of the Arab world under the aegis of Cairo; and the solution of the Palestine problem in terms favorable to the Arabs. The two aims seem to the Israelis to be closely related. Without the elimination of the present state of Israel (or return to the borders of the 1947 partition, which would be equivalent to elimination in the long run), the unification of the Arab world would be made more difficult, if only because of the geographical position of the Jewish state. But unless the unification of the Arab states under new Egyptian leadership begins to be a reality, victory against Israel seems improbable to the Israelis, in the foreseeable future at any rate. President Nasser was believed to be attempting to reach the two objectives by means of several simultaneous maneuvers. Although the Six-Day War of June, 1967, makes a victory against Israel appear even more uncertain, the political, economic, and even military cooperation of the Arab countries since then, however, appears to be more genuine than before.

Until the summer of 1969 it seemed conceivable that certain moderate elements in the Arab world, and especially King Hussein of Jordan, might be prepared, if only for tactical reasons, to consider negotiation with Israel. But the increasing power of the Palestinian organizations over Jordan now makes any separate action by the Jordanian sovereign appear very difficult, indeed. King Hussein now seems to be aligned with President Nasser's policy toward Israel. How can this be defined at present?

In the eyes of most Israelis, the principles of Egyptian policy, as often stated by President Nasser, are: "No peace treaty with Israel; no recognition of Israel; no negotiations with Israel; and no bargaining about the future of the Palestine territory and people." Viewed from Jerusalem, the underlying reasoning seems simple: time is working for the Arabs. Either the great powers will in the end compel the Jewish state to evacuate the occupied territories without an Arab-Israeli negotiated settlement or a signed peace treaty, or else patient military preparation will eventually enable the Arabs to regain by force the territories lost in 1967. In this second eventuality Israel might be obliged to make new concessions which would reduce her power even more. Possibly, the State of Israel would disappear. Such a policy, if pursued, by no means excludes the possibility of another Arab-Israeli conflict in the not-too-distant future.

It might of course be argued that President Nasser's statements were no more than a refusal to recognize the State of Israel, and that they did not contain an implicit determination to resume the battle and to destroy Israel in the foreseeable future. Another argument is that the former Egyptian President's declarations were only face-saving devices which, although intransigent in appearance, hid a wish to avoid another war and to achieve some political settlement in due time. On the other hand, one may wonder if President Nasser would have been able to achieve a political settlement in the face of the growing radicalism of many Arabs influenced by the Palestinian ideologies and of the more extreme elements in the Egyptian armed forces.

Anyhow, those Israelis who believe that Nasser wished to reach a reasonable settlement and could impose it under the right circumstances are a small minority and their actual influence on policymaking is practically nil.

The Policies of the Great Powers

The creation of an Israeli State was made possible because U.S. and U.S.S.R. views coincided. The Russians enabled the Israelis to hold out during the first few months of the 1948 war of liberation, yet the Americans compelled the Israeli forces to leave the El-Arish area in Sinai at the end of the same war. Neither Russian nor American nor any outside pressure succeeded in restoring peace after the 1949 armistice agreements of Rhodes. The U.S.-sponsored Baghdad Pact (1955)[3] may have contributed indirectly to the Arab-Israeli tensions that flared out again in 1955 and were brought to a head in 1956 by the arms supplies delivered to Egypt from the Communist-bloc countries. An American error led to the nationalization

[3]An agreement of military cooperation at first between Iraq and Turkey, the Baghdad Pact was acceded to in 1955 by Pakistan, Turkey, Iran, and the United Kingdom. Iraq withdrew March 24, 1959, and the pact was redesignated the Central Treaty Organization (CENTO) by resolution August 21, 1959. The United States has been an observer and an informal participant, but never a formal member.

of the Suez Canal and gave Israel the possibility and the pretext of joint action with Great Britain and France against Egypt. The concurrence of U.S. and U.S.S.R. views at this time is thought by some Israelis to have saved Egypt from breaking down and to have enabled her to transform her military defeat into political and psychological victory. Since 1956 Soviet arms supplies and the provision of Russian technical and military instructors have strengthened the military potential of both Egypt and Syria. The United States, on the other hand, both ensured its position in Lebanon and Jordan and strengthened Israel's military potential by direct and indirect arms supplies.

The Russians, although no doubt pursuing their own objectives, are believed by the Israelis to have helped to trigger the chain reaction leading to the June, 1967, war. Since then, neither the Russians nor the Americans have decisively changed the situation created by the war. In view of the considerable influence that both the United States and the U.S.S.R. exert in the region, it seems justifiable to ask whether the interests of these countries will prompt them to prolong the Arab-Israeli conflict, or to seek a settlement soon.

U.S.S.R. Policy. Soviet policy in the Middle East appears to the Israelis to be a direct inheritance from that of the czars. Like the pressure which they once exerted on the Ottoman Empire, the present penetration of the Russians into the Arab countries seems to be fundamentally aimed at controlling the maritime approaches to southwestern Russia, as well as the resources of the Middle East and the strategic routes between Europe and the Indian Ocean. From the Bolshevik Revolution until Stalin's death, Russian activity in this region remained cautious. It was concentrated on the U.S.S.R.'s neighbors, namely, Turkey and Iran. Then in this era of "peaceful coexistence," the Russians changed their policy, reacting no doubt against the Baghdad Pact set up by the Americans. Ever since this pact, Russian penetration into the Arab world has been increasing year by year. Under these circumstances, let us consider the Israeli view of the significance of the present conflict in the global strategy of the U.S.S.R.

The advantages which the Soviet Union could derive from a prolongation of the conflict are evident. If there were peace, the Arab countries would probably devote a large portion of their energies to the economic and technical development of their territories and to raising the living standards of their peoples. The United States would in that case take at least an equal share with the Soviet Union in the supply of technology of equipment and, above all, of funds. As long as the conflict continues, the Arabs would urgently need armaments and instructors which only the Soviet Union and the Communist countries are willing to supply (apart from the weapons which the Americans are providing for Jordan and Saudi Arabia).

These supplies of military matériel and instructors have enabled the Russians to establish themselves more prominently in the region, as has been seen in the past few years, especially since June, 1967. From now on Syria, Egypt, Yemen, Algeria, the Sudan, and probably Libya, will be subjected to varying degrees of Soviet influence. Egyptian and Syrian ports are facilitating the concentration of a considerable Russian naval force in the eastern Mediterranean. This military and naval foothold certainly has some immediate aims: (1) to prevent the Western powers from regaining control in Egypt and in Syria in case of a change in their controlling regimes, (2) to neutralize the American Sixth Fleet and to bypass the entire NATO defense system in Europe, and (3) to compel the Americans to accept the division of the Middle East into zones of influence [4] which would establish the presence of the Soviet Union in the region over the long term. Both for long-range and immediate policy aims the Russian hold on Syria and Egypt seems essential and the cooperation of these countries is ensured by maintaining the tension with Israel.

Until the spring of 1970 the Israelis, along with many Western observers, believed that, nothwithstanding the advantages reaped from continued tension in the Middle East, the Soviet Union would follow a cautious policy because of the risks involved in the escalation of a local conflict. Direct military involvement of the U.S.S.R. did not seem plausible. But the appearance in April, 1970, of Russian-manned SAM-3 antiaircraft missiles on Egyptian territory and the acknowledged participation of Russian pilots in operational missions over Egypt introduced an entirely new factor into the situation. It is now difficult to evaluate the further course of Russian policy in the Middle East. It may still be a defensive one, aiming mostly at bolstering the Russian positions in the Arab world, but it may as well, in Israeli eyes at least, be one of dangerous brinkmanship that could upset the whole strategic balance in that part of the world. In both cases, its ultimate course will be greatly influenced by the forthcoming reactions of the United States.

U.S. Policy. But how is the policy of the United States viewed in Israel?

As early as the end of World War II, the United States began to replace Britain in the eastern Mediterranean and in the Middle East. Since then, their policies in this part of the world have seemed somewhat contradictory to Israeli viewers. On the one hand, the Americans support their own economic, diplomatic, and strategic interests in the Arab countries; on the other, they support Israel, both for ideological reasons (Israel being a liberal democracy attached to Western values) and for the sympathy

[4]In October, 1968, Andrei Gromyko, Foreign Minister of the U.S.S.R., in a speech delivered to the U.N. General Assembly, for the first time designated the Middle East as a "security zone" of the Soviet Union.

a large portion of the American people feel for the Jewish state as well as for the part the Jewish electorate plays in American political life. To this day, American policy appears to be torn between these conflicting demands. Since the end of Eisenhower's Presidency and especially during the Kennedy and the Johnson eras, the links between Americans and Israelis have become closer, despite the opposition of a considerable section of the State Department. Although some American statements made in December, 1969, and at the beginning of 1970 suggested a shift to a harder U.S. policy line toward Israel, the new Russian military activity in Egypt may well compel the United States to reassess its policies again.

At this stage it seems to Israel that American policy may develop in three directions: (1) attempting to reach a global settlement with the Soviet Union in order to avoid any risk of armed confrontation; (2) bolstering the defenses of Israel, mostly through plane deliveries, if a global settlement does not seem possible in the near future; (3) furthering concessions from the Israelis in order to minimize in the Arab world the effects of weapons deliveries to Israel.

If there were a serious divergence of views between Washington and Jerusalem concerning the concessions to be accepted by Israel, the United States could theoretically compel the Jewish state to comply without reservation. Most Israelis think that such a course is hardly conceivable. They do not believe that the United States will try to compel Israel to abandon elements of its policy which it considers as vital. If, however, the U.S. government wishes to force Israel to abandon these elements, it would have to exert drastic political, economic, and financial pressure. But to the Israelis it seems unlikely that American public opinion could accept such governmental pressure under present circumstances, as long as the attitude of the state of Israel is considered by many as rational.

The Military Factors

The Israelis see the enemy's response to the situation as the determining factor in the options before Israel. There are three types of military response to be considered. How do the majority of Israelis envisage the possibility of another conventional war? In Israeli opinion, what are the possible effects of Arab guerrilla war? What of the introduction of nuclear weapons into the area?

The Possibility of Another Conventional War

Two different situations have to be taken into consideration in this context: (1) a war between Israel and the Arab states alone, or (2) the intervention of the great powers.

A War between Israel and the Arab States Alone. Within three years after the Six-Day War, the Egyptian army had not only re-established its military potential in terms of equipment, but had perhaps increased it. Further, systematic training is now being given to the army of the U.A.R. by several thousand Soviet instructors. But does the reconstitution of the Egyptian arms potential mean that their actual military power is greater than it was in June, 1967? The results of the operations of the Israeli commandos in the past year and the air battles of 1969 and 1970 leave room for doubt about this. How can this continued weakness under fire be explained?

The behavior of Egyptian officers and soldiers during and since the June, 1967, war indicates both intellectual and psychological shortcomings, revealed by their difficulty in controlling and operating very modern equipment under complex fighting conditions involving hundreds of planes and tanks, thousands of vehicles, and tens of thousands of troops. Obviously, a society which is underdeveloped to a great extent cannot conduct a modern war with all its technological and scientific demands.

Before the beginning of the war, the Israelis themselves had been mistaken about the ability of the Arabs to use the ultramodern equipment at their disposal. They were convinced that with the help of Soviet training, the Arab armies would be far more efficient in 1967 than in 1956, not to mention 1948. However, no fundamental improvement was noted.

Even more serious than their technical failures, the psychological shortcomings of the Arabs appeared mainly in the officers' behavior under fire. They fled from the enemy, abandoned their troops, invented unrealistic reports on the development of the situation, exhibited profound mistrust of their comrades, and demonstrated an inability to act effectively as a team. It appears that this latter difficulty, an inherent mistrust of the various members of a group, is a fundamental feature of Arab society, and that the behavior of troops and officers is a characteristic expression of this.

According to an Israeli specialist in Arab affairs another cause contributing "to the Arabs' breakdown is their attitude towards truth and reality. It is stupefying to see how frequent lies are in their public life. . . . An example of the 'big lie' technique was the allegation that American and British attacks had caused the destruction of the Egyptian air force. . . . In Sinai, Egyptian units from behind the lines were sometimes captured be the Israelis because of false statements on the Egyptian radio announcing the success of Arab armies. . . ." [5]

In contrast to the severe weaknesses of the Arab armies, the psychological advantages of the Israeli Defense Force (IDF) are obvious. The IDF has

[5]Y. Harkabi, "Basic Factors of the Arab Collapse During the Six-Day War," *Orbis,* Vol. XI, No. 3 (Fall, 1967), pp. 677-691.

increasing technological superiority, a remarkable level of general training, and originality of the strategic and tactical conceptions of the command. The army's fighting spirit is no less obvious. In fact, the qualities of the Israeli Defense Force reflect the level of development and the values of the society as a whole.

It is true that the qualitative advantages of the IDF might be outweighed by a considerable quantitative imbalance in armaments, but it seems that this may be offset by Israeli ingenuity. It has indeed been shown that Israel's external sources of supply were sufficiently varied to enable her to overcome such measures as the French embargo; further, the Jewish state is thought to be progressing rapidly toward self-sufficiency in the manufacture of armaments.

Under these conditions, Israeli observers of the situation believe that as long as there is no radical change in the structure of Arab society, the qualitative difference between Israeli and Arab military potential will persist and will perhaps increase to the detriment of the Arabs. But, one might ask, what about the effect of the systematic activities of the Soviet instructors?[6] First of all, no training, however excellent, can radically change the influence of debilitating social structures and primitive ways of thinking. Second, the experience of the Israeli raids of 1969, seems to show that the Russians have again instilled in the Egyptians a strategy based on static defense lines which, when opposed to the extreme mobility of the Israelis, can only lead to catastrophe.

These arguments taken together, even when viewed with all due caution, suggest to most Israelis that, in the event of a conventional attack in the course of the next few years and in the context of a general war fought by the Arabs alone against Israel, the Arabs would again be defeated. But would the Arabs have to fight alone? Nothing is sure at the present stage.

The Intervention of the Great Powers. Little can be said here about the prospects of a conventional war in which Soviet Russia would intervene on the side of the Arabs. To overcome Israel with conventional means only, the Soviet Union would have to bring into the Middle East much stronger forces than those stationed in Egypt or carried by the Soviet fleet in the Mediterranean, at the beginning of the summer of 1970. The Soviet Union can do it. But, it is hard to believe that, under such circumstances, the United States would choose not to interfere. The ensuing Russo-American military confrontation is a type of situation which need not be analyzed here. Since the Russian move of April, 1970, however, it remains a possibility.

[6]According to information published by the Israeli press during the summer of 1970, there may have been as many as 14,000 Russian instructors and experts in Egypt alone.

The Possibility of Arab Guerrilla Action

Most of the Israelis share similar views about the possible actions of Arab sabotage organizations. They believe that one of the major aims of the first Palestinian sabotage organizations appearing in 1965 was to draw the Arab countries into a war against Israel through sabotage, escalation, and reprisals. These organizations helped, along with other factors, to trigger the 1967 Six-Day War, but that war did not end with the expected results.

The guerrilla warfare that has developed since 1967 seems to aim at more ambitious objectives. Today two principal and competing organizations dominate Arab sabotage activity: *al-Fatah,* directed by Yasir Arafat, whose military organization is called *al-Assifa,* and the Popular Front for the Liberation of Palestine (PFLP). Both organizations aim, primarily, for the "destruction of Zionist identity," that is, the "destruction of all the political, economic, social, and military structures of Zionism."[7] The difference between the two organizations lies mainly in their ideology. PFLP claims to be based on Marxism-Leninism, while *al-Fatah* claims to be above any ideology, aiming only at the destruction of the state of Israel as a sovereign entity. As suggested earlier, most Israelis believe that the avowed intentions of the sabotage organizations do indeed represent their genuine aims.

Israel must consider the present and, above all, the future possible courses of action of these Palestinian sabotage organizations. Let us be careful to distinguish between military and political or psychological activities. Although the possibilities of military action by the sabotage organizations seem limited, their attacks may have considerable psychological and political repercussions.

For three months following the Six-Day War, the sabotage organizations were almost completely paralyzed. Their cadres who had served in auxiliary units with Arab forces had been killed during the fighting, their bases were occupied, and their networks dismantled. But in September, 1967, with the help of the various Arab governments, they resumed their activity. They have met with only limited success in the last three years.

Arab extremists did not choose to allow Israel's occupation of the West Bank of the Jordan and of Gaza to continue unhampered for any length of time. The idea of a Palestinian national will would have been severely affected by it. Guerrilla operations attempted to resume as soon as possible after the end of the Six-Day War. For such operations to be efficient, supporting networks must be set up patiently and effective hiding places for armaments need to be devised. For various reasons, this does not seem to have been the case. Guerrilla warfare cannot be carried on in the desert

[7]*L'Orient* (Beirut), February 14, 1969.

of Sinai—any more than it could be in the Sahara. It must be limited
to regions of the West Bank, Gaza, and Israel's Jordan Valley and Upper
Galilee. This terrain is open and its natural shelters inadequate. (In Palestine there is nothing comparable to the Algerian Aurès or the Vietnamese
jungles.)

The Arabs had conducted a relatively efficient guerrilla war on this
ground against the British in 1936 and 1937. But the Israelis have two
advantages over the British. They are not foreigners, being as much at home
in Palestine as the Arabs; they know the terrain as well as the saboteurs.
Further, the Israelis are fighting on what they consider to be their land;
they know that they will not leave. The fight, therefore, is waged with far
greater stubborness than it would be by a colonial occupant who can return
home if it comes to the worst.

To these advantages must be added their intellectual ability, their
aptitude for fighting, and the superior training of their soldiers over the
Arabs.

To prevent the guerrilla war from spreading to the Arab populations
of the West Bank, Israel has from the start succeeded in combining
a liberal occupation policy with severe measures against anyone helping
the terrorists. After some hesitation, the Israeli Defense Forces have
responded to guerrilla activities with the combined tactics of static defense
and extreme mobility. Static defense, the whole efficiency of which did
not make itself felt until the beginning of 1969, means setting up a line
of barbed and electrified wire equipped with electronic detection devices
along the zones where penetration is particularly easy (the Beisan Valley,
for instance). The mobility of antiterrorist fighting units has already
yielded results. Helicopter-borne commandos can act with considerable
efficiency both in the West Bank and in the neighboring countries, if necessary. The method of massive reprisal the Israelis have used since 1953
to dissuade the inhabitants of an area or even a government from helping
infiltrators is applied with many variations: sometimes sending powerful
units across the frontier, sometimes long-distance artillery or aircraft.

The Israelis believe that in the near future, Arab sabotage organizations
will not obtain any significant military successes. It is not inconceivable,
though, that their efficiency will increase slightly if they succeed in setting
up networks in the occupied territories and if their recruitment improves.
Because the Palestinians have succeeded in giving their struggle the ideological stamp of a war of liberation, in Western Europe in particular, the
participation of foreign volunteers cannot be discounted. The Israelis
believe, however, that their success can only be limited.

What does the continued operation of the Arab guerrilla organizations
mean to Israelis? Their major concern is for the mounting psychological

and political pressures which these activities bring to bear upon Israel and the Western world. At the lowest end of the scale of threatening pressures, the saboteurs, mostly Palestinians, bring into reality the question of decisive advantages.

Next, by shifting the fight from the level of "Arab states against Israel" to the level of "Palestine Arabs against Israel," they transform its image in the eyes of the world from a "war of aggression" into a "war of liberation." Unless Israel reacts in time by countering this threat with information, the image of a "war of liberation" may gain sympathy for the Arab cause in the developing countries as well as in a majority of the new Left and in liberal circles of the Western world. In this way, the sabotage organizations will have been able (and will no doubt continue) to isolate Israel from an important section of world opinion.

Further, the actual or fictitious operations of the sabotage organizations permit the Arab world to overcome the humiliation of defeat and to believe in the possibility of revenge. These organizations are already a powerful remedy against frustration and despair in the Arab world.

The heaviest threat of all is that the sabotage organizations may prevent, through their action in the field or their threats, any idea of a *rapprochement* between certain Arab circles (mainly in the West Bank and in Jordan) and the state of Israel. They may put obstacles in the way of a peaceful settlement of the conflict, if such a settlement were to appear on the horizon.

There are further dangers.

For more than a year after the June, 1967, war, Arab sabotage organizations were unsuccessful in organizing significant attacks against the civilian population, especially in the large towns. Since August, 1968, however, some attacks against Israeli civilians have succeeded.

Finally, some of the most extreme of the terrorist organizations, especially the Popular Front (PFLP), attack Israel's communication system with the outside world, as well as Israeli representations in foreign countries.

Since Israel would not remain passive if the rhythm of attacks were to increase, she therefore runs the risk of facing the classic escalation of terrorism and repression.

The Strategic Advantage of the Occupied Territories

Both in antiguerrilla warfare and in the possibility of another conventional war, the occupied territories provide Israel with undoubted and perhaps decisive advantages.

In antiguerrilla warfare, the occupied territories of the Gaza Strip and the West Bank offer the advantage of dispersing sabotage groups before they can become active, and of intercepting parties on their way to Israeli territory before they have managed to cross the former frontier. Before the

Six-Day War the Israelis had to try to intercept sabotage groups on Israeli soil, which will again be the case if the occupied territories are evacuated without a general peace. Today, with the exception of the Beisan Valley and an area south of the Dead Sea, the Israeli army is fighting the sabotage groups in Arab territory; this obviously lessens the risk for the Israeli population.

In the event of another conventional war the strategic importance of these territories would be crucial. The Golan Heights lie directly above the Israeli villages in the Sea of Galilee area and the Jordan Valley. For 20 years the Israeli populations of the valley and the seashore were targets for the Syrians who were settled on the heights above. Israeli control of the Golan Heights is therefore a security guarantee for these villages. If hostilities with Syria were to start again, this small territory—less than 1000 square kilometers—would provide the Israelis with a strategic springboard for an advance on Damascus. It would also enable them to take Jordan by a pincer movement.

Control of the Golan Heights also means control of the Banias River and the Mouheiba Dam, which means preventing any renewed Arab attempt to alter the course of the Jordan River (another source of conflict) and possibly also to exert pressure on Jordan.

There are many direct strategic advantages for Israel in controlling the whole of Sinai including the Gaza Strip, an extension of Sinai toward Tel Aviv. Egyptian control of the whole of Sinai would enable any Cairo government desirous of resuming hostilities to concentrate troops near the southern frontier of Israel, threatening to cut the Negev in two at any moment, isolating Eilat, and to advance as far as the coastal area of Tel Aviv. The Straits of Tiran might again be closed. Lastly, the Israelis would have only four minutes' warning in the case of an air attack from the airfields in the north of Sinai.

Before June, 1967, the Egyptian radar stations at El-Arish and in other spots of northern Sinai were theoretically able to follow any aircraft movements in Israel. Now the Israeli radar stations on the bank of the Suez Canal detect aircraft movements in the areas of the Nile Delta and the Egyptian capital.[8] In the case of a land attack against Israel, the Egyptians would first have to overcome the major obstacle of a Suez Canal reinforced by a line of fortifications. They would then have to cross nearly 200 kilometers of desert before arriving at the Israeli border. The Israeli

[8]The time of warning in the case of an Egyptian air attack is now 27 minutes. If the Egyptians were to adopt the Israeli tactics of flying at low altitude over the sea, they might perhaps take some Israeli planes by surprise on their runways (this is a purely theoretical possibility), but they would not threaten the Israeli towns, since they would then have a minimum bomb load.

army would have at its disposal enough maneuvering space to reorganize its troops, should the enemy achieve an initial success. The inhabited areas of Israel are now more than 200 kilometers from the Egyptian lines, while some of the vital Egyptian centers, especially Port Said, are within firing range of the Israeli lines.

These military assets also provide Israel with a considerable political advantage. Faced with a threat from Egypt, Israel may now adopt a defensive strategy and avoid the opprobrium of a preventive attack which was essential until 1967. Yet this defensive strategy would not necessitate the maintenance of large forces on the alert. Indeed, the Suez Canal and the Israeli fortifications on the eastern bank are such an obstacle that Israel will be able to avoid costly mobilization until the very last moment, even in the case of a serious crisis. In fact, it is highly unlikely that the Egyptian forces would risk crossing the Israeli lines along the Suez Canal in the foreseeable future.

To these strategic and political advantages must be added the economic asset of possession of the mineral resources of Sinai, especially the oil fields, whose present production is double the current requirements of Israel.

The advantages for the occupation of the West Bank of the Jordan are very similar to those concerning Sinai. A well-led Jordanian army might have cut off Jerusalem from the rest of Israel at Latrun or, worse still, cut the state of Israel in two along a line running from Tulkarem to Netanya, where the width of the Israeli territory between the Jordan border and the coast was 14 kilometers. Israel's occupation of the West Bank eliminates these dangers and shifts her defense lines to the heights west of the Jordan River, forming a line of defense which is easy to hold, like the Suez Canal.

Although the occupation of the Golan, Sinai, Gaza Strip, and the West Bank implies a considerable lengthening of the Israeli lines of communication and certain complex logistic problems, the frontier that now has to be defended is shorter than it was before the June, 1967, war.

The Introduction of Nuclear Weapons into the Middle East

According to press reports which have become frequent since the early 1960s, Israel is said to possess the knowledge and the technical means to manufacture nuclear weapons if she wanted them, and the Jewish state of less than three-million inhabitants is usually placed on a par with West Germany, Japan, or India.[9] Although there is no explicit Israeli doctrine concerning the manufacture and use of nuclear weapons, Israel has stated on several occasions that she would not be the first country to introduce

[9] In October, 1968, W. R. Taylor, the publisher of Jane's *All the World's Aircraft* wrote that by 1970 Israel would possess missiles of about 500-km. range, equipped with nuclear warheads.

such weapons into the Middle East.

The following discussion represents the author's own views. Let us suppose, first, that Israel acquires nuclear weapons and that the Arabs do not. In this case, Israel would have an absolute advantage, because her enemies would no longer dare to launch a massive attack. The threat of military destruction of Israel by the Arabs would disappear, although it is true that this would not stop the guerrilla warfare. Further, if the Soviet Union gave the Arab countries a nuclear guarantee, Israel's advantage would be partly neutralized, although she would still retain some dissuasive power.

Let us suppose, second, that by some means the Arab states also succeeded in acquiring nuclear weapons. In this situation a balance of terror might establish itself in the Middle East, in which any intensive military action of the June, 1967, type would not be possible. Furthermore, Israeli massive reprisals against Arab guerrilla operations would involve greater risk than before. The distrust between Arabs and Israelis would increase. In such a situation of tension, Israelis might find it difficult to foresee the behavior of Arab leaders. Nuclear dissuasion would be ineffective and overall ruin might even be a possibility.

Let us suppose, third, that the Arabs were to acquire nuclear weapons while Israel had none. Such a possibility would entail very grave danger for the survival of the Jewish state.

If the reports on Israel's technological means are to be believed, then the country faces the following possibilities:

1. To acquire nuclear weapons and ensure her security in military terms for a foreseeable future, at the risk of being caught in a process of general destruction should the Arabs acquire the same weapons and, remembering their less rational behavior patterns, should be driven to use them.

2. To risk not acquiring nuclear weapons in order to avoid the danger of general destruction, on the assumption that the Arabs will also not obtain such weapons if Israel does not have any, and to continue to trust to her superiority in conventional military maneuvers.

3. To risk not acquiring nuclear weapons, based both upon the arguments just put forward, and upon pressure from the United States who, as is well known, is firmly intent on preventing the extension of the nuclear club.[10]

[10]It may have been noticed that I do not mention the treaty of nonproliferation of nuclear weapons. For countries such as Israel, the importance of this treaty depends entirely on the intentions of America in this field. The treaty in itself has about the same value as the famous Briand-Kellogg Pact of 1928, which outlawed wars of aggression and was signed by almost all states.

It is probable that if she had the means, Israel would soon try to acquire or work toward the possibility of manufacture of nuclear weapons if it became apparent that either the Arabs were on the same path, or the ratio of conventional armaments inclined too much in favor of the Arabs, or the divergence of views between Israel and the United States reached a point where Israel no longer decided to take any account of American desires. This last alternative would imply Israel's freeing herself from the political and financial pressure of the United States, as well as from dependence on the Americans for conventional weapons. Thus, if Israel were to acquire nuclear weapons in two, three, five, or ten years' time, any forecast about her subsequent physical survival would depend upon Arab actions, assuming that the Arabs would in the end have the same weapons.

Should nuclear weapons be introduced into the Middle East, the strategic importance of the territories which are now occupied by Israel would be minimal, although Sinai would perhaps be more appropriate than the Negev for any nuclear tests, as well as for the setting up of missile bases.

The Refugee Problem

Today there are nearly 1,300,000 Palestinian refugees, 500,000 of them under Israeli control and 800,000 living in the neighboring countries, mainly in Jordan. These refugees yearn to return to their homes. Only a minority finally emigrate to the oil states of the Persian Gulf or even overseas. And even these consider their emigration as "temporary."

The new generation of refugees who were born in the camps and who did not experience pre-1948 Palestine are even more extreme in their attitude toward Israel than their parents' generation, both because their level of education is higher and because of systematic and constant indoctrination.

Although some of the refugees have become integrated into the economic life of the Arab countries, most of them continue to live at the expense of the United Nations Relief and Works Agency (UNRWA) and rebel against the possibility of permanent settlement outside the frontiers of Palestine. Further, the Arab countries, with the exception of Jordan and to some extent Lebanon, refuse to grant the Palestine refugees the status of permanent residents.[11]

In fact, the hatred of the refugees toward Israel and their determination to return to Palestine is increasingly assuming the aspect of a mystical obsession bearing no relation to reality and the actual possibilities of repatriation. According to some Arab authors, a new "Zionist" movement is being

---

[11]Rivka Bar-Yosef, *Sociological Surveys Carried Out in the West Bank of Jordan and Gaza. Conclusions and Suggestions* (Jerusalem: Hebrew University, February 26, 1968).

formed. The very intensity of their determination to return, which is further strengthened by the refugees of the 1967 war and the physical impossibility of resettling most of them in their places of origin are among the most threatening obstacles to a long-term settlement of the Israeli-Arab conflict.

III. The Possibilities before Israel

Having thus described various aspects of the situation which Israel has to face, let us now turn to the possibilities which offer themselves to the state of Israel.

Peace Negotiations

Most Israelis conceive of Arab attitudes toward them as dominated by humiliation and hatred. In response to this hatred, most Israelis exhibit extreme mistrust toward Arab intentions. They believe that the Arabs will accept the reality of Israel's existence only if they are totally convinced that it cannot be destroyed by force. Consequently, the immediate physical defense of the Yishuv[12] and then of the state of Israel has always had priority over long-term preoccupations concerning peace. In fact, ultimate peace is considered to be the result of efficient defense.

Israeli Emotional Attitudes

In Israel the impression prevails that the Arabs are far from convinced that the use of force has no chance of success whatsoever. One rule the Israelis consider to be essential: nothing which contributes to security of the nation should ever be abandoned before it has been ascertained that the Arabs really intend to recognize the existence of Israel and to live at peace with her.

Many Israelis also have a feeling of superiority over the Arabs which makes them accept the Arab "refusal" to live in peace with them with equanimity. There are many Israelis who consider Arab society as primitive, backward, even degenerate, and the Jewish society of Israel as modern and dynamic. As individuals, this feeling of superiority shows itself in the relations between Israeli Jews and Arabs living in Israel;[13] as a group, it impregnates official propaganda and sometimes even education, especially at the primary level. In the body politic this superior attitude may be expressed as follows: "If the Arabs refuse peace, Israel can wait; if they try once more to use force, they will be beaten once again."

[12]The Jewish community in Palestine before the state of Israel was formed. Ed.

[13]In this connection, see the paper (in Hebrew) by Y. Peres and Z. Levy, "Jews and Arabs — The One in the Eyes of the Other" (Jerusalem: Hebrew University, 1967).

As for the "good conscience" of the Israelis, Y. Harkabi wrote a most accurate definition of this on the eve of the Six-Day War:

"We have a tendency to pay no attention to those of our actions which we dislike, and conversely, to place the whole burden of accusation on the Arab's shoulders as if we on our part had only good intentions toward them. Our identification with Zionism, the pride which we feel in its achievements and the ethnocentrism peculiar to every human group are all elements which may impair the objectivity of our vision. All the virulence of our criticism is reserved for our opponents, while our self-criticism remains weak."[14]

The consequences of the Six-Day War have merely strengthened this attitude, because most Israelis consider that it is they who constantly speak of peace and the Arabs who, unrelentingly, refuse it.

For many Arabs, humiliation and hatred give rise to the vision of a conflict which will end only with the total destruction of Israel and Zionism. For many Israelis, distrust of the Arab world leads to a vision of the future which some consider to be fatalist, others realistic, but which at any rate is but a prospect of more fighting. Quoting Arthur Ruppin of 30 years ago, General Dayan stated in September, 1968: "The Arabs refuse to recognize our achievements. If we want to continue our work despite their attitude, we cannot avoid the sacrifice of human lives; fate imposes upon us perpetual war with the Arabs. This may not be a desirable situation, but such is the reality."[15]

Israeli Political Attitudes

Before defining the political attitudes of the majority of Israelis, let us briefly describe the extreme positions. At one extreme there exists the pro-Soviet Communist Rakah Party, made up of Israelis who fully adopt the Soviet position on the Middle East and a tiny group of a few hundred Israelis called Matzpen, whose position is similar to that of Rakah. Other groups of Israelis who would be prepared to favor a policy of extreme conciliation toward the Arab world in the hope that, faced with much good will, the Arabs might themselves be ready for a reasonable compromise include these various small parties: Aveneri's Haolam Hazeh, the Siah (the Israeli new left), the Israeli Communist Party led by Sneh (Maki), and various groups without direct party affiliation.[16] The attitudes of these

[14]Y. Harkabi, Les temps modernes, No. 253 bis (1967), p. 473.

[15]The text of General Dayan's speech was published as "Ourselves and the Arabs," Haaretz, November 22, 1968.

[16]One of the most active of these groups is called the "Movement for Security and Peace."

groups range from a simple declaration of intentions about the return of all occupied territories in case of peace, to the idea of a unilateral initiative by Israel concerning territories or refugees. In some cases these views are also linked to overall conceptions advocating a de-Zionized Israel and a Federation of the Middle East.[17]

The total numerical strength of these groups is very low. While Rakah polled almost 3 percent of the total votes in November, 1969, because of the influx of Arab voters, Haolam Hazeh, the Peace List, and the Israeli Communists taken together did not poll more than 2.75 percent of all votes. Haolam Hazeh has two members in the Knesset (out of 120), the Israeli Communists have one, and the Peace List none.[18] It should be noted however, that when, in the spring of 1970, the Israeli government did not allow the President of the World Jewish Congress, Dr. Nahum Goldmann, to meet President Nasser, some 30 to 40 percent of the population took a stand against the government. The attitudes widely expressed at that time could mean that, under given circumstances, the groups which are ready to give back all the conquered territories in exchange for a peace treaty may gain greater support than in the 1969 elections.

At the other extreme, a larger group was formed around the slogan "the Whole Land of Israel." Of heterogeneous origin, this group includes left- and right-wingers, some of whom had no contact with each other before the Six-Day War. The common mystique of a "liberated" Palestine suddenly brought them together; they have become zealots trying to recreate the historical fatherland in its entirety. Within this group some use "realistic" arguments, others "mystical" ones, but on the whole their attitude toward peace is the following: peace, yes, provided it is based on a territorial status quo, at least in Palestine; but if peace implies the restitution of territories, then it is preferable to give up peace.

The elections of November, 1969, do not permit a clear assessment of the strength of this movement because many people who advocate its views voted, out of old loyalty ties, for parties without annexationist programs. But on the whole the Gachal, the State List, the Free Center, and an important section of the National Religious Party may be considered as being favorable to "the Whole Land of Israel" conception which, according to the November, 1969, election results, amounts to nearly 30 percent of the population. Allowing for the fact that inside the Avoda Party (Israel Labor Party) itself some elements are favorable to this position, one may reasonably suggest that between 30 and 40 percent of the Israeli population today is annexationist.

[17]This latter is Aveneri's position.
[18]The Peace List has disbanded since then.

Let us now turn to the attitudes of the majority of the population and of the members of the national-coalition cabinet. In exchange for the explicit recognition of Israel by the Arab countries and for peace treaties to be duly signed by them with the Jewish state, Israel is prepared to abandon part of the occupied territories on condition that the new frontiers are compatible with the country's security. Failing explicit recognition and a peace treaty, Israel will not evacuate the territories occupied in June, 1967.

The central factor which conditions all the other aspects of Israel's attitude toward the Arabs is a determination to compel the Arab countries, this time, to recognize the existence of Israel. The tangible expression of this determination is the persistent demand Israel has voiced ever since the end of the war: that any arrangement with the Arab states should be the result of direct negotiations between the parties concerned. It is true that since October, 1968, Israel adopted a somewhat more lenient attitude on this point and that the Israelis would perhaps be prepared to accept indirect negotiations in a first stage, under the aegis of the United Nations envoy. Nevertheless, the fundamental attitude of Israel has not changed: the final stage of negotiations will have to be direct and must end in a peace treaty. The Israelis demand this initial guarantee of a real change in the Arab attitude toward the Jewish state and explicit recognition of its existence.

A peace treaty signed by the Arabs, while being an indispensable condition for the evacuation by the Israelis of part of the territories occupied in June, 1967, would in itself perhaps not be considered as sufficient proof of Arab good faith. This is why Israel demands that the new frontiers should be not only "recognized" but also "secure": that is to say, they should offer Israel various strategic advantages in case the Arabs should change their minds once again.

Failing Arab recognition of Israel's existence, "security first" is the main preoccupation. Since the occupied territories represent major advantages for Israel in the event of another military conflict, there can be no question of their being evacuated as a preliminary step: evacuation can only be the consequence of a peace treaty.

But while there seems to be an agreement among a majority of the members of the Israeli government about the fundamental principle of secure borders, the views concerning the new frontiers which are to meet the requirements of the country's security are by no means in harmony.

It seems that all members of the Israeli government agree that the Arab part of Jerusalem and the Golan Heights cannot be restored to the Arab countries. They also seem to agree that the Jordan River must remain the "security frontier" of Israel, which means that no Arab military forces can be stationed west of the Jordan River. But there the agreement ends.

A majority in the government, mainly opposed by the Mapam ministers, seems to be in favor of retaining Sharm-el-Sheik and of keeping a territorial link between Israel and that strategic outpost.[19]

The Gaza Strip would not be returned to Egypt, although its final status has apparently not yet been decided upon. The main discussion concerns the fate of most of the West Bank. The Mapam ministers consider that practically the whole West Bank should be given back to the Arabs. According to Yigal Allon, Deputy Prime Minister, Israel should keep the Jordan Valley with the exception of a narrow passage near Jericho, as well as the southern approaches to Jerusalem, while the remainder of the West Bank could be returned to the Hashemite kindgom in the case of a peace treaty. It appears that Golda Meir and Sapir are close to Allon's views. Defense Minister Dayan has a different idea. Without excluding the possibility of administrative and political control of the West Bank, he seems mainly to be opposed to the idea of a definite frontier between Israel and this area, and he advocates military control over it by the creation of Israeli bases in various strategic points. As for the ministers of the Gachal, who are implicitly supported by ministers of the Labor Party (such as Galili), they seem to favor annexation of the West Bank. When Levi Eshkol intimated in an interview with *Newsweek* in February, 1969, that Israel did not wish to keep the major part of the West Bank, the Gachal ministers compelled the Prime Minister to retract his statement by threatening to leave the government.

The policy of the Israeli government concerning the fate of the West Bank is therefore not well defined, and an attempt to define it at the present stage would probably lead to a severe internal crisis. The official attitude is that since the Arabs have so far refused to recognize Israel explicitly and to negotiate a peace treaty, any policy concerning the territorial adjustments in case of peace would be premature.

Israel's attitude toward the Security Council Resolution of November 22, 1967, must also be considered in this context. Israel's reluctance is due to the fact that this resolution does not imply the formal recognition of the Jewish state by the Arabs and of a peace treaty. This fundamental condition being absent from the resolution, Israel refuses to accept it without reservation, since with even a formal acceptance of the resolution she would also

[19]The retention of Sharm el-Sheik seems vital to Defense Minister Moshe Dayan, who tried to have this officially stated in the election program of HaMaarach (the Labor Party plus Mapam). As far as any official pronouncement is concerned, General Dayan's efforts have failed until now, but his views on this issue seem to have been tacitly accepted by a majority of the group in August, 1969.

be compelled to define "recognized and safe frontiers," something that cannot be done without considerable difficulties.

Israeli policy is thus, in a way, an "all-or-nothing" policy. But what if Israel were faced with a compromise proposal presented by the great powers (or the United States and the Soviet Union alone) which, while not offering Israel all the guarantees of security that she wanted, would give her some of them, that is, a compromise which, although short of a peace treaty, would offer her some sort of contractual agreement with the Arab nations? Israel's reply would probably depend on the nature of the security guarantees offered. If the Jewish state could keep the Golan Heights, Jerusalem, and Sharm el-Sheik, it might accept a compromise even without a formal peace treaty, but it is difficult to foresee the Soviet Union recommending a solution that would be unacceptable to Egypt (Sharm el-Sheik under Israeli control). If the compromise solution presented by the great powers excluded the control of Sharm el-Sheik, the present government in Jerusalem would probably oppose such a proposal with all possible means: the demilitarization of Sinai would not be an acceptable alternative. Everything would then depend on the degree of pressure which the United States decided to exert.

As of now a separate arrangement between Israel and certain moderate elements of the Arab world seems entirely out of the question, but this was not so for almost eighteen months after the Six-Day War, and, theoretically, the same situation could appear again if King Hussein succeeds in crushing the Palestinian organizations.

What would the attitude of Israel be if one of the most moderate Arab countries, Jordan, were to decide that, after all, peace negotiations were the only way out? Would Israel be prepared to negotiate with Jordan alone?

A Partial Peace

At first glance, peace between Israel and the Hashemite kingdom would seem advantageous, even if Egypt were to refuse to associate herself with any negotiations. An Israeli-Jordanian settlement would prove that coexistence between the Jewish state and an Arab country of the Middle East is possible. The united front which the Arabs seem to have been building up against Zionism and the state of Israel for several decades would be modified. The guerrilla activities in the West Bank territories and in Jordan might disappear. Lebanon and Saudi Arabia might perhaps join in the peaceful solution, and thus a zone under American influence as well as American protection could be formed in the Middle East: Israel, Jordan, Lebanon, and Saudi Arabia. If there were a new war with Egypt, the IDF would not have to worry about the eastern frontiers. Lastly, these neighboring countries would provide vast outlets for Israel's economy. Israel would no doubt have to restore the West Bank and to accept concessions in Jerusalem, but would such favorable prospects not justify some concessions?

Many objections have been raised against a settlement with Jordan alone. The opposition of Egypt and the bellicose majority of Arab opinion might make any settlement with Jordan alone a very short-lived affair. Above all, King Hussein would have to eliminate from his territory the various Palestine sabotage organizations as a preliminary to any agreement. But would he have the means for such an action? In the present state of affairs, the Hashemite King might well run the risk of being assassinated, as did his grandfather under somewhat similar circumstances. If King Hussein were to be assassinated after the signing of a treaty with Israel, the compromises which Israel would have consented to make would become mere gratuitous sacrifices, and she might again find herself facing a uniformly hostile Arab world, without the advantage of strategic control over important areas of the West Bank.

One view suggests that it would be in the interest of Israel to avoid any agreement with the Hashemite King, whose position is very precarious, and, instead, to hope for the arrival of a government at Amman headed by Palestinians who, together with the West Bank Palestinians, could become genuine partners for discussion, representing to some extent a more real social entity than the Hashemites. Such a possibility has been debated on various occasions in the Israeli press[20] and it may even have been considered in political circles. Advocates of this line claim, correctly it seems, that "Palestinian presence" is henceforward part of a reality that cannot be ignored.

But opponents of such a view have no difficulty in defining the dangers it would involve both in the short and in the long term:

1. The Palestinians from Jordan are the least inclined to negotiate with Israel in the near future, and if they came to power would only aggravate incidents along the eastern frontier of Israel in the near future, and encourage raids by sabotage groups.

2. King Hussein's disappearance would still further weaken the American position in the area and would risk (a) at best, increasing Soviet power (which for Israel would be a great disadvantage, since she would then be surrounded by countries under Soviet influence), and (b) at the worst, facilitating the penetration of Communist China into the area.

These remarks lead to the conclusion that if the idea of a partial peace with King Hussein is not based on a very realistic outlook and may even

[20]See in particular Shimon Shamir's excellent article, "The Palestine Challenge" in *New Outlook,* March-April, 1969.

seem undesirable, any reasoning based on the arrival in power at Amman of the Palestinians is even less so.

In the Israeli view, even supposing that Jordan would accept a settlement, it is believed highly unlikely that the Egyptian President and the Palestinian organizations would do so, and hence any agreement with Jordan appears as doubtful and difficult in the future as it is now.

One final point: the Israelis are aware that, all other considerations put aside, a treaty with Jordan could not be achieved without some compromise over the status of Jerusalem. For the Jews, Mount Moriah (the Mount of the Temple) and the Wailing Wall are at the heart of their historic consciousness. Over the centuries Jerusalem was the center of the dreams and the prayers of the dispersed Jewish people. It is difficult to believe that the Israelis would accept another division of the city and that some new Arab authority might one day obstruct their access to places which for them are the holiest of all. But Jerusalem is also, together with Mecca and Medina, one of the three great holy cities of Islam; and for the Muslims, it is a real profanation to leave the Omar Mosque or the Al Aqsa Mosque under Jewish control. After the fire in the Al Aqsa Mosque, the intensity of these emotions became apparent to all. While for many Arabs the signing of a peace treaty with Israel may be a symbol of defeat, it seems that for many others, Jewish control over Jerusalem is a symbol both of defeat and of humiliation.

What, in fact, are the possibilities sometimes mentioned about Jerusalem?

To internationalize the whole of Jerusalem seems out of the question for practically all Israelis, because this would amount to internationalizing a city which, for them, is the capital of Israel.[21] There remains the possibility of internationalizing the Arab city where all the holy places are. In theory, this would be an acceptable solution, but the history of Jerusalem proves that in the absence of a strong authority and a clear policy, the holy places where the demands of several religions are literally intertwined over an area of a few hundred square yards may be a continuous source of friction leading to serious conflicts. The authority of a single municipality having at its disposal the means required for the maintenance of order seems to be a safer solution. In order to prevent the Muslim holy places from being under Jewish control, one possibility would be to provide for the representatives of each religion to have complete control over its holy places, flying the Jordanian or Palestinian flag on the dome of the Omar and the Al Aqsa mosques, while the state of Israel would undertake to

[21]It should be noted that many countries, including the permanent members of the U.N. Security Council, have not adopted de jure Israel's position on the status of Jerusalem, although they accept it de facto.

respect the free access of all to the holy places. Israeli sovereignty would not extend to the non-Jewish holy places themselves: the status of the Muslim and Christian sanctuaries would be an exterritorial one.

Initiatives toward De-escalation

Failing realistic possible options which might lead to general or partial peace, is there any initiative which Israel might take toward de-escalation of the conflict?

There is one possibility often mentioned among those Israelis who are definitely opposed to an annexation of the occupied territories and who feel that a breakup of the national coalition government would not be a disaster. Israel should make a clear declaration that in exchange for recognition by the Arab nations and the ultimate signature of peace treaties, she would be prepared: (1) to forsake direct negotiations, and (2) to return practically all the occupied territories, with the exception of some minor strategic holdings. This actually seems to be the only serious initiative that Israel could take at this stage to de-escalate the conflict. We have already pointed out why the Israeli government opposes such a step.

Another theoretical possibility could be for Israel to allow the clearing of the Suez Canal and its reopening to navigation. But this possibility seems unrealistic for the following reasons:

1. Israel may not accept the reopening of the Suez Canal if her own ships are not to obtain their internationally recognized right of passage. The Egyptians have said that they would accept this right of passage only if all territories occupied in June, 1967, were evacuated and the refugees repatriated.

2. The Egyptians would not agree to open the Canal to navigation as long as its eastern bank were occupied by the Israeli forces. But an Israeli withdrawal of even a few miles may be difficult (although not inconceivable) for strategic reasons: the Canal is important as an obstacle to the invasion of Sinai, hence the importance of the fortifications erected on the waterside.

3. Finally, the clearing of the Canal might be detrimental to Israel from a military point of view, since it would enable Soviet naval units from the Mediterranean to enter the Red Sea, thus rendering the position of Israel in Sinai more precarious.

Thus, in the present circumstances, a realistic initiative on the part of Israel which might lead to a de-escalation of the conflict is hardly in sight. It seems reasonable to consider the political, military, and diplomatic options facing Israel in the context of continuance of the present tension or even of its aggravation.

Unilateral Political Choices

In the territories she now occupies, Israel has been conducting a day-to-day policy with immediate and limited objectives: (1) avoiding any serious disorder that might impair the safety of the occupation forces and of Israel, (2) avoiding the formation of any opposition and sabotage networks in the territories, (3) promoting economic contacts between the occupied territories and Israel, and between the occupied territories and the Arab world, in order to maintain a living standard comparable to that before the June, 1967, war.

To achieve these various immediate objectives the Israeli authorities are giving the local Arabs a maximum of privileges in the administration of society, and are fostering an open-door policy, that is, promoting contacts between Arabs from the occupied territories and the surrounding Arab world.

There are various divergent views on the future of the occupied territories of Palestine. Before examining them let us briefly consider two aspects of a demographic problem the Israelis will have to face in their planning for the future.

The Fate of the West Bank and of Gaza

When Israel occupied the West Bank, the Golan Heights, the Gaza Strip, and Sinai, over 200,000 Arabs fled from their homes. Since then, the exodus has slowed down considerably and by September, 1969, it had practically ceased. Over 1,000,000 Arabs now live in the occupied territories. Counting the 300,000 Arabs now living in Israel, the Arab population under Israeli control at present amounts to more than half the Jewish population of Israel. But since the natural rate of growth of the Arab population of Palestine is approximately twice that of the Jewish population (if the difference between these rates of growth is maintained and barring substantial Jewish immigration or another Arab exodus), the Arab and the Jewish population living in the territories which are now under Israel's control will become numerically equal within 25 to 30 years, after which the Arab population will become the majority.

The prospects of Jewish immigration are extremely difficult to assess. After the large waves of immigration following the creation of the Jewish state, the movement slowed down considerably. During the two years preceding the Six-Day War immigration had dropped to an average of 15,000 persons per annum. Would-be emigrants in the poor countries had become fewer and fewer, and various psychological and economic obstacles occurred in Israel to lower immigration. Further, in 1966 and 1967 emigration almost equaled immigration. Immigration in 1968 more than doubled as compared with 1966. In 1968 approximately 30,000 immigrants arrived as compared to 14,000 in 1966. Forty thousand arrived in 1969, coming from Central Europe as well as from France, Great Britain, the United States, and Canada. United States and Canadian immigration has more than doubled over the annual average of the pre-Six-Day-War period, but the total figures remain very low. There were 4000 immigrants in 1968 from the United States and Canada as against a previous annual average of 1800. Immigration from France seems to reflect the direct influence of the events of June, 1967. The monthly average rose from 30-50 immigrants to 180 for the period July, 1967, to July, 1968. After July, 1968, French immigration jumped again to 400 immigrants per month, where it has remained ever since.

Including immigrants at the rate of 25,000 per annum, the total Jewish population of Israel would be about 3,500,000 by 1985, while the Arab population, which was 1,300,000 in 1968, would be above 2,600,000. Assuming that Jewish immigration is maintained at an optimum rate during the years to come, Israel will have to face the problem of integrating almost equal numbers of Jews and Arabs.

Therefore, assuming that Israel will not evacuate the occupied territories unilaterally without a peace treaty, the possibility of such a treaty being concluded seeming slight, and considering the demographic problem, what are Israel's options in the occupied territories?

A Palestinian Entity? Israel might create an autonomous Palestinian entity comprising either the West Bank and Gaza or the West Bank alone.

Critics of this plan maintain that an autonomous Palestinian entity is not feasible because of lack of Palestinian national feeling among the West Bank Arabs. There has indeed never been a Palestinian nation, but until recently, there was no Jordanian or Saudi nation either. In Iraq also, the "national" sentiment is very recent. There is a growing Arab national sentiment with local variations, among which the Palestinian community feeling is certainly one of the most powerful, if only as a consequence of the direct and constant clash between Arabs and Palestinian Jews or between Arabs and the state of Israel.

A Palestinian entity under the aegis of Israel would be refused by practically all Palestinians. During the year which followed the Six-Day War, there appeared to be a chance of an agreement between Israel and certain West Bank notables. Today, although some of these Palestinians are faithful to Jordanian King Hussein, a much larger section of the population looks to Egypt and the majority, or so it seems, identify themselves, theoretically if not actively, with the Palestinian terrorist organizations.

The possibility of creating a Palestinian entity under the aegis of Israel seems dimmer than before.

Let us now consider annexation or the maintenance of the status quo.

Some Consequences of Annexation. If Israel annexed the occupied territories, any peaceful settlement of the conflict would probably be finally excluded. Israel might be completely isolated internationally. Further, there would be internal economic and social consequences from such a decision.

By the autumn of 1969 over 20,000 Arabs from the occupied territories were already working in Israel. All unskilled, they already represented a threat to the employment of Jewish unskilled labor, since the Arabs will work for lower wages. This problem, only beginning now, may well increase rapidly.

The principal threat to Israeli society would come from the progressive transformation of the proletariat into an essentially Arab class, with the Jews a "ruling class." This would end not only the Zionist ideal, but also Israel as a socialist and humanist society. Labor conflicts would develop if social claims were to interfere with national claims. Every strike would then become part of the Israeli-Arab fight.

Because of the short distance between the West Bank territory and Israel's industrial centers, it would seem possible for the Palestinian worker to travel both ways every day, but in practice this would be difficult, and in the long run it would be hard to avoid the formation of Arab districts on the outskirts of Israel's large towns. The concentration of large portions of urban Arab population might lead the observer to forecast racial problems similar to those of the American black minority.

The Arabs of "Greater Israel" would sooner or later become full-fledged citizens, enjoying the same right to vote as the Israeli Arabs today. But there can be no doubt as to the violence of their anti-Israeli feelings, something hardly likely to improve in the future. An Arab nationalist party might be formed which could send united deputies to the Knesset, with the intention of entirely stopping normal parliamentary procedure. If it came to the worst, when the Arab and Jewish populations reach numerical equality, Arab nationalist deputies might, for instance, attempt to submit for approval a law limiting Jewish immigration into Israel. In short, such a situation would involve all the hazards of a binational state, quite apart from the fact that in the event of another war with the Arab world, 2 million or more Arabs within the Israeli frontiers would pose difficult security problems.

Further negative consequences can be imagined as a result of such an annexation. The presence of a vast Arab population within Israel might cause Jewish extremists, both on economic and on religious or national arguments, to demand the expulsion of all the Arabs or the application of a regime of "apartheid." Should this happen, the Jewish state would not only cut itself off from the international community, but also from the Jews in the Diaspora. Finally, while it is probable that in a state comprising a vast Arab population, the "Oriental" Jews would have a tendency to integrate themselves more rapidly into a "Western" population, thus differentiating themselves from the Arabs, it is not entirely inconceivable that the poorest Jews might not be attracted both culturally and socially by the Arab proletariat. The Arab population might thus become an active element of disruption of the Jewish society.

Stabilization under the Status Quo. Here again, the policy which has been followed is not clear and the exponents of various theories within the government are at loggerheads with one another. The government, preoccupied with maintaining the unity of its coalition, has been reluctant to set up any program that might provoke hostile reactions outside or disturbances among the population of the occupied territories. Some public clashes between members of the government have already occurred.

Four of the existing positions are more clearly defined than others: the view of the Gachal party; that of the Mapam, supported by Sapir and a few other members of the Avoda party; that of General Dayan; and that of the Deputy Prime Minister, Yigal Allon.

The Gachal, a minority party, openly advocates the creation of *faits accomplis,* the object of which would be to prepare for the annexation of the occupied territories.

It is precisely in order to avoid the possibility of political integration that the members of the Mapam and Sapir among others are opposed to a policy of economic *faits accomplis,* because in their eyes economic integration would infallibly lead to political integration with all the undesirable consequences which we have outlined above.

In Yigal Allon's view, certain *faits accomplis* should be created for reasons of security in the strategic areas of the occupied territories, which Israel should continue to control in the long term (the Golan Heights, the Jordan Valley with the exception of Jericho, the Hebron, and the north of Sinai).

As for Defense Minister Moshe Dayan, whose ideas have sometimes been criticized by Sapir in particular, he advocates increasing economic integration of the occupied territories, to maintain order by creating an adequate living standard to develop the Israeli economy, and to establish links of dependence between the Palestine Arabs and Israel. Such bonds might subsequently make any open political and military hostility a difficult matter. Lastly, in his view, economic cooperation among Israelis and Arabs in the occupied territories might be a "bridge" toward a wider Israeli-Arab understanding.

In spite of opposing principles and divergences as to the long-term policy to be followed, it appears that the Israeli government has decided in favor of a stabilization of the status quo to some extent; this trend, which could be reversed, appears as a gradual application of some of Allon's and some of General Dayan's views. Kibbutzim (collective villages) of the Nahal are being established on the Golan Heights, along the Jordan Valley, and in the north of Sinai. The government has considered creating larger urban centers in the occupied territories. Certain limited economic measures have been taken which, admittedly, have not yet transformed the economic life of the territories in question, but which might, if continued for a few years, lead to the integration of the economy of the occupied territories into that of Israel, in accordance with General Dayan's views.

Prospects for the Antiguerrilla Activities

Antiguerrilla Action. The Israelis must try to keep sabotage activities within narrow limits, because if a certain ceiling of destruction and a certain number of victims were exceeded, harmful psychological and political consequences would not fail to arise. What could Israel do if her present methods of antiguerrilla fighting and of action in the occupied territories became inadequate? Let us consider several alternatives that seem possible, both singly and in combination.

1. Occupation of the Arab territories (especially in Jordan or in Lebanon) in order to eliminate the bases for concentration and training of terrorists near the Israeli frontiers.

Such an initiative would be absurd, for it would mean even more Arabs within the lines controlled by Israel, and the formation of more sabotage groups within these lines would soon follow; moreover, any prolonged occupation of new Arab territories is hardly conceivable from the point of view of international politics.

2. More frequent dissuasive raids against the Arab countries which give shelter to the terrorists.

Experience has shown that such actions yield only temporary and limited results and that they are risky politically.

3. Massive eviction of the Gaza and the West Bank inhabitants, in order to facilitate control of the remaining populations and regions and to avoid the formation of resistance networks in these areas.

Such a policy would be not only impractical, since the Jordanians would need only to close their bridges over the Jordan River to prevent the Palestinian exodus, but also morally inexcusable: it would mean that tens or hundreds of thousands of innocent people would be made to pay for the acts committed by a small minority. Some decisions, which may be dictated by reasons of state in other circumstances, the Jewish state cannot undertake to shoulder.

4. Evacuation of the occupied territories.

This would simply enable the terrorists to organize themselves along all the frontiers of Israel, as before 1967.

There does not seem to be a single clear-cut solution to the problem of the antiguerrilla activities.

To stop incursions from Lebanese or Jordanian territory, Israel may start patrols on both sides of the borders. This new method, used together with static defenses and commando operations against the Palestinian bases, could have far-reaching results.

As far as sabotage within the occupied territories is concerned, Israel hopes that this can be kept within bearable limits through a combination of political measures granting the local Palestinians in the West Bank and in Gaza a maximum of autonomy, with social measures (active Israeli participation in the rehabilitation of the refugees and in the raising of the peasants' living standard), plus repressive measures against anyone attempting to assist the terrorists. It would appear that intensification of a liberal and generous policy toward those Palestinians who are prepared to avoid terrorism, and increased severity toward those who do not, should lead to relative calm in the West Bank and Gaza.

If these measures do not stabilize the area, however, a firmer policy might have to be chosen: maintaining strict military control of the occupied areas, *while isolating them from Israel*. In this situation Palestinians would not be allowed to travel in Israel; Israeli civilians would be forbidden to enter the territories of Gaza and the West Bank. If necessary, these regions would be separated from Israel by mine fields and electrified barriers of the kind which have been set up in the Beisan Valley in order to stem terrorist infiltration from Jordan. Although such measures would no doubt make sabotage activities more difficult in Israel itself, they would mean the surrender of the liberal view which, in spite of everything, has held open the hope of peaceful coexistence between the two communities. Further, it is far from certain that Israeli reprisals against Arab interests paralleling Israeli interests abroad now under attack by the Popular Front would stop those attacks.

As a matter of fact, as long as sabotage organizations exist, they have not lost the battle. The important thing for those struggling against guerrillas is to keep their activities within bearable limits. Will Israel achieve this by the methods used until now? At this stage the answer seems to be Yes, but no precise forecasting is possible.

Harassment along the Suez Canal. Sporadic harassment of the Israeli forces along the Suez Canal is the Egyptian equivalent of and substitute for the sabotage acts committed by the Palestinians. Israel can respond with one of three possibilities:

1. A massive reaction aiming at the complete destruction of Egyptian forces concentrated along the Suez Canal.

This would mean, in fact, another general war.

2. Heavy air raids linked with commando operations.

Such raids cause considerable damage to the Egyptians and have an undoubted psychological effect.

3. An essentially static defense based on the fortification lines along the Suez Canal.

The adoption of such an essentially static defense seems unlikely both because of the spirit and tradition of the Israeli army,[22] and because such a policy would leave the advantage with the Egyptians. But a massive attack aimed at the destruction of the whole Egyptian army is also not easily conceivable in the present international contest. It is therefore probable that the Israelis will continue with the strategy inaugurated in the summer of 1969: heavy air raids against the Egyptian positions on the Canal and some rear bases, as well as limited commando operations. To be fully efficient, this Israeli strategy employed air raids against Egyptian military bases in the Nile Delta, attacks which had to stop because of the danger of Russian intervention. It remains to be seen if the Russians will try to interfere with Israeli raids in the Canal Zone. If they do, Israel may probably choose a showdown instead of retreating one more step. She shall then be faced with the problem of direct Russian military involvement in the fighting against her, a problem which cannot be analyzed here.

Diplomacy

Since the Six-Day War, the margin within which Israeli diplomacy can move, never very large, has become even narrower. Israel no longer has any diplomatic relations or even unofficial contacts worth mentioning with the Soviet Union and the Soviet-bloc countries, with the single exception of Romania. The relations between Israel and France, after reaching their nadir at the

[22]How far do the military options considered as optimal by the Israeli army influence Israeli decisionmaking at the highest political level? The answer cannot be clear-cut. On the one hand, notwithstanding the state of war, Israel is basically a civilian society and there is no doubt about the fact that the Israeli Defense Force has no direct influence on the decisions taken by the government. On the other hand, some key members of the government are ex-generals (Dayan, Allon, Weizmann), and all members of the government are intensely security-minded, for obvious reasons, so that military considerations brought up by the Chief of Staff or by the Minister of Defense as optimal from a purely military viewpoint may weigh heavily on their overall considerations.

beginning of 1968, have improved since the departure of General De Gaulle, although they continue to suffer from the increasing interests which France is acquiring in the Arab world. Great Britain hardly represents an influential factor any longer on the Middle Eastern scene. As for the United States, Israel's entire diplomatic policy is now concentrated on the maintenance of a certain American position, in the belief that if the United States will agree to support the broad lines of Israel's position, the detrimental influence of Soviet support for the Arab world will be neutralized.

Objectives

In outline, Israel is defending the following points of view in Washington:

1. No matter what the American interests in the Arab world, the maintenance of a strong and independent state of Israel is the best guarantee the United States can have to stop total control of the area by the Soviet Union. In respect to Soviet penetration into the Middle East, American and Israeli interests are therefore the same.

2. Israel would be considerably weakened and would become vulnerable if she were to be forced to abandon the occupied Arab territories without explicit recognition of the Jewish state by the Arab countries and without formal ratification of peace treaties. A return to the *status quo ante* of June 4, 1967, which is more or less what the Arabs and the Russians demand, could only encourage the Arabs to make another attempt at destroying Israel. This would represent a final success for the U.S.S.R. in the Middle East. Obviously, an Israeli withdrawal without peace would elicit Arab responses which the Russians would not fail to exploit, so that the bonds between the Soviet Union and the Arab world would become more firmly cemented. The maintenance of the status quo, however, by showing the Arabs the limits of Soviet means, may drive some Arab governments in desperation to abandon Soviet protection and to turn to Washington. The possibilities of imposing real peace in the region and of evicting the Russians from some of their positions would then be more real than before.

3. An arms equilibrium is, the Israelis believe, an essential condition to avoid another general Middle Eastern war. To enable Israel to defend her position effectively, she hopes to encourage the United States not only to neutralize those diplomatic efforts of the Arabs and the Russians which are aimed at an unconditional application of the Security Council resolution of November 22, 1967, but also to provide the Israelis with military equipment and supplies to maintain the fundamental security requirements of Israel. This latter point, rendered important by the massive Russian armaments sent to Egypt and Syria and by the maintenance of France's embargo on the jet planes bought by Israel, has become essential since Russian-manned missiles and Russian pilots were spotted in Egypt.

Prospects

If the divergence of views between Washington and Jerusalem were to increase and if the United States were to accept a form of settlement which would be too far from the Israeli position, the Jewish state would be confronted with a difficult dilemma. Israel might indeed either submit to the "suggestions" of Washington in order to avoid total diplomatic isolation, which would be dangerous to her in view of the Russian attitude, or accept such isolation by running the risk of losing American support in the event of Soviet pressure.

In spite of the risks involved, it is probable that, under present thinking, Israel would choose this latter alternative. It is clear that any form of settlement that would avoid an explicit recognition of Israel by the Arabs and compel the Jewish states to evacuate the occupied territories would make Israel almost as vulnerable as in May, 1967, while still permitting Soviet assistance to the Arab states. By keeping her position, Israel would have strategic advantages over the Arab world; at the same time, she could reckon that in the event of a *direct military involvement by the Soviets, the United States would not, in the last resort, remain passive.* It might be argued that in the case of a deep divergence of views between the United States and Israel over a compromise settlement, the American government would not necessarily intervene in order to give Israel military assistance, if the Arabs supported by the Soviet Union were to try to recover the occupied territories. In this eventuality there are two possibilities to be considered:

1. The Arab states would benefit only from indirect Soviet aid.

In this case, it is probable that the Israeli army would overcome them without any help from the United States.

2. The Soviet Union would take part in the conflict directly.

In that case, American abstention is hardly conceivable, whatever her divergence of views with Israel.

War

When evacuating the occupied Egyptian territories in 1957, Israel explicitly stated that the closing of the Straits of Tiran to her navigation would be a *casus belli;* and on May 23, 1967, when President Nasser ordered the closing of the Straits to Israeli ships, many Israelis were convinced immediately that war would break out at short notice. They were right.

Israel's *Casi Belli*

Today, this specific *casus belli* no longer exists, but other factors which contributed to Israel's decisions in October, 1956, and June, 1967, are still present. These are, first, the attacks by Arab saboteurs from bases situated in the neighboring Arab countries; second, a potential imbalance between the armaments of the Arab countries and those of Israel, which, past a certain point, would eliminate Israel's qualitative advantage in the military field. In 1956 it was the overwhelming superiority of the Arabs in terms of armaments as well as the activities of the Egyptian Fedayeen that induced the government of Ben-Gurion to launch a preventive attack. In 1967 the quantitative disparity between the Arab and the Israeli air forces no doubt induced Israel to take the first step, although the actual *casus belli* was a different one.

It is difficult to assess the influence which another fundamental imbalance in military armaments, especially between the Israeli and the Arab air forces, might have on Israeli decisionmaking. Although present strategic positions enable Israel to decide in favor of a defensive strategy that avoids the opprobrium of preventive attack in most of the contingencies which may be envisaged, a fundamental imbalance in armaments could bring about another preventive action. Today such a situation does not seem plausible, mainly because of the danger of Soviet reaction.

The *casus belli* mentioned most often is that of a significant intensification of attacks by Arab commandos from one of the neighboring countries coupled with an increase in Egyptian harassment along the Suez Canal. That Israel would no doubt react by launching limited raids of increasing force has already been stressed. Such a course of action might, of course, start an escalation process that would lead to another general war, without actual premeditation.

Israel's Stand on Nuclear Weapons

I have suggested that Israeli acquisition of nuclear arms would be a long-term security guarantee, assuming that the Arabs were to show a minimum of rationality in their response. I have also indicated that if, in one way or another, the Arabs succeeded in providing themselves with nuclear arms without Israel having any, the Jewish state would be in a serious situation.

This being said, it seems to me that one of the central objectives of both Israel's diplomatic policies and her technological efforts would be to put herself in a position to manufacture nuclear arms very rapidly in case of need. If it appeared to be technologically possible for Israel to manufacture nuclear arms, but difficult politically because of U.S. pressure, her government might be prepared to make very large sacrifices indeed in other ways in order both to keep this option open and to remain the sole judge of the need to implement it.

From this point of view, the situation before Israel is not fundamentally different from that facing India, for instance; only the consequences of a nuclear-arms option would not be comparable.

Rehabilitation of the Refugees

Officially Israel's policy toward the refugee problem has not changed: a solution to it is possible only within the terms of a general peace treaty or, possibly, in *ad hoc* discussions between Israelis and Arabs outside of formal negotiations.[23] Yet, unofficially during 1969 and 1970 the Israelis have been studying some experimental and unilateral rehabilitation measures.[24] They discovered that the refugees' determination to "return" was intimately connected with their particular status. The existence of and life in the camps perpetuated the refugees' ideology, while economic and social integration among the local populations seemed to soften their attitudes toward returning.

It would be in Israel's interest to integrate the refugees among the populations of the West Bank and to dismantle the camps gradually.

In order to achieve this, Israel would need to offer the refugees extremely cheap lodgings in various towns and villages in the area, to lend them the sums needed by the traders in the camps to set up shops in the towns, to ensure the integration of camp teachers and officials in the urban life of the occupied territories, and to provide for the entire population a level of wages and medical care superior to that offered by UNRWA. The Israelis would have to create economic and social conditions that would induce the refugees to prefer integration to sterile camp life.[25]

It may be argued that a rise in the refugees' standard of living would increase their ideological consciousness and, hence, their nationalism. This may be true if the rise in the living standard were to occur within the camps, that is, within the context of the present refugee life.

But Israel could therefore contribute socially and economically toward a solution of the problem of the West Bank refugees by taking the measures just mentioned. Although requiring some sort of Israeli presence in the West Bank, such activity under the present situation would be possible.

The rehabilitation of the nearly 300,000 refugees from the Gaza Strip is more difficult. Their living standard in the camps is higher than that of the population of the area, which makes any integration practically impossible. And these refugees are more extremist in their attitude toward Israel, because Egyptian indoctrination has been far more systematic and intensive than that of the Hashemite kingdom. The most rational solution for Israel would be to allow these refugees to emigrate to the oil countries of the

[23]In this connection, see Abba Eban's statements of October, 1968, and April, 1969.
[24]In 1970 Shimon Peres, Minister without Portfolio, was put in charge of all matters linked with the refugee problem.
[25]See Y. Ben-Porath, E. Marx, and S. Shamir, *A Refugee Camp in the West Bank,* Jerusalem, April, 1968. (Mimeo)

Persian Gulf, which can offer well-paid work to hundreds of thousands of
people. Israel has not discouraged the trend toward such emigration which
had started, and has given financial help to the refugees who wished to leave.
But Jordan has closed its doors to this type of traffic and the refugees from
Gaza can therefore no longer leave the areas controlled by Israel. Although
the West Bank might absorb a few thousand of them, a massive migration
from Gaza to the West Bank can hardly be encouraged, since there are
limits to the numbers of newcomers the West Bank can support, and because this area should be devoted mainly to integrating local refugees.

In fact, the only solution to the problem of the Gaza refugees would be,
however utopian this may seem, the creation of entirely new settlements[26]
in this, and especially in the El-Arish area. It goes without saying that
Israel alone could not finance and implement such a gigantic enterprise,
but it is not inconceivable that the United States and various international
organizations might be prepared to contribute to such a scheme. It is true,
though, that the fundamental problem of irrigation in these desert regions
seems to be difficult to solve.

In any case, these are merely theoretical possibilities; it is unlikely that
the Israeli unilateral initiatives will go beyond the experimental stage
during the next few years.

IV. Possible Outcomes

At the end of this survey, a few brief remarks about the possible evolution
of the present situation in the next few years are called for.

Two extreme possibilities may be excluded from the outset in this discussion of the possible evolution of Israel because of their degree of probability in the next ten years or so remains very low, although not theoretically
impossible: the advent of general peace and of harmonious relations between Israel and her Arab neighbors, on the one hand, and the physical
destruction of Israel, on the other. Let us consider the future in the light
of an extension of the conflict. In this view the trends outlined in the course
of this survey permit a number of extrapolations but confront the observer
with a number of imponderables. Some developments seem likely over the
next few years:

1. A strengthening of extremist elements in the Arab world and hence
a weakening of the moderate regimes.

2. The maintenance of Arab sabotage operations within limits which
will not affect Israel's power in economic and military terms.

[26]A plan for the settlement of 10,000 refugee families at El-Arish was prepared for
  Golda Meir by the former head of the settlement department of the Jewish Agency,
  Dr. Raanan Weitz. Various aspects of this plan have been sharply criticized in the
  Israeli press and there are serious doubts about its economic feasibility.

3. The maintenance of Israel's military superiority in relation to the Arab world as a whole and Egypt in particular, as long as the Soviet Union does not get directly involved in the fighting on the Arab side.

The two major imponderables are the possible evolution of Russian military involvement, on the one hand, and, on the other, the eventuality of a temporary settlement imposed by the great powers. As for Russian military involvement, no forecasting is possible at the present stage. Concerning a temporary settlement imposed by the great powers, the reader will be aware that it is the author's opinion on this point that they will not succeed in doing so, but any forecast is of course perilous.

If one admits the possibility of a settlement imposed from the outside, real de-escalation of the conflict cannot be excluded, but it is equally possible to imagine merely a period of calm with serious dangers for Israel in the long term. If, however, a settlement is not imposed from outside, which seems probable, two lines of evolution appear possible and also plausible. First, the present situation might continue for several years with limited military activity along the cease-fire lines and antisabotage fighting. This prolongation would not remedy the unsettled situation in the occupied territories, but would lead to an increasing administrative and economic integration into Israel of part of these territories. It would not remove internal problems arising out of the presence of a large Arab population under the control of the Jewish state. There might perhaps be an increase in Jewish immigration up to a level of about 45,000 to 50,000 people per year. It is not impossible that a situation of this kind might enable Israel, in the long run, to undertake unilateral projects for the rehabilitation of Arab refugees living under her control; this could perhaps lead to a more open attitude on the part of some Arabs toward the Jewish state. In any case the prolongation of the present situation would probably imply an increasing strengthening of Israel in relation to the Arab world and, failing a real peace, this position is clearly the most desirable one to a large majority of Israelis.

But the probable exacerbation of extremist elements within the Arab world might also push the Arab states, Egypt in particular, into some military initiative which might lead, directly or indirectly, to another general war. Without interference by the Soviet Union, Israel would no doubt carry off another military victory. But it is hard to believe that, in its present stage of involvement, the Soviet Union would allow another Arab defeat without intervening directly. Anyhow, the present writer believes that even another victory against the Arab armies would not bring about a peaceful solution and that the situation, after another successful war, would not necessarily be different for Israel from what it is now.

It appears therefore that in the short and middle term, Israel and the Arab countries alike are at an impasse from a political and military point of view. The most logical possibility in this context is a prolongation of the present situation, since another war would probably not lead to peace and might mean heavy destruction. Whether or not Israel will be able to hold out in a situation of prolonged conflict, not only militarily, which seems likely, but psychologically and spiritually remains to be seen.

CHAPTER 5

Israel's Internal Politics and Foreign Policy

Nadav Safran

I. Introduction

This chapter analyzes the structure and dynamics of the internal politics of Israel and their bearing on Israel's foreign policy, particularly its position regarding the postwar Middle Eastern crisis.

The chapter focuses on the country's political party system as the principal mechanism for aggregating opinion and articulating positions, both because Israel is an effective democracy and because this democracy expresses itself through an exceptionally clearly delineated party system. As Section II of this chapter shows, sharp divisions of opinion on a wide variety of issues are manifested in numerous strong, ideologically formulated and institutionally buttressed parties. Therefore, the system involves not only intense competition but also laborious interparty dealings and alignments to produce ruling coalitions based on specific programs. This multi-party system has had four main consequences for the total Israeli political system: it has reduced voter influence on policy by concentrating decisionmaking power in the hands of party oligarchies; required *seemingly* cynical postelection compromises; permitted Mapai, the party nearest center, to dominate all coalitions; and allowed the religious parties, Mapai's staunchest allies, to influence policy more strongly than their real electoral strength would justify.

Section III examines the evolution of the party system and its adaptation to the internal and external pre-1967 Israeli experiences, which combined to eliminate or reduce differences of opinion among parties and erode the ideological and institutional buttresses that supported these differences, thus fostering a trend toward consensus and expanding the circle of parties capable of collaborating in governmental coalitions.

Section IV deals with the impact of the June, 1967, war, including its prelude and aftermath, on the Israeli political system, and the consequences of that impact in terms of Israel's position vis-à-vis the postwar issues. The crisis that led to the war culminated the trend toward consensus among parties, while the issues opened by the war and its aftermath presented new grounds for the division of opinion and a total realignment and reformation of the parties.

The leaders of the existing parties, particularly those of pragmatic socialist Mapai, which has always occupied a strategic center position in the
whole political system, found it politically desirable to avoid formulating
specific positions on the new issues, testing them within the constitutional
bodies of the parties, and presenting them to the electorate. They chose
instead to preserve and prolong the national coalition government embracing virtually all parties on the basis of an agreement to avoid decisions on
the new issues as long as no group felt that an option it favored was being
foreclosed. This decision forced the Israeli government to formulate its
position in terms of insistence on negotiations aimed at peace and greatly
restricted its capacity to maneuver diplomatically. Internally, the absence
of authoritative leadership by parties and government has encouraged the
emergence of individual charismatic leaders and allowed strong and well-
placed ministers to influence affairs personally by a cumulation of administrative decisions.

This situation could evolve only because external pressures were too
weak to override the essentially internal political considerations that determined it. The fifth and last section, which treats the future of the Israeli
political system and the Middle Eastern crisis, begins there and examines
the interplay between the two (external pressures and internal considerations) on the basis of a series of assumptions:

1. If external pressures should continue at the levels that have prevailed
since 1967, the economy, society, and polity of Israel could withstand
them without serious damage in the foreseeable future, but the present
political system may collapse under the strains inherent in it. If it does not,
the present external position of Israel will remain the same; if it does, the
reshuffle would produce a more homogeneous government capable of taking
a definite position and better able to maneuver, but it would insist on peace
and considerable territorial changes over the 1949 armistice lines.

2. If the level of external pressure should change because the superpowers urge a settlement plan involving firm peace, but without any significant territorial modifications over the prewar armistice lines, then the
national coalition would disintegrate, most parties would split internally,
and the resultant political upheaval and realignment of forces would probably produce a majority favorable to the plan. The Arab-Israeli conflict
may then, at last, begin to be concluded.

3. If the superpowers pressed a plan with similar territorial provisions
but some kind of *ad hoc* formula instead of a firm contractual peace provision, the result would be almost diametrically opposite. The present
precarious formal unity would solidify, Israel would resolutely resist, and
the military conflict would escalate rapidly into all-out war. In the process,

Israel would probably produce nuclear weapons to reserve as a deterrent, if necessary. The speculation stops here.

Participation by Soviet personnel in military pressure on Israel in all three contexts above is briefly considered.

II. The Party System in the First Years of Statehood

The party system with which Israel began its internal political life bore the marks of its origins in the Zionist endeavors to create a national home for the Jews, then a Jewish state in Palestine. These circumstances endowed the system with four distinguishing major characteristics: an extraordinary multiplicity of parties, a very strong ideological party orientation and extremely intense party politics, extension of party activities to all spheres of life, and centralized party authority.

In the January, 1949, elections to Israels' first 120-member, unicameral Knesset, or parliament, 24 parties and organizations competed with separate lists, and 16 elected one or more candidates to the 120 seats. Of the successful lists, ten represented "major" established parties; the rest were ephemeral. This multitude of parties, listed in Table 1 (pp. 158, 159), can be attributed to the same causes underlying any multiparty system: the multiaxial division of opinion and a system of proportional representation.

The Political Divisions

In 1949 Israeli opinion was divided over five major issues, all inherited from prestatehood experience and minimally modified to accommodate the establishment of the state: socioeconomic doctrine, religion, the definition and prerogatives of the Israeli state, foreign policy orientation, and relations with the Arab countries, and the "communal problem."

The first issue, basic socioeconomic doctrine, differentiated five leftist parties—the Palestine Communist Party, Mapam, Mapai, Hapoel Hammizrachi, and Poalei Agudat Yisrael—from five rightist parties—the Progressive Party, the General Zionists' Party, the Cherut movement, the Mizrachi Party, and Agudat Yisrael. Within each group of parties, too, were important differences of doctrine and practice on socioeconomic issues, such as those separating Mapam's dogmatic Marxism from Mapai's fluid pragmatic socialism, and Cherut's national managerialism from the Progressives' free enterprise. But among some parties—for example the Communists and Mapam, Mapai and Hapoel Hammizrachi and Poalei Agudat Yisrael, Cherut or the Progressive Party and all of the other rightist parties—socioeconomic differences were minimal or absent. Other topics differentiated them. Religion caused the second main axis of opinion.

Table 1
Israeli Political Parties

Party	Evolution	Policy and Aims	Supporters	Seats in 1965 Knesset	Seats in 1969 Knesset	Percent of Votes in National Elections: 1955	1959	1965	1969
MAPAM	Composed of HASHOMER HATZAIR and ACHDUT HAAVODA; split in 1954; allied with MAPAI to form HAMAARACH since 1968.	Orthodox Marxist-Zionist; in 1949 favored publicly owned enterprise, guaranteed wages, progressive taxation, equal rights for Arabs, neutralist foreign policy.	Urban workers, professionals, 74 kibbutzim.	8		5.8	5.5	5.3	
HASHOMER HATZAIR	Component of MAPAM.	Leftist; before 1947 advocated binational Jewish/ Arab state.							
ACHDUT HAAVODA	Former component of MAPAM; allied with MAPAI in 1968 to form HAMAARACH, then the ISRAEL LABOR PARTY.	Leftist Zionist-Socialist; nonconformist policy.	Trade unions, Histadrut, and kibbutzim.	45	56	8.1	5.5	36.9	46.2
MAPAI		Centrist pragmatic socialist; in 1949 favored "positive neutralist" foreign policy.	Labor; communal and cooperative agricultural villages.			32.1	39.1		
RAFI	The ISRAEL WORKERS' LIST; 1965 breakaway from MAPAI, with which it reunited in 1968.	Leftist; favors modernizing economy, reorganizing education, reform of electoral system toward constituency representation.	Founded by D. Ben-Gurion.	10				7.9	
POALEI AGUDAT YISRAEL	Left-wing offshoot of AGUDAT YISRAEL, allied with it.	Leftist Orthodox Judaist party; favors Israeli state based on Jewish religious law.	Wage-earners.	2	2	14.2*	14.7*	14.1*	14.7*
AGUDAT YISRAEL		Rightist Orthodox Judaist party; favors Israeli state based on Jewish religious law.		4	4				

Table 1
Israeli Political Parties

Party	Evolution	Policy and Aims	Supporters	Seats in 1965 Knesset	Seats in 1969 Knesset	Percent of Votes in National Elections: 1955	1959	1965	1969
PROGRESSIVE	Merged in 1961 into LIBERAL PARTY BLOC; in 1965, INDEPENDENT LIBERAL PARTY portion seceded when LIBERAL PARTY merged with CHERUT.	Centrist; favors equal rights for various economic sectors.		5 I.L.**	4 I.L.**	4.8 I.L.**	4.9 I.L.**	3.9 I.L.**	3.9 I.L.**
GENERAL ZIONIST	PARTY merged with CHERUT.	Rightist; favors strengthening political and economic ties with new African and Asian states; economic reforms.				12.7	7.0		
CHERUT	Descended from hardline IRGUN; merged with LIBERAL PARTY in 1965 to become GACHAL.	Rightist; hopes to extend frontiers to historic lines on both sides of the Jordan; private enterprise; direct political action (e.g., civil disobedience).		26***	28***	14.9	15.2	23.6***	22.9***
MIZRACHI	Merged in 1956, becoming NATIONAL RELIGIOUS PARTY (MAFDAL), to apply Judaism in everyday life.	Zionist religious party; right-wing; favors Israeli state based on Jewish religious law.	Religious traditionalists.	11	12				
HAPOEL HAMMIZRACHI		Zionist religious party; left-wing; favors Israeli state based on Jewish religious law.							
COMMUNIST PARTY OF ISRAEL (MAKI)	Previously known as PALESTINE C. P.; broke up in 1965.	Favors secular government; nonalignment with West; peace with Arab states; recognition of national rights of both Arabs and Israelis.		1	1	4.1	3.0	1.3	1.2
NEW COMMUNIST LIST (RAKAH)	Seceded from MAKI.	More pro-Soviet and hostile to government than MAKI.	Mainly Arab Communists.	3	3				

*Includes MAFDAL (National Religious Party) and AGUDAT YISRAEL.
**Independent Liberals.
***Includes Free Center Party which seceded from Gahal; these groups together held 4 seats in 1965 Knesset and 2 in 1969 Knesset.

The issue of the place of religion in the state separated Hapoel Hammizrachi and Poalei Agudat Yisrael from the other left-wing parties, and the Mizrachi and Agudat Yisrael from others of the right. All four sought to establish an Israeli state based on the Jewish religious law; but the Mizrachi and its labor offspring, Hapoel Hammizrachi, had for many decades participated fully in the Zionist enterprise, while Agudat Yisrael and its workers' offspring, Poalei Agudat Yisrael, had totally opposed Zionism as an encroachment upon the idea of redemption through miraculous divine intervention. Members of both Agudat Yisrael parties had come to Palestine for purely religious or practical considerations. However, most members accepted the establishment of the state, now concentrating their efforts on influencing its policy.

All other parties were opposed to a theocratic state, though all but the Communists recognized the national cultural value of the Bible and certain elements of Jewish tradition. On matters specifically relating to religion, attitudes differed *within* the other parties on a range extending from considerate tolerance to mild anticlericalism, except for Mapam and the Communists, who were militant atheist secularizers.

A third divisive issue stemmed from the definition of the national and territorial claims of Zionism. This issue was greatly weakened by the establishment of the state of Israel. Until the Soviet Union announced its support of partition and the establishment of a Jewish state, the Communist Party of Palestine had totally opposed the Zionist aspiration to statehood. This opposition had defined that party's main difference from the other component of Mapam, the Zionist Hashomer Hatzair that also espoused Marxism and worshiped the Soviet Union. Hashomer Hatzair had also distinguished itself from the other left-wing parties by advocating a binational Jewish-Arab state.

On the other side of the sociceconomic divide, Cherut's antecedents, the Revisionist Party and its underground military offshoot, the Irgun, had differentiated themselves from the General Zionists with whom they shared very similar socioeconomic tenets and from the other parties in general by their claim to the whole of Palestine west and east of the Jordan and by their readiness to fight alone for their goal outside the framework of the Zionist institutions. The latter disposition had confronted the Yishuv (the Jewish Community) with the threat of civil war and had led Ben-Gurion, the Prime Minister in the provisional government, to order the shooting and sinking of an Irgun-mustered arms ship, the *Altalena,* a few weeks after the establishment of Israel.

The creation of the state and the imposition of its authority impelled the Communists, Hashomer Hatzair (united with Achdut Haavoda in Mapam), and Cherut to adapt themselves to these facts, but their past attitudes found new forms of expression that continued to distinguish them. The Communists, for example, while accepting Israel, continued to reject the underlying Zionist doctrine that viewed Israel not just as a Jewish state but as the state of the Jews, and to oppose all its theoretical and practical implications. Mapam, while abandoning the idea of a binational state, considered itself the guardian of the rights of the Arab minority and pressed for the easing of security restrictions. Cherut, while repressing open talk about Israeli *irredentism* and submitting its armed forces to the authority of the state after the *Altalena* showdown, pressed for greater militancy in the country's relations with its neighbors and continued to favor direct action to achieve its goals and oppose the government, for example, with street demonstrations and civil disobedience.

Foreign policy orientation reinforced the division on the previous question and gave it an added justification. The Soviet Union's initial active support of Israel appeared to Hashomer Hatzair finally to vindicate its own long-nurtured faith that the Socialist Motherland would eventually recognize the merits of Zionist Socialism and thus remove the one reservation in its otherwise complete identification with and boundless devotion to the Soviet Union. Consequently, even before the actual establishment of Israel, Hashomer Hatzair impelled Mapam to advocate a pro-Soviet foreign policy orientation and to look askance at any American or bourgeois-Zionist influence in Israel. At the other end of the spectrum, Cherut and the General Zionists were profoundly anti-Soviet and favored open alignment with the West. Between the two groups stood Mapai, whose nondoctrinaire socialism committed it to neither East nor West. Mapai took a tentative positive neutralist orientation (which it called "nonidentification"), adopted and open to change on pragmatic grounds.

Relations with the Arab countries were not then a major issue, since everyone expected the 1949 armistice agreements to lead to peace. But implicit in some parties' perception of the recent war with the Palestinian and the Arab states was an attitude that would soon engender divisions over foreign policy. Mapam thought the armed opposition of the Arabs was instigated by the effendis and pashas for their own benefit to the detriment to the toiling masses, whose interests lay in peace and cooperation with the Jewish working class. Therefore, when the Arab governments refused to conclude peace agreements with Israel, Mapam professed not to be surprised and anticipated the takeover by Arab revolutionary regimes as the prerequisite for peace. Cherut, on the opposite extreme, viewed the war as well as the preceding strife as a kind of Darwinian struggle for survival between two ethnic groups, that could end only in the triumph of one and the submission of the other. Consequently, strength and toughness were the only assurance that the Jewish side would win.

Between these two extremes, Mapai typically occupied a middle ground. It believed that the Arab masses would benefit from cooperation with the Jews and were hostile to Zionism only because incited by their leaders who feared the example set by the progressive Yishuv and Israel. Thus, it hoped that social change in the Arab countries would result in better Arab-Jewish understanding. At the same time, Mapai suspected that something more elemental, like a clash of cultures or national aspirations, might be involved and that therefore only strength and diplomacy would convince the Arabs to accept the Jews.

The fifth topic creating political divisions was the "communal problem." In 1949 the Arabs formed several small parties to publicize Arab grievances and demands. Long before, Sepharadi, Yemenite, and Central European Jews had set up separate political groupings to advance their interests with the ruling Ashkenazi and Eastern European Jews. Never did separate, ethnically based political organizations become important political forces. But the "communal problem" itself soon became a serious issue of social integration and threatened a new political division.

Ideological and Institutionalized Politics

The division and redivision of opinion was largely caused and sustained by the extreme ideological character of Zionist politics. Each party had its own daily newspaper, at least one organ devoted to discussions of "fundamental questions," recognized ideologues, itinerant speakers, seminars and study days, a youth movement, cultural committees and clubs, and training centers for leaders and activists. This phenomenon is based in the environment in which Zionism developed.

Because Zionism emerged among a widely scattered people who were everywhere a minority, because it lacked means of enforcing its dicta, and because it had no substantial foothold in the territory it claimed until long after the movement began, it initially relied on persuasion and moral pressure to achieve its aim. It needed to convince the persecuted Jews that its program was the only solution to their suffering, the emancipated and assimilated Jews that it offered them the only guarantee of security and dignity, and the traditionalists that its scheme was in the best spirit of Judaism. It had to persuade some world powers that it was in their best interest to support Zionism, and convince all and sundry that its project was realizable. To accomplish all this and to answer the objections of both Jews and Gentiles, the Zionists had to develop a whole sociology on the nature and causes of anti-Semitism, reinterpret the history and eschatology of Judaism, and continually reassess political events as they might affect or be affected by Zionism and Palestine. From these studies, the Zionists quickly evolved an ideology on which all parties in the movement drew and to which each added.

Under the leadership of Theodor Herzl, the Zionist movement acted first as an international lobby to obtain a charter for the Jewish national home prior to organizing a general exodus of Jews from Europe. But once this grand scheme failed, the movement concentrated on slow, piecemeal colonization in Palestine with small numbers of pioneers. Because of the difficult conditions and the requisite hardships and sacrifice, candidate pioneers could be recruited only through prior intensive indoctrination or ideological self-intoxication. As the Zionist endeavor progressed and succeeded, the original pioneers became the founders and leaders of most of the country's institutions and parties and imprinted on them their predilection for ideology.

The most fundamental reason for the addiction of Israeli parties to ideology probably lies in the East European environment in which they were generated at the turn of the century. At that time, Judaism there was confronting a severe crisis due to the Enlightenment and the deterioration of the conditions of Jewish existence. Many Jews in Czarist Russia and Poland who had acquired a modern education during the short period of relative liberalism in the sixties and seventies became convinced, like many Christians around them, that their religion was obsolete, superstitious, false, opposed to progress, and harmful. The initial reaction of many was to substitute for their faith a fervent belief in one of the many current liberal, populist, or socialist philosophies, and to join groups of Russians of similar persuasion in seeking to transform Russian society.

However, the reaction that began after 1881, particularly the outbreak of pogroms that were often tactitly condoned by Russian "progressive" and revolutionary groups, made many of these Jews realize that their Jewishness inevitably set them apart. They were thus alienated from both their own still-Orthodox brethren and the Gentiles. Other educated Jews, who had attempted to redefine Jewish identity on the grounds of a self-created enlightened secular Jewish culture, found their goals menaced by the uncertain conditions and prospects of their people. Both groups saw in Zionism a timely resolution of their problem: it allowed them to discard traditional Judaism for their preferred alternative while remaining Jews. Thus grew the multitude of hyphenated Zionist groups with ideologies that were not merely political doctrines but religion-surrogates.

Because Zionist commitment filled the role of religion for a generation of people who had lost their inherited faith, Zionist politics assumed a total, passionate, explosive character that was carried over into Israeli politics. People fought with a bitter relentlessness reminiscent of religious controversy when both contestants believe that salvation is at stake. The knowledge that they must preserve at least the semblance of unity vis-à-vis both the enemies and the potential supporters of Zionism on the outside limited the extent to which the parties might push their warfare; but these restraints merely heightened the intensity and drama of the struggle within the vague boundaries of the permissible.

Illustrations of the passion with which Israeli parties have carried their politics are embarrassingly abundant. A left-wing faction seceded from Mapai in 1946, for example, and two years later united with the extreme left-wing movement Hashomer Hatzair to constitute Mapam, which became the chief rival of Mapai for the labor vote. The struggle between these two socialist parties became so intense that many kibbutzim (collective villages) split apart. Whichever group was in the majority expelled the minority; in some cases, sections of one kibbutz had to be segregated by barbed wire. Lifelong friendships were broken, children who had grown together in children communities were separated, families were sundered. All this over such issues as whether or not Mapai had sold out to the capitalists and whether or not Mapam had sold out to the Soviets. Ironically, within a year after the climax of this controversy, Mapam itself spilt three ways over the implications of the anti-Semitic Prague trials and Moscow Doctors' Plot.

The sinking of the *Altalena* has already been mentioned. This act, which violently climaxed the long struggle between the Irgun and the organized institutions of the Yishuv, may perhaps be defended by reasons of state; but Ben-Gurion's gloating over it and his designation of the gun that sunk the ship as a "holy gun" certainly displayed the fanatic zeal that, along with hyperbole, passion, and cataclysmic oratory, constituted the stuff of everyday politics in the Israeli tradition.

The manifold division of opinion was stimulated and enlivened by a strong addiction to ideology; it was institutionally buttressed by the ramification of party activity. In the system inherited by Israel, most party energies, staff, and financial resources were used not in electoral contests but in multitudinous daily activities nowhere else associated with parties. Parties built agricultural settlements, industries, schools, and clinics; they had their own publishing houses, issued newspapers and periodicals, established cultural centers and synagogues, developed housing projects, maintained sports clubs, and sponsored youth movements. Long after the establishment of the state, some even supported their own military and paramilitary organizations.

To perform all these activities, the parties employed relatively large permanent staffs; to finance them, they founded banks and credit organizations and collected funds in the country and abroad. The most remarkable manifestation of this tendency was the Histadrut—the General Federation of Hebrew Workers — founded in 1920 by two socialist parties. So immense, varied, and ramified were the activities directly or indirectly sponsored by the Histadrut that some of its leaders in the late fifties still claimed for it parity with the state itself.

This characteristic of the Israeli parties results from the fact that Israel was a new society as well as a new state. Men banded together in Palestine to build a new society on the basis of definite ideas as to what that society should be like. As the total endeavor progressed and central institutions endowed with funds from Zionists and Jews everywhere were established, these small groups became political parties competing for influence over the institutions. Newcomers who did not already belong to a party abroad were immediately absorbed into one so that, when Israel was created, most of the population was politically affiliated and strongly integrated in the system.

While addiction to ideology stressed the differences among parties and the ramification of party activity made party affiliation a way of life, the extreme centralization of party authority further perpetuated the divisions by emphasizing party discipline and by centralizing party control in the hands of small oligarchies that personalized the differences and animosities. The key to this characteristic is the system of pure proportional representation, wherein the voters choose party lists rather than individual candidates, and the "democratic-centralist" structure of internal party organization, which allows the leaders to compile the lists. The system was first adopted by the World Zionist Organization and the self-government institutions of the Yishuv because these were voluntary associations without fixed territorial constituencies, eager to maximize member participation but lacking the capacity to enforce majority decisions on reluctant minorities. It was automatically extended to the state because the vested interest of small parties in proportional representation precluded the formation of a sufficient majority in favor of an alternative system.

The Effect of Party Character on the Political System

The collective characteristics of the Israeli party system had several effects on the Israeli political system as a whole. First, the party system has diluted voter influence on policy, leaving policy determination largely in the hands of party oligarchies. True, the multiplicity of parties and the wide variety of ideological coloring offered the Israeli voter an unusual choice of programs and orientations. However, having chosen the party that best expressed his wishes, he could never see that program fully realized because, under the existing system of proportional representation and firm party allegiance, no single party could obtain the necessary majority to enact its program. The necessary coalition governments were always based on bargaining and compromises by the party leaders *after* the elections.

Second, because the compromises had to be made after the elections, they were more difficult to achieve, less enduring, and more repugnant to the voter. Elections everywhere, especially in Israel, stress the differences rather than the common elements among the various parties, involve bitter attacks against the opposition, impel the parties to rededicate themselves to their original principles, and generally intensify the spirit of partisanship and belligerence. Any compromise after the bitterness of an Israeli election discredited the sincerity of the leaders involved; to compromise easily was to seem cynical. Hence, the formation of a government in Israel after elections was a long, painful, wearing process that demoralized the public and aroused resentment of the system. Moreover, since no compromise program could provide for all contingencies, the governments tended to have a short and contentious existence ending in a storm long before their formal appointed time. The average life of a government has extended to less than half of its term; the average life of a Knesset, less than two-thirds of its term. Most Knessets have deadlocked and had to be dissolved to permit new elections.

A third and probably the most crucial effect of the party system is Mapai's domination of all coalitions, which somewhat counteracts the inherent governmental instability. By far the strongest party, Mapai has continually taken about one-third of the Knesset seats. Moreover, Mapai has always occupied the center position between two extremes in the Israeli political spectrum. Mapai was able to draw coalition partners from both the right and the left and from all the religious parties. Its opponents, on the other hand, could not muster a majority unless they all coalesced, which they could not because they differed too greatly.

The dispersal of Mapai's opponents had another equally important consequence for the political system: it ensured the absence of a constructive and responsible opposition, capable of presenting a coherent alternative program. Thus, again and again the majority of Israeli voters had had quite enough of Mapai rule, but saw no alternative.

Finally, another effect of the party system has been to give the religious parties stronger influence on policy than their real electoral strength would justify. The religious parties together never pulled more than 15 percent of the vote, yet the state has always placed matters of personal status under the exclusive jurisdiction of religious courts, supported the institution of the chief rabbinate, created a Ministry of Religions, promulgated national Sabbath and dietary laws, and given official recognition and financial support to religiously oriented schools.

To be sure, much of the government's willingness to concede so much to the religious interest results from the novelty of the religion-state problem in Jewish experience, the historical centrality of religion in defining Jewish identity, the desire of many secularists to preserve Israel's religious link to many Jews abroad, the symbolic national-cultural significance of many religious features, and finally the desire to avoid a *Kulturkampf* when the country was confronted with grave external threats. But as much if not more of that willingness is also due to the religious parties' peculiar balance-of-power position in the Israeli political system, wherein they constituted Mapai's perennial coalition partners.

In principle, Mapai favored the formation of broad coalitions because this made any single partner dispensable and therefore more tractable. In practice, however, Mapai had to rely greatly on the religious parties because the others, especially in the early years of statehood, were too distant from it on issues of foreign and internal policies it considered crucial. The religious parties, on the other hand, were content to follow Mapai's lead on these matters as long as it conceded to them on religious issues, which Mapai then considered to be of relatively secondary priority.

III. The Adaptation of the System until 1967

Although the original Israeli party system had inherent and powerful forces of inertia, the realities of Israel's experience provided no less powerful counterpressures for change. The interaction between the two sets of forces caused a gradual adaptation that has greatly altered the character and effects of the system (although it has retained its original form and external appearance), including the elimination or reduction of most of the differences among the various parties and the lowering of the intensity and heat of party struggles, better enabling the parties to work together. Three forces were primarily responsible for the change: the creation of the state and the activities it assumed; the massive immigration and the forced-pace economic development it entailed; and the imperatives of Israel's perceived security needs. A reflection of the change could be seen in the repeated attempts at fusion among groups of parties and in the increase in the number of parties able to associate in a coalition, a process that culminated in 1967 and after.

The Effect of the State

The establishment of Israel eventually reduced differences among parties by eliminating hypothetical options that had divided opinion and by converting others into practical policy options that could be tested. Ideological addiction and the habit of abstract thinking delayed but could not prevent adjustment to reality. For example, the creation of the state settled an issue that had previously divided Hashomer Hatzair, which wanted a binational state; the two Agudah parties, which opposed a Zionist state; and other parties to which these were otherwise close.

The establishment of the state also provided a positive common focus of loyalty and emotional attachment that overarched particularistic loyalties to parties. So strong had these loyalties been that party members at first submitted state loyalty to party loyalty and assumed that what was good for their party was good for the state; but, with time, the weight of the state, the richness of its symbols, and the rapid influx of hundreds of thousands of immigrants whose loyalty was exclusively focused on the state brought it to the primary position. The state made itself felt through its assumption of many functions previously performed by political parties: education, social security, the labor exchanges, unemployment insurance, housing, frontier settlement, and immigrant services.

The Effect of Immigration

Immigration contributed to the change in a variety of ways. During the first four years of statehood, more than 700,000 immigrants poured into the country, nearly doubling its Jewish population; a comparable number followed in the next 15 years. The absorption of these masses into the existing system could not but alter it fundamentally. To begin with, half of the new immigrants came from Muslim countries and brought no doctrinaire political tradition; most of the other half came from Communist Eastern Europe, where they had mostly known ideology as a cover for repression and therefore shied away from it suspiciously. Since all acquired the right to vote the moment they landed in the country, the political parties had to appeal to them increasingly on terms that were relevant to them, such as national sentiment, the personality of the leaders, and bread-and-butter issues. This gradually replaced the parties' neo-religious ideological fervor with pragmatic goals and ideas that blurred the differences among them. Illustrative of the change is the answer that Yossef Almogui, campaign manager for Mapai in an election in the fifties, gave to criticism that his down-to-earth appeal and methods alienated the intellectuals and the ideologically sensitive people from the party: "How many of them are there?" he asked rhetorically, "About one *ma'barah* worth?" (A *ma'barah* is an immigrant transit camp, of which there were many at the time.)

Immigration also affected the party system by its effect on the economy. The massive influx of mostly destitute people had to be sorted out, housed and cared for, and above all given productive jobs. Two critical questions had to be faced: where to get the necessary capital, and how to provide the organization and enterprise to use it. At first the various parties answered these questions each according to its abstract ideology. Mapai, which was responsible for the government, initially relied on socialist planning. It sought to raise capital by printing money with one hand and regulating demand with the other; it relied for organization and enterprise on the cadres of the existing collective and cooperative sector and on a burgeoning new state bureaucratic apparatus. This approach worked for a while but then collapsed entirely as controls broke down, inflation mounted, and hundreds of thousands of immigrants jammed miserable reception camps month after month in costly idleness due to shortage of jobs and housing. By 1952 Mapai was supporting all massive capital import and exploiting and encouraging any enterprise that could work and make work. These conditions and this outlook were behind Mapai's willingness to sign the reparations agreement with West Germany in the face of fierce widespread emotional opposition. They also underlay Mapai's agreement to ally with the "capitalist" General Zionist Party.

The participation of the General Zionists in the government signaled an adjustment on their part too, since Mapai's new pragmatic orientation still required investing substantial public resources through the "labor sector" of the economy and state direction of the activities of the "private sector." Other parties, however, took longer to free themselves from ideological dogmas. Cherut, for example, violently opposed the reparations agreement with Germany on purely nationalist grounds, though it ceased to object to its application once it was ratified. Mapam not only opposed the agreement but also objected to the entire economic policy of Mapai and continued for some years to advocate its own wholly unrealistic, ideologically inspired plan that envisaged capital formation mainly through a domestic effort by organizing the masses of immigrants into collective agricultural and industrial enterprises and socializing large private capital resources. The tenuousness of this approach was evident in the fact that even its own kibbutzim had trouble recruiting enough personnel to allow them to expand production through the cultivation of newly acquired state lands. Like the kibbutzim and the moshavim (cooperative villages) of other movements, Mapam's own had to resort to hired labor, thus in fact turning the strongholds of pure socialism into collective capitalist enterprises. Ultimately, reality cured Mapam of its theoretical economic doctrines.

Massive immigration and the character of the immigrants eroded not only the doctrinal boundaries of the parties but also many of the practices and institutions they had established on the basis of doctrine. Besides the necessity of hired labor in kibbutzim and moshavim, for example, the egalitarian wage structure established by the Histadrut from Yishuv days was gradually eroded by the economy's increasing demands for highly trained personnel when unskilled labor was abundant among the new immigrants. Still other examples included the breakdown of the monopoly of cooperative marketing agencies due to the resistance of new immigrant farmers, and the practical loss of control by Histadrut central bodies over their burgeoning industrial enterprises. The collective effect of these changes was to loosen up all the parties, undermine their self-assurance and intolerance, and transform interparty struggles to resemble, not fights among tight sects but, rather, wrangles within one church (to borrow a Weberian distinction) wherein doctrine still mattered but the claims of the world also were acknowledged and accommodated.

Immigration also blurred the division concerning the relationship between religion and state. Unlike the other issues differentiating the various parties, no viable middle ground appeared possible on this issue; opinion remained as polarized on it ideologically in 1967 as it was in 1948. Partly for this reason all the parties except Mapam tacitly agreed from the outset to contain the problem by maintaining the status quo that prevailed at the time of independence and postponing resolution of the issue to some indefinite future date. However, even the application of this agreement tended to cause heated clashes that threatened to subvert it and lead to widespread civil strife. In these situations the attitude of the hundreds of thousands of immigrants from Muslim countries was a restraining factor and eventually reduced both the sharpness and the frequency of the conflicts.

This moderating influence of the Oriental Jews derived from their different experience of the religious problem. European Jews came from societies that had long been engaged in fierce ideological and political battles over the issue of church and state, the role of religion in the class struggle, its impact on the minds of men, and so on. These Jews, therefore, viewed the problem in Judaism in comparable terms and arrayed themselves accordingly on the battlefield. The Oriental Jews, on the other hand, came from Muslim societies in which religion had become an issue only recently and in which, because of the different character and history of Islam, the question had not led to any clear polarizations but, rather, to a range of muddled "modernistic" improvisations. Their inclination, therefore, was to view the problem similarly in its Jewish context, and to affirm vigorously the validity of the faith and its prescriptions in principle while supporting or tolerating in practice the widest range of behavior. This "inconsistent" attitude, straddling both poles, was best suited to the *de facto* compromise that prevailed in Israel for tactical political reasons. Moreover it provided a kind of "floating vote" of substantial magnitude on specific issues having to do with religion that forced the entrenched camps to moderate their stands to attract that vote or avoid alienating it.

While mass immigration and the very high component of Oriental Jews in it had these mostly salutary effects on the Israeli political system, it also magnified a problem that had been insignificant in the Yishuv—namely, the "communal problem." With all its intense factionalism, the population of the Yishuv at least had a certain degree of cultural and social homogeneity derived from its common European background. The masses of Oriental immigrants who came after the establishment of the state, and who with their offspring soon constituted nearly half of Israel's population, differed dramatically from the Yishuv's population not only in the respects already discussed but in a host of other ways, too.

Collectively, the Oriental Jews were less educated than the Europeans, had larger families, were more tradition-oriented, and had almost no political experience. In Israel, therefore, they had much lower per capita income than the Europeans, and occupied lower-status positions including those in the government, the professions, and the armed forces. The Orientals blamed their condition on deliberate discrimination by the Europeans (Ashkenazi), while the Europeans attributed the difference to the Orientals' backwardness and their own superiority. Alternatively, the Europeans justified their privileges by invoking their own past struggles in building the Jewish state and defending it before the Orientals had arrived, while the Orientals retorted by citing the sacrifices they made in order to come to Israel and by accusing the Europeans of hypocrisy with regard to their proclaimed ideals of equality and brotherhood. Thus, the objective cultural, economic, and social disparities were overlaid with a dimension of subjective antipathy that gave the problem a dangerous tribal-communal coloring.

The ethnic division did not express itself politically in the same way as other divisions of opinion. No significant ethnically based Jewish political party was able to establish itself nationally even though a few were attempted. The Oriental Jews were not only absorbed into the existing parties, but their distribution did not significantly alter the parties' relative strength—a phenomenon unexplainable on the basis of existing information. The existing parties, in turn, while unanimously ignoring the subjective antipathy aspect of the problem, unanimously and equally favored first equality and integration and then special efforts to remedy the economic gaps between Orientals and Europeans. In short, the problem never threatened to split Israeli society vertically, but it did nearly crack many of its vital institutions horizontally.

Initially, the Orientals' absorption into the existing political parties had led the Israeli leaders to expect them likewise to be quickly assimilated into the Israeli polity, economy, and society because of the integrative mechanisms such as equality and social mobility, national education, service in the armed forces, and membership in the Histadrut. What actually happened was that, as with Black Americans, the partial integration only made the Orientals more aware and resentful of the remaining gap. Before the government and other concerned authorities finally recognized the need for and initiated *special* efforts to meet the problem, there were demonstrations, sit-ins, sporadic outbreaks of violence, defiance of the authorities and resistance to law enforcement in slums where Orientals crowded, a few desertions from Zahal (the Israeli Defense Force), and studies that showed that the gap tended to perpetuate itself rather than narrow. A particularly effective spur for the political parties was the Orientals' promotion of several ethnic lists on the local municipal level, though they developed no viable national party. In some instances, this totally disrupted previous political patterns and warned party leaders what might happen on a national scale if no effective adjustments were made. By the mid-sixties the substantive and, no less important, symbolic responses made by the authorities over a wide range of institutions had controlled though not solved the problem.

The Effect of Threats to National Security

National security was the third and probably the most important countervailing force that modified the characteristics of the Israeli party system. The general concern with this topic not only prevented Israeli factionalism at its worst from tearing the whole political system asunder, but it also contributed more than any other factor to the development of a positive consensus on some specific perceptions, policies, and procedures. All parties soon shared the perception of Israel as engaged in an inescapable confrontation with its neighbors. They all agreed that building Israel's deterrent power was the main, possibly the only, assurance against destruction and constituted a condition *sine qua non* for eventual peace. All parties, therefore, agreed that the requirements of building Israel's military capacity should have the first claim on the country's resources, and that security considerations should be the chief guide of its foreign policy. The armed forces of the state should be insulated from politics, and all disagreements on specific security issues should be resolved *in camera* in the appropriate constitutional bodies and not be fought out in public.

The agreement on these questions and their many ramifications was not at all easily achieved and required much adaptation by most political groupings. The various parties differed greatly in their perceptions of the conflict with the Arabs and the desirable foreign policy orientation of Israel, according to ideological predisposition rather than experience. Experience, however, eventually asserted itself over ideological predilection and forced the various parties to meet on its ground.

The first perceptual adjustment made by all parties was to renounce their expectation of a prompt peace through treaties and to recognize that the Arab reticence on this score created an immediate though at first not urgent security problem. This adjustment was accomplished easily, because it did not clash with any ideological inclination. All parties also agreed at the same time that the security problem should be met by a combination of national armed power and international support, capable of deterring potential Arab aggression. The divergences and difficulties began with views about the practical application of this principle.

Mapam, who felt its long attachment to the Soviet Union vindicated by that country's diplomatic and material support of the creation of Israel, naturally advocated the cultivation of Soviet friendship as a buttress for Israel's security while opposing cooperation with the United States. It denounced the government for accepting an American loan in 1949 and condemned it for welcoming the May, 1950, Tripartite Declaration by which the United States, Britain, and France made themselves the guarantors of the armistice between Israel and its neighbors and proposed to enlist the countries of the area into some regional defense scheme. However, Mapam persisted in its policy even in the face of mounting Soviet hostility to Israel, the launching of a Soviet campaign against Zionism that degenerated into anti-Semitic agitation, the liquidation of Jewish cultural institutions, mass arrests, and the elimination of Jewish writers and artists. Not even the Prague Trials of December, 1952, or the notorious Moscow Doctors' Plot of January, 1953, dissuaded Mapam. On the contrary, it defended its position so passionately against the outraged attacks of members of Mapai that kibbutzim including people of both political persuasions had to split up. In March, 1953, when Stalin died, Mapam went into official mourning, and its organ bemoaned the loss of the "Sun of all Nations."

By a strange process well understood by specialists on Communist affairs, it was Soviet "liberalism" rather than harshness that began to erode Mapam's faith. Stalin's hard line could always be blamed on the "provocations" that the Mapai-dominated government of Israel perpetrated by selling-out to American imperialism. But when, by mending Stalin's actions, repealing some of his sanctions, and restoring reasonable relations with Israel, his successors implied that these provocations had after all not been so serious, Mapam's faithfuls were confused. One consequence was that Achdut Haavoda seceded from the party in 1954. Another was that the remainder of the party, torn by dissent, began to find Soviet policy and action less than impeccable even before the shattering revelations of Khrushchev in the Twentieth Party Congress.

The ground was thus prepared for the about-face that occurred after the conclusion of the 1955 Soviet-Egyptian arms transaction. With Israel facing its most serious security crisis since statehood, Mapam joined the government for the first time in a coalition with Mapai and, incredibly, the religious parties. Several months later when Ben-Gurion, together with the British and French imperialists, prepared to attack Egypt, Mapam voted against the action in the Cabinet, but nevertheless remained in the government and abstained from publicly opposing the attack. Subsequently, whether in the government or out, Mapam persisted in this method of balancing the dictates of its ideological conscience with the demands of Israel's security, which was more than enough to permit alliance with Mapai.

This alliance was due to some adaptation by Mapai also. Mapai initially advocated positive neutrality through which it had hoped to retain the favor that both the United States and the Soviet Union had shown toward Israel at the outset, and to elicit from both powers maximum support for the goals of security, immigration, and economic development. However, because the United States gave Israel economic aid and the Soviet Union did not, and because the United States was better placed by its position in the Middle East to help Israel in its search for peace and security, Mapai's pursuit of its proclaimed policy inclined Israel more and more toward the United States. This inclination was particularly resented by the Soviet government, which at the time was intolerant of even genuine, balanced neutrality and which had internal reasons having to do with its own "Jewish problem" for keeping some distance from Israel. As a result, it turned violently against Israel, leaving Mapai little choice but to give up neutrality and turn more completely to the West.

After turning Israel to the West, however, Mapai realized that the West was not prepared to accept Israel fully. In 1954 NATO refused a request for membership and the United States declined a formal proposal for a mutual defense treaty that Israel had made in an effort to counterbalance a projected Western-Arab alliance that resulted eventually in the Baghdad Pact. Moreover, in 1955, after the Soviet Union had concluded its massive arms transaction with Egypt, the West refused for many critical months to supply Israel with weapons to counter those acquired by Egypt, until France provided some secretly. It was then that Mapai, disabused of its illusions about the West, decided that Israel could rely for its security only on its own military strength and on the influence of that strength on outsiders. On the basis of this new policy, Mapam, which had been disabused of *its* illusions about the Soviet Union, agreed with Mapai.

The other parties with initial definite ideological inclinations about foreign affairs could rally to the new ground more easily than Mapam and Mapai. Achdut Haavoda had to begin with less enthusiasm than Mapam (or Hashomer Hatzair) about the Soviet Union and was more inclined toward "activism" in defense. The General Zionists, pro-American before Mapai, were even more disappointed than it by the rebuff of the West. Cherut, with its extreme nationalism and its predilection for toughness, was comfortable in the new orientation and in the war to which it immediately led. In the face of what it regarded as a general vindication of its outlook, Cherut was even willing to act with a greater sense of responsibility—by respecting, for example, the reasons of the government in agreeing to withdraw from Sinai in 1957 to the extent of confining its opposition to the parliament.

The Soviet-Egyptian arms agreement and the ensuing security crisis and war rallied the various parties to a common ground with respect to both the perceptions of Israel's relations with the big powers and the dynamics of the Arab-Israeli conflict. The critical factor here was the new Egyptian regime's change of attitude on the Palestine question, from apparent moderation to mobilization of Egypt's military resources to lead the Arab countries in an assault on Israel. Strangely enough, this change presented fewer problems of adjustment for Cherut and Mapam than for pragmatic Mapai. Cherut, with its nationalistic, power-oriented perspective, had seen the new Egyptian regime from the outset as more dangerous because more effective than the corrupt monarchy. Mapam, with its classical Marxist approach, never regarded the military coup as the real revolution of the working classes prerequisite to a new Arab approach to the conflict. At most it might have been inclined to follow the Soviet lead and consider the new regime as an anti-imperialist nationalist-bourgeois revolution. It was Mapai, with its vague populistic perception of Arab hostility as fanned by antiprogressive forces, that had the most hopeful expectations of the new Egyptian regime and was most shocked by its intensified anti-Israelism. The initial hopefulness was reflected in the appointment of Moshe Sharett as Prime Minister, replacing the more militant Ben-Gurion, and in the secret contacts he entertained with the Egyptian regime in an effort to promote a settlement. After the Soviet-Egyptian arms transaction, however, Ben-Gurion returned to the government leadership and Sharett was dropped from even his previous post—Foreign Minister. In accordance with the consensus procedure for settling disagreements on security matters, the grounds for the removal of Sharett from any role in the government and the extent of the breach that this action caused within Mapai were not disclosed at the time by anyone and became dimly apparent only ten years later.

Fusion and Coalition

All these processes of adaptation, begun in the 1940s and 1950s, were consolidated in the sixties before the 1967 crisis. The weakening and crumbling of barriers between the various parties—prerequisite to reconciliation—were reflected in widespread attempts at formal party fusion. Thus, the four religious parties at one time combined in a formal political alignment called the National Religious Front. The two veteran Zionist religious parties of the right and left, Mizrachi and Hapoel Hammizrachi, merged in 1956 to constitute the National Religious Party (Mafdal). The centrist Progressive Party united with the General Zionists to its right to form the Liberal Party; the latter in 1965 merged with right-wing Cherut in the Cherut-Liberal Block (Gachal). Finally, in 1965 Achdut Haavoda and Mapai entered into an alliance, the Alignment (Hamaarach).

Even more indicative of the growing *rapprochement* of parties was their increasing capacity to work together in coalition with Mapai. The religious parties were Mapai's first partners and have worked with it almost without interruption. The basis of this partnership was, as pointed out above, an agreement to maintain the status quo in religious affairs and the political convenience of both sides. Next, the experience with economic development and immigrant absorption prepared for a coalition of the General Zionists with Mapai, the Progressives, and the religious parties. The same experience and the weakening of differences in the sphere of security and foreign affairs subsequently enabled Achdut Haavoda and finally Mapam to enter into a coalition with Mapai that included the religious parties. With the participation of Mapam, all the parties except the Communists and Cherut became in principle routinely "coalitionable"; even Cherut was on its way to partnership through its merger with the Liberal Party, which had qualified earlier.

In spite of the adaptation of the party system to the Israeli experience, opposite developments simultaneously demonstrated the remaining strength of the original tendencies of that system. Thus the National Religious Front broke up after a brief experience and was never revived; Achdut Haavoda seceded from Mapam after eight years of unhappy unity; a segment of the Liberal Party refused the merger with Cherut and set itself up as the Independent Liberal Party; and Mapai itself broke up from within as Ben-Gurion and a number of followers including Moshe Dayan and Shimon Peres seceded to form the Israel Workers' List (Rafi).

The last split was particularly important because it struck the party that had been the mainstay of Israel's little political stability, and could have had far-reaching consequences had it not been compensated by Mapai's alignment with Achdut Haavoda. Moreover, the split was the outcome of a crisis that stemmed from the worst features of Israel's political system. In 1964 Ben-Gurion insisted on reopening the Lavon affair, a complicated tangle that had been bitterly fought out once before in 1960-1961, and the only crisis in Israel's history that had entangled the defense establishment in partisan politics.

The revived crisis pitted Ben-Gurion, recently retired after thirty years of undisputed leadership of Mapai and the nation, against Prime Minister Eshkol, Ben-Gurion's long-time collaborator and his handpicked choice as successor; and when Eshkol won at the party convention, Ben-Gurion seceded. The electorate rebuffed the national hero by giving his Rafi list only 20 percent of Mapai's vote in the general election. This, together with the timely alignment between Mapai and Achdut Haavoda, which compensated for that loss almost exactly, not only saved the party and the political system, but also dramatically demonstrated the public's impatience with the stormy old-style politics. But that the crisis occurred at all showed how deeply entrenched this style of politics still was.

Thus the trend toward fusion of parties was in large measure offset by a countertrend of fission, the healing of old antagonisms amid an increasingly pragmatic atmosphere did not prevent the frenzied disputes surrounding the Lavon affair in 1960-1961 and 1964-1965, and the gradual qualification of old pariah-parties for participation in the government did not prevent the emergence of a new pariah-party in the form of Rafi led by Ben-Gurion. In this context the May, 1967, crisis and war exploded, bringing in their wake momentous change in the political dynamics of Israel.

IV. The Impact of the June 1967 War and
Its Prelude and Aftermath

The 1967 war, together with its prelude and aftermath, had a powerful and far-reaching impact on the Israeli political system. Very quickly this cluster of events culminated the trend toward growing consensus in public opinion and increasing interparty collaboration; redivided opinion on new issues it raised and challenged the parties to redefine and realign themselves in terms of these issues; and impelled the parties to avoid the challenge by agreeing not to compete on the new issues as long as certain conditions dependent on outside factors did not arise. The result was a system in which many substantive divergences of views were barely contained within a framework of formal unity on the intraparty as well as the interparty coalition level—a system therefore nearly incapable of taking the initiative on basic issues and whose evolution from its present inertia depends primarily on the course of outside events.

The Effects of the June 1967 Crisis and War

The basis of the development of the Israeli political system since 1967 is the May-June crisis preceding the war. Fairly accurate and detailed descriptions of that crisis have been published, so here we will merely note a few highlights. By the last week of May, nearly all Israelis perceived a clear and imminent danger of destruction for their state, and for themselves as a people and even as individuals. In the light of the subsequent course of events, these fears may appear highly exaggerated and unjustified; nevertheless, they were experienced as real, and thus not only guided the Israeli actions at the time but left a lasting imprint on subsequent behavior.

The main focus of the crisis from the Israeli perspective was not so much the actions of Nasser or the position of Washington, Moscow, London, and Paris, as it was the timid reaction of their own government under Eshkol's leadership. This reaction, in the view of Israelis, could be interpreted only as a sign that either Zahal might be incapable of meeting the Arab military threat, or that civilian leadership was weak and indecisive. Because, first, faith in Zahal had been nurtured for 20 years and, second, doubts about Eshkol's competence as Minister of Defense had long been fostered by political opponents such as Ben-Gurion, most Israelis were inclined to take the latter view though still apprehensive about the former. Discontent reached its peak after Eshkol's speech on May 29, 1967, in which he declared the government's decision to continue exploring the possibilities of solving the crisis without war. The popular restlessness stimulated a project initiated previously by some politicians: replace Eshkol as Minister of Defense with General Moshe Dayan.

The success of the maneuver dramatically demonstrated the change that the crisis had wrought in the Israeli political system. The proposal for the appointment of Dayan originated outside the coalition altogether, in consultations that brought together leaders of the two pariah-parties, Rafi and Cherut, including sworn enemies like Ben-Gurion and Begin who had never even exchanged a greeting. It was endorsed by the National Religious Party, a partner in the ruling coalition, and was forcefully presented by this party's leader in the Cabinet, against strong opposition by Eshkol. Finally, as the popular dissatisfaction peaked, the proposal was endorsed by a majority vote of the leadership of Mapai, leaving Eshkol with no choice other than to accept his party's decision or resign. After this disintegration of traditional political allegiances, alliances, and hostilities, the formation of a national coalition government embracing all parties except the Communists was a logical sequel.

The actions of all those involved in the resolution of the internal political crisis, from the grumblings of the masses to the feverish caucusing of politicians, were clearly impelled by the sense that the country faced a life-and-death situation. Once taken, however, the actions created conditions that profoundly affected the subsequent course of Israeli politics. Thus the brilliant victory in the war that followed the emergency actions confirmed the erosion of political loyalties and Eshkol's leadership. Although Zahal was undoubtedly given the chief credit for victory, Dayan was seen as the one who had no doubt about Zahal's might and who knew how to exploit it. He emerged as a national hero with a political stature that far transcended his identification with Rafi. At the same time, the relative ease with which Zahal won made the hesitations and doubts of Eshkol and some of his governmental colleagues retrospectively appear all the more unjustified and due to weakness. The subsequent public revelations as to what had really happened in the government sought, among other things, to prove that Eshkol had favored military action all along and to explain the reasons for the pursuit of diplomatic courses; instead, they merely demonstrated that Eshkol believed himself in a politically weak, defensive posture.

Eshkol's sense of weakness gravely detracted from his ability to lead the nation in exploiting the political prospects opened by victory. The first necessary task was to define Israel's postwar aims and the method by which they were to be pursued. Israel, like the United States in World War II, was well prepared to win a war but not ready to utilize victory to achieve certain definite goals. Clearly, the military operations executed during the war, including the capture of enemy territories, had been very carefully planned; but the question of how to use the conquered territories had apparently never been given serious consideration. Perhaps everyone had assumed that they would be exchanged for peace, without deciding whether everything would be traded back, and if not, what would and what would not be traded.

During the war, Eshkol tentatively attempted such a decision by issuing a declaration that Israel sought no conquest and no annexation from the war but had lasting peace as its only aim. Two days later, however, Dayan, in a solemn moment before the Wailing Wall right after the bloody capture of the Old City of Jerusalem, announced that the Israelis had returned to Jerusalem and would never be parted from it again. Dayan's oath received immediate universal Israeli endorsement and proved to be the first of many unilateral statements and deeds by Dayan and others that, though they did not command this kind of support, expressed nonetheless widespread dissent from Eshkol's definition of Israel's aims.

Had the Prime Minister been someone other than Eshkol, or had Eshkol not recently been partially repudiated by his own party, his political allies, and the nation, he might have maintained his own position and sought to impose it on party and government. After all, Ben-Gurion had done so on several critical occasions, such as in 1948 when he insisted on the proclamation of the state of Israel; in 1951 when he signed the German Reparations Agreement; and in 1957 when he ordered the withdrawal of Israel's troops from Sinai and Gaza after he himself had led the opposition to retreat. However, Eshkol remained silent to avoid another crisis in the government and the party, hoping that his own declaration would be forgotten. In the absence of firm leadership, an unchecked debate developed over goals and means that increasingly fragmented Israeli opinion.

Three basic positions and numerous variants emerged from the debate and split opinion across existing party lines. Perhaps particular positions could be associated with Gachal and Mapam more readily than with other parties, but in all instances the deviation was too great to permit accurate extrapolation of strength from position to party or vice versa.

The basic positions were: annexing all the occupied territories; returning them with exceptions to the Arab states in exchange for peace; or ceding some to a "Palestinian entity" rather than to states from which they were seized. Annexationists ranged from extreme left-wing idealists who still desired a binational state to extreme right-wing nationalists who dreamed of a "greater Israel" occupying both sides of the Jordan. In between were pious Jews and romantic atheists, people who sought a Jewish-Arab symbiosis, those who desired *lebensraum* and incentive for massive immigration, hard-nosed realists who mistrusted peace treaties, and "de-Zionizers" who wished to see Israel become a Middle Eastern state. Those who favored exchange of territory for peace differed greatly as to which territories should be kept and which returned, including at one end those who would return practically everything (the "minimalists") and at the other end those who would retain so much as to approach the total annexationists. Similarly, those who favored a Palestinian entity were divided among themselves as to the scope and character of the country: whether sovereignty for all the occupied Jordanian territory plus the Gaza Strip—a position very close to the minimalists within the previously cited approach—or mere internal autonomy for a portion of the Jordanian West Bank—a viewpoint close to some of the annexationists. In addition to the divisions and subdivisions about ends, there were considerable differences about means and tactics. Almost the only point on which there was general agreement was the opposition to withdrawal for the sake of a "patched-up" settlement. Thus, even the minimalists insisted on firm peace as the price.

The consequences of Eshkol's failure to press his own views of the postwar aims of Israel might have been corrected in the course of the elections scheduled for October, 1969, had his party been willing to prepare for these elections by developing a specific, concrete program regarding the postwar issues. Such action by Mapai would have forced the other parties to do likewise; opinion would therefore have reaggregated around a set of alternative programs. However, after a few initial attempts to find a program, Mapai sought other ways to approach the impending national poll.

One reason Mapai was reluctant to pursue its initial course was the record of some of its leaders in the government during the crisis, especially the nearly fatal hesitation of Eshkol. A party effort to justify it might alienate some of the electorate and perhaps predetermine unnecessarily some policy choices; while an attempt to disavow it would estrange the leaders associated with it, besides being a politically damaging admission of fault. Another reason was non-Mapai Dayan's enormous popularity due to his role in the war. Attempts were made to deflect some of Dayan's glory to Zahal or General Rabin, and to build up Yigal Allon, a hero of the 1948 war, as a rival popular leader; but these were proved abortive by the development of a "Dayan for Premier" movement that quickly gathered an impressive number of adherents. A third reason was the unknown effect on the public of the participation of Cherut (Gachal) in the government for the first time in Israel's history. Since 1955 the drift of Israel's orientation in matters of security and foreign policy had been toward greater toughness and reliance on the nation's armed forces, generally associated with Cherut. However, the political gains that might have accrued to Cherut from this "vindication" of its approach were restricted by the memory of its past defiance of the majority of the Yishuv and by the political ostracism that had condemned it to permanent ineffective opposition. Now that Cherut was at last respectable and the big victory of Israel's armed forces permitted the expansion that Cherut had long advocated, the danger of a major shift in political strength in an electoral showdown based on specific programs appeared particularly grave. With this danger, the Dayan phenomenon, and the mishandling of the prewar crisis, any general reaggregation could permit a majority coalition composed of Rafi (Dayan's party), Gachal, and the religious parties, thus dislodging Mapai from its central position in Israeli politics. One need not be cynical to understand why Mapai's leaders sought to avoid such a possibility; most probably believed that this would be disastrous for both their party and the entire nation.

Thus Mapai attempted to combine the other parties on the basis of abstention from clear and openly contested alternatives. On one level, this effort involved deliberately prolonging the national coalition by agreeing that the government would take no position on the basic options and issues facing the country as long as none of the partners believed its own option was either ripe for realization or being foreclosed. In effect, the government committed itself to insisting on negotiations aimed at achieving peace and leaving all options open as long as the Arabs did not accept the proposed procedure and its aim.

On another level, Mapai used essentially the same principle to promote a union with the left-wing parties. Ignoring the great diversity of views among leaders and masses by postponing indefinitely the elaboration of a specific program on the postwar issues, but taking advantage of the reduction of past differences and of the left's dream of "unity of labor," Mapai succeeded in merging with Rafi and Achdut Haavoda to constitute the Israel Labor Party, and inducing Mapam to align itself with the new party as a prelude to an eventual fusion. This whole endeavor was almost defeated shortly after its completion, as Eshkol's sudden death triggered a struggle for the succession that threatened not only to split the new party but also to precipitate a policy showdown among the contenders, which would in turn cause a general showdown among all parties. However, the threat was averted by the selection, in the person of Golda Meir, of a compromise candidate who, unlike Dayan, Allon, and Sapir, was known to be firm but uncommitted to any specific position. Moreover, Meir was also, by virtue of her age, clearly a transient leader. The net effect was to confirm and solidify the principle of "keeping all options open" that was the basis of unification.

The success of the efforts to suspend decision on the basic postwar issues was confirmed in the October, 1969, general elections. At a time when opinion in the entire country was so fragmented, these proved to be the least controversial of all Israeli elections. Not only was the number of significant lists presented to the electorate smaller than ever, but the programs proposed were similar and all couched in general terms. Naturally, the returns were no more indicative of opinion in the country than the platforms on which people voted, but the results were nonetheless taken as a mandate for the continuation of the national government and the suspension of decision.

The Effects of Postwar Events

The ability of the leaders of the various parties to agree to suspend any contest on the basic options and issues raised by the war, and the fluidity of public opinion underlying that agreement depended decisively on the absence of an external precipitant that could necessitate decision. When Eshkol declared in the middle of the war that Israel's only aim was to achieve peace, he had assumed that Israel would be forced after the war to take a clear policy stand, either by strong international pressure to withdraw unconditionally or by the necessity of reacting to specific settlement proposals. His retreat from that position, while immediately due to internal political reasons discussed above, was ultimately possible only because the outside factor never materialized; thus he could withdraw. True, the Soviet Union attempted to build up pressure in the United Nations for an unconditional withdrawal, but that pressure was effectively checked by the United States. The Soviet Union then tried to forestall a stalemate by agreeing on the conditions for Israeli withdrawal with the United States (the Gromyko-Rusk talks), but the Arab states, led by Algeria, torpedoed the effort.

Nor did the subsequent course of external events force the Israeli political system to make basic decisions and incur divisions, though three potential pressures might have: an agreement by one or more Arab states to a position acceptable to the "minimalists" in Israel; an agreement by the big powers on such a formula; or overwhelming military pressure. However, no such pressures developed sufficiently to force a decision.

Immediately after the war, the Arab states naturally awaited the outcome of the United Nations efforts to secure an unconditional Israeli withdrawal before committing themselves to any position. When these endeavors failed, they adopted at the August, 1967, Khartoum Summit Conference a decision that authorized any state to seek a political solution to the conflict with Israel provided this involved no negotiations, no formal peace, and no recognition. All Israelis interpreted this position, coming so soon after the war and on the heels of the abortive United Nations exertions, to signify Arab determination to continue the confrontation; therefore, it did not tempt any political group to respond substantively to its positive aspect. The Arab states have essentially adhered to this decision; those that agreed to the November 22, 1967, Security Council resolution read it in the light of the Khartoum formula. Sometimes President Nasser or King Hussein found it necessary to stress willingness to accept a political settlement, and even to stretch its meaning; but at no point did they stretch it beyond the three "no's" of Khartoum, especially the "no peace" that was essential to overcome the universal Israeli suspicion.[1]

[1] In 1970, Nasser said to various Western interlocutors that he would be willing to make peace with Israel; but he always qualified his statement by the condition that the rights of the Palestinian *nation* should be respected, which in effect nullified the concession.

The superpowers did attempt again to formulate the conditions of a settlement after the initial stalemate, and were eventually able to reach an agreement that was expressed in the November 22, 1967, Security Council resolution. Clearly, however, from the outset the resolution was susceptible to widely divergent interpretations—precisely why it commanded widespread approval—and the big powers had subscribed to it in the hope that the United Nations' envoy, Ambassador Jarring, might find it under a common ground for the Arabs and the Israelis. When Gunnar Jarring failed, the Big Four, then the United States and the Soviet Union together, tried to translate the resolution into a specific settlement, but they could not agree among themselves.

The Arab states and the Palestinian guerrillas applied military pressures, but never of sufficient magnitude to force the Israeli government to reconsider its formal stand. Occasionally, the pressure made the country uneasy. For example, after the Israeli raid on Karameh, guerrilla activities and acts of terrorism and civil disobedience in the occupied areas seemed to be constantly increasing; or in summer, 1969, when the Egyptian forces on the Suez Canal began the war of attrition that initially inflicted heavy casualties. However, Zahal always took effective countermeasures before the pressure became too great.

Because the Israeli political system has neglected unity of goals in favor of unity of rank, the government has been unable to respond effectively to external challenges and opportunities, except militarily. Since the government and the parties failed to provide systematic leadership and guidance, the public, perplexed by the multiplicity of views and the complexity of issues, has tended naturally to rely on individual leaders. So far, several have been the focus of attention, including Golda Meir, Ezer Weizmann, Yigal Allon, and of course, Moshe Dayan; but should the situation become critical, especially militarily, the focus will probably concentrate upon one person, who will then emerge as the charismatic leader of Israel.

Moreover, since individual members of the government do have definite views on the issues raised by the war, those who administer functions particularly relevant to these issues—for example current defense, administration of occupied territories, foreign affairs, and the interior—could not avoid subjectivity in the day-to-day management of affairs, even if they sincerely wished to abide by the overall cabinet policy of keeping all options open. Mutual vigilance by the different individuals somewhat ensures that no single administrative decision likely to foreclose or predetermine options is made without Cabinet review. However, the accumulation of many smaller decisions, which could no less effectively determine choices, naturally escapes observance.

Because defense mostly requires nonroutine daily decisions, because defense decisions need to be made quickly, and because defense has a professional-technical character beyond the competence of most others, the Defense Minister has had the greatest capacity to affect the general policy orientation by his administrative decisions. For example, Moshe Dayan decreed the "open bridges policy" allowing movement between the two banks of the Jordan; he originated the policy of using Arab labor in Israel proper; he experimented with "neighborhood punishments"; and he authorized the bombing of targets deep in enemy territory, a decision that has most recently led to a crisis in the whole Middle Eastern confrontation.

V. The Future of the Political System and the Middle Eastern Confrontation

The current Israeli political system is unstable because of the disparity between the actual substantive division of national opinion on the issues arising from the war and the traditional forms of political organization. This disparity has been prevented from breaking up the national coalition government and reforming the parties by an agreement to insist on negotiations aiming at peace that skirted the central substantive issues. However, the adoption and retention of this formula, which has been the only link among the diverse opinions and between public opinion and formal organization, has been possible only because no strong external pressure has forced Israel to adopt a more specific position on the postwar issues. What would happen if this condition should change? What would happen even if this condition did not change? Can the present system endure? What would be the effects on the entire Middle Eastern situation in either case?

A change in the external postwar conditions could be precipitated either by a protracted intensification of the military pressure on Israel, or through an attempt by the superpowers to impose a specific settlement worked out by themselves.

The first of these possibilities does not seem very likely in the foreseeable future. Nothing in the relation of forces between the two sides or in the strategic and tactical options available to them portends any significant rise in Arab military capabilities. Increased exertions along past lines or experimentation with new types of operations may, as in the past, initially hurt the Israelis; but again the Israeli armed forces would probably soon find ways to ease the pressure to a bearable level and to counter the new approaches. However, the Russians could participate more actively in the Arab war effort, starting with Soviet pilots and air defense personnel. Such action would change the entire configuration of the problem and set different conditions for the Israeli reaction, discussed below.

An agreement between the superpowers is conceivable in the foreseeable future only on the basis of withdrawal of Israel's forces from virtually all the occupied territories. On this point the Soviets have insisted and to it the United States has publicly conceded in the Rogers Plan. But the critical feature of any superpower agreement from the perspective of its effect on Israel is whether it would achieve a formal peace (involving a treaty or an equivalent contractual agreement, such as the post-World-War-II agreement between the Soviet Union and Japan), as the United States has insisted so far; or whether it would envisage only an *ad hoc* settlement, as the Soviets have urged at their most accommodating moments. The two alternatives would have almost diametrically opposite effects on the Israeli political system, which in turn would have vastly different consequences for the Middle Eastern confrontation.

A superpower agreement that aims at achieving firm peace presupposes the prior acquiescence of Egypt, or the Soviets would not consider it. The plan would also provide for both Arab and Israeli security and for navigation, refugees, and so on, as envisaged in the November 22, 1967, Security Council resolution. The superpowers would presumably support the agreement with positive measures, such as joint or separate security guarantees and arms control measures, and would press hard for its acceptance. They might even condone Arab use of force and condemn Israeli responses as long as Israel does not accept the plan.

Under such circumstances *only,* the proposal would quickly shatter the national coalition government. The relative group sizes of those who would accept and those who would reject the plan would most likely not permit the government to drop some members, reshuffle, and then continue the coalition. Moreover, the division would probably cut across party lines, thus forcing the representatives of the various views in the government to return to their respective parties for arbitration. Thus some parties would disintegrate, especially the large, inchoate, diverse Israel Labor Party. Simultaneously, national opinion would stridently support or oppose the plan. In short, a superpower agreement under the terms and the circumstances here envisaged would cause an upheaval in the Israeli political system leading to a complete redistribution of strength and realignment of parties on the basis of support for or opposition to the agreement.

The substantive outcome of the upheaval would depend greatly on when the plan is thrust upon Israel. Two years ago, for example, a firm majority would have accepted. At the time of writing, on the eve of the third anniversary of the war, there is only a probability that such a majority would emerge. The difference results from a combination of several influences. Israel's sacrifices and losses from the fighting since 1968, while not great enough to wear down the spirit of most who have always insisted on the need for territorial revisions in addition to peace, have been sufficiently important to make many who in 1968 would have accepted peace without such revisions insist now on changes to justify the suffering. At the same time, Israel's ability to hold the conquered territories for three years has converted many who were initially prepared to accept peace without territorial modifications on the grounds that no practical alternative existed. Finally, the emergence of the Palestinian guerrillas as a political if not a military force has caused some Israelis to question the viability of any agreement reached with the Arab states alone and induced them to regard a settlement with the Palestinians as perhaps more worthwhile.

Withal, the concrete prospect of peace with Egypt, Jordan, and Lebanon; the desires to be accepted, to escape psychological confinement, to achieve normal international relations, and to divert the energies invested in defense and warfare to other uses—all these combined with the alternative prospect of having to continue fighting alone, being branded as warmongers, incurring international sanctions, and losing much support even among world Jewry seem sufficient to secure a majority, however reluctant, in favor of acceptance.

Should the superpowers attempt to force such a plan on Israel at some more remote date, for example in three years, the effect on the political system would probably be the same but the outcome of the upheaval would be much more difficult to predict. The strength of the acceptors would be further weakened by the same influences that have reduced their strength since 1968; and the capacity of Israel to resist may be significantly increased by the development of its military industries. On the other hand, war weariness, the strain on the economy, the erosion of Israel's moral position, and the probable reduction of doubts caused by the Palestinian factor would probably leave Israel as prepared to accept the plan in the years ahead as now. At any time, such a plan would open a real prospect for a more peaceful and more hopeful era in the region.

A superpower agreement designed to achieve an *ad hoc* settlement would presumably involve the same features supposed in the peace plan minus, of course, a treaty or some equivalent contractual agreement. That is, it would presuppose prior acquiescence of Egypt, would include provisions for demilitarized zones, free navigation, refugee settlement, and so on; would be either "guaranteed" by the superpowers or supported by an American security guarantee for Israel; and its acceptance would be forced by the superpowers.

Such a plan would almost certainly transform Israel's formal political unity into substantive unity—a common determination to resist it. Some politicians might acquiesce in the plan for fear of the political consequences of rejection and because they were attracted by the American security guarantee. However, this would only slightly diminish the national coalition, leaving it essentially intact and actually stronger. Some members of the Israel Labor Party might quit, for example, and align with a segment of a more badly broken Mapam and a few intellectuals and dropouts from other parties to constitute a new political grouping advocating acquiescence; but there would be no major party reformation.

As with pressure on behalf of a peace plan, time is also a factor here—but unequivocally. An *ad hoc* settlement plan vigorously pressed by the superpowers immediately after the war might not have elicited a majority acquiescence, but it would probably have shattered the national coalition and forced a far-reaching political realignment. Since then, many factors produced the current situation. The Arab states' prolonged resistance to peace has ruled out any hope that an *ad hoc* settlement could be a prelude to peace; at best, it would be a truce before the next war. An *ad hoc* settlement more or less along the lines assumed here has been attainable, in the Israeli view at least, since the November, 1967, resolution; to accept it now would be to admit to a defeat unjustified by the facts, and to acknowledge that all the casualties and all the sacrifices borne in the subsequent war have been in vain. No government accountable to the public would accept that before exhausting first every possible means of resistance.

In addition the Israeli government has acted since 1967 on the assumption that it would accept nothing less than peace. On the basis of that premise, it has established facts that restrict its capacity to accept another. For example, it has established more than two dozen rural and urban settlements in occupied territories while denying that this necessarily indicated an intention to annex the areas concerned on the grounds that nothing should preclude these settlements' being in Arab territory under a formal peace. Also, the government has encouraged an investment of hundreds of millions of dollars in a 42-inch oil pipeline from Eilat to Ashdod and in tankers and tank farms to utilize it in the conviction that the whole project will be protected either by Israel's armed forces or by an unequivocal contractual agreement with Egypt. Finally, the Israeli economy has been increasingly linked to the economy of the West Bank and the Gaza Strip, particularly through the employment of tens of thousands of Arab workers in Israel, on the grounds that such arrangements were workable under a peace treaty. An *ad hoc* settlement has thus become almost unanimously unacceptable for practical as well as for political, psychological, and security reasons.

In resisting attempts to impose an *ad hoc* settlement on it, Israel would also be fortified by a sense of righteousness. Here Israel would be fighting for the elementary right to peace while its opponents would be trying to force it to accept less. This would allow Israel to ignore United Nations resolutions against it with greater equanimity, to hope that public opinion in the United States and the world at large would deter the superpowers from a vigorous application of sanctions against it and eventually induce a reversal of policy. Most important, Israel would be able to rely on massive moral and material support from world Jewry, which it could not in the previous scenario.

Israel's physical capacity to resist outside pressure has greatly increased even since the beginning of 1968 and will continue to grow in the few years ahead. Israel's GNP has grown by 25 percent in 1968-1969 alone, and its defense allocations in these years have been at double the prewar rate. Of the nearly 3 billion dollars allocated to defense since the end of the war, a considerable percentage—probably as much as half—has been invested in military industries designed to make Israel self-sufficient in all kinds of armaments. This program has already reduced Israel's dependence on the outside; at the present rate of development, it should approach its goal of self-sufficiency in a few years.

The consequences for the Middle Eastern confrontation of a superpower attempt to impose an *ad hoc* settlement under these circumstances can be easily imagined. Depending on how the crisis arising from such an attempt would unfold, either the Arab or the Israeli side would profit from an acceleration in the fighting to provoke a general showdown. If pressure against Israel should seem to be building up effectively, the Arabs might prefer to forgo battle and allow the superpowers to become more embroiled with Israel, or they might seek to precipitate wider fighting to force a decision while the external situation appeared most favorable; but the Israelis would in either case probably favor a pre-emptive large-scale action to change the whole situation by military means. If, on the other hand, the pressure campaign should decrease or if Israeli resistance were stalling it, the Israelis would probably wish to abstain from general war and the Arabs would wish to precipitate one in order to reactivate the pressure or to achieve the maximum advantage before the pressure stopped completely. In any case, large-scale military operations would introduce grave and unforseeable complications.

A possible and even probable related development could be Israeli production of nuclear weapons as soon as pressure was applied. Then, depending on how the pressure was applied and the course of the military operations it would precipitate, they might either keep the possession of these weapons secret or proclaim the fact in order to use them as a deterrent. A less likely alternative—in view of the enhanced confidence in their conventional warfare capacity since 1967, their military industrial program, and their awareness of the complications that might ensue—is that the Israelis should use the nuclear weapons as a *deterrent* as soon as they become available, regardless of the course of the external pressures and military operations.

Whatever the situation, an *ad hoc* settlement would clearly be the most likely to precipitate the kind of violence and complications that the super-powers are trying to avoid. The superpower agreement would, in turn, be most unlikely to survive the crisis, and its disintegration could further deteriorate their relationship.

Superpower pressure for an *ad hoc* settlement might also develop if the Soviet Union were to enhance the capacity of Egypt to exert military pressure on Israel through participation of Soviet personnel in the air war, while the United States abstained from providing Israel with means to counter that pressure. This would in fact amount to a *tacit* joint superpower pressure, which may or may not be accompanied by separate American advice to Israel to accept an American-elaborated *ad-hoc* plan along lines agreeable to the Soviets. The likelihood of such a situation is rather low, be-cause the Soviet Union would then be the predominant power in the region; however, it cannot be altogether excluded in view of the embroilment of the Administration in Indochina and the possibility of at least an initial mis-perception. In any case, the Israeli reaction would be essentially the same as toward an explicitly concerted plan, with all the more reason, since the hope of reversing the United States' position through staunch resistance would be much greater.

If the American position were reversed, or if the United States should initially react to Soviet participation by providing Israel with additional weapons, one of two conditions would develop. If the Soviets should respond to the American move by increasing their participation, a very dangerous situation like Vietnam in reverse would evolve, the consequences of which defy prediction at present, except for the certainty that it would be faced by a solidly united and determined Israeli government and people. If, on the other hand, the Soviets should freeze their participation at a level designed to protect the rear of the Egyptian front against deep Israeli air incursions in order to protect the regime itself, then the situation would resemble the one that has actually prevailed since 1967 with important differences to be presently noted.

A continuation of the circumstances that have prevailed since 1967— that is, relatively weak external pressure without direct military involvement by either superpower—would entail the continuation of the present Israeli political system, but on a more precarious basis. The extended adaptation of the Israeli political system has eliminated or checked *basic* sources of division that might have caused the system to disintegrate under prolonged pressure of the kind it has endured since 1967. On the other hand, the particular configuration that system has assumed since the war is unstable.

Several related sources of potential basic Israeli weakness under prolonged pressure have often been cited. The curve of defense expenditure has reached the astounding level of 25 percent of GNP, has brought the absolute gap in the balance of payments well past the fabulous amount, for Israel, of 1 billion dollars a year, and has already nearly eliminated the country's foreign currency reserves. Such a rate of defense spending, it is argued, cannot be sustained for long, let alone increase, without the adoption of measures that would cripple economic growth, impair the economy's capacity to sustain future expenditures, and impose a heavy strain on the taxpayers. These consequences would trigger social conflicts that could stimulate the latent communal problem, causing grave intercommunal strife. The necessary countermeasures might involve a combination of formal and informal repression and jingoistic propaganda that would generate an oppressive, intolerant, embattled atmosphere in the country. Add the effect of the guerrilla action, urban terrorism, and civil disobedience on the part of the Palestinian Arabs and the increasingly drastic countermeasures of the Israeli authorities, and you have a nightmarish garrison state.

Our previous analysis allows us to correct the distortions in this picture fairly quickly. The rapid increase in defense expenditure is largely associated —perhaps half the total—with a program of investment in military industries. At the present moment, when Israel must import most of its equipment while making the necessary investments, the burden is at or near its heaviest; but as the new assembly lines begin to produce hardware, it should not only substitute for the imports but provide a considerable output for export.

Other things being equal, such industries should ease the balance-of-payments problem and allow the rebuilding of the reserves. Moreover, the investment in military industries is already stimulating rather than crippling economic growth and the capacity for additional future investments, and is positively affecting nonmilitary industrial growth. The realization of a high rate of development from the present fairly high economic base by comparison with the economies of its opponents should allow Israel to spend increasingly larger absolute amounts on defense in the future without damaging its economy. There will still be problems with inflation, balance of payments, income distribution, and so on, but an Israel in which sharp, ideologically founded, socioeconomic divisions no longer exist should be able to handle these problems better than at any other past time.

So too do the threats of social conflict and intercommunal strife prove unreal. We previously distinguished between the "objective" aspect of the communal problem in the form of disparities between Europeans and Orientals in income, education, representation in the professions and high state positions, and its "subjective" aspect in the form of mutual antipathies based on differences in world-view and experience, and justification of privilege on one side and resentment on the other. The war and the subsequent national experience have done little to change the objective aspect beyond continuing the slow trend toward closing the gap. But the war and its aftermath accomplished a near miracle in bridging the subjective gulf. A full explanation of the transformation must await systematic inquiry, but certain elements are apparent even now: the sharing of a traumatic experience; the impeccable performance in the war of the Oriental soldiers who constituted half of the armed forces; the ability of the Orientals now to answer proudly the question, "Where were you when . . . ?"; the placing of cultural differences in perspective by the sharing of a common peril; and perhaps also the occupied-territory Arab's position as "bottom dog." Whatever the explanation, this phenomenon bodes greater rather than less future social cohesion for Israel.

Chauvinism and repression as by-products of economic penury, social conflict, and intercommunal strife cannot be more likely than the products themselves. As for the consequences of the Palestinian insurgency and the Israeli counterinsurgency measures, these would depend on the future level of insurgency. Should the guerrillas succeed in polarizing the Arab masses, establishing bases in the occupied territories, and terrorizing urban centers, especially Jewish cities and towns, official measures of repression and unauthorized Jewish counterterror and mob eruptions could combine to produce a climate reminiscent of Algerian days, though in no way presaging an Algerian conclusion. However, the record of the first half of 1970 seems to indicate that the insurgency has passed its peak without achieving the conditions cited, and that the trend, if not headed downward, has settled on an unthreatening plateau.

In short, then, the substructure on which the present political configuration rests is firm enough to endure and even prosper in future years under the conditions here assumed. On the other hand, the political configuration itself has enough inherent weaknesses possibly to shatter it, even under these same conditions. The unity of both the national government and the individual parties is primarily formal. Within that framework of unity, individual leaders express very different and often highly antagonistic views.

Some are in a position to make administrative decisions that establish *faits accomplis* vis-à-vis both their own colleagues and the outside world. This system is so prone to accidents or incidents—for example, calculated leakages of Cabinet decisions, distortion or excessive criticism of a colleague's views, deliberate or innocent overstepping of the limits of individual ministerial discretion in word or in deed, disagreement in the Cabinet over the adoption of a specific action or reaction—that it would have soon disintegrated without a certain deterrent: the uncertainty of the outcome of "going to the country" or even of going to the ruling institutions of some of the big parties. This deterrent, however, is not absolute and the likelihood of breakdown remains high.

Another weakness of the system is its heavy dependence on personal rather than institutionalized leadership, characterized by possession more of the qualities of a chairman or an arbitrator of disputes than of those of a chief with authority and independent ideas. Golda Meir certainly has the requisite qualities, but she is advanced in age and weak in health; a suitable and generally acceptable successor may not be readily available. In that case a struggle for the succession could develop involving men like Dayan and Allon, who are of the "chief" rather than the "chairman" cut, and destroying the system.

The implications for the future of the Middle Eastern confrontation are as follows:

1. If the existing superstructure weathers the accidents and incidents to which it is prone and avoids a crisis of succession, then Israel would certainly continue to adhere to the formula at the root of the formal unity of the system. The longer this situation lasts, the more difficult it will become for the two sides to negotiate a peace treaty involving no substantial territorial modification. In effect, this would mean that for peace to be achieved, the continuation of the status quo must generate enough pressure to force the Arabs not only to agree to peace, but also to make considerable territorial concessions.

2. If the existing superstructure collapses as a result of its inherent weaknesses, the new Israeli government would probably have a concrete position on the substantive issues and enjoy considerable flexibility in pursuing it. The showdown that would follow the collapse would force all political groupings to define their stands, and a more homogeneous and therefore maneuverable government would follow. However, on the assumptions under discussion here (i.e., no strong external pressure and no concrete peace option available—the existing unity having broken down as a result of purely internal factors), the new government's position would almost certainly exceed the one of peace without substantial territorial modifica-

tion. By comparison with the previous subscenario (continuation of the national government), the achievement of peace would require the Arab side to take the same two steps, except that here it would clearly know what would be expected from it in advance of the negotiations.

A limited direct involvement of Soviet personnel in the ongoing partial war on the Arab side would not basically alter the substructure. It would raise the level of violence, of Israeli casualties, of expenditure on current defense, and of the temperature of the conflict as a whole; but these effects would be unlikely to cause any serious fissure in Israeli society and might indeed further consolidate it. On the superstructural level, however, it would almost certainly eliminate the chances of the system's toppling due to internal strife by uniting government and people in the face of greater danger. At the same time, it would reduce the occasions for the kind of initiatives that could disrupt unity through the concentration of attention on meeting that danger. More important, perhaps, the involvement of Soviet personnel would so enhance the already favorable conditions for the emergence of a charismatic leadership that the advent of such a leader would become almost inevitable. The effect would be a tremendous increase in the capacity of Israel to decide and to maneuver; but the decision and the maneuvering would be unlikely to favor a minimalist solution.

CHAPTER 6

The United Arab Republic: The Domestic, Political, and Economic Background of Foreign Policy

Malcolm H. Kerr

I. The Revolution and Its Legitimacy

The legitimacy of the U.A.R. regime should not be confused with the charismatic image of its late leader, nor with the popularity of its general policies and objectives. The test lies with public acceptance of controversial or unpopular measures, decided upon and carried out by public officials of lesser breed than former President Nasser, acting in accordance with the authority and responsibility vested in their offices. It lies with their transferability of roles, up to the highest political level, among alternative individuals chosen by some form of due process understood and accepted as proper by the public. It means, in other words, the effective institutionalization of the leadership of the late Gamal Abdel Nasser and the group of several hundred high-ranking officials (vice-presidents, ministers, deputy ministers, industrial and economic managers, ambassadors, press editors, and so on) whom the revolution has installed in power and who seek to bend the bureaucracy to their will.

During the first 15 years of the revolution, this institutionalization was only partial and ineffective. Political power was widely understood to lie elsewhere than where it was officially declared to rest. The official formulas characterizing the sources and distribution of public authority underwent several successive sweeping changes, each one pointing implicitly to the unconvincingness of its predecessor, and also coming about in a manner that cast doubt upon its own credibility.

A glimpse of this problem can be obtained from a brief recitation of constitutional revisions since 1952. From July, 1952, until June, 1953, Egypt remained officially a monarchy. It then became a republic, with General Muhammad Naguib as President; on his ouster in the fall of 1954, the Presidency remained vacant until Prime Minister Nasser finally assumed it in June, 1956. At that time a new constitution was implemented, and the Revolutionary Command Council—an inner circle of officers led by Nasser, who had engineered the coup in 1952, and whose formally declared powers in relation to the Cabinet had remained nebulous—was abolished. Both Nasser's election and the adoption of the constitution were approved, with near unanimity, in a plebiscite. A parliament was elected in 1957, from among candidates closely screened by a committee of former Revolutionary Command Council members; but a few months later the whole structure was abolished on the occasion of the union of Egypt and Syria in the United Arab Republic, in February, 1958. Again Nasser, and the union itself, were endorsed by plebiscite. A new provisional constitution was adopted and a new Syro-Egyptian parliament was finally selected in July, 1960, this time by presidential appointment. Again, its life was short, for the Syrian secession from the U.A.R. in September, 1961, caused Nasser to declare the parliament dissolved and the constitution inoperative. Still another provisional constitution was promulgated, and a new parliament elected, in March, 1964. As of January, 1969, these were still in effect although only of limited consequence.[1] In February, 1965, Nasser was elected to a new seven-year term in another nationwide plebiscite, this time with only 65 dissenting votes. The drafting of a permanent constitution was indefinitely delayed by the war of June, 1967.

Each of the three constitutions, and each of the three parliamentary elections, was decided upon and organized in its details by presidential decree. None of the parliaments has had an appreciable impact upon public policy. The first two were in any case too shortlived, and the third, during its four and one-half years, conducted some lively debates on a number of selected domestic questions but never posed any notable challenge to the views of the President and his Cabinet. Three times Nasser replaced his Prime Minister and reshuffled the Cabinet (September, 1965; September, 1966; June, 1967), but parliament did not play any part in the decision or even receive a serious explanation. Parliament owed its own life to the President; it was efficiently presided over by Nasser's trusted associate, Anwar al-Sadat—a fellow conspirator in 1952, and member of the Revolutionary Command Council afterward. The electoral rules provided by Nasser forbade independent political parties and private local constituency organizations and required one of the two candidates from each district to be a certified worker or peasant. Thus it was assured that the members elected would be mostly inexperienced men without any political base of their own, honest and intelligent perhaps but dependent on the good will of the President, his ministers, and the governors of the provinces in which their districts lay.

In any case, even on formal terms parliament and the constitution were of limited importance, for they were declared to be subordinate to the single official party, the Arab Socialist Union, and to its official statement of guiding political and ideological principles, the Charter of National Action. The Arab Socialist Union was declared to be the organization through which the public would participate in political action on a day-to-day basis,

[1]The parliament was re-elected in January, 1969.

at the local levels, and—through a hierarchy of local, district, provincial, and national assemblies—provide a channel of communication between popular opinion and the regime. At different times this channel has been described as being intended primarily to enable the public to influence the regime, or for the regime to indoctrinate the public, or both equally. The ambiguity of overt intention is not really very important, however, for the formal structure is one of "democratic centralism" familiar in mass-mobilizing single-party systems in many countries, in which in practice the flow of communication from the top down is inevitably the preponderant function, and the significant questions are how effectively this can be accomplished, and whether its accomplishment enabled the party leadership to operate as a more important locus of power than the ministries of government.

In Egypt the Arab Socialist Union has not thus far succeeded to any great extent in developing this downward-communicating function, and it remains a passive adjunct of the state, with little institutional vitality of its own. It suffers from two obvious liabilities. In the first place, it was called into being from above, by the ruling group of ex-officers whose position of power in the land had already been secured by other means. It was implausible to imagine that somehow they might remain in power, but transfer their base of support from what it already was—the confidence of the military officer corps and the emerging caste of technocrats in them—to a new organization with roots in the revolutionary will of the urban and rural populace. Those who ran the government also ran the Arab Socialist Union. Its supreme executive council, which in due course was to be chosen by democratic means from below, was "temporarily" composed of Nasser and his designees who already sat in the government with him. Nasser seemed well aware of this anomaly and eager to rectify it, but his opportunities were limited.

The second liability arose from the need to develop a cadre of militants who would exercise leadership in the Arab Socialist Union. These militants would be both loyal to the existing regime and yet morally independent enough to breathe life into the party. Here, of course, was an implicit contradiction. Meanwhile, in the absence of such a cadre, the work of the local committees elected in Egypt's villages, urban quarters, and places of work lacked direction and purpose. The election and convening of the National Congress of the Arab Socialist Union (comparable in designation to the All-Union Party Congress of the Russian Communist Party) and its Central Committee was repeatedly put off year after year. It finally came into being in the summer of 1968 as a result of the war with Israel the year before.

At the time the Arab Socialist Union was called into being in 1962, as Nasser remarked subsequently, there had been consideration of the idea of restricting its membership to a small minority of the population; the figure of 300,000 was mentioned.[2] This idea was dropped, Nasser explained, out of reluctance to face the invidious choice of who should or should not be accepted to membership; instead, the rolls were open to virtually everyone, with the result that 5 million joined. The 5 million, comprising the bulk of the male adult population in a country of 30 million inhabitants, were of course a conglomerate mass incapable of playing any distinctive collective role. They could hardly make an impact on the populace, for they *were* the populace. Any leaders they elected from among themselves, through the pyramidal structure of committees of the Arab Socialist Union, were more likely to play the role of representing their demands as consumers of government services than that of instilling them with revolutionary discipline and zeal. Thus there was the prospect—largely borne out in the years up to 1968, at least—that the supposedly mass-mobilizing Arab Socialist Union would do little mobilizing of popular energies and enthusiasms, but would merely enhance the existing air of passive expectancy with which the masses looked to the military regime. The regime could thereby hope to gain political credit in the short run, but the credit would have been borrowed, and repayable with interest.

To fill the breach, in 1964 the Nasser regime declared its intention to create a "political apparatus" or cadre of militants within the Arab Socialist Union. These would be carefully selected, from above, from among the "sincere revolutionary youth" of the country, given special political training, and sent out to work in various endeavors throughout the Arab Socialist Union. Their identity would remain secret, and this gave rise to speculation that their real function would be an intelligence one. In 1965 an Institute of Socialist Studies was opened, enrolling several dozen trainees at a time for courses of a few months' duration. Officials vaguely alleged that the work of constructing the "apparatus" was moving forward, and by 1966 they were claiming that several thousand militants were on the rolls. Two years later, however, they were quietly acknowledging that nothing had really been accomplished; the Institute of Socialist Studies was disbanded; and the whole effort had come to naught.

We have already mentioned the basic problem behind the failure to

[2]*Mahadir Jalsat Mubahathat al-Wahda* (Cairo, 1963), p. 163. This is the text of the minutes of the abortive Egyptian-Syrian-Iraqi negotiations for unity in 1963, as released by the Egyptian government. An excerpted English translation was published in *Arab Political Documents 1963* (American University of Beirut, n.d.), pp. 75-217. A full translation of the record of the first few sessions appeared in *New Outlook* (Jerusalem), September, October, and November-December, 1963.

generate leadership and institutional vitality within the Arab Socialist Union: the organization was designed as a prop to an already existing national power structure. Related to this was another problem, which has plagued the revolution in a variety of contexts and which will be discussed with economic and ideological problems later on: the unanswered, the unanswerable, question of precisely what kind of revolution it was, for whose benefit, and at whose expense. The regime had been deliberately equivocal about this since the beginning, attempting to cast its appeals for popular support as widely as possible. From what elements would the militants be drawn, and what precise objects would they be militant about? The Marxist left, or the neo-Islamic right, if given the chance, could well supply organizational talent and ideological zeal; but the regime was hardly about to turn initiative over to either of them.

In the absence of a militant and independent cadre, the Arab Socialist Union was left with a residual function, an essentially negative but not unimportant function it shares with the parliamentary constitutional system. The institutions of party and state serve to pre-empt the field of organized political activity and political representation, on behalf of the regime, from all potential challengers. They serve to head off conflict and disruption. They provide objects of hope for those who would like to see the revolution take more determined directions, and opportunities for petty career-building for several thousand people who relish the sensation—if not quite the reality—of being where the action is. For those citizens who thus far have been satisfied with the revolution's accomplishments, and for those who live in hopes of what it has promised them, the existing institutional structure of representation, participation, and procedural legality are enough to stave off any submerged uneasiness they may have about the new class of soldiers and technocrats who are actually running the show—as long as nothing goes disastrously wrong. This is only a passive kind of support, however, provoking only a tenuous form of legitimacy for the regime. The necessary incremental margin of enthusiasm cannot be gained by bolder and more vigorous internal reforms without dividing the society and replacing the present acquiescence with mass anxiety. Instead, therefore, the margin has been provided by nationalism, which Nasser's regime cultivated and expressed through its activist foreign policy. That the activism has been more apparent than real does not matter in this context. It is sufficient for this purpose that Egypt and its revolution should be seen to be threatened by foreign forces whom President Nasser, with his superior skill and vigilance, held at bay. Doubts and divisions and recriminations within the ranks of those on whom Nasser's regime had come to depend for at least passive endorsement would naturally increase the pressure to cultivate this image of its international position.

Conversely, however, because the support has been passive and the legitimacy tenuous, those in power must feel particularly sensitive about existing areas of actual or potential disaffection in Egyptian society. They must worry about the ability of these groups to undermine the regime, and particularly about their receptiveness to subversive appeals and connections abroad—with other Arab regimes on the left and right, and at a further remove with the great powers. It seems hardly coincidental that the Egyptian Communists should have been jailed en masse from 1959 to 1964, a period during which Nasser was in sharp contention with the fellow-traveling regime of Qasim in Iraq and, on occasion, with the Soviet Union, and also when he was engaged in introducing his "Arab socialist" economic and political reforms.[3] Nor is it coincidental that roundups of the Muslim Brotherhood, and the execution of several of them in the fall of 1965, should have been linked to tension in relations with Saudi Arabia and the United States.

At the same time, given his internal uncertainties, Nasser must have worried all the more about the designs on Egypt by the great powers themselves, and their efforts to mount pressure on him from within the other Arab states. Such considerations serve to reinforce the tendency, already present for other reasons, for the Egyptian government to attempt to pre-empt influence in the surrounding states before the great powers can build up their own (see Chap. 2, above).

Something of the relationship between domestic insecurity and foreign policy may be observed during the first two years following the defeat of June, 1967. It was obvious that simply on grounds of military weakness and vulnerability, as well as grounds of economic hardship, the U.A.R. was under great pressure to make substantial concessions to Israel working toward some form of settlement, in return for evacuation. At some times and in some ways, the Egyptians indicated their receptiveness to such concessions. It was also clear that Nasser faced considerable internal difficulty, that the whole moral reputation of his regime had been called into question in consequence of the defeat, and that this had the effect of increasing his intransigence toward Israel. Throughout these two years, observers of the Egyptian bargaining stance differed widely in their perceptions, and in the net it was not at all clear which of the contradictory signals coming from Cairo, suggesting either moderation or intransigence, was to be taken most seriously. Perhaps the most plausible explanation is that the U.A.R. authorities did not know the answer themselves. Nasser's

[3]Before and after this period, when relations with the U.S.S.R. were much more cordial, many Egyptian Communists were treated well. Particularly, many of them were assigned to attractive positions in the news media.

position was somewhat comparable to that of the Wafdist government of Premier Mustafa Nahhas in 1951-1952 vis-à-vis the British army in the Canal Zone—a materially weak bargaining position, coupled with an insecure domestic political base, resulting in an unstable policy both of intransigence and of keeping lines of communication open.

The legitimacy of the Nasser regime was shaken in two major respects after June, 1967. First, the public realized that the leadership of the armed forces, which as they knew at heart had always been the real backbone of the government regardless of formal appearances, was professionally incompetent; if the army could not defend the country, it lost its moral claim to rule it. Second, there were myriad tales of personal ambition, jealousy, selfishness, and corruption throughout the upper echelons of the regime that came tumbling out in the series of court trials. These involved not only soldiers but some prominent civilians as well, and not only incompetence but a jungle atmosphere of mutual mistrust within the leadership. They were followed by student and worker demonstrations in February, 1968, voicing the demand for change both in faces and in the system of rule itself. All the gaps of credibility in the regime's claim to be solidly based on popular support and democratic procedures, which had been covered up by the façade of formal institutions, official pronounce-ments, and inspired press commentary, were now uncovered. Nasser's response was to temporize. He reshuffled his Cabinet; he carried out fresh elections to the local committees of the Arab Socialist Union; and in July, 1968, at long last he convened the National Congress of the Arab Socialist Union and arranged for it to elect its Central Committee. None of these steps was altogether responsive to the disaffection of the demonstrators, but together they induced enough of a wait-and-see attitude to buy time for Nasser and strengthen his control. To reinforce these limited steps and to revive his own image as an indispensable national protector, begin-ning in the spring of 1968 Nasser in his public declarations struck a strong note of preparation for renewed warfare with Israel to recover the Sinai ("inch by inch") and of support for the Palestinian commandos. A time of public unrest was hardly a time to advise the Egyptian people that the longstanding refusal to treat with Israel must now be abandoned, that Israel's position in Palestine must be accepted, and that her ships must now be allowed to pass through the Canal.

II. The Military and Their Concerns

What difference does it make to Egyptian foreign policy that since 1952 the country has been governed by a regime of military origins and is implicitly dependent upon army support? It is difficult to formulate very detailed hypotheses about this, let alone demonstrable conclusions, if only for the reason that the precise character of the regime's political relationship with the army has been informal and hidden from public view. It was surprising to many, for example, in the wake of the death of Field Marshal Abdul Hakim Amer in September, 1967, to hear the allegation that Amer had succeeded some four or five years before in establishing a measure of independence from President Nasser in military matters, and that an ongoing struggle for control of the War Ministry had raged between them.[4] Were the corps of officers genuinely loyal to the person of Nasser, or only at Amer's bidding? If this varied by faction, how were the factions defined? What issues mattered to them, outside of purely military issues, and in what manner was the pressure of their opinion felt in the government? And were their views governed by their military status, or by other considerations such as their social background? We simply do not know the answers to these questions.

Two general matters of common knowledge, however, may help us to construct some reasonable hypotheses. One is the widespread presence, within the administration of the state and of the economy, of retired military officers. Anouar Abdel-Malek, a respected and independent Egyptian expatriate scholar, states that "about fifteen hundred officers came within this category between 1952 and 1964."[5] Whether or not this is an accurate figure, there is no doubt that the number at least runs well into the hundreds and that ex-officers abound in the establishment. The presence of the soldiers begins at the top with Nasser himself, all of the onetime vice-presidents, prime ministers, and speakers of parliament (Abd al-Hakim Amer, Zakaria Mohieddin, Abd al-Latif Baghdadi, Hussein al-Shafei, Ahmad Hussein, Hussan Ibrahim, Ali Sabri, Mohammed Sidki Suleiman, Anwar al-Sadat) and a large number of Cabinet ministers. But in addition there have been countless ambassadors, provincial governors, undersecretaries, directors of state-owned corporations, and so forth who were men of military background.

This state of affairs had built-in tendencies of self-perpetuation. The more the military officer caste was pampered in terms of their pay, perquisites, and social prestige by comparison with the run of the mill of civilian bureaucrats, and the more their numbers grew within the upper reaches of the civil administration (*not* at the run-of-the-mill level), the more it was natural for the armed forces to take both their élite status and the special importance of their mission of national defense for granted, and consequently to insist on deferential treatment from the government.

[4]See Nasser's interview with *Time* magazine, May 16, 1969, p. 31, for confirmation of this.
[5]*Egypt: Military Society* (New York: Vintage Books, 1968), p. xx.

In turn, of course, this could only undermine President Nasser's efforts to legitimize the regime as a civil and constitutional authority, and to develop the Arab Socialist Union as a base of political strength that could be invoked as a counterweight to the army.

The role of the army in Egyptian politics since 1952 has sometimes been considerably oversimplified by casual foreign observers who have seemed to imagine that the military were in direct and completely unrestricted control of the government. This ignored not only the successive constitutional arrangements (Presidential and parliamentary elections, the one-party system, and so forth) expressly designed to provide a civilian base for the regime, but also the presence of a number of civilian ministers, advisers, diplomats, and technocrats close to the top of the pyramid of power. These civilians have been drawn from various sources. Some were senior public servants before 1952; many others were recruited from university faculties. The majority of them have been selected for their technical expertise or organizing ability, especially in the field of finance, economic planning, and foreign affairs. They have commanded considerable public respect, but have had no constituency or base of influence outside the administration to support them in their positions; they have come and gone at the President's convenience, often to be replaced by other nonpolitical civilians. By contrast, it would be surprising indeed were the selection of army officers for civilian positions not to pass at least informally through a screen of review within the army, with an eye to factional representation and rivalry.

Egyptians speak of the "New Class" with varying implications. Sometimes the term simply refers in a neutral way to the rise under the revolution of managerial élite, comprising officers and civilians alike, whose careers are founded upon the new military, economic, political, social, and cultural enterprises of the state. In this latter sense, what distinguishes officers from civilians is not of great importance. What matters is the rise of a group of several thousand men in responsible positions in and out of uniform who owe their careers to the revolution and its programs and who would provide a collective deterrent to any sweeping dismemberment of those programs under a new regime. In that sense the New Class is there to stay, and will no doubt continue to grow, as an indispensable group of directors of Egypt's modernization.

More often, however, the New Class is an expression directed against the privileged and pervasive character of the military establishment. The presence of large numbers of retired officers in civilian jobs is regarded as being at the expense of qualified civilians. It also suggests that those remaining on active military duty have been blessed with a host of personal connections in the civilian hierarchy, and that apart from whatever influence military officers might seek to exert directly on the President and his Cabinet, their interests have had a broad base of back-door political support from within the governmental structure. Military budget requests, for example, or the performance and objectives of the Egyptian forces in Yemen from 1962 to 1967, were much less likely to attract consistent criticism or complaint, or competition for attention, from the civilian agencies of the government and nationalized economy, when those agencies were themselves sprinkled so liberally with military men.

The other matter of common knowledge is partly a corollary of the first. From 1955 onward the Egyptian armed forces were the beneficiaries of very large shipments of Soviet arms and equipment: more, as it turned out, than they were capable of absorbing effectively. It should go without saying that there were important foreign policy needs, conceived by the government in terms of the public interest, that pointed in the direction of strengthening the armed forces as a priority objective. But the powerful position of the Egyptian military in domestic politics naturally reinforced the readiness of the government to allocate its scarce resources to defense.

Military-dominated regimes are hardly inclined to de-emphasize defense commitments, even when large numbers of officers have become responsible for factories, schools, and farms. The Egyptian army under any regime could make a strong case for larger budgetary appropriations than were readily at hand; under a regime of their own making, they simply ran away with the game, and other public needs came more and more to be calculated after theirs had first been met. The advent of the Yemen war strengthened this tendency still further; according to one well-informed estimate, defense expenditures rose sharply after 1962, climbing from a more or less steady level of about 5.6 percent of gross domestic product (GDP) in the preceding several years to about 11 percent in 1966;[6] and when mounting balance-of-payments difficulties led to budgetary cutbacks after the completion of the first Five-Year Plan in mid-1965, these cutbacks were not made in military spending but in economic development investment and other civilian areas.

Thus it seems likely that arms were acquired, and the ranks of the military services expanded, not only because of demonstrable national need but also to satisfy the organizational appetite of the corps of military officers. But once these resources were in their hands, it behooved the military leadership, politically and psychologically, to justify what they had received, and it behooved the political leadership to justify what they had given, by emphasizing the utility of Egypt's military power as an instrument of foreign policy. Two notable kinds of utility—intervention and

[6]B. Hansen, *Economic Development in Egypt* (RM-5961-FF, The Rand Corporation, October, 1969).

prestige—thus gained added (indeed, dangerously exaggerated) emphasis.

As for intervention, the primary and obvious case is the Yemen war. The U.A.R. had at hand large numbers of ground troops and considerable air and sea transport to move the troops to Yemen; a rapid involvement following the *coup d'état* in Sanaa was easy, and it was therefore tempting to become involved. Because of the availability of combat aircraft, tanks, land transport, artillery, and the like, it was also natural for the Egyptian forces to attempt to fight a modern, conventional style of war, emphasizing sheer destructive capabilities, however unsuited to local military and political conditions. The heavy financial investment of the government in the Yemen war brought about by this type of operation and the heavy investment of organizational energy by the military command were bound to reinforce the feeling that a major political commitment was at stake that could not be lightly abandoned when things went badly. As in the case of the American intervention in Vietnam, so in Yemen, the Egyptians were led by their abundance of military resources to approach their problems in exaggeratedly military terms, which in turn deepened and complicated their political involvement as well.

The frustrations of the military in Yemen may also have had secondary effects in Egyptian policy elsewhere. If the war in Yemen was difficult to bring to a conclusion, inevitably some commanders and defense planners would console themselves with the rationalization that the war was none-theless worthwhile as a training operation, and that therefore, with this experience behind them, Egyptian forces were all the more ready for activity on other fronts. One can certainly speculate that in May, 1967, this led Nasser, his advisers, and his generals to form an exaggerated estimate of their readiness for war with Israel.

Furthermore, Egyptian forces returning from Yemen, like French forces returning from Indochina and Algeria some years earlier, or for that matter like Egyptian troops returning from Palestine in 1948, could be expected to bring back with them some degree of frustration, political disaffection, and compulsion to prove their worth on other fronts. After Indochina and two years of Algeria, French officers reportedly found the Suez invasion a singularly appealing opportunity for catharsis. Did Egyptian veterans of Yemen in 1967, when the crisis with Israel arose, share any of this psychology? Was the reported eagerness of some Egyptian air force officers to strike a pre-emptive blow at Israel, and particularly their apparent confidence in their ability to do so effectively, in any way a reflection of this? We do not know.

Yemen was not the only example of an Egyptian interventionist policy made plausible by the abundance of military resources, although certainly it was the most significant. It might be argued that the manner in which the Syrian-Egyptian union was administered was a modest case in point. The integration of the combined armed forces, inevitably with an Egyptian domination of the process, provided a good part of the cement that held the union together, and correspondingly was the focal point of Syrian resentments that built up during the union and provided the immediate cause of the 1961 secession. Would Nasser ever have consented to the demand for union in 1958 without the resources at hand to send a large cadre of officers to Syria to reorganize and retrain its armed forces, and to play a part in its civil administration as well? Or if the process of integration had had no significant military dimension but had emphasized other fields of endeavor more heavily, would the union have survived? These must remain open questions, but they deserve to be raised.

A further case in point is the Egyptian effort in 1964-1965 to send arms to the Simba rebels in the northern Congo. The arms themselves were of a sort that any minor state might have on hand in abundance—mainly rifles and ammunition—but their transmission required a considerable organizational and transport capacity, as they were airlifted to Khartoum in the Sudan, transshipped by smaller aircraft to Juba, and then delivered to Simba representatives for overland transport across the frontier. The operation was not very successful, as many arms fell into the hands of southern Sudanese rebels and Ugandans along the way from Juba, and eventually it was disbanded. But only a state with the capability of mounting the airlift could think of pursuing a major foreign policy objective of this kind, designed as it was to encourage the collapse of the central Congolese government. The most significant aspect of this affair was that under the circumstances of the time, it put the U.A.R. in clear conflict with the United States, which was engaged in providing military support to the Leopoldville regime; among other things, this conflict led to the burning of the USIS library in Cairo by a mob, which in turn hastened a sharp decline in American-Egyptian relations, the termination of American PL 480 food shipments, and the reactivation of the cold war in the Middle East that had dominated the 1950s.

Distinguished from intervention has been the use of the military machine for prestige purposes. Here, of course, the significant case in point has been the confrontation with Israel. Egyptian military strength before 1967 was widely viewed in the Arab world, by leaders and the public alike, as a major deterrent to Israeli intervention in Jordan or Syria. The circumstances in which the May, 1967, crisis arose, in which Nasser attempted to pose this deterrent on behalf of Syria, illustrate the point precisely. Secondarily, Egyptian strength was viewed—more by the Arab masses than by their leaders—as the eventual spearhead of a future liberation of Palestine.

The greater the military buildup, the greater the opportunity for the

Egyptian government to capitalize on the sentiments mentioned above to cultivate Egyptian political influence in other Arab countries. To be sure, this Egyptian quest for pan-Arab influence had its own rational justification in the policymaking calculations of Egyptian diplomatic strategists. But the possession of a supposedly powerful army and air force gave exaggerated stimulus to the game, and led the government at length into a tangle of moral and contractual commitments to Syria and Jordan, and into a race with Saudi Arabia for leadership and prestige in the Arab world as a whole, that severely limited the U.A.R.'s ability to keep clear of risks of a war with Israel for which she was not really prepared. She did succeed in extricating herself in 1964, at the time of the Jordan water diversion crisis, and in standing aside at the time of the Israeli military raids on Jordan (November, 1966) and Syria (April, 1967); but her diplomatic overcommitment caught up with her in the May-June crisis.

Where does this recitation of past events lead us? The commonsense implication is that the future rise or fall in the predominance of the military establishment in the U.A.R.'s domestic affairs is likely in some measure to affect the magnitude of that establishment itself, and that sequentially, a relative emphasis or de-emphasis on military preparedness may tend to make for a greater or smaller Egyptian inclination to pursue regional policies in the manner of a great power.

However, there are many other variables. Since the 1967 military defeat we have witnessed a severe blow to the army's prestige in the domestic political arena and possibly (though less certainly) a decline in its influence over political decisions. It is not inconceivable that the disgrace of the armed forces will provide a long-run opportunity to civilians—the technocrats of the administration, the activists of the Arab Socialist Union, and perhaps even elected members of parliament—to develop a more genuinely civilian political system. Admittedly, this does not seem the most likely possibility. However, the U.A.R.'s rearmament has proceeded rapidly since the defeat, for obvious foreign policy reasons, at the very time when the domestic position of the military has suffered eclipse. And whatever opportunity the abundance of resources may provide for new political involvements outside the U.A.R.'s frontiers, the sobering lessons of 1967 may more than counteract the temptation.

A long-drawn-out crisis over the future of relations with Israel, continuing from the situation that has persisted since the June war, seems likely to reaffirm the central role of the armed forces in Egyptian national life. This might occur through a military coup overthrowing the present regime, or else simply through a return to past patterns, with the leaders of the armed forces pressing the claim that since diplomacy has failed, Egyptian hopes and resources must therefore be consigned to them—and likewise, a controlling voice in the administration of the country. And pending the never-never day of revenge against Israel, other objects may again be discovered in the Middle East to which available military capabilities can be applied.

Conversely, an early diplomatic solution to problems with Israel would be likely to serve to strengthen the public reaction within Egypt against the influence and claims of the military that has occurred since the defeat. It would then be observed not only that the military had unjustifiably and unconstructively foisted themselves on the civilian life of the country, but that the Israeli occupation of Egyptian soil, which the armed forces had failed to prevent, had now been ended by nonmilitary means. In such an atmosphere, the claims of officers on the government for financial appropriations and for political patronage alike would surely be difficult to sustain.

III. Economic Policy and the Imbalance of Payments

As Hansen notes, the U.A.R.'s balance of payments from 1961 to 1967 showed an annual deficit ranging from 1.2 percent to 6.2 percent of GDP, which had to be made up for by a mounting foreign indebtedness that is now estimated at about £E 1500 million.[7] He estimates that for a steady rate of economic growth to be maintained in future years, one necessity is that a net further increase in the foreign debt be avoided, which is to say that domestic resources will have to be utilized more efficiently than in the past. To this end, he estimates a need to reduce both defense spending and civil administration spending from around 11 percent and 10 percent of GDP, respectively, to about half those figures; for the management of the economy and the state apparatus to be freed from much of their present red tape; for greater attention to be paid to agricultural productivity; and for private consumption to be brought down from about 60 percent of GDP in 1966 to 53 percent in 1980.

To a large extent the roots of these problems are political in character. My main object will be to suggest what some of these political difficulties are, and in what respects they may deepen or diminish in the future. Here my primary attention will be on problems of bureaucracy and of consumption. Second, I shall try to show how these problems are inputs in the foreign policymaking process and are reflected in the dependence of the U.A.R. on foreign economic assistance.

Domestic Political Problems of Economic Development

A sustained and significant growth rate in the U.A.R. economy is regarded as a political necessity. Whether an aggregate rise of 6 percent per

[7]Hansen, *Economic Development in Egypt,* pp. 51, 55, 57-63.

year, or a higher figure, is sufficient, no one can say, at least without knowing how it is to be spent. Nasser himself, by his own account, decided in 1960 that an overall target of doubling the national income in 10 years, and quadrupling it in 20 (an annual rate of increase of 7.4 percent) was politically essential, and when his economic advisers demurred that this was unrealistic, he insisted that nothing less would do, and that planning must proceed on the basis of this objective.

So far, the advisers may feel that they have been proved right. The 1960-1965 development plan came close to target, but the means remaining at hand were insufficient to begin the second Five-Year Plan, and even before the 1967 war intervened it was clear that progress was lagging badly. Nonetheless, this does not indicate that Nasser was wrong in his judgment of what was politically required, in the light of past promises and rising expectations for the future. Rapid urbanization, the rise in enrollments in all levels of education, the mobilization of the population effected (however incompletely) by a variety of political and social reforms, all pointed and continue to point to the mounting of long-run pressures on the regime to deliver an improvement in the standard of living.

Yet the necessary economic measures are impeded by obstacles that are in large part political; and the political obstacles cannot easily be removed. Thus what is politically necessary may well prove to be politically impossible.

No doubt, as Hansen says, the framework of state ownership in the Egyptian economy naturally lends itself to bureaucratic proliferation and wastefulness. Hansen may also be right that in the effort to restrict private consumption, a large bureaucratic establishment tends naturally to resort to more complicated and less effective methods than the free-market rise in prices that he recommends. In both areas, however, the problem goes well beyond ownership and organization, and comes to the question of the regime's political leadership and sources of popular support. This relates in part to the question of institutional legitimacy raised above. Nasser's regime superimposed the representatives of one bureaucracy (the armed forces) on another (the civil administration), co-opted the services of the necessary civilian experts, and provided the country with a remarkably non-political form of leadership, whose most notable instinct in many situations was to follow the path of least resistance, in order to make as few enemies as possible. The goals were ambitious, the rhetoric revolutionary, the general atmosphere of concern for the public welfare commendable, the old ruling class of wealthy landowners swept aside; but invidious political choices among major segments of the society have been carefully avoided.

One broad explanation of this situation would have to do with the social composition of the military officers and the bureaucrats themselves.

Assuredly they were not drawn from the fellaheen,[8] but their social connections appear to span broadly all those levels of the population who
possess at least some modest stake in Egyptian society, including both
those experiencing or aspiring to greater upward mobility and those more
concerned to preserve their present status. This is admittedly a vague
characterization, but not a meaningless one, for on balance it reaffirms an
attitude that is clearly reflected in the policies of the Nasser regime—a
firm approbation of broad but moderate economic and social reforms; a
perception of the need for, but less vigorous insistence on, significant
improvements in the life of the deprived urban and rural masses; and a
pronounced aversion to violence and disruption within the society. Apart
from the old ruling class, who in any case were relieved of most of their
wealth and position in a bloodless and relatively gentle manner, there is
no social stratum with whose claim to a share in the benefits of the revolution a significant number of officers and bureaucrats could not be expected
to identify.

Still, priorities must be assigned and choices made, if the pie is to be
made large enough ever to be worth dividing widely; and inescapably we
are brought back to the political organization of national leadership. Given
the ambitious economic objectives adopted, given the fact of state ownership or control of the leading sectors of the economy, and given the semi-
totalitarian, quasi-Marxist-Leninist ideology that has pervaded the atmosphere of official political discussion since 1961, one might look in the
U.A.R. for some form of tightly knit conspiratorial élite to impose its
discipline on the public. The projected "political apparatus" of Arab
Socialist Union militants, mentioned in Section I, would in theory be the
appropriate underpinning of such an élite.

Indeed, some observers sympathetic to the Egyptian revolutionary regime
have appeared to discern in it the makings of such a system. Even before
the Egyptian nationalizations of 1961 an astute Arab academic observer
contended that the leaders' task in such countries as Egypt

> requires them to establish nationalist resurgence as their mission and
> the state as the only possible agent of this mission. To this end, the

[8]In his study of "Social Origin and Family Background of the Egyptian Army Officer
Class," Eliezer Beeri concludes that the prerevolutionary officers were by no means
the aristocrats they are often imagined to have been, nor have officers recruited after
1952 been of a very much more modest social origin. Both before and after, the
great majority were related by family to salaried employees or to villagers owning
medium-sized farms. (*Asian and African Studies*, II [Jerusalem, 1966], pp. 1-40.)
On the social status of both officers and bureaucrats, see also Leonard Binder,
"Egypt: The Integrative Revolution," in Lucian W. Pye and Sidney Verba (eds.),
Political Culture and Political Development (Princeton: Princeton University Press,
1965), pp. 397-449, especially pp. 419-426.

state must be established as the source of inspiration and of authority for action. Apart from the consolidation of law and order, this means that the state has to have a "presence"—its image must be built up as a source of power, knowledge, wisdom, resourcefulness. The state knows best and is surest to succeed: this becomes the philosophy of economic action [and many other areas of social activity, one might add] and the bridge of communication between ruler and ruled.[9]

"The state must be established as the source of inspiration and of authority" —but who represents the state, and what is *his* source of inspiration and authority? In the absence of clear answers, inspiration and authority are necessarily diffuse. The Marxists understand this[10]; so do the new wave of American specialists in comparative public administration.[11] Nasser himself also appears to have sensed it, but to have been incapable of acting accordingly.

The practical consequence of running the revolution by a combination of consensus and administration has been that Nasser's regime felt inordinately compelled to alleviate the social and economic insecurities of certain segments of the population. This explains something of its inability to cope with two of the most serious problems of economic development: an overgrown bureaucracy and an irrepressible marginal propensity to consume.

The overstaffing of the bureaucracy is part of a vicious cycle that long predates the 1952 revolution, but has grown worse since then. The modernizing autocrat Mohammed Ali (ruled 1805-1849) introduced modern secular education in order to provide trained manpower for the administration of the state; his successors continued in this vein until at length the logic was reversed and the administration acquired the function of providing employment for the continually expanding class of educated people. In a country whose economy offered limited career opportunities for university and secondary school graduates (and in which modern commercial establishments were preponderantly owned and staffed

[9]Yusif A. Sayigh, "Development: The Visible or the Invisible Hand?" *World Politics*, XIII (July, 1961), 573.

[10]Abdel-Malek, *Egypt: Military Society*, p. xxxiii, declares: "It is impossible to build a modern state in the absence of a 'political class' in the Gramscian sense of the term; yet this is precisely what the military regime has tried to eliminate [presumably, in suppressing the Egyptian Communists] since 1952." Furthermore, he adds, "It is impossible to initiate a socialist revolution and to build a popular state in the absence of socialists."

[11]See James Heaphey, "The Organization of Egypt: Inadequacies of a Nonpolitical Model for Nation-Building," *World Politics*, XVIII (January, 1966), 177-193, for criticism of the efforts of the Egyptian regime to attack basic problems of reform through administrative means.

by foreign and religious minorities), the prospect of state employment offered invaluable economic security, combined with respectable social status. Already in the 1930s and 1940s the enormous expansion of university enrollment added unusable manpower to the ranks of the bureaucracy; but it was the revolutionary regime in 1962 that took the step of actually guaranteeing jobs to graduates.

This step was greatly facilitated by the introduction into Egypt of a socialist economy. Following the Suez war of 1956 the state assumed control of a large number of businesses owned by British and French citizens, which it placed under the authority of a single public holding company. Concurrently, a drive for industrialization was instituted which involved the creation of new state-owned enterprises. In 1959 the government embarked upon what was to be the largest single enterprise in the economy, namely the construction of the Aswan High Dam. The most dramatic step was the series of sweeping nationalization decrees in July, 1961, by which the great bulk of the modern commercial and industrial sector of the economy above the shopkeeper's level was taken over and reorganized under a series of large-scale public corporations. Still further nationalizations followed piecemeal, and another lengthy list of them in 1963.[12]

Other measures accompanied these: for example, the nationalization of the press in 1960, and the sequestration of the property of several hundred wealthy Egyptians in the fall of 1961. Tight controls were placed on all foreign trade, on currency exchange, and on foreign travel. The construction of new industry under state ownership proceeded apace, especially during the period of the 1960-1965 Five-Year Plan.

There was an obvious economic rationale to many of these measures, which presumably played the major part in the decision to undertake them. They offered the government the prospect of controlling and manipulating the leading sectors of the economy more effectively for purposes of development planning.

Whatever the motive and whatever the validity of the rationale from the standpoint of an economist, however, the nationalizations and other measures formed an integral part of the process of centralizing authority over many aspects of Egyptian life in the hands of the state. One result

[12]A number of excellent studies of the development of socialist economics in Egypt have been published. Most notable are: Charles Issawi, *Egypt in Revolution* (London: Oxford University Press for the Royal Institute of International Affairs, 1963); Bent Hansen and Girgis Marzouk, *Development and Economic Policy in the UAR* (Amsterdam: North Holland Publishing Company, 1965); and Patrick O'Brien, *The Revolution in Egypt's Economic System* (London: Oxford University Press for the Royal Institute of International Affairs, 1966).

has been an extension of the already heavy bureaucratization of the country, to the point where the bulk of the educated class has been absorbed and molded into a society of civil servants. In this respect, the political implications of economic centralization have been as significant for the U.A.R. as the economic ones.

Bureaucratization has had two notable political effects. First, it has undercut the potential for the development of sources of power and influence in society independent of the state, since the latter is now the predominant employer, entrepreneur, organizer, and dispenser of ideas. Second, however, the new demand of the state for professionally qualified personnel has brought together an ever-growing group of well-educated men whose talents and horizons cause them to become highly critical of the stultifying mediocrity of the bureaucratic life into which they have been thrust, and of the personal faults of those in authority over them. For the run-of-the-mill employees who fill the ranks of the government and its enterprises, such tendencies are no doubt vastly outweighed by the consideration of the security of livelihood that their jobs provide; but among those upon whose superior professional abilities the system really depends for its operation, a certain level of alienation is inescapable. Thus there is a tension between their dependence upon the system and their resentment of its failings. This may be only latent under normal circumstances when things are going tolerably well; these men, like others, have certainly been in sympathy with much that the system stood for and, as already mentioned, could feel that they had a stake in its reforms. Their reaction to major failures on the part of Nasser's regime, such as the military disaster of 1967 or perhaps even the mounting economic problems of the two preceding years, however, is a different matter. Although they lack the political or personal base from which to oppose or criticize the government openly, any sharp decline in their morale can only bode ill for both the effectiveness of the revolution's programs, through the emigration of some of them to other countries and a drop in the performance of those who remain. Should an alternative regime come clearly into view, it may find among these men a ready and waiting source of support.

The bureaucracy remains cumbersome and inefficient, and the attachment of its members to job security and routine procedure has attracted public complaint and ridicule for many years. Although this is obviously an obstacle to many of the regime's reforms, the bureaucracy is in some ways a political asset. It enables the business of the country to proceed without more vigorous political activity, and it facilitates the extensive organization of Egyptian society in a manner that keeps initiative out of hands other than those of the bureaucracy enabling Nasser's regime to assert a tangible authority over all questions of public concern. Further-

more, although most things are apt to be done poorly, the availability of so
much trained manpower and organizational framework means that at any
given time the regime possesses the means to accomplish a few top-priority
tasks very well indeed: the management of the Suez Canal, the construction
of the High Dam, the supervision of banking and currency, and—not least
of all—the maintenance of a vigorous internal security service.[13] Also,
whether they are done well or not, some administratively complex undertakings such as land reform and the nationalization of private properties
and businesses, which are important to the regime for their political effect,
are at least made possible by the existence of the bureaucracy.

The bureaucracy's ability to soak up the initiative of members of the
public, however, is an asset only if the government's purpose is to conduct a holding operation. The more extensive the bureaucracy, the more
it is overstaffed as time passes, and the more alienated its most capable
members become—the more difficult it must be not only to instill entre-
preneurial dynamism in the economy but also to instill political dynamism in
the Arab Socialist Union. This is a vicious cycle, inasmuch as without the
kind of vigorous political discipline over the society that the Arab Socialist
Union is expected to furnish, no one is in a position to challenge those
processes that feed the bureaucracy, particularly the virtually unrestricted
movement of young men into the higher education system and on from there
into public employment. The authorities recognize that the university
admissions system is out of control, and that the assurance of jobs to
graduates is an evil; but it is also widely taken for granted that it is
politically impossible to do anything about it, so great is the pressure
within expanding middle-income stratum of the population for continuing
upward social mobility and greater economic security.

Today's student is tomorrow's bureaucrat, and this fact instills in students a conflicting set of concerns comparable to those of the professional
classes whose services the government already commands. The conditions
of the job market put the student in a highly vulnerable situation in which
it behooves him to work the ropes of the system as diligently but as
circumspectly as he can; but the very system that makes him vulnerable
is bound to be the object of some resentment on his part. As the men of the
professions have their standards and their urge for mental and economic
independence of the authorities, so the students, like students anywhere
else, have theirs—as they frequently showed in their high degree of political
activism in prerevolutionary times, and as they showed again, under the

[13]If this is so, one might ask, why not also the armed forces? But the armed forces
are too large to benefit dramatically from the assigning of special priority. Unlike
the other cases, authority over the army is bound to be widely delegated and
redelegated.

stress of Egypt's humiliation in the 1967 war, in their demonstrations of February and November, 1968.

The problem of the overexpansion of higher education leads us into the economic manifestations of the U.A.R's consensus politics; for higher education and public employment, to the extent that they are unproductive, are of course items of consumption. Like a number of other third-world countries, the U.A.R. has sought to combine rapid development with expanding welfare, under the official slogan of "sufficiency and justice." The patterns of capital formation through mass deprivation characterizing the European industrial revolution and the Stalinist era in the U.S.S.R. are explicitly excluded as morally unjust and politically unworkable. Thus far, the alternative sought in Egypt has proved economically workable only with certain windfalls, and these cannot go on growing indefinitely. One such windfall was foreign aid, about which more later.

The other windfall was the sequestration of the property of the wealthy class in 1961. As they were a small and isolated group of a few thousand, and many of them were foreigners or Copts, this was an easy measure, politically speaking, and was readily approved by the bulk of the population. It could not have been extended much farther down the ladder of economic classes, however, without cutting into the regime's own membership as well as its broad national clientele, and therefore without undermining its consensus politics.[14]

If the expansion of the welfare state is to be arrested and private consumption held constant, as Hansen has urged, then we are no longer speaking of blows against an unpopular class of prerevolutionary pashas but against the aspirations of large segments of the population upon whom the regime feels dependent, and from whom it lacks the force or persuasion to extract sacrifices. This is indeed a political problem and not simply one of economic and administrative planning, and it is striking to hear not only liberal economists but also Marxists complain about the incompatibility of the welfare state with the development objectives.[15]

[14]In January, 1962, when Nasser formally decreed that those affected by the land reforms of 1952 and 1961 should lose their political rights, he attached a list of some 1257 persons exempted from this penalty. It seems highly probable that this list included a good many senior civil servants, army officers, industrial managers, other members of the establishment, and their relatives.

[15]Abdel-Malek, *Egypt: Military Society,* p. xix. It is a common contention among Egyptian Marxists, in the author's experience, that middle- and lower-class Egyptians would readily accept greater economic sacrifices under a regime providing more moral leadership and effective political organization. It is alleged, for example, that in the wake of the February, 1968, riots, labor union members were prepared to contribute a portion of their fringe benefits to national defense, and were disgusted when the government instead sought to alleviate their disaffection by actually increasing their benefits.

The welfare state, of course, comprises a range of benefits aimed at different strata. A rise in food prices, for example, or in the cost of lower-class urban housing and transportation, would hit the largest number of people but not the most politically significant, and it might be judged that the Nasser regime could manage to weather the controversy that such measures would produce, especially if the post-1967 international crisis were somehow ended successfully. But that is a questionable judgment; the Mohieddin Cabinet in the fall of 1965 adopted a few such measures only with great difficulty within the regime itself, and after a year in office Mohieddin was forced out. In fact Zakaria Mohieddin, whom no one would call a sentimentalist, felt compelled upon taking office not only to declare that the economy was overstrained and that it was necessary to "squeeze consumption," but simultaneously to add to the strain by allotting additional funds for public housing. Even if the urban and rural masses are still politically passive on the whole, Nasser and his colleagues have clearly thought it important over the years to cultivate their support; and who could say that Nasser was wrong, after the night of June 9, 1967, when it was the mobs that filled the streets of Cairo who kept him in power following his resignation?

Alternatively, we may consider the welfare state in terms of those benefits reaped not by the popular masses but by the urban-centered middle class who staff the civil service, the professions, and the administration of the modern sectors of the economy. These have been favored by relatively low income taxes, controlled rents, and modest prices of a wide range of household goods, petty luxuries, and other items not consumed by the masses. In some lines of work, though not many, they still earn comfortable salaries; a good number draw significant income from the 20 or 30 acres of farmland they still own and occasionally visit on the weekend. (It is noteworthy that the liberal ceiling placed on land ownership by the reform laws, allowing for the retention of private plots of up to 100 acres, preserves the interests of a substantial number of middle- and upper-middle-class city dwellers.)

The great majority of the white-collar class are very poorly paid, and restrictions on foreign travel and on the importation of many goods cramp the style of those who are financially better off. Still, a policy of maximum austerity could readily be devised that would significantly reduce the aggregate consumption of the middle classes. One could talk of higher taxes, of slashed university enrollments and civil service appointments, of the reduction of maximum land-ownership to 25 acres, of the cancellation of bonds issued for nationalized property. Under the present political system, however, such a program is unthinkable. It would embitter a much wider segment of the bourgeoisie than did the earlier reforms, and would mean renunciation of the principle of respect for private property and activation of the idea of class war. The civil service, the army officer corps, the nationalized economy, the universities, and the professions are staffed primarily by people who would either be affected themselves or feel strong kinship with others who were. The resentment, the sacrifice of talent, and the fear that could be expected to result from this kind of program could only be manageable for a regime disposing of a much tighter, more exclusive, class-conscious, disciplined, ideologically minded apparatus of party militants than the present Arab Socialist Union can produce. Systematic police intimidation and the resort to mass violence (in a society that craves public order as it craves air and water) might also be required.

In the past 30 years, many thousands of Egyptians have risen to a social status superior to that into which they were born. They live in psychological proximity to the way of life they left behind, and in awareness of the vulnerability of their present status. To a large measure it is people of this category to whom the revolution carries its most effective appeal. The fact that they have risen from the bog and must fear that they or their children may be sucked back into it has inevitably had a moderating effect on their responsiveness to revolutionary reforms and ideological propositions. Expropriation of millionaires is one thing; distinctions of favor at any lower level can only seem invidious because of their uncertain implications. Thus insecurity breeds its own brand of tolerance, and creates great distaste for the prospect that violence, vengefulness, or forceful deprivation might be exercised even against groups other than one's own.

Foreign Policy Implications

The moral of this unhappy picture is that Egypt's success in obtaining foreign credit, reflected in her chronically adverse balance of payments, has been an inescapable political safety valve for the revolutionary government. It has enabled both economic growth and (by Egyptian standards) a high-consumption welfare economy to proceed at the same time; and as long as greater economic belt-tightening was not urgently necessary, political belt-tightening, for which the regime was poorly equipped, could be avoided as well.

On the other hand, this has obviously meant that the procurement of loans and assistance from abroad was a primary diplomatic necessity for the government. Foreign policy had to be devised in a manner calculated to facilitate such arrangements—either by throwing the U.A.R. into a close embrace with one superpower or the other, and establishing the claim of a client on the patrons' protection, or by playing a shifting game of tactics calculated to arouse competitive hopes and fears on the part of Moscow and Washington and thus induce them both to cultivate Egyptian favor through aid agreements. This latter was the pattern that Nasser adopted, whether by initial accident or design.[16] Nasser's relationship with the Soviet Union and the United States have been shaped more than anything else in the light of his regional policies toward the other Arab states and Israel, and consequently his desire to sustain the superpowers' competitive interest in the U.A.R. reinforced both his heavy involvement in regional affairs and the frequency with which he shifted individual policies.

It is tempting, but a little too easy, to think of the Nasser regime's commitments to domestic modernization and to the cultivation of international influence as mutually incompatible. To be sure, a heavy military budget means less money for economic development projects, and at times the latter have had to be curtailed to make room for the former. But in general the political outlook of the revolutionary government has been one that conceived the foreign and domestic fronts as complementary, and that has not shrunk from the prospect of overcommitment. We have seen that within the economic sphere itself there has been an ingrained reluctance to make clear-cut choices between consumption and investment. The same reluctance has obtained in weighing domestic against foreign policy priorities, although for somewhat different reasons.

Nasser was an activist by temperament. He was also a nationalist, who evidently believed that only a vigorous resurgence of Egyptian society at home will enable it to make its own way in the outside world, and conversely that only the strongest affirmation of Egyptian independence in the international arena would protect his domestic program of reforms.[17] Whether the U.A.R. possesses the necessary resources for this two-pronged effort is open to serious doubt, especially in the light of such foreign policy misfortunes as the Yemen expedition and the Six-Day War. For the first dozen years of the revolution, however, the effort had gone rather well: as late as 1964 it could be said that the U.A.R.'s position both internationally and domestically was vastly more impressive than it had been in 1952—not in spite of such risky ventures and the drive for regional leadership, but because of them. In the aftermath of 1967 Nasser and his associates could well reason that they had made a horrible miscalculation and that their luck

[16]These tactics are discussed further in Chapter 2, above, "Regional Arab Politics and the Conflict with Israel."

[17]For an astute and imaginative discussion of this combination of objectives in the conception of Nasser and his fellow Free Officers, see Maxime Rodinson, "The Political System," in P. J. Vatikiotis (ed.), Egypt since the Revolution (New York: Praeger, 1968), pp. 87-113. "The motivating ideas they had in common," writes Rodinson, "can be related to two main aims: national independence and modernization. The latter is not even conceived as an independent aim but as a necessary condition to achieve the independence of the nation" (p. 87).

had failed them at a crucial juncture, but that the basic policy of ambitious commitments, despite the risks involved, had been necessary and sound.

Nasser's successor may not share his predilection for foreign ventures, and may wish to concentrate more heavily on domestic concerns; but it seems very doubtful that he could think seriously of abandoning the ambitious development programs of the past, and in his search for ways to finance them he cannot lightly discard the strategy of maximizing the U.A.R.'s international influence and seeking to cash in on it for foreign aid —unless some major windfall comes into his hands, such as the discovery of very large oil deposits. Nor can he lightly assume that if he pursues an unobtrusive foreign policy, the rest of the world will leave him alone.

In the aftermath of the June war, Nasser cut his ties with the United States and thereby renounced for the time being any hope of renewing the American aid agreements that had lapsed in 1966. Apart from the subsidy granted him by the Arab oil states to cover his war losses, Nasser's payments gap was now a baby on Moscow's doorstep; and with this sudden acceleration of economic (as well as military) dependence on Soviet good will, the U.A.R. came into serious danger of losing its long-proclaimed freedom of maneuver in the international arena. This would seem to have given Nasser's regime a new and urgent reason to bring the domestic economy under greater control, in order to produce a modicum of independence in dealing with the Soviets. This was presumably at least part of what was in the mind of the Egyptian government in the first year following the 1967 defeat, when it adopted a number of limited austerity measures, cut its development expenditures, negotiated a consolidation of its debt with European commercial creditors, and came to an agreement with the International Monetary Fund (whose terms, calling for domestic deflationary measures, it had previously been unwilling to satisfy) to entitle it to additional drawing rights.

These, however, were emergency measures. There is considerable cause for doubt that the political basis of the Nasser regime allowed for more substantial ones, and therefore for a reduction of the economic stimulus for an activist foreign policy that enhances the U.A.R.'s nuisance value on the great-power diplomatic market. What might save the day, of course, would be a substantial increase in oil discoveries. Were oil income to rise to a level sufficient to cover the country's foreign-exchange needs, both the national economy and the political system would be relieved of potentially dangerous problems, and by the same token Egyptian international involvements would be shorn of one of their principal motivations.

IV. The Prospects for Alternative Regimes

I have maintained that the regime of President Nasser was inhibited by its social composition and weak political organization from making a funda-mental attack on the problems of bureaucratic waste and high consumption rate that plague the economy. What conceivable change in the character of a new regime could make a lasting difference? Certainly not the mere disappearance of Nasser himself and his replacement by some other ortho-dox nationalist of military background who would have to rely on a more or less similar base of support. It is true that the military junta that has operated since 1952 has comprised various tendencies within its ranks. A contrast has frequently been drawn, for instance, between Ali Sabri and Zakaria Mohieddin as men of the "left" and the "right" respectively, with Sabri more interested in expansion of the socialist system and cultivating the Soviet Union, and Mohieddin more interested in balanced budgets and good relations with the United States. But neither these nor other main-stream variants of nationalist-revolutionary outlook, especially if coupled with dependence on the broad backing of the officer corps, seems likely to lead outside the confines of Nasser's basically ambivalent consensual approach on domestic reforms, while juggling rival sets of friends and enemies abroad.

Nor does it make sense to anticipate any return from the dead of the unreconstructed prerevolutionary class of politicians, as happened in Syria in 1961, for these would find no genuine base of support in Egyptian society at all.

Forceful political leadership in the U.A.R., capable of subjecting the society to the cold shower it requires, could probably come only, if at all, from the neo-Marxist left or the neo-Islamic right—but in each case, at the expense of other aspects of public life. By the left we have in mind not so much the members of the now disbanded Communist organizations, the Egyptian Communist Party and the Democratic Movement of National Liberation, who have suffered a moral decline after five years' compliant service as house propagandists for the regime that had previously kept them in prison.[18] A more likely source of dynamism on the left would appear to be among intellectuals, students, young professionals, and perhaps some young trade unionists, who may prove capable of building on the disillu-sionment with the regime expressed in the demonstrations of February and November, 1968, and constructing a more truly radical, civilian-based revolutionary movement than either Nasser and his Free Officers or the veterans of the two Communist parties were able to mount. One thinks of Fidel Castro as a rough model, at least in terms of successful political mobilization and organization if not in terms of economic success.

[18]Both these organizations formally disbanded themselves in 1965 and declared the readiness of their members to work in support of the regime.

What the neo-Marxist left might do with its political triumph, if it should ever have one, is highly conjectural. We can imagine some of the general objectives that they would be likely to set for themselves: the creation of a tightly knit, conspiratorially organized, élite-led political party to whom the government and administration would be held strictly accountable; the collectivization of a good part of Egyptian agriculture, and the lowering of the maximum private holdings to a much more modest level than the 100 acres per family allowed at the present time; a wide-ranging purge of the ranks of the civil service, particularly in the economic and financial agencies, where men of Marxist tendencies have been systematically excluded; likewise, a purge of the national cultural establishment (the universities, information media, subsidized literary and dramatic arts circles) and a cutback on higher education outside the technological fields; and an abandonment of the commitment to an early rise in mass living standards, together with the imposition of greater austerity on the middle classes. Yet we can never discount the possibility that in time the things that distinguished the leaders of such a movement from the Nasser regime might simply evaporate under the pressures of the fundamental need of the Egyptian economy and administration not to let the boat be rocked too vigorously, and of the need of the men in power to find some minimal basis of popular support beyond their own thin ranks.

As for the neo-Islamic right, again we are not thinking of the Muslim Brotherhood of the mid-1950s, still less of the fossilized class of Azharite religious dignitaries, but of a class of men not altogether different in their social composition and political outlook from many of the more conservative Free Officers of 1952 themselves. They may include a good many of the men we have described earlier as the newly expanded group of highly qualified administrative and technical specialists who chafe at the bureaucratic system.

The neo-Islamic right is not known to exist as an organization in Egypt today, but it is unmistakably present as a political outlook. It is an attitude of criticism of the regime, not for most of its reform measures, but for its alleged moral poverty, its synthetic and opportunistic ideology of quasi-Marxism and Arab nationalism for the educated plus religious demagogy for the masses, its manufactured institutions, the corruption of some of its leading members, its business-as-usual conduct of public affairs behind a façade of self-proclaimed virtue, its reliance upon the security apparatus in dealing with opposition, and last but not least, its readiness to consort with the Soviet Union. Were men of this tendency somehow to come to power, their appeal would be likely to assume the character of a kind of Islamic Moral Rearmament, initially directed against corruption and permissiveness at home and overinvolvement abroad, and seeking to mobilize the conservative moral and social instincts of the great mass of Egyptians of all classes: puritanism, sobriety, respect for virtuous leadership, and—alas—paternalism. This, of course, is precisely where Nasser started out; and like him, these men would find that this was not enough. Unlike him, they might well prove capable of exercising discipline and imposing unpopular policies, through a tightly knit and militant ideological leadership; they might force the country to live within its means, and channel its human resources into more productive employment. But if they did achieve these objects, it would be likely to be at the cost of introducing a retrograde and violent totalitarianism in place of the present permissive system. On the other hand, like the neo-Marxists, should they fail in their most distinctive objectives, they could well drift back toward a middle position somewhat like that of the Nasser regime.

Each of these alternative groups echoes tendencies that were present in the junta of 1952, and yet we have been projecting differences between each of them and the regime that the junta produced. How successful either of them could be in imprinting its own distinct political personality on the Egyptian state might depend crucially on the degree of its dependence upon army support. For either of them would surely need a military coup to bring it to power in the first place. It may be that any military coup will simply introduce another military regime, but that is not inevitable; for there is always the chance that an incoming junta may be dominated by a group of a particular ideological persuasion, whose links with like-minded civilians were stronger than those with other officers. Conceivably, this could provide an avenue to power for a preponderantly civilian movement.

In turn, to the extent that such civilians were free of dependence on a military or other external interest group, their base of political support would have to be built from scratch, beginning with the motive force of their own convictions. This would provide them with some prospect of sustained moral independence and creativity, and would enhance the likelihood that their policies would not be pre-emptive and consensual, following the line of least resistance, like that of the Nasser regime. But conversely, the more they are beholden to the armed forces as a body for maintenance in power, the more they must expect to be responsive to the paralyzing national consensus that the officer corps reflects, and therefore the more we can expect them to drift back to the present regime's incapacity to make invidious choices between national priorities.

The implications of these three possible regimes—the present system, the neo-Marxist left, and the neo-Islamic right—for the future of Egyptian foreign policy are manifold, inasmuch as each one would bring to bear its own preconceived notions of what mode of foreign alignment was ideologically desirable, and each would also have its own distinctive domestic strengths and weaknesses steering it toward or away from the active pursuit of regional and international objectives. The ideological atmosphere that has grown up around the program of the revolutionary regime since 1952, and the composition of factions and groups in the U.A.R. arrayed in support of the regime and against it on the basis of varying outlooks, have always encouraged an activist but shifting involvement with the great powers. The common denominator has been nationalism, which has meant a vigorous role for the U.A.R.; but the alternative prospects of drawing closer to the Soviet Union or the United States have elicited conflicting aspirations and insecurities among the groups of whom the regime has had to take account (including elements within its own ranks). This situation has made for instability in the U.A.R.'s own conception of its international alignments; and, given a seizure of power by either of the two above-mentioned potential contenders, it would be an open question whether it could impose its own preferences in the face of criticism from its rivals.

While it may seem simple enough to point out that the neo-Marxists might welcome a major break with the United States, and the neo-Islamists likewise with the Soviet Union; and that each might tend in inter-Arab affairs to line up consistently along ideological lines with the most likeminded Arab regimes, their probable approach to Israel is less easy to forecast. Although the left tends to view Israel as an adjunct of American imperialism, it also is less nationalist-minded and a good deal less sentimental than are garden-variety Nasserists. Conversely, the right is unlikely to welcome a stance toward Israel that relies on close involvement with Soviet sponsors, but is nonetheless capable of great inflexibility on issues in which rights and honor are felt to be involved. However, the politically conservative Egyptian Muslim, much more than his counterpart in the Fertile Crescent countries, does possess an isolationist streak: Egypt is a complete nation, unlike Syria and Iraq, culturally and politically sufficient unto itself, and the interests she pursues elsewhere in the Middle East tend to be practical and rationally definable and therefore capable of limitation, rather than simple reflections of the sense of political unfulfillment. The Egyptian Marxist, on the other hand, is part of an ecumenical and messianic movement and for him there is bound always to be unfinished business. Also, although a neo-Marxist regime in the Castroite mold might develop the political discipline needed to make Egypt economically viable, it seems doubtful that it would possess much good sense in economic matters with which to put the discipline to use; it would be likely to become at least as heavily dependent on Soviet trade and aid as the present regime is, and serve correspondingly as a medium of Soviet hopes for influence in neighboring countries. Such a situation would point to a continuing heavy Egyptian involvement in the politics of the area.

CHAPTER 7

The Politics of the Fertile Crescent

P. J. Vatikiotis

I. Introduction

The countries of the Fertile Crescent—Syria, Iraq, Jordan, and Lebanon—
exhibit in varying degrees politically significant social, ethnic, sectarian,
and economic fragmentation. Major communal divisions exist, such as that
between Muslims and Christians in Lebanon and between Sunnis and Shia
in Iraq. Ethnic splits are also common in Iraq and Syria, while in Jordan a
major dichotomy is that between Palestinians and East Bank Jordanians.
Cutting across these lines are regional and economic cleavages.

Constraints acting on policymakers in the states of the Fertile Crescent
are generated by domestic forces, inter-Arab relations, and the behavior of
the great powers. Domestic constraints stem from civil military relations,
ethnic fragmentation, and ideological considerations. The Palestine Liberation Movement (PLM) injects itself into the politics of Jordan and Lebanon
particularly, reducing the range of choice for the governments of these two
countries. Communal discontent, such as the Kurdish rebellion in Iraq,
tends to undermine government capabilities in domestic and foreign
endeavors to some degree in all four countries.

Regional politics also impinge on these four governments. Inter-Arab
tensions, the conflicting demands of Arab nationalism and state interests
add to internal cleavages and the Arab-Israeli dispute puts these demands
in further conflict besides imposing difficulties of its own on these regimes.
Finally, the great powers inject their demands and preferences into the
political arena, further complicating political life for rulers in Amman,
Baghdad, and Damascus. Despite these common constraints, however, each
country has developed a distinctive political culture.

II. Syria

Syrian political life over the last decade has been dominated by the Syrian
army officer corps. It would be misleading, however, to assume that a
homogeneous, unified military establishment rules from Damascus. The
officer corps, in fact, has been divided in composition, purpose, and
ideology. Its fragmentation reflects the diversity of sectarian, ethnic, and
economic interests found in Syrian society.

The sectarian, ethnic, socioeconomic amalgam which consitutes the

Syrian "nation" is as artificial as the frontiers fixed by the French in the period 1920 to 1924. The Sunni Muslim majority flourished under the Ottoman Empire as merchants, religious teachers, provincial administrators, and Ottoman army officers who considered themselves the progeny and heirs of the first Umayyad Arab Kingdom in Damascus. Among the Sunni Muslims, the most sizeable ethnic minority is the Kurds, estimated at between 150,000 and 200,000 in a population of about 5½ million. In the northern and western regions there are not only Kurds, Armenians, and several Turkish-speaking communities, but also Christians, pagans, and so-called heretical Islamic sects including about a half-million Alawis (Nusayris) and Ismailis who make up about 10 percent of the total population of the country. In the extreme southwestern part of Syria, there are about 120,000 to 150,000 Druze, another Muslim heretical sect. These sectarian, somewhat secretive, inward-looking and nearly inbred communities have periodically been persecuted by the established Sunni majority. Minority settlement in these mountainous regions was motivated in part by the search for defensible security. This in turn led to a stronger communal cohesiveness. The Alawis and Druze have been traditionally agrarian people. Recently, and particularly since the French Mandate, they have been disproportionately prominent in the military profession. The sizeable Christian minority living in Syria, which makes up another 10 percent of the population, is further fragmented into Greek Orthodox, Catholic, and several branches of the Uniate Church.

In addition to these major religious communal divisions, certain fundamental geographical and ethnic divisions of political significance still exist in Syria. These are roughly:

1. *Damascus*: the old Sunni political leaders, many of them linked to commercial, financial, and industrial interests;

2. *Aleppo*: a largely commercial Sunni establishment (with a sizeable Armenian minority) who differ from and clash with the Damascus one because of their regional orientation, mainly toward Mesopotamia;

3. *Hama-Homs*: a sort of middle-Syria "presence" in Syrian politics, comprising an old landowning "aristocracy" in the Hama area, often pitted against tenant farmers and large agricultural worker groups; and a rising (since 1959) industrial force in Homs comprising not only skilled laborers, but also technicians and managers, especially in the oil-refining industry.

4. *The West, Northwest*: a traditionally poor agricultural area consisting largely of socially and economically deprived religious minority communities (Nusayris and Ismailis lumped under Alawis); now being joined by (and transferred into) a rising industrial workers force in Latakia and Tartus.

5. *The Druze*: concentrated in the southwest with fierce sectarian insularity, and disproportionate representation in the army officer corps;

6. *Other ethnic minorities* in the north and northeast: Kurds, Turkmans, and other;

7. *Desert Areas to the East*: steadily declining Bedouin and other tribal groups.

Typical sectarian-ethnic-regional divisions may erode with the rise of industrial groups in Latakia, Homs, and Tartus (mainly as petroleum, port, and general transport workers); and glass and textile industry workers, including perhaps old artisans and craftsmen, in Damascus.

The east, with its steppe and desert, and only 20 percent of the population, has until recently been isolated from the western, Levantine parts of the country. Nomads and seminomads populate its interior. Yet Syria also manifests characteristics of concentrated urbanism: Damascus has over one-half million inhabitants; Aleppo just under one-half million; Homs about 200,000; Hama almost 200,000; Latakia, 100,000, and Deyr ez Zor about 70,000.

The urban social structure includes merchants, family combinations of investors, owners of industrial concerns, landowners, and growing numbers of industrial workers. Hama and Homs have always been agriculturally oriented, with a large concentration of landowners, tenant farmers, and agricultural workers in their surrounding areas. Latakia now has an industrial transport orientation and has traditionally welcomed Alawis and other refugees from Alexandretta. Rising groups of industrial workers are concentrated in Latakia and Tartus (highly Alawi), the Homs area and Damascus.

The Social Basis of Politics

The conflicting forces in the society at large are mirrored, perhaps magnified, in the Syrian officer corps. Politics at the nation-state level in Syria remains a very limited phenomenon, engaged in by only a few participants who are highly fragmented into factions and cliques. Together, these groups make up the army officer corps with its internal factions. Regimented participation on a wider scale is strictly subject to the heavy hand of the army internal security services.

For minority officers, allegiance to their sectarian-communal and/or ethnic identity takes precedence over a wider political loyalty to Syria, the nation-state. This clash of loyalties is the key to army politics and ultimately to Syrian politics in general. Such primary loyalties have repeatedly been exploited by officers with political ambitions to construct personal clienteles within the officer corps, even controlling whole brigades which could play a crucial role in any attempt to seize power. The more exclusive the clientele in terms of these primary loyalties, the more cohesively it reacts against all outsiders.

It must be made clear from the outset that the army groups which have seized power in Syria by way of more than a dozen coups since 1946 (not to speak of a similar number of abortive ones) comprise minute officer cabals, wresting power from one another. Violence in these seizures of power has never been widespread. It has been confined again to narrow circles of officers and occasionally to a few of their civilian patrons or clients.

Because the personal factor outweighs all others in the Syrian experience, prescriptive ideology and institutional affiliations have limited relevance in Syrian politics. The political outlook, orientation, or even party membership of officers only partially explains their political behavior and the state policies they might initiate or support. One must also study their sectarian, communal-ethnic affiliations, and their military careers.

Syrian Politics since Independence

It is often assumed that the involvement of the army in Syrian politics dates from the *coup d'état* led by Colonel Husni al-Zaim in 1949. In terms of the direct access of army officers to political office, this is correct. Yet the political involvement of the military antedates this coup. For example, one must ascribe political significance to the French Mandate practice of recruiting religious and ethnic minorities for the Syrian security forces, such as the Nusayris in western and northwestern Syria, and the warlike Druze in the southwest. The Alawis had never felt secure under the hegemony of the Sunni majority centered in Damascus and Aleppo. They have been traditionally anti-establishment and antigovernment. The French used these sectarian and ethnic minority recruits as a counterweight to the Sunni Arab Nationalists. Immediately after independence in 1945-1946, the Homs Military Academy shifted its admission criteria in favor of the politically ascendant Sunni majority, the new rulers of Syria. Graduates of the academy for the years 1947-1950 were active in the formation of the union with Egypt in 1958, as well as in Syria's secession from that union in 1961. Friction between Alawi and Druze officers, on the one hand, and Sunni, especially Damascene, officers, on the other, has become a constant in Syrian political life.

The political system inaugurated by the old Sunni nationalist notables disintegrated between 1955 and 1957. Outside forces that might have maintained the authority were neutralized by the so-called leftist forces in which sectarian and ethnic minority officers were prominent. Union with Egypt (1958-1961) further institutionalized the opposition of army officers to the old Sunni bourgeoisie. The "Socialist laws" passed in the last days of union with Egypt further alienated the Sunni bourgeoisie. Individual officer conspiracies and small cabals opposed to the Sunni-dominated *ancien regimes* were replaced by wider conspiracies of officers operating on the periphery of the political system and within radical groups such as the Ba'ath (Resurrection) Party. These groups of officers tended to join radical political movements, some of them even more radical than the Ba'ath, such as the old PPS (Parti Populaire Syrian) and the Communist Party led by the Kurd, Khalid Bekdash. This predilection for political radicalism may have been due in part to resentment of the minority groups and desire for revenge against the Arab Sunni Nationalist élite that was favored in the 1940s and 1950s.

The original Ba'ath Party under Aflaq[1] and Bitar confined its appeal and following to groups such as teachers, students, and a few radical "intellectuals"; it was very much limited to Damascus, Beirut, and Baghdad. The Ba'ath was the first Arab radical "leftist" party in modern history whose arena of political activity was to span the whole Arab world. Yet in seeking a Syrian power-base for its wider Arab activities, the Ba'ath first sought the cooperation of a peculiar political group: the Arab Socialist Party of Akram Hourani, based in the Hama area. Hourani was a known PPS sympathizer, whose socialism was motivated less by ideology than by his desire to undermine the political hegemony of certain large landowning families. Hourani's appeal to peasants and agricultural workers should be viewed in that light. Recognizing that his socialist "peasants' movement" could not come to power without the help of younger army officers, Hourani therefore brought together the army and the rural Hama areas of central Syria. However, as the Ba'ath's involvement in Syrian politics increased, its pan-Arab pretensions tended to confuse Hourani's programs and policies. At the same time, Aflaq's mixture of romanticism and idealism in a national, socialist pan-Arab ideology (based primarily on love and the assertion of the will) was too diffuse for army officers who, by 1956, had become the arbiters of power in the Syrian polity.

The canvassing and use of army officers by politicians for support in their political struggles was not confined to the Ba'ath. Practically every party (Shaab, National Bloc, Nationalists) had its military adherents who were

---

[1]Michel Aflaq, co-founder of the Ba'ath, sought to articulate an ideology of Arab nationalism that would extricate the Arabs from the disabilities of a basically Muslim religious ethos and resolve the problem of minorities. (Aflaq is Greek Orthodox in religion.) The party, therefore, had little appeal outside the socially disadvantaged and economically deprived minorities in the Fertile Crescent. This partly explains why most of the Ba'ath followers in Syria and elsewhere were Alawis, Druze, Christians, and members of other religious and ethnic minorities.

motivated, again, not so much by party or ideological considerations, as by personal considerations such as family, ethnic, economic, sectarian, and regional interests and affiliations. The use of the officer corps by politicians to intimidate, weaken, and oust their opponents became accepted political practice. Thus in April, 1949, Quwwatli sought to destroy the Druze power base of the Atrash family. He enlisted the military assistance of Colonel Husni al-Zaim, a Kurd, for this purpose. Zaim, who took power in August, 1949, tried in turn to intimidate the Druze in their Jabal area for his own purposes. Sami al-Hinnawi overthrew Zaim by another military coup primarily because he successfully manipulated the resentful Druze armored unit commanders. The pattern continued in December, 1949, when Adib al-Shishakli used mainly Druze officers in his coup against Hinnawi, as well as, perhaps for the first time, other minority elements in the PPS through Hourani's cooperation. Druze officers were involved again in leading the coup against Shishakli in February, 1954.

After the merger between Hourani's Socialist Party and Aflaq's Arab Ba'ath in 1953, rural and lower-class urban elements from the north and northwest began to join the party ranks, particularly from among the disaffected sectarian and ethnic minorities. Especially within the Syrian army, these became the most active elements in political conspiracies. Thus, even the least prestigious and most economically deprived groups in Syria, such as the Alawis, have nonetheless had long experience in the Syrian armed forces.

Ba'ath Military Conflicts

There were three levels of conflict between the Ba'ath and the military in Syria: (1) between the National Executive group and the Ba'ath military committee (or officers committee) in Syria, (2) between the National Executive group and the Regional Executives in both Syria and Iraq, (3) between the Syrian Regional Executives, both civilians and army officers, and the military committee. The crucial conflict occurred between the National Executive and the Regional Executive groups. It began roughly with the return of the Ba'ath to power on March 8, 1963, and exploded to the surface at the Eighth Party Congress in April, 1965. It was then that the army under General Amin al-Hafez effectively took over the party leadership in Syria. The authority of the National Executive in Syria was thoroughly undermined, generating further conflict among army officers in the party leadership, culminating in the ouster of Hafez in February, 1966.

The Ba'ath Party suffered from in-fighting and conflicting factions. The Ba'ath claimed that, even though temporarily confined to Syria, the national struggle had pan-Arab significance. But, in fact, the party's ties to Syria were stronger than this claim implies, for the founding civilian leaders (Aflaq and Bitar as well as their later colleague, Hourani) were all Syrians, who quite naturally sought power in Damascus.

Further conflict within the party resulted from its apparent agreement to dissolve during the union with Egypt in deference to the newly formed National Union in February, 1958. This period of Egyptian-decreed *la-hizbiyya* (nonpartisanship) permitted the rise to prominence of a strengthened Egyptian-supervised bureaucracy, as well as the Syrian pro-consul Abdul Hamid Serraj, whose security services controlled the armed forces for a while. Resentment among Syrian officers led to conspiratorial cabals directed against both the Ba'ath leadership and the army command. It produced pro-Nasser and anti-Nasser splits in the Ba'ath itself. Most important, it led to the rise of a militarist wing in the party interested in freeing itself from Egyptian control, and later of party control.

The party's organization was replaced by the covert and overt organs of the Serraj, or Egyptian, state apparatus. But in fact, the party leadership still existed ostensibly as part of the Egyptian-dominated compromise. By September, 1958, came the first major purge of Ba'athist leaders. This meant that effective opposition to Egyptian domination had to come from the more militant, resentful, conspiratorial Syrian army officer who could work in secrecy. The "sell-out" to Egypt discredited the party's civilian leaders, and some army officers must have decided at this time to exclude the civilian leadership from their machinations. During the same period (1958-1961) new factions of one kind or another (e.g., regionalist, leftist, pseudo-leftist, conservative Damascene, and Aleppine) coalesced around the regional and/or sectarian affiliation of the officers themselves.

Serraj's secret agents, often counted in the thousands, infiltrated trade unions and syndicates, student organizations, etc., and the various internal state security services. The units of the Syrian army organized as the First Army of the United Arab Republic, were politically controlled by Egyptian officers. Senior Syrian officers, moreover, resented the appointment of junior Syrian officers to important administrative posts.

It is clear that these junior officers who had been co-opted to ministerial positions in Syria under the union, lost their following in Syrian army units. Moreover, the "number two" officers (e.g., chiefs of staff of divisions, brigades, and regiments) were Egyptians assigned to watch the Syrian unit commanders. By September, 1961, the senior staff officers of the Syrian First Army were also overwhelmingly Egyptian. Yet the presence of Syrian staff officers in the various branches of the First Syrian Army GHQ permitted them to create a network of opposition leading up to the secession coup. Colonel Nahlawi, Deputy Director of Officer Affairs, could arrange appropriate transfers of loyal Syrian officers to key combat units, especially in the Damascus area, that would be crucial to the success of any coup.

The role of intelligence and counterintelligence services in this period is highlighted by Zahr al-Din, who reproduced signals and telegrams regarding the surveillance of officers and the payment of large sums of money from special secret funds to various officers without explanation.[2] A climate of hostility and mistrust surrounded the Syrian military. "The buying of consciences" that Zahr al-Din speaks about may be the most practical and expedient technique in such circumstances.

When Serraj fell out with Nasser's personal representative in Syria, the opportunity for a Ba'athist coup was too good to be missed. Egyptian-controlled military intelligence, apparently concentrating on breaking up Serraj's network in the country, paid scant attention to the conspiring Syrian officers who were unconnected with Serraj.

Party developments after Syria's secession from the United Arab Republic in September, 1961, corroborate these assertions. While the Ba'ath Party Conference held in Brummana (Lebanon) resolved to defend the union with Egypt but to oppose the system of rule in the United Arab Republic, Army officers led by Abdul Karim al-Nahlawi and his fellow-Damascene officers mounted the secession coup. These extreme secessionists were mostly members of the old political parties' establishment, businessmen, and officer supporters. They wanted to discredit former Ba'ath leadership, and so they denounced the national Ba'ath leaders (Aflaq, Bitar, and Hourani) for failing to extract any guarantees from Nasser before agreeing to dissolve the party.

The Ba'ath in 1961 included four groups: (1) the National Executive group, (2) the more leftist socialist unionists (pro-Nasser), both of which favored a revised union with Egypt, (3) the regionalists, and (4) Hourani's group who intransigently opposed any union with Egypt. The fortunes of the party were at their lowest during this so-called period of *infisal* (secession).[3]

Even by the end of March, 1962, when there was an abortive coup in

---

[2]Abdel-Karim Zahr al-Din, *Mudhakirat an fatrat al-Iifisali fi surya ma bayna 28 Aylul 1961 wa 8 Adhard 1963 (Memoirs)*, (Beirut: Dar al-Andalus), 1968. Abdel-Karim Zahr al-Din,general politician, army officer; was Commander-in-Chief Syrian armed forces 1961-1963; Syrian Minister of Defense 1962-1963 (*Who's Who in the Arab World*, 1967-1968).

[3]Oddly, the period September 29, 1961-March 8, 1963, is referred to as "the period of secession" although no revised union with Egypt had taken place. However, during *infisal* Sunni old-guard politicians, especially the presumed pro-Iraq Shaab Party, made a brief comeback.

Homs and Aleppo, the various Ba'ath factions in the military tended to be independent of the party's official civilian leadership. In fact, Ba'athi officers in the Homs Military Academy generally supported Akram Hourani.[4]

Restoration of civilian rule after September, 1961, did not ease, let alone resolve, the problem of civil-military relations in Syria. The fundamental reason for this was, and remains, the conditions under which a civilian government must function following an army *coup d'état*. No such government could survive, given the constant demands of officers in the National Command Council, the highest policymaking body in the country with a veto over all government actions. At the appearance of a rift between the civilians and the military, the government must compromise or fall. Neither the President nor his Prime Minister and Cabinet could withstand this military pressure. In these circumstances, further conspiracies within the officer corps flourished.

Undoubtedly the Ba'ath takeover in Damascus on March 8, 1963, was strongly related to the party's accession to power in Baghdad exactly a month earlier. Yet the Syrian party, as became quickly evident, had no united or effective organizational base in the country at large. Its strongest support came from the officer corps; and the officers by then sought power for themselves. It is clear that the coup was purely a military operation mounted by an uneasy alliance of mixed officer elements—Ba'athis, Nasserites, so-called Arab Nationalists, and others—prompted by the success of the coup in Iraq. Lacking any united purpose or program among themselves, once in power these elements called in Bitar to form a government.

Bitar and the rest of the Ba'ath civilian leadership wrongly assumed that the time had come for a real Ba'athi regime based on party organization and discipline. They tried to neutralize the ever-interfering military through appropriate purges, retirements, and transfers, including appointments to civilian posts, especially the diplomatic corps. These efforts to impose party discipline and control over all political groups eventually precipitated the extremist officer coup led by Jadid on February 23, 1966. Bitar's fundamental mistake was in granting the military a sizeable representation in the party executive group (7 officers to 15 civilians)—a concession that institutionalized the perennial tug-of-war in Syrian civil-military relations.

While the civilians thus permitted the military to be represented in the ratio of one to two in the party executive group, the military excluded all civilian participation in their own political organization.

[4]Salah Jadid, Muhammad Omran and Hafez Asad, the so-called extremist Ba'ath officer cabalists who attempted the March 31, 1962, coup in the north, were already alienated from the Party Executive group.

After March 8, 1963, there were in fact two competing Ba'ath parties in Syria. The so-called National Command, led by Aflaq and Bitar, was hesitant about implementing the party's socialist ideology. They were, on the other hand, willing to negotiate a conditional *rapprochement* with Egypt and Iraq in the hope of strengthening their position at home. The younger, more radical military wing of the party, dominated by minority officers, favored faster radical social reform. It adamantly opposed any accommodation with Egypt or Iraq, and continuously purged its ranks of any officers suspected of Nasserite leanings, especially after a suspected pro-Nasserite abortive coup on June 18, 1963. When Aref overthrew the short-lived Ba'ath regime in Baghdad, the civilian party leadership in Damascus had no defense against the military extremists. The military cabalists revived the old accusation against the civilian party leadership of having sold out to Nasser, and bitterly resisted the efforts of Bitar and Aflaq to neutralize military influence in the party.

In February, 1964, General Amin al-Hafez became Prime Minister and chief of the party's military committee. Soon the military purged the party in Syria of "undesirables." The civilians tried frantically to check military control over the party; Aflaq's resignation from the post of General Secretary was considered an appropriate compromise.

Victory over the civilian wing of Ba'ath failed to resolve factional struggles within the triumphant military leadership. General Jadid, who had supported Hafez's rise to power, challenged the Prime Minister's growing independence from the party's Military Committee. An attempted compromise failed, and the two rivals took measures to strengthen their respective positions. Hafez formed a powerful clique of officers around him, led by Colonel Salim Hatum. These cohorts did not necessarily rally round Hafez because of any strong attachment to him, but because they opposed Jadid. Hafez also attempted to create a popular public image. He accused Jadid of *ta'ifiyya* (anti-Nationalist sectarianism) and of undermining the party. But in assuming that his popularity was more important than strength in the army, Hafez erred, for although his charge of *ta'ifiyya* against Jadid was well founded, Hafez was defeated precisely because his own *ta'ifiyya* proved weaker.

Jadid, on the other hand, quietly built up his own personal, sectarian following. Through his network in the army, he managed to effect the appropriate transfers of officers, always with a view to consolidating his solid base of support among officers who belonged to the Alawi and other minorities, including the Druze. These groups were still smarting from the purges of the September, 1961–March 8, 1965, period when Damascene-Sunni officers had been politically ascendant. Jadid was also in a good position to elicit civilian support among the rural minorities in the west and northwest. These too held a grudge, for they viewed the Ba'ath leadership as an anti-Sunni group centered in Damascus.[5] The earlier efforts of Hourani in the Hama countryside against landowners also helped Jadid. The older Sunni leadership versus sectarian-ethnic minority division thus continued to be a major factor within the new military-political establishment.

In this sense, one can consider the Hafez-Jadid power struggle in 1965-1966 as an Alawi-Sunni conflict. Personal loyalties actually became paramount, moreover, so that Syrian politics for a year centered upon the struggle between the Jadid and Hafez factions in the army, and what was left of the Aflaq-Bitar group, that is, friends of the Ba'ath National Executive group.

As a counterweight to military power, the Bitar government created a new National Revolution Council including representatives of trade unions, farmers' organizations, feminist organizations, syndicates of lawyers, doctors, university teachers and students, merchants, and others. To forestall trouble from the army, the government also announced the postponement of elections for the Regional Party Executive which had been scheduled to take place after the Syrian Party Congress on February 26, 1966.

However, these desperate moves failed to prevent a successful coup on February 23, 1966. The military arrested Hafez, Aflaq, Razzaz (Secretary-General of the National Executive), Muhammad Omran, the Druze leader Mansur al-Atrash, Bitar, and effectively abolished the Regional Executive group of the party and dissolved the National Revolution Council. The rebels announced that those arrested would be tried by a party tribunal. It accused the National Party Executive and particularly the Bitar government of reversing socialist and nationalization measures and of trying to purge revolutionary socialist elements from the army, the government, and other organizations.

The Lebanese press opined that the February, 1966, coup was prompted

[5]Munif Razzaz bitterly commented on this kind of power struggle in Syria: "Alliances and alignments (among officers) in this type of struggle take very strange forms. These have no connection with political or other principles. . . . Thus Hafez, Jadid, and Hatum are against Omran. Then Colonel Hatum's clique appears against Jadid. This is followed by a period during which General Jadid joins with Colonel Hatum against Amin Hafez; something resembling a game of chess when only the 'Shah' is left on the board. As for the ideological or other principles behind which the struggle occurs, they are no more than weapons for use against rivals. . . . Moreover, these principles change from one stage of the power struggle to the next. Thus 'revolutionary solidarity' (with other states) under Amin Hafez and the party National Executive is a crime; under the February 23, 1966 regime, it is a progressive policy" (Al-tajriba al-murra [The Bitter Experience] [Beirut: Dar Ghandur, 1967], p. 138).

by Aflaq's remarks a few days earlier regarding the deviationism of Ba'athi officers and their attempt to control the party. It was known that Hafez had agreed with civilian leaders to carry out certain army purges and especially to exile General Jadid.

In contrast the new regime claimed that the February revolution had resulted from a conflict between the right wing of the Ba'ath represented by the civilians and the revolutionary Ba'ath of the officers. Assuming a conspicuous left-wing posture, the new leaders paid more attention to popular ideology than had been given in a decade. One of them, a prominent labor leader, Khalid al-Jundi, harangued the workers in Latakia about the "workers and peasants' revolution." The new regime emphasized that party policy would henceforth be established by the regional leadership, which was introduced in late March. Its declared policies included national unity, furtherance of the socialist program, solidarity and cooperation with revolutionary progressive regimes, and a belief in "people's democracy."

In mid-April, while celebrating the nineteenth anniversary of the founding of the Ba'ath, the new regime deplored all rightist tendencies in the party and announced the intention to expand land redistribution affecting over 170 villages and about 485,000 dunums (about 10,000 acres) of land. Khalid Bekdash, exiled leader of the Syrian Communist Party, returned to Syria and immediately announced his party's participation in the new government. The regime vilified the so-called Islamic bloc alliance of Faisal, Hussein, and other monarchs, while strengthening its relations with the Soviet Union.

In inaugurating the Euphrates Dam project, the railway network to and from it, the building of a northeastern pipeline from the new Syrian oil field, the regime explained that it was constructing the economic base for the people's struggle. It extolled the immediate benefit of these projects in increased employment. Moreover, the regime explained, a modern economic base would reflect the new political order, because old backward economic conditions reflected conservative political regimes. Similarly, the military regime produced new legislation to reorganize local government administration, trade unions, and to set up a new Youth of the Revolution Union, as well as local Defense Committees, asserting that Syria was in the forefront of the third world.

This move to the left began to falter when, at the end of October, 1968, the first relatively serious rift in the military leadership occurred with the removal of Youssef Zuayyin as Premier. The rumor was that Jadid's rivals advocated a more diplomatic approach to both Iraq and Jordan and, especially after the June war, a more cautious relationship with the Soviet Union. The rift, it was suggested, had widened by early 1969. These circumstances provided an opening for officers of Damascus origin and other anti-Jadid elements.

The events of February and March, 1969, confirmed this view of Syrian politics. General Jadid and his supporters apparently committed the mistake of their predecessors. Another attempt by the Ba'ath Executive to impose discipline on the military wing of the party had backfired, as it had in the coup of February, 1966. Ideological differences over relations with Moscow or Baghdad or over the Arab-Israeli conflict would appear to be only incidental to the Ba'ath's eternal struggle to control its military wing. The game of power—"political" in only the narrowest terms—remains limited to a very small circle.

The Role of Ideology

In Syria individual military officers and factions identify (even in the sense of socioeconomic interest) with sects, ethnic minorities, or a Sunni majority that shelters regionally disparate groups. None of these military groups, however, has made the kind of consistent long-term ideological commitment that could seriously reorient Syrian policy. Consequently, military governments which have succeeded civilian *ancien regimes* manifest a similar domestic political inaction. Despite rhetorical differences in ideology between one military regime and another, each is almost totally preoccupied with internal problems of control, security, and survival.

It may be misleading to discuss the nature of Syrian officer-level conflicts in terms of right and left. "Left" in Syria (as in most other Arab states in the area) implies no more than a leaning toward the Soviet bloc. In terms of domestic politics, however, one can only refer to such short-lived regimes as "pseudo-left." In short, despite proclamations about "masses" and "popular forces," the aims of conspirators are usually obscure. Successive sets of "sacred principles" have constituted the "ideology of the revolution" with little enlightenment as to their significance.

A desire for modernity and a higher standard of living are the least controversial tenets of Ba'athist ideology. Syrian leaders share an understanding of economic development goals with other Middle Eastern Arabs: increasing per capita income and GNP through industrialization, redistributing wealth and raising living standards—all of this to produce their hoped-for social revolution via greater economic independence, culminating in political change.

Yet inherent in this understanding has been the political paradox reflected over the past dozen years by successive Syrian regimes, whether Ba'athi, non-Ba'athi, semi-Ba'athi, or Egyptian-Syrian. State planning of economic development has been manipulated primarily to displace old privileged economic groups and structures. These regimes have utilized bureaucratic control for purposes similar to those of their predecessors; and the economic diversity that industrialization is supposed to produce is denied its most essential sociopolitical component, that is, the rise of new social, economic, and political groups. Traditional institutions of state control—the army, the police, and the bureaucracy—continue to serve whoever happens to rule . . . until the next successful coup.

When the Ba'ath government in 1966 sought mass support as a counterweight to its dependence on the military, it undertook to implement the party's socialist ideology, including effective nationalization under laws passed in 1965. The Ba'ath's decision to strengthen its civilian support met determined opposition from both the army and the merchant class. Thus the lingering National Command of the Ba'ath in Syria was caught between the hammer of their military opponents and the anvil of a still relatively well-organized mercantile bourgeoisie.

Many had hoped that the young military Saviors on Horseback came as the leaders of a new class to usher in revolutionary changes in all aspects of Syrian society. But although these soldiers constituted a different group or class from their predecessors in power, the young officers did not carry a long-term revolutionary commitment.

Students of modernization argue that economic development will eventually produce genuine classes in the European sociological and Marxist senses of the term. Yet, at present, an analysis of Syrian politics does not reveal any class-struggle pattern. Instead, regional religious and ethnic orientations continue to bedevil (if they do not actually supersede) any supraparticularistic class consciousness or identification of class interests in the economic-political sense.

Foreign Relations

Ideological differences are relevant in three major areas of policy: inter-Arab relations, the Arab-Israeli conflict, and, to a lesser degree, the East-West conflict, that is, the position of the superpowers in the Middle East. We have thus far argued that domestic social and economic policies depend heavily on the personal factor in internal politics. However, the context and content of domestic policies involve relationships with one or another of the superpowers, particularly over the question of foreign aid.

Inter-Arab Relations

How to ensure the continued existence of an independent Syria, a Syria not subject to the influence or submerged under the hegemony of neighboring Iraq, remains a perennial and common concern of all Syrian rulers regardless of their political orientations, predilections, and interests. The old fear of Hashemite designs and ambitions in the forties and fifties has continued under the so-called radical regimes of the Ba'ath and its military allies, despite the fact that the Hashemite dynasty in Iraq came to a brutal end in 1958.

By July-September, 1966, the Syrian regime had re-established the familiar pattern of relations with her neighbors. There were reports of trouble on the Jordanian borders, and both Jordan and Iraq were accused of encouraging Colonel Salim Hatum to undermine the Syrian regime. While on this diplomatic-propaganda offensive against Jordan and Iraq, the Damascus regime cited the danger from Israel in concluding its negotiations for a closer relationship with Egypt. On November 14, 1966, it was announced that a Joint Defense Pact had been signed with Egypt. At the same time, Syria proclaimed the need for a further radicalization of the struggle against Israel (at a time when the Egyptians were cautiously nurturing steadier relations with their erstwhile enemies, Saudi Arabia, and Jordan) by the adoption of a people's national liberation war. The regime also sought a closer identification with the Boumedienne regime in Algeria. The diplomatic offensive against Jordan gathered further momentum during the first months of 1967 just before the June war, with reports of plots and counterplots. As late as May, 1967, Jordan was accused of actively planning the overthrow of the regime in Damascus.

The Arab-Israeli Conflict

Syria's performance in the June, 1967 war was at best controversial. The Jordanians, in statements by their King and in a book by the then Prime Minister Saad Jumaa,[6] accused the Syrian regime of noncooperation, especially in the matters of air cover and joint command. More devastating allegations have been made regarding the regime's desire to weather the storm by retaining its two best-trained brigades around Damascus and Homs.

However, the regime's behavior immediately after the war was unequivocal and predictable. The Syrians essentially rejected the Egyptian-Jordanian preference for a "political solution" to the Arab-Israeli conflict. Instead they lined up alongside the distant Algerians in calling for a "National War of Liberation" to be conducted by the Palestinians themselves, preferably from the remnants of Jordanian territory.

On the other hand, the Syrians have at times clamped down on and excluded Palestinian irregular groups such as al-Fatah and al-Jabha al-Sha'biyya (PFLP)[7] from their territory. Al-Sa'iqâh, however, which is Syrian-controlled, is now represented in the Executive Committee of the PLO, chaired by al-Fatah's Arafat, which was elected in February 1969.

[6]Saad Jumaa, Al-Mu'amara wa ma rakat al-masir (Beirut, 1968).
[7]Popular Front for the Liberation of Palestine.

Yet the Israeli presence in the Golan Heights, coupled with the new forces active in Jordan, as well as the rise of the so-called moderate wing of the Ba'ath (actually its military wing) in Baghdad in July, 1968, again confronted the Syrian rulers with the perennial question of their relationship to the other Arab states. A feeling of isolation was reflected in their nervousness about the Baghdad regime in late 1968 and early 1969 and their allegation that Amin al-Hafez in Baghdad had been plotting their overthrow. In fact, the Syrians isolated themselves from the so-called "popular liberation forces" of the Palestinians, despite the verbal extremism found in the speeches of the leadership from June, 1967, to June, 1968.

By October, 1968-February, 1969, Salah Jadid was displaced by Hafez Asad, commander of the Syrian air force and Minister of Defense, as the effective leader of the Syrian Ba'ath. Hafez Asad appeared to recognize the constraints placed upon Syria's domestic and international policies. Under his leadership an approach to both Iraq and Egypt was renewed. Also Syria attempted to avoid too close an association with and dependence upon the U.S.S.R. Finally, the possibility that Syria will align with the position of Egypt and Jordan vis-à-vis Israel seems enhanced under Hafez.

The East-West Conflict and Foreign Aid

Economic development in Syria has, typically, depended on foreign capital, technical assistance, and expertise. Since 1957 the former almost total dependence on the West shifted to the acceptance of Russian and Eastern European long-term credits at a low (2.5 percent) average rate of interest. Yet trade, foreign borrowing, oil and mineral concessions, contracts to build industrial and infrastructure bases, have never followed an exclusively Eastern or exclusively Western pattern. It was not until development of the oil fields in the northeast, the completion of needed pipelines, the further development of the fertilizer industry in Homs, the expansion of rural and other electrification schemes, and the development of communications that Russian and Eastern European financial, technical, and other aid increased.

The trade pattern roughly in 1965 indicated only 35 percent of Syrian exports going to Russia and Eastern Europe. Half of its marked rise in cotton exports in 1965 went to Western spinners, especially France and Italy, as well as to Lebanon. Negotiations with Russian interests in connection with the oil industry did not take place until 1967. Moreover, during the *infisal* period, September 29, 1961, to March 8, 1963, loans mainly for agricultural development came from France, Poland, and the United States, including an IDA grant of $8.5 million for the construction of roads in 1963. Similarly in 1963 a West German credit offer was accepted and then dropped when that country indicated its intention to recognize Israel.

Yet it is not safe to assume that the Syrians will accept development aid from any source. For example, as in Egypt, regimes under military control since 1958 have advocated agrarian reform not so much to benefit the peasants, but to eliminate their landowning oligarchic predecessors. One would assume that because the 1966 5-year plan calls for priority of the Euphrates Dam project, which inevitably involves the riparian states of Turkey and Iraq, Syrian rulers would at least try to remain on speaking terms with the governments of those countries. This has not been true, however, which indicates that narrow "ideological" considerations may override even the paramount goal of national economic development.

One could argue that in Syria, because the Soviet navy has shore facilities at Latakia, tensions between the U.S.S.R. and Damascus are possible. After all, the essential nationalist aim has been complete sovereignty and the removal of all foreign bases from Arab lands. Syrians could in the future complain that French and/or British bases of the past have been succeeded by Russian, and so embarrass their governments. So long as the Arab-Israeli conflict continues, however, any Syrian government could claim that the Soviet presence is necessary. But if it becomes clear that the Russian presence makes no perceptible difference in that conflict so far as Syria is concerned, the Soviets could become unpopular, and internal conflict might follow. Political trouble might erupt, for example, were Syrians to discover that Soviet shore facilities are primarily a dimension of a wider Russian strategy in the Mediterranean, the Red Sea, and the Indian Ocean, not unlike that of the British in the Middle East earlier. One may cautiously view recent Syrian and Iraqi flirtations with China in this light. Beyond propaganda gestures, however, China is not yet in a position to act seriously as a "third force" in the U.S.-U.S.S.R. rivalry in the Middle East. Thus any Syrian—and increasingly any Iraqi—government will, for the foreseeable future, continue to depend for its military needs on the Soviet Union.

Constraints of Syrian Politics

Events and developments in Syria are constrained by certain constants in the country's foreign relations. First, because Syria depends upon foreign financial, technical, and military assistance, her domestic and other policies will continue to be subjected to the external pressures of other nations, including those of its immediate Arab environment.

Second, like all other Arab states since June, 1967, Syria will also be affected by two emergent trends in the Arab movement and its orientation to the Arab-Israeli conflict:

1. The widespread wave of conservative reaction led by the oil-rich states (who now pay huge subventions to their erstwhile revolutionary enemies), as well as the widespread public revulsion against the dramatic failure of

the so-called radical Arab Nationalist-Socialist revolutionary leadership of the Nasser-Syrian camp prior to June, 1967.

2. The emergence of the radicalized Palestine Liberation Movement and its sharpening rift with established Arab governments anxious to reach a political settlement of the Arab-Israeli conflict. Contrary to widespread belief, Syria seems to be among these Arab states.

A third source of political maneuvering of the future is the potential shift of conflict in the Arab world to Arabia and the Persian Gulf in the 1970s. This development is complicated by the possible confrontation between Arab and non-Arab (Iranian) interests, including possible Soviet involvement.

And finally the continued general struggle between Arab states has left its impact on Syria. Egypt's gradual *debarrassement* from pan-Arab questions may confine the consequences of this struggle to the Fertile Crescent.

III. Iraq

The Social Basis of Politics

Iraq, more than any other Arab Middle Eastern state, suffers from national and political disunity. In its historical heyday, the Baghdad government often ruled over territory substantially different from that now encompassed by the Iraqi state. As a province of the Ottoman Empire, Iraq comprised basically three vilayets: Baghdad, Mosul, and Basra. Before the mid-nineteenth century Ottoman administrative reforms filtered down to Iraq, the authority of local governors in these vilayets rarely extended beyond the confines of the city, the town, and their immediate surroundings.

About two-thirds of Iraq's 172,000 square miles are inhospitable. A million Kurds, who constitute a distinct ethnic-national group, live in the northern mountain belt. To the west and southwest lie the desert, steppe, and Jazira running into Syria. This area is the home of two great Arab tribes, Aneiza and Shamar. Finally, over half the population of the country, sharply divided between Sunni and Shia Muslims, lives in the Euphrates and Tigris valleys. Northern and central Iraq are predominantly Sunni (divided between Arab and Kurd), but also include smaller religious minorities— Yazidis, Assyrians, Nestorians, Armenians, and Jews. Part of central and practically all of southern Iraq is overwhelmingly Shia.

The Shia constitute just under half of the total population of 7.7 million (1967); the Sunni Arabs account for about one-fourth of the total. The Kurds and other minority groups make up the remaining quarter. Basic social divisions are four: Shia versus Sunni; Arab versus Kurd; tribal versus settled community; and, more recently (since statehood in 1920), traditional social-religious-economic-political groups versus modern, mainly Western-educated social-economic-political groups.

Iraq is not a tribal society in the literal, romantic sense of the term. Kurds, Shia, Turkmans, Assyrians, and others are mostly rural and mountain peasants. Yet a majority of them trace their origins to tribal groups who gradually settled on the land. Many of these groups retain perceptions, customs, and political conventions that tend to perpetuate an earlier tribal ethos. The family remains the most significant unit of individual, social, and political relationships.

The patterns of Baghdad's rule in this century derive from two fundamental experiences: the latter-day Ottoman administration until 1918; and the British Mandate of 1920-1932, as well as British influence from 1932 until 1958. Administrative and economic reform in the Ottoman Empire after the mid-nineteenth century helped to create a local Sunni aristocracy of religious and administrative officials in Baghdad, Mosul, and Basra. It also produced a cadre of trained Iraqi officers in the Ottoman army. After the Young Turk revolt of 1908 in Istanbul, Arab Sunni Iraqis became involved in Arab separatist and nationalist movements. The further administrative effort to extend provincial control over a wider area of the country also gave rise to what many have called the *effendi* class, the new bureaucrats. The British reinforced these processes. In the countryside, agricultural poverty, absentee *shaykh* landlords, and a Kurdish feudal warrior caste of *aghas* were consequences of Baghdad's attempted centralization for greater administrative control. This also led to peasant emigration to the towns and cities, resulting in urban ghettos and crime.

Since 1920 Iraq's fragmented diffuse polity has lacked any single focus of loyalty. Rather, it has roofed many elements hostile to the state. The economic and administrative evolution under the British Mandate integrated some Shia notables, rich merchants, and senior army officers into a Sunni ruling elite. But the Mandate did not undermine the particularistic loyalties of Iraqis to tribe, religious sect, or ethnic community, nor dissipate Shiitic suspicion of the Sunni establishment.

The diversity of political forces expressing these social realities remains. Despite the adoption of a constitutional system calling for national parliamentary government based on proportional representation, the actual political arrangement has been based on a majority-minority principle, on communal and ethnic representation. This perpetuates a nonunitary, nonnational identity among Iraqis. Minorities continue to harbor their fears and suspicions of the politically ascendant Sunni establishment in Baghdad, of central government in general. Yet outside the proverbial Baghdad mob (a legacy of ninth- and tenth-century *futuwwat*), the newer political groups with progressive notions do not move the masses. The vast majority of the population remains uninterested and insulated from political activity.

Given these social and political divisions, the army's importance as the supreme agency of internal security and necessary broker for any government's administrative control becomes obvious. Formed in 1921 before the kingdom of Iraq was proclaimed, it grew under the British Mandate to a strength of 10,000 to 15,000. A military academy was founded in 1924, and a staff college in 1928. It was officered initially by Iraqis who had served in the Ottoman army. An air force to quell tribal uprisings and frequent rebellions was first formed in 1930. The army remained a volunteer force until 1935, when national conscription was introduced despite Kurdish and Shiitic opposition.

Until 1940-1941 the army was the major prop of the monarchy and politicians of the *ancien regime*. Its crucial role in dealing with minority and tribal challenges to the regime (e.g., the Assyrian uprising of 1933-1935; the Kurdish troubles of 1937; and the tribal uprisings throughout the 1920-1940 period) placed the army in a position to dictate policy to civilian governments, beginning with the first coup of Bakr Sidqi in 1936.

By this time, however, new political groups and parties supporting radical socioeconomic and political reform came into existence. Such were the Ahali (later, the NDP or National Democratic Party) led by lawyer Kamil al-Chadirchi and M. Mahdi Kubba, the Istiqlal (Independence Party) of Shinshil and Hadid, and the Communist Party of Iraq (ICP). An upper class of ministers, high government officials, religious leaders, and rich landowners constituted the ruling elite. Several other significant groups emerged at the same time: (1) a class of merchants, tradesmen, and petty government officials; (2) a new group of Western-educated professionals, managers, technicians, and army officers; and (3) an incipient working class in petroleum transport, and minor industries.

The nationalist movement in the period 1937-1957 developed two new dimensions. Partly as a result of the Palestine Question, Iraqi nationalists became more pan-Arabist and anti-British. The new urban intelligentsia, moreover, introduced democratic-socialist reform programs in their party platforms. They associated the monarchy and *ancien-regime* politicians with a pro-British policy abroad and a conservative socioeconomic policy at home. Yet neither the Ahali nor the Independence Party, representing these new urban elements, commanded wide popular following throughout the country. The Communist Party was small, recurrently purged, pursued, and persecuted by the government, and therefore weak. The Kurds patronized their own political organization.

The Iraqi Ba'ath (founded about 1954), together with the NDP, ICP, and Independence parties formed a United National Front (UNF) in 1957 to oppose the Nuri al-Said regime. In fact, it was the army which succeeded in overthrowing the government in 1958 by conspiratorial means. The more conservative, religious elements in the country did not present a united front as the Shia invariably separated from the Sunni orthodox establishment.

Repression of opposition political groups in the 1950s was the major stimulus for the formation of the UNF. However, the short-lived honeymoon between Qasim and the coalition of opposition parties proved that political divisions in the army were more important than civilian politics. Although the opposition had some following among the economically deprived urban mobs and poor peasants, their success depended—as in several other Arab states—on the extent of their infiltration in the officer corps. The NDP and other progressive elements distrusted military government largely on the basis of their bitter experience with Bakr Sidqi in 1936-1937. Orthodox Sunni and Shia leaders opposed all radical groups, especially the Communists. The Ba'ath and sundry extremist Arab nationalist groups could operate only as secret societies against the tightening control of successive military regimes. As for the Kurds, their political movement acquired even greater momentum and ferocity when their alienation from the military regimes in Baghdad became complete. Finally, the evolving patterns of inter-Arab and superpower politics in the area has put intolerable pressure on recent Iraqi regimes.

Domestic Politics since 1958

Following the overthrow of the Iraqi monarchy in 1958, the national coalition of General Abdul Karim Qasim began to break down barely three months after his military regime assumed power. Military and civilian leaders of the coalition differed over Iraq's attitude to the six-month-old United Arab Republic. The immediate result of these differences was the dismissal of Colonel Abdel Salam Aref from his military and Cabinet posts, followed by the departure of six ministers, generally thought to have shared Aref's desire for the political integration of Iraq with the United Arab Republic. Thus, Qasim ousted a major political group which enjoyed wide support within the rank and file of the Iraqi armed forces.

Qasim's rupture with the pan-Arab nationalists of Iraq led him to rely increasingly on left-wing groups and the Communists, particularly after the Shawaf revolt in Mosul in March 1959. This in turn alienated not only the Ba'ath, the most important and the best organized of the pan-Arab nationalists, but the considerable anti-Communist segment of Iraqi society. The opposition was directed not only to the Qasim regime, but to the Iraqi state as it embodied Qasim's anti-union policies. By the very nature of their beliefs, the pan-Arab Iraqis worked not only for the overthrow of Qasim but for the disestablishment of the state of Iraq and its subsequent merger as a region in the United Arab Republic. Such political objectives were bound to arouse the suspicions and the active opposition of political groups such as the Communists and the Iraqi nationalists as distinct from the pan-Arabists, ethnic groups like the Kurds, and the religious Shia community. Thus when the pan-Arab nationalists under the Ba'ath leadership seized power in 1963, they had to suppress the opposition or conciliate it. The mass killing of Communists and the bloody suppression of the Kurdish rebellion left no room for conciliation. This harsh policy decision split the Ba'ath movement, and it lost control to President Abdel Salam Aref, who assumed power in November, 1963.

This strife hastened the process of disintegration and caused the almost complete disenchantment of various political and social groups that ranged themselves in opposition to the Aref regime. Aref attempted to check this trend by appointing a civilian Prime Minister, Abdel Rahman al-Bazzaz who sought to alleviate the stagnant economy by easing tight government control and amending the harsh nationalization measures of 1964. However, Aref relentlessly pursued a military solution to the Kurdish problem until his death in an air crash in April, 1966.

Though Aref's brother, Abdel Rahman Aref, acceded to the Presidency peacefully, the new President was a compromise candidate who did not enjoy the support of military factions which had had their own candidates for the office. His rule was never a happy one. He lacked his late brother's dynamism and single-mindedness. With Prime Minister Bazzaz, he attempted to conciliate the opposition at home and improve Iraqi's relations with her neighbors. He also wanted to solve the Kurdish rebellion peacefully, and Bazzaz secured a cease-fire when an agreement to end the Kurdish rebellion was signed in June, 1966. This agreement provided for the introduction of political and administrative reform under which the Kurds would be granted local autonomy and Kurdish would be recognized as an official language in their areas. The Iraqi military opposed the agreement. From the beginning they resented Bazzaz's political activities, particularly when he called for the return of the military to their barracks. They successfully pressured the President to dismiss his Prime Minister only two months after the signing of the agreement with the Kurds.

The departure of Bazzaz exposed Aref's weaknesses in controlling the military. Under his regime Iraqi politics had become so factionalized and personalized that any combination af the military and political opposition could have overthrown him. His indecisive and ineffective leadership alienated a great number of Iraqis and led him to rely increasingly on his new Prime Minister, Tahir Yahia, a man whose personal integrity was questioned by many Iraqis. The Iraqi failure to take an active part in the June, 1967, war gave rise to a number of rumors about spy rings operating in Iraq for the Americans and the Israelis. The arrest of few officers and their release a few days later confirmed these rumors. To counter this wave of public criticism, the government adopted an extremist position in Arab ministerial conferences following the war, but was relieved by the resolutions of the Khartoum summit conference.

The Aref regime tottered toward collapse when a group of Ba'athist officers under the leadership of Ahmad Hassan al-Bakr, with the cooperation of the chiefs of military intelligence and the Republican Guards, carried out a bloodless coup on July 17, 1968. A fortnight later, the Ba'athist officers ousted their collaborators from the cabinet and assumed full control. The Kurdish problem is still unresolved; the menace of civil war, economic stagnation, the long-standing dispute with the oil companies, as well as the social and political fragmentation are factors which plague not only the current Ba'ath regime, but threaten the very foundations of the state of Iraq. The regime seems to compound its own problems through rivalry between its military and civilian wings, and clashes among the military leaders themselves. Faced with these conflicts, the regime has been driven to suppress all opposition and to rely on secret trials, public hangings, political assassination and kidnaping in order to survive.

The basic political problem of Iraq, national unity, remains unresolved. Iraq, more than any other Arab country, faces the prospect of disintegration, especially if the Kurds succeed in carving out a state of their own. This eventuality could be forestalled if Baghdad were to give the Kurds some form of autonomy. The recent efforts of the present regime (1969) to split the Kurds does not appear successful. One ray of hope exists in this gloomy situation. The preservation of an independent Iraq is a common commitment of both the military and the civilians—of both Sunni and Shiitic Arabs. A united, nationally harmonious Iraq remains the unanimous goal of the most powerful political factions in the country.

Iraqi-Syrian Relations

Iraqi interest in Syria dates back to the Arab kingdom of Faisal, which was set up in Damascus in 1918 and driven out by the French in 1920 when the Mandate for Syria was awarded to France. Faisal could not readily forget his old capital, nor did his supporters—Iraqis as well as Syrians—who continued to campaign for Syrian independence. After 1921 the Syrians looked to Iraq, the center of pan-Arab nationalist agitation, for help in their struggle against the French Mandate. Iraqi leaders under

Faisal's guidance nurtured plans to unite Syria, Lebanon, Palestine, and Transjordan in a Greater Arab kingdom under the leadership of Iraq. This Fertile Crescent unity plan competed with the Greater Syria evisioned by Amir Abdullah of Transjordan. Syrian enthusiasm waned after the British suppressed the pan-Arab pro-Nazi regime of Rashid Ali al-Gaylani in 1941. Nuri al-Said in 1942 proposed a two-stage plan for an Arab union. He recommended, first, the formation of a single state (unitary or federal) including Syria, Lebanon, Palestine, and Transjordan, wherein the Christians of Lebanon and the Jews of Palestine would be granted special autonomous positions. Second, Nuri proposed an Arab confederation including the new state and Iraq, plus any other Arab state that wished to join. Iraq's rivals for Arab leadership, Egypt and Saudi Arabia, took up the call for Arab unity with British encouragement. The resultant Arab League in 1945 had little resemblance to Nuri's earlier plan. Iraq's ambition for union with Syria was frustrated by the League's recognition of independent sovereign Arab states.

Following the creation of the Arab League, two external factors governed Iraq's relationship with Syria. The first was the opposition of Egypt and Saudi Arabia to the extension of Hashemite authority to Syria. The British, who had considerable influence in Iraq, were reluctant to support the union of the two countries in the face of objections from Iraq's Arab rivals as well as the French, who regarded Syria as their sphere of influence. However, a second external factor drew the two countries closer together, namely, the creation of the state of Israel with its implicit threat to the territorial integrity of Syria.

Iraq was also encouraged by the internal division in the Syrian nationalist movement. Support for union came from the People's Party (PP) based in Aleppo, as opposed to the National Party with Damascus as its stronghold. The People's Party represented the business interests of the city of Aleppo and enjoyed the support of the landed families of Homs. The merchants and bankers of Aleppo felt closer ties to Mosul and Baghdad than to Damascus, and therefore lent their political weight to abolition of the Syrian-Iraqi frontier and the destruction of trade barriers between the two countries. However, the PP was by no means a Hashemite instrument or indeed a monarchical party; it was as attached to Syria's republican institutions as its Damascus rival. The PP was essentially an Aleppo party, and it attempted to use its Iraqi support as political leverage just as the National Party used its Saudi and Egyptian backing.

The Arab loss of the first Arab-Israeli war in 1948 and the creation of the state of Israel impelled the Syrian military under the command of Colonel Husni al-Zaim to seize power in March, 1949. Zaim initiated talks on a military defense pact with Iraq first to strengthen his hands at the coming armistice negotiations with Israel, and second, to offset Egyptian and Saudi opposition to his takeover. The PP, which had advocated an Arab federal union—in effect a union with Iraq—to counter the Israeli threat before the war, supported Zaim in his effort. Zaim was also supported by the small but significant Ba'ath movement. The Syrian talks with Iraq alarmed her Arab rivals, who quickly offered the new regime in Syria diplomatic recognition as well as military and financial aid. Thus the Iraqi effort was checked once more by Egypt and Saudi Arabia. Henceforth, an objective of Iraqi policy was to help friends in Damascus to seize power in the expectation that they would declare a union with Iraq. Iraqi intervention took the form of subsidies to Syrian politicians and newspapers, and contributions to the sectional interests of such communities as Aleppo, Homs, and Jabal al-Druze. Such patronage was channeled through the office of the Iraqi military attachés in Damascus and Beirut.

In this manner the Iraqis managed to have the Zaim regime overthrown in 1949, and that of Shishakli in 1954. Following Zaim's overthrow, the PP controlled the Presidency and dominated the Cabinet, but both were subject to such conflicting external pressures and internal divisions that they lapsed into indecision. The Ba'ath leaders in the Cabinet and the Muslim Brotherhood defended Syria's Republican institutions and opposed the introduction of a monarchy under the Iraqi regent. They also expressed grave reservations about Iraq's commitments to Britain under the Anglo-Iraqi treaty of 1930. However, before any concrete step toward union could be taken, Adib al-Shishakli seized power in December, 1949. Hashemite hopes for union with Syria were blocked when Egypt proposed a pact to coordinate the defenses of all Arab states against Israel and so render bilateral agreements unnecessary. Although the pact was approved by the Arab League Council in April, 1950, Iraq demonstrated her displeasure by not signing it until February, 1951.

In the early 1950s the Arab world was motivated toward neutralism, in reaction to the growth of the cold war. Iraq became associated with the Western-proposed Regional Defense Alliance by signing the Baghdad Pact in 1955, while Egypt under Nasser adopted the Bandung policy of neutrality. Iraq, concerned about the safety of the pipelines, was anxious to prevent Syria from falling under the control of a hostile power. Shishakli's overthrow in Syria coincided with the emergence of Nasser as a major political force on the Arab political scene and the Ba'ath and Communist parties as significant elements in Syrian politics, all of which were regarded as dangerous threats to Iraqi political interests. The Iraqis, disappointed with their Syrian supporters, concluded that a military invasion of Syria was necessary to redress the situation. Thus, the Iraqi high command with the cooperation of several Syrian leaders planned for an invasion in October,

1956, presumably to coincide with the Anglo-French-Israeli attack on Egypt. However, the Syrian security service learned of the plot and arrested a number of the ringleaders. The aftermath of Suez transformed Nasser into an Arab national hero. He won the confidence of many Syrian leaders, especially the Ba'athists. By 1958 his considerable inroads in Syrian politics made possible the union between Syria and Egypt, the United Arab Republic. Iraq countered by declaring a Hashemite Federation with Jordan.

Hashemite opposition to the United Arab Republic ceased when General Qasim overthrew the monarchy in Iraq in July, 1958, and immediately effected a *rapprochement* between Iraq and the United Arab Republic. However, when the ruling junta in Iraq dismissed Colonel Aref, a stanch supporter of President Nasser and Iraq's union with the United Arab Republic, the old rivalry over Syria was renewed, and a war of words ensued. In March, 1959, Syrians and Egyptians supported the military rebellion of the Mosul garrison against the Qasim regime in Baghdad.

In September, 1961, however, Syria seceded from the union with Egypt. Qasim welcomed the restoration of Syrian independence and concluded a treaty of friendship and economic cooperation with the secessionist regime. Neither Qasim nor the secessionist regime lasted long, however. Qasim was overthrown by the Ba'ath Party in February, 1963; his old colleague and rival Abdel Salam Aref became President of the republic. A month later Ba'athist officers seized power in Damascus. In April, 1963, Iraq, Syria, and Egypt initiated talks to set up a tripartite union; but the negotiations proved inconclusive and led to considerable recrimination. The Ba'athists of Syria and Iraq, on the one hand, and Nasser of Egypt, on the other, exchanged charges of opportunism and the desire to dominate the proposed union. The Ba'athists, facing considerable pressure externally from Egypt and internally from their political opponents, drew closer and concluded a joint defense pact in October, 1963, between Iraq and Syria. This pact lapsed when a month later President Aref, supported by army officers, ousted the Ba'athist regime in Iraq. Aref quickly realigned Iraq with Egypt, and once again Syria became the center of a power struggle. The Syrian Ba'athists, however, have managed to retain their control. The return of the moderate-wing of the Ba'ath Party to power in Iraq in July, 1968, and the emergence of Hafez Asad as the strong man of the Ba'athist radical regime in Syria could lead to some kind of cooperation between the two countries. However, serious ideological differences still exist between the two ruling factions.

The failure of Iraq's effort to unite with Syria may be attributed to the evolution of a Syrian vested interest in the continued sovereignty of their own state. This may also explain the breakup of the United Arab Republic as well as Ba'athist particularism despite their ideological commitment to Arab unity.

In this connection one must note a definite consequence of the June, 1967, war in Syria and in the other Arab states most directly involved in the Arab-Israeli conflict: the near disappearance of any references to *al-gawmiyya al-arabiyya* (Arab nationalism). This is due, in part, to the rise of the so-called Palestine Resistance (or Liberation) Movement with its emphasis on a national war of liberation by the Palestinians, whose loyalty attaches to a lost land. But it is also partly due to the accentuated problem of protecting the respective territories of existing Arab states. One can for the moment surmise that there has been a shift from thinking in terms of that abstract plane of "Arab nationalism" to a more concrete priority of the "territorial state."

IV. Jordan

The Political Background

Before the annexation of Palestine's West Bank into Jordan (1948-1950), the population of Transjordan was about 400,000. It was basically divided into nomads and seminomads of the desert, and peasants who traced their descent from tribes that had settled in the area as early as the fourteenth century. To a great extent, these peasants retain their tribal customs, conventions, and perceptions, particularly in the south where several families have played a leading political role in the short history of the state.

Prince, later King, Abdullah administered the state with the financial assistance and political supervision of the British from 1921 until 1946. Abdullah ruled autocratically. He imposed his authority from Amman over recalcitrant, often murderous tribesmen through dual tactics of negotiation and force. While he cajoled, bribed, and persuaded tribal chieftains to abandon their feuds and their opposition to his rule, he offered them a share of power. Meanwhile, his British-trained, -financed, and -led Arab Legion pacified marauding tribes with the assistance of the RAF. The principality also relied heavily on an annual British subsidy to the ruler, on transit and other trade with Mandated Palestine and neighboring Arab states during the interwar period.

Specifically excluded from the Balfour Declaration regarding a Jewish national homeland, Transjordan did not face conflict-generating political issues with Britain, apart from Abdullah's wider Arab ambitions. Transjordanians felt detached—albeit physically near—the anti-Zionist anti-British political activities of the Palestine Arabs.

The major political dichotomy in Transjordan remained the one between favored tribal leaders and others at court plus the Prince's army, on the one hand, versus an emerging small bourgeoisie of educated townsmen in Amman, Irbid, and Salt. This split was reflected in the first significant opposition, the Palestinian-Syrian Independence Party of the early 1920s (handily destroyed by the Nationality Law of 1925), and the opposition political parties of the period 1928-1935. The latter cautiously refrained from challenging the Prince's legitimacy or Transjordan's autonomy. They sought only to curtail the power of the ruler, who governed through his Executive Council, with the veto power of the British lurking behind the throne. Thus, when a Legislative Council was instituted, its actions were subject to approval by the monarch and the British Resident in Amman.

Nevertheless, Transjordanians acquired a parochial state identity during this period, separate and distinct from pan-Arabism. The small, fairly homogeneous Transjordanian population developed its own political style in relation to the ruler, his family, political courtiers (including tribal leaders), British officials and advisers. "Transjordan" began to express a special state nationalism symbolized by the ruler, his political establishment, his administrative conventions, and traditional interests.

After World War II Jordan was dragged into the wider arena of inter-Arab and regional politics. The framework of this involvement was essentially set by two external sources: the Palestine question and Arab nationalist unity. Changes in Syria and Lebanon, the emergence of the state of Israel, the incorporation of nearly 1.5 million Palestinian Arabs into the state (over one-third of them refugees) began to undermine the social fabric of the kingdom.

The overwhelming majority of Palestinians who became Jordanian citizens after 1948 were Sunni peasants. The mass of these Palestinian peasants followed their traditional leaders of the religious, administrative, landowning, and merchant hierarchies because, first, they were conservative Muslims and, second, they had little alternative.

However, the Palestinian ranks of better-educated, skilled technicians, professionals, administrators, merchants, and entrepreneurs far outnumbered their Transjordanian counterparts. These newcomers were bitter not simply over the loss of their homes to the victorious Israelis, but also because of Abdullah's alleged treachery in the national struggle against the Zionists and British. Much of this attitude stemmed from the earlier conflict between the Palestinian Husseinis versus the Hashemites, the latter of whom cooperated with Britain and associated themselves with British policies and interests in the Middle East. In fact, given their experience and psychological disposition, these élite Palestinians presented one of the most fertile recruiting grounds for the radical ideological groups which began to acquire momentum in the late 1940s and 1950s.

Despite sustained efforts by the monarchy to integrate the Palestinians in the ruling establishment and the state in general, the newcomers remained only superficially loyal Jordanians. The problem of security and state control plagued the regime for twenty years. Palestinians were always receptive to outside currents and influences of the wider Arab region.

Yet, in Amman and on the West Bank, enterprising Palestinians soon prospered. They had been enfranchised immediately after 1948, although they were not welcomed into the army. Members of their upper class soon became cabinet ministers, members of parliament, and heads of civil service departments. By 1967 most observers felt that these Palestinians were finally becoming reconciled to their Jordanian political identity; that they were exhibiting clear signs of loyalty to the Hashemite ruling house and its state.

Clearly, the parochial and conservative Muslim groups in East Jordan, despite their differences, tended to support the Hashemite regime. The Palestinians, on the other hand, disillusioned and abandoned by the Husseini leadership, were drawn toward two new major political forces: the Syrian Ba'ath and Nasserism. Ramallah, Jerusalem, Salt, Irbid, and Amman became centers of radical political agitation. By inclination and experience, these pan-Arabist centers challenged the very existence of the state by 1956. However, both radical groups attracted mainly urban, educated, middle- and upper-class nationalists as well as members of an enlarged petite bourgeoisie. The rural peasants remained conservative Muslims, socially insulated from politics until the PLO became active in 1964-1965 and *al-Fatah* since 1967. The working class was small and confined to major urban centers; the most skilled of its ranks entered the army. Nonetheless, some were proselytized by local Communists and Marxists who initially came from the Christian intelligentsia.

The regime was able to neutralize the impact of the new political parties (the Ba'ath, the National Socialists, the Communists, the Islamic Liberation Party, the Muslim Brotherhood) by the mid-1950s. In this connection the role of the army was crucial. The monarchy could rely on the loyalty of tribal elements in the army when anti-status-quo parties attempted to infiltrate the officer corps. To some extent, this generalization accounts for the failure of the attempted coup of April, 1957.

While Britain retained a relatively strong political and military presence in the country, the regime felt justifiably secure. After 1957, it managed to maintain its power with the support of a tribal East Jordanian political establishment, which rather boldly admitted more and more Palestinians into its ranks. A vastly expanded, strengthened army, of course, supported this whole edifice until the June, 1967, war.

Following the June, 1967, war and the loss of the West Bank to Israeli occupation, Jordan faced major difficulties: (1) an economic crisis which quickly abated with massive aid from Arab states and outside powers, (2) a swollen refugee population in camps, (3) shattered defenses resulting from the destruction of the country's small air force and nearly half the effective strength of its army, (4) several Palestine guerrilla organizations operating from its territory against the Israeli-occupied West Bank, thus provoking Israeli retaliation against East Jordan, and (5) continuing dilemmas in inter-Arab relations.

Economic Crisis

With the West Bank under Israeli military occupation, Jordan lost a rich agricultural area and its flourishing tourist trade. The West Bank had provided annual income of over $40 million in foreign exchange from tourism and remittances by Palestinians working abroad. (Some 120,000 Palestinian Jordanians work in Kuwait and elsewhere in the Gulf.) The region, moreover, comprised 25 percent of the country's arable land, which produced 35 percent of its agricultural output, consisting mainly of fruit and vegetables.

However, despite its great political significance, the loss of the West Bank does not, in retrospect, appear to have been economically disastrous for East Jordan. Whatever manufacturing industry Jordan had in 1967 was already concentrated and developing in the East Bank, if the country's Seven-Year Plan (1964-1970) is any indication. Thus all mining, road construction, and water irrigation schemes are located in the East.

Undoubtedly, the general impact of the territorial loss has caused economic stagnation mainly in the private sector, after a sustained phenomenal expansion in 1958-1967. Yet, thanks to the annual Arab subsidy of over $100 million (Kuwait, Saudi Arabia, and Libya), Western aid[8] and gifts, East Jordan has been able since June, 1967, to adjust its economy by expanding the public sector, especially in the form of public works (schools, housing, roads, etc.). It continues to export phosphates, as well as its agricultural products, many of which come across the river from the West Bank. Private consumption has been depressed, and imports have been cut by over a quarter.

Two new sources of economic expansion have appeared in the private

[8]Hussein's first and only visit to Moscow, in October, 1967, was designed as leverage against the West. It did not reflect a serious commitment by Hussein to seek material and other aid from the U.S.S.R.

sector: (1) imports for Saudi and Iraqi troops stationed in Jordan, and (2) the provision and supply of Palestine guerrilla units by Jordanian contractors (food, clothing, etc.). This situation encourages East Jordanians, including the King, not to be apprehensive about a possible return to the old, original East Jordanian entity.

Refugees

The loss of economically important territory comprising some 750,000 Arabs was aggravated by the gain of additional refugees who fled to the East Bank (estimate: 125,000). Before the June war, Jericho and its rich agricultural environs had reached a population of 100,000 (including the refugee camps). At the end of the June, 1967, hostilities, only about 7000 were left in Jericho. It is from this area that most of the refugees initially crossed to the East Bank: they were the nearest to the river. A few from Wadi al-Tuffah and the Ramallah camps ventured out briefly, only to return.

On the other hand, this time around, there was far less readiness on the part of Arabs to flee their homes. Those who left did so for financial, family, and personal reasons. Moreover, the disoriented masses of West Bank refugees were in no mood, spirit, or physical condition to mount any "popular" attacks on the regime. They simply had nowhere else to go.[9]

One immediate impact of the June war has been the renewed feeling of resentment between East Jordanians and Palestinians. The former were effectively pushing forward a local-traditional Transjordanian patriotism which, they argued, had suffered ever since they became involved in the affairs of Palestinians. They resented having to fight for the Palestinians who, they charged, had for twenty years tried to undermine their state. Unofficially, there was talk in East Jordan for a return to old Transjordan.

Shattered Defenses

One need hardly emphasize the impact of the June, 1967, war on Jordan in this respect. The destruction of its committed army in the West Bank by the Israeli forces was total. Nevertheless, capitalizing on his stand in the war, Hussein spent most of June and July, 1967, in search of economic aid from other Arab states, for arms and equipment from the West to rebuild his army and air force. His success was remarkable, and defense spending continues at a high level of 50 to 55 percent of total government expenditure.

In one instance, however, this foreign aid has developed into a mixed

[9]On the refugees, see the study, *al-Nazihun,* by Halim Barakat and Peter Dodd of the American University of Beirut (1968).

blessing for Hussein. Jordan's internal security and power structure are simultaneously supported and potentially threatened by the presence of an Iraqi division in the Mafrak-Irbid area of northwestern Jordan.

Guerrillas and Israeli Reprisals

It is clear that Jordan's future is linked to the evolution, development, and activities of the Palestine guerrilla organizations. A new relationship between the Palestine guerrilla organizations and Hussein emerged after the clashes of November 4-5, 1968, in Amman. Even though the so-called criminal group destroyed by the Bedouin units of the Jordan army was identified as *Kataeb al-Nasr* (Contingents for Victory, formerly al-Sa'iqâh), there is no doubt that these were elements of the extremist wing of the Arab Nationalist Popular Front for the Liberation of Palestine (PFLP). In this confrontation, Hussein tested three things: (1) he tested the loyalty of the army; (2) by this action against al-Sa'iqâh, he indirectly hit at all guerrilla organizations and reasserted his primacy in the country; (3) he warned the Israelis not to dismiss him so readily: on the contrary, a future political settlement with him as head of state would be meaningful.

For their part, Palestinian leaders, especially Yasir Arafat, were only too willing to conclude some agreement with Hussein, for they were not prepared to forgo the following advantages: (1) operating from an Arab country whose regime and head of state are recognized by other Arab states of the world; (2) receiving massive financial aid from other Arab rulers (e.g., Saudi Arabia and Kuwait) without which their movement would collapse. Moreover, without Hussein, the Palestinian guerrillas would expose themselves to more severe reprisals by Israeli forces, and they would have to seek cover elsewhere. Finally, a showdown which might eliminate Hussein would embroil the Palestinians in the succession problem in East Jordan and a first-class political mess.

The agreement between Hussein and *al-Fatah*'s Arafat concluded on November 18, 1968, involved mutual concessions. Hussein, for example, agreed to the guerrillas' maintaining training camps in the Salt Valley, Jerash, and Karak areas. The guerrillas agreed to "disappear" from Amman's public view. However, many Transjordanians were visibly irritated by the trouble Palestinians continued to bring to the country. The settled, though originally tribal, communities of Salt, Jerash, and Kerak were particularly annoyed.

In effect, the guerrillas would let Hussein rule East Jordan unhindered by them, provided he would permit them a free hand in their operations against Israel. This constituted a new challenge to Israeli policy. When the guerrillas in the same month blew up the market in Jerusalem with serious loss of Israeli life, Israeli forces retaliated with their new commando-style attack deep inside Jordan. First, they disrupted communications between Amman and Aqaba, seriously impairing exports and therefore the economy. When Iraqi artillery subsequently shelled Israeli border settlements, the Israeli air force hit back in the Irbid populated sector (Kafr Asad). It appeared then that the Israelis intended (1) to force Hussein either to dissociate himself completely from the guerrillas or to throw his lot in with them; (2) to force the Iraqis to withdraw from Jordan or, better still, to encourage Hussein to demand their withdrawal on the grounds they were drawing heavy Israeli fire against his country; and (3) to isolate Jordan from the Arab countries by destroying communications to the south, the north, and the northeast.

After the Israeli attack on Karameh, Hussein seemed to opt for a policy of a closer identification with the Palestinian guerrilla organizations, especially the strongest among these, *al-Fatah*. The latter found this equally convenient once they realized that East Jordan must be their major base of operations in the face of opposition from the Syrian regime, the distance of Iraq, and the "clever" policy of the Egyptians.

Arafat's election in February, 1969, as chief of the PLO Executive produced typical consequences, not unhelpful to Hussein. The extremist PFLP declared its dissidence. They contended that the Palestine Liberation Movement (PLM) should constitute the basis for the radicalization of the whole Arab world. George Habash and particularly his rival, the extreme leftist Arab Nationalist Nayef Hawatmah, even referred to the leaders of *al-Fatah* as "feudalists." Arafat, who had previously eschewed any political involvements, will have to direct much of his energy and effort (as well as those of his colleagues) at external and internal political action. In addition to the internal pressures and conspiracies of any movement, Arafat exposed himself to the vast conspiratorial resources and experience of heads of Arab states, most of whom at the moment seem to desire a political settlement. The important question for Jordan's immediate future is: Will the PLM succeed in infiltrating at least one of the Arab state armies? Assuming a settlement is reached between Israel and Egypt and/or Jordan, both parties would feel agreement-bound to bear down heavily upon the activities of the Palestinian groups.

Guerrilla activities from Jordan declined in December, 1968-January, 1969. This was partly due to the air-strikes of the Israelis, especially against the Iraqi army units in Jordan. These strikes further alienated East Jordanians from the guerrillas. Attention moved to Lebanon (the Israeli commando raid on Beirut airport) and to Egypt, where the Palestinian Liberation Movement was getting ready for its meetings.

While the Nasser-sponsored Second Solidarity Conference of the Arab People concluded its meetings at the end of January, 1969, the Palestine National Council met to reorganize the PLM. By February 4 the latter elected a new Executive for the PLO, chaired by al-Fatah leader Yasir Arafat. Briefly, the new Executive is overwhelmingly controlled by al-Fatah. While the new policy is further removed from official Egyptian and Jordanian attitudes to the Arab-Israeli conflict, the PLM paradoxically became more dependent on help from the Arab states.

The Arabs in early 1969 were at a crossroads regarding the Palestine Question. The Arab states (especially Jordan and Egypt) clearly wanted settlement. The Palestinians under al-Fatah leadership wanted no less than the total destruction of Israel by force. The gulf between these two camps has been widening. The powers have become involved on the side of the states. This conflict could lead to a widespread conservative reaction in Jordan and Egypt, leading up to a suppression of the Palestine Liberation Movement by forcing it to accept whatever arrangement the states come to with Israel. This is not so much because the "official" Arabs do not wish the Palestinians to get their own land back, but because the Palestinians in typical Arab style, feeling their current popularity, are proclaiming, or at least implying, that their movement will come to constitute the only genuine revolution in the Arab world. This is nothing less than a veiled threat to established Arab governments.

Finally, the recent hardening of the official Jordanian and Lebanese attitudes and measures against the PLM reflect three external constraints: (1) tacit approval of Egypt and perhaps indirectly Russia, (2) continued Israeli military capacity to deal effectively with trouble on the armistice lines, and (3) continued American patronage of these two states, and the presence of the U.S. Sixth Fleet in the Mediterranean.

Inter-Arab Relations

Arab attacks on Jordan virtually stopped in the first year after the Six-Day War, as did most inter-Arab verbal strife. As the Palestine Liberation Movement became more active and its attitude to the Arab-Israel conflict more intransigent (and therefore removed from the official position of the Egyptian and Jordanian governments), so did the relationship of Jordan with some of the Arab states undergo a change. Thus, even though relations with Syria were strained before the June war, they worsened at least until February, 1969. Since the Ba'ath regime took power in Baghdad in July, 1968, relations with Iraq have also deteriorated. We know, for instance, that Hussein had requested former President Abdel Rahman Aref of Iraq to replace the known Ba'athi officer, General Hasan al-Naqib, commanding officer of the Iraqi division in Jordan, primarily because he was giving too much fire-cover to Palestinian guerrillas. Aref complied; Bakr, however, returned Naqib to his command in Jordan against Hussein's wishes.

However, since the war, Hussein found in Nasser—another hard-pressed Arab ruler—a close associate and ally; and together they managed for almost two years to maintain an official line favoring the political or diplomatic settlement of the Arab-Israeli conflict. Thus, whereas Jordan's relations with Egypt improved after 1965-1966, they became close and cordial only after the June war—a condition which had never prevailed since the country became an independent kingdom in 1946.

Many observers expected Hussein's kingdom to collapse after the June, 1967, war. To suggest that this has not occurred because of Hussein's political ability alone would be ludicrous. What is interesting is that after June, 1967, no Arab state has been in a position to undermine the existence of any other Arab state—a distinct departure from pre-June, 1967, days. To be sure, Hussein's successful search for security in "collective" Arab action (the Khartoum Conference and after), together with the financial and military assistance he has received from some Arab states and the West, have helped him to retain his kingdom. The very close relationship Hussein established with Nasser also helped. Until the Israeli raids against Karameh in March and April, 1968, the Palestine guerrilla organizations were in no position to threaten seriously his authority; Hussein's Bedouin army units could have dealt decisively with dissident armed groups. Above all, the Palestinian organizations themselves were undergoing change in a still-unpublicized power struggle whose protagonists and nature have become clearer only recently, and specifically in February, 1969.

In this connection, the loyalty of army officers is crucial. The survival of present-day Arab regimes rests in their hands. Hussein, who continues to re-equip and retrain his army, is likely to maintain his position of at least equal internal strength vis-à-vis the armed Palestinians. So long as he is diplomatically supported by Nasser and some of the Western powers, his position is fairly secure.

A source of added strength for Hussein in contrast to the Palestinian Liberation Movement was that socioeconomic policy and action continued to be the prerogative of the national government. There was no evidence that the PLM pretended to be more than a political-military organization and operation. Until very recently, it did not offer wide-scale social-action programs to its people. Thus UNRWA still shares most of the cost for refugees. The government sponsors, directs, and implements public housing, schools, and other social programs.

The inability of the PLM so far to establish an extensive political base in the occupied territories suggests that a further division between them and the West-Bankers is not unlikely.

During the early postwar period when the Israelis felt that Hussein was expendable, the idea of an autonomous Palestinian entity on the West Bank, tied to Israel, was put forward. It briefly appealed to some Palestinian leaders and West Bank notables, for example Anwar Nuseibeh of Jerusalem, Jaabari of Hebron, Hamdi Kanaan of Nablus, and others. But the idea was soon relinquished by Israel, partly because of international diplomatic objections, and partly because suddenly the Palestinians on the West Bank began to identify with Jordan by expressing their loyalty to Hussein. This was perhaps one of the war's most interesting consequences, for it gave Hussein a moral-political claim for the return of the West Bank to his kingdom.

The political evolution of East Jordan depends to a large extent on events in the surrounding countries of Iraq, Syria, and Lebanon. In Lebanon, the Karameh government in 1969 clearly clamped down on security in its southern border region with Israel. Only residents of that area were allowed there without military authorization. Moreover, the new Israeli military tactic of hitting Palestine guerrilla centers in the Arab states seriously affected their training and morale. In addition, as soon as say, Saudi Arabia feels strong militarily, Hussein's Jordan might further dissociate itself from the PLM. On the other hand, so long as East Jordan remains the most convenient base of operations for the Palestine guerrillas, *al-Fatah*-controlled PLM will continue to coexist with Hussein's regime.

Since that time, in view of further development in the relations between the PLM and the Lebanese government (e.g., the crisis of October, 1969) there have been indications of a shift in official Israeli attitudes towards the Palestinians and Jordan. Israel has moved closer to a recognition of the existence of a Palestinian national entity, and may have even, via press and radio directed at the Palestinians, encouraged them on both sides of the Jordan to view themselves as such and therefore separate from King Hussein's Jordan. Implicit in this new approach is perhaps an Israeli attempt to nurture a Palestinian entity distinct from both Hussein's Jordan and the PLM.

Jordan's essentially conservative orientation is not in question. The same conservative orientation probably prevails in the rank and file of the *al-Fatah*-PLM organization, whose vast majority consists of Muslim peasants. The avowed Marxist, radical revolutionary PFLP is too small a group to constitute any meaningful constraint on Jordanian policy, domestically or externally. So long as outside help continues to pour in, East Jordan under Hussein can carry on indefinitely in the near future.

V. Prospects

The four countries of the Fertile Crescent were directly affected by the Arab-Israeli war of June, 1967. Syria and Jordan lost territory now under Israeli occupation. Lebanon suffered a massive retaliatory raid against its international airport and civilian air fleet; and the delicate Muslim-Christian balance which constitutes the Lebanese political system has been threatened by the emergence of Palestinian militants intent on operating against Israel from Lebanese territory. In Jordan the old Palestinian versus Transjordanian (West Bank vs. East) dichotomy has acquired new significance. In Syria the extreme "leftist" military regime isolated the country from the other Arab states with its radical stand against Israel, while exposing the country to the long retaliatory arm of Israeli military power. Fifteen months after the war, these factors forced Syria to realign its position vis-à-vis its Arab neighbors. Even Iraq, most remote of the four states from the immediate arena of the war, suffered Israeli strikes against its air force and its troops stationed in Jordan. At the same time, Iraq must deal with its permanent problem of internal sedition, engendered by the separatist Kurds.

The general overall constraint on the policies of the Fertile Crescent countries is, for the moment, the massive Israeli military presence in the area. The most vexing aspect of the ongoing Arab-Israeli conflict (aside from the possibility of another June, 1967) is the prospect of a confrontation between these states and the Palestine Liberation Movement. The PLM must either compromise its radical goal to destroy Israel or risk an armed clash with the security forces of the Arab states. The argument often invoked against such an eventuality is that no Arab ruler dares test the loyalty of his army and its officers. This hypothetical formulation assumes that Arab army-officer loyalty to the PLM is a foregone conclusion, an established fact.

Yet King Hussein has declared that he would consider it against his country's best interests should the guerrillas attempt to use Jordan as a permanent base.

Even if the Arab-Israeli conflict miraculously dissipated, however, powerful internal constraints will continue for the present to shape the political future of the Fertile Crescent: (1) social fragmentation within the states, (2) inordinate power in the hands of army officers, and (3) stunted ideological development. It is misleading to approach each factor in isolation, for the fact is that they are mutually reinforcing. For example, the exposure of Syria and Iraq to military government in the last decade has revived the political significance of the social divisions within these states. *Ancien regimes* of conservative Muslim politicians and native middle classes have been effectively destroyed, along with their fledgling parties. They have been replaced by military rulers whose ethnic and sectarian rivalries constitute one of the major sources of internal conflict. These divisions weaken state authority and render long-term policymaking, the kind resulting from clearly defined ideological bases, very difficult.

One is thus inclined to doubt the effectiveness of the nation-state as a definable political unit, even for purposes of political analysis, in the Fertile Crescent. Yet it is the only political unit now in existence. The weakness of the local basis for a state national entity has made it easier for its inhabitants to opt for an abstract Arab nationalism in order to assuage their national-identity problem. The lack of proper means to achieve the latter and the absence of a real basis for the development of the former have kept these societies in a perpetually weak political state. Rulers can largely ignore their people, safe in the knowledge that their fragmented societies cannot act collectively. The people fall back on old ethnic and communal affiliations that still offer them some sense of cohesiveness and identity. The game of politics is played among and within limited political officer groups. After the defeat of the Arabs in June, 1967, scarcely a ripple of protest was heard against military leadership, an indication of a weak and divided society. Perhaps the main obstacle to development, the most powerful restraint on any Fertile Crescent government, is the very weakness of a society that stubbornly resists true nationhood.

The roots of military power-struggles run deep. Sedition in the Iraqi army occurred four years after independence (1936); in Egypt four years after the end of British control over certain aspects of army training; in Syria three years after independence; in Jordan two or three attempted coups failed for reasons peculiar to the civil-military relationship in that country.

When older indigenous social institutions and political arrangements were replaced by imported postindependence forms, the resultant chaos invited military pre-eminence in politics. For example, even the greatest early political party, the Egyptian Wafd, failed to formulate a socio-economic program beyond opposition to foreign control. The dissipation of the Wafd's influence during discouraging postindependence difficulties led to the rise of the military in Egypt.

The ideological factor is mixed and often fused with the personal factor in Syria, Iraq and Jordan, where primary loyalty belongs to the family, the sect, the ethnic group. Even the polarity of Lebanese politics primarily reflects the Muslim-Christian communal division, rather than ideological preferences.

Culturally, socially, and emotionally, the ethos of Islam prevails on a mass level in Syria, Iraq, and Jordan. Religious dignitaries and teachers continue to enjoy informal influence over the rural masses. National political leaders avoid minimizing the importance of Islam. To this extent, Islam and the conservatism that is associated with it constitute a constraint on policy. Yet Islam has historically done the bidding of the ruler of the day; in this sense, a forceful ruler may neutralize Islamic sources of opposition.

On the other hand, there is another revolutionary-populist kind of Islamic conservatism which could conceivably influence political evolution in the Fertile Crescent states. Why it has not done so, and why it is not likely to do so in the future, is that the realities of the power structure demand non-Islamic appearances, appurtenances, and friends. Thus, *al-Fatah* is basically a Muslim Palestinian Arab organization. By this token *al-Fatah* can claim pre-eminence over other Palestinian guerrilla groups such as the PFLP, which subscribes to an alien non-Islamic ideology.

Another consequence of the June, 1967, war has been the conservative reaction in Egypt and other Arab states. This phenomenon is buttressed by subvention from Arab rulers and regimes long considered conservative. To this extent, further attempts to restructure radically the power bases in these states are unlikely for some time to come.

The independence movement in the postwar period provided the basis for a dynamic of state survival. This dynamic served to brake wider pan-Arab nationalist movements and aims. But the identification of Arab nationalism with a Sunni élite presented serious problems for the Shia in Iraq, the heterodox minorities in Syria, and the Christians of Lebanon, who viewed the Sunni notables with suspicion and fear. When this Sunni leadership became the governing group in Iraq and Syria upon independence, the minorities were consequently attracted to both the PPS and the Ba'ath. In the PPS, the minorities saw a non-Muslim Syrian nationalist movement which could act as a counterforce to the Muslim-dominated Arab nationalism of the ruling classes. The Ba'ath, on the other hand, was attractive to both the town Sunni intelligentsia and the minorities because of its forcefully articulated (though ambiguous) secular arguments for nationalism.

The greatest limitation on any such integrative development is the fact that no Arab state disposes of the kind of military and political strength which could bring it to fruition. Vested state interests that have coalesced over the last quarter of a century instinctively oppose Arab unity. One must conclude that the verbalized ideological premise of the 1950s and 1960s—an abstract Arab nationalism—has existed only as a superficial consensus between societies lacking sufficient social cohesion to cooperate at much less ambitious levels of integration.

The Refugees as a Special Issue

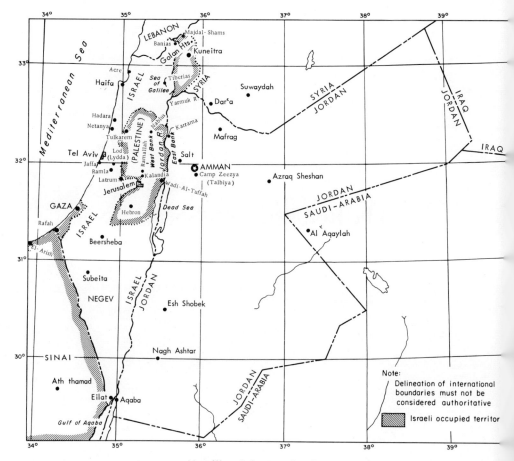

Map III — Palestine, Israel, and Jordan

PART III. The Refugees as a Special Issue

The two chapters in this part concentrate upon a specific dispute between Israel and the Arabs, the fate of the Palestine refugees. Peretz surveys the dispute since its inception in 1947, while Dodd and Barakat report on and analyze their own field research. Both chapters treat the refugee problem as a genuine conflict of interest, that is to say, as a political issue. At the same time, both are ameliorative and to some extent conciliatory, singling out component issues that can be handled analytically and that, if clarified or resolved, might contribute to a solution. For one thing, they assess the personal costs of displacement to the refugees. For another, they deal with the long-standing question whether and at what costs the Palestinian refugees could be absorbed into the states of the region, rather than meeting their demand for a separate Palestinian state. Peretz in general terms and Dodd and Barakat on the basis of their own survey data do this by examining the social, psychological, and political pressures that inhibit or sometimes induce economic absorption into the Arab state's economy.

Both chapters depict the refugee movement as much more than an issue of economic absorptive capacity, one that is rooted in sentiment and not easily placated. Chapter 8 considers the salient political question of the future of Palestine as it exists in the operations of Palestinian refugees. Chapter 9 presents data on two conditions important to the feasibility of the refugees' return to their homes: (1) the extent to which the refugees, both "new" and "old", were economically integrated in their communities prior to June 1967; and (2) whether those refugees who wished to return immediately, even under Israeli occupation, were 'mild' or 'militant' in their attitudes toward Israel.

None of this is to deny that the political nature of the issues involved, the conflict of interest over the national aspirations of the Palestinian Arabs, overrides the options of employment and political acceptance within existing states. Some protagonists claim that the Arab states could have absorbed the refugees into their economies but perpetuate the human misery involved for their own political purposes. Yet all the Arab states involved have to live with a great deal of human misery among their own populations. Leaving aside the issue of Israel's moral responsibility, the Arabs' failure to deal with this humanitarian issue has been no more conspicuous than their failure (or the failure of other low-income states) to deal with other humanitarian issues that are less unmistakably their own.

Efforts to solve the refugee problem also run afoul of an Arab objective to avoid conceding juridicial standing to Israeli control over territory claimed by and on behalf of the refugees. The Arab states are not the first to use *de jure* nonrecognition to oppose *de facto* political changes of which

267

they disapproved. Their diplomatic position with respect to Israel is comparable to the American diplomatic stance of nonrecognition, adopted with respect to the expanding hegemony of Japan on the Chinese mainland during the 1930s, to the Communist takeover in Russia in 1918, to the Axis power takeovers in Europe in the 1930s, and to the Communist Chinese takeover on the mainland of China in 1948. Neither, for that matter, has Israel been the first state to change the status quo unilaterally by a series of political *faits accomplis* which use time to erode the will of the opponent to resist the new status quo.

Don Peretz is Professor of Political Science and Director of the Southwest Asian and North African (SWANA) Program at the State University of New York at Binghamton, and author of "Israel and the Palestine Arabs" in *The Middle East: Selected Readings* (Boston: Houghton Mifflin, 1968).

Halim Barakat and Peter Dodd are both on the faculty of the American University, Beirut. They are coauthors of *River without Bridges* (Beirut: Institute for Palestine Studies, 1968).

CHAPTER 8

The Palestine Arab Refugee Problem

Don Peretz

I. Introduction

For many years the Palestine Arab refugee problem has loomed large in the Middle East. It first attracted international attention just a little over two years after the end of World War II, in November, 1947, when strife between Jews and Arabs erupted into armed struggle. At first only a few Palestinians left their homes for neighboring Arab countries, but the number grew until at the end of the Arab-Israeli war of 1947-1948 the vast majority of Arabs in Israeli-held territories had left. The problem became a focal point of world concern and has remained so during the more than 20-year struggle between Israel and the Arab states.

From 1947 until the present the refugee problem has been a symbol of failure to resolve the Arab-Israeli conflict. To the Arabs the continuing problem represents the injustices to which the Palestine Arabs have been subjected by the Western powers and by Israel; to Israelis its existence symbolizes the adamant refusal of the Arab world to come to terms wth reality and to accept responsibility for a problem the Arabs themselves created; to many Americans the problem is typical of the frustrations her policy-makers have encountered in trying to deal with the Palestine dilemma and, in a larger context, with the whole Middle East.

Many Westerners compare the Palestine refugee problem with other refugee problems such as those which arose during the Greek-Turkish war in the 1920s and the India-Pakistan war following partition in 1947. In the latter instances the respective nations were willing to accept within their borders hundreds of thousands and millions of refugees who fled from enemy territory, permitting them to become citizens. The Palestine situation differs because of refusal by most Palestinians to accept other nationality (except in the case of Jordan, but even in Jordan where most have become citizens of the Hashemite kingdom, they continue to identify themselves as Palestinians). Furthermore, the host countries, except Jordan, have refused to grant citizenship to the Palestinians for a variety of reasons that will be examined. Not only are most countries reluctant to extend citizenship to the Palestine refugees, but they seldom extend it to each other's nationals; thus tens of thousands of Syrians are not accepted as citizens of

Lebanon, nor did many thousands of Lebanese who had lived for generations in Egypt become citizens of that country.

Perhaps because the refugee situation is always visible, it has attracted
more attention than other less obvious, but potentially more disruptive,
problems plaguing the Middle East. Certainly until June, 1967, the refugee
problem had received greater attention at the United Nations than most
other problems of the Middle East. It has appeared on the agenda of every
session of the General Assembly since 1948, when it was emphasized in the
reports of the United Nations Mediator, Count Folke Bernadotte. The
United Nations Conciliation Commission for Palestine (UNCCP) spent
much of its time and efforts, although with little avail, on attempts to resolve
the refugee dilemma, leading finally to the nearly complete inactivity if not
total demise of the Commission.

Throughout its involvement in the Arab-Israeli conflict, the United
States government has repeatedly sought to ease tensions in the area by
"rational" amelioration if not solution of the refugee plight. Often American
"rational" approaches to problems of the Middle East have either over-
looked or discounted the extent to which they have involved deeply held
emotions that are not susceptible to Western-oriented concepts of what is
"rational." This has resulted in a tendency to dismiss non-Western and, in
this case, Middle Eastern concepts of principles such as "justice" or "equity"
as mere abstractions inapplicable in the "real" or "traditional" world of
power politics, science, and technology. From the early days of the Clapp
report in 1949[1] through the various schemes projected by John Blandford,[2]
Eric Johnston,[3] and Joseph Johnson,[4] American policymakers have singled
out the refugee problem as the one whose solution is most urgent in ending
the Arab-Israeli conflict and in bringing stability to the region.

It is the purpose of this study to examine the refugee situation in the
context of various Middle East problems, to analyze many of the proposals
that have been offered for solution, and to inquire into prospects of these
proposals as contributions to solution of larger problems in the Palestine
conflict and in the Middle East.

From the genesis of the problem until the present, it has been difficult to
determine many of the pertinent facts: the causes of refugee flight, the
number of refugees, the conditions under which the refugees have been

[1]Gordon Clapp, former chairman of the TVA, was chairman of the U.N. Economic
Survey Mission in the Middle East established by the UNCCP in 1949.

[2]John Blandford was one of the early Directors of UNRWA.

[3]Eric Johnston was appointed as a Special Representative in the Middle East by President Eisenhower in 1953.

[4]Dr. Joseph Johnson was appointed as a Special Representative of the UNCCP in
1961.

living, the actual desires of the refugees, political organization among them, and the extent to which they have or have not been absorbed in the host countries in which they found refuge. Reasons for lack of information or for varied interpretations of available data are many. Precise information about the Palestine Arab community of which the refugees constituted a major part was lacking when the problem arose. Population figures were based on estimates compiled by the British Mandatory government, derived from the last census conducted in Palestine during the 1930s. In the turmoil and upheaval of the Palestine war and in the unsettled conditions of the surrounding areas to which the refugees fled, it was difficult to gather accurate statistical data. Indeed, in many of the host countries there existed only scanty statistical data for the indigenous population. Furthermore, as conditions became better organized, collection of such information, although theoretically possible, was regarded as politically suspicious. Neither the host countries nor the United Nations gathered precise data about the refugees between 1948 and 1968, and much information concerning the numbers of refugees and their conditions was based on projections from earlier estimates under uncertain and unstable conditions.

The data that were collected were frequently suspect as being partisan by both Arabs and Israelis. Since neither Arabs nor Israelis placed great confidence in the United Nations or its employees, there were frequent charges that those administering the U.N. refugee relief programs were biased toward one side or another. Because of the great suspicion, the deep emotions, and the hostile atttitudes engendered by the Palestine problem, outsiders, or those who were involved but sought objectivity, were frequently attacked for their views or for simple observations. For this reason the United Nations and many scholars were deterred from undertaking examination in depth of certain aspects of the refugee problem. Nevertheless, it continued to be regarded by many as the chief obstacle to stability in the Middle East.

Without some solution of the refugee problem, it was held, regional as well as national development would be stymied. Since plans for regional development involved use of the labor, capital, and land and water resources of countries that were centers of refugee concentration as well as those that had only small numbers of refugees, such plans could not be conceived and executed without progress toward the solution of the refugee problem.

Throughout the 20 years of attempted negotiations on Middle East problems, a vicious circle seems to revolve around Arab inisistence that other problems cannot be managed unless the refugee fate is first resolved, and the Israeli determination that progress toward solution of the refugee problem cannot be made unless the Arab states accept the political realities of Israel's existence, Arab responsibility for the displaced Palestinians, and initiation of attempts to resettle the refugees within the context of overall regional development.

The dimensions of the refugee problem were radically altered by the Six-Day War in June, 1967. Not only were the numbers of refugees suddenly increased, but several categories of newly displaced persons were created by the fighting and by subsequent military or paramilitary actions. Attention, during the previous two decades, had focused on the Palestinians classified as refugees in Gaza, Jordan, Lebanon, and Syria, but new groups of displaced persons included several hundred thousand who had crossed on international frontier, such as Syrians who fled the Golan Heights and Egyptians who evacuated the Suez Canal Zone. There were also now various categories of Palestinian refugees. They included those who remained in their camps or residences from the 1948 era; those who fled during the first Arab-Israeli war and who again fled in 1967-1968; and those who were "new" refugees, displaced from their homes for the first time in the June war or its aftermath. Thus, the term "Palestine refugee," or "Palestine Arab refugee," covers only some of the persons displaced in the Palestine conflict, with almost as many displaced Arabs excluded from the category as are included.

In addition to the Arabs there are several hundred thousand Jews who emigrated from Morocco, Tunisia, Libya, Algeria, Egypt, Yemen, Aden, Syria, and Iraq since 1948 as a direct consequence of tensions created by the conflict between Zionist and Arab nationalism. The exodus of Jews from Arab countries was also substantially increased as a result of the Six-Day War with thousands departing from their ancestral lands.

Not only were hundreds of thousands of persons newly displaced, but the political and strategic aspects of the Palestine problem were altered by the June war. Israel became a principal Arab refugee host government through occupation of Gaza and the West Bank of Jordan; the whole of the territory disputed in the Palestine conflict fell under Israel's control; and the political dispute between Israel and the Arab states was greatly intensified as Palestine Arab consciousness became inflamed. The new situation altered the range of political choices available in the search for solutions to the Palestine problem of which the refugees had become the most visible symbol. These aspects of the situation will be discussed at greater length in the next section.

II. Origin of the Problem

Examination of the origins of the refugee problem is important because of the great emotions stirred by the myths, the realities, and the half-truths surrounding events leading to the flight. Neither Arabs, Israelis, nor their protagonists would deny that the refugee problem is no isolated phenomenon. Although during the past 20 years attempts have been made to deal with the refugees in isolation from larger issues, the problem has, since its beginning, been an integral part of the Palestine conflict. Had there been no violence between Arab and Zionist nationalisms, there probably would have been no Arab refugee problem, no problem of Jews displaced from Arab countries, nor the mass dislocations caused by the June, 1967, war.[5]

An aspect of the whole Arab-Israeli conflict frequently forgotten in contemporary discussions is the extent to which the Western world is both involved in and responsible for the conflict. Although both Arab and Zionist nationalists charge the West with betrayal of promises of assistance, both received assistance from the West at one or another stages of their development. The Zionist movement received encouragement and aid from Great Britian through the Balfour Declaration in 1917, the establishment of the Mandate for Palestine after World War I, and in the development of the Jewish national home in the early days of the Mandate. This assistance was rendered in the furtherance of Bristish imperial aspirations despite opposition from the then Arab majority of Palestine. During World War I, Great Britain also, to further its ambitions and to strengthen its position in the Middle East, a vital hinterland to its Indian and other eastern imperial outposts, gave political and other support to the budding Arab nationalist movement. Support for Zionist aspirations in Palestine and for a controlled Arab nationalist movement confronted the British with their most serious and most irreconcilable dilemma resulting in policies

[5]In discussion of the Palestine problem and the Arab-Israeli conflict there is often confusion of the terms "Jewish" and "Zionist." Until the 1960s many Jews attempted to differentiate between them, using "Jewish" as a term referring to religion, and "Zionist" as a term referring to a national movement, most of whose partisans were of the Jewish faith. More recently, especially since the 1967 war, the government of Israel and the World Zionist movement have tended to de-emphasize any such distinction and there is increasing emphasis on equating the terms "Jewish" and "Zionist." This tendency is supported by the wide extent to which Jewish communities and organizations all over the world rallied to Israel's support in the war which seemed to large number of Jews a war for Israel's survival of paramount, even of prophetic, importance in the history of Judaism. Prior to World War II there were other Jewish nationalist movements, but since the war these movements, such as the Bund in Eastern Europe, have lost their identity and their following, with the result that today the only Jewish nationalist movement of any consequence is Zionism, which in turn has increasingly come to be identified with any Jewish group identification, particularly of a nationalist character. On the other hand, many Arab officials, who at one time failed to distinguish between the terms "Jewish" and "Zionist," have in recent years put more stress in government statements and propaganda on the distinction.

that seemed, at best, inconsistent to the parties concerned and, at worst, as outright favoritism toward the "opposite side." During World War II, Great Britain further encouraged controlled Arab nationalism through support for the newly formed Arab League. The ambivalence of British policy was evident in the postwar era when British officers were supplied to the Jordanian Arab Legion and British military equipment to several Arab armies engaged in the war with Israel.

American policy has been no less inconsistent or ambivalent. On one hand, the so-called King-Crane Commission designated by President Woodrow Wilson to investigate the wishes of inhabitants of the Middle East after the war reported widespread Arab hostility to Zionist aspirations. On the other hand, numerous U.S. Congressional resolutions and Presidential pronouncements or acts since 1918 have supported Zionist aspirations. The apex of American support for Zionist aspirations was reached after World War II when it became evident to what extent the Nazis in Europe had exterminated the Jewish population of the continent. While continuing to express sympathy for Arab nationalist goals, the American government also gave support—political, moral, and material—to postwar Zionist goals and to the newly formed state of Israel, thus earning the suspicion if not the enmity of the Arabs. Nevertheless, it becomes obvious that as a result of their respective policies in the region both Great Britain and the United States have become not only involved, but in large part responsible for the Arab-Israeli conflict and the resulting refugee problem.

When Great Britain, beset by a myriad of domestic and foreign troubles, decided in 1947 to place the burdens of the apparently insoluble dilemma on the United Nations, Zionist and Arab nationalist claims had already become irreconcilable. There was no longer a point of compromise between Arab nationalist insistence on an independent Palestine governed by its Arab majority and Zionism whose goal was now proclaimed in the Biltmore Program[6] to establish Palestine as a Jewish commonwealth. The United Nations General Assembly, unable to find any other seemingly rational compromise, recommended that the disputed country be divided into a Jewish state, an Arab state, and an international enclave to include Jerusalem and Bethlehem.

Although the great majority of Palestine's Jewish population and their supporters abroad were willing to accept the U.N. recommendation as a compromise, the leaders of the country's Arab majority and nationalists in the surrounding Arab nations declared the U.N. decision unjust, contravening the fundamental principle of self-determination, and they organized to resist it. Throughout Palestine tensions between Jews and

[6]Named after the Biltmore Hotel in New York City where the American Emergency Committee for Zionist Affairs approved the program in May, 1942.

Arabs grew to an angry pitch. What little cooperation had existed between the two communities soon came to a halt. Few members of either group dared venture into territory of the other. In such a hostile atmosphere it took but a small spark to ignite widespread flames of violence. Within hours after the United Nations partition recommendation in November, 1947, the first incidents occurred. Small bands of agitated Arabs demonstrating against the resolution ran into groups of Jews celebrating their United Nations victory. The situation was much like that in other post-World War II cases of intercommunal stress such as existed between Hindus and Muslims in India and Greeks and Turks in Cyprus. Blows with fists and sticks and stones were followed by retaliation which soon escalated into arson, dynamiting of homes and public buildings, and armed ambushes. Armed Arab bands searched out and attacked Jews traveling on public highways or in isolated settlements, and Jews reciprocated with attacks on Arab individuals, villages, and sectors of several larger towns and cities. The violence burst into a civil war with the British maintaining an official position of nonintervention except in instances where British lives were involved. Actually there were varied responses in some of which British officers or officials aided the Arab forces and in others they assisted the Jews.

During the civil war phase of the conflict the Palestine Arab forces were assisted by volunteers and paramilitary units from surrounding countries while the Jewish community encouraged and received assistance, both Jewish and non-Jewish, from Europe and the United States. Within hours after proclamation of the Jewish state of Israel on May 14-15, 1948, the armed forces of Egypt, Syria, Jordan, Iraq, and Lebanon came to assist the Palestine Arab units. The British had withdrawn to small enclaves in preparation for final evacuation within a few weeks. The conflict, which began as a civil war between Palestinian Arabs and Jews, now erupted into an international war involving armed forces of at least half a dozen nations.

As the fighting spread throughout Palestine it engulfed increasing numbers of noncombatants until no person in the country could feel free from danger. Neither Arabs, Jews, nor neutrals could be assured of safety if they traveled from one settlement to another. Those living along the borders of urban areas divided between Jews and Arabs were often the targets of snipers from one side or the other. The country was for all practical purposes divided between Jewish and Arab armed forces. By the end of 1948 each side had tried to clear its territory of those considered as security risks. Arabs generally considered Jews as "the enemy" and most Jews regarded both individual Arabs and large concentrations of them as potentially subversive. In such an atmosphere it was inevitable that many people who were not directly involved in military activity would become victims of violence.

Throughout the period of civil war, between November, 1947, and the military action by the neighboring states in May, 1948, local Arabs attempted to dislodge small enclaves of Jews settled in heavily populated Arab areas, such as those who lived in the Old City of Jerusalem or in the Etzion block of settlements near Hebron. Jewish forces attempted to root out heavy concentrations of Arabs believed to be endangering their sectors of urban centers as those in the corridor between Tel Aviv and Jerusalem, or along the border between Tel Aviv and Jaffa. In Haifa the Jewish mayor attempted to persuade the Arab inhabitants to remain. However, after the defeat of Arab forces in the area by the Haganah[7], most Arab residents, fearing their fate in Jewish-controlled territory, fled or were encouraged to depart rather than remain under Jewish armed control. After the outbreak of full-scale war there was no longer any ambivalence among either Jews or Arabs about the enemy. Each side fought to consolidate under its control as much territory in Palestine as possible.

Reports of incidents, both true and false, spread like wildfire through the Palestine Arab community, and many thousands of villagers fled without ever seeing an Israeli soldier. Furthermore, many notables of the Palestine Arab community were already absent, leaving most of the common people without leadership. In many Arab areas essential municipal and social services, which had been operated and managed by the Mandatory government, collapsed on the eve of the British departure. With schools closed, and water, sanitation, health, and other public services inaccessible; with no effective leadership present; and with widely circulated stories of Jewish atrocities prevailing in the Arab community, the atmosphere was conducive to flight. Little heed was paid to pleas, warnings, or threats broadcast from neighboring Arab capitals against abandoning the homeland. Strong impetus was given to flight psychology after the Deir Yaseen slaughter of Arab villagers early in April, 1948, by Jewish armed forces. Although leaders of the Jewish Agency[8] denounced the Irgun Tzvai Leumi[9] for its role in the massacre, the action was seized upon by Arab propagandists as evidence typifying Zionist attitudes toward Palestine's

[7]The underground defense force of the Yishuv (Jewish community) in Palestine under the British Mandate; the forerunner of the present Israeli Defense Force.

[8]The Jewish Agency was established in the 1920s to enlist support of world Jewry in developing the Jewish national home in Palestine. Although non-Zionists were represented, it was dominated by Zionist groups, with the greatest representation from Palestine.

[9]National Military Organization, an outgrowth of a dissident Zionist group which broke with the Jewish Agency.

Arab population. Word of Deir Yaseen spread through the whole Arab world, greatly exacerbating the fears of villagers and townsmen and speeding up their hasty departure for more secure regions. By the end of hostilities and the armistice agreements in 1949, more than three-quarters of the Arab population in Israeli-held areas had departed, radically altering the demographic patterns of the Jewish state. According to the U.N. partition plan nearly half of Israel's population in 1947-1948 was to have been Arab.[10] As a result of the Arab flight, the remaining Arab minority constituted only about 10 percent of the population. Most of the approximately 170,000 Arabs remaining within Israel's armistice frontiers lived in areas that had been rapidly incorporated during the period between the truces, or within villages acquired along the Jordanian frontier as a result of the armistice agreement.

Why, it may be asked, did the Jewish population not flee from areas of heavy fighting? The Yishuv, or Palestine Jewish Community, was far better organized and had much more central direction than the country's Arab community. Before the end of the Mandate the Yishuv had established its own shadow government including military and security forces, and even its own postal system. When fighting engulfed Jewish settlements they were much better prepared to deal with emergencies and were able to continue day-to-day functions of civil life that had disappeared from many Arab towns and villages. Furthermore, the Jews had no place to withdraw to, unless they were to evacuate the country completely and cross the Mediterranean. Most Jews in the new state of Israel regarded the struggle as one of life or death, whereas Arab residents of the country could depart to neighboring regions with the hope that they would return to their homes after the war.

The fate of the Palestine refugees soon became a major issue in the dispute between Israel and the Arab nations. Most refugees fled to avoid the cataclysm of war and to seek temporary safety. The refugees, the Arab host countries, and the international community expected that most of them would return to their homes at the conclusion of hostilities. The host countries had not anticipated so large or so long-term an exodus. None of them was prepared to deal with the tens of thousands of Palestinians who flocked across their borders, crowding urban centers and generally creating a crisis atmosphere. It soon became evident that the

---

[10]In the partition plan Jewish-Arab Jerusalem was separated from both the Jewish and the Arab states, although Arab and Jewish populations of Jerusalem could become citizens of their respective national entities. The leadership of the Jewish state assumed that the more than 340,000 European Jewish refugees interned in Cyprus would immigrate to Israel as soon as independence was achieved, thus immediately altering the ratio of 66 percent Jews and 33 percent Arabs.

meager resources of Lebanon, Syria, Transjordan, and Egypt could not cope with this emergency situation. Not only were the refugees an economic burden, but they were also a source of potential political and social unrest, likely to disrupt already restive societies. Furthermore, acceptance of the principle of resettlement was tantamount to acceptance of defeat at the hands of Israel.

Arab attitudes toward the problem were formed during its early stages and have by and large remained unchanged. The Arabs charge that the exodus was caused by Israeli atrocities, therefore Arabs are not responsible. Since the international community, through the United Nations, was an accomplice in the creation of Israel, the United Nations must bear responsibility for care of those displaced as a result of its recommendation. Initially the host countries urged that all refugees be permitted to return to their homes in Israeli-held territory. By the early 1950s official Arab attitudes had somewhat modified. Rather than insistence on complete repatriation, the official position has changed to emphasis upon U.N. General Assembly Resolution 194 (111) of December 11, 1948, which resolved that:

> The refugees wishing to return to their homes and live at peace with their neighbours should be permitted to do so at the earliest practicable date, and that compensation should be paid for the property of those choosing not to return and for loss or damage to property which, under principles of international law or in equity, should be made good by the Governments or authorities responsible.

Arab interpretation of this clause in the resolution is that all refugees be given opportunity to choose whether or not they desire to return to their homes.

Language of the U.N. resolution was adopted from recommendations of Count Bernadotte's final report.[11] Bernadotte forcefully pointed out the need for emergency assistance and urged that the refugees be repatriated as soon as possible. Not only were his recommendations incorporated into U.N. resolutions at this early stage of the conflict, but the wording of paragraph 11 concerning refugee repatriation and compensation was either repeated or recalled at every subsequent session of the Assembly in the context of discussion of the annual activities of the United Nations Relief and Works Agency for Palestine Refugees in the Near East (UNRWA). The problem discussed annually at the United Nations thus became the focus of international attention as the most visible aspects of the Palestine problem.

Resolution 194 also established a United Nations Conciliation Commis-

[11]U.N. General Assembly, 3rd Session, A/648.

sion for Palestine,[12] which was charged with taking "steps to assist the Governments and authorities concerned to achieve a final peace settlement of all questions outstanding between them" and to "facilitate the repatriation, resettlement and economic and social rehabilitation of the refugees and the payment of compensation." From its creation in 1949 to the present, the major thrust of UNCCP's activities has been to resolve or to ameliorate the refugee situation. Although UNCCP still maintains a shadowy existence with an office at U.N. Headquarters in New York, its activities have been sporadic since the early 1950s. Its various subsidiary missions and investigatory groups have met with so little success in dealing with the major tasks assigned them that the organization has for all practical purposes ceased to exist, especially since the June, 1967, war. The activities of UNCCP, in which the United States played a significant and generally a major role, tended to reflect the strength of U.S. desires at any particular time to do something about the Palestine problem, and especially about the refugee question which was seen as the most critical aspect, and key to solution, of the Arab-Israeli conflict.

The position of the Israeli government since 1948 has been that the refugee problem is subsidiary to larger issues, without settlement of which there can be no solution to the refugee problem. Most important for Israel has been the question of national security, which is tantamount to the country's continued existence. Israel has resisted accepting recommendations by the United Nations or by the great powers that her security authorities believe would endanger the country's existence. Initially the Israeli government's Arab refugee policy was ambiguous, attempting to forestall any definite decision on a mass Arab return. In 1949 the Israeli government offered conditionally to take back as many as 100,000 refugees provided the return was part of an overall settlement. Other similar Israeli offers included possible acceptance of responsibility for the refugees in Gaza, if the area were turned over to Israel. However, these early offers were withdrawn when the Arab states insisted that repatriation of all refugees must precede any peace settlement. Israel's security authorities feared the return of hundreds of thousands of Arabs so soon after hostilities. Israelis generally had serious doubts about the prospects of Arab loyalty to the new Jewish state. Within months official policy had solidified against a mass return of Arabs without an overall peace settlement. The Arab states, not Israel, it was charged, were responsible for the flight. Attempts were made to produce data proving that the Arab leaders, in Palestine and in the neighboring countries, had encouraged the refugees to depart. The Israelis claimed that radio broadcasts from Arab countries

[12]Present membership of UNCCP, although inactive, includes France, Turkey, and the United States.

had stirred up fear, calling upon the Palestine Arab community to leave their homes in the hope of returning to reap the fruits of a great victory (attempts to track down such broadcasts have not proved successful despite repeated requests made to both Arab and Israeli officials).

Between its creation in 1948 and June, 1967, Israel and the territory it controlled contained a number of Arabs small enough to control yet large enough in absolute numbers to constitute a distinctive minority group with an identity of its own. Although the Arab minority about doubled during this era from some 160,000 to over 300,000, they were not considered a major threat to national security. In the early days of statehood strict security measures were imposed on areas containing large concentrations of Arabs, but these measures were gradually modified until by 1967 they applied to only a small number of suspects considered dangerous by the security forces. Within the armed forces of Israel, in its border patrol units and other security bodies there were Arabs, mostly Druzes; and a significant number of lower-ranking police officers were also Arab. Israeli self confidence vis-à-vis the Arab minority was the result of its relatively small size and the scarcity of subversive acts attributable to Arab residents. Those responsible for national security or for policies pertaining to the Arab minority were thus not eager to create problems that might accompany any substantial increase in the number of Arabs under their jurisdiction. Small numbers of Palestinians were permitted to return from neighboring countries after strict security clearance, as individual cases within the framework of a family reunion scheme, but there was no authorization for large-scale resettlement or re-establishment of Arab communities formed from returning refugees.

Also significant in determining policy was the Jewish character of the state. Popular sentiment and national leadership conceived of Israel as a Jewish state, created to fulfill Jewish needs and to achieve cultural, political, and social goals of the world Zionist movement. Symbols of national loyalty and slogans used to create unity and national consciousness were Jewish-Zionist, based on political and cultural movements established in the European Diaspora in the decades preceding establishment of the Jewish state. Of what significance could the picture of Theodor Herzl (founder of the Zionist movement), found in most schoolrooms, be to the country's Arab citizens? How could the slogan, "ingathering of the [Jewish] exiles," have meaning to Arab children? How could an Arab minority respond to national holidays related to events commemorating great moments in Jewish history such as the exodus from Egypt or destruction of the temple? The policy of encouraging large-scale Jewish immigration while discouraging the return of significant numbers of Arab refugees was highly consistent with the country's general political, social, and cultural orientation.

In addition to the security and political-cultural basis for Israel's Arab refugee policy there was also an economic rationale. The property abandoned by the Palestine Arabs was a valuable resource helping to make room for hundreds of thousands of Jews who replaced the Arab refugees. The abandoned Arab fields, orchards, vineyards, homes, shops, factories, and businesses provided shelter, economic sustenance, and employment for a significant percentage of the nearly 700,000 new immigrants who came to Israel between May, 1948, and the end of 1951. Israel would have found it far more difficult to more than double its population during this period had it not had access to abandoned Arab property.

The UNCCP estimated that although only a little more than a quarter was considered cultivable, more than 80 percent of Israel's total area of some 20,000 square kilometers represented land abandoned by the Arab refugees (three-quarters of the 16,000 square kilometers counted as former Arab land was submarginal or semidesert state-owned land in the Negev, subject to Bedouin use and tenure rights). Of the 370 new Jewish settlements established between 1948 and the beginning of 1953, 350 were on absentee property. In 1954, more than one-third of Israel's Jewish population lived on absentee property, and nearly a third of the new immigrants (250,000 people) were settled in urban areas abandoned by Arabs. The refugees left whole cities, including Jaffa, Acre, Lydda, Ramleh, Beisan, and Majdal; 388 towns and villages and large parts of 94 other cities and towns, containing nearly a quarter of all the buildings in Israel at that time. Ten thousand Arab shops, businesses, and stores were left in Jewish hands. At the end of the British Mandate, citrus holdings in the area that became Israel totaled about 240,000 dunums (about 50,000 acres), of which over half had been Arab-owned. In 1951-1952, former Arab groves produced 1.25 million boxes of fruit, of which 400,000 were exported, constituting about 10 percent of the country's fruit exports.[13]

Although abandoned Arab property was rapidly absorbed into Israel's Jewish economy facilitating the large influx of immigrants, ownership was initially vested in a Custodian of Absentee Property. Later, large portions

[18]Figures on absentee property documented in Don Peretz, *Israel and the Palestine Arabs* (Washington, D.C.: Middle East Institute, 1958), pp. 164-167; from Israeli sources such as *Ha-Arez, Ha-Boqer, Jerusalem Post, Israeli Government Year-Book;* and A. Granott, *Agrarian Reform and the Record of Israel* (London, 1956). According to the *Israel Government Year-Book,* 5713 (1952), (Jerusalem, 1952), p. 380, the value of all exports for 1951 was 15,983,483 Israeli pounds, of which some 3,800,000 cases of citrus fruits accounted for 5,707,632 Israeli pounds.

of the property under the Custodian's control were parceled out in varying legal forms of ownership. The Custodian received payment, either actual or theoretical, which was supposedly held in account for possible payment of compensation to original owners. The Israeli government's policy toward compensation and some related problems will be discussed later in this study. This section has emphasized the importance of the economic factors shaping Israel's policy toward the return of Arab refugees. Had there been a large-scale return of refugees to their property during the early years of Israel's existence, the character of the Jewish state would have been substantially different.

III. Nature of the Problem

Numbers

From the time the refugee problem became an international concern, there has been great controversy about the number of Palestine Arabs who departed from Israel-held territory. Generally, Israelis or their supporters have intended to make estimates some 20 to 50 percent less than those of the United Nations or Arab observers. Such estimates are not only beclouded by political considerations in which a smaller number would be favored by Israel and a larger one by the Arab host countries, but by technical problems, and those of definition. When the problem arose, statistics were generally unreliable in most Arab countries and procedures for collecting such data were rather unsophisticated. In Arab communities there was general suspicion of the motives behind official collection of population and income information.

The United Nations Economic Survey Mission for the Middle East (known as the Clapp Mission) established by UNCCP in 1949 to examine possibilities of refugee integration, basing its calculations on the population of Palestine in December, 1946 (which in turn was based on previous British Mandatory estimates derived from the 1931 census),[14] estimated that as of September 30, 1949, there were some 726,000 refugees (persons who fled from Israeli-held territory), but a total of 1,019,243 "alleged relief recipients." The difference was accounted for, according to the Mission, by "duplicate registrations, destitute persons and other non-repatriable relief recipients in the different areas." In Arab Palestine alone, the Mission estimated that of the 431,500 alleged relief recipients, only some 280,000 were persons who had fled from Israeli-held territory. The difference was attributed to 69,157 local villagers who were being fed

[14]Although subsequent censuses were planned, they were not carried out because of internal disturbances and administrative difficulties caused by World War II.

by the United Nations and to a 20 percent duplication in the remainder.[15]

Shortly after it began operations in 1950, UNRWA adopted as a working definition of refugees eligible for assistance, a needy person who as a result of the Palestine conflict "lost both his home and his means of livelihood," and whose "normal residence had been Palestine for a minimum period of two years preceding the outbreak of the conflict in 1948. . ."[16] Not all Palestinians who left their homes in 1948 were defined as needy or as eligible for relief. The Clapp Mission estimated that about 652,000 were in need, of whom 17,000 were Jews and 31,000 Arabs living within Israeli-held territory. When UNRWA operations came to a halt in Israel during July, 1952, through an agreement between UNRWA and the Israeli government, the few refugees remaining there became the responsibility of the Israeli government and the problem was no longer considered an international responsibility.

Throughout its existence UNRWA has established varying criteria for need and set different levels at which refugees could receive all or partial UNRWA services. At one end of the spectrum are those entitled to all UNRWA facilities and services; at the other end are those entitled merely to possession of an UNRWA identity card, but to none of the rations, health, education, social welfare, or other benefits. The Agency has attempted with varying degrees of success to eliminate from its ration rolls or as recipients of its assistance those who were neither refugees or who, although refugees, were not qualified to receive assistance according to the various levels of need established. Although over the years more than 500,000 names were deleted from the ration rolls, the degree of success in rectification of refugee estimates depended in large measure upon

---

[15]United Nations Conciliation Commission for Palestine (UNCCP), *Final Report of the United Nations Economic Survey Mission for the Middle East, Part I, Final Report and Appendices*, Report No. A/AC25/6, United Nations, Lake Success, New York, December 28, 1949, p. 23.

[16]United Nations, *Report of the Commissioner-General of UNRWA*, 1 July 1964-30 June 1965, Supplement No. 13, Doc. A/6013 (New York, 1965).

UNRWA limited eligibility or assistance to those in need who were:

"(a) Palestine refugees who, as a result of the conflict, took direct refuge in 1948 in Lebanon, Syria, Jordan, or the Gaza Strip;

"(b) Palestine refugees originally registered with UNRWA in Israel who before 1 July 1952 took refuge in Lebanon, Syria, Jordan, or the Gaza Strip and whose basic rations were removed from the ration roles in Israel;

"(c) Children of the above born after 14 May 1948;

"(d) Palestine refugee women fulfilling the conditions under (a) or (b) above having married unregistered non-refugees, when divorced or widowed."

cooperation from the host countries.[17] In Lebanon during recent years there was systematic review and verification of ration rolls involving cooperation of the government, with the result that they could be considered reasonably accurate in regard to need as well as presence and existence. A similar situation existed in Gaza until 1967 where, according to the Commissioner-General of UNRWA, "a steady, though limited, flow of rectification of the ration rolls was maintained with the cooperation of the government authorities." In Jordan, "for years past the issue of rectification has been deadlocked because of the authorities' apprehension of adverse reactions among the refugees and of the effect which this would have on public order." The Syrian government, "for many years past ... has not permitted systematic investigations to ascertain whether ration recipients were genuinely in need of this form of help. In other respects, however (such as the verification of existence and presence in the country), the rolls are believed to be reasonably accurate."

In an attempt to counterbalance inflation of ration rolls by unqualified beneficiaries of UNRWA assistance, no new names were added to existing lists for a number of years. Thus several hundred thousand[18] children who were, according to UNRWA's definition, entitled to rations were prevented from receiving them in an effort to strike a balance between the actual number of refugees and the inflated rolls. If all nonrationed children and other bona fide claimants were to be given rations, and all ineligibles including absentees, dead persons, false and duplicate registrants, and families with high incomes were to lose their rations, it is impossible to estimate where the balance would lie.

A census conducted by the Israeli government in Arab areas occupied after the June, 1967, war showed a considerable disparity from the number of refugees listed by UNRWA, even after taking into account the departure of over 200,000 Palestinians during and after the war. A year after the war, UNRWA estimated that 245,000 registered refugees remained on the West Bank (including Jerusalem), of whom 140,000 were normal ration recipients. In Gaza the Agency estimated that about 265,000 refugees remained, of whom 206,638 received regular rations and 2,435 were emergency cases. The Israeli census enumerated only 105,700 refugees on the West Bank, or 139,000 fewer than were listed by UNRWA a year later; and 207,300 in Gaza, or some 58,000 fewer than the number

[17]United Nations, *Report of the Commissioner-General of UNRWA*, 1 July 1966-30 June 1967, General Assembly, 22nd session, Supplement No. 13, Doc. A/6713 (New York, 1967), pp. 7-8.

[18]By June, 1969, this number, according to UNRWA's annual report, reached 308,038; *op. cit.*, 1 July 1968-30 June 1969, General Assembly, 24th session, Supplement No. 14, Doc. A/7614 (New York, 1969).

listed by UNRWA in 1968.[19] Attempts were made to account for disparities through joint committees of UNRWA officials and representatives
of the Israeli government. Part of the variation in statistics can be attributed
to differences in the definition of "refugee," and part to separation
of Jerusalem from the West Bank in the Israeli census, while UNRWA's
figures continued to include Jerusalem refugees as part of the West Bank.
The Israeli definition strongly emphasized birth-locality of household heads
rather than using the UNRWA definition. Other reasons for the disparity
might be difference in census techniques, types of questions asked, and
temporary absence of some Palestinians whose rations cards were available
to relatives still living in Israeli-occupied areas.

The Agency maintained that it was unable to continue normal rectification in East Jordan and the West Bank after the June war because of confusion created by mass population movements. Nevertheless, a substantial
number of ineligible persons were removed from the rolls. "Considerable
progress in this respect has been made in Gaza and the West Bank, but
much remains to be done," the Commissioner-General reported in 1968.
In all areas of UNRWA operations, 72,433 persons, including 61,877
ration recipients, were removed in the year ending June 30, 1969. In place
of refugees removed from the ration rolls, 23,463 rations were issued
to children on the waiting list whose families were in extreme need.[20]

According to the annual report of the Commissioner-General for
1968-1969, the total number of registered refugees in all host countries
as of June, 1969, was 1,395,074.[21] Of these, over 121,000 were members
of families receiving no rations or services from UNRWA. In all, about

[19]Compare: Israel Government, Central Bureau of Statistics, Census of Population,
1967, Publication No. 1, *West Bank . . . Gaza Strip and Northern Sinai . . .*
(Jerusalem, 1967), p. XVIII, and *Report of the Commissioner-General of UNRWA*,
1 July 1967-30 June 1968, Supplement No. 13, Doc. A/7213 (New York, 1968),
pp. 4-8.

[20]UNRWA, 1 July 1968-30 June 1969 Doc. A/7614, pp. 14-15.

[21]*Ibid.* As of the end of June, 1969, refugees registered with UNRWA were distributed
as follows:

TOTAL REFUGEES REGISTERED WITH UNRWA

Refugees	June, 1968	June, 1969	Receiving Rations 1968-1969
Lebanon	166,264	171,517	103,727
Syria	149,537	154,285	100,503
West Bank	245,000	271,796	140,000
East Jordan	455,500	489,762	
Gaza refugees in East Jordan	38,500		350,000
Displaced persons registered by Jordan government	246,000		240,000
Gaza	265,000	307,714	206,638

60.2 percent of the registered refugees received food rations from UNRWA. However, this number does not give a total picture of individuals displaced by the Palestine conflict, for it omits those displaced from the Suez Canal Zone, the Golan Heights, and other persons displaced as a result of the June, 1967, war. These cases will be examined later in this study.

1948 Conditions

At the time of the Palestine flight in 1947-1948, the overwhelming majority of refugees were rural peasants with few if any highly developed skills. In areas to which they fled they constituted a serious economic liability, since these places were already overburdened with surplus unskilled peasant populations. The largest concentration was in areas controlled by the Hashemite kingdom. There the 730,000 refugees constituted over a third of the population. The effect on Jordan might be compared to the impact of a refugee influx of over 70 million people to the United States within a few weeks time. A major difference is that Jordan's preparedness for this influx was even less than that of the United States. In 1947-1948 Jordan was far from a developed nation with none of the social services, relief organizations, economic infrastructure, or government administration necessary to cope with so large a problem in so short a time. Furthermore, the country was riddled with political instability, and its government could not command the popular support necessary to galvanize public effort for the economic and social tasks required in dealing with such precipitous change. Although there were potential resources available within Jordan, development of which could greatly expand the country's economic productivity and absorptive capacity, it was to be some years before Jordanian society could undertake the effort required to begin economic integration of its surplus population.

The refugees who crammed into the Egyptian-occupied 135-square-mile Gaza Strip outnumbered the native Palestinians there by nearly 3 to 1. Gaza itself was hardly viable, cut off from the hinterland to which its economic life had been tied. Large numbers of native inhabitants of the Gaza Strip-owned property that was no longer accessible since it was now held by Israel. The Gaza region was separated from Egypt by the Sinai Peninsula, which was not then prepared to absorb even a few hundred new settlers. Egypt was itself already overburdened with one of the world's most critical population problems, a very high birth rate and a slowly declining per capita rate of national income. Characterized as one of the outstanding examples of an undeveloped and impoverished nation, Egypt, crowded into the Nile Valley, had no room for additional thousands of unskilled rural laborers. Cairo has, accordingly, strictly controlled refugee immigration into the country. Although several thousand Palestinians have settled in Egypt, its government has prevented any large immigration from Gaza during the past 20 years.

The Palestinians who arrived in Lebanon in 1947-1948 increased that country's population by nearly 10 percent. A comparison might be the arrival in the United States of 15 to 20 million refugees. The economic impact of the refugees on Lebanon was less acute than in Jordan or Gaza, but the repercussions were severe. The country was only a little better prepared to care for or to absorb so sudden an influx of outsiders. Furthermore, since an estimated 90 percent of the refugees were Muslim, their presence created political embarrassment to the Lebanese government which was based on a delicate balance between Christians and Muslims. No population census had been taken since 1932 for fear of undermining the supposed Christian majority of 1 to 3 percent. The whole fabric of Lebanese society and politics was based on a quota system in which there was assumed to be approximately 5 Muslims for every 6 Christian inhabitants. Government posts from presidency, prime ministry, and speaker of the Lebanese parliament down to clerkships and junior officer grades in the army and police forces were allocated according to this ratio determined by religious origins. The influx of tens of thousands of Muslim Palestinians threatened to upset the balance and to jeopardize the basis of the communal system under which Lebanese life operated.

Even in Syria where refugees constituted less than 2 percent of the population, they were at the time of their arrival in 1948 neither an economic nor a political asset. Syria was politically volatile, extremely hostile to outsiders, and not yet ready to initiate the development efforts which within a few years made possible economic absorption of large numbers of the country's unskilled agricultural labor.

Not only were the principal refugee host countries unprepared to absorb large numbers of outsiders in 1948, but adjoining Arab countries were also politically unstable, lacking competent governmental and administrative machinery and a public sufficiently well organized to undertake massive development efforts. Although land, water, and other natural resources were available in sufficient quantities to give hope for the future, the Arab East of 1948 was unprepared to undertake the tasks necessary for either absorbing or temporarily caring for hundreds of thousands of unskilled peasants. Gordon Clapp, chairman of the U.N. Economic Survey Mission for the Middle East, warned in his final report:

> The region is not ready, the projects are not ready, the people and Governments are not ready, for large-scale development of the region's basic river systems or major undeveloped land areas. To press forward

on such a course is to pursue folly and frustration and thereby delay sound economic growth.[22]

U.N. Responsibility

Since no Arab country was willing or able to acknowledge responsibility for the refugees, Count Bernadotte suggested establishment of a U.N. emergency relief program. Within a year it became obvious that U.N. organized relief would have to continue, or political instability might topple the host governments. Upon recommendation of the Clapp Mission, the General Assembly established UNRWA to organize an integrated operation containing a program for public works intended to improve economic productivity in the Arab countries, and to continue relief. In its final report, the Clapp Mission outlined a plan of works projects and relief at a total cost of $54.9 million, which, it believed, could resolve the refugee problem within eighteen months.

By December 31, 1950, the date the Clapp Mission had fixed for ending relief, not more than 12,287 of the 878,000 refugees on the rolls were employed. Little progress was made on any of the major projects outlined by the Mission because of failure to obtain cooperation from Arab governments. Their spokesmen charged that projects intended to resettle refugees outside Palestine would undermine rights to repatriation in Israel. After completion of a few projects benefiting the host governments, the refugees returned to their tents and ration lines. UNRWA reported to the General Assembly at the end of 1952 that it found itself financing and operating labor camps to build public works that the governments themselves would have built the following year. When the public works fund began to run out, UNRWA decided to terminate that phase of its program. It had created neither permanent benefit for the refugees nor financial relief for the United Nations. Instead, it had spent five times the amount necessary for simple relief.[23]

Despite the initial failure to find an economic solution, another attempt was made when the General Assembly established a $30 million reintegration fund in November, 1950. The Assembly took into account Arab fears of compromising refugee rights by carefully emphasizing that establishment of the fund did not prejudice these rights. Arab governments also demand assurances of sustained and substantial international support for

---

[22]UNCCP, *Economic Survey Mission*, Part 1, p. 3.

[23]For descriptions of early efforts at economic integration see Peretz, *Israel and the Palestine Arabs;* Rony E. Gabbay, *A Political Study of the Arab-Jewish Conflict— The Arab Refugee Problem* (Geneva: DROZ, 1959); Fred J. Khouri, *The Arab Israeli Dilemma* (Syracuse: Syracuse University Press, 1968).

any new projects. On the other hand, there was deep suspicion that any large-scale development assistance would become an entering wedge for foreign interference or control.

To assuage Arab fears, John Blandford, the Director of UNRWA, negotiated with various Arab capitals between 1951 and 1953. Finally a new program was proposed in which $50 million would be appropriated for relief and $200 million for reintegration. Relief was to be progressively reduced until it would cost the United Nations only $5 million a year by 1954. A gradual transfer of responsibility for both relief and rehabilitation projects from UNRWA to the Arab states was projected, with guarantees that refugee rights to repatriation and compensation would not be compromised.

By 1954 not even 8000 refugees were made self-sufficient through the program. Of the $200 million appropriation, only $45 million was ever raised for the fund, less than $10 million had been used, and signs of progress on major developments were absent. A solution of the refugee problem now seemed so remote that the General Assembly extended the mandate of UNRWA for 5 years, until June 30, 1960. It was now becoming evident that the problem was not one of temporary relief measures, and that UNRWA's services could not be dispensed with in the near future.

During the Eisenhower Administration, still another attempt was made to bypass a political solution of the Palestine and the Arab refugee problem through an economic approach. Under strong congressional pressure to resolve the refugee problem, Eric Johnston, chairman of the International Advisory Board of the Technical Cooperation Administration, was sent to the Middle East as a special emissary of the American President with plans for unified development of the water resources in the Jordan River Valley. A major intent of the scheme was to resettle large numbers of refugees, thus lessening tension created by their conditions. The so-called Johnston plan envisioned irrigation of about 936,000 dunums in the Jordan Valley at an estimated cost of $121,000,000. Implementation of the plan would make possible generation of 167,000,000 kilowatt hours of electric power at about $53,119,000. The undertaking would support 224,000 workers and their families, 160,000 directly from agriculture, and 64,000 more from ancillary employment. This was 143,000 more people than were employed in the valley during 1953. As a result of numerous visits to Egypt, Syria, Lebanon, Jordan, and Israel, Johnston came close to achieving "technical" agreement. However, by 1955 the Johnston proposals were blocked despite American financial inducements and schemes for protecting political positions through a neutral supervising authority.[24] Although not rejecting the plan outright, the Arab governments continued what seemed to be an indefinite delay on formal acceptance of any arrangement that could contribute to Israel's development. Egypt at the time supported the plan's general outline as contributing to improvement of refugee conditions and urged other Arab governments to accept it. Lebanon balked for internal political and economic reasons. Neither Jordan nor Syria were then prepared to enter into any direct agreements with Israel. Outweighing all other Arab objections was fear of American schemes that might ultimately weaken the Arab states to Israel's advantage. Some Arab spokesmen depicted the whole Johnston proposal as a devious plan to increase immigration to Israel and to deprive the refugees of their rights. While agreeing to the ratio of water distribution recommended by Johnston, Israel would not accept those parts of the plan calling for international or United Nations control of storage areas within its borders. Although there was no formal termination of the Johnston enterprise, Arab officials could come to no agreement, and finally referred the plan back to their technicians.

By 1957 major efforts at a large-scale economic solution of the refugee problem seemed to have borne no fruit. The Jordan-Yarmuk and Sinai Peninsula[25] schemes had failed to win support from the governments involved. Furthermore, the Suez-Sinai war in 1956 and UNRWA's precarious financial situation brought to a halt a number of experimental programs of lesser scale. Henry R. Labouisse, then Director of UNRWA, pointed out in February, 1957, that little change had occurred in the refugee situation because:

> ... of politics, and ... deep-seated human emotions. It [the reason] does not lie simply in the field of economics. UNRWA can, to be sure, enable some hundreds of refugees to become self-supporting each year —through small agricultural development projects, grants to establish small businesses and the like. But it cannot overcome the fact that the refugees as a whole insist upon the choice provided for them in General Assembly resolution 194—that is, repatriation or compensation. In the absence of that choice, they bitterly oppose anything which has even the semblance of permanent settlement elsewhere. Officials of the host Governments, with but few exceptions, openly support the refugees

[24]*Ibid.;* also Georgiana G. Stevens, *Jordan River Partition* (Hoover Institute, Stanford University, 1965); Kathryn Dogherty, *Jordan Waters Conflict,* International Conciliation, No. 553 (New York: Carnegie Endowment for International Peace, 1965).

[25]The Sinai plan envisioned use of Nile River surplus water for Sinai desert irrigation, facilitating resettlement there of several thousand refugees. The plan fell into abeyance as Egypt later developed its own plans for use of the water in the Nile Valley.

in this position and oppose the large-scale resettlement projects. On the other hand, in the matter of repatriation and compensation, the government of Israel has taken no affirmative action.[26]

A decade had now passed with little if any prospect of solving the refugee problem or of lessening tensions between Israel and its Arab neighbors. The dilemma continued to appear on the annual agenda of the General Assembly—and United Nations relief operations, which had been initiated as short-term emergency measures, now seemed to have become institutionalized under UNRWA direction. The situation was considered of such a critical nature that it required direct and concentrated attention of the Secretary-General. The General Assembly accordingly requested him, in December, 1958, to submit proposals.

In June, 1959, Secretary-General Dag Hammarskjöld recommended continuation of UNRWA services but also noted that unemployed refugees should be regarded as an asset, not a liability, in future development of the region. Economic absorption of refugees in the economies of Israel and the Arab states presented problems similar to those involved in all cases of reintegrating a large, unskilled, and unemployed population. In a general economic analysis of the potential development capacities of the Middle East, the Secretary-General laid out a broad-ranging plan that assumed economic obstacles were as great as the political difficulties in blocking progress.[27] Most refugees were still surplus labor, and only by increasing absorptive capacity in the area would integration become possible. Hammarskjöld's approach treated Egypt, Syria, Lebanon, Iraq, Jordan, the Arabian Peninsula, and Israel as a single economic unit. Provided, "in the long run . . . there is a fair degree of mobility of capital or labour, or both, among at least some of its parts," the region was considered economically viable. Surplus labor from overpopulated Egypt and Jordan should be free to emigrate to areas of potential labor shortage such as Iraq and Syria. Part of this population movement would include Palestine refugees who would be free to cross international frontiers into Syria, Iraq, or Israel.

Equally necessary would be mobility of surplus capital from oil-producing Iraq, Saudi Arabia, Kuwait, Bahrein, and Qatar to nations such as Jordan and Egypt, which would require far larger investment sources than could be financed from capital sources within their boundaries. At the time, countries with the largest needs for external capital bore the heaviest

[26]U.N. Press Release PM/3369, February 11, 1957.

[27]United Nations, Doc. A/4121, June 15, 1959. The plan was significant because its general premises—that the refugee problem can be resolved through economic development—have been the basis of most Western and Israeli approaches to a solution.

population burdens, and also contained the greatest overconcentration of Palestine refugees. The financing of their development within the decade in order to create absorptive capacity for at least some of their present surplus population would depend in part on outside capital.

To maintain employment at the 1959 relationship to the working population, and to raise living standards by about 2 percent each year during the next decade, a total of 4 million job opportunities would have had to become available by 1970 in Egypt, Syria, Lebanon, Jordan, and Israel. Only if this number of jobs could be created for the indigenous populations would it be possible to find employment for 500,000 Palestine refugees who would enter the labor market by 1970. Given favorable political conditions and free transit across borders, part of the surplus labor could be shifted to capital-surplus countries that would face labor shortages by 1970, and part to Syria and Israel, provided the latter received sufficient outside capital to ensure success of their development programs and absorption of their own increased labor supply.

The estimated cost of development between 1960 and 1970 sufficient to maintain existing employment levels, to absorb natural population increases plus the refugees, and to raise living standards by about 2 percent a year would be approximately $14 billion. Capital investment would be largely in agricultural and industrial projects. To remain competitive, agriculture would have to become highly mechanized; therefore new agricultural production areas, or new nonagricultural opportunities, would have to be created at fairly high cost to absorb the agricultural population freed by mechanization. Of the proposed $14 billion, about $12 billion was required to accommodate the net cumulative increase in the labor force (exclusive of the refugees), and another $2 billion to absorb the refugees. (The estimated cost of providing employment for each refugee added to the labor force was about $3300.)

The Secretary-General envisioned two major sources of funds: domestic savings, and various foreign funds and investments. Non-oil-producing, capital-deficit countries of the region would require approximately $9.5 billion in investment by 1970 to absorb the total estimated labor force including the refugees. Since these states could produce less than half this amount, they would be short by some $5.1 billion. Given favorable political conditions and capital mobility, this amount could be supplied by the oil-producing capital-surplus countries as they found increasing investment opportunities among their poorer neighbors.

An initial 5-year effort would be required to begin the projected development process during which time large capital transfers from the surplus to the deficit countries would be insufficient. Pump-priming capital from outside the Middle East would be required to initiate operations. Within five years the non-oil-producing Arab states would require capital investment of $5.4 billion to absorb an additional indigenous labor force of about 1,800,000 plus the refugees. Domestic saving and anticipated foreign investment would provide about $2.4 billion, leaving a shortage of $3 billion. The oil-producing Arab countries would probably be able to provide about $1 billion in investment capital within 5 years; thus an additional investment of nearly $2 billion would be required from outside the Middle East.

If outside funds were available to support sufficient Middle East investment, demands for labor would be great enough to absorb expanding labor forces in Egypt, Lebanon, and Jordan, as well as those Palestinians who could be rehabilitated. Upon completion of the pump-priming operation, foreign investment would be less necessary. Decline in requirements for outside monies would depend on the pace of economic expansion and the rise in domestic savings induced by the general development process and increased oil production.

The Secretary-General noted that despite initial progress toward economic regionalism, large scale capital and labor mobility within the region was still a long-range objective rather than an immediate possibility. By 1959, each of the countries had made considerable progress in internal economic development, but regional development had not increased at the same rate because of political difficulties, inter-Arab rivalries, and great economic and social disparities among the countries of the area. Only through a gradual approach to political problems could regional progress be attained. To direct attention primarily to relationships between these problems and the refugee dilemma would be inadvisable. "A solution," he warned,

> ... should be sought, *inter alia,* in order to create conditions for a sound economic development ... irrespective of its significance for the reintegration of the refugees. If the problems are solved sufficiently well to provide for such conditions, the proper political setting would probably *ipso facto* be created for a solution of the refugee problem in its political aspects.[28]

In the decade since Hammarskjöld's report, few conditions he considered as prerequisite for massive rehabilitation have been established. Although there has been some mobility of capital and labor, it has taken place outside the framework of any large-scale rationalized plan. More than 100,000 Palestinians are estimated to have left areas of refugee concentration

[28]*Ibid.,* p. 6.

to seek employment in the Persian Gulf. But few of them have become politically integrated in countries such as Kuwait, Saudi Arabia, or the Persian Gulf. A certain amount of capital has been sent by these Palestinians as remittances to families still living in Gaza and Jordan. Furthermore, establishment of the Kuwait Fund for Arab Economic Development has made possible transfers of capital to Jordan and Egypt. After the June, 1967, war, Kuwait, Libya, and Saudi Arabia provided Jordan and Egypt with subsidy payments to compensate for war losses, but these subsidies are hardly more than token amounts when compared with the large-scale transfers that would be necessary as part of a major regional development scheme. Israel is as remote from becoming an integral part of a single Middle Eastern economic unit as it ever was, and relations between the so-called conservative and revolutionary Arab governments are as much an obstacle to economic integration as in 1959. Neither internal political conditions nor relations among states of the area have favored implementation of a regional plan along the lines proposed by Hammarskjöld in 1959.

IV. The Changing Refugee Problem
Economic Development

Although efforts specifically directed at an overall economic solution of the refugee problem have been unsuccessful, changing economic, political, and social conditions in the Middle East have not bypassed the Arabs of Palestine. In Egypt, Syria, and Iraq, revolutionary socialist governments replaced the laissez-faire regimes described in the 1949 Clapp report.[29] Although there was little if any regional planning, economic developments within individual countries substantially changed the material position of many refugees. In Lebanon, Syria, and to some extent in Jordan and Gaza, refugees were finding full- or part-time employment within the framework of expanding economies despite opposition by host countries and the refugees themselves to resolution of the Palestine problem through an economic solution.

During the decade before Syria became part of the United Arab Republic it experienced what some economists described as phenomenal growth. Despite *coups d'états,* an antiquated social structure, and aversion to accepting Western economic and technical aid, cultivated land doubled, grain production increased by nearly 75 percent, and newly introduced cotton output expanded to eight times the pre-World War II average.[30] Total out-

[29]UNCCP, *Economic Survey Mission.*

[30]Doreen Warriner, *Land Reform and Development in the Middle East: A Study of Egypt, Syria and Iraq* (2nd ed.; London: Royal Institute of International Affairs, 1966).

put was increasing at a much more rapid rate than the rise in population. Most surprising was that this economic expansion occurred without foreign capital and experts, extensive development of public services, or long-term planning including agrarian reform. Agricultural growth was being financed largely by the urban merchant class which was turning its new-won profits back into the Syrian soil. New regions were opened to development in the northern parts of the country, near Aleppo, and in the Jezira, the "island" area between the Tigris and Euphrates rivers. As these formerly semiarid zones were put under the plow, their populations changed from sparsely nomadic to a settled peasantry, mostly working for agricultural wages. Labor shortages in the country resulted in the economic integration of a large proportion of Syria's more than 100,000 Palestine refugees.

In Iraq, where per capita output increased, but at a much slower rate than in Syria, there was a lesser degree of economic integration of the country's small number of Palestine refugees (about 7000 in 1949). Many of them provided basic skills such as those of file clerks, auto mechanics, or sanitary technicians. Iraq, like other underdeveloped countries, has a surplus of unskilled workers, but a drastic shortage of technicians and skilled labor. After initiation of a development program in 1950, the shortage of skills became acute so that Palestinians who could provide them were welcomed. However, since the 1958 revolution political instability in Iraq has made difficult implementation of long-term development planning. Given present conditions it will take years before the country can absorb its own indigenous unskilled workers, to say nothing of additional thousands of unskilled Palestinians from labor surplus areas such as Gaza and Jordan. The outskirts of Baghdad are overpopulated with encampments of Iraqi peasants who have flocked to the capital seeking employment. Many studies have indicated that Iraq has the potential absorptive capacity for hundreds of thousands, if not millions of additional people, but political turmoil and lack of any well-directed central planning has kept Baghdad's slums a constant reminder of the country's internal dilemmas.

Economic developments in Lebanon's free economy during the decade between the Clapp Report and the 1958 civil war also favored economic absorption or partial absorption of thousands of refugees. Although the Lebanese government officially excluded foreigners from entering the labor market in large numbers, Palestine refugees provided black market labor below established minimum wages in the country's rapidly expanding construction industry and in some agricultural areas. Many who succeeded in obtaining working permits also found employment at substandard wages in various types of services and service industries. Since neither UNRWA nor the Lebanese government generally recognized refugee labor because it was illegal, it is difficult to obtain accurate data on the numbers who supplemented their UNRWA rations or services in this manner. Furthermore, in Lebanon the refugees were a political embarrassment to the government because most of them, as Muslims, constituted a threat to the country's political and social balance.

The rate of economic growth in Jordan, where half the refugee population lived during the decade and a half following acquisition of the West Bank, was more rapid than in any of the neighboring Arab countries except Saudi Arabia. Gross domestic product rose from 51 million Jordanian dinars in 1954 to 140 million in 1964 at current prices but without inflation, just over 10 percent a year. Foreign exchange earnings quadrupled in this period, despite an earlier estimate by a World Bank economic mission that they would merely double. School attendance in the country rose from 110,000 in 1950 to over 320,000 by 1965, with the result that illiteracy declined from 69 percent to only 15 percent of children between 6 and 14 years old. National income per person was higher in Jordan during 1966 than in Syria and Egypt, and about half of that in Lebanon.[31] Political stability and foreign aid had made possible development of widely expanding infrastructure, extensive irrigation and agricultural projects, and a small amount of industry. A new network of roads linked most of the inhabited parts of the country; expanded education included a new national university in Amman; the country was less dependent upon overland transport with the opening of a modern port at Aqaba; an active and well-trained civil service was beginning to function effectively; and perhaps most important, a great expansion of tourism and the Jordan Valley development scheme were increasing foreign currency earnings and absorbing large amounts of refugee labor.

Although no formal agreement had been reached on implementing the Johnston plan for division of Jordan Valley waters, both Israel and the Hashemite kingdom proceeded to carry out those phases that most directly affected them. Israel initiated and completed its project to divert water from the Jordan River north of Lake Tiberias to the Negev, and Jordan carried out and completed the first phase of the East Ghawr scheme. In implementing their respective river diversion plans, both Jordan and Israel kept within the limits of water usage proposed in the Johnston plan. By 1963 the first phase of the East Ghawr Canal had extended irrigation 40 miles south

[31]*World Bank Atlas* (Washington, D.C.: International Bank for Reconstruction and Development, 1968). GNP per capita for calendar year 1966, in U.S. dollars:

Iraq	— 270	Lebanon	— 480
Syria	— 180	Jordan	— 220
Egypt	— 160		

of the Yarmuk River to some 120,000 dunums on the east side of the Jordan Valley. Approximately 100,000 people, most of whom were refugees, lived from employment created by the newly irrigated areas.

Economic absorption of refugees in Jordan was facilitated by the Hashemite kingdom's policy of granting citizenship to all Palestinians who desired it. Not only did the government refrain from placing obstacles in the way of refugee economic integration, but it actively encouraged projects that would provide employment, sought foreign capital and assistance to carry them out, and maintained the political stability necessary to implement them. Despite the apparently optimistic picture of Jordan's developing economy, there was still a substantial proportion of the labor force that could not yet be absorbed by 1967. Although in 1955 the World Bank mission had projected an unemployment rate of some 20 percent by the end of the next decade, the actual level was only 12 to 14 percent, still quite high.[32] A large part of the country's labor force (mostly Palestinians, many of them refugees—some estimates as high as 100,000) was employed outside Jordan, in the Arabian Peninsula and Persian Gulf. Remittances from Jordanians abroad helped in large measure to increase the country's foreign currency earnings and to provide the difference that made possible a subsistence income level for many families.

Generally, conditions in the Egyptian-occupied Gaza area did not change greatly between the time of the Clapp Report and 1967. Although the economy of Gaza expanded, it was unable to absorb as large numbers of refugees as other areas. By 1967 the economy of Gaza had grown as a result of extensive development of citrus exports, Egypt's decision to make the town a free port, remittances from abroad (mostly the Arabian Peninsula) and employment provided to thousands of residents by the United Nations Emergency Force (UNEF) and UNRWA. U.A.R. policy toward admission of large numbers of refugees was still restrictive since Egypt's population problem had become even more acute after 1949. Despite restrictions on Palestinian immigration, the U.A.R. government had permitted 6000 to 7000 refugees to settle in the Nile Valley. At one time the Cairo government recruited about 4000 high school and college graduates for administrative and teaching positions. However, by 1967, the Gaza refugees, numbering over 200,000, were still those most in need of the basic rations and services provided by UNRWA.

Living Conditions and UNRWA

Over the years as a result of excellent organizational abilities and personal

[32]*The Economic Development of Jordan* (Baltimore: Johns Hopkins Press for International Bank for Reconstruction and Development, 1957).

dedication of both Palestinian and international UNRWA officials, life was made bearable for the refugees. The most extensive changes occurred by 1957-1960. During this era resistance to transfer from temporary tent camps to more permanent structures had dissipated. Realization developed that UNRWA was not a foreign imperialist organization, but a service enterprise largely staffed, managed, and operated by Palestinians. The UNRWA identity card lost its stigma as a sign of displacement and became a symbol of "Palestinianness." Indeed, many individuals who were to forgo UNRWA rations and services as a result of economic success retained their UNRWA ration card as a sort of Palestinian passport.

Many once-dismal tent encampments, surrounded by dust storms in summer and wallowing in mud during winter, became extensions of adjoining urban centers, complete with the infrastructure of town life. Cement and concrete, wood, adobe, or other permanent material replaced canvas; often UNRWA supplied permanent or weatherproof roofing, and many refugee camp homes were equipped with normal home furnishings. In most camps the main streets were paved; many were supplied with electricity and water for public or private use. As the camps acquired a relative permanence, local transportation services often linked them with urban centers, making it possible for those with jobs to commute.

From the beginning of UNRWA's responsibility for the refugee problem in 1950 until the present only a minority of refugees has lived in United Nations camps.[33] As of June, 1969, the overall average number in camps was under one-third, from a low of 5.9 percent in Syria to a high of 62.4 percent in Gaza. Although there had been considerable improvement of living conditions over the years, limited space still made it necessary for a camp family of four to five to live in a single room 3 by 4 meters. Often as many as 10 to 20 people lived in a single shelter, creating serious social if not health problems. Refugee daily living conditions, though far from idyllic, were generally superior to life in a typical Nile Valley village. According to a survey of facilities conducted by the Israel government after the June war, there was little difference between refugees and nonrefugees living in Gaza and the West Bank in ownership of such amenities as stoves, indoor toilets, electricity, running water, radios, and television sets.[34] The

[33]The registered population of the 53 established UNRWA camps was 434,952 in June, 1969, although the number of persons actually residing in these camps was estimated at approximately 490,000. There were also six emerging camps in East Jordan and four in Syria establised after June, 1967, with a total population of some 100,000.

[34]Israel Government, Central Bureau of Statistics, Census of Population 1967, Publication No. 2, *Housing Conditions, Household Equipment, Welfare Assistance and Farming in the Administered Areas* (Jerusalem, 1968).

same survey also showed little disparity in income levels between those living in refugee camps and the indigenous population (using income figures based on the prewar situation and including UNRWA provisions and services).

Since UNRWA was established in 1950, its operations have become considerably more sophisticated than administration of simple relief programs. Although its annual budget, now over $40 million, permits expenditure of about ten cents a day on each registered refugee, less than half this amount is used for basic relief services such as food, supplementary rations, and the like. Even with the burden of added hundreds of thousands of refugees to care for during the 1967-1968 fiscal year, relief amounted to less than five cents a day per displaced person. By far the largest proportion of the budget was allocated to health and educational services. Considering the Agency's limited funds, the physical conditions in which the refugees lived, and the problems of nutritional inadequacy facing them, health standards were relatively high. Throughout the history of the problem there have been no major serious epidemics, although fairly large numbers of children and some older people suffer from malnutrition, a condition which the Agency attempts to rectify, although not always successfully, through its supplementary feeding program for nursing mothers, infants, children, and some aged.

In general it can be stated that medical services available to registered refugees are superior to those accessible to the average villager or urban slum dweller in host countries. While UNRWA medical services are rather primitive by Western standards, they have prevented the disastrous spread of disease which could have decimated the refugee population. UNRWA clinics, hospitals, and laboratories, the nursing services, and the program for health education, control of communicable disease and environmental sanitation, supervised by the World Health Organization (WHO) and assisted by private voluntary organizations, have established standards and developed models for dealing with health problems which have assisted in raising conditions generally in the area.

The Agency has also provided social services through its welfare staff, youth activities programs, and preschool play centers. The most important permanent contribution of UNRWA has been its general and vocational educational programs. In the year ending June, 1969, the Agency operated 466 elementary and preparatory schools, of which 275 were Agency-built. Refugee children enrolled in UNRWA and other schools covering the first nine years of education totaled over 242,059 in 1969. The annual increase in UNRWA school population was on the order of 14,000 by 1969 with the cost of education rising at the rate of about $1 million a year. With a little less than half of UNRWA's budget expended on education, the cost amounted to less than $100 a year per child. Although the Agency does not operate upper secondary schools of general education, it has helped support some 15,000 children in mostly governmental institutions, and the main burden of their cost has been carried by the host governments. About half the Agency staff were teachers employed by UNRWA, totaling 5790 men and women. UNESCO professional staff supervises and directs UNRWA's educational program under terms of an agreement between the two international agencies.

The Agency teacher-training program includes pre-service preparation of secondary school graduates in 2-year courses at UNRWA or government centers, and an in-service program for teaching staff supervised by the UNRWA/UNESCO Institute of Education operating out of the Agency's Beirut headquarters. The general and teacher-training program, operated in conjunction with UNESCO, are relatively high level, and compare favorably with the educational systems of the host countries. Although UNESCO plays a role in the UNRWA school system, educational standards and curriculum are generally determined by the host governments. This has created problems for UNRWA because of the nationalistic content of parts of the curriculum. UNRWA, as an international agency, has been criticized because of references deprecatory of Jews in general and Israel in particular which have frequently appeared in texts used by children attending school under its auspices. Some observers have been critical of the extent of nationalist indoctrination not only permitted, but openly encouraged by the largely Palestinian teaching and supervisory staff. It has not been uncommon to find UNRWA schools decorated with slogans and symbols intended to arouse the Palestine consciousness of students, or to discover texts or lessons glorifying guerrilla fighters against Zionism and Israel. There is no doubt that children who have passed through the UNRWA school system are Palestine patriots who have deep resentments against the Jewish state, nor are such attitudes inconsistent with the environment and the situation in which the refugee youths mature.

The UNRWA system has prepared thousands of youths for both higher and vocational education, making possible their entrance into the economic life of the region. Especially qualified refugee students are awarded university scholarships at various institutions throughout the Middle East. In 1967-1968, 718 received awards for higher study.

As early as 1950 UNRWA began to train young men and women in skills that could lead to partial or complete self-support. Initially there was training in carpentry, shoemaking, weaving, bookbinding, mechanics, and domestic skills. By 1953 the first UNRWA vocational training center was opened at Kalandia, Jordan (near Jerusalem) to train young men as electricians, radio mechanics, wiremen, fitter mechanics, blacksmiths, welders, plumbers, carpenters, builders, draughtsmen, and automotive mechanics, which were in short supply in the Arab world. By 1969 about 2300 youths were being trained yearly in seven such vocational training centers located in Syria, Lebanon, Gaza, and East and West Bank Jordan.[35] The initial intent of the vocational training program was to train a substantial number of the more than 30,000 refugee youths who reach maturity each year without skills or experience, and with no visible prospects for future employment. Despite this goal, less than 10 percent of refugee youths receive vocational training of the type that would ensure them a secure place in the developing economies of the region. Although nearly all graduates of the vocational centers are employed in the trades for which they were trained, it has not been possible to raise sufficient funds to increase these opportunities. Because of the need to provide basic relief, health, and educational services, UNRWA has been unable to divert more of the 10 cents a day per refugee from fundamental needs to more sophisticated programs such as the vocational training centers.

With the modest resources at its disposal, UNRWA experimented in developing a number of self-support projects between 1950 and 1960, including both grants and loans in Syria and Jordan. The largest program was directed through the Development Bank of Jordan, which began operations in 1951 with an authorized capital of $1.4 million, later increased to $2.8 million, of which some $2.1 million was subscribed for and paid in shares. UNRWA controlled 85 percent of the Bank's shares, and Palestine refugees were the chief beneficiaries of its activities. By 1967 the Bank had made 764 loans in agriculture, industry, and construction totaling almost $4 million. It was estimated that more than 3000 refugees were directly employed and that some 13,000 benefited from these activities. While UNRWA's economic programs in Syria were too limited in scope to affect the local economy, it is probable that in Jordan during the 1950s the Agency's larger and more diversified economic programs played a significant role in that country's progress and development. By 1960-1961 UNRWA had decided to devote such money as was available beyond fundamental needs to improving education and vocational training as more productive expenditure of limited funds in preparing refugees to become self-sufficient. In 1967 the Jordan Development Bank was dissolved with its remaining assets and liabilities transferred to the Jordanian government's Agricultural Credit Corporation. UNRWA was to receive for its investment

---

[35]The total number of courses rose in 1969 to 38, also including training in commercial and paramedical trades and professions, and including nearly 300 women.

in the Bank, $1,813,000 in installments to be used for school construction.

The nature of the economic, political, and social changes after the 1940s and early 1950s in several countries of the area has been briefly outlined. As the environment of the host countries changed, there was also change in the refugee community itself. Having left the land as unskilled agricultural labor, most refugees raised families that were no longer illiterate fellaheen. The younger generation, taking advantage of opportunities offered by UNRWA, broke out of the framework of traditional Arab society. Much of the refugee population has lived in or near urban centers and is rapidly adjusting to modern city life. They have the same aspirations for upward mobility and economic security found in nearly all modern urban societies. This explains the hunger for education among the younger generation and the orientation toward city life rather than toward work on the land.

The meager assistance provided by UNRWA through the years has often made the difference between refugee ability to subsist at an average local income, or mere existence at a starvation level. Obviously, few refugees could have lived for 20 years on foodstuffs worth less than five cents a day; it was not so much the UNRWA ration, therefore, as the extensive network of services provided by the Agency that helped to keep alive refugee aspirations for mobility and security.

During this era, UNRWA itself was transformed from a temporary relief-dispensing agency to a more or less permanent social service organization providing needs the host countries were not yet able to provide. In areas such as Syria, Lebanon, or parts of Jordan where it might have been possible to dispense with all or much of the basic ration, the other health, welfare, and educational services were valuable assets contributing not only to refugee development, but to the growing infrastructure of the whole society. It is true that during this era many officials, both local and international, developed vested interests in continuation of the Agency, but this does not lessen the value of the work contributed by approximately 13,000 staff members (of whom a mere 110 were international in 1969). An appraisal of UNRWA's activities by a team of Israeli professors made after the 1967 war observed that its orientation is

> that of an international service agency which sees its main task in improving the lives of the population which it serves, in this case the Arab refugees. As in other similar international organizations, a strong ideology pervades the Agency and its staff to work with dedication for underprivileged peoples for whose sake the Agency has come into being.[36]

[36]From a proprietary source.

Since UNRWA was organized in 1950, its total income was a little over $667,420,000, a relatively small sum in the context of the amounts required for economic development outlined in the Hammarskjöld proposals. Had UNRWA funds been used totally for projects of the type envisioned by the former Secretary-General, they would have theoretically provided money for rehabilitation of about 200,000 people. However, such rehabilitation could not have taken place outside the framework of the overall plan which was estimated ten years ago at a cost of $14 billion (of which $2 billion was calculated to be the cost of refugee rehabilitation). A large part of UNRWA budgets have been allocated to programs which in reality added to, if they did not actually create, new infrastructure in the host countries. It is difficult to indicate how much of the 10 cents a day per person expended on refugees over the 20-year period under discussion was also a contribution to economic development of the region.

V. The Political Constant

Simultaneously with attempts to improve refugee living conditions and to seek an economic solution of the Palestine dilemma, there were political attacks on the problem. These have concentrated largely on efforts to effect a compromise between Israel's reluctance to take back large numbers of refugees and Arab resistance to resettlement. Initially Count Bernadotte recommended that the general principle of repatriation be accepted. His suggestions were incorporated into U.N. Resolution 194, adopted in 1948, establishing UNCCP; the principle of repatriation was repeatedly pressed in UNCCP by Western powers, and accepted or pressed by individual mediators. (Israel was not yet a member of the United Nations when Resolution 194 was adopted, but was understood to have accepted it when admitted to the organization.) Israel's initial response was that the refugee problem could be considered within the framework of a general peace settlement. Under American pressure in 1949 Israel was persuaded to agree that 100,000 refugees be returned as part of an overall peace settlement; at another point it seemed that the Israeli government would accept responsibility for the Gaza Strip refugees, provided the area was also incorporated into Israel. With Arab hostility to the Jewish states remaining as intense as ever, and with internal conditions making absorption of many Arabs more difficult, Israeli attitudes toward extensive repatriation hardened until any suggestion of a large-scale Arab return was rejected. The only Israeli concession on repatriation was permission granted for some 10,000 to 50,000 former Arab residents to reunite with families remaining in Israel. By the early 1950s Israel's official policy strongly emphasized refugee integration in the Arab world with possibilites of compensation payment for abandoned property as part of an overall peace settlement.

Despite numerous transformations in the Arab world and changing economic and social status of the refugees, political attitudes toward Israel and the refugee question remained unchanged. At the Lausanne meetings held under UNCCP auspices during 1949, there had been indications that participating Arab governments were willing to discuss a peace settlement to include refugee repatriation and surrender of substantial areas on the Israeli side on the armistice demarcation lines. Through the 1950s and most of the 1960s, however, the official Arab position has been that there can be no peace with Israel not based on the 1947 partition resolution and implementation of those sections of Resolution 194 calling for refugee repatriation. The Arab diplomatic position has strongly emphasized implementation of the United Nations resolutions, but there has also been strong support for organizations and policies aiming at liquidation of the Jewish Zionist state,[37] repatriation of Palestinians, and re-establishment of their country as part of the Arab world. The latter approach has been strongly emphasized in the public press, the communications media, in school curricula, and in the internal and some external pronouncements of most political leaders throughout the Arab east. Support for Palestinian Arab irredentism was most clearly enunciated in backing given by the Arab League and most Arab governments to the Palestine Liberation Organization (PLO) after 1964 and more recently to *al-Fatah,* which merged in 1969 with the PLO. The principal objective of these organizations was stated to be reconstitution of Palestine as a secular state governed by Palestinians, an objective recognized as legitimate by the Arab governments.

Arab attachment to Palestine was strengthened by the social setting in which the refugees lived. Many resided in large concentrations where their principal contacts were with other Palestinians, often from the same villages in which they had been born. Refugees more often than not married other Palestinians and raised their children as Palestinians. In camps or urban areas, schools and other facilities were often named after towns and villages from which the refugees had fled. Buildings were frequently decorated with maps of the homeland and with slogans and symbols intended to keep alive Palestine consciousness. In much the same way that Jewish refugees in European displaced-persons camps after World War II were reminded of their associations with Palestine, Arab refugees were also

[37]The Arab position was that a Jewish or Zionist state was contradictory to the principle of self-determination, since it meant the exclusion from national life of the Palestine Arab majority which had been forced from its country during the 1948 Arab-Israeli war, resulting in displacement of the rightful owners of the country by an influx of foreigners who were establishing a new state on the basis of religious-ethnic identity.

reminded of their homeland. School texts not only emphasized Arab attachment to the land but also underscored deep animosity to the state of Israel, to Zionism, and to Jews in general. International attention was focused on this indoctrination after the June, 1967 war, when a UNESCO commission was appointed to examine UNRWA/UNESCO textbooks, and to report in 1969 whether or not they conform with the objective of promoting "understanding, tolerance, and friendship among all nations, racial or religious groups, and . . . the activities of the United Nations for the maintenance of peace."

The Commission reported in November, 1968, that some materials used in UNRWA schools were "often inspired by a preoccupation with indoctrination against Jews rather than by strictly educational aims. Many of these exercises should be removed or entirely rewritten," the Commission recommended (UNESCO. 82 EX/8, Paris, April 4, 1969. Annex I. First Report, p. 3). In commenting on textbooks for Muslim religious instructions the Commission noted that in relating the history of Islam, many texts emphasized that "the Jews as a whole have worked hand in glove with the enemies of Islam" (Annex II, p. 6). It stated that "liar, cheat, usurer, idiot —terms applied to Jews in certain passages, and part of the deplorable language of international anti-semitism—cannot be tolerated" (Annex II, p. 9).

In many texts there were calls to "liberate the usurped homeland," "to evict Israel and give Palestine back to its rightful inhabitants," or to attack "Imperialism and Israel [which] are endeavoring to weaken the Arabs, who will never rest until they have exterminated their enemies" (Annex II, p. 3).

"Palestine," the Commission noted, "is always in people's thoughts, even if not always mentioned. It influences the choice of poetry or prose for anthologists, the kind of examples and exercises pupils are set, as it conditions the tracing of maps and the wording of their captions" (Annex II, p. 9).

Palestine consciousness among the refugees was also intensified by host populations' hostility to them on numerous occasions in times of internal political stress. There were frequent instances where refugees were singled out by security authorities and by hostile host populations as an untrustworthy element, likely to cause political and social disruption. Against the background of marginal economic conditions under which refugees lived and the economic exploitation they suffered, many become embittered, feeling that they had been betrayed by all outsiders, including other Arabs.

Many refugees have been exceedingly successful in rising far above the mere subsistence level. Palestinians can be found in significant technical and administrative positions throughout the Arab world. They have ascended to cabinet, ministerial, or ambassadorial roles in Libya, Saudi Arabia, Syria, Jordan, and the Persian Gulf principalities. Palestinian contractors, merchants, bankers, and other businessmen have made major contributions to rapid development in these countries. They have been a general leavening agent in the development process throughout the whole Middle East. This has been due in large measure to their relatively greater sophistication, higher literacy, and better training, the last a heritage retained by many who had been Arab officials of the British Mandatory government, and to more keenly felt aspirations for upward mobility among an educated group considered by many as outside the mainstream of national identification. Despite their successes in the material world, few Palestinians have abandoned attachment to their homeland. Indeed, it is often the successful who are the most outspoken advocates of irredentist policies, providing substantial financial support for guerrilla activities against Israel such as those of *al-Fatah*. Often, like Jewish nationalists who settled in America or Europe, Palestinians who have gone abroad, or who have become successful in countries distant from their homeland have been most militant in support of nationalist aspirations.

Thus, although thousands of Palestine refugees have been integrated within the expanding economies of the Arab world as an unplanned and unconscious aspect of the development process, there has been little political or social integration. Whereas schemes primarily calculated to absorb large numbers of refugees have usually failed, some development programs that have had as their chief goal a solution of the refugee problem have absorbed tens of thousands. In large measure UNRWA has succeeded in helping to provide the fundamental physical necessities of its charges, a task assisted by the pace of economic development in the region, but neither UNRWA nor any other agency has been able to stimulate programs that would help solve the refugee problem in isolation from the overall process of regional development. The essence of the matter is that there has been little correlation between the extent of economic integration of the refugees in the Arab world and their social or political absorption.

Efforts to mitigate Arab, particularly refugee, hostility to Israel through such schemes as release of blocked accounts remaining in Israeli-controlled banks or negotiations for payment of compensation for abandoned property have not succeeded in lessening tensions, nor have they gone far in their own terms. Between 1951 and 1956 UNCCP labored through a maze of intricate negotiations involving Israel, the Arab states, the refugees, and several British banks to unfreeze a little over 6000 Arab accounts held in Israel with a total value of some 12 million Palestine pounds. Although finally successful in its efforts to obtain Israeli agreement to the release, the effort did little if anything to lessen hostility between Israel and the Arabs, nor did it contribute substantially to economic improvement of those who received the released funds. Israel regarded the release as a concession, and the Arabs viewed it as an inherent right, long overdue.

From the beginning of its involvement in the refugee problem, the United Nations has attempted to work some easement of tensions by effecting a process for payment of compensation by Israel for refugee property. But there have been both political and technical obstacles to such plans. Both the Arab states and Israel have been ambivalent in their attitudes toward the compensation issue. At times the Israeli government has expressed willingness to consider the question outside of and before a general peace settlement. On the other hand there have been government statements implying that compensation would be paid only as part of an overall peace settlement, to include consideration of claims for war damages, counterclaims by Jewish immigrants from Arab countries, guarantees that such compensation would be used to integrate Arab refugees in areas outside Israel and that payment would free Israel from all other Arab claims against the Jewish state. In general the official position of the Arab governments has been to insist that payment of compensation is directed by Resolution 194, and that without prior implementation of provisions of the resolution pertaining to the refugees, offering a genuine choice between repatriation or compensation, there can be no peaceful settlement.

The technical complications in carrying out any compensation scheme include both identification and evaluation of Arab property. UNCCP's refugee office estimated that more than 80 percent of Israel's pre-1967 total area of 20,850 square kilometers represented abandoned Arab property, although only a little more than a quarter was considered cultivable. Much of this area was unregistered, with ownership identified by cadastral survey. During the British Mandate efforts were made to register land holdings under the Land Settlement Acts, but by 1948 much Arab property was still registered under the old Ottoman system which usually defined properties without a survey. Property entries in the Register of Deeds could rarely be identified with the parcel of land to which they purported to refer. Much land was held by private contracts drawn up in accord with local customs outside the official Land Registry Office. After the 1948 war, there were also difficulties in locating records of land registered according to the British system. For several years UNCCP devoted a large part of its activities to tracing land holdings, and then to evaluating them.

Since such a large part of former Arab property was uncultivated or uncultivable, difficulties arose in land classification for purposes of evaluation. A UNCCP global evaluation of Arab property in 1950 based on a theoretical formula placed the value at 120 million Palestine pounds of purchasing power. Arab valuations of the original value of this property were 10 to 20 times the UNCCP estimates. Furthermore, Arabs have added to the 1948 value of their property the loss of income that would have accrued to the former owners during the past two decades totaling over $5 billion.

Whereas Israel has expressed willingness to consider, within the framework of a general settlement, some form of global compensation with appropriate deductions for losses sustained by her citizens, the Arab approach to the problem has been that compensation must be paid to individuals who suffered losses, and that such payments are a right which must in no way carry implications of surrender by Palestinians of political rights, Occasional efforts by Israel to settle property claims with individual refugees or groups representing them have been attacked by Arab governments, and those who entered into such negotiations have found themselves in difficulty, if not in serious trouble, sometimes resulting in imprisonment or exile from one or another of the host countries. Efforts to bypass the fundamental question of Palestine Arab irredentism through schemes such as release of blocked bank accounts or payments of compensation have so far foundered on the political problems. Such efforts have not been regarded by Arabs as concessions or as indications of good will by Israel. Rather, they have been considered as attempts to obtain fulfillment of inherent Arab rights which must be realized before any basic settlement is even discussed with Israel.

Shortly after the beginning of the Kennedy Administration, one more attempt was made to explore possibilities of compromise. Again, efforts were concentrated on effecting a formula to resolve the refugee question through negotiations conducted by Dr. Joseph E. Johnson, president of the Carnegie Endowment for International Peace, who was appointed a special representative of the UNCCP in August, 1961. Dr. Johnson's proposals centered on a plan under which each Arab refugee would be given an opportunity, under U.N. supervision, to express his preference for repatriation to Israel or resettlement in the Arab world, or elsewhere. Under the proposal, Israel would be free to reject return of individuals for security reasons and each Arab refugee would be informed of the changes in life awaiting him in Israel. Repatriation and resettlement would be carried out simultaneously over a long period, and would be assisted by a special fund, to which Israel would contribute compensation payments for abandoned Arab property. The United Nations would play a central role in supervising the various stages of the program. Although some Arab governments were willing to consider the Johnson proposals on a pilot basis, refugee organizations and more militant nationalist groups regarded steps necessary to carry out the plan as likely to undermine or to compromise their rights. Nor could Israelis be persuaded to accept any plan threatening them with the return of substantial numbers of Arabs.[38]

Johnson's rationale was that the question of repatriation or resettlement is largely theoretical since, if given a choice, few refugees would return to Israel. The question is essentially a psychological one, in which most of the refugees, if offered an opportunity to determine their own fate, would probably accept resettlement in the surrounding Arab countries with large amounts of economic assistance as an inducement to start life anew in favorable circumstances. However, refugee attitudes during the 20 years up to 1967 seemed to indicate that regardless of whether or not the Palestinians were given such a choice, attachment to their homeland would remain, as would their deep resentment of Israel. These attitudes are not only passed on from one generation to another, so that children of refugees who have never seen Palestine regard the country as their homeland, but they have also been transmitted to Arab peoples throughout the whole Middle East and North Africa. The crucial question for the Arabs is thus not repatriation or resettlement, not compensation, nor even the boundaries of Israel, but the existence of a Jewish state created to carry out the program of Zionism in an area regarded as vital to Arab national aspirations. This became clearly evident in Arab popular reactions to the June, 1967, Six-Day War.

VI. Consequences of the Six-Day War

Political Effects

The Six-Day War greatly altered both the dimensions and the nature of the refugee problem in the Middle East. In addition to more than one million Palestinians who were already classified as refugees, there were hundreds of thousands of additional people displaced by the war or by subsequent continuation of the conflict. About 100,000 Syrians, most of whom are under care of the Syrian government, are estimated to have fled from the Golan Heights. Between 300,000 and 500,000 Egyptians were evacuated from large urban centers such as Suez and Ismailia in the Canal Zone after the war because of frequent artillery duels, and most of them are cared for by the Egyptian government. There are some 250,000 displaced persons from the West Bank and Gaza who crossed to Jordan, some under UNRWA care and some receiving aid from the Jordan govern-

[38]Joseph E. Johnson, "Arab *vs.* Israeli: A Persistent Challenge," *The Middle East Journal,* Vol. 18, No. 1 (Winter, 1964), pp. 1-13; *Christian Science Monitor* (October 4, 1962), Wm. E. Frye, "Mideast Peace Goal of U.S. Plan."

ment. About 162,000 became refugees for a second time during the June war or because of subsequent activities resulting from the conflict. Thus the total number of newly displaced persons is about one million. Furthermore, many refugees and inhabitants of the Jordan valley fled as many as four times since June, 1967, because of the postwar military actions and shelling in the area or because of economic and social dislocations resulting from these hostilities.

About 25,000 Jews left North African countries for Europe and Israel with assistance from various Jewish organizations and the International Red Cross. They fled in response to widespread outbursts early in June, 1967, against Jewish property and lives and against certain Western diplomatic outposts. Those mass uprisings indicated that popular hostility to Israel was not limited to the Arab East but was widespread through the whole region. Incidents occurred not only in countries where there had been constant anti-Israel and sometimes anti-Jewish propaganda but in Tunisia as well where the government had attempted to play down the Palestine question and to keep public emotions in hand.

The causes of recent large population movements were similar to those which created the Arab refugee problem in 1947-1948. Most Palestinians moved because of danger, war rumors both true and false, and for economic reasons resulting from upheaval in the region. About 20,000 Palestinians living in six villages along the former armistice demarcation line between Israel and Jordan were forced by the Israeli army to leave their homes during June, 1967. Large parts, if not all, of the villages were destroyed, because, according to Israeli authorities, they had been used as Arab military bases, although this was denied by the villagers. In Jerusalem some 200 Arab families were given only a few hours' notice before being required to leave their homes to make room for a large plaza before the Wailing Wall. Many of the village evacuees became refugees on the East Bank, some found refuge with Arab families in Israeli-held territory, and others were provided with makeshift shelter by UNRWA. According to the Israeli government all those displaced in Jerusalem were provided with alternative dwellings or funds to find such dwellings.

Two sociology professors from the American University of Beirut conducted a survey on the East Bank among 100 refugee families. It indicated that they fled because of physical fear of the Israelis and a sense of honor. "... There is a very deep-seated fear of Israel specifically ... but even deeper and in some ways more important, it is a fear for honor; the honor and dignity of the family, especially of the women." Although the professors noted few signs of outright atrocities in the accounts of the refugees, "They talked of gestures: the rounding up of persons, searching of homes, not respecting the women's quarters, forcing old men to take off their hats and shoes which is very shameful in the Arab world.[39]

The Special Representative of the U.N. Secretary-General in a report submitted after the war, found it difficult

> to determine the line between physical and psychological pressure. . . . [He indicated] that the local population felt frightened by incidents such as shooting in the air, or the rounding up of civilians. . . . [He] felt that it was likely that many such incidents had taken place and that the Israel forces had not viewed unfavorably the impact of such incidents on the movement of population out of the area.[40]

While UNRWA operations continued with little change in Lebanon and Syria, the Agency faced new situations in East Jordan, the Israeli-occupied West Bank, and the Gaza Strip. During the war and in the months that followed, there was considerable movement of refugee population, including many of the UNRWA staff from Gaza and the West Bank to East Jordan. Established camps with places for tens of thousands of people and facilities such as schools, health centers, and feeding centers remained unused on the West Bank, while in East Jordan thousands of new and second-time refugees were trapped without shelter or access to facilities. These population moves created confusion, since it became difficult to separate "old" and "new" refugees. As of June, 1968, in addition to nearly 500,000 registered refugees shown in UNRWA records in East Jordan, the Jordanian government had registered some 237,500 displaced persons from the West Bank plus several additional thousands from Gaza.[41] Although there was believed to be some duplication between the UNRWA and Jordanian government registrations, as well as rather large duplication within government registration, the actual number of rations issued during June, 1968, in East Jordan was 590,000. The total number of refugees and displaced persons in the country was officially estimated to be about 740,000 people, or about one-half the country's post-June, 1967, population. However, independent observers believed that this figure was inflated, and that 600,000 refugees and displaced persons was more accurate.

Although the United Nations Security Council, General Assembly, and

[39]*Christian Science Monitor,* October 30, 1967.

[40]*Report of the Secretary-General,* Doc. A/6797 (September 15, 1967), pp. 8-10.

[41]The actual number from Gaza is unknown. However, early in 1969 UNRWA was issuing 23,500 rations to UNRWA-registered refugees from Gaza then in East Jordan; and another 22,800 registered DPs from Gaza in East Jordan also received rations, provided by the Jordan government and distributed by UNRWA. These were obvious duplications which were acknowledged by UNRWA but which the Agency, as of January, 1969, had been unable to sort out.

various U.N. agencies endorsed resolutions calling for return to their homes of persons displaced as a result of the June war, only a handful found it possible to go back to territory occupied by Israel. During July and August, 1967, about 14,000 persons returned to the West Bank under a scheme worked out by Israel, Jordan, and the United Nations. Since then another 2000 were permitted to return on grounds of special hardship or family reunion, and Israel has announced plans for permitting still another 7000 to return. In general the position on return of persons displaced by the June, 1967, war is identical to that followed by the respective parties between 1948 and 1967. Despite U.N. Security Council Resolution 242 of November 22, 1967, which called "for achieving a just settlement of the refugee problem . . . ," no progress had been made toward its implementation by the end of 1969.

In October, 1968, Israel's Minister of Foreign Affairs, Abba Eban, told the U.N. General Assembly that the refugee problem could be resolved within a "new peace structure in the Middle East," including secure and recognized boundaries, pledges of mutual nonaggression, open frontiers, free navigation through the area's international waterways, mutual agreements on protection of holy places in Jerusalem, recognition of sovereign integrity, and cooperation in resolving regional problems. With regard to the refugee problem, Eban stated that it had been "caused by war and can be solved by peace." He proposed an international conference of Middle Eastern states and the U.N. specialized agencies, with governments contributing to the refugee relief, to "chart a five-year plan for the solution of the refugee problem in the framework of a lasting peace and the integration of the refugees into productive life. This conference can be called in advance of peace negotiations," he stated. Under the peace settlement, "joint refugee integration and rehabilitation commissions should be established.[42]

While general international reaction to Eban's suggestions was favorable, less because of their novelty than because of their reasonable tone, Arab reaction was hostile. In general, Arab governments in their official positions continued to emphasize full implementation of all U.N. resolutions, particularly the November 22, 1967, resolution and Resolution 194. With regard to the refugee question this meant immediate return of all those displaced by the June, 1967, war, and implementation of paragraph 11 in Resolution 194 as a solution of the pre-June, 1967, refugee dilemma.

Arab reaction to the Six-Day War brought sharply into focus the wide disparity between official government policies as presented in the United Nations and other international diplomatic forums and popular feelings. While the governments were ostensibly working for a return to the pre-

[42]*New York Times,* October 9, 1968.

June, 1967, frontiers, or arguing for those of the 1947 partisan resolution, public sentiment ran in terms of eliminating the Jewish character of the state of Israel, as embodied in the Fedayeen programs. A major consequence of defeat was to intensify Palestinian irredentist sentiments and to rally support, both governmental and popular, for Arab guerrillas or commandos, particularly for the three principal groups: the Palestinian Liberation Organization, *al-Fatah* (whose military activities were undertaken by *al-Assifa*), and the Popular Front for the Liberation of Palestine. All gained widespread support and greatly escalated their activities against Israel after the war. The extent of backing for the Palestinian guerrilla forces was evident in the wide display throughout Arab cities and towns of posters and slogans calling for redemption of Palestine, in the favorable reaction to their activities in the Arab press, in refugee camps, and among university professors, students, intellectuals, and government officials. Their stated objective was not restoration of the pre-June, 1967, armistice frontiers, nor of the boundaries laid out in the 1947 U.N. partition resolution, but total defeat of Israel so that Palestine would again become an Arab country. Although commando leaders had no clearly defined policy concerning the future of the country's Jewish inhabitants, some advanced a secular Palestinian state with guarantees of equal rights to all Jews who lived there before 1948; some urged that, in addition, all Jews from Muslim countries who arrived after 1948 be given equal rights; still others placed no restrictions on citizenship in a secular Palestine. Few if any supporters of the commando movements seemed willing to accept a Palestine Jewish or Zionist state in any form or under any conditions that might have been remotely acceptable to those in Israel who led public opinion or who were responsible for creating government policies, or to the population at large. The political conflict created by differences between Zionist nationalism and Palestine Arab irredentism was not in any way lessened by the June war, but intensified to a pitch higher than ever.

Israeli reaction to intensification of Arab nationalism was increased determination not to relinquish territory acquired during the June war, nor to permit any large scale return of refugees, if such actions seemed to threaten the country's security. Growing resignation to continued Arab hostility was perhaps most clearly evident in the policies and statements of Israel's Minister of Defense, Major-General Moshe Dayan, who was chief architect of occupation policies. Quoting from the writings of Dr. Arthur Ruppin, a Zionist leader who was active in the country during the 1920s and 1930s, General Dayan stated:

> The Arabs do not agree to our venture. If we want to continue our work in Eretz Israel against their desires, there is no alternative but that

lives should be lost. It is our destiny to be in a state of continual warfare with the Arabs. This situation may well be undesirable, but such is the reality.[43]

While placing primary emphasis on security considerations derived from Arab resentment at its existence, Israel also sought to normalize the economic and social life of Arabs in the occupied areas. Shortly after the war, frontiers between Israeli-held territory and East Jordan were opened, expediting movement of thousands of people and of trade and commerce across the Jordan River to the extent permitted by Jordan. This facilitated sale of agricultural produce from the occupied West Bank in Jordan and from other Arab markets to the east. Although actions of the military authorities responsible for the occupation were strict, and at times arbitrary or harsh, local Arab authorities were permitted to continue their functions under Israeli supervision in accordance with the Geneva Convention. Terrorist activities by the commandos against civilian populations in Israel's large urban centers sharpened security measures by Israel's armed forces and so threatened to undermine Arab freedom of movement in the occupied areas to a point where relationships between Jews and Arabs would be jeopardized if not broken off. This was, of course, a prime objective of the commandos, and Israel's response in part accorded with the Fedayeen objective to isolate the country even further from its Arab neighbors.

Within Israel, both public opinion and government policy reflected differences in reaction to the problems created by acquisition of one million additional Arabs. The one million Arabs on the West Bank and in Gaza added to the Arab minority within the 1949 armistice frontiers of about 300,000, brought the number of Arabs under Israeli jurisdiction to over one-third the total augmented population.[44] With growing limits on potential sources of Jewish immigration and the high Arab birth rate, many Israelis feared that permanent incorporation of the occupied areas would within a few years leave them a minority, and thus undermine the Jewish state. Various proposals were put forward for dealing with this quandary, euphemistically referred to as the "demographic problem." They included establishment of heavily Arab occupied areas as an autonomous state in which Israeli armed forces would have security bases; the return of parts of the occupied areas, especially the West Bank minus Jerusalem, to Jordan

[43]*Jerusalem Post*, Weekly Overseas Edition, No. 414, September 30, 1968, p. 7.
[44]Estimated Arab population under Israeli control early in 1969:

Israel	300,000	
Gaza	350,000	$\pm$ 25,000
West Bank	650,000	$\pm$ 50,000
Total	1,300,000	$\pm$ 75,000

as part of an overall peace settlement; establishment of a binational state in which political power would be divided, not on the basis of population but by a fixed ratio; or some variation of these alternatives.

Economic Effects

The economic impact of the Six-Day War on the Arab countries seriously affected progress made during the previous two decades as well as immediate future prospects for continued refugee economic absorption. Jordan was the country most drastically affected. Almost 40 percent of the current East Bank population of about 1.8 million consists of refugees and displaced persons. The influx of about 400,000 people from the West Bank and Gaza increased the East Bank population by about one-third, greatly expanding demand for food, shelter, and basic services. Since most of the recently added population were poor and unskilled, they could not be regarded as an addition to East Jordan's productive capacity, at least not within the immediate future. According to a recent U.N. study, [45]

> The magnitude of the loss in Jordan's economic potential because of the Israeli occupation of the West Bank accounted for 38 percent of Jordan's total gross domestic product, with particularly high percentages for services (55 percent), transportation (47 percent) and wholesale and retail trade (43 percent). The contribution of the West Bank to Jordan's output of some agricultural products was even higher (e.g., over 60 to 65 percent for fruits and vegetables and 80 percent for olives) and, although the share of the West Bank in total industrial output amounted only to about 20 percent, the number of industrial establishments there represented about 48 percent of the total for the Kingdom . . . employing 37 percent of the Jordanian labour force engaged in industry. Income from tourism and remittances from Jordanians working abroad—two major sources of foreign exchange earnings—have declined about 85 percent and 50 percent, respectively . . . implementation of the "Seven-Year Programme for Economic Development of Jordan, 1964-1970" has suffered a major blow. Several major projects have had to be suspended and others re-examined in the light of the new circumstances, special emphasis being placed on labour intensive projects which can alleviate the increasing unemployment.

Not only was work on the major East Ghawr irrigation canal halted, but parts of the completed waterway were severed in the frequent artillery duels fought between Israeli and Jordanian forces since June, 1967. Furthermore, nearly all inhabitants of the east Jordan Valley, once considered

[45]*Studies on Selected Development Problems in Various Countries in the Middle East,* United Nations, ECOSOC, Doc. E/4511 (Summary), May 15, 1968, pp. 14-15.

a principal area for refugee resettlement, have fled. Jordan's gold and foreign exchange reserves have actually increased, mainly because of financial assistance of 40 million sterling, pledged by Kuwait, Libya, and Saudi Arabia at the 1967 Arab Summit Conference in Khartoum. Despite uncertain political conditions, the economic impact of the war, and the influx of refugees, there has been some revival of the Jordanian economy, especially in construction widely evident in Amman and in the expansions of small industry and trade.

Although Iraq, Kuwait, and Saudi Arabia were not directly involved in the war, suffering no major economic reversals, their budgets and development programs were adversely affected. The temporary cutoff of oil shipments from these countries resulted in reduction of revenue with consequent contraction of development budgets. According to the above-mentioned U.N. report, Iraq's development program was revised, reducing allocations for agriculture and industry by some 12 percent. The anticipated expansion of the Kuwait Fund for Arab Economic Development was postponed indefinitely. Diversion of funds by Saudi Arabia, Kuwait, and Libya to Jordan and the U.A.R. also was responsible for contraction of development programs by the donor nations.

As a result of the disrupted pattern of tourism in the Middle East, the number of travelers to Lebanon decreased during 1967. The departure of many foreigners as a result of the war, the lag in tourism, and a decline in construction culminated in a general decline of confidence in Lebanon and contraction of economic activity. According to the U.N. study:

> The June hostilities also affected capital movements within the countries studied, and between them and the rest of the world in an adverse manner which cannot yet be ascertained. Most important, however, it is not the physical damage and the reconstruction tasks confronting these countries. It is that a very large number of people live in conditions of precariousness or increased precariousness and in a climate of uncertainty which pervades the economic and social life of their nations. This uncertainty and the diversion of resources for increased military expenditure casts a shadow on the pursuit of development efforts.[46]

Insofar as economic absorption of refugees displaced by continuing hostilities between Israel and the Arab nations is a function of regional development, solution of the problem has been seriously retarded. Insofar as a political solution of the refugee problem is determined by the state of hostility between Israel and the Arab world, it too has been set back farther than ever before. While Palestine irredentism has been intensified to a higher degree, thus casting doubt on possibilities of resolving the con-

[46]*Ibid.*, p. 17.

flict between Arab nationalism and Zionism, there remains a residue of hope that the economic developments prerequisite to creating absorptive capacity may again be generated in the near future. The U.N. study cited above concluded that the Arab governments "have shown themselves conscious of the importance of sustaining and intensifying these [development] efforts. At the Arab Summit Conference in Khartoum, renewed interest was expressed in the establishment, on a cooperative basis, of an Arab institution for the financing of economic and social development projects and in achieving closer trade cooperation among the countries." However, such resolutions in the past have produced few if any results. Only the Kuwait Fund for Arab Economic Development has initiated successfully any major inter-Arab economic development.

VII. Can the Arab Refugee Problem Be Solved?

Discussion of solutions to the refugee problem often becomes involved in circular argumentation. On one hand, it is asserted that if the refugee problem is resolved, the broader issues of the Palestine conflict will become manageable; on the other hand, there are those who maintain that only if there is an overall resolution of the Arab-Israeli conflict will it be possible to end the refugee dilemma. Both approaches emphasize the close interconnection of the refugee fate with the struggle for Palestine, but neither sufficiently emphasizes what to this observer appears to be the most crucial issue in the dispute, that is, whether or not Arab nationalism will or can accept the existence of a Jewish or Zionist state in the Middle East. If the various strands of the Arab nationalist movement do not in the near future accept the state in its approximate present form (but not necessarily present frontiers) then neither the Arab nationalist movement nor the various Arab governments are likely to agree to any specific solutions of the refugee problem acceptable to Israel or capable of eliciting support from the Western powers, particularly from the United States. To those Arabs who seek to end the existence of Israel, the refugee problem is less a humanitarian than a political or a national problem; therefore, any solution that includes continuation of Israel's existence, whether it involves refugee resettlement, repatriation, compensation, or some combination of these, is for them not a solution because it would prevent control of all of Palestine by the Palestine Arabs.

Since June, 1967, the passage of time has not had a therapeutic effect on tensions between Israel and the Arab nations. Although the Arab states sustained a defeat which shook the whole Arab world and undermined possibilities of destroying Israel through military means in the foreseeable future, Arab nationalist antagonism to Israel has become so intense that until now no Arab government has been able to resist popular pressures against a negotiated and definitive peace settlement. Both the governments of the United Arab Republic and the Hashemite kingdom of Jordan have indicated in statements to the United Nations and to interested governments that they would be willing to come to terms with Israel on the basis of the November 22, 1967, Security Council resolution which, *inter alia,* calls for solution of the refugee problem; however, both governments also overtly support Arab commando movements whose stated objective is Israel's destruction, including termination of its Zionist nationalist institutions and character. The ambiguity of positions taken by all Arab governments toward the commando movements also makes implementation of theoretical solutions to the refugee problem rather remote.

Assuming, however, that the governments of the U.A.R. and Jordan could resist the commando movements and the popular pressures these movements have generated (a doubtful assumption at best) and that they could achieve a peace settlement with Israel, how would this affect the refugee problem?

To spell out prospects of solving the refugee problem within the context of a peace settlement, the nature of such a theoretical settlement must be postulated. It would be necessary to end all hostilities between Israel and the neighboring states; to terminate the state of belligerency, boycott, and blockade which the Arab states have imposed upon Israel; to set fixed and mutually agreed boundaries between Israel and its neighbors; to determine a mutually agreed status for Jerusalem; and to halt the Middle East arms race, establishing mutually acceptable methods of arms control and inspection (including nuclear capabilities). These would be prerequisites in any peace settlement that would also include resolution of the refugee problem.

It must be assumed that settlement of the refugee problem would involve compromise between Israel and the Arab states based upon consideration of refugee desires and aspirations. A first step would be to determine these desires and aspirations through a plan such as that proposed by Dr. Joseph Johnson. Without conditions of peace such as those outlined above it would be impossible to establish an environment in which a creditable survey of refugee views could be undertaken, or to establish conditions in which large scale economic development, specifically aimed at facilitating resettlement, could be undertaken. Without the stable environment of peace, it would be difficult if not impossible to persuade refugee leaders to permit their followers to make an honest choice, or to cooperate in resettlement programs intended to resolve the problem. Furthermore, without peace, those responsible for the security of Israel could not be persuaded to accept any form of free choice that might involve return of thousands, or possibly tens or hundreds of thousands, of Arabs to territory under Israel's control.

Most of those who propose offering the Arab refugees a free choice between repatriation and resettlement maintain that only a small number would opt for return to Israel; that by far the larger number of refugees would choose resettlement in some area not under Israeli control. This is a speculative thesis not yet tested by any extensive public-opinion sampling. However, many observers, including this one, believe that as a result of the June, 1967, war, a large number of 1948 Arab refugees who remained under Israeli control and who had opportunity to observe at first hand the changing conditions in the country during the previous two decades through visits to former homes and property would prefer equitable individual compensation to settlement in areas under Israel's jurisdiction.

The previously mentioned study, conducted by a team of sociologists from the American University of Beirut, indicated that the vast majority of refugees who fled during the June, 1967, war would prefer to return under any conditions to their pre-June, 1967, homes. The study did indicate that the proportion of "new" 1967 refugees who desired to return to their homes (82%) was larger than that of the "old" 1948 refugees who desired to return regardless of conditions (64%). Those among the new refugees who wished to return conditionally was 16 percent and among the old, 21 percent.[47] Thus it becomes obvious that peaceful solution of the refugee problem is inextricably tied with the status of the West Bank and the Gaza Strip. If these two areas were returned to some form of Arab control as part of a general peace settlement, it would be far easier to carry out the wishes of old and new refugees who lived in them before 1967. If they remain wholly or partially under Israeli control (not a likely possibility as part of a mutually agreed-upon peace settlement), then it would be more difficult to determine the fate of refugees who left the areas in 1967, or of the old refugees who remained there after the June war.

The conditions of peace outlined above would be necessary in order to divert the large sums of money now expended on military security to the costs of regional economic development, which would make possible refugee rehabilitation. Although diversion of large amounts of money from arms expenditures to economic development would lessen the need for outside assistance, most estimates of the region's economic potential indicate that foreign aid would still be required for the development projects necessary to solve the refugee problem.

[47] Peter C. Dodd and Halim Barakat, *River without Bridges: A Study of the Exodus of the 1967 Arab Palestinian Refugees,* Monograph Series No. 10 (Beirut: Institute for Palestine Studies, 1968).

Even under the most favorable conditions there would remain a hard core of refugees who could not be economically rehabilitated. They are older adults who prior to 1948 were mostly unskilled agricultural laborers, who during the following two decades by and large lived in refugee camps, and who were either totally or mostly unemployed. They owned little or no property, thus would benefit marginally, if at all, from payment of individual compensation. The group includes most men and women in their late forties or older, of whom there are several tens of thousands. Few of them could be retrained to participate in the development process even if opportunities for employment were available. Most would be social welfare cases who would probably remain under the care of the host countries should United Nations refugee operations be halted in the area. This would not be an especially difficult burden for the host countries, given the theoretical prospects of general economic improvement envisioned within the context of the peaceful conditions postulated above.

More likely than a general peace settlement is continuation of some form of belligerency along the lines of the existing status quo. Without a settlement that not only ends hostilities, but also terminates the state of belligerency and all uncertainties that accompany it, it is unlikely that Israel's security authorities can be persuaded to accept any large-scale return of refugees beyond the present minute, almost token, reunion of families. Short of an overall settlement, it is unlikely that Israel will surrender security control of any substantial part of Arab territories it now occupies. Continued Israeli occupation of Arab territories will considerably increase prospects of a growing commando movement uncontrolled by the neighboring Arab countries. Continued political influence of the commandos in these countries will probably be a major obstacle to implementing any large-scale development plan specifically intended to facilitate extensive refugee rehabilitation.

Continuation of even a modified status quo in which hostilities were either terminated or contained, but in which the state of belligerency continued, would mean prolongation of the arms race, border confrontations, and attempts by each side to escalate its military prowess. Continued arms competition would divert a substantial amount of resources which otherwise might be invested in regional development and either direct or indirect refugee rehabilitation.

Given the political, the military, and the economic uncertainties of the status quo, it would be difficult to postulate with any reasonable degree of accuracy possibilities of large-scale refugee resettlement in the Arab world. Theoretical calculations of refugee economic absorption as a marginal by-product of long-term regional economic development or of development in Jordan, Syria, Iraq, Lebanon, and the Persian Gulf states might be postulated. Guidelines for such an exercise were laid out by Dag Hammarskjöld in his 1959 analysis of the problem. It should be emphasized, however, that because of the many uncertainties in such a situation, because of the uneven pace of development likely to occur under these conditions, only the most tentative estimates can be made of possibilities for refugee integration. Above all, such integration would, because of political considerations, be marginal to other more direct development efforts.

Within the framework of the status quo, in which Israel continued to hold substantial Arab-inhabited areas such as Gaza and the West Bank, it might be possible for the Israeli government to initiate a number of pilot projects for refugee resettlement. If successful they would to some degree lighten the burden of the refugees upon Israel, the United Nations, and Israel's friends, while improving the economic status of the refugees who cooperated. On the other hand, Arab governments would regard unilateral involvement by Israel in the affairs of the Palestine refugees with a jaundiced eye and the commandos would probably attempt to sabotage such efforts. But, unless given a free hand to experiment, Israel would be unlikely to initiate projects of this type in areas under its jurisdiction.

After occupation of the West Bank in the latter half of 1967, a number of committees were established by the Israeli government to examine possibilities of refugee rehabilitation. Organized from Israeli officials, scholars, and technical experts, the committees had no Arab representation. Although a number of preliminary draft surveys were completed, the government never carried out any major projects for Arab refugee resettlement in the occupied areas. Lack of agreement among the various parties in the coalition government on long-term policy for the West Bank and its Arab occupants was believed to have been the chief obstacle to carrying out the projects, although high-level government committees met as late as the spring of 1969 to discuss them.

The Israeli government has adopted a policy of permitting local Arab West Bank authorities to carry out their duties, and Israeli ministries subsidize functions such as public health, agriculture, education, and the like, without imposing any major structural changes on the society or economy of the West Bank. This policy seems most likely to be pursued for the immediate future, unless there is a decision to change the political status of the West Bank. Changes might occur if the territory is incorporated into Israel (as was the case of Arab Jerusalem), or if a separate Palestine Arab government is established in the West Bank area. If Arab areas are integrated into Israel, there would probably be increased opposition from Arabs living under Israel's jurisdiction and from the neighboring Arab states, thus making difficult, if not impossible, any development programs that would facilitate refugee rehabilitation.

Still another rearrangement of the existing political situation might establish the West Bank and the Gaza Strip as Palestinian entities, separated from jurisdiction of either Israel or any of the existing Arab states. Since June, 1967, many Palestine Arab nationalists and a few Israelis have called for establishment of a Palestine entity to be governed by Palestine Arabs. The rationale is that the people who inhabit these areas, although Arab, do not desire return to Jordanian or Egyptian control, but prefer to govern themselves. In essence, this would mean reconstitution of the concept, although not the actual boundaries, of the 1947 U.N. partition plan that envisioned division of Palestine into a Jewish state, an Arab state, and an international enclave including Jerusalem and Bethlehem.

Under the variety of present proposals the largely Arab-populated areas of Palestine would be turned over to Arab civil jurisdiction. Plans range from the so-called Allon scheme, with Israeli security outposts along the Jordan River, to Arab proposals for return to the full original partition plan. They all have in common the concept of an Arab Palestine closely linked with the Jewish state through economic and other ties. In some measure the *de facto* situation is evolving along these general lines, especially in the West Bank. Although Israeli military authorities have final control, and Israeli civil authorities exercise decisive authority in many matters pertaining to agriculture, education, and the like, there is a relatively large measure of Palestinian local administration at the village and town level.

If the Israelis could come to terms with the Palestine Arabs, either as part of an overall peace agreement including the neighboring states, or separately, it might be possible to terminate or to greatly diminish commando activity thus facilitating evacuation from the occupied territories. Some mutually satisfactory arrangement would have to be agreed upon for Jerusalem, since no Arab government, and especially a Palestine Arab government, could surrender authority in the entire city. Within the context of a peace settlement resolution of the Jerusalem problem might make the city a joint Arab-Israeli capital, or a city in which Arab areas are returned to Arab jurisdiction and those with predominantly Jewish population would remain in Israel, but the city would be unified in common municipal services such as water, eletricity, sanitation, transport, and the like. Jerusalem would be semi-international in that it would be under control of a Palestinian Arab state and an Israeli state with equal access and rights for all citizens of both.

Without arrangements such as those outlined above, involving Israeli evacuation from heavily Arab-inhabited areas of Palestine including Jerusalem, it is difficult to postulate that a peace arrangement can be made with Palestine Arab nationalists. If such an arrangement is arrived at, it is quite possible that the Palestine Arab and Israeli Jewish sectors of the country might evolve toward some form of economic and political fusion along the lines of a federated, cantonized, or binational entity. It may be argued that it is somewhat visionary, given the deep antagonisms between Arabs and Israeli Jews, but the prospect of peace generally is visionary considering the psychological and emotional cleavages between the two peoples. If emotions are cooled sufficiently to make possible cooperation in a peace settlement, there is no reason why they cannot continue to cool to a point where Arabs and Israelis find peaceful cooperation in a multinational venture preferable to political, social, and economic isolation behind the walls of separatist enclaves.

Given possibilities of initial Palestine Arab separateness, leading through peaceful coexistence toward cooperation and eventual fusion with Israel, settlement of large numbers of refugees would be facilitated. To begin with, the new refugees, who left their homes on the West Bank and in Gaza since June, 1967, would be able to return, thus lessening the burden on Jordan and on the international community. Within a new Palestine state, other Palestinians could also be "in-gathered" and efforts made at rehabilitating the Palestine community which was uprooted beginning in 1948. Many of the Palestinians who have contributed so much to development of countries in the Arabian Peninsula and elsewhere in the Middle East would find opportunities for their creative talents in their own homeland. Their return in large numbers to a reconstituted homeland would diminish the widespread irredentism that has infected the whole Arab world and has become integral to the ideas of Arab nationalism.

Rehabilitation efforts might be financed with large amounts of assistance from capital-surplus, Arab oil-producing countries, the United States, and the international community, and through individual compensation payments for property left in Israel. Economic assistance would also help to sustain the hard-core refugees who cannot be rehabilitated, but who would greatly appreciate opportunity to return to their homeland or as close to their original homes as possible.

The variable conditions outlined above—that is, an overall peace settlement between Israel and the Arab states, a separate peace with the Palestine Arabs and reconstitution of a Palestine Arab state, or continuation of the status quo—will depend in large measure on forces outside the Middle East. The extent to which countries in the area continue to resist alternatives to the status quo is strongly affected by attitudes of the United States and the Soviet Union, by the extent to which arms supplies of the antagonists are replenished by their great-power supporters, and by the degree of political support the great powers give to status quo positions. Although the great powers cannot force the Arabs and the Israelis to make peace, they can do much to create an atmosphere in which the benefits of a peaceful solution to the Palestine and to the refugee problem become the wisest policy for governments in the area to follow.

In conclusion, a final caveat: wisdom and rational calculations are not the decisive factors in determining policies of governments on matters such as the Arab refugee dilemma. One has only to compare it to the Cyprus conflict between Turks and Greeks. The dimensions of the Cyprus problem are much smaller than those of the Palestine encounter, yet there has been no more success in resolving the clash between Greeks and Turks than in settling differences between Israel and the Arabs. In Cyprus there are no more than 100,000 Turks living among some 400,000 Greeks. The Turks there number a little more than the population of a Turkish provincial city. Economic problems of resettling them among over 30 million Turks cannot be described as insurmountable, especially if international economic assistance were forthcoming, a possibility for which the United States would certainly be willing to pay if it would end the dangers of war between two NATO allies. Yet this problem also continues to plague international relations and to threaten the peace of the region—not because there are no rational answers, but because of deep emotional and psychological dilemmas. The Turks, like the Arabs, oppose any large-scale transfers of populations, not because of material difficulties, but because they insist on "national rights" and fear the intentions of their rival. The Turks fear Greek imperial aspirations much as the Arabs fear Israeli expansionism. Although the Palestine and the Cyprus problems may not be precisely parallel, they both indicate that in the immediate future in the Middle East deep-rooted fears and historic rivalries are more likely to shape the course of events than the "rational" calculations of Western economists or political scientists.

CHAPTER 9

Palestinian Refugees: Two Surveys of Uprootedness

Halim Barakat and Peter Dodd

I. Summary

This chapter summarizes two surveys made of Palestinian refugee families: one of a lower-class population in a camp setting, the Camp Zeezya sample, the other of a largely middle-class population not resident in camps, the Amman sample. These two samples were drawn from the 1967 refugees in Jordan, that is, those who left their homes in the wake of the 1967 war.[1] This population, then about 200,500, is about one-eighth of the total number of Palestinian refugees in the Middle East.

Prior to June, 1967, the majority of these families, both lower and middle-class, were well integrated into their home communities. Many of those who were uprooted for the first time in 1967, called new refugees in this study, owned houses and lands in communities where their families had long resided. Others uprooted once before in 1948 and called old refugees in our terminology, although handicapped by their earlier displacement, had also acquired property and a measure of stability in their second homes before being uprooted in 1967. There is little indication that these families were marginal to their communities.

The exodus was caused by the events of the war and the subsequent Israeli occupation of the West Bank. The wartime occurrence that the refugees found most terrifying was the aerial bombardment. The subsequent occupation brought with it the destruction of homes and villages, threats to members of the family, the shaming of respected persons, and economic dislocation. The adverse effects of the occupation were especially evident in the Amman (the middle-class) sample.

We obtained data on political attitudes and expectations from this sample. While 90 percent of these families wanted to return to their homes, only one-third of them expected to be able to return peacefully. The majority thought that there would be no political solution to the Palestine problem and that only military action could achieve a solution. They distinguished between Jews and Zionists, directing their hostility toward the latter. If the situation were improved, they indicated willingness to coexist with Jews as "ordinary citizens."

[1]For a more complete presentation of this material with methodological information see Peter C. Dodd and Halim Barakat, *River Without Bridges: A Study of the Exodus of the 1967 Arab Palestinian Refugees,* Monograph Series No. 10, Institute for Palestine Studies, Beirul, 1968.

The majority of families in both the Zeezya and the Amman samples expressed the desire to return to their home communities. Many wanted to return immediately; but others, especially in the Amman or middle-class sample, wanted to return only after Israeli withdrawal. When new refugee families are compared with old refugee families, it appears that the new refugees are more likely to want to return immediately, and the old refugees are more likely to want to return later. The new refugee families tend to have stronger ties to their home communities than the old refugees, reflecting higher socioeconomic status and the presence of relatives in these communities. Families with strong ties want to return immediately; those with weaker ties, want to wait until after Israeli withdrawal.

Political attitudes also influence the desire to return. Mild attitudes toward Israel are concomitant with the desire to return immediately, while militant attitudes accompany the desire to return after Israeli withdrawal.

The question of resettlement is extremely sensitive and was not approached directly in our interviews. It is our impression, based on the interviews, that the families in both samples are strongly opposed to resettlement. The desire to return home precludes willingness to resettle elsewhere.

We have not discussed any of the proposed solutions to the problem of the Palestinians, refugees as well as nonrefugees. It is our conclusion that two of our findings bear directly on any proposed solution. One is that more than 90 percent of the refugees want to return to their homes, often with an intense longing. The other is that the refugee families, prior to the war of 1967, were well integrated into their home communities. They owned houses and land, had relatives about them, and held respected positions in these communities. Their desire to return, therefore, is supported by the evidence of pre-1967 social integration.

II. Background

In June, 1967, large numbers of Palestinian Arabs crossed the Jordan River seeking safety. They left behind them their homes, their lands, their properties, and their livelihoods and, by doing so, became refugees. Some, less than half the total number, became refugees for the second time in their lives, having already been refugees before in 1947-1948.[2] The major-

[2]Between 1948 and 1967 only one field study was published of the 1948 refugees, and it covered only English-speaking refugees, an atypical sample: see F. C. Bruhns, "A Study of Arab Refugee Attitudes," *Middle East Journal,* Spring 1955, 30-38. Preliminary results have now been published on an Israeli study of refugees from 1948 who remained in the West Bank after the June war: see Yoram Ben-Porath, "Some Economic Characteristics of a Refugee Camp—Preliminary Results," *Middle East Development,* Hebrew University, Harry S. Truman Center for the Advancement of Peace, Jerusalem, 1968, pp. 32-63.

ity, however, were new refugees, Palestinians who had never before been forced to leave their homes.

By the end of July, 1967, the number of these refugees in the kingdom of Jordan was estimated to be over 200,000.[3] Of these, about 14,000 were permitted to return to the West Bank in August, 1967.[4] The flow of refugees into the East Bank sector of Jordan continued throughout 1967 and 1968. Many of them come from the West Bank sector of Jordan, presently occupied by Israel. Others come from the Gaza Strip, also under Israeli occupation. The total number of 1967 refugees in the East Bank sector of Jordan is estimated by some authorities to be as high as 400,000, in an area whose pre-1967 population was less than one million.

About one-third of these new refugees are housed in tent camps provided by UNRWA for Palestinian refugees, by the Jordanian government, and by charitable agencies. The remaining two-thirds reside in the towns and villages of East Jordan. Their living conditions, in or out of the camps, have been and continue to be poor and their future uncertain.

III. Methodology

In order to gather information on the interests, attitudes, experiences, and living conditions of the refugees, we conducted two surveys with the assistance of students from the American University of Beirut and the University of Jordan. The first survey, made in the late summer of 1967, samples the camp population of Camp Zeezya, now renamed Talbiya, about thirty miles south of Amman. The second survey interviewed out-of-camp refugees families living in Amman in the summer of 1968.

The differences between refugees living in camps at the time of interview and those living elsewhere is a major point of comparison. Information about the attitudes of the camp refugees comes from the Zeezya sample; that of the out-of-camp refugees, comes from the Amman sample.

We divided the 1967 refugees into two groups, old and new. The old refugees are those who were displaced in the 1948 crisis and again uprooted in 1967. Most, but not all, of these were registered with UNRWA before June, 1967. New refugees are those who were uprooted for the first time in 1967. Until June of that year they had lived in the towns and villages

---

[3]United Nations, *Report of the Commissioner-General of UNRWA* (United Nations Relief and Works Agency), July 1, 1966-June 30, 1967, General Assembly, 22nd session, Supplement No. 13, Doc. A/6713 (New York, 1967), p. 11. See also the *Report of the Commissioner-General of UNRWA*, July 1, 1967-June 30, 1968, and July 1, 1968-June 30, 1969.

[4]Fred J. Khouri, *The Arab-Israel Dilemma* (Syracuse: Syracuse University Press, 1968).

of the West Bank districts of Nablus, Jerusalem, and Hebron. These two groups differ in a number of respects. Their differences and their similarities form a second point of comparison.

Both surveys were carried out under unusual conditions. The Camp Zeezya survey took place shortly after the Arab-Israeli war in June, 1967, which had disastrous consequences for the kingdom of Jordan. Half of the country had been occupied by the Israeli army. The unoccupied section, the East Bank, was crowded with refugees, and the milieu, one of suspicion, fear, and rumor. The second survey, in Amman, took place under slightly improved conditions. The country had begun to recover from the shock of war. Israeli raids into Jordanian territory were frequent, however, and the people were living in a state of nearly constant alert. Because of these conditions, it was not possible to obtain exact information about the location and distribution of Palestinians, or to apply the sampling techniques that are customary in survey research. The authors tried to obtain as diversified a sample as possible, and especially in the case of the Zeezya survey, to establish a rapport with the respondents to ease the climate of fear and suspicion.

Camp Zeezya was selected as representative of the tent camps, which numbered 11 in September, 1967, housing approximately 70,000 camp refugees, or one-third of all 1967 Palestinian refugees. We selected a random sample of one-third of the tents in Zeezya. The unit of study was the family, defined as a household unit: persons related by a kin tie and sharing common living facilities. Since some of the families occupied more than one tent, the Zeezya sample of 100 families occupied a total of 120 tents. This sample represents the population of Camp Zeezya, and, by extension, appears to be reasonably representative of the tent-camp population of refugees.

Most of the refugees do not live in the tent camps. The main reason for remaining in them seems to be financial necessity. Families who had a source of income or relatives with whom they could live chose to stay outside the camps. In the fall of 1967 these out-of-camp refugees numbered approximately 140,000, or two-thirds of the refugee population. By the time of our second survey in July, 1968, this number had increased substantially. These refugees were more difficult to locate; drawing a sample of this refugee population presented special problems. Not only more numerous than the in-camp refugees, these refugees were also likely to be of higher socioeconomic status.

We concentrated the interviewing for the second survey in Amman, working in as many different neighborhoods as possible. We located respondents with the assistance of friends, relatives, and relief officials, instructing our assistants to obtain interviews from persons of different social classes, districts of origin in the West Bank, religion, and previous refugee status ("old" and "new" refugees). This procedure was relatively successful, as judged by the available criteria.

The Amman sample contains a large number of middle-class families, so large that it is referred to as the middle-class sample. Because the Zeezya sample, which was finished first, was found to include only a few middle-class families, we chose to concentrate on the middle-class refugee in the Amman sample.

All interviews took place in Arabic, conducted by teams of interviewers working in pairs. We made every effort to train the interviewers in objectivity and full reporting, and to identify and explain possible sources of bias. One of us also reviewed the interviews before accepting them. In Zeezya, the interviewers worked as volunteers; in Amman, they were paid standard wages. There were no refusals to be interviewed in Zeezya, while in Amman the refusal rate was less than 5 percent.

The interview schedule consisted of 45 questions organized into 10 major topics: the composition of the refugee family; their previous residence and property; family income and sources of livelihood; the social bonds with their home community; family educational level and plans for education; experiences and feelings before the 1967 war; during the war; and after the war; present situation of the family; and attitudes toward the crisis and toward the future. All questions were open-ended, permitting a flexible style of interviewing. In Zeezya, the interview took the form of a visit and all responses were recorded after the interview. Repeated visits were often necessary to complete the interview. In Amman, the interview was more formal and responses were recorded in the presence of the respondent. The Amman interviews included additional questions on the likelihood of return to Palestine, the possibilities of a political solution, and attitudes toward Israel.

The refugee's community of origin is one of three districts that comprised the West Bank of Jordan before June, 1967. Table 1 shows the distribution of refugees by district of residence before becoming refugees. The distribution is shown for three populations: the Zeezya sample, the Amman sample, and the entire population of 1967 refugees as of July of that year, taken from a Jordanian governmen report.[5] The 1967 refugees include only those persons who left their homes because of the June war and moved to the East Bank districts of Jordan. They do not include persons who left their homes because of the events of 1948 and were already located in the East Bank districts. In all three populations the governorate of Jerusalem is the place of origin for more than half the refugees; the

[5]Joint Ministry Commission for Refugees, *Official Report* (unpublished) obtained from the Ministry of Information, Jordanian Government, August, 1967.

governorate of Nablus second in frequency, and the governorate of Hebron, third.[6]

Table 1

District of Residence in the West Bank before June, 1967

(%)

District	Zeezya Sample (N = 100)	Amman Sample (N = 135)	All Refugees as of July, 1967* (N = 200,000 persons)
Governorate of Jerusalem	74	54	58
Governorate of Nablus	14	25	29
Governorate of Hebron	10	08	13
Gaza Strip	(00)	12	(00)
No information	02	01	—
Total %	100	100	100

Note: N = Number of families unless otherwise indicated.
*Source: Joint Ministry Commission for Refugees, *Official Report,* Amman, Jordan, August, 1967.

Table 1 shows that both of the samples are roughly similar to the parent population in terms of the district of residence. The Amman sample appears to resemble the parent population more than does the Zeezya sample. The parent population shows that 58 percent of the refugees came from the district of Jerusalem; the comparable figure for Amman is 54 percent and for Zeezya 74 percent. The Zeezya sample and its parent population do not include any persons from Gaza. Refugees from Gaza did not come into the East Bank until early fall, 1967. The parent population was reported as of July 31, 1967, but the Zeezya sample was made in September. Accordingly, neither of these groups includes people from Gaza.

Our survey samples show a higher proportion of new refugees to old than does the report of the Jordanian government. In the Zeezya sample the proportion of new to old refugees was 61 percent; in the Amman sample, 59 percent, while the government report gives this proportion as 51 percent. It is not clear whether this is a sampling fluctuation or the Jordanian report has underestimated the true proportion of new refugees.

IV. Socioeconomic Status and Integration in the Home Communities

What kind of people became refugees in 1967? It is important to know the distribution by social class, as well as the occupation, education, income,

[6]See also *Statistical Guide to Jordan,* Department of Statistics, Amman (1965), for the total population of each governorate.

and ownership of property. This will help to answer questions of deprivation and marginality. How different is their present status as refugees from their status prior to June, 1967? To what extent, prior to the war, were these refugee families already marginal to their communities? Or were they well integrated into these communities? We included questions in the interview on the structural ties linking the families to their communities, and we suggest the basis for the refugees' desire to return to their homes.

Each sample is presented separately. In each sample we compared the new and old refugees, a meaningful distinction since the old refugee had been handicapped in terms of economic status and community integration.

The old refugees have not forgotten their original homes occupied before 1968. In the present discussion, however, the home communities of the old refugees means the places where they were living in June, 1967, immediately before the outbreak of war. Many of these refugees had established themselves in the cities, towns, and villages of the West Bank. Many more were located in refugee camps.

Table 2

Occupation, Education, and Income, Zeezya Sample

(%)

Occupation	Old Refugees (N = 37)	New Refugees (N = 58)	Total (N = 95)
Farmer, peasant	24	40	34
Manual worker	22	10	15
Semiskilled worker	19	19	19
Skilled and clerical workers	6	7	7
Salesman, shopowner	22	14	17
Professional	0	2	1
Retired, unemployed, not classifiable	7	7	7
Total, %	100	100	100

Educational Level	Old Refugees (N = 30)	New Refugees (N = 47)	Total (N = 77)
Illiterate	70	49	57
Some elementary schooling	17	26	22
Completed elementary schooling	6	10	11
Secondary schooling or more	7	15	10
Total, %	100	100	100

Monthly Income of Family in Jordanian Dinars	Old Refugees (N = 28)	New Refugees (N = 50)	Total (N = 78)
0-20 dinars	50	26	35
21-40 dinars	25	36	32
41 dinars or more	25	38	33
Total, %	100	100	100

The Zeezya Sample

The occupational distribution in Table 2 reflects the village origin of many of the Zeezya refugees. The occupation and level of education shown is that of the head of the family. Two-thirds (68%) of the men belong to one of three occupational groups: peasant-farmers (34%), unskilled (15%), and semiskilled workers (19%). There are few skilled and clerical workers (7%) and only one professional man, a village *mullah*. Salesmen and shopowners (17%) complete the categories of workers; another 7 percent are retired, unemployed, or not classifiable.

Table 2 also shows the highest level of education reached by the head of the family; illiterate, without schooling (57%); some elementary schooling (22%). Eleven percent have completed elementary and 10 percent have had secondary schooling or more. Of the Zeezya men, 43 percent are classified as literate. It would appear that the literacy rate for the Zeezya sample is not markedly lower than that in the districts in Jordan from which these families came.

The income figures in Table 2 also reflect the rural origins of the families. In the interview, income was defined as total family income, but families may not have reported income received from members working in other towns or countries. The median monthly income per family was about 30 Jordanian dinars, or $84.00. If one allows about seven persons per family, the median per-capita income was about 52 dinars per year.

Comparison of old and new refugees shows that the new refugees have more peasant-farmers (40% compared to 24%). The old refugees have more manual workers (22% to 10%) and more salesmen and shopowners (22% to 14%). The other occupational categories are about equal.

The new refugees tend to have more education and a higher income than do the old refugees. Sevently percent of the old refugees are illiterate as compared to 49 percent of the new refugees. Fifty percent of the old refugee families had an income of less than 20 dinars as compared to 26 percent of the new refugee families.

Table 3 shows ownership of homes and land. Eighty percent of the Zeezya sample reported owning the houses that they lived in prior to June, 1967. Twenty percent reported renting their homes. Ownership probably includes property belonging to a member of the kin-group for which no rent is paid. The houses were about equally divided between small houses (1-2 rooms) and larger ones (3 rooms or more).

[7]This literacy statistic can be compared with statistics on literacy for the districts in Jordan from which the refugees came. The *Statistical Guide to Jordan* (1965, p. 17) reports the following literacy figures for men 15 and over: district of Nablus 56 percent, district of Jerusalem 55 percent, and district of Hebron 40 percent. The Zeezya sample has a literacy rate lower than that of two of the three, but higher than the third. It should be noted that the Zeezya sample consists of heads of families, most of them aged 30 or more. Literacy rates in his age group are known to be lower than the rate for younger age groups.

Table 3

Housing and Land Ownership, Zeezya Sample

(%)

Ownership of House	Old Refugees (N = 30)	New Refugees (N = 56)	Total (N = 86)
Owned their house	73	84	80
Lived in rented house	27	16	20
Total %	100	100	100

Number of Rooms	Old Refugees (N = 33)	New Refugees (N = 56)	Total (N = 89)
1-2 Rooms	67	45	53
3 rooms or more	33	55	47
Total %	100	100	100

Ownership of Land	Old Refugees (N = 35)	New Refugees (N = 59)	Total (N = 94)
Owned no land	69	22	39
0-10 dunums*	12	22	18
11-20 dunums	8	12	11
21 dunums or more	8	34	25
Owned land, amount not specified	3	10	7
Total %	100	100	100

*One dunum = 0.22 acres.

Sixty-one percent said they owned land. Thirty-nine percent reported that they owned no land; 18 percent owned less than 10 dunums, 11 percent owned 10 to 20 dunums, and 25 percent owned more than 20 dunums. Although they did not specify the amount, 7 percent reported owning land.

Tables 2 and 3 suggest that Zeezya families were about average in socioeconomic status in the communities from which they came. Their occupations are those typical of village families and their literacy rate is near the average. Most of them owned their homes and many owned land.

The higher economic status of the new refugee families is evident on all three indices in Table 3. They were less likely to live in rented houses than the old refugees (16% compared to 27%). Their houses were larger: 55 percent had three rooms or more compared to 33 percent of the old refugees. They were more likely to own land: 78 percent of them owned land compared to 31 percent of the old refugees.

We can see from this that the new refugee families are markedly higher in status than old refugees. Fifty-one percent of the new refugee men were literate but only 30 percent of the old refugees. Seventy-four percent of the new refugee families had a monthly income in excess of 20 dinars, compared to 50 percent of the old refugees. Seventy-eight percent of the refugees owned land, compared with 31 percent of the old refugees.

Table 4

Occupation, Education, and Income, Amman Sample

(%)

Occupation of Head of Family	Old Refugees (N = 56)	New Refugees (N = 79)	Total (N = 135)
Farmer, peasant	13	11	12
Unskilled worker	11	10	10
Semiskilled worker	3	5	5
Skilled and clerical workers	19	22	21
Business	13	18	16
Professional	20	25	23
Unemployed	16	2	7
Others (students, estate owners, etc.)	5	7	6
Total %	100	100	100

Educational Level Attained	Old Refugees (N = 56)	New Refugees (N = 79)	Total (N = 135)
Illiterate	36	20	27
Elementary	23	32	28
Secondary	25	29	27
University	12	18	16
No information	4	1	2
Total %	100	100	100

Monthly Income of Family in Jordanian Dinars*	Old Refugees (N = 56)	New Refugees (N = 79)	Total (N = 135)
0- 20 dinars	34	16	23
21- 40 dinars	29	31	30
41-100 dinars	14	29	23
101 dinars or more	18	20	19
no information	5	4	5
Total %	100	100	100

*One dinar = $2.80 U.S.

The Amman Sample

The middle-class nature of the Amman sample is evident from the data presented in Tables 4 and 5. Table 4 shows that 60 percent of the sample is comprised of the professional men (23%), the skilled and clerical workers (21%), and the businessmen (16%). In Zeezya these occupations total 24 percent. Peasant-farmers, who were 34 percent of the Zeezya sample, are only 10 percent of the Amman sample.

To classify by education and by income also shows the middle-class nature of the Amman families. Seventy-one percent are literate compared to 43 percent in Zeezya. Forty-three percent have had secondary education or more, compared to 10 percent of the Zeezya sample. Forty-two percent had a monthly income of more than 40 dinars, compared to 33 percent in Zeezya. A number of families reported monthly incomes in excess of 100 dinars (49% compared to 32% in Zeezya). Comparison of old and new refugees reveals that the old refugees are more likely to be unemployed (16% *vs.* 2%).

Table 5

Housing and Land Ownership, Amman Sample

(%)

Ownership of Home	Old Refugees (N = 55)	New Refugees (N = 79)	Total (N = 134)
Rented	34	20	26
Owned	46	80	66
UNRWA-owned	20	0	8
Total %	100	100	100

Number of Rooms	Old Refugees (N = 55)	New Refugees (N = 77)	Total (N = 132)
1-2 rooms	33	29	31
3 rooms or more	67	71	69
Total %	100	100	100

Land Ownership	Old Refugees (N = 56)	New Refugees (N = 78)	Total (N = 134)
None	70	15	38
10 dunums or less	9	24	18
11-20 dunums	9	14	10
21 dunums or more	16	47	33
Amount not specified	1	0	1
Total %	100	100	100

Table 5 classifies refugees by ownership of house, size of house, and ownership of land. Many of the Amman families (66%) owned their homes before June, 1967. More of the Amman families live in houses of three or more rooms (69% as opposed to 47% of Zeezya families). About the same proportion (61% of Zeezya and 62% of Amman families), reported owning land. In these two respects, the Amman families do *not* show higher status than the Zeezya families. The proportion of Zeezya families that owned land is 61% and the proportion that owned their homes (80%) is actually higher than in the Amman sample. At first thought, this appears to contradict our finding, in Table 4, that the Amman families are higher in status. The apparent contradiction is resolved by the data in Table 6 concerning the place of origin of the Amman sample. About half of these families (57%) came from the cities and larger towns of the West Bank. Much more than the Zeezya sample, the Amman sample tends to be urban in origin: only 35 percent came from villages and 14 percent from refugee camps. The urban family is less likely to own its home and to own land, even though its socioeconomic status may be relatively high. For this reason, the indicators of home and land ownership are less meaningful for urban residents than for village people.

Table 6

Community of Origin, Family Size, and Religion, Amman Sample

(%)

Community of Origin	Old Refugees (N = 56)	New Refugees (N = 77)	Total (N = 133)
Camps	34	0	14
Villages	21	45	35
Towns and cities	45	55	51
Total %	100	100	100

Size of Immediate Family	Old Refugees (N = 56)	New Refugees (N = 77)	Total (N = 133)
Small (4 or less)	24	20	22
Medium (5 or 6)	23	32	28
Large (7 or more)	53	48	50
Total %	100	100	100

Religion	Old Refugees (N = 56)	New Refugees (N = 77)	Total (N = 133)
Muslim	88	92	90
Christian	12	8	10
Total %	100	100	100

Table 6 also shows that half of the Amman families were relatively large, seven or more persons; about one-quarter are middle-sized, with five to six persons; only 22 percent have four persons or less. Comparison of the new with the old refugee families in Table 6 shows that there are few differences with respect to community of origin, family size, and religion. The main difference is that 34 percent of the old refugees, but none of the new refugees, came from refugee camps in the West Bank and Gaza. The great majority of the sample, 90 percent, is Muslim; 10 percent is Christian. When compared with those for the population of Jordan,[8] 94 percent Muslim, 6 percent Christian, we see a somewhat higher proportion of Christians in the Amman sample.

Tables 4 and 5 compare old and new refugee families in the Amman sample. The new refugees are more likely than the old to have had some form of education (79% compared to 60%); to have a monthly income in excess of 40 dinars (49% compared to 32%); to have owned their homes (80% compared to 46%); and to own land, (85% compared to 30%). It is clear that even in this middle-class sample the socioeconomic status of new-refugee families is higher than that of the old. It would seem that the period between 1948 and 1967 was not sufficient to permit the refugees of 1948 to attain the socioeconomic status of Palestinians who had never been forced to leave their homes.

[8]*Statistical Guide to Jordan* (1965), p. 16.

Ties with the Home Community

This discussion on socioeconomic status shows the extent of home and ownership in the lower-class Zeezya sample and the middle-class characteristics of the Amman sample. Ownership of property suggests that these families before June, 1967, were established members of their village and urban communities. Such families are likely to retain strong ties with their previous homes.

It is possible to pursue this question further by considering two additional items of information: the length of time that the family has lived in the community and the presence of relatives in the community. Each of these items is an indicator of the structural ties linking the family to its home community. For instance, a family that has lived in the same place for a long time usually has stronger ties to that place than a family that has moved in recently. Geographical mobility is likely to result in decreased attachment to specific places.

A similar argument applies to the presence of relatives in the community. Those families with relatives nearby are more firmly established than families without relatives. This is especially true in Arab society, where kin-ties carry great importance and relatives support each other in many ways.

Table 7 indicates the intensity of these structural ties for the Zeezya sample. While over half of the families (59%) had always lived in their home communities, the remainder had moved only once, as a sequel to the war of 1948. There is virtually no other residential mobility among these families. In Table 7 the presence of relatives in the home community is reported by the great majority (86%) of the families. Virtually every

Table 7

Ties with the Home Community, Zeezya Sample

(%)

Length of Time Lived in Home Community	Old Refugees (N = 37)	New Refugees (N = 61)	Total (N = 98)
Two years or less	3	0	1
3-10 years	0	2	1
11-20 years	94	5	39
21 years or more (including "always")	3	93	59
Total %	100	100	100
Families Having Relatives in Home Community	Old Refugees (N = 26)	New Refugees (N = 48)	Total (N = 74)
Had no relatives	31	4	14
Had relatives	69	96	86
Total %	100	100	100

new-refugee family (96%) had relatives in their community of origin.
Of the old-refugee families, 69 percent had relatives in their community of
origin. This is another index of the ties linking these families to their
homes.

Table 8

Ties with the Home Community, Amman Sample

(%)

Length of Time Lived in Home Community	Old Refugees (N = 56)	New Refugees (N = 79)	Total (N = 135)
Ten years or less	7	10	10
11-20 years	89	5	40
21 years or more (including "always")	4	85	50
Total %	100	100	100
Families Having Relatives in Home Community	Old Refugees (N = 56)	New Refugees (N = 78)	Total (N = 134)
Had no relatives	39	28	33
Had relatives	61	72	67
Total %	100	100	100
Did Any Members of the Family, Including Relatives, Have a Position in the Community?	Old Refugees (N = 56)	New Refugees (N = 77)	Total (N = 134)
No	73	47	58
Yes	27	53	42
Total %	100	100	100

Similar patterns may be observed in Table 8 for the Amman sample.
There is little residential mobility. The new-refugee families had always
lived in their home communities, while the old-refugee families had moved
only once. Over two-thirds of the families had relatives with them in these
communities. Judging by this index, the Zeezya sample has even stronger
structural ties than does the Amman sample: 86 percent report relatives
with them, compared to 67 percent in the Amman sample. This is an index,
too, of the number of urbanized families in the Amman sample, since kin-
ties tend to be less important in the city than in the village.

Another indicator of structural ties in Table 8 shows the number of
family members who have had a position of importance in the community.
Forty-two percent of the families reported members occupying such
positions as member of town council, leader (sheik) of a kin-group,
religious leader, and mayor. This proportion is higher among the new-
refugee families (63%) than among the old refugees (27%), and the
difference shows the stronger structural ties of the new refugee families.

The extent of the structural ties between the refugee families and their
home communities leads us to agree with a conclusion reached in 1955 by

another investigator. In trying to understand the attitude and ideology of middle-class Palestinian refugees, "... the greatest significance must be given to the factor of social uprooting.[9]

V. The Exodus, 1967

Since the refugee families were generally well established in their home communities, why did they leave? Further, since the manner of their departure—flight or expulsion—is relevant to their desire to return, what were the circumstances of their leaving?

Table 9

Date of Arrival in the East Bank Sector

Date Family Arrived in East Bank	Zeezya Sample (N = 71)	Amman Sample (N = 133)
June 5-8 (during the war)	56	27
June 9-10	25	40
June 11-30	19	
July or later	0	33
Total %	100	100

The Date of Departure

One piece of evidence to be considered is the date when the families reported leaving their homes. If the family left during or immediately after the war this suggests that the decision was made suddenly. If the family waited for a while and then decided to leave, this suggests a more careful and deliberate decision. Table 9 shows a sharp difference in departure date between the two samples. The Zeezya families either left their homes during the war (56%) or immediately after (25%). The Amman families did not leave so soon. One-quarter left during the war and 40 percent left during the month of June, but after the cessation of hostilities. An additional 33 percent did not leave their homes until July or later. More of the old-refugee families in the Amman sample came during the war (36%) than of the new (20%). Further, more of the new refugees (36%) than of the old (29%) waited until July or later.[10] Apparently a large number of families, mainly lower class, sought refuge in the wake of the war.

[9]F. C. Bruhns, "A study of Arab Refugee Attitudes," *Middle East Journal* Vol. IX (Spring, 1955), p. 137.

[10]Table 10 provides date of arrival in the East Bank rather than the date of departure from home. The precise date of departure was not recorded for the Amman sample. For the Zeezya sample, the date of departure and the date of arrival on the East Bank were the same for most of the families. A few spent one night on the way, but most made the journey in a single day, even in a few hours.

Table 10

Experiences during the War, Both Samples

(%)

Experience	Zeezya Sample			Amman Sample		
	Old Refugees (N = 37)	New Refugees (N = 59)	Total (N = 96)	Old Refugees (N = 56)	New Refugees (N = 79)	Total (N = 135)
Contact with Israelis						
Yes	32	58	48	59	85	74
No	68	42	52	39	14	24
No answer	0	0	0	2	1	2
Total %	100	100	100	100	100	100
Description of Israeli Behavior	Old Refugees (N = 11)	New Refugees (N = 33)	Total (N = 44)	Old Refugees (N = 31)	New Refugees (N = 65)	Total (N = 96)
Negative	64	84	80	97	95	96
Neutral	36	13	18	3	5	4
Positive	0	3	2	0	0	0
Total %	100	100	100	100	100	100
Injury or Death of Relatives	Old Refugees (N = 37)	New Refugees (N = 58)	Total (N = 95)	Old Refugees (N = 56)	New Refugees (N = 79)	Total (N = 135)
None	92	81	85	88	78	82
Injury	8	9	9	5	6	6
Death	0	10	6	7	14	11
No answer	0	0	0	0	2	1
Total %	100	100	100	100	100	100
Injury or Death of Others in Community	Old Refugees (N = 34)	New Refugees (N = 53)	Total (N = 87)	Old Refugees (N = 56)	New Refugees (N = 79)	Total (N = 135)
None	82	64	71	25	27	26
Injury	6	8	7	7	13	10
Death	12	28	22	68	58	62
No answer	0	0	0	0	2	2
Total %	100	100	100	100	100	100

Experiences during the War

Refugee families were asked about their experiences during the war and the occupation that followed. Their answers are reported in Table 10. The refugees were asked specifically whether they had seen any Israeli soldiers or civilians. If they had seen Israelis, they were then asked what the behavior of these Israelis had been. In other words, they were asked to tell what they had seen, not to report hearsay accounts. Of the Zeezya sample, 48 percent reported that they had seen Israeli soldiers or civilians, while 74 percent of the Amman sample reported actually seeing Israelis. In both samples, new-refugee families were more likely to have seen Israeli forces than were old-refugee families. In Zeezya, 58 percent of the new refugees reported contact with soldiers; in Amman, 85 percent.

A large number of the refugee families, therefore, witnessed the arrival of the enemy, and most of these families report the behavior of these forces as frightening. Instances of frightening behavior include the eviction of civilians from their homes, looting, the destruction of houses (and in some cases entire villages), the rounding up and detention of male civilians, the deliberate shaming of older persons and of women, and the shooting of men suspected of being soldiers or guerrilla fighters. Eighty percent of the Zeezya sample and 96 percent of the Amman sample reported incidents of this type.

In both samples, a few families reported that Israeli behavior had been neutral, neither threatening nor reassuring the population (18% of the Zeezya sample and 4% of the Amman sample).

The families were also asked about injuries and deaths among their relatives and about injuries and deaths in their home community. Table 10 shows that about one-sixth of the sample reported either injuries or deaths among their relatives. Some of these were members of the immediate family; others were members of kin-group.

Reports of casualties in the community differ between the samples. Only 29 percent of the Zeezya sample said that there were casualties in their communities, while 72 percent of the Amman sample reported casualties. The families in the Amman sample, in general, stayed longer in their communities and so were more likely to hear of injuries and deaths to persons outside the kin-group. Furthermore, the home communities of the Amman sample are larger than those of the Zeezya sample. The larger the community, the more likely it is that casualties would have occurred. Another frightening experience that many of the families reported, especially those from the area around Jericho, was aerial bombardment. The families sought shelter from the bombs, often in orchards and caves, and then were unable to return to their homes. Knowledge of the use of napalm increased their terror.

This summary of experiences during the war and the occupation does not convey the force of the experiences, but it does indicate their extent. Most of the families, especially the new refugees, had direct contact with the enemy forces. Most of them report frightening occurrences. About one-sixth report the death or injury of members of the family.

Table 11
Causes for Leaving Home, Both Samples

Causes for Leaving Home	Zeezya Sample (N = 100)	Amman Sample (N = 135)
Fear		
of airplanes	57	27
of dishonor (al-'ird.)	30	7
of massacre	8	6
other fears	0	11
Psychological pressures of enemy occupation, including threats	43	71
Mass behavior (seeing army retreat, others leave)	51	9
Destruction of villages; destruction of homes; eviction	19	18
Economic pressures; sources of income being cut off	10	26
Total	218	175

Note: The table gives the number of families mentioning each cause for leaving home. The total number of causes therefore exceeds N, since many families mentioned more than one cause.

Causes for Leaving

In the interviews, the families were asked to describe their departure from their homes, including their thoughts about leaving. Table 11 identifies five causes of departure: fear of such events as airplane attack, psychological pressures of Israeli occupation (including threats), mass behavior (seeing the army retreat and others flee), destruction of homes and villages, and economic pressures.

Events that were feared varied from such realistic occurrences as aerial attack to such imponderables as the mention of massacre of civilians. The "realistic" fear of aerial attack was mentioned by 57 of the Zeezya families and 27 of the Amman families. Eight of the Zeezya families and six of the Amman families feared civilian massacre. A major source of fear, especially to 30 Zeezya families, was the dishonor that would come to the family if any of its women were insulted or molested. The value of the family's honor (al-'ird), as represented by the dignity of its women, was seen as seriously threatened because the enemy was not Arab and would not observe Arab customs of modesty.

Psychological pressures of enemy occupation differed from the fears cited above. They were based on the behavior of the Israelis in occupation rather than wartime events. These were mentioned by half of the Amman sample (71 families) and by about 40 percent (43 families) of the Zeezya sample. One of the pressures most frequently mentioned was threats to members of the family, especially to the young men. Other pressures included the searching and dynamiting of houses, the shaming of older persons, and mass arrests.

Under "mass behavior" have been listed such causes of departure as seeing the Jordanian and Iraqi armies retreat and seeing many others in the community leave. Such mass behavior was much more frequent in the lower-class families of Zeezya (51 reported it) than in the middle-class Amman families (9 reported it). Behavior characteristic of wartime confusion was especially prevalent in the camps of 1948 refugees.

Destruction of home and village was reported by about one-fifth of the Zeezya sample and one-eighth of the Amman sample. The destruction in most cases was carried out deliberately by Israeli forces after the war was over.

The fifth cause of departure, economic pressure, was reported by 10 of the Zeezya families and 26 of the Amman families. Economic pressure includes the loss of income from persons outside the occupied area and the loss of income from the war and the occupation.

In summary, the most important causes of departure for the Zeezya families appear to have been the fear of airplanes, the example of others leaving, and the psychological pressures exerted by the occupying forces. For the Amman families, psychological pressures of the occupation appear to have been much more frequent than any other cause. Apparently, the middle-class families resisted the initial impulses of fear and panic, but were strongly influenced by the actions of the occupying forces.

Indirect Causes for Leaving

In addition to the direct causes reported by the refugees, there were indirect causes of the exodus. These indirect causes are connected with the social structure and values of the communities of origin, as well as the political events of the area. Four indirect causes have been identified as important for the Zeezya sample: the element of surprise, the lack of other-than-family loyalties in the villages, Arab values connected with honor and the family, and the atmosphere of doubt and mutual distrust. Two of these are not applicable to the Amman sample. The Amman sample, being partly urban and largely middle class, had more other-than-family loyalties than did the Zeezya. Also, the Amman families were less affected by traditional values connected with honor and the family, as is evident from Table 11.

Only seven of the Amman families mentioned fears connected with dishonor, whereas 30 of the Zeezya families did so.

Two of these indirect causes, the element of surprise and the atmosphere of mutual doubt and distrust, were operative among the families of the Amman sample. Most of them (74%), like the Zeezya families, expected that the Arab nations would win the war. About two-thirds (64%) were surprised by the actual outbreak of war. In the wake of surprise and defeat, they were unable to trust any official source or leader. The surprise and distrust, while widespread, did not always result in the immediate preparations to leave.

Table 12
Attitudes Toward the Palestine Problem, Amman Sample

Question	Answer	%	Number of Respondents
"Do you think that the Jews will permit the Arabs to return without a war?"	Yes, without reservations	1	1
	Yes, possible with reservations	15	21
	No	72	95
	Don't know (includes "God knows")	11	15
	Total		132
"Do you think that there can be a political solution to the Palestine problem?"	Yes, without reservations	13	18
	Yes, with reservations	19	26
	No	61	80
	Don't know (includes "God knows")	7	9
	Total	100	133
"In your opinion, is there any difference between Zionists and Jews?"	Yes	56	73
	No	32	42
	Don't know	12	16
	Total	100	131
"In the event of an Arab victory, is coexistence as ordinary citizens with the Jews possible?"	Yes, without reservations	26	34
	Yes, with reservations	45	59
	No	28	36
	Don't know	1	1
	Total	100	130

VI. Political Attitudes

It was possible to include in the Amman interviews several questions concerning the Palestine problem. These questions, shown with answers in Table 12, are of interest because they reflect the attitudes of a middle-class sample of Palestinians. The questions deal with the return of the Arabs to Palestine, the possibility of a political (i.e., nonmilitary) solution to the problem, the possibility of Jews and Arabs living peacefully together, and the distinction between Jews and Zionists.

Only 1 percent of the Amman sample agreed without qualifications that Israel would permit the Arabs to return without a war. Fifteen percent said that a peaceful return might be possible, but qualified this with comments such as, "strong pressure from outside would be necessary." Almost three-quarters of the respondents (72%) said that no peaceful return was conceivable. In other words, most of the sample thought that only military action could restore their homes to them.

The Amman refugees were asked whether there could be a political (i.e., nonmilitary) solution to the Palestine problem. Their answers show a relatively pessimistic outlook: 13 percent said, without reservations, that there could be such a solution. Nineteen percent thought there was some chance of a political solution, but placed strong reservations on their statements. Sixty-one percent said that no political solution was possible, implying that only a war could bring about an end to the problem.

Two questions dealt with attitudes toward Jews. One asked whether there was any difference between Zionists and Jews. Over half the sample (56%) replied positively, while about one-third said that there was no difference. The other question was a hypothetical one, designed to measure basic attitudes toward Jews. It asked whether, in the event of an Arab victory, coexistence between Jews and Arabs as "ordinary citizens" would be possible. One-quarter of the sample said Yes, without reservations. Another 45 percent said Yes, coexistence was possible, but qualified their opinions by statements such as these: only with the Jews who were in Palestine before 1948; or with the Eastern Jews now in Israel; or if we (the Arabs) are careful; or if the Jews stop being Zionists. About one-quarter of the sample (28%) said that coexistence would not be possible under any conditions.

These political attitudes lead us to describe our sample as pessimistic about the chances for a nonmilitary solution, but relatively tolerant toward Jews. Much of the refugees' anger is directed toward Zionism, and toward Israel as an occupying power.

VII. The Desire to Return

The question most frequently asked about the Palestinian refugees is whether they really want to return to their home communities. The interviews in Table 13 for both samples provide information on this question. A very high percentage of the Zeezya sample (93%) and 90 percent of the Amman sample expressed the desire to return to their homes. Only 7 percent of the Zeezya sample and 4 percent of the Amman sample said that they did not want to return.

For many families, this desire to return is not without qualification. They wanted to return, but not to a community under Israeli rule. The qualification "only if the Israelis withdraw" was stated more often by the Amman families (50%) than by the Zeezya families (18%).

Table 13

Desire to Return Home, Both Samples

(%)

Nature of Desire	Zeezya Sample		
	Old Refugees (N = 33)	New Refugees (N = 55)	Total (N = 88)
Definitely wish to return	64	82	75
Wish to return, conditionally	21	16	18
Do not wish to return	15	2	7
Total %	100	100	100
Wish to Return	Amman Sample		
	Old Refugees (N = 56)	New Refugees (N = 77)	Total (N = 133)
Will return whether Israelis withdraw or not	32	50	42
Will return only if Israelis withdraw	52	45	48
No	7	1	4
Don't know, uncertain	9	4	6
Total %	100	100	100

The Zeezya families were more willing than the Amman families to return even under the adverse conditions of Israeli occupation. But the Amman families were interviewed later, one year after the Israeli occupation of the West Bank, and the conduct of the occupation may have influenced their attitude toward return.

In two respects, the new-refugee families showed more eagerness to return than the old refugees. More of them were willing to return without waiting for Israeli withdrawal: in the Zeezya sample, 82 percent *vs.* 64 percent; in the Amman sample, 50 percent *vs.* 32 percent. Fewer of the new refugees said that they do not want to return: in the Zeezya sample, 2 percent *vs.* 15 percent; in the Amman sample, 1 percent *vs.* 7 percent.

Before the war, the new-refugee families tended to have stronger ties to their home communities than did the old refugees, as has been shown above (Tables 7 and 8). They had higher socioeconomic status and more of them had relatives in these communities. It may reasonably be asked whether there is a direct relationship between these structural ties and the desire to return. Table 14 shows that the answer to this question is affirmative for the Amman sample. For each of five indicators of the ties between the family and the home community, there is a positive relationship: the families with the stronger ties are more likely to want to return immediately. The families with the weaker ties are more likely to want to wait until after the Israeli withdrawal. Strong ties and higher socioeconomic status go with the desire to return soon, while weak ties and lower socioeconomic status accompany a reluctance to return under Israeli occupation.

Table 14

Structural Ties and the Desire to Return, Amman Sample

(%)

Land Ownership	Nonowners (N = 51)	Owners (N = 83)
Return, unconditionally	31	47
Return, only if Israelis withdraw	47	48
No return	8	1
Don't know, uncertain	14	4
Total %	100	100

Homes with Utilities	No Utilities (N = 27)	Some Utilities (N = 107)
Return, unconditionally	22	46
Return only if Israelis withdraw	67	43
No return	7	3
Don't know, uncertain	4	8
Total %	100	100

Approximate Monthly Income	0-30 Dinars (N = 50)	31-60 Dinars (N = 31)	61 Dinars or more (N = 42)
Return, unconditionally	34	55	38
Return only if Israelis withdraw	59	35	45
No return	2	0	7
Don't know, uncertain	5	10	10
Total %	100	100	100

Family Member Having Important Position in the Community	No (N = 77)	Yes (N = 55)
Return, unconditionally	34	51
Return only if Israelis withdraw	50	45
No return	4	4
Don't know, uncertain	12	0
Total %	100	100

Relatives in Same Community	No Relatives (N = 44)	Relatives (N = 90)
Return, unconditionally	30	47
Return only if Israelis withdraw	59	42
No return	4	3
Don't know, uncertain	7	8
Total %	100	100

As a middle-class group, the Amman families in general should be more eager to return immediately. They are not, however; in spite of their higher status and generally stronger ties, more of them are reluctant to return while the Israeli occupation continues. Perhaps the year of Israeli occupation has discouraged many from wanting to return while the occupation continues, although a large number still wish to return immediately.

Other factors also influence the desire to return. One such factor is the presence in the family of a man who has had military training. The refugees said that men with military training are likely to be interned by the Israeli occupation authorities and that it is therefore unwise for such men to return while the occupation continues. Since these men are also the wage earners in the family, the family is not willing to return without them. Of the 75 families in Table 15 who had a member with military training, 33 percent wanted to return immediately, without waiting for Israeli withdrawal. Of the families who did not have any one with military training, 51 percent wanted to return immediately.

Table 15

Military Training and Desire to Return, Amman Sample

Attitude/Response	Military Training (%)		Number of Families Queried
	Nobody in Family (N = 59)	Somebody in Family (N = 75)	
Will return whether Israelis withdraw or not	51	33	55
Will return only if Israelis withdraw	37	56	64
Will not return	3	4	5
Don't know Uncertain No answer	9	7	10
Total	100	100	134

Another factor influencing the willingness to return while the Israeli occupation continues is the political attitude held by the respondent. Table 16 indicates that, in general, those who are optimistic about a peaceful or political solution are more likely to want to return immediately. Those who are pessimistic about the possibility of a peaceful solution want to return only when the Israeli occupation of their home communities ends. Also, those who see some hope of Arab-Jewish coexistence are more willing to return immediately than those who see no such hope. In short, "mild" attitudes toward Israel are related to the desire to return immediately, while "militant" attitudes are related to the desire to return *after* Israeli withdrawal.

The refugee families were not asked about their willingness to resettle outside Palestine. The question of resettlement is an extremely sensitive one; to ask about it directly would have created suspicion and prejudiced the entire survey. It is our impression, based on the interviews and especially on the answers regarding the desire to return, that the general attitudes of the families in both samples were strongly opposed to resettlement. This opposition extended to actions that implied resettlement, such as the construction of permanent shelters in the refugee camps. In general, the desire to return to their homes precluded willingness to resettle elsewhere.

Table 16

Political Attitudes and the Desire to Return, Amman Sample

(%)

Possibility of Peaceful Return and Desire to Return

Israelis will allow you to return peacefully.	Will return whether Israelis withdraw or not	Will return only if Israelis withdraw	Will not return	Don't know, uncertain, and no answer	Total
Yes (N = 22)	64	36	0	0	100
No (N = 95)	32	56	5	7	100

Possibility of a Political Solution and Desire to Return

There can be a political solution	Will return whether Israelis withdraw or not	Will return only if Israelis withdraw	Will not return	Don't know, uncertain, and no answer	Total
Yes (N = 43)	60	33	2	5	100
No (N = 80)	33	56	5	6	100

Zionism-Judaism Differences and Desire to Return

Any difference between Zionism and Judaism	Will return whether Israelis withdraw or not	Will return only if Israelis withdraw	Will not return	Don't know, uncertain, and no answer	Total
Yes (N = 73)	45	44	5	6	100
No (N = 42)	36	55	2	7	100

Possibility of Arab-Jewish Coexistence and Desire to Return

Coexistence in case of future Arab victory	Will return whether Israelis withdraw or not	Will return only if Israelis withdraw	Will not return	Don't know, uncertain, and no answer	Total
No (N = 36)	22	72	6	0	100
Yes, with reservations (N = 59)	42	44	4	10	100
Yes (N = 34)	59	32	3	6	100

The Regional Bystanders

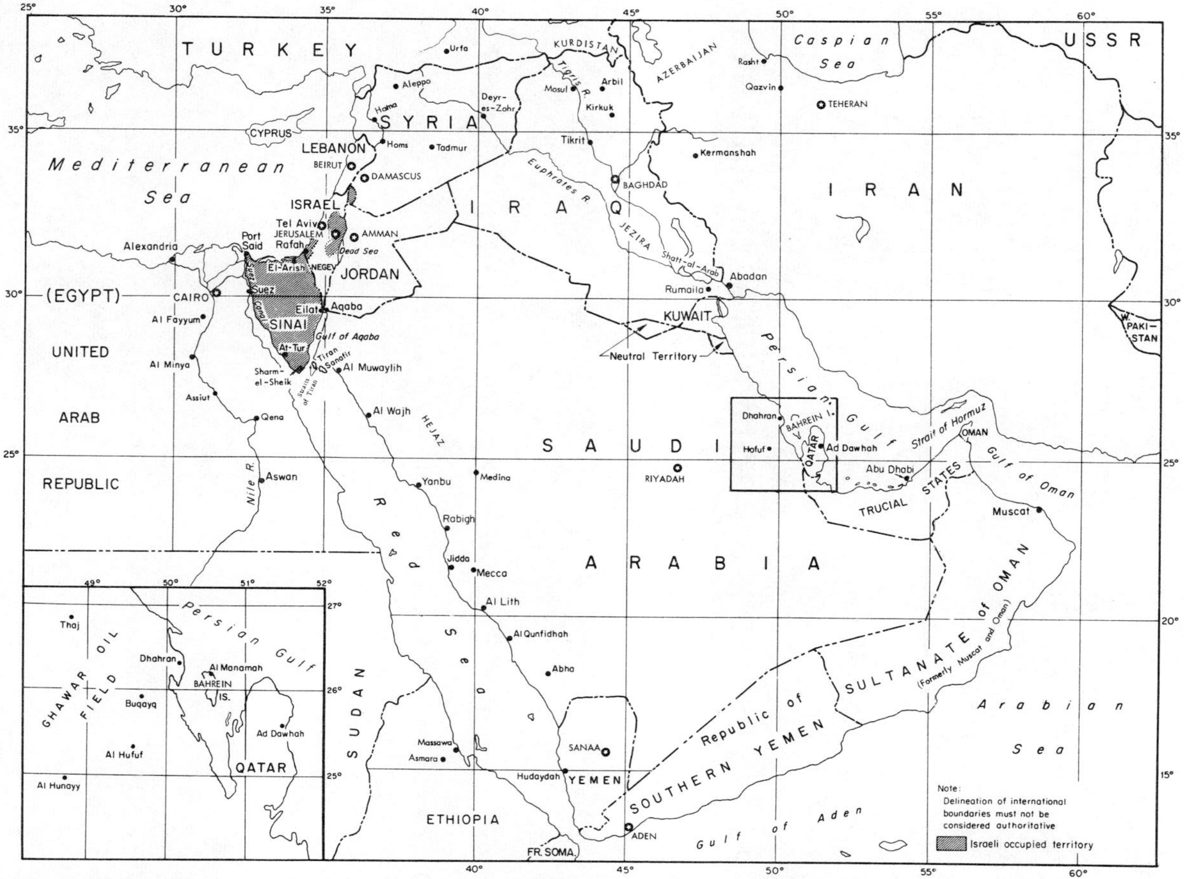

USSR

Caspian Sea

TURKEY

Urfa
Aleppo
Homs
Tadmur
Deyr-z-Zohr

SYRIA
DAMASCUS
BEIRUT
LEBANON
CYPRUS

Mediterranean Sea

Alexandria
CAIRO
Al Fayyum
Al Minya
Asyut

UNITED ARAB REPUBLIC (EGYPT)

Port Said
Suez
Suez Canal
ISRAEL
Tel Aviv
JERUSALEM
Gaza
El-Arish
Rafah
At-Tur
SINAI
Eilat
Aqaba
Dead Sea
AMMAN
JORDAN
Gulf of Aqaba
Strait of Tiran
Sharm el-Sheik
Al Muwaylih
Al Wajh

Nile R.
Qena
Aswan

SUDAN

Red Sea

HEJAZ
Yanbu
Rabigh
Medina
Jidda
Mecca
Al Lith
Al Qunfidhah
Abha

Turtur
Mosul
Kirkuk
Arbil
KURDISTAN
Tikrit
Tigris R.
BAGHDAD
JEZIRA
Euphrates R.
IRAQ

IRAN
Rasht
Qazvin
TEHERAN
Kermanshah
AZERBAIJAN

Abadan
Shatt-al-Arab
Rumailia
KUWAIT
Neutral Territory

Persian Gulf
BAHREIN
QATAR
Dhahran
Hofuf

SAUDI ARABIA

RIYADH

Ad Dawhah
Abu Dhabi
TRUCIAL STATES

Strait of Hormuz
Gulf of Oman
Muscat
SULTANATE OF OMAN

Arabian Sea

PAKI-STAN

Republic of SOUTHERN YEMEN

YEMEN
SANAA
Hudaydah
ADEN
Gulf of Aden

ETHIOPIA
Massawa
Asmara
FR. SOMA.

Masira

Note:
Delineation of international
boundaries must not be
considered authoritative

▨ Israeli occupied territory

Persian Gulf
Dhahran
Al Manamah
BAHREIN IS.
Buqayq
Al Hufuf
Al Hunayy
QATAR
Ad Dawhah
GHAWAR OIL FIELD
Thaj

Map IV. The regional survey

The Regional Bystanders

This part deals with Iran and the Maghrib states, Tunisia, Algeria, and Morocco. Iran has not been involved in the Arab-Israeli conflict, and the Maghrib states, although ethnically and culturally Arabic, have maintained a certain detachment from that conflict and from other Arab nationalist objectives. Both the Maghrib group and Iran, then, have been bystanders in the region; but in few other respects have their regional roles been parallel.

Iran's energetic monarch is heavily committed to economic modernization and growth, and he relies upon oil revenues for the foreign exchange that makes his economic plans feasible. A modernizing, military-backed regime rules Algeria. It also is committed to economic development with the aid of oil revenues, although they are less sizeable than Iran's. Morocco and Tunisia are less favorably situated for economic development than Algeria; their political structures are different and their modernizing objectives have been less ambitious. All three Maghrib states have remained aloof from Middle East regional issues, and the prospects of their assuming a major role in the Middle East are not conspicuous.

Iran's prognosis is quite the opposite. Binder shows in Chapter 10 that Iran may become during the 1970s one of the most assertive indigenous powers in the region, while Gallagher in Chapter 11 draws a quite contrary conclusion about the Maghrib states. He holds that they are regional isolates. Certain forces draw them eastward; other forces now on the increase draw them toward Europe. The vector that results probably has a stabilizing effect in the Middle East because it limits the power of Arab nationalism as a revisionist or revolutionary force at the same time that it resists Soviet penetration. By the same token, however, the Maghrib states could become a source of change if France, as their main European mentor, were to assume an aggressive diplomatic role in the Mediterranean. Iran's ambitions could grow into a major regional imperial force. Which course these states take will not depend entirely on internal factors, but will be affected by regional and international conditions that will be treated in Part V.

Leonard Binder is Professor of Political Science at the University of Chicago, and author of *Iran, Political Development in a Changing Society,* Berkeley, U. of California Press, 1963.

Charles F. Gallagher, Director of Studies of the American Universities Field Staff, Rome, Italy, is the author of *United States and North Africa: Morocco, Algeria and Tunisia* (Cambridge, Mass.: Harvard University Press, 1963).

CHAPTER 10

Iran's Potential as a Regional Power
Leonard Binder

I. Iran in the Twentieth Century

In less than 10 years, Iran's international position has been transformed from one of ludicrous heroic posing to one of substantial political and possibly even military significance in the Middle East. Over this period, a large measure of domestic political stability has been achieved; important economic advances have been made; organized, legitimate domestic political opposition has collapsed; the religious authorities have been driven into disarray; and the Queen has produced an heir to the throne. Iran has backed away from a forlorn foreign policy based upon the remnants of the Baghdad Pact and has constructed a new and more pragmatic policy based in part on opportunism but also upon a real responsiveness to the shifts and reorientations among the great powers. Iran has moved to an assertive foreign policy position from a regionally defensive position, constructed out of its uneasiness about Iraq's policy in the Shatt al-Arab and in Kuwait, about Afghanistan's close ties with the Soviet Union and her hostility toward Pakistan, about Egypt's constant reference to the Arab irredentists in Khuzistan, about the potential Soviet military threat and the existing Communist subversive threat, and, above all, about the tentativeness of the American commitment to regional security. The causes of this remarkable transformation are manifold and complex, domestic and foreign, consciously purposeful as well as accidental.

Since the June war of 1967, the great powers and most of the regional powers apparently earnestly desire Iran's friendship or, at least, assiduously avoid antagonizing it. Iran is in a position to intensify Iraq's Kurdish problem. It can relieve some of the Arab nationalist pressure on Saudi Arabia and Kuwait. It can help police the Persian Gulf when the British leave. It may be able to induce the Russians to avoid a show of force in the Gulf. Iran has, in fact, acquired influence with the Soviet Union, has purchased arms from the Soviet Union, now ships goods via the Soviet Union, sells natural gas to the Soviets, and intends to increase its economic involvement with them. Iran has enhanced its independence of U.S. policy without really weakening its ties with the United States.

Far from viewing Iran as a weak and dependent client in an unstable region, the United States has come to see Iran as an important potentially stabilizing force in the Middle East. Iran can help to achieve many of the

355

goals America finds desirable without the need to intervene in the region. Thus far, at least, even the improved Soviet-Iranian relations have reduced the intensity of U.S. concern for Iran rather than increased it. This same improvement in Soviet-Iranian relations has also diminished the possibility of friction with Afghanistan because of the close relations that the Soviets have had with that country. As Iran strengthens its position among the powers, the Iranian-Turkish alliance, through the CENTO agreement, becomes more valuable to Turkey, which is also readjusting the character of its association with the West and with NATO. The Iranian alliance with Israel, though implicit and not by treaty, has been mutually advantageous. Israeli cooperation gives Iran great political and military maneuverability in the region, especially against threatening Arab states. Moreover, Israel's relative isolation from other regional powers has made this tacit alliance asymmetrical in Iran's favor.

Even Great Britain, in the process of withdrawal from the region and somewhat apprehensive about Iran's claims to Bahrein, can view Iran's presence in the Gulf as essentially benign insofar as the remainder of British petroleum interests are concerned. Iran's is by no means a politically stable regime, and there is still much to fear from a Soviet invasion or from U.S. pressure. So Iran has not yet moved from the old policy of exploiting its weakness to one of aggressive imperialism. The attitude is buoyant rather than uneasy. Pride is beginning to replace plaintiveness. Courage is beginning to supplant cunning. But it is only a beginning and it all depends, thus far, on the Shah. Nevertheless, the direction of change is toward independence, aggressiveness, and probably imperialism.

There are many reasons for this far-reaching change in Iran's international position, but none is more important than the achievement of a high degree of domestic political tranquility. This situation may be changed by certain situational factors to be discussed later, but the achievement of the 1960s is important. Recent years have seen the Shah establish his political supremacy after a shaky, if not all but hopeless, beginning in 1941. He has gained control of the gendarmerie, the army, the police, the Cabinet, the parliament, and lastly, the bureaucracy. The relevant events are referred to, however briefly, below. For the gendarmerie, assistance came from U.S. foreign aid and the work of General Schwarzkopf; for the army, Generals Zahedi and Bakhtiyar after August, 1953; the police (in Teheran) were easily managed after the army was purged and SAVAK (secret police) strengthened, but the task was more directly achieved by Asadullah Alam in 1954 as Minister of the Interior; the Cabinet was more fully controlled under Eghbal; the parliament since the creation of a puppet two-party system 1957-1963; and the bureaucracy, including the Plan Organization,* have been better controlled since the establishment of the Iran-i-Novin (New Party) as the party in power.

The Reza Shah

The rhythm of Iranian history remained unbroken until the Allied occupation of World War II. Despite the involvement of European politics from early in the nineteenth century, despite the growing foreign control of Iranian finances toward the end of that century, despite the importation of foreign manufactures, the importation of a constitution, and the importation of a form of Kemalism, Iran faced the world in 1941 as it had for centuries before. The Reza Shah thought he was pulling Iran into the twentieth century; the little band of incredibly romantic nationalists at Teheran University produced a dozen improbable paper revolutions in the decade of the thirties; and the Trans-Iranian railroad was built. But Iranian society and conceptions of government were largely unchanged. It is no fault of the heroes of Iran's awakening that they failed to make a deep impression. Jamal al-Din al-Afghani left followers in Egypt, but not in Iran. The martyrs of the constitutional movement had no later imitators. The survivors of those turbulent days now appear as little more than docile notables, political anachronisms. Even the great Qajar lords of the kingdom have preferred opulent seclusion to entering the political fray. The Reza Shah ran the puppet show of Majlis (parliament) and Council of Ministers; he subdued the clergy or exiled them; he held down the tribes; he built some factories and the railroad; he elicited a revision of the D'Arcy oil concession from the British. These things he did as would any of the great Shahs of the past. Beyond the accumulated experience of Iran he could not go, because he knew nothing else. Had he lived even a century ago, things might be different for Iran, but in the interwar era even a Shah Abbas in military uniform could do little.

With the Allied occupation, violent, abrupt, and merciless change burst upon Iran. In September, 1941, Britain and the Soviet Union invaded Iran to prevent the further growth of German influence and to open a secure supply line to southern Russia. At the first, the Reza Shah was disposed to resist, but his army quickly collapsed. The aging but still proud Shah abdicated in order to save the throne for his twenty-year-old son, Mohammad Reza. Soviet troops occupied the northern and most heavily populated third of the country down to Teheran, and the British resumed

*A group responsible for economic and social planning in Iran; by law the Plan Organization controls the planning and execution of short- and long-range economic projects; see Richard W. Cottam, *Nationalism in Iran*, (Pittsburgh, Penn., U. of Pittsburgh Press, 1964), pp. 272, 289-290.

their control of the southern part where lay the oil fields, tribal allies, and the ports on the Persian Gulf. Over a year later American troops arrived and built up these ports, all but took over the railroad, set up a truck assembly plant, and constructed the road over which millions of tons of war materiel were delivered into Russian hands at the Iranian city of Qazvin.

In return for the Reza Shah's prudent withdrawal, the transparent fiction of Iran's cooperation with the Allies was created; and later Iran was admitted to the wartime United Nations, and its independence and territorial integrity were guaranteed in the famous Teheran Declaration of 1943. In this manner and under the exigency of a war that threatened the very existence of both Britain and the Soviet Union was one of the most politically anomalous situations of our time created. If such words had meaning, we might say that Iran's was a government in exile without ever being exiled. To all intents and purposes, Iran's international existence was extinguished. Internally, neither Britain nor the Soviet Union took real responsibility for the administration of government. Each of the occupying powers contented itself with limiting what the government of Iran might do. The United States tried its best to act as though its troops weren't really there.

Little more than Teheran itself came under the administrative power of the Iranian government, and even in the capital city there were many substantive areas, particularly those of economics and supply, that were controlled by the Allied ambassadors. Iran's parliament, the Majlis, was permitted to meet and Cabinets were regularly appointed to manage affairs, to deal with the occupying powers and to requite the demands of an urban population now mobilized by wartime conditions.

Within this limiting framework, Iranian politics were supposed to go on as though nothing had happened. But a great deal had happened. One of the first acts imposed upon the young Shah was the declaration of an amnesty for all political prisoners and the nullification of censorship regulations. The immediate beneficiaries of both were the Tudeh Party (a Communist organization) and the pan-Iranism groups. The political arena was opened to the extremist groups that the Reza Shah had suppressed, and it was further opened to many traditional groups that had remained quiescent throughout the previous 14 years. Of even greater long-range importance, however, was the intellectual and cultural opening of Iran resulting from the relative freedom of the press which now prevailed. Nationalism, democracy, socialism, equality, economic development, Western art, and modern literary criticism were the themes and subject matter of a host of new journals, pamphlets, newspapers, and books that suddenly addressed themselves to the attention of the educated youth. Though these ideas were poorly presented and often dogmatic or naïvely unequivocal in their revelation of the modern world, the intellectual impact of all this inked paper was massive. After the near seclusion of Iran, its aspiring middle classes were subjected to the cold douche of Western idealism and liberalism, an experience that left them contemptuous of the achievements of the Reza Shah and floundering about seeking an explanation of where Iran fit into this rational, nonreligious world seemingly without history, or at least unburdened by its memory. The sum total of this experience was no less than a cultural shock.

Under the circumstances, political normalcy could hardly be expected, yet abnormal conditions consequent on foreign intervention have been more or less consistently a part of Iranian political life since the end of the nineteenth century, with the exception of the reign of the Reza Shah, that is, from about 1924 to 1941. The special conditions produced by foreign intervention were of two sorts, depending upon whether only a single one or two foreign powers were exerting influence within Iran. Prior to 1906 it might be said that Russia alone influenced Iranian government. From 1907 to 1917 Russia and Britain shared influence. From 1917 to 1924 British influence was dominant. From 1941 to 1951, that is, the beginning of Mossadegh's prime ministry, Soviet Russia and Britain shared influence. Since that date no outside power has held exclusive influence nor has any enjoyed the degree of influence previously prevailing, but the United States has clearly been more influential than any other foreign power.

During periods of dual influence the Iranian political system exhibited the characteristics of a competitive, almost open political system, with a substantial proportion of the major urban populations participating in both political movements and party activities, with vigorous electioneering for the Majlis seats from Teheran, and with an outspoken press. There is a certain artificiality in this situation because opposition middle-class groups and intellectuals who thus become politically active are inherently weak in numbers, cohesion, and both ideology and specificity of the interests they pursue. Not all are propped up by foreigners, for the competition for influence permits a degree of initiative in the formation of political groups that can act either as spokesmen for quiescent or unarticulated interests or as political brokers. These free-lance politicians are open to overtures from any real power center, the Shah or a foreign embassy, or a traditional autocratic dignitary. Newspaper editors and guild officers act in much the same way.

When only a single foreign power is influential, that influence tends to sustain the prevailing autocratic tendency, but interaction between Shah and ambassador appears to induce the Shah to create political structures of a democratic appearance that he can use to conteract undesirable pressures. This has been the case since the constitutional movement of 1906.

After prolonged periods of foreign influence broken only by the sixteen years of the Reza Shah's attempt at integral nationalism, if there is any norm to which Iran might return, it is a monarchical absolutism. But even this absolutism must take account of both traditionally powerful elements and the modernized classes in the cities. There is little sense in trying to describe such a rarely occurrent norm, and instead we shall be concerned with the actual working of the present system, which, as a consequence of the tenuousness of American influence, is the nearest approximation of the norm available for empirical observation.

The Present Shah

First, however, it is important to understand that the present Shah, whose reign has now lasted some 28 years, took the throne under circumstances which all but completely discredited his father's efforts and, as pointed out, provided for an artificially competitive situation under dual foreign domination. The prestige of the new dynasty was at a low after the army failed to react against occupation and after the Reza Shah accepted abdication. There were many individuals and groups who had suffered under the heavy-handed rule of the Reza Shah and most of these looked forward to settling old scores with the new Shah.

Among those who had been severely dealt with were those associated with the previous Qajar dynasty, provincial landed dignitaries, the ulama or Shiite clergy, a nascent Communist group, and even a proto-Fascist organization. The military, which had been reconstituted of non-aristocratic elements by the Reza Shah, and which had served as the major prop of his regime, was all but broken in both morale and influence by foreign occupation.[1] The never very efficient bureaucracy inherited and reformed by the Reza Shah was further weakened by foreign interference. Finally, wartime conditions brought new elements into political participation that had had no previous association with the Pahlavi dynasty. Transport and supply requirements brought into existence important new groups of wage earners and opened new opportunities to enterprising contractors and truck owners. The free importation of books and movies, coupled with the example of the way of life of the numerous foreigners who now resided in Teheran, had a deep and continuing effect on the attitudes and ideologies of the younger aspirants to civil service or other middle-class positions. For the first time in Iran the idea of modernity was definitely linked to Western

[1]General Hassan Arfa, *Under Five Shahs* (New York, Morrow, 1966), pp. 300f.

styles, cultural motifs, and organizational standards. That traditional Shiite Islam was not modern had already been established by the Reza Shah's favorites among the cultural elite and by such vigorous writers as Kasravi.

When the present Shah assumed the throne he had no real army to support him; his legitimacy was not sanctioned by the ulama; his Cabinet was not of his own choosing; the Majlis was an independent, almost anarchic body; and a host of new political parties have suddenly emerged: clique-oriented parties of notables in the Parliament as ideologically oriented parties among the young nationalists. Sustained neither by love, respect, self-confidence, nor legitimacy, Mohammad Reza Pahlavi strove to re-establish the foundation of royal authority and to continue to pursue the modernizing goals of his father. But these ends were pursued at first within the political framework created by the dual occupation. That is, the Shah was compelled to enter into the now competitive political arena to win support. This required compromise, bargaining, favoritism, occasional swallowing of pride, indirection, intrigue, and the playing off of rivals against one another. On the other hand, the stakes were not only the re-establishment of the new dynasty, but actual control of the government. At the present time the two are inseparable in Iran. The demand that the Shah reign not rule, voiced during the Mossadegh period, was really no more than the first step in the direction of republicanism or dictatorship.[2] Control of the government, to be effective in the sense of not permitting rivals to manipulate sections of the administration and security forces to their own advantage, required further measures of rationalizing reform. To put the matter simply, even in a traditional monarchy where the legitimate authority of the King is unchallenged, much of the royal effort is spent on improving the organization and central control over both the military and the bureaucracy. In such a traditional system it is relatively rare that ordinary political activity is aimed at changing the dynasty and it is almost never aimed at changing the regime. In Iran the legitimacy of the monarchy was undermined before the Reza Shah took the throne. His son rightly understood that even the most routine of political activities could lead to his unseating. If this monarch goes the dynasty may go. If this dynasty goes, the institution of monarchy will go with it.

In his search for support the Shah had to compromise with his desire for administrative rationality and efficiency. Gradually, the Shah won over a section of the military, a section of the old aristocracy, and a section of the ulama. The institutional inertia of the army, the bureaucracy, the religious institution, the police, and the gendarmerie helped to keep

[2]*Ibid.*, p. 395. "I knew that the real purpose of Musaddiq [Mossadegh] coming to power was the elimination of the Pahlavi dynasty . . . ."

routine government, law, and order operating. During the period of Allied occupation, however, the allegiance of the younger generation had been irretrievably lost. In their capacities as civil servants or as junior officers, these younger educated city dwellers carried out specific duties. Nevertheless, in their private capacities they were opposed to the regime and increasingly convinced of the impossibility of improving conditions in Iran without doing away with that regime. As opponents of the dynasty they were, under the conditions of the occupation, incapable of organizing a revolution, but the groundwork was laid. At the same time the Shah's efforts bore some fruit in the sense that the postwar political system of Iran was shaped by the progress of his struggle to maintain and improve his postiton.

Iranian Political Style

Against this background we can understand why concern with political and ideological hypocrisy is so central a feature of the Iranian political style. In the first place, the central symbol of authority and legitimacy, the Shah, had lost prestige. In the second place, he regained for the throne much political power by working in the manner of the traditionally influential elements of the élite and accepting their support. These elements, if aristocrats, had stronger attachments to the previous dynasty; if religious, had grave doubts about the religious sincerity of the Shah; and if in the military, were well aware of the differences in personality between the present Shah and his father. In the third place, the younger nationalists performed their bureaucratic roles in a routine manner while harboring strong feelings of alienation. In the fourth place, the Shah himself sought efficiency and progress but controverted his own ideals in the interest of maintaining the support of the disunited, faction-ridden traditional leaders.

From 1941 to the fall of Mossadegh in 1953, the Shah was simply one of the more important contenders in a competitive free-for-all. His importance depended upon the permanence of his position, a permanence which at the start was tenuously based only upon Allied recognition and the provisions of the constitution. Although he had the support of those who were so close to his father, these had been in part discredited by the abdication. Gradually, however, he re-established ties with the rebellious Bakhtiari. Concessions were made to the ulama, and the Shah was able to maintain control over the military budget, though he could not determine its size.

In the Majlis, traditional dignitaries struggled with one another for the loaves and fishes, while bringing down governments with regularity and with an asperity born of long subjection to the will of the Reza Shah's puppet ministries. The political game was being played on the level of the distribution of graft, prestige, and positions of influence in the form of seats in the Majlis and Cabinet posts, but much more was at stake. The nationalist intelligentsia watched this game, from which they were largely excluded, with increasing frustration; and their reaction produced a pattern of irrational and sometimes pointless street demonstrations. Violence, intimidation, and gross corruption took their place beside traditional conspiracy and intrigue and beside vague ideological protest during this most confused and directionless period of Iran's political history. Birds of many different feathers flocked together in a most amazing display of tactical flexibility, ideological doubletalk, and crass manipulation.

At the end of the war attention was focused on three issues: the position of the Shah, the perennial problem of who was to be Prime Minister, and the evacuation of Soviet troops from Azerbaijan. The position of the Shah, though clearly defined in the constitution, was politically unclear. There were some who wished to establish a republic, although the great majority who were willing to keep the monarchy had no desire or expectation that the old despotism of the Reza Shah would be restored. The real issue, then, was whether the Shah would be an actual party in political affairs or merely an instrument of some group or individual. The problem of who was to be Prime Minister touched on issues of policy, for the Prime Minister would determine fiscal matters, cope with the trade unions, and decide on petroleum affairs. Perhaps more important to most influential politicians was the likelihood that the Prime Minister would allocate most of the Cabinet posts, import licenses, and other sources of prestige and wealth. The third problem entailed more than Iranian-Soviet relations for, even if the United States did not take a clear stand on the issue, it was clear that Great Britian was prepared to pressure Iran at least to the point of weakening central government control over the south.

Iranian Prime Ministers

In order to resolve the third of these problems the second was exacerbated by the appointment of the most skillful, courageous, and traditionally imposing of Iran's prime ministers in this century, Qavam al-Saltaneh, an outstanding member of the Qajar aristocracy. During his ministry, the Soviets were induced to leave Azerbaijan, some of the younger reform- and efficiency-minded nationalists were brought into the Majlis and Cabinet, and the position of the Shah was rendered dependent upon the resolution of the incumbency of the prime ministry.

Until this time, the Shah had concentrated upon building his support in the army and had merely played the parliamentary game of helping to unseat ministries. Qavam's skillful avoidance of facing the Majlis, his domination over his Cabinets, his building of at least a semblance of a mass party, and his development of the gendarmerie over against the army shifted the emphasis within the Iranian political system so that it appeared that relations between the Shah and the Prime Minister were its most important aspect. Through all subsequent changes a central objective of the Shah has remained the desire to choose the Prime Minister; to prevent his gaining full control over the Cabinet; to exclude military, foreign, and oil affairs from thorough Cabinet consideration. At first the Shah was unable to accomplish any of these purposes, primarily because he could control few of the Majlis factions. Full control of the Majlis did not come until 1945, and it was not stable until after 1963.

There were two other strong prime ministers: Ali Razmara (1951) and Mohammed Mossadegh (1951 to 1953). Prior to 1954 the Shah, by convention, appointed as prime minister whoever had received a "vote of preference" from the Majlis. The sole exception was General Razmara whom the Shah appointed in July 1950, and who served until his assassination in 1951, when he was succeeded by Mossadegh. In appointing Razmara without prior consultation of the Majlis, the Shah was attempting to assume leadership of the political life of the country. However, the Shah grew to fear Razmara himself and, it is reported, did not mourn him after his assassination. If Qavam's ministry raised the danger of subordination of the throne to the Qajar aristocracy, Razmara's ministry raised an alternative danger of a military coup similar to the one the Reza Shah himself had accomplished. Mossadegh's ministry began as a reassertion of Majlis independence, complicated by the fact that the Shah turned to the Majlis on the "rebound," as it were, from a military solution, and further by the fact that members of the Majlis, though not solidly behind Mossadegh, were themselves recoiling from the pressures of street mobs and the nationalist parties.

These three strong prime ministers represented three of the major threats to the Shah and the dynasty. Mossadegh doubtlessly presented the greatest threat of all, and his ministry, from April 1951 to August 1953, effectively molded the form of Iranian political attitudes and set the pattern for the political dynamics of the Iranian system. Ostensibly, the issue that dominated the period was Mossadegh's attempt to nationalize Iranian oil. The real issue was the place of the Shah in Iranian politics, and indeed the place of all other important forces.

Mossadegh permitted nearly unbridled political activity of all organized parties, movements, and front groups, fanatical religious groups, Fascist and paramilitary groups, as well as bazaar groups in the guise of political fronts. At times newspapers were suspended and occasionally police action was taken against certain groups. The Tudeh Party, proscribed in

1949, remained outlawed but was nevertheless extremely active. Street fights and demonstrations by rival groups were a common feature. But Mossadegh did not associate himself with any party. He even went so far as to permit his own National Front to dwindle to little more than a name. He sent Allah Yar Saleh, the leader of the Iran-i-Novin Party, to the United States as Iran's ambassador. He did not maintain any effective liaison with the Tudeh Party or with any other. He did not keep his Cabinet well informed, nor did he consult them on policy. He appealed to the people over the heads of the members of the Majlis and terrorized or cajoled many of them into submission. He intervened in the bureaucracy, especially in the Ministry of Justice, with a free hand. He tried to build up the Teheran police as a security force and attempted to gain control of the army by winning over officers and more directly by demanding that control over the military budget be turned over to him by the Shah. He disliked working with the radical parties and preferred instead to bargain with guild groups, professional associations, and others on a direct basis. He tried to hold an election and proved to be a more cynical manipulator in this than either Qavam or Razmara had been.

The Struggle between Mossadegh and the Shah

The struggle between Mossadegh and the Shah probably mobilized more groups into political activity than had the war and Soviet propaganda. Each antagonist strove by bargains, intrigues, speeches, and any other available means to win over cliques, groups, parties, military formations, intelligence units, individual ulama, and even hooligan gangs. Three important dates mark turning points in this struggle and they have since become the most significant symbols of Iranian politics. The thirtieth of Tir (July 20, 1952) marked Mossadegh's resignation over the question of the military budget. The Shah attempted to install Qavam again; but faced with popular demonstrations in Mossadegh's favor, Qavam demanded control of the armed forces. The Shah demurred and Qavam resigned and fled the country. Mossadegh returned to office and the struggle for power resumed with even greater intensity. On the ninth of Esfand (February 28, 1953) the Shah held a public meeting at which he threatened to leave the country, and a demonstration of royalist forces was held to implore him to remain. The consequences of the demonstration might have been very bad for Mossadegh had not the Teheran Chief of Police (subsequently murdered) acted to save the situation. The third date is the twenty-eighth of Mordad (August 19, 1953), the date on which Mossadegh was deposed. Less than a week before, the Shah had attempted to dismiss the Prime

Minister. Mossadegh defied the order and the Shah fled the country. Hussein Fatemi and Dr. Shayegan, two important Nationalist Front figures, called for a republican form of government. Then the elements that the Shah had won over were moved to rise against Mossadegh and his support (which turned out to be only a segment of the educated middle class and a section of the bazaar). *Mullahs*, hawkers, laborers, and others marched mob fashion from south Teheran. They were supported by a small section of the army under General Zahedi. Later in the day they were joined by the Teheran police. The Tudeh Party appealed to Mossadegh for weapons, which he declined to give them. By mid-afternoon Mossadegh was in prison, Radio Teheran broadcast the restoration of the Shah, and the troops coming from the provinces under General Bakhtiyar in support of Zahedi were no longer needed.[3]

Nearly everyone who was in Teheran on the twenty-eighth of Mordad has his own version of what actually occurred. The official, legitimate version of those events is contained in the memoirs of the Shah, and another loyalist version is contained in General Arfa's autobiography.[4] These stress the loyalty of the common people to the Shah and to traditional institutions. The popular reaction in favor of the Shah on the ninth of Esfand is also given prominence, while the culturally alien and socially estranged character of the middle-class revolutionaries is given contrapuntal emphasis. Arfa, himself, participated in some of the events of the day, directing small military units and haranguing the *sans-culottes* of Teheran.

Bahman Nirumand gives another version of those events, denying that there was any spontaneity on the part of the Teheran masses;[5] Nirumand attributes the events to an American or CIA conspiracy. He makes much of the facts that General Schwarzkopf visited Iran at that time, that Ambassador Henderson made a trip to Switzerland, and that General Zahedi went into hiding. He argues that Schwarzkopf, who had built up the Iranian gendarmeries just after the war, was, in 1953, representing the CIA and that he was a friend of Zahedi. He cites newspaper sources in asserting that Henderson met with Allen Dulles, then Director of the CIA, and with Princess Ashraf "on the slopes of the Swiss Alps." He implies that Schwarzkopf met with Zahedi and concludes that Zahedi must have been hiding in the U.S. embassy. Nirumand goes on to cite *Le Monde* as the source of the information that "American agents" had

[3]Arfa has an interesting description of the events of the 28th of Mordad from the royalist point of view (*ibid.*, pp. 406 f.).

[4]Mohammad Reza Pahlavi, *Mission for My Country* (London, Hutchinson, 1961).

[5]Bahman Nirumand, *Iran: The New Imperialism in Action* (New York: The Monthly Review Press, 1969), pp. 83 f.

cashed a check for nearly $400,000-worth of Iranian rials on August 18. The "lumpenproletariat" of Teheran was set in motion by bribery distributed by the *mullahs*. But even Nirumand concludes: "Now the CIA would not be the CIA if one could prove by documents that it was guilty of such an enormous crime as the overthrow of a foreign government."[6]

Despite the divergence of emphasis, certain features of all versions seem to coincide. There were plots and maneuvers on both sides. The United States favored the Shah. Most of the religious authorities favored the Shah. When Mossadegh and Kashani split, parts of the bazaar and of the lower middle class left Mossadegh's support. The army was infiltrated by the Tudeh Party but traditionally oriented senior officers with Qajar dynastic connections, tribal connections, or with personal ties to the Shah's father sided with the Shah. Mossadegh had no desire to win over the army, or at least he thought that an impossible goal. Instead he intended to weaken it because it was a strong support for the Shah's regime. Hence self-interest strengthened conviction and cultural inclination in inducing many officers to side with the monarchy. The lack of Tudeh Party action, either among the armed forces or among the intelligentsia, further permitted the actions of a relatively small number of pro-Shah officers to succeed. Nirumand seems to indicate that the decisive act was simply the arrival of Zahedi with a couple of tanks at the front gate of Mossadegh's home. Mossadegh refused to arm the Tudeh Party workers. Popular support for the anti-Mossadegh coup grew during the day and did not have city-wide support until late afternoon. On the other hand, it does appear that the mass support was the crucial variable. If there was active American intervention it was probably financial, as indicated by all the speculators, and hortatory—for the chances did not appear to be very good at the time.

The Security of the Shah's Regime

In this manner, the Shah was relieved of the threat of Mossadegh. All political parties were banned. The Tudeh Party was smashed and over 500 of its members were rooted out of the armed forces by effective police work. A *rapprochement* was effected with the highest religious authorities. When the Majlis was reconstituted it was little more than a rubber stamp. All important groups, the Bar Association, the Chamber of Commerce, the guilds, the teachers' association, and more were purged and favorable leadership installed. The bazaar was forcibly threatened and brought into line. All those who had supported the Shah were handsomely rewarded. The police, like the army and the gendarmerie, were purged and rewarded with increased benefits. How well these policies, and careful

[6]*Ibid.*, p. 88.

policies of screening and surveillance, have worked it is difficult to say. The Shah has been most obviously successful in dealing with a handful of senior officers.

But the Shah was, in 1954, too dependent upon General Zahedi, his Prime Minister, and General Bakhtiyar, the head of the Security Agency. Zahedi's son was married to the Shah's daughter, and the loyal General was given a handsome pension and retired to a palatial villa in Switzerland. General Bakhtiyar remained on until 1961 when he was finally replaced as Security Chief.

Since the removal of General Zahedi as Prime Minister, the Shah has sought for a stable solution to the problem of providing for the government of Iran while securing his own position. For the most part his attempts have taken the form of institutional and personnel manipulations which have hardly touched the surface of Iranian politics. After Zahedi there was a short prime-ministerial interregnum during which Hussein Ala, perennial Minister of Court (head of the Shah's personal administrative apparatus), served in the former capacity. After Ala, Dr. Manuchehr Eghbal was made Prime Minister; and a close associate of the Shah, Asadullah Alam, was permitted to form an opposition party called the Hizb-i-Mardom (Mardom Party). This opposition did not really oppose, but it was useful in drawing off some elements hostile to the Shah and also permitted the political rehabilitation of some ex-Tudeh Party people. Its existence also suggested that Alam was to be the next Prime Minister. Eghbal formed a government party, Hizb-i-Melliyun (Melliyun Party), clearly intending to hold power if possible, and the Shah sanctioned a puppet two-party system. Eghbal used the government party to organize the Majlis to some extent. He managed to gain control over the Plan Organization and to extend his control over the Cabinet. Eghbal dominated the 1960 elections, but so crude was his manipulation of those elections that even Alam had to protest publicly, and the Shah then obliged the protesters by annulling the elections.

It is not entirely clear why the Shah allowed this general public protest against the elections of 1960, but barring the real possibility of miscalculation or simple ineptitude, it is obvious that the major consequence of this action was to end the prime ministry of Dr. Eghbal. Other consequences were to end, at least for a time, the two-party experiment, and to allow popular political participation by means of street demonstrations. It is difficult to understand why the Shah allowed a situation that was so well in hand to get so completely out of hand. The steps back to political repression and control were halting. Sharif Imami, a political enemy of Eghbal, was appointed Prime Minister. Subsequent (exaggerated) charges of corruption against Eghbal suggest that there may have been some desire to get rid of him.

But there was no sign of any decisive new political direction warranting so important a shift in political tactics to accomplish a change of personnel. So great is the mystery regarding the political motivation behind the domestic policy of the period that one feels compelled to speculate further that the Shah may have been persuaded that the time was right for a liberalization of the regime. If so, it was doubtlessly American well-wishers who persuaded him of what was clearly a premature policy. New and fair elections under the two-party system were promised, and under conditions of disorderly campaigning, political intimidation, and crude manipulation such elections were held in January, 1961. The election moved things more toward the Mardom Party Candidates, but the real consequence of the two elections was the re-emergence of the National Front and the parties and political style of the Mossadegh period. None of the elements of the Front seemed willing or able to work things out with the Shah. The Front had boycotted the elections of both 1960 and 1961 and contrived to attack their validity and to demand new, fair elections. Street demonstrations continued and extremist groups sprang up on the left of the Front.

In May, 1961, the Cabinet was dismissed, the parliament prorogued, and Dr. Ali Amini appointed Prime Minister. Amini, though of aristocratic background, had been connected with the National Front and with Mossadegh, and was known as a liberal. He had also served as the chief Iranian negotiator in working on the oil agreement of 1954. He set about trying to introduce reform measures, primarily ending corruption and stepping up land reform, but his major task in ruling without parliament was to co-opt or suppress the National Front. Since he could co-opt the National Front only at the expense of his government, he pursued the latter course of suppression.[7] He attempted to counterbalance this unpopular policy by reducing the land-reform pressure on the aristocracy and increasing government development expenditures, much of which would go to the educated middle class. To offset these expenditures Amini attempted to persuade the military to agree to a budget cut, in the expectation that American military assistance cash payments would be sufficiently increased to counterbalance the cut.[8] The disappointment of this expectation contributed to Amini's dismissal in July, 1962, after an important but ineffective National Front demonstration.

[7]*Ibid.*, pp. 156-157.

[8]For the interrelations of foreign aid and domestic politics, see L. Binder, *Iran* (Berkeley: University of California Press, 1963), pp. 340 f.

Amini, at the expense of his own popularity, had managed to bring political affairs under control, the military (and the Shah with them) had reasserted their supremacy, and now the breathing space was extended by the appointment of Asadullah Alam as Prime Minister. Alam, who later became Minister of Court, prepared the way for the most recent and most successful phase of the Shah's struggle to secure his regime and complete his father's revolution. This phase was the period of the "White Revolution" inaugurated by the Shah's six-point program of January, 1963—a program which included a serious land reform (originally proposed under Amini) and the symbolically significant grant to women of the right to vote.

Important opposition was manifested in June, 1963, instigated by the landed classes and led by some of the Shiite clergy. The cooperation of these two conservative groups was based on more than ideology and cultural affinity, for the land reform was to encompass religiously endowed lands which were an important source of religious revenue. The opposition was surprisingly violent and well supported by the Teheran masses. It was, nevertheless, swiftly and brutally suppressed.

These three steps to a new monarchical stability—suppression of the National Front in 1962, announcement of the White Revolution in early 1963, and suppression of the religiously led opposition in June, 1963— were completed with the holding of new elections in the fall of 1963. Asadullah Alam's supporters won handily. They were a coalition of various groups most of which were pragmatically and developmentally oriented. Outstanding among them was the Iran-i-Novin Party which had been formed earlier in 1963 as a party, but which was linked with an earlier group of ambitious, American-oriented (culturally) and efficiency-minded technicians of upper-middle- and upper-class backgrounds.[9] Alam remained as Prime Minister until March, 1964, when Hassan Ali Mansur, another Qajar with a long and distinguished administrative career, was appointed Prime Minister. Mansur was more closely identified with Iran-i-Novin. Mansur immediately increased the development budget and devoted himself to advancing the White Revolution, improving relations with the Soviet Union, and increasing oil production.

There is, of course, significant ideological and social opposition to the regime, both in Iran and among students and political exiles abroad, but little of this has been evident in Iran where politics have been well controlled, except for the two assassination plots of 1965. The first of these was successfully perpetrated by a fanatical religious group and

[9]Apparently there is some connection between this group and the Iran-i-Novin group described in L. Binder, *Iran*, p. 197. See also Nirumand, p. 161.

resulted in the death of Prime Minister Hassan Ali Mansur. His finance minister, Amir Abbas Hoveida, was immediately appointed in his stead and remains Prime Minister today. The second assassination attempt was on the life of the Shah and it was unsuccessfully plotted by an extreme left-wing group. During this period the Shah's land-reform program has achieved some signal successes, economic development has proceeded at an annual compounded rate of 7 percent, oil revenues have increased substantially, and Iran has finally responded favorably to constant Soviet pressure for more friendly relations on a broad front.[10]

II. Iran's Domestic Political and Social Situation

The new international position of Iran described in the introduction to this paper is in large part due to the reality or convincing appearance of the domestic political success of the Shah. It is certainly plausible to conclude that after 28 years the impossible has been achieved and that Iran is on its way to becoming a prosperous, stable, modernizing autocracy, and it may even have a chance of becoming a bourgeois-nationalist constitutional monarchy.[11]

More important than these speculations, however, is the point that having achieved these related domestic and international positions, it is hard to conceive of any but a satellite regime living up to the advantageous position that Iran thus attained. It might even be argued that this new international role, extended to Iran gradually with the development of its internal political strength, is so valuable to Iran's allies and so threatening to Iran's enemies that circumstances will force this new role on any successor regime. Hence, even if the regime is not as stable as it might appear, Iran's international position is probably quite stable.

[10]Despite his deep suspicion of Soviet motives, Donald Wilber gives a good summary of persistent Soviet efforts to work out their relationships with Iran, emphasizing the Soviet fear that Iran might allow the United States to set up missile bases on Iranian soil. (*Contemporary Iran* [New York, Praeger 1963] pp. 197 f.).

[11]Marvin Zonis summarizes the situation according to a widely held view in his unpublished thesis, "Iran: The Politics of Insecurity" (MIT, 1968), pp. 17-18.

"Now, at last, the throne appears secure. Organized international opposition has been decimated, while even the expression of anti-regime sentiment is absent. International support for the Shah's rule has been broadened to include not only the United States and its Western allies, but also the USSR and other communist nations as well. With a firm grasp over the political process, the Shah has devoted himself and Iran's continually increasing oil income to internal development. A mounting gross national product, social reforms, educational development, land distribution, and even a massive program of heavy industries have been the rewards."

Domestic Political Forces

These assertions regarding the low probability of domestic political change affecting Iran's foreign policy will have to be sustained by an examination of the potential sources of domestic political change. The political ideological spectrum in Iran has undergone but modest change in the last decade. The assassination of Hassan Ali Mansur in 1965 evidenced the continued vigor of the religious extremist Fidayan-i-Islam, as did the rioting of 1963 evidence the continued vigor of the influence of the traditional religious leaders. The attempted assassination of the Shah, also in 1965, brought to light a Peking-oriented Communist group. Here and there, from an occasional arrest or from propaganda broadcasts, the continued existence of the Tudeh Party and of a Moscow-oriented group of Communists is confirmed. These two tendencies comprise the ideological extremes. In between it is important to note the decline of the National Front centrist elements and the emergence of a more stridently anti-regime group called the Freedom Movement of Iran.[12] The movement was active in 1961 and after, but the last few years its activities in exile and among students studying abroad have been more significant than its activities in Iran. The symmetrical opposite of the Freedom Movement of Iran is the Pan-Iranism Party, a right-wing nationalist and irredentist party, which is allowed freedom of action by the Shah but not overtly endorsed or legalized.[13] In the center there are also two tendencies, one predominantly technocratic, bureaucratic, and rationalizing, and the other aristocratic, enterprising, and traditional. The first is represented by the Iran-i-Novin Party of Prime Minister Amir Abbas Hoveida, and the second by the residuals of the once official Mardom and Melliyun parties. It goes without saying that such formally organized groups do not comprise all the adherents of one view or another.

The extreme leftist- and rightist-religious oppositions deny the legitimacy of the regime and see little benefit in anything short of its complete destruction. For the remaining groups, and for the Shah, there is a central issue on which they can differ and on which compromise may emerge: that is, whether a king should reign or rule, whether the parliament of Iran in an efficient or only an ornamental part of the constitution, and whether elections are to be "cooked" or consumed *au nature*.

[12]The Freedom Movement of Iran is briefly described by Wilber, *Contemporary Iran*, p. 152: "The Freedom Movement of Iran appears to contain at least two factions: one allegedly of individuals holding pro-Communist views and the other with a religious orientation."

[13]See Leonard Binder, *Iran*, p. 219, for additional information on the Pan-Iranism Party.

The Shah has more or less turned away from "positive nationalism," so named to distinguish his policy from positive neutrality, to the White Revolution. The doctrine of the White Revolution is primarily oriented to domestic politics, and since it emphasizes land reform, electoral reform, economic development, and literacy, it symbolizes the Shah's commitment to parliamentarism, to democratic process, and to more effective political participation by the masses. But the Shah's commitment has been expressed through controlled elections, certified party organization, and parliamentary discipline. None of these aspects of a liberal regime has been allowed to interfere with centralized control and bureaucratic domination of Iranian life. Thus the Shah continues to invoke the legitimacy of the constitution of Iran while sustaining an autocratic, paternalistic, and technocratic regime.

The Free Iran Movement and many less radical groups have been driven to demand republicanism because they do not believe that the Shah will be willing to play a subordinate political role. The Shah does not believe that these groups would respect his throne, nor does he believe that they will pursue his goals of development efficiently. The outlook of the Iran-i-Novin Party, the group or deputies and administrators actually in power, is that technologically and economically efficient development will eventually allow the expansion of effective political participation, the decline of ideological politics, and the free operation of a multi-party system and a politically competent parliament. The more general goals of nationalism and modernization are shared by nearly all of the groups in the center, as well as by the great majority of unaffiliated members of the educated middle class in Iran and abroad.

One of the more remarkable aspects of Iranian politics, noticed by a good many observers, is the small number of Iranian students abroad who support the Shah, and the number, vigor, and intensity of those who oppose him. There have been important incidents of protest and demonstration against the Shah when he has visited foreign countries. There are also a few opposition newspapers or newsletters issued abroad and distributed among students. It is hardly reasonable to draw conclusions from the distribution of sentiment among these groups, but at the least, we must be cautious of overestimating the Shah's popularity among the younger intellectuals in Iran. The hostility of a majority of the young educated is not fully counterbalanced by the support of the army officers and those members of the aristocracy who are either connected with the army or who have made the transition from landowner to entrepreneur.

Social and Ideological Forces

But the vigor of even the most hostile groups is open to question, for in most cases, ideological groups or, rather, tendencies, are informally organized at best. If they can be said to have memberships, these vary greatly in size from time to time, and only on rare occasions can their adherents be expected to act in accordance with their erratically expressed convictions. The ideological spectrum is not at all significant as a guide to the parties or movements or even social segments that are likely to act politically and in a concerted and consistent manner. These ideological perspectives are merely available to the politically aware and potentially participant groups. So long as they persist in inaction or in acquiescence in the present regime, there is no need to resolve the ideological dilemma of whether the ultra-traditional or ultra-modern critique of the regime is more correct. If an upheaval does take place, however, then we can expect increasingly large numbers of people to be forced to choose a specific political orientation and to act accordingly.

The pattern of Iranian ideologies is simple because that pattern does not reflect the highly complex society of Iran. Too many observers will describe the society in terms of the few known ideological tendencies or worse yet, according to some simple model of a developing society. Even though recent years have seen an increasing number of publications on Iran and there have been two censuses, really imaginative studies of Iranian society that go beyond stereotypes are still lacking. Of the main divisions of society into nomads, peasants, and townspeople there is no argument. There is much variation, however, among the nomads regarding tribal structure, pattern of nomadism, extent and type of national identity, willingness to submit to local authority, degree of religiosity, willingness to fight outside of the tribal region, and availability for sedentarization.[14]

The same sort of complexity is to be found in the peasant villages. The land-tenure, cropping, and tenancy customs vary from place to place. While the unit of landownership is the village, village size and hence village social organization varies greatly. Villages on the major highways have many amenities, yet more remote places are quite primitive. Some villages have resident religious leaders and some do not. In some villages the Kadkhoda (village headman) is the undisputed political head; in others he may have to compete with notables, landowners, religious dignitaries, civil servants, or gendarmerie officers. Water rights, the source of irrigation water, and the financing of production are further bases of difference.

Of the complexity of social organization in the towns and cities we know much more, but too often it is assumed that the overwhelming majority of

[14]Arfa, *Under Five Shahs*, pp. 444-451, has a fascinating rundown of "The Situation in the Tribal Regions and Zones Outside the Central Government's Control in 1921" in which he proceeds counterclockwise around the Iranian plateau with a description of the rebellious tribes.

this population belongs to the educated middle class.[15] The middle class is not politically or socially homogeneous. There is a modern middle class and a traditional middle class; a commercial middle class, an intellectual middle class; a professional middle class, and a managerial middle class; there is a national middle class, and a middle class of the minorities and foreigners; there is an urban middle class and a rural middle class. There are others besides the middle class in the cities: aristocrats, workers, artisans, casual laborers, hawkers, porters, policemen, streetsweepers, army officers, drivers, and many more. To complicate matters some of these people are related to others so that their political loyalties and personal loyalties are not immediately revealed by their class affiliations, and, of course, many identify their interests with either their family or their occupation rather than with their class.

It is widely assumed that the tribesmen are sullenly disloyal to the regime, that the peasants are indifferent, and that the intellectual middle class is actively hostile. Only the casual laborers, bazaar people, artisans, hawkers, police, and so on are said to be loyal. Of course, the establishment is loyal: the army officers, religious leaders holding official positions, important bureaucrats, government technicians, and the leaders of the minority communities. The old aristocracy, the landowners, the clergy, and the old middle class of scribes and the "respectably poor" do not favor the reforms of the Shah, but they have nowhere else to go.[16]

[15]Wilber, *Contemporary Iran*, pp. 159-164, describes the middle class in Iran, citing the fact that most Western observers look upon this social element as crucial to the political future of Iran. Wilber expresses a reasonable skepticism, "Not all these appraisals can be correct and they are in the category of personal opinions, since there is simply no reliable information on this class" (p. 159). On the other hand, James A. Bill in his unpublished paper, "Social and Political Development in Iran: Implications for Contemporary United States Foreign Policy," presents a table showing the growth of the Iranian professional-bureaucratic intelligentsia from 1956 to 1966 (p. 9). He concludes, "The professional middle class now confronts the traditional system" (p. 11).

[16]In discussing the Lebanese middle class, Fuad I. Khuri, in "The Changing Class Structure of Lebanon," *Middle East Journal*, 23/1 (Winter, 1969), 37, distinguishes between the *masturin* and the affluent. "These masturin include small landowners and shopkeepers, teachers, technicians, tradesmen, and those who earn their living independently by owning and managing their own capital and resources. They also include minor clerks, secretaries and ordinary soldiers, often employed by the central administration, the commercial and industrial firms, and the army. Implied by the term masturin is the honorable means by which these men earn their living." Note the similar usage in H. Ammar, *Growing Up in an Egyptian Village* (London, Rontledge, Kegan, Paul), p. 35: "The main ideal for which every family strives is to be 'mastourah,' which literally means to be covered, or, in other words, to be balanced and publicly approved and not exposed to outside shaming."

Such is the stereotypical view of the political orientations of the various segments of Iranian society, and this view was not altogether inadequate for a situation in which political matters were decisively determined in Teheran long before the rest of the country could do anything about it. But the rapid progress of development, the stepped-up rate of migration and of demographic changes in general, the improvement of transport and communications, and the success of the land reform all prove the necessity of a new dynamic analysis.

Thus all the tribes have been more or less quiescent for the last four or five years, but the Kurds have supported the Shah's policies, the Bakhtiyari have shifted away from their super loyalism to a more neutral attitude, and the largely sedentary Arab tribes of Khuzistan were a growing source of concern (even though we have no information about uprisings) until Egypt's defeat in June, 1967. Land reform has deprived the great nobles and chiefs of a ready source of political support. One may well ask whether politicization of the countryside will inevitably result in increased opposition to the regime or in a new source of support for the Shah.[17] It is entirely possible that a new breed of politician will emerge from the agricultural areas in the form of either the local notable or the co-op director, not to speak of the independent freeholder. In the cities, the traditional religious leaders still wield great power over the masses, but so do the police. Students are hostile to the regime, but there are significant rewards that await them upon the successful completion of a degree.[18] Civil servants are opposed to autocracy, but life is becoming easier and there are so many social obligations to fulfill that one has little time for politics. In other words the cross pressures are great even while the burdens of acquiescing in the continuation of the present regime become less difficult to bear. And they are also becoming less difficult to bear in a psychological sense, as the country gains in international prestige and power, and particularly as it develops an almost believable policy of nonalignment. It is too early to say whether emerging urban groups will support the Shah or some more liberal

---

[17]Jay C. Hurewitz, *Middle East Politics: The Military Dimension,* (New York: Praeger, 1969), p. 291, comments with regard to these rural programs: ". . . it was a growth not only in the rural economy but in the politicization of the peasantry." He makes a similar point: ". . . and when the peasants come to political life, the rural areas are likely to enlarge the breeding grounds of anti-royalism." Bill, "Social and Political Development in Iran," p. 19, reports: "This has begun to alienate many of the villagers who are told that they are to begin new lives but who in fact see themselves as the victims of government agents."

[18]Marvin Zonis has written on education in Iran in "Educational Ambivalence in Iran," *Iranian Studies,* Vol. II (Autumn, 1968), pp. 132 f., and elsewhere in unpublished papers. See also Lawrence M. Brammer, "Problems of Iranian University Students," *Middle East Journal,* 18/4 (Autumn, 1964), 443 f.

interpretation of the constitution, but the possibility ought not to be excluded. For these reasons, the growth of the middle class, the politicization of the peasants, the increased number of students, the increased number of industrial workers, the increased migration to the cities, the rapidly increasing population, the expropriation of the landlords, and the restrictions upon the economic resources of the clergy are not all unequivocal danger signs for the regime.[19]

These are the incipient social structural changes that are often pointed out as the "inner contradictions" of the system under the White Revolution. There is no doubt that it is difficult for any political analyst to observe the Iranian scene for long without experiencing a profound sense of uneasiness about the future of the Shah's regime. Observers are bound to look for the sources of dysfunctional change simply because there is such a low level of overt verbal support for the regime in spite of its doubtlessly effective performance in recent years. This improved performance is obviously a product of the last few years, whereas the ideological context is of long standing, and rhetorical habits are difficult to change. Yet it is also often the case that ideas of political reality are constructed out of prevailing political cultural tendencies and seldom out of statistics on rising national income. Even those who argue that the White Revolution is succeeding in winning support for the regime display an uneasy lack of confidence in their own long-term predictions.

But pessimism seems to afflict all observers of the Iranian scene equally, including those who earnestly desire the most complete revolutionary change. Rather than judging a completely corrupt regime to be ripe for revolution, many opponents of the regime estimate that the chances for successful revolution diminish with the increasing despotism of the government. Opponents of the regime do consider the White Revolution to be a new and more subtle form of tyranny. Hans Enzensberger, a commentator on Nirumand's tract, sums up the situation thus: Iran is neither a poor country nor an overpopulated one; geographically it is favorably situated; it has an intelligentsia and an indubitable national identity; the reactionary force that has kept Iran backward cannot be diverted because there is no "widespread illegal organization in the country's villages . . ." and "the urban proletariat is weak. . . . Iranian Islam is unable to release revolutionary energies . . . ." He says further, "nor can aid be expected from the bourgeoisie . . . , and . . . equally dim is the prospect for aid from

[19]Bill, "Social and Political Development in Iran," p. 8, calculates that in ten years the middle class has grown by 60%. On p. 19 he writes: "One of the deepest unintended consequences of the White Revolution is the accelerating growth of the professional middle class. Yet this is the very class that threatens the ongoing system." "Opposes" might be a better word than threatens, for the moment anyway.

the outside." He expects no help from the countries of the third world, from Russia, or even from China.[20]

This paradoxical lack of confidence in the future on both sides of the Iranian political fence can best be explained by noting that it is characteristic, if infrequently admitted, that the most underdeveloped aspect of underdeveloped countries is the availability of accurate information. In this regard, I do not believe that the Shah himself is much better off than the rest of us. From a slightly different perspective, however, it might be argued that the most volatile groups in Iran are simply available for mobilization under political circumstances that cannot yet be foreseen. At the moment these forces appear to be in suspended animation.

Not all of the vital political forces in Iran are in such suspended animation. The most significant institutional structures, the *mullahs*, the army, and the bureaucracy, are not "available" to anywhere near the degree that other groups may be. The Shah has striven to weaken the religious institution as an autonomous force without alienating his traditional religious support. Typically, the religious leaders who are most prominent at the Court or in Teheran are unwilling to accept the leadership of the more bookish clergy at Qumm. After the death in the early 1960s of Ayatullah Burujirdi, the last national head of the religious institution, rival *mullahs* prevented any successor from becoming the acknowledged head of the Shiite sect in Iran. Khomaini, who was prominent in the disturbances of June, 1963, was probably making a bid for such leadership. By successfully putting down religious opposition in 1963 and by preventing anyone from being acknowledged as "Ayatullah al-Uzmah" or chief *mullah,* the Shah strengthened the relative position of his friends and supporters among the clergy, even though it is now more than ever known that the Shah is not a friend of orthodox Shiite Islam.

The Army and SAVAK

The army is the most important institution of all, and the one that both supporters and opponents of the regime believe is responsible for the stability of the Shah's government. Most observers explain the army's support of the Shah by pointing to the material benefits enjoyed by the officers. This is correct but possibly an incomplete view. Nirumand believes that the officers are so brainwashed by their training that they are in fact devoted to the Shah.[21] A further consideration is the fact that some families still own a good deal of land, some have "noble blood," some maintain a military tradition, and some are politically connected with the Shah or

[20]Nirumand, *Iran . . .* , pp. 183-189.
[21]*Ibid.,* p. 93.

his father. Younger members of these families are available for co-optation, and they will make fairly reliable officers. A second element that is constantly courted by the Shah is the group strongly oriented to the latest technological advances in military techniques and the more highly trained branches such as the air force. That the system is not foolproof was amply demonstrated by the inroads that the Tudeh Party was able to make into the army. These inevitable lacunae are made up for, in part, by assiduous secret police work. At any rate, it is highly unlikely that the army as a whole would move against the Shah, so that any attempted coup would be opposed by some elements of the military who share a genuinely traditional heritage. These military forces are likely to try to keep the monarchy and the dynasty going.

The sort of control that the Shah has over the bureaucracy is of a similar nature. Salaries and benefits, even the prospects for promotion, for most classes of civil servants have improved. There is, paradoxically, more hierarchy and less camaraderie in the bureaucracy than in the military officer corps so that the formal structure itself offers a relatively effective means of control. But most important of all is the effort of the Shah to create a group of senior bureaucrats and administrators who have the same sort of personal and ideological attachment to himself as does a segment of the traditional clergy and segments of the military. These elements are of the Iran-i-Novin Party or possibly aspirants to influential membership in that party. The Shah presents himself to these people as a modernizer, interested in rational, scientific, and modern technological progress. To them the Shah emphasizes his desire for reform and his reliance on well-trained, highly skilled, formally educated, self-reliant administrators who are able to demonstrate their loyalty in however discreet a manner. These leading administrators and some members of parliament are few enough to be carefully screened and tested before co-optation. Furthermore, unlike the military officers, the highest administrators are asked to perform every day rather than merely prepare for future action, so they are probably even more reliable than the military officers.

It is unlikely that the loyalty of these groups is assured by the activity of the secret police, or SAVAK as it is more popularly known. It is even unlikely that subversive and conspiratorial activity would be far more extensive than they are if the SAVAK were inoperative. It is true, however, that SAVAK is extremely active in all phases of Iranian political life. SAVAK's omnipresence adds to prevailing anxieties, inhibits some activities, and as Nirumand indicates, sometimes apprehends army officers or students whom it accuses of plotting against the regime.[22] SAVAK assists

[22]*Ibid.*, pp. 155, 158, 162-168.

in control of the media of mass communication, and it has some interest in the activities of students who study abroad. But SAVAK is also an official Persian institution, blended into both the military and the administrative institutions. It offers another and not unattractive career line, it functions as a source of access for the usual kinds of political demands, even occasionally for some of its victims.

Opponents of the regime insist that it is sustained by means of force and oppression, while the most that sympathetic foreign observers will say is that stability has been purchased with a policy of repressive benevolence. Surely the situation is complicated and aspects of both interpretations are true. Yet it seems to me that the more violently repressive aspects of the regime appear only transitionally when a measure of political liberalization is seen to have backfired and is being withdrawn, as in 1953-1954 and 1962-1963. At other periods the law of anticipated reaction prevails, and the regime, in the face of the political discretion of its opponents, practices benevolent repressiveness by attempting to buy off or co-opt the intelligentsia.

III. Iran's New International Position

The present domestic political situation is a very fluid one, but certain features stand out: (1) the Shah has gained control of all important institutions; (2) the army and the police are loyal and effective; (3) the urban political culture, including many mass elements, is still unequivocally opposed to the regime; (4) economic development is proceeding at a very satisfying pace; (5) oil revenues are still increasing; (6) private entrepreneurship is growing; (7) an economic, technological, and bureaucratic élite of substantial competence and with a certain character of political neutrality has emerged; (8) the organized political opposition is quiescent.

An important conclusion to be drawn from all of this is that, although the gravest danger to the existing regime is assassination of the Shah, it is no longer as certain as it once was that such an event would end the monarchy. An assassination would be the desperate act of one of the extremist groups, but these are not capable of taking over the government. It is more likely that a regency would be established under the aegis of the military or some group of the Iran-i-Novin, or both in combination, and that these forces of the establishment would rally many who have a stake in the existing order. Until recently the Shah was less concerned with providing for an orderly succession in case of an emergency than he was with reducing the possibility of an emergency by leaving it unclear who would succeed if he were removed from the scene. After the birth of a male heir, however, the Shah's view changed, and the Queen who produced the heir has been crowned and designated as regent in the event of the prince's succession during his minority. Those who do have a stake in the existing order now have a symbol about which to rally in case of need. The only thing that would weaken Iran's international position would be the failure of any group to achieve reasonable control, but there is no evidence that the security forces and central bureaucracy will fragment with the first revolutionary impact.

The uncertainty I have emphasized must cast doubt upon my own conclusions just as it has thrown doubt upon the alternative conclusions of other observers. The problem of this analysis, however, is rather more one of explaining why all the dire predictions of other careful observers have not been fulfilled. It is to some extent the function of these uncertainties to explain, or at least to leave room for an explanation of, how the Shah managed to gain such extensive control, to achieve political stability, to institute relatively far-reaching reforms, and to greatly increase the country's prosperity. It is also noteworthy, if not surprising, that the Shah has done all this without achieving popularity or winning political support outside of the army.

Internationally, I believe that Iran's position is far more stable than it is domestically. The most persistent feature of Iran's foreign policy is its close involvement with the Soviet Union. Beginning with the loss of its Caucasian provinces at the end of the eighteenth and the beginning of the nineteenth centuries, Iran has been subjected to pressures of varying forms and intensities from the north. An Iranian defeat in 1824 led to the establishment of the capitulation treaties. The middle of the nineteenth century witnessed an extensive expansion of Russian sovereignty in Central Asia which alarmed the British in India. Their concern was not eased until the signing of the Anglo-Russian treaty of 1907. Preceded by thirty years or more of relatively intense British-Russian rivalry, that treaty divided parts of Asia and sections of Iran into spheres of exclusive Russian and British influence. Western observers do not tire of referring Soviet interests in Iran to the so-called legacy of Peter the Great, but there is little evidence of such an insatiable imperialistic appetite in earlier Russian policy.[23]

British interest in Iran was largely derivative of concern with India and of the intent to prevent other powers from gaining influence there. After encouraging the Constitutional Movement of 1906, the British abruptly ignored Iran's domestic affairs until the outbreak of World War I. British interest grew with the prospect of dismemberment of the neighboring Ottoman Empire, with the conversion of the British navy from coal to oil use, and with the outbreak of the Soviet revolution. Nevertheless, British interest was still secondary and largely negative, so that when in

[23]Wilber, *Contemporary Iran*, p. 135, cites the testament of Peter the Great.

1919 Iran was offered a treaty that would have made Britain dominant in Iranian affairs, the major pressure brought to bear on Iran was the payment of a substantial bribe to the Iranian negotiators.

The Soviets, in turn, though denouncing Czarist imperialism in Iran, brought revolutionary pressure to bear in the northern provinces during 1919 and 1920. The British encouraged tribal risings in the south near the oil fields and further toward the Indian border. The Reza Khan, the father of the present Shah, came to power in 1921 and decisively repudiated the proposed British treaty and countered it with a Soviet treaty that recognized Iranian sovereignty with the proviso that, should Iran allow its territory to be employed by a foreign power threatening an attack on the Soviet Union, the Soviet Union could exercise a right to invade Iran. Though the Soviet Union encouraged the local Communist Party during the interwar period, its behavior was more or less correct up to 1941.

During and after the Soviet occupation there was ample evidence of a Soviet desire to detach some parts of Iran under pro-Soviet regimes, but it is also clear that these goals were secondary to acquiring oil concessions in northern Iran, to acquiring broader political and economic influence, and to preventing Iran from becoming a threat to Soviet security. British and American support and counterpressure helped Iran through the early postwar crisis in Azerbaijan and Kurdistan, but from there, through the Mossadegh period to the founding of the Baghdad Pact and perhaps even later, the Soviet Union provides a classic example of a paper tiger.

When Mossadegh nationalized the British-owned oil company[24] and allowed the Tudeh Party almost free rein in Teheran, the Soviet Union did not take advantage of the situation. Stalin died in March, 1953, which may explain why nothing was done in August when Mossadegh fell. More significant, however, is the fact that after Iran joined the Baghdad Pact in 1955 Soviet policy emphasized pressure on Iran to leave the Pact or to guarantee that its soil would not be used as a base to attack southern Russia. In particular the Russians demanded that no American missile bases be set up on Iranian territory.

Of course, Soviet policy may have been limited by circumstances and so more far-reaching aspirations were not expressed. If this was the case, then it is also the case that the United States was more apprehensive about these purported Soviet aims than was Iran. American conclusions differed also in that they advised the Persians against provoking the Russians. The

[24]The Majlis passed the Oil Nationalization Act in May, 1951, immediately after Mossadegh's appointment as Prime Minister on April 30, 1951. The pressure of enforcing the act eventually caused the complete withdrawal of the Anglo-Iranian Oil Company.

Persians were not really afraid of provoking the Russians, but they hoped to play on American fears in order to get increased military aid. The United States did not strongly encourage Iran to join the Baghdad Pact because Iran's internal position was thought to be too weak and America was worried about encouraging an intensified Soviet pressure on Iran. The Shah was evidently less worried about the Soviet countermeasures than he was about a potential situation in which there would be no reliable force counter-balancing the Russians. The United States was immediately subject to increased pressure from Iran for some sort of commitment: adherence to the Baghdad Pact, a bilateral treaty commitment to counter the Iranian-Soviet treaty of 1921, or arms, and in particular missiles, to commit America to Iran's defense even without additional contractual guarantees. To overcome U.S. reluctance, the Shah commenced negotiations with the Soviets in 1958 with a view to a nonaggression pact. The United States broke up these negotiations in a particularly crude way, and the Shah sent Soviet Ambassador Pegov off in a similar manner early in 1959.

Iranian-U.S. Relations

The bilateral treaty was signed on March 3, 1959, but the United States did not agree to supply Iran with missiles or to join the Baghdad Pact. In recognition of an explicit or implicit reluctance to tie American policy to an unpopular head of state, and because of his disappointment in the failure of political liberalization to please either the Americans or the Iranians, the Shah began to reconsider his policy toward the Soviet Union.[25]

The Soviets had alternated very aggressive propaganda policies with conciliatory efforts that emphasized their desire to prevent the United States from acquiring a position in Iran that the United States was in any case reluctant to assume. After his abortive experiment with a modicum of political liberalization in 1959-1962, immediately following the decline in relations with the Soviet Union (and following the frightening *coup d'état* in Iraq), the Shah adopted the domestic policy of the White Revolution, and friendship (short of nonalignment) with the Soviets. According to Donald Wilber, at the end of 1959 the Shah had given his personal assurances that no foreign power would be permitted to set up medium or

[25]Bill, "Social and Political Development in Iran," p. 24, argues: "Political leaders and elites must be encouraged, even pressured, to revolutionize and modernize their socio-political systems." But see Samuel P. Huntington, *Military Intervention, Political Involvement, and the Unlessons of Viet Nam,* Adlai Stevenson Institute of International Affairs, (Monograph) (Chicago, 1968): "If the Vietnamese won't reform and change their own society, we must reform it for them. And few phenomena are more unsettling in their consequences than masses of energetic and highminded Americans intent on doing good." One is inevitably reminded of Morgan Shuster, Millspaugh, and the rest.

long-range missiles in Iran.[26] The same source records that the Soviets moved to a softer position on this issue toward the end of 1962, whereupon they took official cognizance of the Shah's assurances. John Marlowe phrased the situation as follows:

> Officially, Irano-Russian relations have remained correct, if not cordial, with each side expressing the desire for friendship with the other, and each side making sporadic and ineffectual efforts in that direction. It is unlikely that Russia really apprehends the danger of Iran's being used by the West as a base for an offensive against Russia; it is unlikely that Iran really apprehends any danger of being invaded by Russia. . . . In conversations with the West, it is Iran, and not the Western Powers which pleads the seriousness and urgency of the communist menace.[27]

Normalization of relations with the Soviets was declared to be an integral part of the policy of Hassan Ali Mansur.[28]

Progress in improving these relations was more rapid after the beginning of 1964. Iranian-Soviet trade increased, and in June, 1964, a payments agreement was signed. In August a civil air agreement was signed. In September Dr. Eghbal, Chairman of the National Iranian Oil Company, visited Moscow and made an agreement on the exploration of various oil-bearing regions in northern Iran. In October an agreement was reached whereby Iran could ship goods to Europe via Russia, and Russia could ship goods to the Far East via Iran. The following June the Shah himself visited Moscow, and at the end of an extended and highly successful visit it was announced that the Soviet Union would build a steel mill for Iran and that Iran would sell natural gas to the Soviet Union by means of a pipeline that the Soviets would build. Further agreements followed in 1965 on the Caspian fisheries, on freight rates, on the steel mill, and on the pipeline, while other agreements for cultural and economic cooperation were signed with most of the countries of Eastern Europe. But the most outstanding development of all came in February, 1966, when a Soviet-Iranian deal for certain types of military equipment and arms was revealed.[29]

Iran continued to purchase more sophisticated weapons from the United States and Britain, and the Iranian government was careful to make clear

---

[26]Wilber, "Social and Political Development in Iran," p. 201.

[27]John Marlowe, *Iran: A Short Political Guide* (New York, Praeger 1963), pp. 132-133.

[28]Hassan Ali Mansur, *The Middle East and North Africa, 1966-1967* (London: Europa Publications, 1966), p. 235.

[29]Soviet policy appears to have disgusted many Iranian Communists. I heard a report that the Soviets delivered to the government of Iran, for execution, the Tudeh-affiliated officer who had allowed the condemned Tudeh leaders to escape after Mossadegh's downfall.

that it was not turning toward complete reliance on the Soviets for arms. But in return for continued trade relations with the West the Iranian government insisted on the opportunity to purchase highly sophisticated weapons of the latest design, and in August, 1967, after the disastrous defeat of the Arab armies by Israel, the United States agreed to sell a squadron of Phantom jets to Iran. The United States continued to be uneasy about the matter, but rather than being in a position to pressure Iran, the U.S. officially ended the Point Four program, and is now responsive to Iranian threats that they will purchase advanced jets from the Russians or that they will move even more toward nonalignment.

Relations with Neighboring States

During this period of Soviet-Iranian friendship lasting from about the end of 1962 and still continuing, Iran has not been drawn into satellite status, the Tudeh Party has not flourished, the Soviets have not supported their Arab allies against Iran, and Iran has not weakened its close ties with the West. When coupled with the success of the White Revolution and with what Charles Issawi has called "Iran's Economic Upsurge," this new relationship with the Soviet Union has transformed Iran's international position.[30]

At the very least Iran has learned how to play the buffer state with greater skill and initiative than Afghanistan, and it has learned how to accomplish the nonaligned balancing act with almost as much skill as Nasser used to display. At this juncture the United States and the Soviet Union believe that they will benefit from a strong and independent Iran. Both sides have more to gain than security, for as the ultimate anxiety declines, the economic benefits from Iranian and Persian Gulf oil loom even larger. However, as Iran grows in prosperity and military strength, the price that the superpowers must pay to maintain this buffer will include not only preferential increases in quantity of oil marketed annually but also a measure of support for Iran's political interests in the region.

In the years since the Iraqi coup of 1958, Iran's relations with Iraq have deteriorated. The major points at issue are navigation in the Shatt al-Arab, offshore oil rights, the status of minority communities of Arabs and Persians, Iranian support for the Iraqi-Kurdish revolt, Iranian access to the Shiite holy places, and political hegemony over the Persian Gulf. For a brief period when Abdul Karim Qasim favored the Iraqi Communists, the Soviets supported Iraq. At other times they have supported the Kurds, though more to hedge bets than to help the Kurds win. Iraq looks to the

[30]Charles Issawi, "Iran's Economic Upsurge," *Middle East Journal*, 21/4 (Autumn, 1967), 447 f.

West still, to Egypt until 1969, and now to Syria for its political orientation, and to Europe for its petroleum markets. Even before Iran's relations
with the Soviet Union improved it was able to cope with the Iraqi threat,
but now Iraq has been thrown on the defensive and has much to fear from
Iranian pressure.

This new relationship is not due to Soviet friendship alone, but to the
decline in the military and political power of the U.A.R. Before the June,
1967, war Nasser was fighting in Yemen, threatening Saudi Arabia, encouraging nationalist revolution in South Arabia, creating anxiety in the
Trucial sheikdoms and in Kuwait, and claiming Khuzistan as an Arab
province. Iran attempted to win allies in the Persian Gulf and found some
encouragement because of the Iraqi threat to Kuwait and the Egyptian
involvement in Yemen, both in the early 1960s. But her attempted friendship met with only modest success because she still maintained claim to
Bahrein even in the late 1960s. Iraq's threat was countered by the United
States, but Iraq has since been supported by Egypt in its pressure on Iran.
Cairo Radio attacks the Shah, and along with the accusation that Iran is
aiding Israel (which is true), Nasser tried to encourage the extremist
religious groups in Iran against the Shah. Iran, of course, has countered
by seeking close relations with Saudi Arabia, with Kuwait, and with the
rulers of other Muslim states.

It was against this background that Iran apprehensively viewed the
Egyptian preparations for war with Israel in 1967. If the prewar pronouncements were to be believed, Israel was about to be annihilated. Iran
temporized and began to consider its brotherly connections with the Arab
states. An Egyptian victory would have resulted in tremendous pressure
on Iran, but that was not to be the case. Instead, the rout of U.A.R. forces
removed all regional pressure from Iran and more than vindicated the
Shah's policy of cooperation with Israel. The U.A.R. could not support
Iraq, had to withdraw its troops from Yemen, and was forced to accept
financial assistance from Saudi Arabia and Kuwait. Iraq had to shift important forces to the Israeli front. Iran began to take a very hard line in
dealing with Iraq, Syria, and even Lebanon—not to speak of the U.A.R.

In the Gulf, the situation was also transformed as a result of the June
war. The closure of the Suez Canal kept the Soviet navy out at a time when
the British were withdrawing and when Egypt had lost its near access. Iran
is now attempting to fill the vacuum, and it would seem that the great
powers as well as the Gulf states are not averse to this. Iran has built up
her Gulf ports. She has agreed to ship Soviet goods through them. She has
purchased a number of modern ships from Great Britain. She has declared
her willingness to cooperate with all regional powers for defense of the

Gulf to the exclusion of outside powers. She has worked out agreements on offshore areas with Kuwait and Saudi Arabia.

It is not easy to foresee the future pattern of international relations in the Persian Gulf region because the present situation appears to be based on the consequences of the June war. So long as the present situation in the region as a whole is viewed as temporary, unstable, or dangerously bordering on war, then the derivative situation in the Gulf must be seen as quite impermanent. It is easy to draw the moral that any overall settlement should be carefully examined for the possible consequences it may have for the Gulf. Nevertheless, not all aspects of the Gulf situation are dependent on other regional factors. At the present it appears certain that the United Kingdom's influence will decline in an overt political sense while British commercial and especially oil interests will continue effective. It is unlikely that the Arab rulers of the region will be able to establish an effective political organization of their own. Although it is probable that Iranian efforts to develop good relations with Kuwait and Saudi Arabia will continue to succeed, the smaller sheikdoms are vulnerable and wary. It is unlikely that Egypt will soon again be able to put great pressure on the Arabian Peninsula countries, but Kuwait and, to a lesser extent, Saudi Arabia, will be subjected to Syrian and Palestinian pressures.

If the Suez Canal is opened a Soviet presence of some sort will be established in the Gulf. This presence is likely to be achieved with Persian assistance. Any countering move by the United States may rely on Saudi Arabia, but the dangerous implications of such a competitive arrangement ought to be borne in mind. A preferable arrangement would be one in which both the Soviet Union and the United States encourage Iran to play a role in the Gulf that will protect great-power interests, prevent violent conflict, encourage regional economic and political cooperation, and regulate migration and navigation in the Gulf. Iran's interests do not, however, always coincide with those of her neighbors, and it is likely that Iran will demand a stiff price for such cooperation—not excluding annexation of Bahrein, but more likely being content with a more advantageous share of the annual world oil export quota.[31] Any Iranian encroachment on Arab territory will lead to widespread objection and efforts at countermeasures, the success of which will depend upon the positions of Egypt and Iraq at the time. The Soviets will be hard-pressed to formulate a policy that will satisfy the demands of both the Egyptians and the Persians, as will the United States (assuming that it succeeds in restoring good relations with the Egyptian regime). Iraq may then find it sensible to explore the possibilities of support at Peking. All of this is, of course, highly speculative

[31]Iran gave up her claim to Bahrein in May, 1970.

and possibly remote from the more prosaic eventuality that everything will continue as it is. Still, the most imperative idea to emerge from this speculation is the danger that the United States may find itself acting against Iran and the Soviet Union in the Persian Gulf precisely when Iran has become the paramount power in that part of the world.

Relations with Israel

Iran continues its *de facto* recognition of Israel and maintains friendly if not warm relations with the Jewish state. Iranian-Israel cooperation extends to the fields of petroleum export, development projects, trade, air transport, military training, technical assistance, the training of co-op managers, and tacit political support in relations with the Arab states. Iran has, however, expressed its deep sympathy for the Arab refugees and has called for Israeli evacuation of the territories occupied in the June war. Like the United States and like the Soviet Union, Iran too wishes to see peace in the region so long as that peace is not based on the total victory of either Arabs or Israelis. Israel would be an important counterweight to a peaceful and unified, or even partly unified, Arab world.

In its relations with Israel, Iran has successfully avoided undertaking any formal political or military commitment, while still defying almost all Arab pressures to withhold from any cooperation whatsoever with Israel. Actually, the extent of Iranian-Israeli cooperation has been significant, as in the training of cooperative managers, or in the Qazvin regional development project, or in the training of Israeli pilots in Iran in the use of American aircraft. But cooperation is based on the expectation that Israel will continue to be a formidable opponent of any combination of Arab countries. Thus, Iran will not go to the aid of Israel in case of a conflict with the Arab states, but it is likely that Israel will aid Iran in such a case. There is in any case little that Iran can do for Israel, given the distance between the two and their relative strengths, but Israel does desire the legitimacy of formal recognition which Iran will continue to refuse.

There is scope for the expansion of Iranian-Israeli cooperation in the field of military training, and in some operations in Kurdistan. A more delicate area is that of petroleum refining and marketing beyond the present commercial arrangements. Doubtlessly there are many less politically sensitive areas where cooperative efforts may be fruitful for both sides, but, in general, the potentialities and instruments for the implementation of a close alliance are limited by culture, geography, strategic situations, economic circumstances, and domestic political structure.

A partially silent participant in this tacit Iranian-Israeli alliance, and a participant who helps to make it work, is the United States. It is the U.S. military assistance program, the petroleum politics, the support for Israel, and the support for Iran, among other things, that have made this arrangement work and partially make up for the failure, from Iran's point of view, of the Baghdad Pact. There are many implications in this situation for the future of U.S. relations with Israel, but for present purposes it will suffice to stress the conclusion that U.S. involvement with Iran is a product of regional forces and not alone determined by formal agreements of a bilateral nature. It is for this reason that the United States can view with equanimity the change in U.S. relations with Iran.

Relations with the United States

Iran's relations with the United States have not deteriorated. Though America is much less involved in Iranian affairs, and even proportionately less involved in Iranian petroleum now, she is as deeply interested as before. Her attitude is a bit less paranoid these days, perhaps because she tends to overestimate the domestication of the Russian Bear. America has been able to see the end of the substantial AID program to Iran. She has also taken somewhat less responsibility for the Iranian armed forces. America has been pleased not to be blamed for every change in the Cabinet and for every financial crisis, and to be less morally identified with the ruling autocracy, even though she has come to benefit much more from her more active international role than in the past when she was passively dependent on herself. With good reason, the Shah still makes intensive public relations efforts in the United States, and I think that he, too, prefers a situation in which he can influence America without being dictated to by her.

But Iran's new role and new ability to take the initiative is particularly gratifying to the United States in the light of Congressional reactions to the Vietnam war, and in the light of her long-standing unwillingness to tie support for Iran to personal support for the Shah. America has welcomed the increased political stability which Iran has gained without further U.S. involvements as though it were a political windfall. This change has tested America's preference for a world of multilateralism and of independent nation-states. But like all former trustees, the United States has been somewhat disappointed that her aid is not as necessary nor as urgently demanded as in the past, and some observers are afraid that America may even lose Iran's friendly cooperation. America's original involvement with Iran was based on the assumption that U.S. forces might have to intervene to save Iran from a Soviet invasion or to delay a Soviet advance until there could be some suitable NATO riposte in another area. As American reluctance to do any such thing in the Middle East has grown with her experience in Southeast Asia, she has been much relieved to see Iran emerge as an international actor with a degree of independence and a relationship with the Soviet Union that is not likely to require anything but tolerance on

America's part. Iran will continue to demand military equipment from the United States. She will also insist on an expanding share of the market for her petroleum products, and she is likely to demand more liberal credits and more favorable trade agreements from America, as from other nations in the West. Not only will it be in America's interest to help Iran in these ways; America must also provide a counterweight to Soviet influence at least in the areas of petroleum exploitation and arms supply. Should the United States become petulant about the recently improved Iranian-Soviet relations, she might reduce even further her influence in Teheran. The United States might even start to think seriously of a bona-fide cultural exchange—if America could only bring herself to a sense of respect for the venerable culture of Iran.

IV. Iran's Economic Position and Future Policies

Finally, we must give some brief consideration to the economic advance which has strengthened the change in Iran's international position. The main facts, as given by Issawi, are that Iranian oil production has increased from 32 million tons in 1957 to about 130 million tons in 1967, and government revenue has gone up four times. Industrial growth from 1960 to 1967 has been at the rate of 10 percent per year. Gross national product has increased, from 1962 to 1967, at the rate of 7 percent per year.[32] Although three bad agricultural years coincided with the early land-reform years of 1962/3-1964/5, the three following years of 1965/6-1967/8 were good, and they helped the Third Plan to succeed.[33]

It is readily apparent from the preceding discussion that Iran's international position is more internationally determined than domestically, but it is also true that, had there been no domestic transformation, Iran would not have been in a position to take full advantage of the new regional situation. Economic prosperity and optimism for the future are probably less responsible for the present international position of Iran than they may be for a future intensification or elaboration of current policies. An economic decline would hurt, but it might bring greater domestic than international changes, or, in view of the importance of Iran to both the U.S.S.R. and the United States, America might have to produce an artificial prosperity.

Despite this discounting of the possible foreign policy effects of an economic downturn or of a deflection of the developmental upsurge, there can be no denying that it would have important political consequences.

[32]Issawi, "Iran's Economic Upsurge," pp. 447 f.

[33]Hurewitz, *Middle East Politics* . . . , p. 290; Issawi, "Iran's Economic Upsurge," p. 455.

It is agreed that land reform, good harvests, and the literacy program have benefited the peasants and increased their political awareness, but has not yet alienated them. An economic decline would hurt them. In the cities the self-interested aristocratic and bourgeois entrepreneurs, the guilt-ridden but passive intelligentsia, and the self-confident technocrats would all be shaken in their political acquiescence by an economic decline. We cannot tell what effect a recession would have on the workers and on the petit-bourgeoisie. If the trouble caused by a recession would not lead to a change of regime, it might still suffice to deaden any initiative.

Given the experience of recent years, there is little reason to suppose that a serious recession is likely to occur. The last Prime Minister to subordinate the development budget to the current budget was Asadullah Alam in 1963, and that was in part due to the poor agricultural performance of those years. There may, of course, be minor problems such as bottlenecks, some exchange difficulties, or a lack of trained manpower, but the current rate of development should continue—unless there is a very large and very unexpected increase in military expenditures.[34]

J. C. Hurewitz anticipated some increase in the size of the Iranian armed forces after the United States ceased to supply free equipment and thereby lost some influential leverage.[35] It has also been noted that part of Iran's independent status has been the result of arms purchases from the Soviet Union, so that increased purchases have a symbolic value apart from the use of the arms or the satisfaction of the military. Another point to consider is the opportunity to use military force at least in the Persian Gulf that Iran now has. On the other hand, Iranian military expenditures are modest by international comparison and should be no cause for alarm—if available figures are correct. Hurewitz shows figures from 1959-1960 to 1965-1966 that range from 4.3 percent to 5.4 percent of GNP.[36] If his figures are correct, military expenditures have increased at a slower rate than has the development budget. Hurewitz's figures are supported by those in *The Middle East and North Africa*.[37] A grossly different picture is given by Manoucher Parvin, who writes that

[34]Issawi, "Iran's Economic Upsurge," pp. 456 f.: "Of the three general shortages impending rapid economic growth—capital, foreign exchange, and skills—only the last may prove to be very serious in Iran." On p. 459 he writes ". . . and although Iranian development may be slowed down, it will not be halted by the sluggishness of agriculture."

[35]Hurewitz, *Middle East Politics* . . . , p. 293: "Once the United States ceased paying for much of the new equipment, the Shah was almost certain to start enlarging his army again."

[36]*Ibid.*, p. 285.

[37]Hassan Ali Mansur, *The Middle East*, p. 241.

"The average percentage of the Iranian national budget spent on the armed forces has vacillated [sic] around the 40% level during recent years."[38] He does not give the figures but *The Middle East* records expenditures on Defense and Security in 1965-1966 as approximately 25 billion rials or less than \$2 billion.[39] The total budget is listed as 176 billion rials (Hurewitz has it at 112 billion), thus rendering Defense and Security expenditures as 14 percent (or 22% according to Hurewitz) of the budget. The 40-percent figure is valid only for the general budget *minus* the development budget. At any rate, in terms of GNP, this recent rate of expenditure is not alarming. What may be alarming is the (unconfirmed) statement that Iran contemplates spending an additional \$600 million (during an undetermined period) to modernize the military establishment.[40] This sort of unproductive use, even if in part dictated by political exigencies, may hurt the development program. Parvin is very critical of this rate of expenditure. He believes it is an indicator of the influence of the military and the high potentiality of a military *coup d'état*. He is also suspicious of the goals of this military expenditure, and his suspicions articulate if crudely with some of the issues discussed above. He writes that there are only three possible reasons for what he considers to be an extremely high rate of expenditure on defense:[41]

(a) The "White Revolution" is not as successful as has been claimed by the present regime and, consequently, a large military force is required to preserve the present political system. [About 200,000 soldiers out of 27,000,000 population.] Obviously acceptance of this hypothesis contradicts the representativeness and progressiveness of the present regime, as publicized by the press and spokesmen of the government.

(b) Alternatively, it can be assumed that Iranian national security is purchased at a higher cost per citizen relative to other nations. This hypothesis implies that the military forces in Iran are unnecessarily large and/or inefficient and that they are growing and flourishing at the expense of the Iranian taxpayers. This implies that either the military establishment has become an

[38]Manoucher Parvin, "Military Expenditure in Iran: A Forgotten Question," *Iranian Studies* (Autmun, 1968), II, p. 154.

[39]Hassan Ali Mansur, *The Middle East*, p. 241.

[40]Parvin, "Military Expenditure in Iran," p. 150. We are not told over what period this expenditure is to be made.

[41]*Ibid.*, p. 153.

autonomous interest group and/or that military policies are anachronistic and must be restudied and changed.

(c) The third alternative hypothesis is that Iran's foreign policy has changed gradually and silently with the result that the Iran of today is pursuing an expansionist policy.

It is useful to remind oneself of the rhetorical style and ideological orientation of opposition elements in Iran, and especially so in the light of the congratulatory satisfaction with which the American press usually celebrates the continuing political stability and economic progress of Iran. Parvin is far more moderate in his expression than is Nirumand, but the purport of his criticism comes through the formal conceits of the pseudo-scientific alternatives of an economic type of analysis: the army has a politically repressive purpose. The army is an autonomous interest group. The army will be used for imperialistic purposes. These three "alternatives" are actually all compatible, so we must conclude that their juxtaposition represents a challenge to the regime to choose its own form of self-condemnation, or else to reduce its military expenditures. The emphasis on the last alternative is meant to appeal to foreign readers as the most likely interpretation and the most objectionable to them.

I do not believe that the gradual and silent change described has taken place, but Iran's new international position permits consideration of a more assertive foreign policy which will require larger and more easily deployable armed forces. Present levels of military expenditure are probably inadequate to some of the possible uses to which Iranian armed forces may be put. These uses might be in the Persian Gulf and Kurdish areas, and far less likely in the Palestine zone or further to the east of Iran. The recent handling of affairs with Iraq by the movement of troops to the border is an indication of an inclination, but not yet of a change.

If a change toward a more militarily assertive policy is to be accomplished, then additional resources will have to be allocated to the military. Additional resources will be necessary to avoid weakening the gains of the White Revolution, to avoid decreasing the "fringe benefits" of the officers corps, and to provide for additional training, new equipment, and increased manpower. Perhaps this is the reason why the Shah has persistently requested an even higher rate of growth of oil revenues from recent levels of 10 percent or less per year to almost double that figure. There may be other reasons as well, for the oil lesson of the Mossadegh period was that, barring the exhaustion of resources and taking account of increased demand, any one country's production increase is at the expense of all other producing countries. This situation is partly due to the relative inelasticity of demand, the limited shipping and marketing facilities at any given time, and the equalizing price structure of petroleum in international trade. It is, consequently, possible that the Shah, recognizing the greater political leverage that Iran has gained, and understanding the relative decline in the influence of the Arab oil producers, is simply trying to get all that the market will bear. Increased oil revenues will be a hedge against any short-run economic downturn as well.

Iran is on the threshold of a profound cultural-identity change in which its self-image as a weak, declining, acquiescent client power will be transformed. There is already a yearning for a revival of the image of ancient imperial glory. The Reza Shah began it by reviving pre-Islamic linguistic and architectural themes. Mohammad Reza Shah has continued it by his coronation as Shah and by his toleration of the Pan-Iranism Party. The appropriate cultural categories are already prevalent in the negative comparison that most intellectuals now make of present-day Iran with the achievements of Darius and Cyrus. If we were inclined to be mystical we might now say something about Iran's destiny. Instead, we will exercise the proper restraint and conclude that a more assertive foreign policy will not be merely the whim of the Shah, but an even more vigorously sought goal for any conceivable alternative government.

CHAPTER 11

The Maghrib and the Middle East
Charles F. Gallagher

I. The Personality of the Maghrib

The areas of northwest Africa west of the Gulf of Sirte form a compact geographical entity which throughout history has demonstrated considerable cultural unity and ethnic homegeneity. Today the area is heavily Arabic-speaking and is culturally a part of the general domain of Arab civilization, while expressing itself through a distinctive subcultural pattern of that civilization. This characteristic subculture has been intensified in modern times in Morocco, Algeria, and Tunisia, because of the massive settler colonialism which left a French cultural heritage that must be taken into account in any assessment of the fundamental postures of those societies. Libya is different, for it belongs to the Maghrib geographically only in its Tripolitanian part, and its modern history during the past century has accentuated rather than reduced the differences between it and its Maghrib neighbors. It is therefore difficult to make valid generalizations about all four countries considered by some sources, but not all, to make up the Maghrib. In this study, unless Libya is explicitly mentioned, general remarks—particularly those having to do with attitudes and institutions formed under French influence—should be considered confined to Morocco, Algeria, and Tunisia.

The geographical position of the Maghrib has had and continues to have important effects on its overall evolution. For 1200 years it has been the remote, western wing of the civilization flourishing in the Arab and Muslim Middle East. Since World War II it has played a much larger and more important role in the political affairs of the Arab world, although not in social or economic aspects of Middle Eastern life. On the other hand, it still receives the greater part of its intellectual and cultural sustenance from Europe, which is closer to it geographically as well as sentimentally, insofar as many of the intellectual élite and the nontraditional bourgeoisie are concerned. Finally, the Maghrib is part of Africa, and in the past decade it has shown a desire, not always realizable, to expand its personality by playing as full a role as it can in the pan-African struggle for identity and in the battle against the remnants of colonialism on that continent.

The basic quest for identity still goes on in the Maghrib, and if communion with Africanism seems a minor factor at present, the problem is really whether to feel wholeheartedly a part of the Arab world or to attempt, with nuances, to take the best of both that and European civilization while asserting itself as something ultimately different from and independent of either. Perhaps the most serious side of this issue today is that it has increasingly become a factor of division in terms of attitudes toward culture and technique. A large and growing number of mostly urban individuals and many of the younger generation who are receiving a quasi-French type of schooling lean toward the modern, scientific, technical, and more "rational" aspects of life associated with Europe. The affective, romantic, and moral aspects of Muslim-Arab life predominate in the world-view of a number of more traditional urbanites, with the highly politicized in all classes and groups, and among the still largely illiterate and semi-literate rural masses.

II. Maghrib-Mashriq Relations

Broadly viewed over the course of history, relations between the Maghrib (North Africa) and the Mashriq (Middle East) have seldom been close or warm for any long period. The main characteristics of the relationship might best be described as cousinly but uneasy, with the root of the uneasiness lying in the suppression of certain feelings about the other member of the family. The outstanding emotion on this score from the North African side is the secret realization that the Maghrib has normally been in a situation of passive acceptance with respect to cultural and intellectual contacts with the Middle East; and until the most recent past these exchanges have been almost wholly one-sided. The converse of this, which is partly a compensation reflex, is the disdain most North Africans with an education in the European style feel for the general social and political climate of the Arab Middle East. To them, the Mashriq has not cut a good figure in recent history, and the events of 1967—like those of 1956 and, indeed, the entire Palestine question, from no matter which political optic they are viewed—merely confirm a long-standing suspicion of Middle Eastern incompetence. As the result of these conflicting pulls in their appraisal of a society which is from many standpoints their own, and which, above all else, is the fount of their religious convictions, North Africans have strong guilt feelings about the Middle East as a whole. For the most part these feelings are internalized, but in times of crisis they break forth with overt expressions of indignation, shame, and irritation at the conduct or attitudes of Middle Eastern leaders and peoples, usually, though, in private conversations. Any observer of the North African scene has encountered such behavior amongst a broad gamut of individuals—fervently pro-Arab Algerians, liberal nationalist Destourians in Tunisia, and conservative nationalists or traditionals in Morocco and Libya—often enough to recognize it as representative of a very basic outlook.

However, it is essential to distinguish between Maghribi attitudes toward the sociopolitical culture of the Middle East—with respect to, for example, political instability, the status of women, the general state of civism noted by returning diplomats or pilgrims—and feelings about Arab culture as a whole, and notably about Islamic culture. Except for a handful of Marxists and secularists, and also leaving aside much of the Tunisian élite, North Africans by and large are stolidly religious in their conservative Maliki Islam, and they hold the spiritual aspects of Muslim-Arab culture in the Middle East in high regard. Likewise, many are passionately enthusiastic admirers of parts of the modern culture of the Middle East—the music of Umm Kalthum and Abdel Wahhab, Egyptian films, and the like—but few admire the Middle East *per se*, and even fewer would dream of taking the area or any one country in it as a model for their own social, economic, or political development.

North Africa broke away from the Middle East soon after the Arab conquest in the eighth century and turned inward to its own problems. In the High Middle Ages it constructed its own empires, reaching as far east as Tripoli on one occasion, and often encompassing much of the Iberian Peninsula. Between the two Arab areas, west and east, there was little trade; the principal link was the steady flow of pilgrims and religious students who learned and practiced a more orthodox piety in the East and often returned to rectify or reform local Islamic practice. From the seventeenth century on, North Africa was either wholly withdrawn into itself, as was the case with Morocco and the Algerian hinterland, or under nominal and distant Ottoman rule in coastal Algeria and Tunisia, engaging primarily in intermittent trade and piracy with Europe. The latter issue was the pretext for French intervention in Algeria in 1830 and the subsequent occupation of that country.

The anticolonial struggle of North Africans under European (mostly French, secondarily Spanish and Italian) domination that began in the first decade of this century was the first phenomenon in some time to bring the two Arab areas together. Even so, as is shown by the reserve with which an Egyptian reformer such as Muhammad Abduh was received in Tunisia toward the turn of the century, and by the tenuousness of the ties between Middle Eastern nationalists and their later Maghribi counterparts, the independence movements in North Africa were intellectually not from the East but within the French tradition and have continued to be influenced primarily by it. The other main source of inspiration for the nationalist revival was much less Arabism than Islam, of which the first political expression came in the Italo-Turkish war of 1911-1912. Islam was later used equally by Destourian quasi-secularists for their own purposes, by religious leaders of the Association of Ulama in Algeria as a first step toward regaining an Algerian identity, and by Moroccan nationalists in order to rally the pious masses and link their cause to the Sharifian legitimacy of the Alawite dynasty. At times the ideals of French liberalism and socialism clashed with the stirrings of a reinvigorated Islam placed at the disposal of nationalism—and in Algeria today they often still do—but, on the whole, during the struggle for independence they formed a working partnership in which each had its place.

The emergence of the Arab League at the end of World War II made a brief impression on North African leaders, but in the pretransistor era the Middle East was still a distant land with which contacts were slim. (The ties of the Algerian nationalist movement to Egypt after the 1952 revolution were an exception explained in large part by the chronology of events.) North African nationalist leaders realized that in the end neither the Arab League nor Arab arms would win them independence; instead they concentrated their attention on the forum of the United Nations, on swaying public opinion in France and the West generally, and —in the Algerian case from 1960 on—on getting support from the Communist bloc. Thus it can be said that Morocco and Tunisia both came to independence in 1956 with no greater feelings of indebtedness toward the Arab Middle East than they had toward all the other nations that had supported their cause at the United Nations. Algeria, which became independent in 1962, did recognize the (truly more substantial) role played by the Arab states, but, as its subsequent foreign policy has shown, it has been careful to cultivate ties that are poth practical and sentimental with France, the Soviet Union, Yugoslavia, Cuba, and others, all of which make it less necessary to demonstrate too openly those feelings of gratitude toward the Arab states that may still exist.

Since Tunisia became independent, its relations with the Arab world as a whole have been marked by a tendency to set itself apart from its neighbors and pursue an independent course. Relations with the United Arab Republic have been strained at all times and nonexistent for long periods. The Tunisians on at least two occasions have bitterly denounced Egyptian interference in their internal affairs, and Tunisia in turn has often been publicly vilified by the Nasser regime, the Voice of the Arabs, and the press generally throughout the Arab Middle East from many of its unorthodox stands, from support of the American position in Vietnam, to equating Hungary and Suez, and on the critical Palestine issue.

The underlying causes of friction, however, are more than political. Tunisians have always considered themselves the intellectual leaders of the Maghrib, equal or even superior to Middle Easterners. Tunisia is conscious and proud of what it prefers to call its "Mediterranean heritage," which draws on Carthage and Rome, Arab and European culture. The Tunisian élite was formed in France or, more recently, in the French style. It has more and deeper ties—often through intermarriage—with French culture than any other North African élite. The active copatronage of *francophonie* (the proposal to form an informal group of French-speaking nations for purposes of cultural interchange), undertaken by President Bourguiba along with Leopold Senghor of Senegal, would be unthinkable on the part of any other Arab head of state. Moreover, the many social reforms of a secularist nature introduced by the Tunisian government since 1956 have convinced many Tunisians that their social evolution has outstripped that of other Arab states, and that it is the latter who should look to Tunisia as a model and not vice versa.[1] The disputes that led to the Tunisian walkouts from the Arab League in 1958 and 1968, although staked to specific issues, were really a reflection of this attitude as well as of the unwillingness of Middle Eastern Arabs to countenance what they considered an unbecoming arrogance.

In the eyes of most Arabs the supreme Tunisian heresy has been Bourguiba's position on Palestine. Even after joining the Arab League, Tunisia took little notice of the problem. Tunisian Jews held high posts in the government and in several semiofficial bodies, the boycott was virtually ignored, and Tunisian Jews were allowed to correspond with Israel and even visit it unofficially. Bourguiba had long cherished the idea of suggesting the application of the gradualist tactics of "Bourguibism" to the Palestine issue, and during a tour of the Middle East in the spring of 1965 he proposed a new approach involving the realistic recognition that Israel existed and calling for negotiations intended not as a capitulation but as a way to force the opposite party to the conference table and win major concessions from it. He pointed out that the intransigence of the Arabs in rejecting all discussion with Israel gave it a considerable propaganda advantage by allowing it to portray itself as eager for a reasonable settlement which its opponents refused to consider. These suggestions were received with violent hostility throughout the Middle East and they were not emphasized publicly again until they appeared in somewhat changed form after the 1967 war.

For its part, Morocco moved in the late 1950s with its customary deliberation toward the formulation of a policy of quiet, disinterested friendship for all. It joined the Arab League at the same time as Tunisia in 1958, but it kept its distance from feuding Arab states and gave no support

---

[1]Tunisia is the only Arab country to have outlawed polygamy completely and to have abolished the *shari'a* (the Holy Law) without exception.

to Tunisia in its quarrel with Egypt, for which it was sharply rebuked several years later. Early in 1960 King Muhammad V made a good-will visit to the Middle East combined with a pilgrimage to the holy places. Undertaken at the height of the Egyptian-Iraqi animosity, this trip was intended to consecrate the Moroccan policy of friendship without favoritism. Hassan II, who came to the throne in 1961 on his father's death, has been a more controversial monarch, less warmly received both at home and abroad. Since his accession, difficulties have arisen on several occasions with Algeria and the United Arab Republic, and to a lesser extent with all the self-styled "progressive" Arab governments. Despite the brief hostilities with Algeria, it is fair to say that these quarrels never reached the level of permanently deep bitterness found in Tunisian relations with other Arab countries. The lack of ideology in Morocco and the ability of the King to maneuver adroitly in its absence have certainly been contributing elements, but this suppleness has been criticized by some as showing essentially a lack of principle. My reading is that this judgment is too harsh, and that a better understanding of Morocco emerges if one keeps in mind the constant tendency of that country to slide back into an almost splendid isolation of indifference if its foreign policy initiatives prove unsuccessful. Certainly Morocco appears to be moving in that direction at this time, after several years of confused activism during which it came to be regarded with suspicion by a number of African and Arab states. The hostility it engendered arose mostly because of its irredentist claims to parts of the Sahara held by Algeria and Mauritania, and the often lightly veiled threats by inspired unofficial spokesmen to act in support of these claims. In particular, the Algerian-Moroccan border skirmishes in October, 1963, alienated opinion in much of Africa and the Middle East, for the Moroccans were challenging the tacit acceptance almost everywhere of the sanctity of boundaries inherited from colonial regimes. The ineffectual Moroccan boycott of international meetings attended by Mauritania, the continuing quarrel with Algeria, and the efforts by Morocco in 1966-1967 to ingratiate itself with the American military all helped to create a situation by mid-1967 in which, quite unlike what was true during the reign of Muhammad V, Morocco had almost no supporters and many detractors in the concert of Arab and African nations.

By the middle of 1967 Morocco was beginning to drift back and away from these dangers. It was not only that the Rabat government recognized the difficult situation it was in, but that the national personality as a whole began one of its periodic phases of withdrawal. The psychological political isolation of the regime triggered a return to the tendency of national isolation. Both factors have been instrumental in shaping Moroccan policy during and after the 1967 conflict.

Algerian relations with the Arab Middle East have been distinctive on two counts: (1) they have evolved in a later time-cycle than those of Morocco and Tunisia; and (2) Algeria, although finally victorious in the revolution for other reasons, received much moral support and a certain amount of material aid from the Arab East, especially the United Arab Republic, and found Cairo a useful base of operations in the early years of the struggle. With all this, though, it cannot be said that personal political relations have been close. The visit of President Nasser to Algeria in 1963 was an uncomfortable reminder to all how different Algeria was and how much the real concerns of the Algerian masses were elsewhere. Moreover, during the first few years of independence under the Ben Bella regime (1962-1965), Algeria gave primary attention to Africa in its foreign policy. For a time Algerian influence in sub-Saharan Africa was felt to be, if not a rival, at least an alternative source to that of the United Arab Republic, although in the end neither has played the role that many experts predicted for them in that area. In inter-Arab politics Algeria has grouped itself from the beginning with the "progressive" states (usually the United Arab Republic, Syria, Iraq, and Yemen), not only out of conviction but because of the leverage this provided in its differences with its Maghrib neighbors.

The overthrow of Ben Bella in a coup in July, 1965, ushered in a period of less vociferous propaganda about making revolutions elsewhere in Africa. From then until the Middle East situation began to deteriorate in May, 1967, the Algerian regime under Colonel Boumedienne out of necessity turned away from most of the picaresque involvements of the preceding years and turned to face domestic problems neglected by the previous government. The Boumedienne regime did not generate much enthusiasm for some time, either with Algerians themselves or among most Afro-Asian leaders, in part because of the relatively colorless character of its chief and the austere approach of his moralistic government to problems that had been colorfully but ineptly treated before. By early 1967 Algeria was rather remote from Middle Eastern problems, but it was showing signs of serious internal strain. The contradictions of the self-management system put into effect on vacated settler estates were unresolved; large numbers of landless peasants were still awaiting a promised land reform; student demonstrations had brought police repression condemned in turn by the Algerian National Students' Association; and the lack of any functioning political organization permitting real participation and dialogue had estranged labor union groups, local party members, many enthusiastic militants, and just about everyone not a part of the group of advisers and technocrats surrounding Boumedienne. The Arab-Israeli conflict of 1967 thus came at an opportune moment for the Algerian authorities, unlike the case in Morocco and Tunisia, where both governments were essentially embarrassed by the crisis. In Algeria, the emergence of a war psychosis permitted the government to restoke the fires of revolutionary zeal without much danger to itself. Its image as a defender of the Arab cause was enhanced, and it could cry shame at Morocco and Tunisia for the clearly lukewarm nature of the official response to the situation in those countries. Thus the Algerian regime, through its controlled press, was already beating the drums of war at the end of May—at a time when Tunisia was insisting, and hoping, that the crisis would fade away—attacking not only Israel but the United States as well, accusing the latter of a variety of misdeeds, most notably of arming Morocco and inciting it to attack Algeria.

III. The Reaction of the Maghrib to the 1967 War

Everywhere in the Maghrib there were reactions of shock, shame, and disbelief when the magnitude of the Arab defeat became known. In each country, however, these emotions—which were popular feelings but were also echoed in official circles except in Tunisia—were associated with other responses. In both Morocco and Tunisia demonstrations were directed against what was felt to be an insufficient zeal on the part of the authorities for the Arab cause, and they were an expression of dissatisfaction with the regimes themselves. Both governments had procrastinated in sending promised aid to the Middle East and were relieved to have been spared real involvement thanks to the rapid cease-fire agreement. A serious riot in Tunis had as primary targets the American and British embassies, both of which were damaged. The Jewish quarter in Tunis was later sacked, partly out of what would appear to be simple anti-Semitism and partly inspired by a desire to loot. The Tunisian government appears to have been taken aback by the size and vigor of the demonstrations, but the surprising absence of police and security forces has led some observers to speculate that the whole scenario was, if not staged, at least allowed to take place by a government anxious to have popular discontent express itself on targets other than the government itself. In Morocco disorders were minor, although a few deaths resulted. A strong speech by Hassan II reproving demonstrations brought attacks from remnants of his political opposition, which led to the arrest and conviction of a prominent labor leader and editorialist. In Tunisia more than one hundred of the rioters were tried some time later and their leaders given stiff prison sentences. The Moroccan government asked for donations to the Arab cause at gatherings and rallies held for that purpose, and this proved to be an effective means for dampening excessive public enthusiasm.

Somewhat shaken by both external and internal events, the Tunisian government felt it prudent for a time to drop the condescending attitude normally used toward the Arab Middle East. It had been surprised by the outbreak of the war, if not by its outcome. But it returned within a month or two to the usual criticisms, directed mainly at the United Arab Republic, charging the Egyptian government with a "lack of seriousness" and, by October, urging President Nasser to resign. The basic lack of respect with which the Tunisian government has consistently viewed Arab political activities was in the end reinforced by the events of June, 1967. And some Tunisian students and intellectuals and a few adherents of the Ba'ath Party or admirers of Nasser were, in turn, confirmed in their hostility to the regime—a hostility stemming from many causes, but to which was now added a feeling that the Bourguiba government was guilty of nothing less than treason to the cause of the Arabs. This is a distinctly minority sentiment, however, which does not appear to be shared by many Tunisians of any status.

Although numerous declarations about the Palestine problem have been made over the years by Bourguiba, the Tunisian position was perhaps best outlined by him in a speech given before the National Press Club in Washington in May, 1968. In this discourse he stressed the theme of "United Nations legality," pointing out that the "difficult, uncomfortable situation in which the Arabs find themselves" arises from their rejection of the partition decision of November, 1947. The three-phase plan for settling the present impasse suggested by the Tunisian President consisted of: (1) the replacement by U.N. troops of Israeli forces in all territories occupied since June, 1967; (2) negotiations with the parties concerned through the Special Representative of the Secretary-General; and (3) withdrawal of U.N. troops following an eventual decision by the Security Council. The reference to the legality of the partition decision is an important point in the Tunisian position with regard to acceptance of the November 22, 1967, resolution of the Security Council. The Tunisian President has gone farther than any other Arab leader in pressing for a political solution based essentially on the original 1947 partition plan and recognizing the "reality" of Israel. Nevertheless, his present position is not without shadings, for at the same time that he deprecates the past record of Middle East Arab governments regarding Palestine, he is constrained—like all statesmen today—to give the Palestine guerrilla fighters moral encouragement, something which does not necessarily contradict the views he has already set forth on the question as a whole.

Morocco for its part was even less affected in the long run by the war. There too, student opinion—to the extent it could be openly expressed— was strongly activist, but the lack of freedom and the generally low tenor of Moroccan intellectual life meant that agitation soon petered out. Unlike the Tunisian government, which by its post-1967-war walkout from the Arab League has now virtually eliminated itself from efforts to coordinate joint Arab policies regarding Palestine, the Moroccan government has officially expressed its willingness to support negotiations through the Jarring mission, and to take part in any summit meetings held. Under the surface of this policy, which—as with the recent voyage of Hassan II to Turkey, Iran, Saudi Arabia, and Tunisia—seeks to strengthen the dimension of Islamic rectitude and solidarity which the King would introduce into all facets of his policy, foreign or domestic, there has been a return to the traditional Moroccan aloofness discussed above on the part of the palace. This is paralleled, however, in a widespread indifference toward Middle Eastern affairs shown by the bourgeoisie and even by much of the urban proletariat.

The Algerian government might be said to have added disillusionment and a degree of disgust to its feelings of astonishment and shame. The inheritors of a doctrine holding that since the Algerian revolution was won by persisting in guerrilla warfare all other wars should be similarly fought to a victorious conclusion, the Algerians considered the cease-fire agreements a capital error. The Algerian position is that the Arabs should and could have gone on fighting, even with the loss of much more territory; indeed, by ultimately overextending Israeli forces, the loss of territory would have been beneficial (this viewpoint is, of course, easier to maintain in Algiers than in Cairo). The Algerians further held that no concessions were to be expected from Israel once it consolidated its position with cease-fire lines. And finally, they insisted that a further military confrontation was inevitable. This engagement would have to be undertaken primarily by the Palestinians themselves, albeit with military help from the Arab states. The Algerians say that they are prepared to assist in the training of guerrillas—and they are in fact now doing so—but they were the first of the Arab countries to point out that psychological leadership must come from those directly involved, the Palestinians themselves. Drawing on their own experience in the 1954-1962 revolution, the Algerians have recently convinced the al-Fatah movement of the usefulness of extensive public relations and propaganda activity. A former Minister of Information, Mohammed Yazid, has helped the Palestinian organization establish information offices in European cities to present the Palestinian case as seen by Palestinians to world opinion. On the occasion of the convening of the International Islamic Conference in Kuala Lumpur, Malaysia, in the spring of 1969, similar efforts began in Southeast Asia. The evolution of events by early 1969 indicates that the Algerian assessment of the probable shape of things to come was far from inaccurate.

Meanwhile, the Algerian government took advantage of the situation created by the war to stabilize its own position and to mobilize the population on its behalf. Demonstrations and strikes were forbidden, high school students were called for military training of a dubious nature on a crash basis, compulsory military service was introduced in 1968, and a general atmosphere emphasizing a wartimelike austerity and stressing the need for unqualified patriotism was created. Relations were broken with America and for several months the press and radio cried that Algeria was in danger of attack by the United States, Britain, and other unspecified imperialists.

These dangers failed to materialize, but an effort to overthrow the government was made by dissident officers in December, 1967. The attempted coup was put down with some bloodshed involving the use of tanks and aircraft, and it underlined the need to pay greater heed to internal political and social problems. As events in the Maghrib became relatively normal once again in 1968, all the countries of the region began gradually to take a more balanced, long-range view of their position in the light of their fundamental internal problems; of their relations not only with the Middle East in continuing crisis but with all the outside world; and of the cross-linkages between these two spheres of problems.

IV. The Basic Problems of the Maghrib

All the Maghrib states share a number of fundamental socioeconomic problems, both as a consequence of their status as developing countries and more specifically because of their heritage of settler colonialism and the deep implantation of a "total" European system on the indigenous culture. The result has been the formation of societies characterized by a dual economic infrastructure and a dual sociocultural outlook of an intensity rarely found in ex-colonial countries. It is really this duality, slowly declining in some respects and being sharply modified in others, but having everywhere left a profound sense of dislocation and insecurity, that distinguishes the Maghrib from the Arab Middle East. It has often been pointed out that Algeria in the 1960s was a nation with an unusually developed, modern infrastructure whose trained human skills and capacities were almost completely inadequate to handle the material plant abandoned by France. In the same vein, the fact that more than 20 percent of the cultivable land of Algeria and Tunisia, and 10 percent in Morocco, were in the hands of European settlers just before independence, has meant that a vast effort has had to be made almost overnight with regard to land tenure reorganization, economic adaptation, and new kinds of agricultural training methods. Moreover, the extremely close ties of the recent colonial period included export markets for both local agricultural products and for surplus local labor, and they were also built into an educational system that was either an identical copy of the metropolitan version or its intimate spiritual protégé.

It is clear of course that complex links in so many domains could not be severed immediately even if desired; and, despite the strong psychological pressures and the political oratory calling for an ever greater immersion in Arabism and a break with the colonial past, the deeds of North African leaders indicate that in most cases they view economical and cultural cooperation as an advantage as well as a necessity. Probably most vital, illustrating this problem well, is the question of negotiating some kind of associational or free-trade agreement of an apolitical nature with the European Economic Community (EEC).

Tunisia, the most vulnerable of the Maghrib countries on all counts, has long felt this need. It began talks in 1963; Morocco followed with its usual hesitancy shortly afterward; and Algeria, relying on the *de facto* privileges of access to the Common Market it continued to enjoy by having been legally part of France in 1957 when the Treaty of Rome was signed, after some indecision chose the alternative of diversifying its trade (as late as 1965 the EEC took 85% of its exports) in other directions rather than seeking any form of economic integration with Western Europe. In this choice it had two advantages not open to the other Maghrib states: growing revenues from oil and the willingness of the Soviet Union to make major economic concessions for political motives.

Tunisia (70% of whose exports went to EEC countries in 1966) has recently come to preliminary agreement with the Community, and Morocco (more than 50% trade with the Common Market) is in the final stages of negotiations. In both cases, intra-Community preference is to be granted for Maghrib industrial products as well as concessions for the more critical 70 to 80 percent of their agricultural products upon which duties will be reduced. The knotty question of North African wine exports may be partly resolved by recent Algerian difficulties on that score, since the much smaller quantity of wine produced by Morocco and Tunisia could more easily be taken up by the EEC. Franco-Algerian relations are complicated on many counts, including the political triangle created by the considerable Soviet influence and activity in Algeria, but economically they may be summed up in two main issues: oil, which France wants and pays for at noncompetitive prices in francs, but which Algeria charges is being sold by French companies to refining subsidiaries at lower than market prices; and wine, which France has been increasingly reluctant to buy, with the result that Algeria finally reached an agreement with the Soviet Union whereby the latter will take 110 million gallons of Algerian wine over a seven-year period at a lower than normal price.

Maghribi emigrant labor has been both another tie to Europe and a source of friction with it. In toto, almost one million North Africans—approximately one-sixth of the active population of the area—work and reside semipermanently, legally and illegally, in Western Europe, mostly in Common Market countries. The emigrants are found mostly in France, but there are goodly numbers in West Germany and Belgium as well. All the Maghrib states have some form of special arrangements with the various European authorities (quotas, guaranteed job requirements, pre-emigration health inspection, and so forth), and all are eager to go on sending surplus labor overseas, for obvious reasons. But the years of easy immigration, often first to France and then on to other European countries, seem over. Restrictions have multiplied as economic growth slowed and automation began to displace many manual workers. The proposals for special labor pool arrangements raised by the Tunisians and Moroccans in their negotiations with the EEC were turned down, and the emigration question has become a factor in Algerian dissatisfaction with France in recent years. Although the free movement of persons between the two countries guaranteed in the agreements on interdependence signed at Evian in 1962 has come to an end, Algerians have continued to enjoy preferential status in moving to France, subject to steady administrative encroachments on this condition. A French quota of 15,000 per year was set in 1966, and subsequently many Algerian immigrants posing as tourists were turned back. Algeria wishes to export at least 50,000 workers annually to Europe from now to 1985, and in 1968 agreement was reached with France to allow 37,000 to enter France annually under specific conditions of control. Early in 1969 the Algerian government made the possession of a passport, instead of a simple identity card, mandatory even for visits to France, in an effort to cooperate in holding down clandestine emigration.

Technical and educational assistance is another domain in which strong bonds have been forged and are still maintained with France. Although each of the countries of the Maghrib is slowly moving toward setting up a genuinely national education system, it is still true as of this writing that bilingualism is a reality, that training in scientific and technical subjects in the secondary schools and universities is conducted only in French and will be for some time, and that progress in education up to now would have been impossible without the massive infusion of French teachers, who still make up more than 20 percent of the total teaching staff, compose half the personnel in technical subjects, and are in a large majority among the university faculties. Tunisia has made an outstanding effort to equip itself in teachers; Algeria has utilized personnel from the Middle East (primarily Syria, the United Arab Republic, and Iraq) and the Soviet bloc; and Morocco has drawn on a variety of sources, including the Peace Corps. But in all cases advanced education in the Maghrib remains an enterprise conducted overwhelmingly in the French mode, either by Frenchmen or their French-acculturated disciples, and it thus helps to perpetuate the already deeply incised Gallic imprint on the face of North African society.

I have dwelt at some length on these problems in order to emphasize several points. The most important of these is that the short- and medium-term material interests of the Maghrib are still so heavily entangled with Western Europe that the North Africans remain enmeshed in a broad socio-economic dependence system. Another is that in a consideration of basic problems of this kind the Arab Middle East need hardly enter the discussion. The only exception to that would arise in an appraisal of the rivalries among the oil-exporting countries of North Africa and the Middle East. Libya, and to a lesser degree Algeria, have both profited from the closing of the Suez Canal. Their oil revenues increased sharply in 1968 with Libya receiving about $500 million and Algeria almost $200 million.

Obviously, however, immediate economic interests are not all, and a sophisticated network of counterbalances has been built by all the Maghrib states in order to reduce the pressures of this dependence system and to provide alternatives to it. Beyond the merely political, one may look on the emotional quotient—at least in popular feeling—in relations with the Middle East as a psychological countercurrent to this heavy involvement with Europe. But one may also legitimately interpret the identification with Europe and things European by so much of the North African élite as a counterweight to the insecurity felt in the Maghrib owing to the religious and cultural pre-eminence of the Mashriq. The contemporary political scene in North Africa appears to be repeating the maneuvers of those Sultans of Morocco and Beys of Tunis who for long periods in history successfully kept threatening foreign forces at bay by astutely playing them off one against the other. The political options of the North African countries today are not so immutably fixed as they might seem at first glance, and some of their subtleties might be worthy of examination.

V. The Foreign Policy of the Maghrib States

Both Morocco and Tunisia achieved independence as the result of a political evolution in which violence played a comparatively restrained role. After the sovereignty of the former protectorates was restored, both retained close ties with France; "independence within interdependence" was the phrase of the day. Most resident Europeans continued living in both countries, and apart from a few minor incidents, relations between France and the new states were conducted for several years in a generally harmonious climate. Nevertheless, both Morocco and Tunisia began searching for forces that would counterbalance French influence.

Tunisia found this readily in the United States, for reasons that include but also exceed the bounds of *realpolitik*. President Bourguiba's view of international politics recalls that of the liberal, Rooseveltian school of a generation ago. He was influenced by World War II, in which he correctly predicted an eventual Allied victory and refused to collaborate with the Axis, and he has assessed the cold war in much the same way. (It is worth remembering that he is the only Arab head of state with any political experience during the 1930s.) Bourguiba fundamentally mistrusts the Soviet bloc, especially China, and is suspicious of those Arab leaders who in his eyes flirt dangerously with it. In a speech early in 1969 he warned that while "one can get rid of the French and the British, it is impossible to free oneself from the Soviets." These apprehensions are at the root of Tunisia's posture in world affairs, for they make it impossible to turn anywhere save to America for the countervailing power sought. The Bourguibist vision of an ideal world might be one where the United States guaranteed protection to Tunisia and supported its indeed outstanding developmental efforts, while Tunisia basked in the glow of French culture and style. The misgivings of the President also account for his hostility to Nasser's Egypt, and to any Algeria, that of Ben Bella or Boumedienne, that by its philosophy and its reliance on Soviet arms is a potential threat to Tunisia.

The American response has been warm. Tunisia represents to American eyes a rational and moderate force in the Afro-Asian world, and the Tunisian stand on many world issues has been of help to Washington. Even more important is the basic ideological similarity of the analysis of the international scene made by both capitals. The United States has made Tunisia a recipient of special attention in the field of economic assistance: in the early 1960s, per capita nonmilitary aid to Tunisia was greater than that given to any other developing country. It has also led to the growth of a special relationship, for the Tunisian president is the only Arab leader whose personal and official relations with Washington have been truly cordial over a period now encompassing four presidents.

As befits a larger and more strategically situated country, Morocco moved into international politics with more deliberate hesitation. Disentanglement from the French embrace was sought but without making commitments as direct as those of Tunisia. Relations with first Washington (1957) and later (1960) Moscow were cultivated, and both were used to offset French influence. At the same time, internal policy was used in the balancing act; internal opposition on the left, of labor and student groups, was neutralized when Muhammad V dismissed the government and formed his own Cabinet in 1960, but it was supposed to be assuaged by a compensating drift from nonalignment to a more pro-Soviet stance in international affairs. When Hassan II succeeded his father in 1961, a change in direction took place; warmer relations have been sought since then with the United States, especially during the 1965-1967 period when France suspended assistance to Morocco in the wake of the Ben Barka affair.

The Moroccan caution under Hassan II vis-à-vis the Soviet bloc has been closely related to the emergence of an Algerian neighbor with whom Morocco's relations have been and still are shaky and suspicious at bottom, openly hostile at some times, and on occasion have degenerated into the support and encouraging of subversive groups by both sides, the massing of troops, and short but bloody border clashes. In 1963 a short-lived border war of some proportions took place, with inconclusive results although the generally admitted superiority of the Moroccan performance has spurred Algeria to acquiring a much increased stock of heavy arms and aircraft. The ostensible cause of tension between the two states has been the Moroccan claim to parts of the mineral-rich Algerian Sahara and Algeria's refusal to discuss the issue. But fundamentally the dispute arises from the near incompatibility of a revolutionary regime with socialist coloration and a state based on a conservative dynastic tradition supported mainly by the religious attachment of rural masses and the interests of a large, propertied bourgeoisie intimately linked with the bureaucracy and the palace. Following the visit of President Boumedienne to Morocco in Janury, 1969, relations between the two states appear to have become more cordial. Given the fundamental dissonance in attitude, style, and ultimate objectives, it would be rash to predict an entirely untroubled future. Still, the willingness to practice mutual tolerance and show respect seems to be more genuine than on earlier occasions of temporary reconciliation. Coincident with this policy of intra-Maghrib détente, Morocco has also recently taken a somewhat warmer attitude toward Soviet overtures of friendship which culminated with the visit to Rabat of President Podgorny in the spring of 1969. This latest tack should also be viewed, however, as a continuation of Morocco's basic policy of not becoming too closely aligned with or dependent on any single power.

When Algeria became free in 1962 it was after an exceptionally bloody revolutionary war; it was almost certain that the main ingredients of its political life would have a much different flavor from those of its neighbors. For one thing, the violence of the 1954-1962 revolution and the conditions under which Algeria separated from France left a legacy of emotional extremism and verbal excess that has marked most Algerian statements— but not deeds—in foreign affairs since then. For another, the almost incestuous complications of the love-hate relationship with France far outstripped the more platonic feelings entertained toward the former metropole by Morocco and Tunisia. And finally, both of those states were already well into the execution of their own foreign policies; the by then firm Tunisian-American relationship and the initiatives of the newly acceded Hassan II were facts that had to be taken into account by the nascent Algerian state. Given the Algerian predisposition to suspicion nurtured by a clandestine guerrilla life, the internal rivalries of postindependence Algeria, and the memory of having been dependent on Morocco and Tunisia during the revolution, it is understandable how both of those countries could be looked on by the Algerians more as threats, however indirect, than as friendly partners.

The Evian Agreements for Franco-Algerian cooperation, signed in 1962 and valid for three years, were more restrictive on many points of national sovereignty than anything signed by Morocco or Tunisia with France. Forced to look for other supports to help establish its identity and integrity and to redress the unequal status of its relationships with France, Algeria turned away from its North African neighbors to the Arab states in the Middle East who espoused seemingly similar approaches to a form of Arab socialism, and away from the West, which had been lukewarm in its support for the revolution, to the Soviet bloc which had early championed the Algerian right to freedom. Moreover, the emotional nature of the Algerian commitment to revolutionary freedom was such that it carried the regime naturally into spiritual communion with those nations it felt had undergone an analogous experience, notably Cuba and Yugoslavia.

This revolutionary ardor led to Algiers becoming the center for any number of sub-Saharan African liberation movements, and even of fringe revolutionary groups in Latin America, Portugal, and other parts of the world. Although verbal encouragement for such activities was substantially reduced after Ben Bella was overthrown in 1965, the Arab-oriented background of Boumedienne and the mythology of the success of the revolution —a mythology being continually shaped into a central pillar of the new national tradition—have combined, especially since 1967, to lay down a policy of disassociating Algeria from a negotiated settlement of the Middle East crisis and of giving encouragement, support, and training to Palestinian guerrillas. It should be emphasized, though, that these are permissive and not mandatory policies. That is, Algeria differs from Syria in holding that if the Arabs wish to commit the mistake of negotiating directly with Israel, Algeria will not oppose this step but neither will it approve it or consider itself engaged by it. The logic of history, it feels, shows the inevitability of a military confrontation with Israel; only the initiative of the Palestinians themselves can redress the situation; the Arab states are psychologically—and morally, because of their acquisition of Palestinian territory—incapable of exercising this leadership; and Algeria is ready and willing to "help those who help themselves." This is an entirely different position from that of Ben Bella and his promises to send thousands of Algerian troops to liberate Palestine.

Algerian antagonism toward the "imperialists" of the West became focused on the United States as early as the Cuban missile crisis of 1962. Since then Algerian-American relations have never prospered, but they remained usually correct on the surface while the temperature underneath varied from cool to frigid. Beginning around 1965 they worsened steadily as the Vietnam war continued, and they were already at a low even before the Middle East crisis erupted in 1967. Immediately prior to and during this period, Algerian attacks on American policy were as bitter as anything in the Arab Middle East or more so, and Algeria was the only Maghrib state to break relations. Later in 1967 it nationalized Anglo-American oil companies operating in the country, but quite recently there have been signs of a thaw. American consultants are cooperating in the current development plan, an independent American oil company has accepted the Algerian oil-monopoly conditions for participation in a joint operation, and a group of American businessmen has been invited to visit Algeria to look into investment possibilities.

Some of this relaxation of tension may be due to the influence of the hard-headed men running the nationalized industrial sector of the economy, who have been openly nonideological. But it also derives in part from the need to pursue a new tack in international relations. Algeria has played off France and the Soviet Union with success for the past five years. Each French withdrawal or lessening of technical and financial aid was compensated for by an increase in the Soviet contribution. France could not complain inasmuch as the foundations of Gaullist foreign policy, as well as France's self-proclaimed position of disinterested magnanimity toward the developing world, was based on successful decolonization in Algeria. In this way the Soviets came to play an important role: they supplied planes, tanks, and other arms to Algeria; they trained cadets for the officer corps; they supplied technicians variously estimated from 3000 to 5000; they contributed to the construction of a steel mill at Annaba (Bône); and they have been reported, without confirmation, to be seeking to use facilities at the naval base of Marna al-Kabir recently vacated by the French ahead of schedule. Still, Algeria is by no means as involved with the Soviets as is the United Arab Republic. Its relative physical security and its increasingly solid financial position have allowed it choices not open to the U.A.R. government. In this category might be included recent unofficial Algerian suggestions that both the American and the Soviet naval presence in the Mediterranean be withdrawn, a proposal unthinkable by the Egyptian government under present circumstances.

As relations with France have reached a point where neither partner is willing to make special concessions of the kind desirable and necessary just after independence, manipulation has become harder. Formerly lavish French aid has diminished sharply, being reduced by half in four years; the recent labor agreement is all that Algeria can hope for in that field for years to come; and French counterpressure is evident in renewed warmth toward Tunisia and the decision to allot development funds to Morocco for the first time since 1965. Even more important over the long haul is the *rapprochement* at a higher level between Paris and Moscow, for this makes France more willing to tolerate a higher degree of Soviet penetration than it might now (as opposed to a few years back when the Soviets were just getting a foothold in Algeria) be willing to admit. In these lights one might view the still hesitant and quiet approaches to the United States as an indication that the Algerian government, which has made clear its determination to preserve its independence of thought and action even though its views may often genuinely coincide with those of the Soviet Union, is giving consideration to finding a new counterweight for the future. All in all, Algeria is much more of a going concern today than it was three or four years ago. Although unemployment remains very high and many social and economic problems are unsolved, the economy shows signs of starting to budge under the joint stimuli of greater rationalism and new investment generated by the now substantial and growing revenues from the well-run oil monopoly. This new degree of stability in Algeria is tenuous, but it may start to be reflected in many aspects of its foreign policy.

VI. Summary and Future Possibilities

The Maghrib has lived through history alongside of or as a peripheral part of nearby great civilizations, a part that has been dependent and autonomous at the same time, and a part never fully integrated in the culture brought to it from outside. Despite the seemingly fashionable political vicissitudes of the moment, this is the most significant and permanent feature of North African life today, as it was yesterday. Its profound contemporary links of an intellectual and cultural as well as socioeconomic nature with modern European civilization confront an ancient and deeply rooted socioreligious, affective adherence to traditional Islamic culture and, to a lesser degree, to the modernist renovation of it being attempted in the Middle East.

North Africa has, however, made one vital contribution in our times to Arab political history—the myth of military victory in the Algerian revolution through persistence in the face of seemingly impossible odds.

It matters little that the legend is false and that independence was won at the conference table after France had simultaneously shown its military capacity to dominate guerrilla resistance and its psychological unwillingness to go on repressing the political ideology that underlay it. For today, not only all Algerians but all Arabs seek to propagate this fiction of battle-field triumph. It is the only military success they can claim out of their recent history, at least since World War I when a somewhat similar legend was created. It is of comparatively little relevance that Algeria is now training a few Palestinians in guerrilla techniques. Much more important is their teaching them the value of propaganda and the usefulness of getting sympathetic reactions from world opinion. And it is of the greatest significance that they have provided the mystique and the model for ultimate success.

Despite this contribution, neither Algeria nor any other North African country can aspire to the "leadership" of the Arab world, as is sometimes suggested. North Africa is too far removed, physically and spiritually, for such a challenge. Algeria has neither the intellectual or material resources nor the geographical position for the task, even if it wished to undertake it, and it clearly does not. Tunisia at times has laid claim to a kind of moral and cultural superiority that would, as it were, give it the right to claim the same kind of leadership among the Maghrib nations as that exercised by Massachusetts at the time of the American Revolution. But this vanity is balanced by a strong tendency to abstentionism—a feeling quickly sensed by the observer that Tunisia is somehow uncomfortable with its Arab neighbors and somewhat embarrassed by them. Intellectual leadership, even within the Maghrib, is thus less tempting than dissocia-tion. And Morocco, for its part, has almost always preferred to lead its own life, the most remote and taciturn of all the Maghrib states.

The policies of states fluctuate but the basic character of societies and nations changes only imperceptibly through the gradual, internal socializa-tion of historical experience. Aloofness in Morocco, the search for a role in Algeria, haughtiness in Tunisia—all still appear to govern the broad approach of these countries to the present and near-term future problems of the Arab Middle East. Certainly if a new Arab-Israeli war broke ont, and especially if the fighting were protracted, popular emotions tinged with the complexities of guilt would demand at least the degree of participation entered into in 1967. But as emotional behavior linked to guilt may often be speedily exorcised by ritual or token deeds, the role would doubtless again be subsidiary and, in the case of Morocco and Tunisia, reluctantly played.

North African interventions in Middle Eastern affairs have been *à la longue* patently unsuccessful. Morocco found that it could not be a distant, impersonal arbiter of inter-Arab problems. Tunisia failed utterly in its efforts to mark out new approaches to a solution of the Arab-Israeli dispute. And now Algeria, too, has soft-pedaled its sometime strenuous efforts to prod the Arab states into maintaining an uncompromisingly rigid posture which would demand a military solution. Thus, no country in the Maghrib has been an active factor for peace in the Middle East, nor is any one of them today a positive stimulus toward a renewal of hostilities. The Maghrib remains in the end, as it has always been, of and for itself— historically chary of stirring outside itself save for fleeting episodes, and then lapsing back into its detachment, its reticence, and its uniqueness.

The Extra-Regional Powers

PART V.

The Extra-regional Powers

The concluding chapters of this book deal with the influence in the Middle East of the Soviet Union, the Western European states (including Great Britain) and the United States.[1]

Peter Calvocoressi (Chap. 12) traces the history of British interests and influence in the Middle East, then describes the general decline of British and European power presence and interest in the region in the twentieth century. Pierre Rondot concerns himself with Italian, French, and West German influence there, mainly since World War II, in Chapter 13. He notes that French commercial and political interest now concentrates mainly on the North African Arabs, that Italy has Arab good will but few tangible assets for exploiting it, and that the Federal Republic's economic expansion assures strengthening commercial links with the Arab states.

Both authors adopt a widely accepted approach in according little weight to the domestic sources of foreign policy. Both treat foreign policy behavior mainly as the rational, tactical response of a given country to its international situation. Both also help to identify an interesting problem in foreign policy behavior that goes beyond the approach they have used and that carries important implications for western Europe's future behavior toward the Middle East: the political adaptation of post-colonial powers to their new international status. Rondot summarizes the cultural and historical basis for France's interest in the North African Arab states, as Gallagher does in Chapter 11 from the Maghrib side, and observes the conspicuous economic interest in oil. Calvocoressi infers from the declining British commitment and interest in the Middle East a corresponding decline in public interest that should be reflected in partisan politics.

The tangible interests of Western Europeans in the Middle East remain as oil consumers and investors. Their governments nevertheless face publics with quite different preoccupations: a fluctuating sympathy for Israel, changing attitudes about cultural ties, and aspirations about status and involvement that are a residue of colonial rule. For the Western

[1] The reader may want to refer back to Chap. 3, which deals with the military balance (and hence the presence of the United States and the Soviet Union, in particular) in the region.

420

European states then, national foreign policy must reconcile these diverse forces: (1) public opinion responses of mood to regional events and issues; (2) private oil interests in the region and the government's interests in oil policy; and (3) the visible response of the government to the international situation. The dichotomous structure of these internal political forces (the public mood, on the one hand, and the specific interest on the other, the one tending to identify with Israel, and the other with the Arab states) indicates that foreign policy behavior will be unstable, very possibly offering the Middle Eastern states the opportunity for high returns on their diplomatic and propaganda activites in Europe.

In contrast to Calvocoressi's and Rondot's approaches, William B. Quandt supplies in Chapter 14, if not a working model of the American political system that can predict foreign policy outcomes, then at least a more explicit description of a model. Arnold L. Horelick and Abraham S. Becker (Chapter 15) examine Soviet foreign policy with a less explicit model of the political system that produces it, reflecting the lesser availability of data in the Soviet Union.

When viewed as the product of private group influence as well as the influence of public officials and bodies, American politics does not distinguish foreign policy from other kinds of public policymaking.[2] The special affection many American Jews have for Israel gives her a special but scarcely a unique place among segments of American foreign policy. Other segments of American public opinion—ethnic as well as social, economic, and geographic—have predisposed American foreign policy to favor one country or another.[3]

It is difficult to establish an objective perspective when comparing American politics with politics in states that are small and politically less cohesive, diversified, and developed. In the United States, ethnic political behavior that is familiar and relatively stable, such as Irish and Jewish politics have been, are perceived as a normal competitive challenge in a

[2]Given the tradition of Congressional oversight of the Executive branch, the decentralization of American politics, the separation of powers, and a relatively diversified press, American public business at the national level is, at least relative to other developed democratic states, and certainly in comparison with other kinds of governments as well, fairly open. These conditions establish an environment of competitive disclosure. In addition, since the Roosevelt political coalition was forged in the 1930s, and even more, since the civil rights revolution began in the 1950s, American politics has dealt openly with the ethnic basis of political association as a fairly widely accepted norm. Perhaps the relative stability of the American political system has made this open handling of ethnic politics practical.

[3]Perhaps the most careful work on this subject is Leroy N. Riselbach, *Roots of Isolationism: Congressional Voting and Presidential Leadership in Foreign Policy* (Indianapolis: Bobbs-Merrill, 1966).

political system that contains many other political groups—including other ethnic groups.[4] Quandt's chapter reflects this dimension in the political literature about the United States, locating the two principal private interests identified conspicuously with Middle Eastern policy, the ethnically centered pro-Israeli interest groups and the economically based Arab oil lobby, in their relationship to the governmental process, particularly to U.S. Executive branch factions.

Quandt also considers several areas of possible Soviet-American cooperation, mainly in limiting weapons acquisition in the region and by agreeing on rules of future intervention. He also considers certain alternatives, taking U.S. involvement and commitment as the main issue.

Every political system keeps some political secrets. It may therefore be something of an illusion for American scholars to assume that, because of the comparative openness of American public life, they can readily infer what the inputs and outputs are that constitute a segment of foreign policy, such as the Arab-Israeli conflict. Students of Soviet foreign policymaking suffer from no such illusion, for comparable public information on the Soviet political system is not available. As a result, Horelick's and Becker's accounts of Soviet Middle Eastern policy are written largely from the outside. Even so, both authors identify some strong restraining conditions that affect Soviet behavior in the Middle East.

China challenges the Soviet Union's Communist bloc leadership by embarrassing the Soviets for supporting non-Communist regimes anywhere. In the Middle East that includes the Arab regimes. These ideological considerations have been visible though not conspicuous in the Middle East and are evidently the source of some constraints on Soviet behavior there. The Soviet Union is also constrained by the quite limited resources available for the pursuit of her worldwide objectives. She has given Arab clients favored treatment recently but in the longer run they must compete with other claimants, a situation that also imposes some constraint on Soviet policy in the Middle East.

Horelick has examined the record of Soviet behavior in and toward the Middle East in an effort to ascribe motives and infer the basis for predictions. Becker has speculated about alternative future conditions and Soviet policies in the Middle East and their possible consequences. The more the Russians become involved in the Middle East and the higher the

[4]In contrast, Indian politicians and elected officials treat communal politics — that is to say, ethnic politics — as a threat to social order. Government-backed self-censorship codes play down Hindu-Muslim rioting, referring only to "groups," disturbances, and "places of worship," for example, in their reports (*New York Times*, June 14, 1970). See also *Lok Sabha Debates*, July 31, 1968 (4th Series, Vol. XVIII, No. 8), col. 2988.

stakes for them, the greater their incentives to control their Arab state clients, he holds. Such involvement for the United States, on the other hand, has been diminishing in a great many places, certainly including Turkey, Iran, Jordan, Ethiopia, and Libya.

Two puzzles concerning the Soviet Union emerge from the discussions in these chapters: (1) the Soviet Union's fluctuating propensity to run the risks associated with involvement in the Middle East, and (2) the prospects of a Soviet-Arab quarrel. As provocateur in 1967 the Russians evidently miscalculated the dangers of war and defeat; but their rapid resupply of arms to the defeated Arab forces and, in the spring of 1970, the participation of Soviet pilots and technicians in the air defense of the U.A.R. have involved them even deeper in the conflict. Their boldness is not wholly consistent with the prevailing characterization of Soviet caution in foreign relations. The risks of this behavior can be discounted on the grounds of Moscow's confidence either that her interests coincide with theirs, that she can control the Arab states, or that the United States will see that Israel backs down. If so, that confidence may be misplaced.

The prospects of Soviet-Arab interest conflicts are real. Great and small powers hardly ever find a complete coincidence of interest. In addition, a conspicuous Russian military presence in the region is likely to run afoul of Arab nationalism and to foster Soviet anxieties about controlling when they are involved. There may also be divergencies over geography and oil. As Hurewitz indicates in Chapter 3, the Soviet Union has an interest in using the Suez Canal for her Mediterranean fleet which she may put ahead of achieving a desirable settlement with Israel for the U.A.R. Moscow also has an interest in denying oil to Western European markets, much as the Arab states have had. Unlike the Arab oil producers, however, the Soviet Union's dependence upon oil revenues for foreign exchange is comparatively small.

These differences and potential differences between the Soviet Union and her clients are important in gauging the prospects of keeping the Arab-Israeli conflict under control and settling it. For any serious effort to settle the dispute must become a test of the will, cohesion, and control of each side, and in the last analysis, of some modicum of mutual confidence.

Peter Calvocoressi, Reader in International Relations at the University of Sussex, England, is author of *World Order and New States* (New York: Praeger, 1962).

Pierre Rondot is former director of the Center of Advanced Administrative Studies of Modern Africa and Asia, (1955-1967), and professor at the Institute of Political Studies of Paris, Lyon, and Grenoble, and at the International Institute of Advanced Administrative Studies, Paris France;

he authored *The Changing Patterns of the Middle East* (New York: Praeger, 1961).

William B. Quandt is a research staff member of the Rand Corporation and author of *Revolution and Political Leadership: Algeria, 1954-1968* (Cambridge, Mass.: M.I.T. Press, 1969).

Arnold L. Horelick is a research staff member of The Rand Corporation and coauthor with Myron Rush of *Strategic Power and Soviet Foreign Policy* (Chicago: University of Chicago Press, 1966).

Abraham S. Becker, also a research staff member of the Rand Corporation, is the author of *Soviet National Income 1958-1964; National Accounts of the USSR in the Seven Year Plan Period* (Berkeley, Calif.:. University of California Press, 1969).

CHAPTER 12

Britain and the Middle East

Peter Calvocoressi

I. The Dual Nature of British Interest

The geographical importance of the Middle East has often been stressed. At the junction of three continents, a narrow barrier between the Mediterranean Sea and the Indian Ocean and penetrated by two lesser waterways, the Red Sea and the Persian Gulf, the Middle East cannot fail to be a prime factor in the calculations of any state whose horizons are not limited to a single continent. Many countries, great and small, which are situated on one or another of its flanks are concerned with what goes on beyond the other flank. Consequently, they wish to be able to pass freely and peacefully across it, for if their way is barred they must either force a passage through it or go a long journey round it. Centuries ago Europe's trade with the East made the Middle East important. Subsequent centuries have increased its commercial importance.

Commerce and Strategy

In the nineteenth century this commercial passageway became an imperial passageway also, and to no state was it more important than to Great Britain. This was because of the British Empire in India, a phenomenon unique not only in the history of imperialism but also in that of British imperialism. The British Empire in India was the base on which Great Britain's Empire, and therefore its world political primacy, rested. Unlike every other major European power, Great Britain was a world power first and a European power second, and (given the state of communications in the nineteenth century) its world power demanded the existence, on the other side of the globe, of a separate army available and acclimatized for operations in half the world. Great Britain was a world power because it held India. Great Britain's position was therefore a dual one, commercial and strategic.

It was dual also in a different sense. It was a characteristic of British attitudes in the age of British predominance that Great Britain looked at certain parts of the world from two sides. This was notably true of the Middle East which was, in British terms, evenly divided into a British and an Indian sphere of influence. The British saw the Middle East from their home base in the British Isles and they saw it no less definitely from

425

India. They continued to see it in these two ways even after they had left India, for habits survive their causes. This dual vision was, moreover, repeated at one remove nearer home, for, having established themselves in the Middle East, the British then looked at Europe from two sides too, from their home base in the British Isles and from the Middle East. The Middle East was therefore both a link between Great Britain and India, and, no less important at the time although less often stressed, a way of approaching Europe and of bringing pressure to bear on Great Britain's enemies in Europe. This latter function of the Middle East was critically important in World War II when the British were thrown out of Western Europe by Hitler and were faced with the problem of getting back after having lost all their Western allies. In both world wars the British spent time and controversy over the question whether to attack their continental enemies from the northwest or the southeast—a debate which few of their American allies, used to thinking of the deployment of power from a single home base only, understood.

The in-betweenness of the Middle East was its main feature in British thinking. The existence of the British Empire in India meant that the British passed through the Middle East not merely to go to market but also to go to what was their second power base, and this duality of interest made it more important for the British than for anybody else to assert and maintain a predominant position in the Middle East.

Power Politics

But the simplest way of doing this was not open to the British. They could not themselves rule over the Middle East. At no time in the nineteenth century could Great Britain have created a Middle Eastern empire because the attempt to do so would have united all the other major European powers to defeat it. Although the Seven Years' War left Great Britain dominant over all other intruders into North America and Southern Asia, no such position was vouchsafed to it in the intercontinental lands of the Middle East until after World War I, when European imperialism was already in decline.

Power politics of the nineteenth century were conditioned by the Vienna settlement of 1815, a settlement based on the redrawing of the map of Europe and the maintenance of the new frontiers by great-power consensus. But although that settlement did not apply to the Ottoman Empire, it was nevertheless clear that the valuable Arab lands of that empire might not be acquired by any European power, least of all by the one furthest removed from the scene. Therefore the European powers were obliged to exercise leverage indirectly, to leave the Turks in control and to establish such good relations with the Sultan that he would not interfere with the free passage of their goods and men through the Middle East or permit any one European power to interdict the lawful activities of another.

Given the special nature of British interests, it was no accident that Great Britain insisted more strongly than any other power on the preservation of the integrity of the Ottoman Empire and expended huge diplomatic efforts on making the Sultan if not Anglophile at least amenable to British persuasion. Only in this way could Great Britain fend off Russian and French ambitions. The Turks might be pagans and sometimes worse, but they were useful so long as they remained strong enough to postpone the crumbling of an empire whose heirs the British could scarcely hope to be. Keeping other powers out of the Middle East, or keeping their activities there within bounds, was a prime consideration in British foreign policy, and the preservation of the Ottoman Empire was, for a time, the most promising means to this end.

The French threat, made manifest by Napoleon himself in 1798, was revived with France's support of the Sultan's overmighty subject, Muhammad Ali of Egypt (who came to rule much Arab land in Asia too). The Russian threat, less immediate at first than the French but geographically more pressing, became a permanent feature of nineteenth-century European politics. The Austrians too competed for European portions of the Ottoman lands, and in the second half of the nineteenth century the Germans competed successfully against the British, influencing the Ottoman's government (the Porte) and then gaining railway concessions in Asia.

Two of the earliest signs of British reaction came from the Indian end of the Anglo-Indian imperium. In 1798, in the immediate aftermath of the failure of Napoleon's Middle Eastern adventure, Great Britain made its first treaty with an Arab prince, the Sultan of Muscat. In 1839 Aden was taken and annexed to the Bombay Presidency. These were outlying parts of the empire where the Ottoman influence was not always certain and it behooved the British to ensure their communications by direct action— diplomatic in the one case, proprietary in the other. By applying the same reasoning under different circumstances, the British later extended their power to Cyprus and to Egypt. Where friendship with the Porte was not enough, either because the Porte's power did not extend far enough, or because its good will was in question, then Great Britain would establish quasi-sovereign rights for itself within the territorial sovereignty of the Ottoman Empire.

There logically came a point when the Porte's own power or its good will toward Great Britain was so reduced that the policy of preserving the integrity of the Ottoman Empire ceased to serve its purpose. This, for Great Britain, was the essence of the Eastern question, and Salisbury for one came to the conclusion that the policy might have to be changed and that British interests might be better served by a partition of the Ottoman Empire. The alternative, he thought, would be war over a corpse, that is, the sort of thing that happened in the Chinese Empire, when European powers vied for privileges and footholds and eventually occupied its capital. This argument was resolved by World War I which produced, among its principal consequences, not only the defeat of the Ottoman Empire but also its dismemberment.

II. British Policy between Two World Wars

The dissolution of the Ottoman Empire in Europe had been gradual and had promoted a number of nations to independent statehood. In Asia, on the other hand, Ottoman rule was ended at a stroke by defeat in war. Its subject peoples, the Arabs, did not constitute a series of successor states: some of them were even dreaming of a single successor state and all of them were quickly made aware of the determination of the European powers to arrogate to themselves part of the Ottoman *potestas*. Russian designs affected the Arabs least, partly because they were directed against Turkey itself, especially Constantinople, and partly because they were frustrated by the revolution of 1917, a circumstance of considerable and unforeseen importance after the next world war when the Arabs had had experience with British and French but not Russian domination. The British strategy was designed to strengthen their position by taking control in the southern, or Palestinian, part of Syria in order to complement their authority in Egypt (declared a British protectorate in December, 1914) and to secure exclusive control over the Suez Canal. They also proposed to dominate the Mesopotamian lands, later Iraq, which the Indian army had conquered from the Turks. These designs required a bargain with France, which claimed and was allotted the rest of Syria, including what later became the independent republic of Lebanon; and as the war progressed the Italians as well as the Russians had to be cut in on the deal. All these wartime arrangements constituted a disposal of the territories of an enemy in the expectation of his defeat, and the settlement, by agreement, of competing claims upon those territories among the victors. None of these powers wanted World War I to be followed by another war over the spoils of the first (as had happened in the Balkan wars), and so they sought to remove by diplomacy and by treaty the possible causes of such a further war. They succeeded. External powers have not yet come to blows with each other in the Middle East.

This method of disposing of the Arab lands of the Ottoman Empire sprang from the strategic and commercial interests of the outside powers in that area. Further, it rested upon an assumption: that the retreat of the Turks left a void into which it was not only desirable but natural that somebody else must step. But this assumption was acted upon only in part, for while the powers took over from the Turks in some areas, elsewhere they were prepared to allow the Arabs to assume the sovereignty which they had hoped to inherit everywhere. Furthermore, the British position in the zones of direct intervention was limited in Palestine and Iraq by the Mandates inaugurated at San Remo in 1920, and in Egypt by the recognition of that country in 1922 as an independent state.

Ambivalent Power Base

Thus the British position between the wars became an ambivalent one. On the one hand, it rested on power, on the British army in Egypt and Palestine, on the royal air force in Iraq, and the royal navy ubiquitously: the independence of Egypt and (later) Iraq was not allowed to interfere with these dispositions, for the price of independence included treaties giving Great Britain special strategic rights and facilities (which were to prove crucial in World War II). But on the other hand, the limits imposed on British authority caused the British to seek a second basis for their rule in the consent and friendship of the Arabs.

It was from the beginning a pecularity of the British position in the Middle East after World War I that theirs was a quasi-imperial position exercised over friends and allies. The British had no quarrel with the Arabs. Their quarrel, if any, was—or could be—with rival European powers. The Arab revolt of 1916 against the Turks had been undertaken in cooperation with Great Britain. But that revolt had introduced an equivocation into Anglo-Arab relations. It implied the reward of independence for the Arabs in all Arab lands subject to the Turks, so far as the British could help to achieve it. It therefore ran counter to the negotiations already in train between Great Britain and France for a postwar settlement of the Middle East in which these two countries would assume part of the Turkish dominion. In 1918 Great Britain, partly as a result of American pressure, publicly committed itself to the sovereign independence of the Arab lands, but by 1920 it was clear that British and Arab interpretations of this pledge could not be reconciled. The Mandate system seemed to the Arabs a derogation from the pledge, which it clearly was. The Anglo-Arab friendship with which the British intended to bolster their power in the Middle East was put under strain by other policies pursued by Great Britain for the same end. But there was also much good will between British and Arabs: the Arabs reflected that the Mandates were temporary and might be short, and they saw the hopelessness of trying to fight the British. The British came to believe that in spite of the 1920 settlement the Arabs were their firm friends and could even be lasting ones.

More than any other power, Great Britain inherited the Ottoman position in the Middle East. But the British position was fundamentally different from the Ottoman. Not only did Great Britain lack the sanction of sovereignty, it had also to make concessions to the French who established themselves in Syria and Lebanon (which were thereby separated from Iraq), and to the Zionist claim to establish a home in Palestine by immigration. Nowhere outside the Arabian peninsula were the Arabs given independence. The boundaries drawn by the mandate system fragmented the Arab world more than had the earlier division into vilayets.

Despite these barriers to growing Arab desire for sovereignty and unity, the British expected the Arabs to be friendly and to forget and forgo for at least another generation political aspirations roused by the intellectual movements begun by their grandfathers and by the growth of wealth and towns in the days of their fathers. In order to master these cross-currents Great Britain was prepared, while maintaining forces in the area, to modify the forms under which it exercised power. The end of the protectorate over Egypt in 1922 and of the Iraqi Mandate in 1932 salved some feelings without entailing the withdrawal of British forces from those countries (including the large Suez Canal Zone). New treaties sanctioned old power. Great Britain also established treaty relations with Saudi Arabia in 1927 and with Yemen in 1934. The former, however, was recognized as an independent state in need of a measure of British protection, while the treaty with the latter was an attempt to avoid trouble in the hinterland of Aden where sundry rulers served as a buffer. In the Persian Gulf the British position, consolidated by a chain of historical accidents and eternal treaties to be examined later, was virtually unaltered.

Palestine

Great Britain might have succeeded, at least for a time, in having the best of both worlds, keeping power in Arab lands and yet not losing Arab friendship, had it not been for Palestine. Zionism eventually drove the British out of Palestine in undignified retreat, but not before British policy had found some justification in terms of British interests when these prevailed in both Egypt and Iraq at critical moments in World War II.

The Zionist movement, founded toward the end of the nineteenth century with the purpose of helping Jews go to Palestine, was equivocal from the start. Its founding fathers proceeded upon the assumption that the territory they wished to occupy was uninhabited. Even when they were obliged to recognize that this was not so, they continued to behave as though it were. The Zionists wished to colonize part of the Ottoman Empire as Megara had colonized Syracuse, or the British, Australia. After the collapse of the Ottoman Empire some Zionists envisaged a Jewish polity under British sovereignty, even perhaps a Jewish dominion within the British Empire. But there were also Zionists who, from the earliest days, looked forward to an independent Jewish state. Their fault, if any, was not that they cherished this means to succor their persecuted race, but that they concealed their intentions in order the better to achieve them. During World War I, at a moment when the British government feared (wrongly) that the Germans were about to endorse Zionist claims and believed (also wrongly) that Zionist influence might keep the revolutionary regime in Russia from leaving the war, the government gave its consent to the Balfour Declaration which recognized the right of the Jews to establish a Jewish home in Palestine. It recognized neither the right to turn all Palestine into a Jewish home nor any right to create a Jewish state there, and it reserved the rights of the native Arabs. After the war it restated, in 1922, its resolution not to allow Jewish immigration to lead to the eviction or subordination of the Palestinian Arabs. The history of Palestine over the next quarter of a century is the history of how the Jews defeated this British policy. It will not be repeated here, though its consequences must be noted. After World War II when the Jews, as in World War I, were good friends to the British (in spite of grounds for enmity), the Jews evicted the British from Palestine by terror and defeated the Arabs by superior skill, superior resources, and superior numbers. After a half-century Zionism had got its state.

For the Arabs (initially the Palestinian Arabs, later Arabs far and wide) this was an unacceptable trespass condoned by the British. The central issue was Jewish immigration, which was controlled by the British. When World War I ended, the Jews in Palestine were fewer than 10 percent of the population. In 1939 they were nearly 30 percent. After the Balfour Declaration Great Britain was under an obligation to permit some immigration. With the growth of persecution in Germany and elsewhere in Europe Britain came under further pressure to increase the influx of immigrants. The Arabs revolted in 1936 in order to reduce this flow and as war in Europe approached, Great Britain first tried to reconcile the irreconcilable and then in 1939 promised that Jewish immigration would be limited to a further 75,000 with no increase beyond that number without Arab assent. (In return the Jews were offered a counterveto on a grant of sovereignty to the Arabs.) This capitulation saved the British position in the Arab world during World War II but not after it. In 1941 Great Britain was able to resist an anti-British government in Iraq, and in 1942 it coerced the

King of Egypt into appointing a government chosen by the British rather than by himself.

III. British Policy After World War II

After World War II the British position appeared at first sight stronger than ever. It had not only survived the war but had contributed to victory; the French had been eliminated; the Russian attempt to keep a footing in Iran had been deflected. But appearances were deceptive. The British will for empire had been ebbing for a long time—perhaps even since it was formed —and their departure from India in 1947 operated like a switch turning off a circuit where the current does not immediately cease to flow altogether. Equally important was the continuing growth of national self-consciousness among the Arabs, causing arrangements such as had subsisted between the two world wars to be unacceptable after the second. This nationalism was divided and confused between a loyalty to the Arab nation as a whole and a growing loyalty to the particular states which, for longer (Egypt) or shorter (Iraq, Syria) periods, figured on the map; but either way it was hostile to British rule. British power, therefore, although still formidable, was increasingly restrained by the circumstances in which it had to operate: the environment was growing more hostile.

Egypt, Jordan, and Iraq

Ernest Bevin's policy after 1945 was to modify but not essentially change the relationship between Great Britain and its semidependent states in the western and northern parts of the Middle East: Egypt, Jordan, Iraq. New treaties were negotiated (the Bevin-Sidki agreement for Egypt and the Treaty of Portsmouth for Iraq) but neither came into effect. There was a third force in Middle East politics and it was now strong enough to impose a veto on arrangements which it did not like. This was the force of popular feeling, a mixture of nationalism and rowdyism. In both Cairo and Baghdad it prevented ratification of new treaties to prolong the old relationship. The touchstone of Middle East politics was the way in which people reacted to the sequence of foreign dominations they had endured for centuries, and a more forthright rejection of this domination, expressed in streets and newspapers, gained acceptance over the more accommodating or Fabian attitudes of the ruling élites.

This failure in the principal centers of influence in the Arab world was compounded by the collapse of British power in Palestine. The British retreat from Palestine opened many eyes, especially since it coincided with the abandonment by Great Britain of tutelary commitments in Greece and Turkey. Together with the failure to refashion and extend treaty relationships with Egypt and Iraq, the British departure left policy in the Middle East in a state of disarray—a condition that contributed to the disastrous throwback to anachronistic attitudes exemplified, and finally exploded, by the conflict of 1956 over the Suez Canal.

In the interval between the disappointments of the immediate postwar years and the Suez war, British thinking about the Middle East was still imprisoned by the past. It was difficult for Great Britain to think of the countries of the Middle East in the same way as other countries. It seemed natural and even necessary to think of them in a special way, as the United States thinks of Central America in a special way. This was partly the imprint on the British mind of the facts of British imperial control in the past, but it was also a consequence of continuing and genuine concern about two issues: bases and stability.

Despite the departure from India, Ceylon, and Burma, Great Britain retained responsibilities and forces in the Far East (it was about to fight a prolonged campaign in Malaya), and the day had not yet come when it would be feasible to send men and supplies to these parts by the west-about route. The Middle East with its air fields and the Suez Canal remained a part of a British imperial system not yet extinguished, and if there were to be no base in Palestine it became all the more important for Great Britain to retain the bases and facilities it possessed along the Canal and at Aden as well as the overfly and landing rights it possessed in Iraq and elsewhere. In terms of what lay beyond the Middle East these rights were still extremely valuable. But in terms of the Middle East itself a new argument arose about the real value of bases whose resented existence bedevilled political relations with the countries in the area and which could even be rendered worthless by hostile activities.

Anti-British riots in the Canal Zone pointed the argument but it was only finally resolved in favor of evacuation and the total relinquishment of a privileged military position when technological change began to offer alternative ways of getting about the world without impinging on the sovereignty of Middle Eastern states. This period therefore was one of gradual acceptance of the need to go, a restless and unsatisfactory search for interim local alternatives (Cyprus), and an attempt to preserve in multilateral form (the Middle East Defense Organization—MEDO—and the Baghdad Pact) the bilateral advantages which were slipping from Great Britain's grasp.

The second major preoccupation was stability. Great Britain, like the Ottoman Empire, had contributed to stability in the Middle East. Stability was not only desirable for its own sake (always excepting underdogs) but was a prerequisite for the steady extraction and flow of oil, a flow that increased spectacularly both in quantity and in importance for Western industrialized countries during these years. In addition, the major operating oil companies included a substantial British capital investment and, as the Iranian crisis of 1951-1954 demonstrated, they employed British citizens whose fate might at times become a matter of active concern for a British government. Given the right circumstances a military presence is the simplest and most effective way of assuring the sort of stability which oil companies and oil consumers want, but in conditions of waxing xenophobia a military presence may create more trouble than it forfends. By the 1950s the political conditions for the exercise of military power had so far worsened that oil companies began to wonder whether they would not be better off without the provocation aroused by their would-be protectors. They were exhorted to remember that other big overseas operators in other parts of the world without such protection had to rely on the economic appetites of local governments to ensure the continuance of a mutually advantageous commerce; and they reconciled themselves to the fact that the withdrawal of British arms from the area was in any case inevitable. British policy in the Middle East became for a period a matter of timetables rather than objectives.

Aden

As British power lessened, the division of the Middle East into distinct fragments became more evident. In Egypt and the Fertile Crescent, Great Britain tried, first, to retain a special relationship and then, when this failed, to move toward a more normal state-to-state relationship, hampered however by the legacy of the unequal past and by the pervasive Arab-Israeli conflict in which Great Britain and other Western states were cast by the Arabs in the role of crypto-imperialist progenitor. The Arabs refused to believe (and after the Suez conflict could hardly be expected to believe) that the West had not connived at the creation of Israel in order to retain a base for meddling in Middle Eastern affairs. This aspect of Great Britain's involvement in the Middle East applied by extension also to bases beyond the immediate area of Egypt and the Fertile Crescent, and notably to Aden, which was regarded by the British as a colony to be retained or emancipated in Great Britain's own good time but was to Egypt just one more British base that, in Cato's insistent phrase, must be destroyed.

Aden was a British colony properly so called, the only one in the Middle East. It was the most visible outward sign of the importance of the Middle East to Great Britain as an Asian power. Before becoming a British colony in 1937 it had for about a century been an appendage first of the Bombay Presidency and then of the government of India. The end of empire in India, Malaya, and Singapore reduced it first from a necessity to a convenience and then from a convenience to an inconvenience. The final solution in 1968 was creditable to nobody. It was complicated by the civil war in neighboring Yemen which brought the conflict between Nasser's Egypt and Faisal's Saudi Arabia into the southwestern corner of the Arabian Peninsula and to the strait which (as Suez guards the northern) guards the southern entry into the Red Sea. The struggle in Aden prolonged anti-British feeling in Cairo for years, while anti-French feeling had been abated by the French withdrawal from Algeria and by de Gaulle's overt anti-American attitudes. Equally, Egypt's help for Adeni nationalists who were trying to throw the British out of Aden in the same way as the Zionists had thrown them out of Palestine prolonged anti-Egyptian bitterness in London. It was an untidy and sorry denouement in which the British felt that they had been cheated of the imperialist's last gratification, that of leaving behind him a stable, working system.

But if the problem of Aden became a particular offshoot of the problem of relations between Great Britain and Arab nationalism, Great Britain's position in the Persian Gulf on the eastern rim of the Arab world had features all its own. Here were oil politics at their most sensitive and here too were British treaty commitments of a special kind. Whereas in Egypt and Iraq Great Britain had been seeking to make treaties, in the Persian Gulf Great Britain came to wish that it had never made the ones by which it was bound: in the Persian Gulf the boot was on the other leg. The sense and fact of obligation, plus the extent of the commercial and financial stake, made the question whether to go or stay in the Gulf a more vexed one than the similar problem in Aden.

The Persian Gulf

The Persian Gulf stretches for 500 miles from the Strait of Hormuz, where the opposite shores approach to within 50 miles of each other, to the head of the Gulf where Iraq marches on the one side with Iran and on the other with the small principality of Kuwait, both of them uneasily. The whole of the eastern shore of the Gulf is uncontested Iranian territory. The western shore belongs mainly but not entirely to Saudi Arabia. Southward from Kuwait are 350 miles of Saudi coastline. Then comes the island principality of Bahrein, the promontory of Qatar and the seven states collectively known as the Trucial States which constitute an arm of land reaching eastward to form the Strait of Hormuz. South of the Strait lies the more extensive sultanate of Muscat and Oman occupying the southeastern corner of the Arabian peninsula and washed by the Gulf of Oman to the east and the Indian Ocean to the south. Thus 13 Arab sovereigns dispute the eastern coastal territories of the Arabian Peninsula and some of them—Iraq, Saudi Arabia, Bahrein—have also been the object of claims by Iran, as has the bed of the Persian Gulf itself. The smaller states, between but excluding

Kuwait at the one end and Muscat at the other, owed their survival to the British presence which prevented the newly established Saudi state from appropriating them in the 1920s. Kuwait survived for similar reasons and also because it was a prize coveted by two nabobs; Muscat because of its somewhat greater strength and inaccessibility. To a cartographer it might appear reasonably obvious that all these states, except possibly Kuwait but including eventually Yemen, would one day be swallowed up by Saudi Arabia. Politics not geography stood in the way of Arabian sovereignty, and politics meant the British, so long as they stayed. But as soon as the British began leaving the nature of politics changed.

Great Britain's commitment in Kuwait was both more recent than its commitments further south and of a different nature. There was no treaty until 1899 and the making of a treaty in that year was not prompted by the need to impose or maintain local order; it was a move in the British game to block German or Russian expansion to the Persian Gulf at a time when Great Britain's direct influence on the Sultan of the Ottoman Empire had declined and was being assumed by other European powers. After World War II Kuwait became fabulously rich and, under the guidance of a sophisticated ruling family, moved to independence and separate membership of the Arab League and the United Nations in 1961. At the moment of independence a threat, or supposed threat, from Iraq caused the ruler to solicit British aid under a treaty on which the ink was scarcely dry, but once this crisis was past the special relationship between Great Britain and Kuwait ended and the 1961 treaty lapsed seven years later. British intervention in 1961 was chiefly significant for the boost it gave to the British feeling that Great Britain still had a role to play in the Persian Gulf.

The basis of this role lay in the origins of the British presence in an area of a rather peculiar nature. The states round the Gulf constitute a system or subsystem within the Middle East as a whole which derives such coherence as it has, not from terra firma, but from its waters. It is a maritime system bounded by shores and not a territorial system defined by the more familiar natural limits of rivers or mountain ranges or seas. Great Britain came to the area to pacify and patrol these waters which were a happy hunting ground for pirates. The Trucial States were then known as the Pirate Coast and the British navy, fumigating what had been a backwater, made life safer for pearl fishers at the same time that it swept its orderly broom along and around Great Britain's imperial routes. But Great Britain was not then concerned with the lands of the Gulf as opposed to its waters.

Great Britain's first formal involvement in this part of the world took place in the eighteenth century when, following Napoleon's excursion into the Middle East, Great Britain made the treaty already referred to with the Sultan of Muscat and Oman. The engagements that were to become characteristic of British activity in the Persian Gulf were not initiated until the middle of the nineteenth century. These concerned the seven Trucial States lining the southern shore of the Gulf; in effect, they turned these states into semidependent protectorates. In return for the protection of their shores against the pirates who interfered with their pearl fishing, the rulers of these states surrendered control of their external affairs (such as they then were) to Great Britain. By a treaty of 1853 Great Britain undertook to suppress piracy and establish a truce in place of continuous maritime brigandage. A generation later, in 1893, these states agreed not to give up any of their territory except to Great Britain. Yet another generation ahead, in 1922, the Gulf states further promised not to grant oil concessions without British assent. By this time piracy had been forgotten and pearl fishing superseded by the whiff of oil, but the British obligation to the rulers remained no more than the original undertaking to protect them from attacks from the sea. What had changed was not the British commitment to the Trucial States, but the nature and extent of the British interest in the Gulf.

To Qatar, however, a promontory that juts northward into the Gulf at the western end of the Trucial coast, Great Britain gave during World War I a more far-reaching promise. In 1916 Great Britain undertook to protect Qatar against attack from the landward side and against any attempt to overthrow its government by violence, which amounted to a promise to defend Qatar against the Turks. But within a few years the Turks had retreated thousands of miles from Qatar, and Qatar was nervously eyeing the new Saudi Arabian state. This contingency was reduced to only comparative insignificance in 1964 when Saudi Arabia and Qatar formally resolved the issues between them.

The British undertaking to Qatar had a precedent in the strategically and commercially more important state of Bahrein, an island lying between the tip of Qatar and the Saudi coast. By a treaty of 1881, reaffirmed in 1951 and 1966, Great Britain promised to protect Bahrein against external attack. In return Bahrein undertook not to part with any of its territory or to grant oil concessions without British assent. The pattern was the same: Great Britain secured a veto on the transfer of land and of oil to any outsider save itself in return for a promise to preserve the integrity and independence of states whose integrity and independence had become in any case a major British interest owing to their commercial potential and strategic location. When, however, Great Britain began to think of leaving the Gulf it was embarrassed by the inevitability, as it seemed, that Iran would revive a latent claim to Bahrein, threaten the independence of the state, clash in consequence with Saudi Arabia, and produce general turmoil in the Gulf. This embarrassing and disagreeable prospect was, however, somewhat reduced when the Iranian and Saudi monarchs resolved to compose their differences before the British departed and in 1968 made an outward show of doing so.

But if a clash between major local powers in the wake of the British departure was rendered less likely by the graduation of Kuwait to viable independence and hopes of a peaceful settlement of Saudi-Iranian differences, the continuing independence of the minor Persian Gulf principalities was clearly endangered. As independent states they were anomalous, too small to defend themselves, too rich (some of them) to be left alone. Geography seemed to have designed them to be a part of a large peninsular Arabian state.

Great Britain's moral and paternal senses revolted against the idea that those whom the British abandoned were being consigned to a fate less than independence. Great Britain therefore sponsored, with a certain painful repetitiveness, the last in the series of its postwar federations whereby the several weaknesses of its former wards in the Gulf might be welded into a jointed strength. After some hesitations the rulers executed, at least on paper, a federation whose sole purpose was to balk Saudi Arabia. It seems doubtful, however, whether any such design can do more than give a few British officials and observers the illusion of having done the right thing. It is also doubtful whether, apart perhaps from the rulers themselves and their close relatives, anybody will be worse off when their principalities lose an independence which in recent times has never been more than formal, and in some cases, no more than an expression of Great Britain's power to arrange the map. There is no law which says that a Trucial monarch makes a better monarch than a Saudi monarch.

The British retreat from the Gulf marked the end of a quarter century of readjustment that began with the surrender of the Palestine Mandate in 1948. There will be debate for a long time to come about whether the readjustment could have been better managed. Presumably it could, since nothing in politics is ever perfectly managed. The record was blackened by the Suez war in 1956, a venture of the most extreme lunacy and also a delict under international law, but apart from this one damaging extravagance the story is of a kind more familiar to historians, a genuinely perplexing variety of interests and events with which statesmen can only grapple with the limited prevision and the fallible sense of timing vouchsafed to them.

In these 25 years Great Britain receded from the position of outstanding power and authority which it had enjoyed as the inheritor of the lion's share of the Ottoman's Arab dominions to one of a number of outside powers with equivalent interests in the area. This shift in the nature of Great Britain's interests and capacities was masked, first, by the comparatively effortless assertion of British power during World War II all the way from Cairo to Baghdad; second, by the half-heartedness of the Arab challenge to the British in a generation still partially dominated by the Anglophile attitudes within Arab ruling élites; and third, by the reluctance of the yet greater powers, the United States and the Soviet Union, to form their own policies and to claim their prerogatives of power in this part of the world.

For a decade the Russians were preoccupied with domestic postwar problems of reconstruction and restoring Communist Party rule, with the creation of a new kind of imperium in Eastern Europe, and with other moves in the cold war. After tentative and unsuccessful ventures in the Northern (non-Arab) Tier they remained, until Stalin's death, spectators. But their concern with the area was well known and not forgotten. For the U.S.S.R. as much as for Great Britain, the Middle East is a pathway to the Indian Ocean and the East; in addition, for the U.S.S.R., it is the route to Africa and a route to southern Europe too. Further, the Middle East is adjacent to the U.S.S.R. itself, so that Turkey and Iran are to the U.S.S.R. what Mexico is to the United States, and the Arab lands have for Moscow the same sort of significance as have the Caribbean islands for Washington.

The British, for whom the Middle East had been for over a century a means for blocking Russian influence and restraining it, found it natural to go on playing this role but wondered how they would be able to do so without American assistance. Churchill thought of converting the British position in the Middle East into an Anglo-American one. He proposed as much to the U.S. Congress. His proposal was received with a stunning silence. For Americans the British position in the Middle East was a colonial one, deplorable and anachronistic. They had no thought of sharing it, for sharing it meant putting American forces into the Suez Canal Zone and aligning themselves with British imperialism. It meant, and they probably read Churchill's intentions correctly, buttressing a position which Great Britain was ready to modify but not to modernize. Americans had had misgivings during the war about major campaigns in the Mediterranean and North Africa which seemed to them designed to preserve British power in the eastern Mediterranean and the Middle East (and French power at the western end). When faced with a direct issue of supporting Great Britain in the Middle East in the Iranian oil crisis of 1951, the Americans did so after considerable hesitation and primarily in the conviction that Mossadegh's challenge to the Shah was opening the way to Communist and Russian influence in Teheran; Mossadegh's challenge to the Anglo-Iranian Oil Company and to the "sanctity of contract" which so flustered the British moved them little, if at all.

IV. The Anglo-American Alliance

Great Britain's imperial past precluded an entente with the United States in areas where the British flag had flown as prominently as it had in the Middle East—except upon the basis of a striking break with the past. The ghosts of gunboats had their say. In order to secure such a partnership Great Britain would have had to make far more radical changes in its Middle Eastern policy than it was contemplating. Yet for the British the alternatives were an Anglo-American presence or, soon, no British presence at all. Both alternatives entailed radical change, but Great Britain saw the former as a way of avoiding radical change. So the chance was, for good or ill, missed. It took some years for Great Britain to appreciate the starkness of the choice (it became inescapable after Suez) and to see that, with the Americans rejecting the sort of dual control which Churchill had in mind, the problem for Great Britain was reduced to how and when to remove its physical presence. By the late 1950s Great Britain was plainly on the way out everywhere in the Middle East. But also in the 1950s American attitudes changed: an Anglo-American partnership in the Middle East was becoming less unattractive. Great Britain no longer seemed bound in imperialistic colonialism and the United States had been driven by the cold war and an overriding anti-Communist attitude to take a more lenient view of its Western European friends. (How could a government in Washington which wanted bases in Morocco, wanted to get France to swallow German rearmament, and was worried about the replacement of French by Chinese influence in Indochina, go on condemning France as an unregenerate colonial power? Was it not redeemed by its anti-Communism? The same applied to Great Britain.) But it was too late to halt the British withdrawal. Great Britain had become convinced not only of the fragility and disadvantages of its traditional involvement in Middle Eastern affairs but also, more generally, that an all-encompassing world role no longer suited its circumstances. Throughout the quarter century under review British and American policies were out of phase.

Yet Great Britain could not leave the Middle East without a backward glance. The habit of regarding Middle Eastern countries as different was ingrained. A special British presence had come to be regarded as natural and beneficent, a responsibility at least as much as an advantage. Abandoning this position was a humiliation which was assuaged by the view that it would go ill with the area after the British had left and that many people would wake up to discover that they regretted the British departure. The chaos and stagnation in Aden in 1968 were not entirely unwelcome to bruised British pride. A year later traditionalists (particularly in the Conservative Party) were striving to persuade themselves that the courtesies extended to them by the rulers in the Persian Gulf amounted to invitations to stay. But such confusion had little relevance to future policy. It was hardly more indicative of future attitudes, for it was plausible to surmise that the British experience in the Middle East would leave them (with the exception of oil men and a few strategists and specialists) peculiarly averse to Middle Eastern affairs. The romance that had played so large a part in forming popular British attitudes, the legends of the Bible lands, of Lady Hester Stanhope, of the great travelers from Palgrave to Philby, of camels and Bedouin, and the silence of deserts and mosques, had been too heavily overlaid by rebuff.

Looking forward, another problem still nagged at the end of the first quarter of a century after World War II. It concerned not specifically the Middle East but the nature of the Anglo-American alliance and Great Britain's role in it. Middle East policies were, or could be, an item in the alliance, since alliance policy, if conceived in one way, could induce Great Britain to accede to American strategic wishes, and these wishes might include British support in the wide area which stretches from the eastern Mediterranean to the western Indian Ocean. The United States might not wish Great Britain to have old-style bases in the Middle East but it expressed alarm and displeasure when the British government announced in 1968 that it would abandon its remaining positions in the Middle East by 1971. British policy in the Middle East, while losing much of its distinctive Middle Eastern motivation, was influenced by British assessments of the weight to be given to American wishes to aid the Anglo-American alliance.

The Anglo-American alliance became an overriding and all-absorbing object of British policy when France was defeated by Germany in 1940. From that point it became impossible for the British to return to the continent and beat the Germans without American help. Compared with this nothing else signified. The alliance was achieved; it triumphed, and it became invested with an emotional and mystic quality over and above its original pragmatic aims. It also acquired fresh pragmatic justification when the cold war began and the support of the United States against Stalin in Europe assumed a paramountcy hardly less absolute than the need for American support against Hitler a few years earlier. For Great Britain the Anglo-American relationship was special because (quite apart from the unusual relationship between Churchill and Roosevelt which was personal and ephemeral) it was seen as an overriding aim of British policy in perpetuity. Both Conservative and Labour governments have adopted this view, or have acted as though they had, in a degree unobservable in any other ally of the United States, whether a considerable European state like Italy, or a dependent like South Korea. Since for so many years Great Britain had handled its alliance with the United States in a special way, it is at the very least possible that it will continue to do so. There is, however, no other reason why Great Britain should act in future in the Middle East or in the seas which reach up to it in any way differently from other leading European states.

The establishment of paramount American influence in the Middle East is not a British interest *per se*. But the prevention of paramount Russian influence may be. Support for American policies and American power in the Middle East will be the more justified in British eyes insofar as it is effective and the only way of blocking Russian hegemony. There are, at least in theory, two other ways of blocking this hegemony. The one, which was favored by Curzon and other British statesmen earlier in this century in relation to Iran, is to come to terms with the Russians, delimit spheres of influence and so prevent the exclusive power of one state by agreeing upon a form of coexistence and partition. This way no longer seems open. The disparity in power between the Soviet Union and Great Britain is probably too great and it is in any case doubtful whether the growth of national self-consciousness within the Middle East any longer permits this kind of veiled, cooperative imperialism. If there are to be spheres of influence in the Middle East as there have been in Europe since the end of World War II, they will be worked out between the Soviet Union and the United States, and not between the Soviet Union and Great Britain. The second way in which a Russian hegemony could be staved off is by the growth of indigenous power sufficiently strong to maintain the independence of the area. Great Britain, which has in the past toyed with Arab unity first as a way of destroying the Ottoman hegemony and then as a way of mediating British hegemony, could now favor Arab unity as a barrier to overmastering Russian power. But this too is a more than doubtful starter. If Arab unity means a single Arab state, it seems to be a remote and receding possibility. If it means continuing joint action by Arab states —a predictable consensus such as the Scandinavians have to a large extent achieved—then this too has so fragile a basis in observable current realities that it can hardly enter into practical policymaking. Nor is it easy to see what Great Britain could do to foster Arab unity, even supposing that this unity were to be adopted as a practical aim of British policy.

Great Britain's day as a military power in and around the Middle East is done—not because Great Britain is not still very much stronger than the states of the Middle East (it is in fact far more powerful than all of them put together) but because the exercise of this kind of power no longer makes sense in terms of British interests or in terms of the political evolution of the Middle East itself. The British will continue to be seen in the Middle East—out of uniform—and they will come to regard themselves, as they are already regarded by Middle Easterners, not as very special people but simply as Europeans—or, as Lucius Aelius Commodus, the Emperor of Rome, called them, Franks.

To speculate further about the British role, even in the near future, is unjustifiable. The base for any such speculation is too slight. It can only produce generalizations which either are obvious or cannot be substantiated. It seems certain that Great Britain will continue to need Middle Eastern oil in large quantities. This assumption is at any rate strong enough to loom large in the minds of politicians and officials responsible for policy-planning. Only one other thing is reasonably certain: that Great Britain has ceased to play an independent role in the Middle East. The renunciation of the British position in the Persian Gulf was the final act and it cannot be retracted. As soon as Great Britain's departure was announced, and before it began to be implemented, the question whether the British should stay in the Gulf or leave it became a historical one, a question for debate by historians not politicians. Although occasioned partly by financial stringency, Britain's departure was not just a decision about the cost of staying in the Persian Gulf; it marked the recognition of a change in the relationship between Great Britain and the entire Middle East.

It follows that Middle Eastern issues are likely to play an ever decreasing part in British politics. This is already observable in relation to the Arab-Israeli problem. Whereas a generation earlier this issue would have been at the heart of British politics, in the 1960s it was restricted to the fervid partisans of one side or the other. Older people, who had known the Middle East or known about it from the period of British dominance, retained a special interest, but their juniors were (partisans apart) concerned only in a more general way: either because war in the Middle East seemed to portend a wider war, or because they deemed it unbecoming for Great Britain to be left out of the diplomatic maneuvering in which the United States, the Soviet Union, and France were engaged. There was also a sense of duty, a feeling that a power like Great Britain with a fleet like the royal navy and a major armaments industry ought to use the one and control the other in the general interest. To this extent self-esteem and international responsibility combine to recommend to Great Britain a contributory role in place of its former independent role, rather than no role at all.

How and how far such a concept may be expressed at a given moment and in a given situation it is impossible to predict, for a contributory role is not only uncharacteristic of Great Britain as a former imperial power (there are neither precedents nor aptitudes), but is also a compromise implying peculiar difficulty in judging which way the compromise will go. This compromise is between, on the one hand, habit and pride which point to action and, on the other hand, circumstances and sense which counsel inaction. The Six-Day War in 1967 showed the British in two minds and showed too how, in that case at any rate, the new mind prevailed over the old. Great Britain had promised to help keep open the Straits of Tiran. It put forward proposals for doing so by sailing ships through them. Yet it did in fact nothing. Why? Not merely because the war ended so quickly, nor because of any calculated preference for one side or the other but, rather, because the issue of war or peace in the Middle East no longer mattered enough to Great Britain. Concomitant with this has come about a change of style in Great Britain's acting in the world beyond Europe— a change of style that is best summed up by saying that the British are fast losing that sense of responsibility which made them policemen in the general interest when and where they find themselves protecting their peculiar interests.

It comes down therefore to the peculiar interests, for it was only upon this basis that the more general role existed. The Middle East was the critical point in the route to India and the East. It still is, but to Great Britain the route itself is no longer critical. Safeguarding the route meant, primarily, keeping the Russians away. But the Russians have now established themselves in the Middle East; they have broken through the barrier; they have the naval bases which the British used to have in the Middle East and they are building up the naval power which the British used to have in the Indian Ocean. Keeping Russians out of the Middle East is a lost cause.

Yet there remains in the end the question of oil. The importance of Middle Eastern oil to Great Britain is uncontested. At the back of the British mind lurks the feeling that something terrible could one day be done to deprive Great Britain of this oil. This is the imponderable in the situation. The continuing need for oil fortifies the romantic reactionaries who want to make a case for continuing British activity and display. The Suez war of 1956 dealt this school a blow which, the decade thereafter, looked like a mortal one. The prevailing view has been that the oil flow will be, or will have to be, secured some other way—by the operation of the market or by the political involvement of the United States which, willy-nilly and like Great Britain in the past, will be securing not only its own interests but also and incidentally those of other countries. The thesis of this chapter is that this view will continue to prevail, in spite of tugs and doubts. If this is so, then the ending of Great Britain's independent role in the Middle East will be total and will not be replaced by a contributory role of any lasting consequence.

CHAPTER 13

Western Europe and the Middle East

Pierre Rondot

I. Western Europe's Attitudes toward the Middle East

The area referred to by the Anglo-Saxons as the "Middle East" is preferably called the "Near East" by the peoples of continental Europe. This term suggests that Europeans feel they are not far away from this area, geographically or otherwise.

For a long time Western Europe nations have taken an interest in the countries of the Middle East. They were rivals in diplomacy, in commerce, sometimes in culture, but never in war. It is indeed remarkable that nations which so often and so vigorously fought each other on the soil of their own continent (and even in Africa) never had occasion to fight in the Middle East. It is tempting to consider this as proof of a certain community of interests more parallel than competitive.

Hence it seems legitimate in the present study to examine the general attitudes of the continental nations of Western Europe toward the Middle East before considering in greater detail particular attitudes among those nations most concerned, Italy, the Federal Republic of Germany (F.R.G.), and France. Great Britain must be considered as a power with special interests and attitudes in the Middle East, and is therefore excluded from the discussion except where mentioned specifically.

But for a few exceptions to be indicated as they arise, the powers of Western Europe all share three aspects of foreign policy in relation to their position in the Middle East: (1) no direct political commitments in the area; (2) no worldwide responsibilities having repercussions or requiring a special attitude in the Middle East; (3) interests that are primarily nonpolitical. It is thus possible for the nations of the Middle East to enjoy free and profitable relationships with the European peninsula; Europe is, as it were, at the Middle East's disposal.

Political Interests in the Middle East

With a few exceptions, the countries of Western Europe are not, or are no longer, politically engaged in the Middle East.

The position of these continental powers is quite different from that of Great Britain, the United States, or the Soviet Union. For several years to come, Britain will still be politically engaged in the Persian Gulf through

her treaty of alliance with Kuwait, the advisory treaties with the states of
the Trucial coast, and her liaison with Muscat; she will also be militarily
engaged through her bases, garrisons, and a small naval force in the Persian
Gulf; she is a member of CENTO which binds her to Turkey and Iran;
and she has military bases at Cyprus. The United States and the Soviet
Union keep powerful naval forces in the Mediterranean and they are considered, rightly or wrongly, as patronizing various Middle Eastern states
(Israel and Saudi Arabia, on one hand; the United Arab Republic, the
Syrian Arab Republic, and Southern Yemen, on the other).

A number of Western European countries, while exerting limited political
influence, have real importance on the cultural, economic, and moral levels;
these include the Scandinavian countries, Belgium, the Netherlands, Switzerland, Spain, and other countries that have never been involved in the
political affairs of the Middle East.

Other countries have been politically involved at various periods, some
of them until recently: Italy and Germany until their defeats of El Alamein
and Stalingrad (1942); France until the crisis of Suez (1956) or, because
of Arab solidarity, until the decolonization of Algeria (1962). The brutal
character of these events has produced a complete change in attitude in
which former attitudes are rapidly being obliterated. Because of an overall
doctrine governing her international relations, the F.R.G. (to be discussed
further below) has entered the Middle Eastern political scene once again,
and is directly involved in local conflicts. Also, a section of French public
opinion has differed with the Paris government's policy of disengagement.

Two other current attitudes deserve mention. Greece is engaged in the
Cyprus case by virtue of Hellenism, and Portugal, while absent from
present-day Middle Eastern affairs, is discredited with Arab public opinion
because of her colonial position in Africa.

No continental power of Western Europe has any commitments of worldwide scope that imply a particular attitude toward the Middle East for
reasons of general policy. It is true that General de Gaulle's attitude toward
the Middle East reflected his wider conception of world policy. But his
view appears to be only an episode in the evolution of French foreign policy.

In this respect the position of these countries differs greatly from that
of the United States or the Soviet Union, for whom the Middle East represents an element of a world strategy. These two great powers are likely to
consider Middle Eastern affairs in relation to events happening in parts of
the world which, for them, are more important—Southeast Asia at present,
for instance.

Although without political involvements on a worldwide scale, some
European states are constrained in their attitudes toward the Middle East
by a certain moral responsibility or a preferential attachment to activities

on other continents. For example, the political attitude of the F.R.G. reflects a moral responsibility toward the Jewish people because of the memory of the Nazi genocide. In France, too, an important section of public opinion is responsive to the Jewish people. While Israel is turning this support to account, the Arabs are complaining about a "worldwide Jewish plot." They are happy to see, as a counterinfluence, that in Spain, among others, there is no sympathy for the Jew. In February, 1970, Spain confirmed again that it does not intend to enter diplomatic relations with Israel. The preferential treatment France gives to the French-speaking states of sub-Saharan Africa in dispensing her assistance restricts a portion of the financial means she may devote to the Middle East.

Nonpolitical Interests in the Middle East

European interests in the Middle East have far more of a nonpolitical than a political character. Although both the United States and the Soviet Union also have many nonpolitical interests in the Middle East, the peoples of the Middle East believe that political interests take precedence for the superpowers, in general, except where petroleum is concerned. In this respect, Britian's position is similar to that of the European states, although a discussion of British interests in the Middle East lies outside the scope of this study.

It is not the writer's intention to compile an exhaustive inventory in this paper; yet, with the reservation that several of the elements mentioned here will be taken up again in connection with Italy, the F.R.G., and France, the writer has provided lists of some nonpolitical interests of Europe's continental powers and the relationships which arise from them to indicate the quality of European interests there. The items are grouped under general subject headings and the countries sharing these interests are included in parentheses at the end of the items.

Economics

1. Exploration and exploitation of oil in the Arab countries. (Mainly France, but also Italy and others.)
2. Purchase of various Oriental products such as high-quality raw cotton from Egypt, Syria, Turkey, etc. (France, Germany, Italy, Belgium, Switzerland.)
3. Citrus fruit from Israel and Arab countries. (Germany, Scandinavian countries, Belgium, the Netherlands, Switzerland, etc. French interest in these products competes with her interest in North African products.)
4. Dried fruit and tobacco from Turkey. (Germany and others.)

5. Arrival of Turkish and other Middle Eastern laborers in Western Europe. (F.R.G., Belgium, Switzerland.)
6. Economic and financial aid. (Various Western powers.)
7. Sale in the Middle East of European equipment, goods, and manufactured products, facilitated for some Middle Eastern countries by the credit balance resulting from the oil, cotton, and other exports.
8. Large public works such as dams, electrification projects, roads, etc. (Italy, Germany, France.)
9. The commerce of airlines. (France, F.R.G., Italy, Belgium, the Netherlands, Switzerland, the Scandinavian countries.)[1]
10. The commerce of shipping. (Italy, Greece.)
11. The application by Middle Eastern countries for membership in the European Economic Community (EEC): for example, Turkey was accepted for a time; Israel has applied seriously; several Arab countries, especially the United Arab Republic, are showing an interest.

Science and Technology

1. Bilateral or multilateral technical assistance.
2. Technical relations necessary for the presence of large companies, including local training of skilled labor and managing personnel.
3. Scientific and technical training in local institutes or universities, or in European institutions.
4. The technical, administrative, and legal know-how acquired during the French Mandate in Syria and Lebanon.

Military Technology

1. The acquisition of the latest armaments developed in Europe, especially from France and Germany, Belgium, Sweden, and Spain.
2. Technical assistance for the local manufacture of armaments. (German specialists, sometimes former Nazis, in the United Arab Republic; a cartridge factory established by a French firm in Saudi Arabia, etc.)
3. The prestige of military training received from certain European

---

[1]Sometimes these economic relations have given rise to political difficulties. After an Israeli plane taking off from the Zurich airport in Switzerland was attacked by PFLP guerrillas on February 18, 1969, the attackers were tried and convicted by a Swiss court in Winterthur. The verdict, passed December 22, 1969, sentenced three Jordanians to 12 years in prison. Later, after two explosions occurred aboard aircraft in flight, one Swissair, the other Austrian Airlines, on February 21, 1970, the Swiss took precautionary measures. A number of Arab countries criticized Switzerland, reacting angrily against the Swiss actions. These occurrences have cooled Arab-Swiss relations, at least temporarily.

countries. (Germany, with which are associated the memories of the former missions of the Ottoman Empire; France, where fairly large numbers of officers and cadets are receiving instruction; Italy.)

Linguistics and Culture

1. Local use of continental European languages (such as Italian, German, Greek). French, especially in Lebanon and among certain élites, is profitable not only for France, but also for Switzerland and Belgium, where French is the mother tongue of a large section of the population.[2]
2. The long-established presence of Catholic and Protestant missionary schools and of hospitals. (Mainly French, but also Italian, German, Swiss, and Danish.)
3. The more recent creation of lay teaching establishments; the activities of the *Alliance israélite universelle,* French foundation which is over 100 years old. These institutions have played a considerable role in the modern intellectual and social evolution of the Middle East.
4. Cultural technical assistance.
5. Archeological missions in the Middle East, excavations, museums, and institutes. (France, Italy, Germany, Belgium.)
6. Visits to Europe by large numbers of students. (France, Germany, Italy, Belgium, Switzerland.)

Personal Relations

1. The existence of small but socially, economically, and intellectually important groups of French, Italian, Greek, and other nationals in the Middle East.
2. Traveling, including tourism, student trips, etc., all of which are encouraged by the geographical proximity, thus establishing basic contacts for personal relationships.
3. Cities like Rome, Geneva, Paris, etc., the prestige of which attracts numerous Middle Easterners for study and from other motives, who on their return make known ways of living and fashions, both by their clothing and by their social and intellectual endeavors.

Religion

1. Islam (followed by the majority in the Middle East).
   a. The prestige of Islamic studies conducted in France, Italy, Spain, Germany, the Netherlands, etc., by such scholars of the past as L. Massignon, Nallino, Miguel Asin Palacios, Noeldeke, Snouck Hurgronje, etc., and by their present-day counterparts.

[2]This is partly true for Canada.

    b. The existence of some religious Muslim centers in continental Europe (Germany, Austria, France, etc.) and the Europeans who convert to Islam. (There was the case of René Guénon in France, and there have been others in Germany, Switzerland, Austria, and the Scandinavian countries.)

2. Judaism (followed by the majority in Israel).
    a. The social weight and the intellectual quality of French and Italian Jewry.
    b. The religious revival of part of the French Jewry under the influence of the practicing Jews who returned from North Africa.
    c. The affinities which the Jews born in Germany, Austria, and other countries kept with their countries of origin.

3. Christianity (followed by four-fifths of the population of Cyprus, half that of Lebanon, and a small but influential minority in Syria, Jordan, the U.A.R., and Kuwait.
    a. The attachment of the Christians from Western Europe to the holy places of Palestine (Jerusalem, Bethlehem, Nazareth), their pilgrimages, and the institutions that derive from them, such as *Custodie de Terre Sainte pour la garde du Saint Sepulcre* (Custody of the Holy Land for the Care of the Holy Sepulchre), a monastic community, primarily Italian, with some French and Spanish followers.[3]
    b. The memory and vestiges of the protection France once provided the Christians in the Middle East, and Austria the Greek-Catholics.[4]
    c. The religious and intellectual activities of Catholic and Protestant religious orders (of French, Italian, German, Belgian, Swiss, Danish, and other origin) among the Christians of the Middle East.
    d. The considerable prestige of Hellenic orthodoxy in Cyprus, and especially on the Levantine coast.
    e. The aura of the Holy See. This high authority is of course world-wide rather than European, yet in its geographical location and the origin of many of its dignitaries it retains a Western European aspect. The Pope is the head of the Catholic communities in the Middle East (including the ecclesiastical law courts which, in Lebanon and Israel, are still the authority on family law, and

[3]The Franciscan "Order of the Friars Minor" has long maintained the guardianship of shrines and holy places. The order is divided geographically into provinces; *Custodie de Terre Sainte pour la garde du Saint Sepulcre* is a provincial subgroup of this order. Ed.

[4]Russia also has extended protection to Orthodox Christians beyond Western Europe from the end of the 18th century.

which in the last resort depend on the Vatican); moreover, the Pope benefits by a lesser or greater prestige with the non-Catholic communities, and even among the Muslim élites.

European Influence

Western Europe continues to occupy a position of some importance in the Middle East. Many of the affinities and interests which have just been described may appear to be minor. It is in fact undeniable that in many areas, whether oil exploration or the wide use of the English language, Western Europe carries but little weight as compared with the Anglo-Saxon world. Further, the considerable power of Russia, which geographically is closer to the Middle East than Western Europe, is strongly felt as compared with the relative weakness of a reduced and divided Western Europe. These elements of the situation, although they cannot be repeated continuously, should always be borne in mind in the course of this study.

The sum of the interests and ties that Europe and the Middle East have shared, and still share, is nevertheless considerable; the European sphere of influence is increased by the fact that its very diversity diminishes the risk of a total break, and that there is no longer any political movement leaning toward supremacy of the West.

The Middle East is not vividly aware of the division between European nations. Quite to the contrary, Britain, which has had many political ties with the Middle East, is increasingly striving to make her presence felt there as a part of Europe, especially now that her political interests and her military presence in the area are waning.

Europe, because of its position apart from the antagonists, the United States and the Soviet Union, and because it has fewer direct or indirect intentions of supremacy than either of these two superpowers, appears to the Middle East as a possible alternative in its relations with the world.[5] The possibility of finding trade exchanges, technical assistance, and

[5]A parallel can be found in Eastern Europe. Romania, a nation now included in the Soviet bloc, has Western affinities through her Romanic origins and language as well as Eastern affinities through her Orthodox religion. After the Six-Day War in Palestine, she refrained from breaking off relations with Israel, but hastened to help the Egyptian people with wheat supplies that were relatively larger than those of the Soviet Union. Her policy is to exchange raw materials from the Middle East and the rest of the third world (Arabian and Iranian oils, Algerian and Indian iron ore) for Romanian industrial products (drilling material, tractors, machinery) thus achieving more economic independence from the Soviet Union. However, elevating to the rank of embassy the Romanian and Israeli diplomatic representations in the summer of 1969 prompted animosity among the Arab states, many of which suspended their diplomatic relations with Romania. Thus, by showing favoritism in view of the Arab states, Romania has lessened the equilibrium of her position.

intellectual openings outside the superpowers is pleasing to the Middle Eastern taste for equilibrium, bargaining and even overbidding. From economic exchange to political exchange, on their own initiative. Middle East nations think of policies such as that of "nonalignment," which aims in fact at excluding the superpowers and their military associates. Some even consider that certain states of Western Europe, such as France, might have their place among the "nonaligned."

But the very reasons that make Western Europe a desirable partner in the Middle East limit its possibilities for even disinterested action there, when important political issues are at stake. This seems to be true for a possible negotiated settlement of the Palestine problem. The F.R.G. is not involved because of her almost exclusive tie with one of the parties; Italy at first modestly but efficiently limited herself to facilitating arrangements of detail, while France, despite her more ambitious aims and possibly because of General de Gaulle's particular political style, was able only to make gestures in the way of conciliation—gestures, moreover, that were presented as part of a mission of the four great powers. (Later, however, France did take action for the limitation of arms supplies to the Middle East.) There are reasons to believe that, in this instance, a united Europe would have carried more weight.

While cautious of Middle Eastern overbidding and local conflicts, the nations of continental Western Europe derive from historical inheritance as well as present conditions the possibility of a limited but real "presence" in the Middle East.

Let us now examine three large states of continental Western Europe in greater detail: Italy, the F.R.G., and France.

II. Italy and the Middle East

Italy has been united for only a short 100 years. But from the Middle Ages on, the citizens of the numerous Italian republics and principalities showed a remarkable presence and activity in the Levant, the countries bordering on the eastern Mediterranean. Despite mixed memories still remaining from the Fascist regime, Italy's long historical continuity in the Middle East operates in her favor.

Relations between Italy and The Levant

Origins of Italian Policy

The Italians were once the only representatives of the West in the Middle East. Genoese, Pisani, Florentines, and Venetians built a "Levantine trade." Until the middle of the nineteenth century, the *lingua franca* on the Levantine coast was Italian (the common language for business and, later, for ideas).

But during the nineteenth century the Italians, occupied with building their own nation and endowing it with international status, were eclipsed in the Middle East by the diplomatic and commercial activities of the English and the French.

After World War I Italy made her political comeback in the Levant with Fascism. This regime impressed the Levantines with its strength and its achievements in general manufacturing of equipment and rural modernization. Fascistic authoritarian formulas are pleasing to certain bents of mind, especially among the Muslims, and they appear as a possible substitute for the parliamentarianism of the French and British. "Green Shirts" in Egypt and "Iron Shirts" in Syria illustrated the favor with which nationalist youth looked upon the "new order."

Fascist Italy nursed great ambitions in the Middle East although these were not immediately perceived, for the policy of Rome was clever enough to disguise them for a long time. Italy seemed to the Middle Easterners to rival Great Britain and France, and this appearance of rivalry, notwithstanding her own colonial enterprises pursued simultaneously, gave her some credit among the North African coastal states. She penetrated into Yemen, but her doctors and technical experts were under close watch from Yahya Muhammad Hamid ed-Din, their suspicious Imam.[6] Next door to Egypt where many Italian citizens had settled and acquired great influence, she brought to a close the conquest of Libya (1912-1930). Although a few Libyan nationalists withdrew to other parts of the Middle East, denouncing Italian imperialism, Italy found an advocate in the person of Chekib Arslan, a great Arab nationalist and Muslim reformer, who supported Mussolini, arguing that the latter might help Libya to fight against the British and French occupation and Mandates. In 1936 Italy seized Ethiopia, but this African country was suspected of oppressing the Muslims, so that in the Middle East the Fascist campaign was viewed not so much as an imperialist expedition as a well-organized and constructive demonstration of force. Italy had held Rhodes and the Dodecanese since 1912, but these Greek islands were quite a distance from the Arab Middle East. Only neighboring Turkey considered this annexation with suspicion, and in the fear of further Italian territorial ambitions drew closer to Britain and France.

Fascist Italy, however, showed her cards by entering the war in 1940 on the side of Nazi Germany. Although the latter country considered that the Middle East was destined to come under Italian influence, Nazi Germany

[6]Yahya Muhammad Hamid ed-Din (b. 1869-d. 1948) was chief ruler of Yemen, inheriting the title of Imam, from 1934 until his assassination in 1948. Ed.

desired that the government in Rome give up its expansionist views in order to retain Arab sympathies. The battle of El Alamein in 1942 soon put an end to such calculations. In spite of this defeat, however, Italy has remained prestigious in the Middle East.

Recent Developments

Italy was the first country compelled to decolonize after World War II, which proved to be to her advantage in the Middle East. With the exception of Count Sforza, who made a brief attempt in 1949 at safeguarding a certain amount of Italy's hold over Libya's destiny, neither the rulers of the new parliamentary republic of Italy nor those responsible for public opinion ever tried to stop Italy's withdrawal from overseas, nor showed any regrets. Italian decolonization was rapid, complete, and sincere, and fairly popular at home. Since Italy had no actual colonial possessions in the Middle East, she had only to become resigned to the eviction of Italian nationals established in Egypt. In the meantime, Eastern Arabism noted with satisfaction her sincerity in the decolonization of Africa. Italy was credited with the same political unselfishness she had shown in Libya ever since the United Nations vote for the Libyan independence in 1949. She was observed to be helping this new state through the rapid settlement of the problems relating to Italian rural property and the withdrawal of the Italian farmers—all of which was made easier by Italy's economic revival. The difficulties arising with Tunisia over the land owned by the Italians were also resolved with all due speed. Furthermore, Italy ceased her tutelage over Somalia in 1960 and instead bestowed a grant of considerable size to the newly independent republic.

In the Middle East itself, Italy refrained from any participation in Western enterprises considered by the Arabs as "neo-colonial" or "imperialist." They did not enter into the steps taken by the great powers leading to the creation of the state of Israel and the establishment of the status quo to preserve it, or attempts to organize a Western defense system in the Middle East, or the Franco-British expedition of Suez.

At a very early stage Italy appears devoid of any political aims or pretensions in the Middle East, while remaining a dynamic and desirable economic partner.

Nonpolitical Factors of Italy's Actions

Language, Culture, and Human Relations

The Italian language is seldom spoken in the Middle East; English and to some extent French take its place. Even in Libya, Italian is not kept up among the younger generation. Efforts are being made to maintain or to promote the knowledge of Italian culture among the élites (there is a Dante Alighieri society, and there have been some successful artistic undertakings). The Italians who live in the Levant are putting their Mediterranean affinities to good use by keeping up effective relations among local society.

Economy

Except for hydrocarbons (Libyan oil and gas are nowadays given preference over Middle Eastern oil because they are geographically closer) and to some extent high quality cotton, Italy is not a very important customer for Middle Eastern products. Italian oil exploration in the Middle East has not been very successful; only a few small fields have been located in Iran and the U.A.R., including some in Sinai that came under Israeli occupation and exploitation in 1967. But the instigator of this enterprise and founder of the Italian state-owned oil agency known as ENI, Enrico Mattei, initiated an audacious and liberal arrangement for the renewal of oil-exploration contracts and development in these areas. He set up a complex system of accepting equipment, supplies, and payment in the form of crude oil in which the conceding state associated with the company agreed to reinvest part of its royalties in the company. ENI gave the oil-rich Middle Eastern countries an even larger share of their already generous profits—75 instead of 50 percent.

As a producer of citrus and other Mediterranean fruit, Italy is in competition with certain Middle Eastern countries, and is therefore somewhat reserved about the association of Israel or of the Arab countries with the European Common Market.

The Italian flag prevails among the ships in the ports of the Levant. The services provided by Italian shipping, airlines, and public-works companies (the technical achievements of which are remarkable) place Italy in a prominent economic position in these service functions. Italian equipment, electric household appliances, automobiles (sometimes assembled locally), some semiluxury consumer goods and, more recently, armaments, now hold a fair proportion of the Middle Eastern market.

Political Factors of Italy's Actions

Italian diplomacy in the Middle East is well-informed and attentive; while avoiding any appearance of interference, it attempts to work discreetly in favor of mediation. Because of the general awareness that Italy is devoid of any political ambitions in the Middle East, she has been able to undertake diplomatic actions that the more involved Western states could not afford. During the summer of 1968 she discreetly brought about the return of the Israeli El Al plane captured by the PFLP and detained in Algiers.

This was the first peaceful and, although indirect and partial, effective settlement reached in the Arab-Israeli conflict after the Six-Day War. Again, in the autumn of 1969 Italian diplomatic intervention facilitated the return of an American Boeing that had been hijacked to Damascus.

On a more general level, the Italian government suggested to the permanent members of the Security Council, on February 5, 1970, that they should adopt measures to limit the armaments race in the Levant. On March 17 and 18 the Egyptian press announced an Italian "peace program" for the Middle East, based mainly on the establishment of a general embargo, subject to control, against weapons intended for this area. Without entering into details about the subject, government circles in Rome then insisted on the fact, especially during the 1969 United Nations General Assembly, that Italy's efforts had always tended in that direction. It therefore seems that Italy's conciliating role in the Middle East might assume greater importance in the future.

III. Federal Republic of Germany and the Middle East

Unlike the Italians, the Germans do not benefit by the historical advantage of constant and long-established relations with the Middle East. Despite the misfortune of two world wars, the Germans nevertheless enjoy considerable prestige because of their technical competence and their country's economic development. But the division of Germany into two states has caused the Federal Republic of Germany, which will be considered here by itself, to employ an extremely difficult Middle Eastern policy.

Relations between the F.R.G. and The Levant

Origins of German Policy

Historically, the Germans took an often brilliant part in Middle Eastern ventures, as in the Crusades. Emperor Frederick II of Hohenstaufen even attempted to achieve a remarkable symbiosis between Islam and Christendom in the middle of the thirteenth century. German troops were later associated with Christians in the fight against the Turks.

After the unification of the German state toward the end of the nineteenth century the Germans initiated an ambitious policy toward the Ottoman Empire. Wilhelm II had vast ambitions. As the Ottoman Sultan's ally, posing as the "protector of Islam," he intended to eclipse British and French efforts at economic and technical penetration. The dimensions of his Baghdad railway scheme (the *Bagdadbahn,* running from Constantinople to the Persian Gulf) did in fact exceed the few networks at the time being built by other European concessionaires. His military expeditions left a profound and lasting impression with the Turkish army. But the Germans were interested exclusively in the decadent Ottoman power and did not concern themselves with incipient Arab nationalism.

After her defeat in 1918 Germany experienced an economic revival followed by a serious inflation, after which came the advent of Nazism, with its fundamental transformation of German thought. But the Third Reich was concerned primarily with Europe; it did not take over Wilhelm II's views about the Middle East. Trade reappeared, mostly with Turkey where Germany bought many local products such as tobacco and fruit, and sold equipment, goods, and manufactured products, for which a market began to develop in the Middle East. The Jews, driven out Central Europe at the start of Nazi persecutions, remained economic partners with the Third Reich until the beginning of World War II. Germany had lost all her African possessions in 1919 and was therefore free of any suspicion of colonialism. The Third Reich, although it became deliriously anti-Semitic, did not take that opportunity to initiate a great Arab policy. Hitler, thinking in terms of Europe, treated the Middle East as an accessory.

Some Arab nationalists of Palestine, Syria, and then of Iraq made advances to Berlin in the hope of finding a natural ally, since London and Paris could not be brought to a compromise, but all they obtained were provisional replies. When World War II began, the Third Reich waited until 1940 before giving some encouragement to Arabism, despite the advice given by Grobba and von Hentig, its experts on Eastern Islam. German diplomacy considered that the Arab countries belonged to the sphere of Italy, although to that nation they advocated the principle of Arab independence.

As the Third Reich continued to hesitate to commit itself fully, the Arab nationalist leaders, such as the Grand Mufti of Jerusalem, Haj Amin al-Husseini; the Prime Minister of Iraq, Rashid Ali al-Gaylani; and others became more and more insistent. Thinking of the forthcoming Russian campaign which would require all possible military strength, the Third Reich would not contemplate massive political and military action in the Middle East before its troops had reached the Caucasus from the North. Germany therefore gave very little help to the revolt in Iraq led by Rashid Ali al-Gaylani in the spring of 1941, which in its view had been launched too early and at any rate without Germany's approval. These hesitations were disappointing for the Iraqi nationalists.

When the British recaptured Baghdad in May, 1941, and entered Iran in September of the same Year, Haj Amin al-Husseini sought refuge with the Germans in the absence of other possibilities. There he served German designs, in areas, however, far away from the Middle East (Tunisia, Bosnia, the Muslims in the Soviet Union), and hence out of reach. In Egypt the nationalists and the Free Officers refused to contribute to the British war effort and did what they could to counter it; in Cairo the crowds were vainly hoping for the arrival of Marshal Rommel's troops, which some officers, among others General Aziz al-Masri, Egyptian chief of staff, tried to join. In the end, the three defeats of Stalingrad, El Alamein, and Tunis, in 1942 and 1943, crushed any prospect of action in the Middle East for the Third Reich even before its collapse.

Recent Developments

Like the defeat of 1918, that of 1949 was followed in Germany, after a few years of crisis, by an extraordinary economic revival; the difference was in the division of Germany.

In the Arab Middle East, West Germany benefits from the prestige Germans generally earn through their qualities. However, the F.R.G. seems unaware that the same prestige also is accorded to East Germans and even to former Nazis. The latter are playing an important part in the United Arab Republic as technical advisers, while East Germans are slowly penetrating into those Arab countries that are open to progressive ideologies. Bonn's attitude toward the outside world is governed by the double preoccupation that the East German government should be thwarted and that a definite stand against the odious memories of Nazism should be taken. Having participated neither in the creation of the state of Israel nor in the Western Defense System for the Middle East, nor in the Suez affair, the F.R.G. has not taken advantage of her availability to the Arab world: while she has neglected to build a local attitude based on the conditions peculiar to the Middle East, she has acted against the latter for the sake of a general policy developed for reasons external to the area. Hence ambiguities arose which gradually caused very serious difficulties to the F.R.G. in the Middle East.

In 1955 the F.R.G. formulated the "Hallstein doctrine," according to which she would not maintain diplomatic relations with governments recognizing the government of East Germany, the German Democratic Republic. In 1957 the F.R.G. decided to pay the state of Israel, in successive annuities, the sum of $831 million, the indemnity which she considered she owed as reparation for the genocide perpetrated by the Nazis against millions of Jews. She was paying compensation in this collective form because it was impossible to determine individual rightful claimants, since entire families had been eradicated.

In spite of this, the Bonn government assumed that the Arabs would maintain normal relations with the F.R.G. to safeguard the highly developed and profitable economic and technical ties already existing. Events first proved this to be true. Although the Arabs resented the compensatory payments to Israel which, by building up the latter's balance of payments, were neutralizing the Arab blockade and boycott, and although some Arab states advocated breaking off relations, others, especially the United Arab Republic, which entertained highly developed trade and technical relations with the F.R.G., delayed the decision. Moreover, the Arab League was of the opinion that the very division between the two German states gave the Middle East some possibility of maneuvering that might enable it to restrict initiatives from Bonn. In 1957 the Arab League was therefore content to inform the F.R.G. that if it granted Israel diplomatic recognition and military aid, they would in turn take up relations with the German Democratic Republic.

This state of things lasted for several years. The German Democratic Republic multiplied informal contacts and increased her economic and technical penetration with the Arab countries. In 1956, however, there was a crisis. The President of the German Democratic Republic, Walter Ulbricht, was officially received in Cairo, whereupon the F.R.G. granted Israel diplomatic recognition and exchanged ambassadors with her, after which the Eastern Arab states and Algeria broke off relations with the F.R.G. Technical aid and assistance agreements already in the process of being fulfilled continued to be honored, but no new agreements were concluded. Private trade continued.

In the spring of 1969 there was another crisis; Iraq, Sudan, Syria, Southern Yemen, and the U.A.R. successively entered diplomatic relations with the German Democratic Republic. The F.R.G. was unable to apply official retaliatory measures since she had not been represented in these states for the past four years. She therefore limited her action to withdrawing the ambassador from Southern Yemen, a country which had achieved independence after 1956 and with which she had subsequently entered diplomatic relations. This left the "progressive" Arab states substituting the German Democratic Republic for the F.R.G., while several "conservative" states were entertaining official relations with neither the one nor the other. Only the "conservative" states of the Maghrib continued their normal relations with the F.R.G., from which they actually received active cooperation.

At the same time the relations between the F.R.G. and Israel were developing in all fields; in particular, Bonn sent Israel armaments valued at $500 million free of charge.

Nonpolitical Factors of the F.R.G.'s Actions

Language, Culture, and Human Relations

Many Israelis who came from Central Europe are familiar with the German language, while it is hardly spoken in the Arab Middle East. Among the

Arabs, only graduates from universities and German institutes speak it, and a few technical experts whom German firms, established in the Middle Eastern countries, have sent back to Germany to improve their technical knowledge, while still employed locally. Germany has some modest cultural associations in the Middle East, such as the *Goethe Institut*. But the Germans develop personal relationships more easily with Turks and Israelis than with the Arabs.

Economics

Since 1965 F.R.G. economic and technical aid for the Arab Middle East has gradually been extinguished, but it is being replaced by cooperation from the German Democratic Republic, a cooperation that has been increasing steadily since the beginning of 1969. Private economic relations, however, continue to be extensive; both West and East Germans are thought of as excellent trade partners who make a genuine effort to know the local market and to adapt to it. F.R.G. private business firms that may send staff members to the Middle East are careful to provide very specialized training, often at university level, for them. The F.R.G. is also acquiring a very important economic position in Israel; in 1966-1967, she received 8 percent of Israel's imports and purchased 10 percent of her exports.

On the whole, economic and technical contacts compensate the F.R.G. in a large measure for the drawbacks of her policy toward the Middle East. These contacts promise a brilliant future for the relationship between the F.R.G. and the Middle East.

Political Factors of the F.R.G.'s Actions

For the past 20 years or so, F.R.G.'s political and diplomatic moves in the Arab Middle East have gradually diminished. While acquiring considerable credit with Israel and maintaining excellent and close relations with Turkey and Iran as well as Morocco and Tunisia, F.R.G.'s diplomatic relations in the Arab Middle East are now confined to Lebanon, Jordan (re-established in the spring of 1967), and Yemen (re-established in the spring of 1969).

A large proportion of West German public opinion now regrets that the attitude toward the third world was not more subtle and better balanced. The Social Democrats in particular are making a point of the fact that the African and Asian states are obliged to take account of various factors that weigh more for them than do the general demands of F.R.G. politics. It would seem necessary for the F.R.G. to act upon individual cases.[7]

[7]At the beginning of 1967 the F.R.G. entered diplomatic relations with Romania even though an embassy of the German Democratic Republic was already established in Bucharest.

The coalition of Social Democrats and Liberals which came to power in 1969 did not set out to re-examine the Hallstein doctrine, but the Middle Eastern Arab states felt encouraged to seek a *rapprochement,* and their initiative has been well received in Bonn. In February, 1970, Bahjat al-Talhouni, Prime Minister of Jordan, obtained notable financial help from the F.R.G. At the same time, the Egyptian Minister of Economic Affairs, Hassan Abbas Zaki, made a statement to the German press agency, DPA, to the effect that "relations between Egypt and Germany should be envisaged in a long-range perspective and not as part of the present political situation. He added that political relations should come back to normal "sooner or later." Trade facilities were again solicited. A spokesman of the F.R.G. Ministry of Foreign Affairs stated on February 11 that the "Federal government completely shared this wish for an improvement in economic and political relations."

However, for reasons of home policy and general morality, Bonn cannot afford to adopt a less favorable attitude toward Israel than before; it must not appear to be giving way to pressure from the extreme right, where occasionally unconcealed anti-Semitism still exists.

In February, 1970, the Israeli Minister of Foreign Affairs paid an official visit to the F.R.G. for the first time. Abba Eban made a point of going to Dachau first "in order to stress the peculiar nature of relations between Israel and Germany." He stated that he was endeavoring to reinforce the ties between Israel and Europe, and that he had first gone to The Hague, Brussels, and Luxembourg, and would then proceed to Rome. During his press conference of February 24, Eban said he was convinced of the F.R.G.'s determination to "maintain and develop her good relations with Israel, independently of the efforts which she accomplished in order to improve her relations with the Arab states and with the Eastern countries; . . . there is no competition and no contradiction." His German counterpart, Walter Scheel, felt that he had shown himself to be "full of understanding" for the German and Arab efforts toward a *rapprochement.*

In spite of the persistently hostile attitude of certain Arab states such as Syria, an improvement in political relations between the F.R.G. and the Arab states is likely in the future. Although this would facilitate another extension of F.R.G.-Arab economic and technical exchanges, F.R.G.-Israeli relations will in all probability remain in the forefront.

IV. France and the Middle East

In order to understand the present state of relations between France and the Middle East it is necessary to consider her history in adequate detail, including the most ancient part of it.

On the one hand, this history has indeed left a psychological mark in the form of authentic and legendary memories, habits, and feelings. On the other hand, it has contributed much to inspiring, recently, the policy of General de Gaulle, who had such a keen sense for history.

France's present attitude toward the Middle East is to a large extent conditioned by the past.

Relations between France and the Middle East

Origin of French Policy

Ever since the early Middle Ages remarkable facts have occurred which are well remembered both in the Middle East and in France, although they are sometimes given different interpretations.

These facts are "European" rather than "French" proper: the relations between Charlemagne, Emperor of the West and Harun al-Rashid, Caliph of Baghdad (9th century); the collective undertaking, with its many aspects, of the crusades, from Godefrey de Bouillon to Louis IX (11th-12th centuries); the first Latin translation of the Koran which was due to the diligence of an abbot of Cluny (middle of the 13th century), and so on.

First Contacts and Increasing Influence. With the advent of modern times, France's policy in the Middle East acquired a more specific character.

In the middle of the fifteenth century, the French King received an ambassador from the Sultan of Cairo: the resultant French trade in the Levant lasted four centuries; it rivaled, equaled, and finally replaced that of Italy.

At the beginning of the sixteenth century, Francis I formed an alliance with the Ottoman Sultan, Suleiman I, the Magnificent (1520-1566), in order to ease the grip of the Austro-Spanish Empire on France. This, the first formal understanding between a Christian state and a Muslim state, stood in complete contrast to the general attitude of Europe at the time. Through the "Capitulations" (small treaties), Francis I moreover obtained from this alliance privileges of security which were at first intended for the French merchants in the Levant and for their chapels, but which were soon gradually extended to all the Christians in the Levant. An official French protection for the latter established itself which was to last until the creation of the present national states. Even before the modern notion of "nationality" came to be conceived in these regions, France was distinguishing more and more between the non-Turkish communities (Middle Eastern Christians of various denominations as well as Arab Muslims) and their masters of Constantinople whose arbitrary action France was endeavoring to restrict.

In the course of the eighteenth century France gradually joined the nations of Europe in a concerted effort against the Ottoman Empire and fought the Turkish and Maghribi Corsairs in the Mediterranean. The French fleet was the only fleet of continental Europe absent from the battle of Lepanto (1571),[8] but the French forces finally went to besiege the Turks at Candia (1665-1669). French protection of the Christians in the Levant has hardly been interrupted.

The eighteenth century ended with Bonaparte's expedition to the Middle East and his declaration that he had come "to restore their rights to the peoples of Egypt"; in Palestine and Syria, he received a hearing from the Sultan's discontented subjects. Stopped by the British, Bonaparte abandoned his Middle Eastern project, but, surrounded as he was by administrators, scholars, and engineers, he opened Egypt to modern influences.

Under the Khedivial dynasty Egypt awakened, turning to France. In the nineteenth century the books of great traveler-writers such as Chateaubriand, Lamartine, Gérard de Nerval, Théophile Gautier, and others gave rise to a general and durable interest in France for the Middle East, where the French language and trade became established. The traditional preoccupation with the protection of minorities gradually widened to become a will for a general guarantee of human rights within an Ottoman Empire being helped in its efforts at modernization. Napoleon III gave orders to write to his ambassador in Constantinople, on March 22, 1867, that "France did not mean to distinguish in any way between the various Ottoman nationalities and that in her concern she did not separate Moslem subjects from Christian subjects." In 1860 France instigated and helped greatly to implement the international intervention which helped Mount Lebanon to re-establish, if not its former *de facto* independence, at least a *de jure* autonomy. The conservative fraction of French opinion regretted that the Emperor did not endow this undertaking with a character of conquest. In 1869 the Suez Canal was inaugurated; it had been built by Ferdinand de Lesseps in cooperation with the Egyptian government, and sponsored by the investments of many French small capitalists.

Establishment of French Influence in North Africa. After Bonaparte's expedition to Egypt, and even more so after the building of the Suez Canal, France's activity in the Middle East was confined to thwarting Britain, which opposed it with increasing vigor. She then turned to the African coast and, following the capture of Algiers taken from the Corsairs of Barbary in 1830, came to concern herself primarily with the Maghrib, by her colonization by settlement in Algeria, and her establishment of protectorates over Tunisia in 1881 and over Morocco in 1908.

From 1880 onward France gradually became resigned to leaving Britain

[8]Or Navpaktos, Greek port and town on the Gulf of Corinth. Ed.

a preponderant diplomatic and political role in the Middle East, in exchange for her freedom of action in the area of the Maghrib. She nonetheless pursued her commercial and cultural activities in the Middle East, as well as her patronage of the Christians there. Moreover, many French people who were opposed both to the arbitrary regime of the Turks and to British ambitions, were discerning and encouraging toward nationalist activities in the Middle East. They approved Egypt's taste for independence (Mustafa Kamel's contacts in Paris), and the incipient national feeling in the Levant as demonstrated by the creation of a "League of the Arab Fatherland" on the French pattern, as well as the publication in Paris, in 1905, of Neguib Azury's design for a working nationalist program *Le Réveil de la Nation arabe*; and the first National Arab Congress held in Paris in 1913.

During World War I France, being engaged on her western front, played a secondary role to Britain in the Middle East. After the war she had to accept less than the general influence she used to exert in various ways in the whole of the Ottoman Empire, and the confinement of her actions to the area of Syria and Lebanon. At the same time that she obtained a Mandate designed to lead these two countries to independence, she was entrusted with the part of the oil concession of Mosul (Iraq), formerly held by Germany. This compensation for the loss of her former concessionary companies (railways, ports, etc.) in the portion of the Ottoman Empire that had become the Turkish national state enabled her to develop her own oil policy.

For various reasons France did not create an important Middle Eastern Arab policy after World War I.

In spite of the intellectual and sentimental ties that a fraction of the French élite had established with Arab nationalism in 1920, French public opinion and most French leaders (in France as well as the Mandate) suspected that this nationalism was an artificial creation of Britain, and certainly an instrument to be used by the latter against the French minorities and the Mandate. They feared, moreover, that the Arab nationalist movement might spread to North Africa, where the maintenance of French authority seemed one of France's major interests.

Thus the representatives of France in the Levant, while accomplishing their Mandatory task of administrative and economic development, conscientiously but too slowly opposed Arab tendencies toward union, curbed the impatient demonstrations of Syrian nationalism, and failed to seize the opportunity offered by the development of a Lebanese nationalism that was Arab but pro-Western. During a brief period from 1936–1937, however, thanks to the clear-sighted statesmanship of Pierre Viénot, treaties were concluded with Syria and Lebanon designed to take the place of the Mandate, and at the same time liberal and evolutive measures were initiated in Tunisia and Algeria. This tendency was checked, however, by the conservative fraction of French opinion supporting the general staff which was reluctant to change French positions in the Mediterranean at a time of imminent danger of war. Hence the government in Paris did not ratify the Franco-Syrian and the Franco-Lebanese treaties of 1936.

During World War II France, suffering from defeat and internal strife, was superseded by Britain in the Middle East even more than during World War I. But as a result of very complex events, things turned to the exclusive benefit of Arab nationalism.

In 1941, with British help, the authorities of Free France were able to take the place of the Vichy government in the tutelage of the Mandated territories. Despite their efforts, they remained subject to various pressures from the British, who were seeking to win over Arab nationalism for the sake of their war effort. In the hope of concluding alliances with these states, Free France granted independence to Syria and Lebanon, to become effective at the end of the war. General de Gaulle at first decreed the independence without elections to avoid intrigues and to ensure moderation in the evolution of events, but Britain eventually imposed popular votes which took place under British pro-nationalist influence.

In 1943 Free France was resigned to the establishment of nationalist parliaments and governments in Beirut and Damascus. As a result of serious incidents and clashes, moreover, in the autumn of 1943 and again in the spring of 1945 she was actually forced to abandon her Mandate without the conclusion of any treaty. In Damascus, where the authorities of Free France had tried to oppose nationalist actions by force, the threat of British arms compelled them to give in. General de Gaulle remarked at the time that he would not forget this act on the part of his British allies. A few years later, his will to reaffirm France's position in the Middle East, in a very different form, was indeed partly inspired by his desire to blot out the memory of the British eviction, an act which was felt even more poignantly after centuries of influence and friendship in the Middle East.

Recent Developments before, during, and after de Gaulle's Presidency

Before General de Gaulle's Presidency (1945-1958). If the Middle East alone had been at stake, or at least if it had constituted, in the eyes of the French leaders, an essential element of their world policy, France could have derived from the cessation of her Mandate the local foundations of a prosperous policy of decolonization as early as in 1945. Instead, no program of decolonization was adopted in the Levant after the cessation of the mandates. Further, because of the weight of French interests in the Maghrib, an understanding with Israel prevailed in the Middle East over a *rapprochement* with the Arab countries.

France's Middle Eastern disaster was in fact more apparent than real. In 1945 she had got rid of the thankless political burden of the Mandate, albeit in painful circumstances. But her achievements of tutelage there had been largely beneficial, and she was far from leaving only bad memories. Fairly considerable elements, moreover, of French influence remained in the Mandated countries and even extended into new areas.

In Syria and Lebanon, France retained commercial habits and economic trade relations, a few prosperous establishments, and provisional participation in financial technical structures, such as the Societé Nouvelle de la Banque du Syrie et du Liban (S.A.L.) the principal Lebanese bank. In the remainder of the area she added to her managerial, technical, and financial participation in the Suez Canal, the exploitation of Iraqi oil and of its outlets on the Levantine coast through a 23.75-percent association in the Iraq Petroleum Company.

Culturally, it is a fact that French influence has gradually declined in most of the area, although it is still found in Egypt and has increased considerably in Syria and especially in Lebanon.

Since France did not succeed in substituting treaties of alliance for any of her Mandates, she was not in any way mortgaging the sovereignty of Lebanon and Syria. They became the most completely independent states of the Middle East. Although she adhered to Balfour's promise of 1917 (mentioning specifically, however, a Jewish "settlement" as opposed to a "national home"), and although she showed no bitterness towards Zionism in Palestine, the French government carefully thwarted every Zionist attempt at buying land in her Mandated territories.

In 1945 France might at last have had a Middle Eastern policy. But despite the value of her ties and her interests there, and regardless of certain liberalization efforts, such as the status of Algeria in 1947 and the granting of internal autonomy to Tunisia in 1954-1955, France continued to safeguard her North African interests against the nationalist claims of the Maghrib.

France was therefore afraid to encourage in North Africa the nationalist tendencies to which she had finally yielded in the Levant, and she continued to imagine and to dread the extension of these to the Maghrib. Hence she abstained from adopting in the Middle East the attitude of decolonization which her local position and circumstances would have enabled her to assume.

In most cases France avoided criticizing and thwarting Western attitudes in the Middle East, which Arabism was exposing as imperialistic. She did indicate, however hostility to the Baghdad Pact (1955) by supporting Syrian independence against what she considered to be British aims. But in general she took part in the important international majority decisions. In

1947 she voted in favor of the partition of Palestine, and in 1948 recognized the state of Israel, although refusing to transfer her embassy to Jerusalem, since she had voted for the internationalization of the city. She aimed at the maintenance of the status quo and, together with the United States and Great Britain, she subscribed in 1950 to the Tripartite Declaration on Palestine.

In various ways, France has taken the opportunity to acquire preferential local friendships. Thus, she hastily drew near Syria in 1949 under the brief regime of Marshal Husni al-Zaim, and she has gradually established closer relationships with Israel in trade, technical cooperation, general staff contacts, and purchases of arms. Inspired in this latter perspective by a fraction of opinion that has influenced most of the governments of the Fourth Republic, French policy tended to consider Israel as a counterweight, or even as an "ally in the rear" against Arab nationalists whose action in the Maghrib gave France increasing fears. This tendency brought about a Franco-Israeli understanding on the eve of the Suez expedition in the autumn of 1956.

In the Maghrib France had finally decided, at Pierre Mendès-France's insistence, to emancipate her protectorates of Tunisia and Morocco (1956). But she regarded Algeria as a portion of the national territory. The Algerian "revolution" of November 1, 1954, therefore appeared to France as an internal rebellion and was opposed as such. The majority of French opinion did not understand Algerian motives for revolt, and attributed the rebellion to instigation and support from the Middle East, especially from Egypt. Hence the *raison d'être* for the Suez expedition of 1956. This operation united France and Britain in the Middle East. It was aimed, as far as France was concerned, much less at defending a questionable legal thesis and minimal material interests (the government in Cairo had promised to pay compensation to the shareholders of the nationalized companies—a promise which it was to keep), than at eclipsing Nasserism, which France considered to be responsible for the disturbances in North Africa.

At this time General de Gaulle, who was not then in power, approved the Suez expedition, attributing its failure regretfully to errors of tactics; he also suggested that Israel should keep the Gaza Strip, since this was "indispensable for her security." De Gaulle's attitude was dictated mostly, it seems, by his policy based on the interests of France alone, the rivalry between the two world blocs, and his desire to escape American patronage even if that patronage were for the defense of the Free World.

The Suez affair had important consequences for France in the Middle East, since it severed her from Arabism and threw her toward Israel. At the injunction of the United Nations France, like Britain, interrupted operations in the Suez crisis and withdrew her troops. All Middle Eastern Arab states excepting Lebanon broke off diplomatic relations with France; she was literally evicted from the Middle Eastern political scene. True enough, she kept her economic ties with the Arab countries; she remained a customer for Egyptian cotton and for oil from Kuwait, Iraq, and Saudi Arabia. And while some of her teaching establishments disappeared from Egypt and Syria, she kept most of her cultural prestige and intellectual influence.

Israel, however, offered France analogous and sometimes even wider possibilities, and she became the best Middle Eastern customer for French industry. Moreover, the absence of Franco-Arab diplomatic relations, the continuation of the Algerian crisis, and the Arab Middle Eastern assistance to the Algerian New Liberation Front promoted the maintenance of an effective Franco-Israeli solidarity. In the military field, contacts between general staffs and considerable sales of arms gave a tangible form to the continuation of a sort of alliance, although this was not corroborated by any public agreement.

During General de Gaulle's Presidency. When coming to power in May-June, 1958, General de Gaulle, constantly inspired as he was by a strictly personal appreciation of national interests, changed Middle Eastern policy very little. Eric Rouleau, an excellent French specialist of Middle Eastern affairs, wrote on the subject:

> From 1958 to 1962 General de Gaulle seemed to ignore the existence of the Arab world. Certainly he missed no opportunity for consolidating French interests in business and the cultural sphere, but he did not try to renew political contacts. His attitude was no different from that of his predecessors; Israel appeared to remain France's privileged partner in the Near East. Until he had cleaned up the Algerian abscess—this was to come with the Evian Agreements in March, 1962—he did not risk losing the substance for the shadow.[9]

General de Gaulle's accession to power in the spring of 1958 and the recognition of Algeria's independence in the spring of 1962 made it possible for France to modify her attitude toward the Middle East. At first this attitude changed but gradually, but after the Six-Day War in 1967, it became distinctly favorable to Arabism.

During these four years Israel indeed supported French policy in Algeria by her votes in the United Nations, being convinced that she would in turn receive complete and durable French support. Following contacts with General de Gaulle, both Golda Meir, the Israeli Foreign Minister in August, 1958, and Ben-Gurion, the Israeli Prime Minister in June, 1960, expressed

[9]E. Rouleau, "France and the Middle East," *The World Today* Vol. XXIV, No. 5, (London, May, 1968).

their conviction in almost identical terms, that Israel's ties with France resulted not from temporary circumstances, but from a true identity of thought and ideas as well as from shared and permanent historical values. In June, 1961, General de Gaulle, after an official luncheon arranged for Ben-Gurion, went so far as to say: "We want to assure you of our solidarity and our friendship, and I raise my glass to Israel, our friend and ally!"

In applying the principles dictated to it by the Algerian affair, however, General de Gaulle's government seemed to be slightly adapting its policy so as to protect French interests against the pure and simple hold of a preconceived plan. The general staff was requested to lessen its collaboration with the Israeli authorities in the field of nuclear information and intelligence. A former ambassador to Cairo, well known for his sympathetic understanding of Arabism, Couve de Murville, took over the Foreign Ministry in an attempt to safeguard future relations with the Arab world. The *Régie des Automobiles Renault* gave in to the pressure of the Arab boycott and interrupted the operation of the assembly line which it had established in Israel; Air France refused to conclude an agreement proposed by El Al; these two companies, the policies of which the state had some means of influencing, thus meant to safeguard their opportunities on the Arab market. A serious incident occurred, however, when the members of a mission sent to Cairo in the autumn of 1961 to initiate new cultural and technical contacts were wrongly accused of espionage.

At the conclusion of the Evian Agreements in 1962, after the recognition of Algeria's independence and the establishment of extensive cooperation with this new state, General de Gaulle was at last able to play the game of decolonization and to corroborate his policy of independence from the United States by making himself the champion of the third world. France immediately drew near Arabism although she did not present this step as a reversal of her policy. Diplomatic relations were taken up again with the Middle Eastern Arab states (Syria, Jordan, and Saudi Arabia in August-September, 1962; Iraq in January, 1963; the United Arab Republic in August, 1963), but no condition was appended to this recognition, and France thus preserved her full freedom of action.

From the start, France did not appear to be building a great Middle Eastern Arab policy. Some proof of this may be seen in the extremely moderate tone of an official document entitled "Special Report Concerning Operations with the Third World" drafted by Ambassador Jean Chauvel and appended to the "Report of the Commission for the Study of the Policy of Cooperation with Developing Countries" (Jeanneney Commission), filed in Paris on July 1, 1963.

Jean Chauvel, who has had wide experience in the Middle East, does indeed note that

> France no longer has any dispute with the Arab world. She no longer has any territorial establishment in this world that might be held against her. She is benefiting by her recent absence which kept her outside the Levant for several years during which, as sometimes happens in these countries, ancient habits, when compared with more recent experiences, recover their flavor. In short, French action is not only acceptable; it is desired.

But the Ambassador went on to point out that

> the French standing in Egypt, which was considerable in every field and preponderant in some cases, has been practically liquidated by the Egyptian government since the Suez crisis. Diplomatic relations, interrupted at the time, have only just been resumed on a minor level. It is too early to foresee their consequences. Investments seem improbable; economic cooperation is theoretically possible.

He concluded that the resumption of relations with Cairo would afford an opportunity, at least in an initial phase, for direct observation. A few weeks after this text was filed, diplomatic relations assumed their normal extension.

Jean Chauvel noted, on the other hand, that "good Franco-Israeli relations work against" the favorable conditions which France is now finding in the Arab world. He concluded:

> It is important not to increase this very real drawback by another, i.e., by taking sides in the conflict which at present opposes Nasserites and Anti-Nasserites in the Middle East. It is difficult to see what advantage France could draw from a triumph by Nasser, and very easy to foresee the consequences which she would have to fear from him as regards in particular her oil interests. But the present quarrels, which may last for a long time and come to the surface again in various ways, are not of the kind in which France wishes to participate. She should guard herself all the more against such engagements since they would not have any decisive effect. She would maintain the point of view that French cooperation, while it supposes and entails agreement with the governments, is not intended for them, but solely for the people, and that her only intention is to provide these peoples with some means of development, i.e., of real independence.

After noting that "the action of France in this area has two poles, one of which is Lebanon, the other Iran," and that "these two positions are traditional," Jean Chauvel expressed the opinion that in these countries the cultural effort "should not slacken. It should moreover be supported by appropriate economic action. In the Levant as elsewhere, culture is no longer possible without economy." After a brief review of French possibilities in the various Arab countries, he formulated this last remark: "It is perfectly clear that French activities in Israel should be considered for their own sake and that on no account do they serve the credit of France in Arabia."

It should be noted, lastly, that the Jeanneney Commission, while recognizing that cooperation with Africa should no longer be exclusive, recommended that it should keep priority. This view was to be endorsed by the French government.

France was therefore unable to make an outstanding effort in the Arab Middle East. Even in the field of technical and cultural aid, requests formulated by Middle Eastern Arab states were sometimes imperfectly satisfied, since the Maghrib and French-speaking Africa were absorbing most of the necessarily limited funds available.

On the other hand, France was also avoiding taking sides in inter-Arab disputes. Thus, in spite of advances from Cairo she abstained from entering diplomatic relations with the new republican regime of Yemen in 1962. This political reserve was modified in only a few cases. For example, General de Gaulle bestowed particular attention on King Hussein of Jordan, to whom he was anxious to point out that "the artificial ill-feeling" that used to divide the two nations was due to "foreign intrigues," a phrase that showed his recollection of past Franco-British dissensions. Moreover, relations with Lebanon, which had never ceased as has been mentioned, were of a particularly friendly nature. Lastly, French interests other than oil, which assumed some importance in Iran, started to develop again in the Middle Eastern Arab world.

Very close relations were maintained with Israel, without any apparent objections on the part of the Arab states. Considerable consignments of armaments were granted to Israel, especially in the field of aviation. During an eight-year period, Israel became the French aeronautical industry's foremost customer, buying Mirage fighter-bombers and helicopters costing over 2½ billion francs. Israel also received, and erected in Dimona, a 20-megawatt experimental nuclear reactor designed in principle for peaceful means, but for which no strict limitation of use appears to have been imposed. It is estimated that Israel would thus be in a position to manufacture six kilograms of plutonium per annum, that is, the amount required for the equipment of a Nagasaki-type bomb. General de Gaulle in July, 1964, amicably received Israel's new Prime Minister, Levi Eshkol, who declared upon leaving the Elysée Palace: "General de Gaulle, from the outset of our talk, spoke of Israel as the friend and ally of France; he repeated this form of words [sic] several times during our meeting."

From 1965 onward, however, a gradual change of direction may be observed in French policy toward the Middle East.

For the purposes of decolonization, General de Gaulle meant to conduct a great policy in favor of the third world. In a policy of "nonalignment" he encouraged the independent states of Asia, Africa, and Latin America to avoid rivalries between the two blocs, and he attempted in particular to protect them and France herself against what he considered to be the United States' will for preponderance. In this respect the Middle East became of increasing interest to him, the more so since he intended to make French oil supplies, which were mostly drawn from Arab countries, as independent as possible of the international trusts.

At the same time General de Gaulle was worrying about the increased tension in the Middle East; and while he was attempting to counterbalance the emotional effects of Nasser's propaganda by showing special interest for the conservative Arab states of the area, it seems that he also endeavored to induce Israel to greater caution.

It should be noted that this evolution in the Middle Eastern policy of France in no way corresponds to a change in public opinion. An important fraction of the conservative and moderate opinion continued to resent vividly the abandonment of Algeria, which made itself felt even more by the resettlement in Paris of nearly one million French people who had returned from North Africa. And while a nostalgia for colonization and traces of anti-Arab sentiment thus remained, a general sympathy, which had nothing to do with considerations of home politics, went to the Jews of Israel. They appeared as the victims of Arab provocations spread by propaganda from Cairo, whose existence was being threatened. In France they might reckon on an atmosphere of sympathy for the Jewish people who had suffered from the recent genocides, on the support of most French Jews, on the activities of various pro-Israeli lobbies (France-Israel Association, presided over by General Koenig, etc.), and lastly on the support of several personalities and certain high officials as well as members of the general staff who were favorably disposed toward them.

The new direction of the French policy became apparent in the reception given to Arab heads of states who were paying more and more frequent visits to Paris. In May, 1965, General de Gaulle received Charles Helou, President of the Republic of Lebanon, to whom he affirmed the sincere friendship of France, and whom he warned against "the new imperialists";

in October, 1965, Marshal Abdul Hakim Amer, Vice-President of the United Arab Republic, expressed his appreciation of French policy toward the third world to General de Gaulle, who replied by praising the economic and social progress of Egypt and the increasing importance of its international role; in December, 1966, he encouraged Youssef Zuayyin and Ibrahim Makhos, respectively Prime Minister and Foreign Minister of the Syrian Arab Republic.

During the autumn of 1966 and the spring of 1967, Israeli reprisals of increasing vigor over Jordan territory aimed at the commandos of the Palestinian resistance movement, or directed against Syria after clashes in the demilitarized zone, were all the more preoccupying for de Gaulle's government in Paris, since the Mirage planes sold to Israel by France were the main instruments for these reprisals. It seems that at the time Israel had been warned that French material was not in any case to be used for general actions of an offensive nature.

In May, 1967, General de Gaulle became very worried about the increase in the Israeli-Arab tension. It appears that the various Arab capitals were then informed of these preoccupations and discreetly requested to refrain from any rash action. When the question of the Gulf of Aqaba arose, General de Gaulle considered it timely to take a peaceful initiative. On May 24 Paris suggested an urgent meeting of the four great powers. Washington and London immediately agreed, but Moscow, after a certain lapse of time, did not.

With the danger of an armed conflict becoming greater, the French government made a last appeal, on June 2, to the antagonistic states "each of which, he affirmed, had a right to live," asking them to abstain from any act which would provoke a war. "France estimates," declared General de Gaulle, "that the opening of hostilities would be the worst possible case. Consequently, the state to first use arms, whichever it be, would have neither France's approbation nor her support." Naturally, this meant that France was thinking of operations of a general nature, since for several months already partial engagements had taken place. The Arab states were confidentially advised that France would not allow Israel to be destroyed, but that she would consider military action as untimely and dangerous. The public warning was repeated privately to Israel, which held armaments of French origin, but its terms clearly showed that it was intended for all. Its aim was, said the French Minister of Information, to have "a calming effect on everyone."

Israel nonetheless launched her military action in the early hours of June 5. General de Gaulle was extremely angry about the disregard shown for his warning. But the majority of French opinion approved Israel's actions.[10] It was thought that the head of the government was wrong in terming as aggressor the state taking the initiative of the fighting, because as a result of the Arab provocations and threats this campaign had a preventive character of self-defense. Some, fewer in numbers, did justify General de Gaulle's attitude by saying that, in this particular case, he had not aimed at defining the aggression but only at warning against lack of caution; he was therefore making a last attempt to save the peace.

Just as the public opinion polls, the demonstrations, private conversations, letters to newspapers, etc., confirmed the sympathy of the public for Israel, so did the volunteers who left to fight at her side. But a possible annexation of the occupied territories did not meet with equally wide approval, and a great majority of citizens continued to trust General de Gaulle.[11]

The embargo on arms intended for the belligerents, said the French Ministers of Information and of the Army in January and February, 1969, for Israel concerned only the Mirage planes, "symbol of the offensive" (J. Le Theule, January 8, 1969); it did not apply to spare parts nor to any other materials, especially helicopters. No delivery was pending for the Arab countries. Fifty Mirage planes, ordered and paid for by Israel, were held back in France; forty others were added during the following months; but among the French public there were rumors that considerable amounts of aeronautical equipment had been sent in various ways on the eve of the battle, and perhaps even subsequently.

In the United Nations French diplomacy supported the Yugoslav draft resolution which was relatively harsh on Israel; France did not succeed, however, in persuading all the French-speaking African states to follow suit, although these used to be administered or Mandated by France, and were privileged beneficiaries of her aid as well as frequent recipients of Israeli technical assistance. Seven of these states voted for the resolution and two against it, while six abstained from voting. Three of them still abstained from voting on the Pakistani resolution adopted on July 5, which

[10]A public opinion poll by IFOP (French Institute of Public Opinion) showed that on the day after the beginning of conflict 54% of the persons questioned considered Egypt and the Arab countries to be the aggressors, whereas 6% designated Israel. A similar proportion, 56% against 2%, were in favor of an Israeli victory. The electors of the democratic center were the most favorable for Israel, followed closely by those of the "Fifth Republic" (Gaullists) and of the Federation of the Left. The Communists were the least favorable.

[11]These last points seemed to confirm the relatively secondary importance of Middle Eastern affairs in the eyes of the French public, as well as its conviction that Israel was able to provide for her own security if necessary by bargaining for the restitution of the occupied territories, and that Israel wished to exclude France from a direct participation in the conflict.

prescribed the cancellation of the steps taken by Israel in respect to Jerusalem. France placed at Israeli disposal the United Nations observers whose duty it was to supervise the application of the cease-fire on the Suez Canal. In the autumn of 1967 she took part in the drafting of the resolution adopted unanimously by the Security Council on November 22, 1967, stipulating the principles of a peaceful settlement. While the English text of this document provided, among these principles, for the evacuation "of occupied territories," the French text, which was more extensive, spoke of the evacuation of *the* occupied territories *(l'évacuation des territoires occupés)*, that is, of all of them, including Jerusalem. Hence the Arab states preferred to refer to the French text.

During a press conference held on November 27, 1967, General de Gaulle mentioned, among other things, that the events in the Middle East justified the Palestinian resistance against Israeli occupation and qualified the Jews as an "élite people, sure of themselves and domineering." This latter epithet aroused considerable emotion among a large sector of French opinion as well as in the Jewish community in France, among whom the memory of the deportations and the Nazi genocide are still vivid. In replying to a letter from David Ben-Gurion, and during a conversation with the Chief Rabbi of France, Joseph Kaplan, the Chief of the French state did his best to point out that he had not intended to give this phrase any pejorative meaning.

At the beginning of 1968 the announcement of projected supplies of fighter planes to Iraq again aroused widespread emotion among the French public. The government justified this step by stressing that Iraq had not been an actual belligerent in 1967.

France's Arab policy was amply formulated by President de Gaulle on February 8, 1968, during the reception of General Abdel Rahman Aref, the Iraqi head of state. France, declared the President, "condemns the war which started in the Middle East [and] which can be ended only by an international settlement establishing a real peace and excluding, of course, any prejudice inflicted on the Arabs." Stating the basic principles of such a settlement, he paraphrased the provision of the November 22 resolution, speaking in particular of the "establishment of peaceful and normal relations among Israel's neighbors and this new state"; he moreover specified that a "worthy fate" should be provided for the refugees who could not be repatriated, "as well as for the minorities"; he added that "France was prepared to participate locally in the application of an agreement which would be founded on such principles." Speaking more specifically of French-Iraqi relations he said, after mentioning Harun al-Rashid and Charlemagne, that "Iraq, having just become a state after the First World War, was placed under foreign influences which kept her away from

France"; he noted that it had also been necessary to "put an end to the affairs of North Africa and their prolongations in the Middle East"; moreover, France had to be in a position again to show "sufficient interest and means" for Iraq "to establish ties with her on a large scale"; he concluded that, "the circumstances which used to provoke a contradiction between the counsels of sentiment and those of common sense had changed profoundly. . . . For the Arab and French people . . . the absorption by the one or the other of the world blocs built around two hegemonies cannot be accepted. . . . They reject any vassalage, be it ideological, political, economic, or military. Hence there is among them an elementary solidarity which they have the best reasons to practice and to organize." It may be noted how much history on the one hand, and the conception of a world policy on the other, contributed to framing General de Gaulle's attitude toward the Middle East.

General Abdel Rahman Aref replied to these words by stating that General de Gaulle's position "had shown to world public opinion the absurdity of a policy of expansionism through force and oppression. . . . There are opportunities for Arab-French cooperation on foundations that will constitute an example to be followed, through their realism, their objectivity, and the understanding established by exchange of common interests in a spirit of friendship and cordiality."

On a practical plane France endeavored to obtain increasing participation in the exploitation of Iraqi national resources, independent of the international trusts. But while *Entreprise de Recherches et d'Activités Pétroliéres* (ERAP), a state-owned oil company, did indeed obtain a contract for oil exploration in the south of Iraq in the form of an association, the *Société Nationale des Petroles d'Aquitaine* (SNPA) was unable to secure the sulphur deposits of Tikrit (these were entrusted to Poland); and the *Compagnie Française des Pétroles* (CFP)[12] had to give up the hope of exploiting the magnificent oil field of North Rumaila, which went to the Soviet Union. In this connection the French public often expressed the opinion, as before in the case of Algeria, that the Franco-Arab *rapprochement* "does not pay." Some thought that General de Gaulle himself felt some bitterness about this during his last months of office.

France again launched the idea of an initiative by the four great powers about the Palestinian conflict. Speaking before the United Nations General Assembly on October 2 and 7, 1968, Michel Debré, French Foreign

---

[12]Although in principle the French Oil Company is a private enterprise, the State owns 40 percent of the stock and the majority of the votes. It is certain that the directors of the enterprise make the most of their advice, and that this is taken into consideration, but in fact the public has the last word. Thus, there are no politics of the French petroleum industry independent of the State.

Minister, recalled that France had adhered to the resolution of November 22, 1967; he thought "that an agreement among the Big Four, if it had taken place in May 1967, would have prevented the conflict from developing," and that such an agreement "remained an indispensable condition for a return to stability." He repeated that France "was prepared to commit herself to a system of guarantees resulting from a general agreement for the application of the just international rule in this part of the world."

From the autumn of 1968 on France again endeavored to bring about a conference between the four powers, and because of a certain *rapprochement* between American and Russian views on the Middle East in December, this idea made notable progress. But after a reprisal by Israeli forces at the Beirut airport on December 28, 1968, in response to an attack on an El Al plane in Athens by a Palestinian commando, the French government, in another special initiative on January 3, 1969, decreed an embargo on all arms for Israel, whatever their nature—this time including spare parts.

This step not only proved very costly for French industry, it also aroused great emotion in France. The embargo was widely criticized, not only by the opposition parties of the center and the Socialists, but even among the ranks of the *Union de la Nouvelle République* (UNR) government party.[13] Jacques Duhamel, president of the *Progrès et Démocratie Moderne* (PDM), the left-center group of the National Assembly, expressed his intention to question the government regarding its arms supplies to the Arab countries, and mentioned an impressive list of them.[14] Couve de Murville, the Prime Minister, curtly replied that "France was not supplying anything to other countries." For a month, the press echoed vehement protests from the most varied personalities and circles.[15]

Despite the impact of these reactions, however, at this juncture French opinion seemed to be more subtly balanced than after the Six-Day War. Sympathy for Israel had ceased to be the majority view, although sympathy for the Arabs had not increased. For many, both sides were equally to be blamed. In the majority, France considered the Israeli reprisals against

[13]Since the 1968 election the government party has been the *Union des Démocrates pour la République* (UDR). Ed.

[14]*Le Monde,* January 10, 1969.

[15]According to some newspapers Israeli orders pending at that time totaled 2 billion francs. Aviation factories had to close down. M. Vallieres, president of *Les Avions Marcel Dassault,* estimated that the embargo would cost the French aeronautical industry 250 million francs and would cause the cancellation of 3000 employments. Some feared that as a retaliatory measure the normal French exports to Israel might also be compromised (450 million francs of nonmilitary supplies from January to November, 1968), and that this step might discourage other customers of the French arms industry.

Beirut to be excessive. But she criticized the embargo decision even more, especially since it was executed without consultation and because of its unilateral nature.[16] It seems that, probably for want of sufficiently accurate information, many Frenchmen had not realized that General de Gaulle's extraordinary gesture was the only available means by which French policy could bring effective help to Lebanon, a country threatened in its national cohesion and hence in its very existence.

Foreign Minister Michel Debré explained and justified the French embargo decision by placing it in the context of general policy:

> By decreeing the suspension of arms deliveries and by placing her diplomacy in the service of procedures likely to direct the Middle East toward real peace, France has given a warning and set an example commensurate with her means. The warning: there is no settlement in the Middle East without tolerance, and the first rule of tolerance, today, is to avoid at all cost an aggravation of the conflict. The example: there will be no settlement in the Middle East if the powers which have responsibilities in the world and especially in the Mediterranean persistently refuse to assume their responsibilities.[17]

Again the French government launched the idea of an action by the Big Four with even greater determination. On January 16, 1969, it suggested to the other three permanent members of the Security Council that an agreement should be reached by means of prior "negotiations and discussions" to promote the implementation of the resolution voted on November 22, 1967, the object being to "open the path for a settlement in which the interested parties should be closely associated".[18] Informal meetings between the delegates of the four states with the Security Council were proposed. The U.S.S.R. acquiesced as early as January 20; the Russian project for a settlement had indeed been considered in Paris as being very close to acceptable; next Britain agreed and, on February 5, the United States followed suit, specifying restrictions on a few points.

[16]IFOP poll conducted from January 6 to 14 for *France-Soir* indicated that 35% of the persons questioned were sympathetic to Israel (as against 56% in June, 1967, and 68% in September, 1967) and 7% to the Arab countries; 19% replied: "neither to the one nor to the other"; 39% did not voice an opinion; 53% disapproved of the raid on Beirut, and 19% approved of it. The results of another poll, *Service de Sondages et Statistiques (SSS)*, from January 14 to 16, according to *Le Monde*, showed blame for the raid by 59% and approval by 28%; 45% against the embargo, and 37% for it. On January 13 *Figaro* estimated that 80% of the letters it had received were disapproving of the embargo; on the same day, *Sud-Ouest* (Bordeaux), after questioning its readers, noted a 93.70% disapproval for the same measure.

[17]*La Nation,* January 10, 1969.

[18]Statement by the Foreign Ministry spokesman, January, 1969.

The Big Four talks opened on April 3 in New York. They were temporarily suspended in July. The discussions took place in an atmosphere of great discretion; according to some rumors, the talks turned into a dialogue between the United States and the Soviet Union; France was said to have somewhat softened her initial position by envisaging, for instance, that the evacuation of the territories might be only partial. The fact that this procedure, suggested in vain by Paris two years before, had now begun, was in itself a success for French diplomacy, which, notwithstanding, did not play an important role in the talks.

After General de Gaulle's Withdrawal (April 28,1969). The referendum of April 27 yielded a negative result and, in accordance with his announced intentions, General de Gaulle withdrew. The object of the popular vote had been to determine the fate of the Senate and a regional reform, but the referendum soon turned into a debate of the general policy and style of government of the head of state. In this respect some may have thought that the "Middle Eastern conflict . . . [had been] the only foreign issue which weighed on the vote of April 27 and contributed no doubt to General de Gaulle's failure."[19] It seems difficult, however, to prove this point, for the General's political attitude as a whole and his demeanor as president were being questioned. The cessation of General de Gaulle's presidential office did not bring about an immediate reversal of French policy in the Middle East, but it did indicate a cautious revision, tending toward a stricter balance and a more discriminating attitude.

From the moment of General de Gaulle's withdrawal, Arab opinion, much dismayed, showed vivid anxiety and fears of a fundamental change in France's attitude toward the Middle East. "We must give France good reason to continue General de Gaulle's policy toward us" wrote Mohammed Hassanein Heykal, who was said to be often inspired by President Gamal Abdel Nasser.[20] Israel saw from the beginning that a revision was probable, and proposed to ask for "an important and fundamental change of French policy."[21]

During the Presidential election campaign the candidates were often questioned as to their position toward the Middle East.[22] Alain Poher, President of the Senate and interim President of the Republic, stated on French television on May 22 that he wanted to "restore the image of an impartial France, faithful to all her friendships in the Middle East [and] to

[19]Philippe Herreman, *Le Monde,* May 29, 1969.

[20]*Al Ahram,* May 2, 1969.

[21]In a statement by Abba Eban, Israeli Foreign Minister, May 17, 1969.

[22]There is a fairly complete survey on this point in *Le Monde* of May 29, 1969, by Philippe Herreman.

admit no discriminatory measure." On the Twelve Items Program, he considered "as unacceptable, the decision of the embargo against one single country. . . ." Yet on June 15, the majority of voters gave preference to one who had shown himself less trenchant, Georges Pompidou, former Prime Minister. Pompidou had said on Radio Europe No. 1 on May 22, "No one is to supply arms to anyone! . . . If the reactions are negative, then France will reflect upon her own positions," a pronouncement which was interpreted by *Le Monde* as a wish to see the United States and the Soviet Union cease arms supplies.[23] Pompidou further defined his position: "For my part, I am quite prepared to suggest that no country is to supply arms to anyone in the Middle East. What we are interested in is the re-establishment of peace. . . . We shall not obtain it if there is a disparity of forces . . . [and] if a solution is sought by means of this disparity, that is, in a victory from superior arms"; he advocated peaceful coexistence with "equitable and secure frontiers guaranteed by the great powers," and a renunciation of the use of force and military conquests; he recalled the resolution of November 22, 1967, which was an "appropriate basis for such a settlement," and wished that it might be applied so that "the talks between the Big Four suggested by France should continue."[24]

Like Alain Poher, Pompidou was questioned by General Koenig, President of the Committee of French Solidarity with Israel; he "reaffirmed the right of Israel to exist as a state . . . in her own right, and to be recognized as such by all her neighbors," and he added that the "problem of the Palestinians [must be] solved . . . [it is] a human problem as well as . . . one of security for the whole of the Middle East"; he confirmed his position about the arms supplies, stating that he wished to "examine with an open mind, in view of a solution compatible with the interest of all," the problem of Israel's association with the European community; and he recalled that "peace was the primary objective."[25]

After Pompidou's election there was agreement in both Israel and the Arab countries that no radical changes were to be expected.[26]

When interviewed on June 27 by Radio Europe No. 1, the new Prime Minister, Jacques Chaban-Delmas, recalled George Pompidou's statement that the embargo must have the "character of an example." Replying to the question of a listener concerning Russian arms supplies to Egypt, Chaban-Delmas pointed out that it was "not in the government's intention to waste time." A commentator thought that this meant that in the eyes of the present government, the embargo had lost the authority of the penalty

[23]*Ibid.*
[24]*Le Figaro,* June 12, 1969.
[25]*Le Monde,* June 11, 1969.
[26]*Al Ahram,* June 16; press conference by Abba Eban, June 25, 1969.

General de Gaulle had wished to give it, and had become, instead, an example. The example not having been followed, the journalist questioned, "What will be the next decision of the French government in this matter?" in an article entitled: "France about to reconsider her position on the embargo."[27]

But during the July 10 press conference, while examining the possibility of reconsidering French policy, the President stated that, "This could in any event only take the form of a return to the 'selective' embargo which existed before January 3," this phrase meaning that the supply of "spare parts, defensive material or material of small offensive capacity" might continue.

Since France was faced with more urgent problems, especially financial ones, several weeks went by without consideration of this question; indeed, there was no new indication of any policy toward the Middle East. It was not until the fire in the Al Aqsa Mosque that the following official text was published:

> The French government was greatly affected by the news of the fire in the Al Aqsa Mosque in Jerusalem. It is aware of the attachment of the Muslim world for this sanctuary of Islam. Whatever the origins of the fire, it sees in the repercussions of this painful incident another reason for believing that, in accordance with what France has constantly proposed, a just and equitable settlement of all the problems arising for the Middle East should be reached in the shortest time. For the immediate future, the government expresses the wish that everything should be done to stop the dangers of an aggravation of the tension.[28]

This document, the moderate tone of which was undoubtedly intentional, seemed to indicate France's intention to pursue actively, but without noisy demonstrations, her cooperation in the international action for peace in the Middle East. In fact, the entreaties of the French government contributed to the resumption of the Big Four talks on December 2, 1969. But the French plan for a settlement suggested on this occasion was considered by the representative of the United States to offer inadequate guarantees for Israel.

At the end of December a resounding incident called international attention to the embargo policy that had been applied by France since January, 1969, against Israel. During the night of December 24 to 25, five gunboats built in France on order for Israel, but retained by virtue of the embargo decision, were leaving the harbor of Cherbourg, headed for Israel

[27]Jean Schwoebel, *Le Monde*, June 29, 1969.
[28]Statement released to the press by a Foreign Ministry spokesman; from *Le Monde*, August 24, 1969.

under circumstances difficult to assess. The French government considered
that the vigilance of the administrative authorities had failed. It suspended
two high-ranking officials and asked for the recall of the head of Israel's
purchasing mission. The French public and French political circles reacted
in various ways: a large sector of public opinion demanded the cancellation
of the embargo applied unilaterally to Israel, and strongly criticized a
project intending sale of arms to Libya, in particular, Mirage planes. News
of the intended sale was first made public by the *New York Times*,
December 17, 1969.

After the Cabinet met on December 13, spokesmen for the French
government stated:

> . . . the President of the Republic has stressed that this incident would
> not in any way change the principles and modalities of French policy
> concerning the problems of the Middle East. . . . In particular, France
> will not modify the rules relating to the limitations of arms supplies
> previously established; she regrets that her example has not been
> followed. She will continue to contribute to the search for a just and
> durable peace through . . . the concerted action of the four permanent
> members of the Security Council in view of the application of the
> resolutions of that Council. (*Le Monde,* December 14)

On several occasions the government was required to give explanations
to parliament. Thus on January 27, 1970, Maurice Schumann, Foreign
Minister, stated before the Senate Commission of Foreign Affairs, "that
there was no such thing as a French policy of arms sales to the Middle East,
but a Mediterranean policy." He added (without, however, receiving the
support of the majority of the Commission), "We are determined not to
supply any kinds of arms to anybody, on any terms." The French government had in fact considered that Libya was not directly engaged in the
Palestinian conflict, that the arms deliveries would not be forthcoming in
the short term, and that every guarantee would be taken concerning the
purpose of their use. Certain commentators added that France thus offered
an alternative to Soviet interference.

At the beginning of February, 1970, Georges Pompidou replied to a
message from the Chairman of the U.S.S.R. Council of Ministers, Alexei
Kosygin; Pompidou insisted on the usefulness of the Big Four talks and
recommended the presence of U.N. forces in the most critical places to
ensure peace. From February 23 to March 3, 1970, Pompidou remained
in the United States, first on an official and then on a private visit. He
hardly succeeded in making an impact on American opinion, and had to
face a few hostile demonstrations by Jewish elements although he forcefully
claimed to be in no way anti-Semitic. In reviewing this trip before the

diplomatic press on March 9, Maurice Schumann assured that nevertheless the talks between Presidents Nixon and Pompidou had been useful: they had helped to bring about the "thaw" of the Big Four talks and had increased the future chances of Dr. Gunnar Jarring's mission.

Before the National Assembly on April 28, Maurice Schumann again justified the contract signed with Libya and stated that regarding the Middle East,

> the main difficulty . . . was a certain incapacity [by Israel] to think of herself in relation to her fundamental problem, i.e., the fate of the occupied territories and of one million Arabs. France had never ceased to proclaim Israel's right to existence, recognition, and security. But she was well aware that only the evacuation of the occupied territories might provide a serious chance to obtain recognition by her neighbors and that they clearly and definitively undertake to live in peace with her within the limit of guaranteed frontiers.

The evacuation, he went on, would be accompanied by the establishment of demilitarized zones held by U.N. forces which could be withdrawn only following a decision by the Security Council. A just settlement, in agreement with the United Nations resolutions, would be applied to the refugee problem and "would make an important contribution toward the solution of another problem which is acquiring greater importance every day, the Palestinian problem." Lastly, the Minister thought that the work done by the Big Four talks "had been discreet but not in vain."

One year after General de Gaulle's departure, it may therefore be concluded that French policy in the Middle East was showing continuity in all areas.

Nonpolitical Factors of France's Actions

Language, Culture, and Human Relations

Only a half-century ago, the French language, culture, and contacts still were preponderant in the Middle East. They influenced a small local élite, but one on which everything depended. The general style of life in this area, however, has changed considerably. The privileged instruments of French influence have now lost ground; French custom has become less desired, less necessary, and less practical, but the various factors listed below continue to make themselves felt, sometimes with increasing intensity:

1. Social upheavals have brought about a rapid renewal of the leading and influential classes which, while increasing the numbers of the élite, are at the same time diminishing its cultural preoccupations and qualifications.

2. The development and modernization of the regional vernaculars, in particular of Arabic, allow them to express the most diverse ideas and some of the most advanced techniques; they have become the official mode of expression, the general vehicle of teaching at an advanced level, and the main instrument of culture.

3. The English language is more extensively employed, as a language easier to learn, more widely spoken in the world, and easier for the conduct of business affairs.

The French language, nonetheless, preserves assets of diverse value and strength:

1. It is still used extensively in some countries (Syria, Egypt, etc.) by the best-trained élites and among the oldest age groups.

2. In Lebanon there exists a type of Franco-Arabic bilingualism that reaches as far as the popular level, which extends beyond the simple use of a second language and provides a truly double culture.[29]

3. The reputation of the French language persists as an instrument of high-level culture and international intellectual contacts.

The nationals of Middle Eastern countries who have a gift for language use Arabic as a vehicle for national culture, official relations, and everyday life; at the same time they speak a more or less primitive English in business, and a frequently better French for outside cultural contacts and for the purposes of acquiring a double personal culture. Knowing both French and English expands their international contacts with continental Europe and French-speaking Africa.

What vestiges of the past prestige of French culture remain cannot be maintained, in the future, by traditional methods and strength of habits; they can be developed by such means even less. A reconversion of attitudes and methods is now taking place. Without this change in attitude, the practice of the French language would become even more precarious and probably disappear completely. These new measures include, among other things, an attempt to reach the present-day élites, in both cultural and technical areas, the care taken to introduce French in the national school programs, the learning of the French language in such local activities as French firms and technical jargon, the use of modern audio-visual methods of the teaching of the language, and a better distribution of books and the press. The necessity for the vulgarization of the French language to a level closer to that of the masses should not lead one to overlook the high-standard contributions maintained among the intellectual élites.

The means required to meet the various demands for promoting French culture are often allocated to the Middle East all too parsimoniously

[29]Some discussion of this point is presented by the Reverend Selim Abu in his thesis (University of Paris).

because of the priority given to French-speaking Africa. This priority should be further reduced in view of the impact that cultural achievements in the Middle East may be expected to have. The Arab countries are not the only ones concerned; Iran and Israel also show great interest in this direction.

Economy

The French economy used to be powerful under the Ottoman Empire in three types of activity: concessionary companies (public works, railways, ports), service companies (navigation, banks), and exports of manufactured products, especially luxury goods. In the new Middle East the French economy, like French culture, encountered greatly modified and often less favorable conditions. France's fairly efficient effort to adapt has been only partially successful, for it depended upon her participation in the exploitation of Middle Eastern oils.

After World War I, through CFP, a state-owned company with some private participation, France obtained a 23.75-percent participation in the Iraq Petroleum Company (IPC), a concessionary company with activities initially in Iraq and then in Qatar, at Abu Dhabi, and elsewhere. Acting sometimes independently of IPC, the French CFP also operated at Abu Dhabi in association with British Petroleum, and in Iran as a member of the International Consortium. Later, under General de Gaulle's Presidency, SNPA, a joint shareholders' Company, and ERAP began activities in the Middle East and other areas. Drawing inspiration from the agreements made with Algeria, the French-owned ERAP has replaced the traditional concessionary agreement, such as that used for the IPC, by an exploration contract in which the state owning the oil fields (in this case, Iraq) can better protect its national interests and properties.

An increasing part of the French consumption and export of petroleum products is thus supplied by crude oils obtained in the Middle East by French companies under very favorable terms of payment. This means that France benefits from the attention paid to an important customer capable of bringing into the transactions original and liberal views.

In other sectors of the economy France's effort in the Middle East has been of much less significance.

France offers a good market for high quality cotton from Egypt, Syria, Turkey, and other producers. Certain French enterprises, in particular public works and financial companies, maintain satisfactory activity in the region. While maritime services, made more expensive by social benefits, have almost disappeared from the Levantine coast, Air France is operating throughout the Middle East and is participating in a national airline company (Middle East Airlines based in Lebanon).

But France's financial aid to the Middle East, and to some extent her technical cooperation, suffer from the relative priority given to French-speaking Africa.

Despite recent French efforts to find expanding production markets (Kuwait, Saudi Arabia, etc.), Middle Eastern countries still spend only a very small portion of the moneys obtained from the sale of oil to France on the purchase of French goods. France's best customers in the Middle East are Lebanon, Iran, and Israel. But the development of trade with the Israelis gives rise to political difficulties because of the conflict with Palestine, Arab boycotts on the sale of arms, and economic retaliatory measures. For example, in order to retain their Arab auto market, Renault had to shut down the automobile assembly line they were operating in Israel.

General de Gaulle's political action also affected France's economic dealings in the Middle East. It tended to make France as independent as possible of the international trusts for her oil supplies, and to facilitate this through an improvement of relations with the producing countries. This policy has had some success. Some companies formed associations with the Arabs that were appreciated (ERAP in Iraq and Iran). But there were also failures like those of CFP and SNPA where the association was not so beneficial. Further, as we have seen, the January 6, 1969, embargo on arms intended for Israel constituted a serious handicap to the French armaments industry. It may be expected that the present French government will revise certain aspects of de Gaulle's policy in this area.

France will have to make a great effort to increase her commerce in the Middle East, especially her exports. The maintenance of her cultural position, developed mostly because of her former economic preponderance, is now largely dependent on the progress of her commercial undertakings and her trade in the Middle East.

Political Factors of France's Actions

It was above all politically that General de Gaulle's action during the past four years modified and no doubt increased France's stake in the Middle East.

While General de Gaulle limited himself to promoting even better relations in Iran and Turkey by endeavoring to turn the prestige of France to better account, his conception of French interests as well as circumstances led him to adopt a decisive position on the Palestine conflict that was, on the whole, favorable to the Arab countries and severe toward Israel. But since French opinion went more or less in the opposite direction, Israel preferred to moderate the expression of her disappointments, making a clear distinction between the action of the head of state and the attitude of the French people, in hopes of achieving an improved position in the future. Conversely, the Arab states are now making efforts not to lose the advantages they derived from General de Gaulle's policy, while, at the same time, suspecting that the same position will never be used again.

Pompidou's government, which took office in Paris in the spring of 1969, therefore benefits from the choice of many possibilities. For varying motives, all states in the area are favorably disposed toward it. Judging by the government's attitude until now, it is bent on a search for equilibrium and prepared to take over from the Gaullist legacy a will to work for peace on a worldwide scale.

The experience of the past few months has provided lessons which will probably not be neglected. It shows the limits of France's action in the course of her political return to the Middle Eastern scene.

Some of these limits were perceived at once by General de Gaulle. Not only was any form of direct intervention impossible—it was only in favor of Lebanon that the General may have thought of direct intervention for a while in June-July, 1958, and in January, 1969—but also since France could not present herself as impartial, she had to renounce any attempt of mediation or even of good offices over questions of detail. It is not inconceivable that henceforward, regarding this latter point, France might put herself in a position to make a few cautious steps toward mediation.

General de Gaulle issued a warning on the eve of the Six-Day War and a penalty by the embargo of January 3, 1969. The warning was not heard: its only effect was to increase French incomprehension of his Middle Eastern policy and Israeli susceptability. As to the penalty of the embargo, it did, indirectly and usefully, strengthen Lebanon, but it did not have an immediate effect upon Israel's combat ability. The present French government has already formulated an interpretation of the embargo, namely, that if its example did not result in the total cessation of arms sales to the antagonists by foreign countries, then the French position should perhaps be revised.

On the other hand, the General had attempted to suggest an international direction for the Arab-Israeli conflict. Within the United Nations, France played a certain role in favor of the Arab position, without always carrying in her wake the North African states having special relationships with her. But de Gaulle paid even greater attention to bringing about an accord and an agreement among the Big Four for peace. His initiative in the spring of 1967 failed because of the Russian refusal. And although in the winter of 1968-1969 he succeeded in initiating the Big Four talks, he was not able to bring them to a successful conclusion. The limits of France's action, which are perhaps due to the inadequacy of her economic means, are clear. Perhaps her political style may be conceived more discreetly in the future.

It remains that in this infinitely myth-conscious area, General de Gaulle's action, with all its arbitrariness, fracas, imbalance, and inadequate yield has had a resonance, the echoes of which will last. What the Arabs will retain from this attitude is that, at a time when the unfavorable dispositions of the West made them aware of their loneliness and compelled them to seek Russian patronage, the dangers of which they perceived in spite of everything, General de Gaulle publicly bore witness to what was justifiable in their cause. Hence all the ambiguities of the past were forgotten. General de Gaulle appeared to the Arabs as a paladin of justice. Even if nothing remains of the provision he tried to make for the Middle East, his personality will be remembered. And the cautious moderation which the French government may show in the future will no doubt derive the best of its persuasiveness and efficiency from the memory of General de Gaulle's legendary figure.

CHAPTER 14

United States Policy in the Middle East: Constraints and Choices

William B. Quandt

I. Introduction

The United States has been actively involved in Middle Eastern affairs since the end of World War II. During this period, Americans, like the British and the French before them, have discovered the complexities and frustrations of trying to devise successful policies for dealing with the states of the Middle East. The experiences of over two decades have demonstrated that the objectives sought by the United States in the Middle East—namely, relative peace and stability, security for the state of Israel, access to the resources and facilities of the region, and the limitation of Soviet influence—have often been in conflict with one another. In trying to ensure Israeli security, the United States has complicated its relations with the Arab states. Moreover, the creation of a defense pact modeled on NATO and designed to prevent Soviet expansion eventually helped to weaken the pro-Western regime in Iraq, thereby opening the door for Soviet influence in the region.

The inability of the United States to achieve simultaneously all its major objectives in the Middle East means that trade-offs must inevitably be made, and some goals must be sacrificed to attain others. To arrive at policy decisions, it is not sufficient merely to enumerate "interests," vital or otherwise, and then to list the steps that should be taken by a rational government to maximize these interests. To understand the process by which American policies in the Middle East are actually formulated, one must analyze the motivations of policymakers, their perceptions of national interest, the bureaucratic interplay of numerous powerful groups and individuals, and the importance of public opinion and pressure groups.[1] These factors are common in any organizational decisionmaking process.

[1] Two recent studies have critically examined the literature on foreign policy decisionmaking and have proposed alternate approaches based on organizational theory, models from bureaucratic politics, and from cognitive psychology. See Graham T. Allison, "Policy, Process and Politics: Conceptual Models and the Cuban Missile Crisis," Ph.D. Thesis, Harvard University, 1968, and John D. Steinbruner, "The Mind and Milieu of Policy Makers: A Case Study of the M.L.F.," Ph.D. Thesis, MIT, 1968. Also see Robert Jervis, "Hypotheses on Misperception," *World Politics*, Vol. 20, No. 3 (April, 1968).

Some of them are particularly important in the analysis of policy considerations in the Middle East. From past examples of American policies in the Middle East, useful insights into the nature of present constraints on policymakers and limitations on their range of choices can be derived.

In the immediate postwar period, United States policies in the Middle East reflected contradictions and dilemmas which continue to plague American officials dealing with that region. On the one hand, the United States was anxious to bring the Arab states into collective security arrangements to prevent Soviet expansion, as had been successfully done in the Northern Tier countries of Turkey and Iran. This policy would have required active cooperation from the Arab states. At the same time, Americans and their political leaders were deeply concerned with Palestine. As developments in Palestine moved toward the creation of a Jewish state, the United States became involved in the diplomatic battle to press for recognition of Israel's legitimacy. The Arab states, of course, were violently opposed to the idea of a Jewish state in Palestine, and some Arabs came to see Israel as a creation of the United States. America's search for Arab allies and its earlier policy toward Palestine illustrate the difficulties of applying a previously successful formula to a new area and the sensitivity of U.S. foreign policy decisions in the Middle East to public opinion and organized pressures.

From 1955 to 1958 the United States faced a new set of problems in the Middle East. Soviet arms to Egypt, the Aswan Dam decision, the Suez crisis of 1956, emergencies in Jordan and Syria in 1957, and the landing of U.S. troops in Lebanon in 1958 all began to undermine assumptions that had guided American behavior since the early 1950s in this particularly troublesome part of the world. By 1959 a renewed effort to deal with the states of the Middle East was under way, supported by a formula for achieving regional stability that showed promise of working for several years. The ultimate failure of this second postwar phase of American policy in the Middle East was highlighted by the Arab-Israeli war of June, 1967. As the search for successful U.S. policies in the Middle East goes on, some lessons may be drawn from earlier experiences.

II. The Nature of Foreign Policy Decisions

Only rarely do political leaders have the leisure, ability, or imagination to select policies according to carefully defined criteria based on critical appraisals of national interest. More often, it seems, policy is the outcome of a complex political process, the product of a momentary constellation of forces that may evaporate soon after the policy is adopted.

Government officials dealing with foreign policy are frequently obliged to respond to crises. U.S. foreign policy is often reactive because many, if not most, events in the world are largely outside of American control. As a global power, the United States often feels compelled to act or to take a stand on issues that other countries can happily ignore. But the American President, while legally responsible for the conduct of foreign affairs, cannot possibly stay abreast of the incredibly complex situations all over the globe.[2]

Policymakers, because of the limited amount of time and information available to them in dealing with any given problem, often make decisions with little consideration of important alternatives and with scant attention to long-range consequences of decisions. At times foreign policy specialists are able to influence decisions in noncrisis periods by capitalizing on their regional expertise. Frequently, however, they are ignored by decisionmakers because of overriding political concerns or dissatisfaction with the narrow focus of the experts' recommendations. In a crisis, responsibility generally shifts to higher levels of the decisionmaking hierarchy. Men who barely understand the ingredients of the crisis may then be called upon to resolve it, often with little knowledge of earlier policy initiatives.

In normal times, authority for the making of foreign policy is widely dispersed. Congress, the President, the State Department, the Department of Defense, the Agency for International Development (AID), and the Central Intelligence Agency (CIA) may all be trying to put across particular views. Coalitions form and disband, negotiations go on continually, occasionally throwing up decisions that gain widespread acceptance as much for the political support that accompanies them as for their intrinsic merits.[3]

Amidst the seeming disorder and chaos of the foreign policymaking process there are nonetheless elements of stability. Americans, perhaps more than other people, share many assumptions about the proper way to behave in the world. Common beliefs often facilitate communication and establish the needed consensus for policy. Notions of "national interest" are widespread and can become unquestioned premises of policymaking. Past commitments are generally taken seriously, especially if they have been expressed in the legally binding form of treaties. All these factors add

[2]Limits on the American President's ability to deal with foreign affairs are well discussed in Theodore C. Sorensen, *Decision-Making in the White House* (New York: Columbia University Press, 1963), Chap. 3.

[3]Stanley Hoffman, in "Restraints and Choices in American Foreign Policy," *Daedalus*, Vol. 91, No. 4 (Fall, 1962), p. 691, says: "The merits on which problems are tackled become the merits of the men engaged in policy-making, and those men represent not so much ideas as tangible bits and pieces of power."

continuity to American foreign policy and help to offset the many sources
of discord and controversy.

These general characteristics of foreign policymaking are supplemented
by other forces that specifically affect policy toward the Middle East. For
example, American public opinion is only occasionally a major force in
determining foreign policy, but sustained public interest in what the United
States does in the Middle East has long been of great significance. This
interest derives primarily from the existence of the state of Israel and the
general concern that many Americans, not only American Jews, feel for
its welfare. This concern is strengthened by the able efforts of leaders of
the American Jewish community to make their views known to policymakers. Finally, there is a very large American stake in Middle East oil,
and U.S. oil companies also attempt to convey their ideas concerning
appropriate policies in the Middle East to official decisionmakers.

The influence of American public opinion, domestic Jewish groups, and
oil companies on U.S. policy in the Middle East has been the subject of
much mythmaking and insufficient objective analysis. In the case studies
that follow, efforts will be made to assess the importance of both the general
bureaucratic environment of foreign policy and the specific domestic forces
related to the Middle East. An understanding of how these variables have
influenced decisions in the past should provide a basis for judging their
importance in future policymaking.

III. U.S. Involvement in the Middle East

Apart from Europe, no area of the world was of greater concern to the
United States after World War II than the Middle East. Two major reasons
for this concern were Soviet pressures on Greece, Turkey, and Iran, and
domestic U.S. pressures to act decisively on the "Palestine problem" to
bring about the creation of a Jewish state. In both of these areas, the
inability of the British to control seemingly dangerous situations that threatened U.S. interests served as a strong impetus to bring the United States
into an area where it had previously been content to let other Western

[4]On the general level of public interest in foreign affairs, see Gabriel A. Almond,
The American People and Foreign Policy (New York: Praeger, 1960), and James
Rosenau, *Public Opinion and Foreign Policy* (New York: Random House, 1968).
Data from several recent opinion polls indicate that approximately 75% of the American population is interested in what occurs in the Arab-Israeli conflict. Forty to 50%
of the population is more sympathetic to Israel than to the Arabs, and 10 to 15%
of the population is strongly committed to Israel. See figures published in *Intercom*,
Vol. 9, No. 6 (November-December, 1967), p. 51, and the Gallup Poll reported in
the *Los Angeles Times*, February 6, 1969.

powers play a dominant role.[5] A brief analysis of how policies were developed toward Iran in 1946-1947 and toward Palestine in 1947-1948 will illustrate some prevalent views of national interest and ways in which domestic political pressures can shape foreign policy.

Iran: The Retreat of Soviet Power

As part of the Allied operations in World War II, British, American, and Soviet troops were stationed in Iran.[6] Pledges to withdraw these troops at the end of hostilities had been made by all three of the Allies, but early in 1946 it became apparent that the Soviet Union did not intend to withdraw its troops by the stipulated deadline. This proved to be the first substantive issue before the newly formed United Nations in January, 1946. It also set the stage for later efforts by the United States to contain Soviet expansion into the Middle East.

The policy of resisting Soviet intrusions into the Middle East, which served as the main guide for U.S. actions in that region until about 1959, was not primarily the result of a careful analysis of Soviet intentions and U.S. interests. Rather, it was at least in part the product of a number of discrete acts that happened to be successful.

In December, 1945, a pro-Soviet regime had been established in Azerbaijan in northern Iran. Initially, Soviet troops were present to support this regime. Pressure was also exerted by Soviet leaders to obtain an oil concession from the Iranian government. While the Shah of Iran was deeply concerned about these Soviet threats to Iran's sovereignty, the Prime Minister, Qavam al-Salteneh, felt that his personal fortunes could be advanced by keeping his contacts open with the Soviet Union. The British, concerned about their own oil concession in southern Iran and still believing it possible to cooperate with the Soviet Union, were reluctant to oppose their wartime ally. Within the U.S. State Department there was also some disagreement over whether to exacerbate relations with Stalin over Iran.

The Iranian ambassador in Washington, a supporter of the Shah, carried his country's case to the United Nations, where the United States supported

[5] An account of early American involvement in the Middle East is found in David H. Finnie, *Pioneers East: The Early American Experience in the Middle East* (Cambridge, Mass.: Harvard University Press, 1967). J. C. Hurewitz, *Middle East Dilemmas: The Background of United States Policy* (New York: Harper, 1953), pp. 127-130, and William Reitzel, *The Mediterranean: Its Role in America's Foreign Policy*, (New York: Harcourt, Brace, 1948), p. 95, both stress the importance of oil and of World War II in bringing the United States into the Middle East as an independent actor.

[6] The following account draws upon the author's interview with former U.S. Ambassador to Iran, George V. Allen, December 3, 1968.

his right to demand the withdrawal of Soviet troops from Iran. Finally, after some maneuvering by Qavam, and perhaps under some pressure from the United States, the Soviets agreed to withdraw their troops in return for an oil concession in the north. Qavam accepted this, subject to the approval of the Iranian parliament.

By May, 1946, Soviet troops had withdrawn across the border, leaving behind the Soviet-established Azerbaijan regime headed by Jafaar Pishavari. By the end of the year, the Shah, with the support of the army, had gained in strength, and he decided to send Iranian troops into Azerbaijan. The army had instructions to take only the first town, then wait to see what Soviet reactions might be.

The role of the United States in what became known as the "liberation of Azerbaijan" of December 1946 was unintended yet significant. Three American journalists accompanied the Shah's troops in a jeep borrowed from the U.S. embassy.[7] When the troops stopped after their success in the first town, the newsmen drove on, a small American flag showing on the fender of the jeep. Rumors spread rapidly, it seems, convincing villagers throughout Azerbaijan that the Iranian army and the U.S. marines were marching on Tabriz, the capital of Pishavari's puppet government. By the time the newsmen reached Tabriz, the Azerbaijani had liberated them-selves, Pishavari and key officials had fled across the border, and his militia had disintegrated.

The Soviets did not react militarily to this setback, but they did redouble their demands for an oil concession, this time going so far as to threaten physically their erstwhile ally, Qavam. Apparently shaken by his encounter with the Soviet Ambassador, Qavam turned immediately to the U.S. Ambassador, George Allen, for help. While declining to offer military assistance, Allen was mildly encouraging.

As Soviet pressure continued, the Iranian parliament was about to vote on the Soviet oil concession. The President of the parliament, fearing that the deputies would be coerced into granting the concession, approached Allen with another request for help. Ambassador Allen responded with a speech in which he mentioned Iran's right to dispose of its natural resources however it wished, free from any threats or coercion. Although the speech itself had not been authorized by Washington, orders were on their way directing Allen to say very much what his own judgment had already dictated. The reaction of the Iranian government to this speech surprised both Allen and Washington, for the Iranian leaders seemed to read into it a

[7]The story of the liberation of Azerbaijan is told by the three journalists in the *New York Times*, December 14, 1946, p. 6. A few days earlier, on December 11, the *New York Times*, p. 22, quoted Dean Acheson as saying that the United States did not want to get involved in an internal Iranian controversy.

guarantee against Soviet pressure that had hardly been intended. The parliament met and decisively turned down the Soviet request for an oil concession.

In short, then, three journalists, an ambassador, Soviet miscalculations, and Iranian shrewdness contributed to two major setbacks for the Soviet Union, first in Azerbaijan and then in the failure to gain an oil concession. For the United States this was an important example, along with other efforts in Turkey and Greece, of how Soviet power could be contained. What began as relatively timid and faltering responses to Soviet probes in Iran soon emerged, with the Truman Doctrine, as a full-fledged policy of containment of the Soviet Union and defense of the Middle East.[8] With successes in Iran, Greece, and Turkey as testimony to how this policy had worked in the past, efforts were subsequently made to extend the scope of the policy and to add a military dimension that had been lacking in the early years. Events, improvisation, and some difficult choices based on an assessment of changing world-power relations had led to successes which then dictated a policy that was applied in various forms in the Arab world, with vastly different results.[9]

Palestine and the Creation of Israel

Few issues received as much high-level U.S. government attention as "the Palestine problem" after World War II. Britain had been responsible for Palestine before and during the war, but as it did in the case of Greece and Turkey, Britain declared in 1947 the desire to relinquish its dominant military role in the area.

Prior to 1947 American policy had been marked by contradictions. On numerous occasions authoritative U.S. spokesmen had supported the idea of a Jewish national home in Palestine. At the same time, the Arabs had

[8]Hurewitz, op. cit., Chap. 7, states that the Truman doctrine marked the end of U.S. interests without responsibility in the Middle East. President Truman, in his memoirs, Years of Trial and Hope (Doubleday & Co., Garden City: 1956), p. 100, gives some of the background to the announcement of the Truman doctrine. Truman's assertion on p. 95 that he had sent a blunt note to Stalin which brought about Soviet withdrawal from Iran has been questioned by some observers and participants in these events. See John C. Campbell, Defense of the Middle East: Problems of American Policy (New York: Harper, 1960), p. 33: "No other available evidence refers to an ultimatum." The simple fact was that the United States had few troops available in 1947 or 1948 for use in the Nothern Tier or in Palestine. While the "containment" policy came to be seen primarily in military terms, its initial successes were brought about by diplomacy and economic aid.

[9]Charles Burton Marshall, The Limits of Foreign Policy (Baltimore: Johns Hopkins Press, 1968), p. 140, has written: "Great errors can be made by grasping some inference from experience, dubbing it a lesson of history, and adopting it as a guideline for another issue under circumstances only partly similar to the antecedent."

been assured that no decision would be made about Palestine without full prior consultations with them.[10] President Roosevelt in particular had seemed relatively optimistic about the prospects for reconciling Arabs and Jews and felt that the United States should play a mediating role.[11]

The complex story of U.S. involvement in the establishment of the state of Israel covers the period of President Truman's efforts to deal with intense and often contradictory pressures aimed at influencing American policy toward Palestine. Truman's final decision to recognize Israel was the successful culmination of a remarkable campaign waged in behalf of a Jewish state by American citizens. This event, more than any other in recent times, illustrates how domestic politics can significantly affect foreign policy.[12] Nonetheless, one should not conclude that Truman's decision reflected merely his desire to win Jewish votes in New York. In some cases the President's highest advisers were able briefly to change U.S. policy from its pro-Zionist stance. Bureaucratic confusion added to inconsistencies in U.S. policy at critical moments. The full story of American policy toward Palestine from 1945 to 1949 has yet to be told, though many of the significant facts are available.[13] For analytical purposes, the period provides a fascinating view of the interaction of public opinion, pressure groups, bureaucratic politics, and the mediating role of the American President in the formulation of foreign policy. A study of the intricacies of policy-making does not support the widespread notion that U.S. policy toward Israel is solely formulated by Zionists or oil companies. Reality, in this case, is much more complicated.

Following the war, U.S. government concern over the Palestine problem revolved around the question of Jewish immigration to Palestine from Europe, especially from refugee camps. Some American officials opposed allowing Jewish refugees to immigrate freely to the United States; to them

[10]See Joseph B. Schechtman, *The United States and the Jewish State Movement* (New York: Yoselof, 1966); H. Bradford Westerfield, *Foreign Policy and Party Politics* (New Haven: Yale University Press, 1958), Chap. 11. Bartley C. Crum, *Behind the Silken Curtain* (New York: Simon and Schuster, 1947), Chap. 2, speaks of the existence of a "secret file" in the State Department which showed that each time promises had been made by the United States to the Jews concerning Palestine, the State Department sent messages to the Arab states promising "full and prior consultation" before any change of policy.

[11]William A. Eddy, *F. D. R. Meets Ibn Saud* (New York: American Friends of the Middle East, Inc., 1954).

[12]Kermit Roosevelt, "The Partition of Palestine: A Lesson in Pressure Politics," *The Middle East Journal*, Vol. 2, No. 1 (January, 1948).

[13]Schechtman, op. cit.; A. M. Lilienthal, *The Other Side of the Coin: An American Perspective of the Arab-Israeli Conflict* (New York: Devin-Adair, 1965), Chap. 5; Richard R. Stevens, *American Zionism and U.S. Foreign Policy, 1942-1947* (New York: Pageant Press, 1962).

Palestine seemed an attractive alternative for resettlement of the victims of Hitler's persecution. The Zionists, while remaining committed to the ultimate objective of a Jewish state, took the immediate step of securing permission from the British for at least 100,000 Jewish refugees to immigrate to Palestine.

As the debate over Palestine shifted more toward the political status of Jews and Arabs once the British withdrew, sharp differences of opinion arose within the U.S. government. Those who were hostile to the Zionist demand for a separate state and who opposed U.S. initiatives designed to bring this about were probably less numerous than the supporters of a Jewish state. Nonetheless, the State Department, and in particular the Secretary of State, the Near Eastern Affairs section, and the Policy Planning Staff were generally opposed to the idea of active U.S. support for a Jewish state in Palestine.[14] The State Department was joined in its opposition by the Department of the Navy, and later by the Department of Defense and the Joint Chiefs of Staff. Much less important as direct sources of pressure against American sponsorship of a Jewish state were American oil companies, some members of the British government, and the Arab states themselves.

Two themes run through the arguments against U.S. efforts to support the creation of a Jewish state in Palestine: oil and the Soviet Union. In some circles, particularly in the Department of the Navy, there was serious concern over oil.[15] It was estimated that U.S. oil reserves were being rapidly depleted and that no future war could be successfully fought without access to Arab oil. Continued access to this oil for U.S. military forces and for Europe required Arab good will, which could be jeopardized by U.S. support for Israel. Despite some naïve thinking about oil as an irreplaceable vital resource, it was true that Middle Eastern oil was necessary for European reconstruction. Secretary of Defense James Forrestal was one of the main spokesmen for the "oil group."

A second, closely related argument against U.S. support for a Jewish state was that the Arabs would turn to the Soviet Union for support if the West sponsored the creation of Israel. The Soviet Union was in fact itself pushing for the creation of a Jewish state as a means of removing the

[14]George Kennan, then on the Policy Planning Staff of the State Department, later wrote: "The establishment of the state of Israel (American military support of which I resolutely opposed) seemed to heighten the danger of Communist infiltration in the Arab countries" *Memoirs: 1925-1950* (Boston: Little, Brown, 1967), p. 380.

[15]The importance attributed to Middle East oil can be seen in Halford L. Hoskins, *Middle East Oil in United States Foreign Policy* (The Library of Congress Legislative Reference Service, Washington, D.C., December, 1950), and Walter Millis (ed.), *The Forrestal Diaries,* (New York: Viking, 1951), p. 323, where Forrestal refers to his concern with ". . . the rapid depletion of American oil reserves . . . ."

British from Palestine. Some American officials judged, however, that Soviet support for the Zionists was only tactical and would readily be abandoned if advantages could thereby be had in the Arab world. Moderate Arab regimes might then be replaced by more radical ones, which would reduce the ability of the West to contain Communist expansion. Strategic interests in the Middle East, including oil, would be endangered. An articulate spokesman for this point of view was Loy Henderson, in charge of the Division of Near Eastern Affairs in the State Department. In time both Forrestal and Henderson became the targets of sharp Zionist criticism and propaganda campaigns.

The forces favoring the establishment of a Jewish state were more numerous and somewhat more diffuse than those opposing it. The Zionist organizations exercised considerable influence through their leaders, Rabbis Stephen Wise and Abba Silver, as well as Chaim Weizmann. But American public opinion also was generally sympathetic to the Zionist demands.[16] Senators and Congressmen such as Robert Wagner, Robert Taft, and Jacob Javits reflected the demands of their constituents. President Truman himself, as a Senator, had expressed sympathy for a Jewish home in Palestine, and there is no reason to think that these sentiments changed when he became President. On Truman's White House staff, David Niles is reported to have played an important role in promoting Zionist demands.[17] Democratic liberals such as Mrs. Eleanor Roosevelt were generally in favor of a Jewish state, and both Democratic and Republican platforms had contained pro-Zionist planks.

From April 2, 1947, when the British formally requested that the United Nations take over "the Palestine problem," until November 29 of the same year, when the United Nations voted in favor of the principle of partition that would establish both a Jewish and an Arab state in Palestine, pro-Zionist forces in the United States were extremely active. Offsetting these pressures were fears that partition would lead to warfare between Arabs and Jews, which might require the United States to send troops to Palestine. President Truman was the object of much direct pressure. In his own words:

The facts were that not only were there pressure movements around the

---

[16] A Gallup survey of public opinion in January, 1946, showed that 75% of those who followed the Palestine problem were sympathetic to Zionist demands. See the *Los Angeles Times*, February 6, 1969. Samuel Halperin, *The Political World of American Zionism* (Detroit: Wayne State University Press, 1961), p. 38, shows that about 80% of American Jews favored the creation of a Jewish state. Young people and those in the professions were slightly less enthusiastic than older, nonprofessional people.

[17] Millis, *op. cit.*, pp. 347, 361.

United Nations unlike anything that had been seen there before but that the White House, too, was subjected to a constant barrage. I do not think I ever had as much pressure and propaganda aimed at the White House as I had in this instance.[18]

The struggle to influence U.S. policy continued, even after the United Nations vote for partition. Secretary of Defense James Forrestal was particularly intent upon "removing the Palestine question from domestic politics."[19] In an election year, he feared, Democrats and Republicans alike would take the easy course of appealing to Jewish voters by fully supporting the Zionist cause rather than analyzing American interests in the Middle East. After two months of concerted activity, Forrestal dropped his public campaign in mid-February, 1948.

As fighting erupted between Jews and Arabs in Palestine, the U.S. representative at the United Nations, Warren Austin, warned of the dangers to peace inherent in the situation, but continued to advocate partition as late as February 24. Loy Henderson and others in the State Department, along with Forrestal, were convinced that partition along the lines of the U.S. resolution would lead to warfare between Arabs and Jews. No matter who won such a war, it was thought, U.S. interests in the region would be jeopardized indefinitely. They therefore chose to interpret the U.N. resolution as a recommendation that was not self-implementing, especially in the absence of a means for partitioning Palestine.[20] Instead, they developed the idea of establishing a trusteeship over all the British Mandated area, thereby postponing for several years any permanent decision regarding the future of Palestine. During the trusteeship, it was hoped, Arabs and Jews might overcome their mutual animosities. This 1948 trusteeship plan, which had the backing of the State Department, was submitted to President Truman. He gave oral approval and left the time of implementation up to the State Department.

Rumors of this change in American policy began to circulate, and Zionist leaders sought to meet with the President. Truman, after having approved the trusteeship plan, tried to insulate himself from Zionist pressures. Finally, an old friend convinced him to see Chaim Weizmann.[21] On

---

[18]Truman, op. cit., p. 158. Secretary of State Marshall is said to have refused to deal with the Palestine question on a day-to-day basis, since he saw it as "a domestic problem." Under-Secretary Lovett therefore was the focus of most pressure. Forrestal notes in his diary that Lovett told him, ". . . he had never in his life been subject to as much pressure as he had . . ." in the days preceding the U.N. vote on partition (Millis, op. cit., p. 346).

[19]Millis, op. cit., pp. 322-323, 344.

[20]Ibid., p. 362.

[21]Truman, op. cit., p. 160.

March 18 Truman privately received Weizmann and led him to understand that the United States still favored partition. In the meantime, the State Department, ignorant of the President's meeting with Weizmann, ordered Warren Austin to present the trusteeship plan to the United Nations on March 19. Needless to say, the speech outraged Zionist leaders, and Truman himself was angry that the speech had not been cleared with him prior to actual delivery.

The trusteeship proposal had little chance of succeeding, for neither Truman nor the Arabs nor the Jews nor the British favored it in the United Nations. Less than two months later the United States, on Truman's initiative, gave *de facto* recognition to the new state of Israel.[22]

President Truman's decisions concerning Palestine demonstrate that organized pressure and personal access to the White House can weigh more heavily than the nearly unanimous recommendations of the President's major foreign policy advisers. The State Department had achieved only a temporary reversal in policy. United States policy toward the Middle East in later years continued to reflect tensions between the advice of the foreign policy specialists, and their proposals based on arguments of "vital national interest," and the demands of public opinion, influential Jewish leaders, and Congressmen. Middle East policy still contains elements of this schizophrenia.

The Arab World: Crises of Involvement, 1951-1958

While Turkey, Iran, and Israel continued to concern U.S. decisionmakers throughout the 1950s, new policy initiatives during these years were primarily directed at the Arab world. Relations with Turkey were extremely close during this period, and Turkey became in many ways the cornerstone of American defense interests in the region. United States involvement in Iran was at times very deep, culminating in active participation in expelling Prime Minister Mossadegh from power in 1953.[23] Thereafter, efforts were made to bring some measure of stability and progress to Iran. With Israel, relations were correct and generally close, but in many circles Israel was still seen as an obstacle to better U.S. relations with the Arabs.

The list of issues which caused strains in U.S. relations with various Arab states between 1951 and 1958 is a lengthy one. The Middle East Defense

---

[22] Even after recognizing Israel, the United States refused to send arms to help the new states. Policies were reportedly suggested by United States officials to retain good relations with the Arabs, especially Saudi Arabia, by promising that Israel would not expand further if the Arabs would agree to recognize the new state, but these proposals were vetoed in Washington.

[23] See the account in David Wise and Thomas B. Ross, *The Invisible Government* (New York: Random House, 1964), pp. 110-114.

Organization (MEDO), the Baghdad Pact, the Soviet arms deal with Egypt, the Suez crisis, the Eisenhower doctrine, the Syrian crisis of 1957 and the U.S. troop landings in Lebanon—all have an aura of failure about them. There were, of course, some limited successes with the Arabs, but the themes of failure, misperception, and inappropriate policies run strongly through most surveys of U.S. relations with the Arab world in the 1950s.

Many of the difficulties faced by the United States in the Arab world were at least in part the result of American policies. Two ideas dominated the thoughts of decisionmakers during this period as they tried to deal with the Arab countries. One was the major objective of "defense of the Middle East" from Soviet aggression and subversion. The success of U.S. policy in the Northern Tier countries seemed to suggest the means for obtaining this objective—namely, military alliances plus economic and military aid.[24] Since Britain's position was constantly threatened with erosion, the United States government felt impelled to become involved in the affairs of the Arab world.

A second theme which ran through American policy during the early 1950s was to contain or settle the Arab-Israeli conflict. Once again the means that seemed appropriate were aid to the Arab countries and Israel, plus elaborate economic projects, such as the Eric Johnston plan, intended to foster a spirit of regional cooperation. By now, of course, the United States was committed to the existence of Israel, and was thus obliged to live with the consequences of this commitment in the Arab countries.

In approaching the Arab world, U.S. policymakers were constrained by a number of preconceptions. The legacy of earlier American policies in both the Northern Tier and Palestine complicated U.S. policy in the Arab world. Problems in Egypt, Iraq, and Syria were not the same as those existing elsewhere in the Middle East, nor could the solutions be the same. United States policy was also strongly influenced by the complex personality of Secretary of State Dulles. From 1953 to 1958 U.S. relations with the Arab world seemed largely to depend on beliefs and desires of two individuals, Gamal Abdel Nasser and John Foster Dulles. While U.S. interests in the rest of the Arab world, particularly in Jordan and Saudi Arabia, were considered important, it was in United States–Egyptian relations that the need for stability and the reality of crises lay.

In trying to deal with Egypt, the United States government was saddled

[24]Ambassador Raymond Hare, in an interview on December 2, 1968, stated: "The Truman Doctrine was distinctly successful in the North, so much so in fact that it was natural to seek a similar approach in the South. The difference was that, whereas the countries of the North understood the communist threat in terms of first-hand experience, the countries of the South were concerned with quite a different set of issues. As a consequence, a policy which had worked in one area failed in the other."

with grave difficulties. Many Americans found it difficult to understand or sympathize with Arab nationalism or the aspiration for Arab unity. If Nasser spoke against the regime in Jordan or Iraq and this was followed by riots, Nasser was automatically seen as responsible for stirring up trouble. Until the Suez crisis of 1956, the United States was also somewhat limited in what it could do in the Middle East by its close association with Great Britain.

The British presence and a distrust of Nasser's regime made American policymakers reluctant to become deeply involved in Egypt. Still, the desire to enlist Egypt in a defensive alignment remained great. These cross-pressures made United States involvement in the Arab world tentative and uncertain. Consistent efforts were made to avoid committing U.S. military forces and to keep from becoming the major arms supplier to the countries of the Middle East. And yet, the United States did make serious attempts to join with the British in establishing defense pacts, to bring about a settlement of the Arab-Israeli conflict, to expedite British withdrawal from Suez, and to help some Arab countries with economic aid.

The question of supplying arms to the countries of the Middle East was common to both the concern for defense against Soviet expansion and the desire for a settlement of the Arab-Israeli conflict. The twin objectives of defense and peace came into conflict in arms policy, for in order to bring the Arab states into a defense organization it would be necessary to offer arms. At the same time, a reduction of arms supplies was thought to be essential if the Arab-Israeli dispute was to be contained or settled.

The Tripartite Declaration of 1950 represented an early attempt to resolve these difficulties. Signed by the United States, Britain, and France, the Declaration reflected American concern for arms limitation and stability along the Arab-Israeli armistice lines. It stated that the allies were opposed to ". . . the development of an arms race between the Arab states and Israel." In addition, the three governments stated their opposition to the violation of boundaries and armistice lines by force, and pledged to take action to prevent such occurrences. The Soviet Union was not yet a major Middle East power, and those drafting the Tripartite Declaration were not immediately concerned with the possibilities of Soviet intrusions into the Middle East. But despite the absence of an immediate Soviet threat to the Arab world, efforts were soon under way to prepare for this eventuality.

The implications of the successes in Turkey and Iran in earlier years were too great to resist, and in 1951 the United States sought to organize, with the British, French, and Turks, a Middle East Defense Organization (MEDO). Why these efforts were made in the Arab world, where the Soviet threat was potential, but not actual, can be partly explained by a bureaucratic tendency to extend a successful policy to new areas, whether appropriate or not. The MEDO plan was short-lived, but the underlying desire to align the Arab states on the side of the West dominated much of U.S. policy well into the 1950s.

Despite these initial misconceptions of what American policy in the Arab world could be, U.S.-Egyptian relations were relatively close, both in the last year of Farouk's rule and in the early days of the Naguib-Nasser regime.[25] Prior to the July 23, 1952, *coup* against the Farouk, the United States actively promoted social and economic reform in Egypt. The momentum in United States–Egyptian relations built up under Farouk and Ali Maher continued under the Revolutionary Command Council.

Meanwhile, the change of administration in Washington led to a new look at the Middle East. In the spring of 1953, U.S. Secretary of State John Foster Dulles traveled to the Middle East to examine the prospects for some form of collective defense arrangements. As a result of this trip, Dulles recognized that the Arab states were much more concerned about the security threat posed by Israel than about any threat from the Soviet Union.[26] Dulles concluded that efforts to organize the Middle East against Communist expansion should be limited to the countries that shared the U.S. desire to contain the Soviet Union, namely the Northern Tier countries, as he was to call them. But despite this overt recognition of the limits on U.S. ability to draw the Arab countries into military alliance with the West, Dulles did not give up the hope of luring Nasser into closer cooperation.

U.S. policy toward the Arab world underwent a shift in emphasis in 1954. While defense was still a major concern, the search for a settlement of the Arab-Israeli dispute began to take precedence. The hope was that if the Arabs could reach a satisfactory arrangement with the Israelis, it would be possible to interest them in joining Western defense pacts.[27] As early as October, 1953, President Eisenhower appointed Eric Johnston to search for an equitable means of sharing the waters of the Jordan River. The purpose of this project was to lessen political tensions between Arabs and Israelis by proposing mutually advantageous economic schemes. Everything seemed to point in favor of the Jordan water project. Water could be made available to increase the amount of arable land, which in turn could facilitate the

[25]The U.S. Ambassador in Cairo, Jefferson Caffrey, was instrumental in bringing about Farouk's peaceful departure from Egypt. Another American, Kermit Roosevelt, identified Nasser as the man to deal with after 1952 and is reported to have become quite closely associated with him.

[26]See E. B. Childers, *The Road to Suez* (London: MacGibbon and Kee, 1962), pp. 120-121, for Nasser's reply to Dulles that nationalism could serve as the strongest barrier to Communism in the Middle East.

[27]Louis L. Gerson, *John Foster Dulles* (New York: Cooper Square Publishers, 1967), p. 257.

resolution of the refugee problem by opening new areas to them for resettlement.

More directly related to Egypt, the United States was talking to Nasser about the possibilities of military aid. After having facilitated, through unusually effective diplomacy, an agreement between Egypt and the British over evacuation of the Suez Canal base, the United States was more eager than ever to bring Nasser into Western defense agreements and to moderate his behavior toward Israel.[28] Arms were to be the primary means of accomplishing this. Initially, Nasser asked for equipment to keep his military establishment happy. The United States hinted at various offers, running from $40 million to $100 million worth of equipment. This, it was thought, would help make Nasser strong internally; then he could afford to take steps to settle matters peacefully with Israel.

Egyptian demands for arms radically changed following Israel's massive surprise attack on Gaza in February, 1955. As the tension mounted, the United States intensified efforts to find a solution to the Arab-Israeli conflict.[29] Extragovernmental initiatives were taken to encourage the United Nations to search for peace in the Middle East. Eventually these suggestions resulted in U.N. Secretary-General Dag Hammarskjöld's visit to the area in February, 1956. In August, 1955, Dulles made a speech to the Council on Foreign Relations that spelled out his views on a possible settlement and what the United States would be willing to do to guarantee frontiers and to settle the refugee problem.

Meanwhile, Iraq and Turkey had agreed in early 1955 to form the Baghdad Pact, and despite the fact that the United States did not join it and had not even played a major role in bringing it about, Nasser placed much of the blame on Washington.[30] Nasser had long been warning the

[28]"The President's Proposal on the Middle East," *Hearings before the Committee on Foreign Relations and the Committee on Armed Services*, United States Senate, 85th Congress, January 14 to February 11, 1957, p. 791, contains the text of a letter dated July 15, 1954, sent by President Eisenhower to President Nasser, stating: ". . . simultaneously with the conclusion of the Suez agreement with Great Britain, the United States would enter into firm commitments with Egypt for economic assistance for strengthening its armed forces."

[29]J. R. Beal, *John Foster Dulles: 1888-1959* (New York: Harper, 1959), p. 252, reports that after a detailed study of the Arab-Israeli conflict, the State Department concluded early in 1955 that the problems could be solved with outside help.

[30]Beal, *op. cit.*, p. 249, argues that after Dulles first suggested a Middle East defense pact in June, 1953, the Turks took most of the initiative, and the United States did nothing to advance the idea. Dulles was apparently surprised when Iraq joined. This latter assessment, however, is partially refuted by the report of the American Ambassador to Iraq in 1954, Waldemar J. Gallman, who claims that Dulles hoped Iraq would join the regional defense arrangements for the Middle East. See Waldemar J. Gallman, *Iraq under Nuri* (Baltimore: Johns Hopkins Press, 1964).

United States in private that he would oppose any Middle East defense pact that included an Arab country. This warning had been passed on to Washington, but many U.S. officials were nonetheless angered by Nasser's vehement opposition to Iraqi participation.

By spring, 1955, Americans began to hear rumors of a possible arms deal between Nasser and the Soviet Union.[31] At the Geneva Conference that summer Dulles and Molotov reportedly discussed Soviet arms to Egypt, but it is not clear whether Dulles considered the arms deal more than a distant possibility. Dulles continued to doubt reports that an agreement had been concluded by August, arguing that this would be "contrary to the spirit of Geneva." When Nasser finally announced the arms deal in September, Dulles acted outraged and even tried to get Nasser to change his mind.[32]

The arms deal provided dramatic evidence of Soviet desires to gain influence in the Middle East. But this did not discourage Western efforts to find a solution to the Arab-Israeli conflict. By October, 1955, although the Johnston mission on sharing the Jordan River water had reached an impasse, other efforts were still being pursued. On November 9, 1955, British Prime Minister Anthony Eden spoke at the Guildhall of the possibility of Israel's making territorial compromises, presumably in the Negev, to reach a settlement with the Arabs. The Israelis were furious. Nasser, of course, responded approvingly. Some U.S. officials seemed to favor this plan.

The most significant American initiative toward Egypt came in December, 1955, when the United States offered to help Egypt finance the construction of the Aswan High Dam. This project appealed to Americans because of its benevolent intent, its boldness of conception, and its prospects of allowing the West to retain influence in Egypt. It was also hoped that Nasser would be discouraged from accepting further arms shipments from the Soviet Union.

The year following the U.S. offer to participate in the construction of the Aswan Dam was perhaps the most confusing in the history of American dealings with the Middle East. It is nearly impossible to sort out all the forces leading first to the U.S. decision to withdraw the Aswan Dam offer in July, and then to the decision to oppose the Anglo-French-Israeli attack on Egypt in October. Enough is known, however, from published sources

---

[31]The actual date of the signing of the Soviet-Egyptian arms deal, which was announced in September, 1955, is unclear. For conflicting evidence, see Uri Ra'anan, *The USSR Arms the Third World* (Cambridge, Mass.: The M.I.T. Press, 1959), pp. 76-82; Kennett Love, *Suez: The Twice-Fought War* (New York: McGraw-Hill, 1969), pp. 83-128; and Miles Copeland, *The Game of Nations* (London: Weidenfeld and Nicolson, 1969).

[32]Ambassador George Allen was sent to Cairo. See the account in Wise and Ross, *op. cit.*, pp. 114-117.

and interviews with participants in the events to estimate the reasons behind these two dramatic decisions.[33]

Following the creation of the Baghdad Pact, the United States had angered the members of the new alliance by refusing to join. This decision reflected American desires to avoid cutting all ties with Egypt. Israel would also have been likely to ask for a security treaty if the United States had joined the Baghdad Pact.[34] In February, 1956, Eden tried to get the United States to "put teeth in the Tripartite Agreement" by giving military backing to the stated guarantees of the armistice lines. The United States again refused.

During this period Dulles became increasingly impatient with efforts to deal constructively with Nasser, especially since Nasser seemed to be using delaying tactics on the Aswan Dam offer to get better terms from the United States. In mid-June Dulles made a speech about the immorality of neutralism which hinted that his attitude toward Egypt was changing.

Finally, in mid-July, the Egyptian Ambassador to the United States, Ahmad Hussein, flew to the United States with the declared intention of accepting the U.S. offer to help construct the Aswan Dam. Before his arrival, some U.S. policymakers had already become discouraged with the possibilities of maintaining good relations with Nasser. Many of Dulles' top advisers on the Middle East no longer favored the Aswan proposal. Congress was clearly opposed to the idea. In addition, Senator Knowland, then Senate minority leader, told Dulles that the Senate would not approve aid for the Aswan Dam, citing competition with U.S. cotton producers as a reason.[35] Congressman Rooney also opposed the plan on the grounds that the United States should not help an enemy of Israel. Others were irritated with Nasser over Egyptian arms agreements with the Soviet Union and for his recognition of Communist China.

While Dulles' own motives in withdrawing the offer are still somewhat unclear, the pressure for him to do so was apparently great. Those who were closest to him at the time, including a U.S. official who attended the meeting between Dulles and the Egyptian Ambassador, have reported that Dulles felt that "the entire developing world was watching" and that the United States was obliged to show that "it did not submit to blackmail."

[33] J. E. Dougherty, "The Aswan Decision in Perspective, "Political Science Quarterly, Vol. 74, No. 1 (1959), pp. 21-45; M. A. Fitzsimons, "The Suez Crisis and Containment Policy," The Review of Politics, Vol. 19, No. 4 (October, 1957), pp. 419-445; Anthony Nutting, No End of a Lesson: The Story of Suez (London: Constable, 1967); Hugh Thomas, Suez (New York: Harper, 1967).

[34] Dwight D. Eisenhower, Waging Peace: 1956-1961 (Garden City: Doubleday & Co., 1965), p. 27.

[35] Ibid., p. 32.

The complex events following the withdrawal of the Aswan offer are still not fully understood. Nasser nationalized the Suez Canal in what seemed to be a moment of outrage at the United States; Eden became obsessed with deposing the "Mussolini of the Nile"; the French desperately hoped to solve their problems in Algeria by eliminating Nasser; and the Israelis saw an opportunity to attack Egypt in concert with Britain and France so as to achieve long-standing objectives of eliminating guerrilla bases in Gaza and opening the Straits of Tiran to Israeli shipping.[36]

With ample warning of the possibility of an attack on Suez, Dulles understandably sought to gain time by proposing various diplomatic solutions to the crisis. As in the case of the Soviet arms deal, he seemed to dismiss the intelligence reports that a joint British, French, and Israeli attack on Egypt was in the making. This may have reflected wishful thinking, for with elections approaching in November, American officials above all wanted to avoid being drawn into a war in the Middle East.

It seems that Dulles was somewhat less indignant and surprised by the British, French, and Israeli attack than he appeared.[37] An important element in bringing about U.S. disapproval may have been Selwyn Lloyd's assurance to U.S. Ambassador in Britain Winthrop Aldrich the day before the attack that the British had no knowledge of an impending Israeli strike against Egypt.[38] In addition, Dulles and Eisenhower were apparently irritated by the immediate British request to help defend the pound. The secrecy and collusion of the entire operation were distasteful to many Americans, as was the clear violation of the U.N. charter, in which Dulles, as a lawyer, continued to believe.[39] Whether or not Dulles was hoping to delay the U.N. resolution calling for a cease-fire until the British had at least disposed of Nasser is open to question. But on November 2 Dulles fell ill, and it was left to Henry Cabot Lodge, perhaps with the encouragement of Herbert Hoover, Jr., to push the resolution rapidly through the United Nations.[40] However ambivalent Dulles may have felt at the time, he claimed to a close aide near the end of his life that his opposition to the attack on Suez was the only deci-

[36]Moshe Dayan, *Diary of the Sinai Campaign* (New York: Harper, 1966).

[37]Gerson, *John Foster Dulles*, p. 283, implies that Eisenhower set the course of American policy by ruling out military action as early as July 28, 1956, at a White House meeting held in Dulles' absence.

[38]Thomas, *Suez*, p. 119. See, also, W. W. Aldrich, "The Suez Crisis: A Footnote to History," *Foreign Affairs*, Vol. 45, No. 3, (April, 1962), pp. 543-545.

[39]According to Emmet John Hughes, *The Ordeal of Power: A Political Memoir of the Eisenhower Years* (New York: Atheneum, 1963), p. 219, Eisenhower was most angered by the poor *military* judgments shown by the British and the French.

[40]Gerson, *op. cit.*, p. 297, says that Lodge, unlike Dulles, did this "without a 'heavy heart.' "

sion of his career that he was completely certain was correct. For the rest, he said, history would have to judge.

The actions of the United States in the Suez crisis illustrate several important aspects of policymaking. Eisenhower and probably Dulles as well seemed to feel that the failure of the British and the French to consult with their major ally was a betrayal of trust that should be condemned. Also, there was a strong feeling that the venture could not possibly succeed in view of Britain's difficulties in the preceding years in holding her base at Suez. Finally, the moral and legal principles invoked by some of the major actors should not be underestimated in any assessment of the dominant factors shaping the American decision to oppose two of its closest allies.[41] Evidence is lacking that decisions at the peak of the crisis were strongly motivated by concerns with domestic Jewish reaction, the New York vote, the desires of the President of Standard Oil, or any other organized domestic interest.

From the time of the Suez crisis to the landing of American troops in Lebanon, the United States was searching for new policy guidelines in the Middle East. Serious efforts were made to undo the consequences of the Suez crisis, and the United States finally brought about Israeli withdrawal from Sinai by using various threats and promises.[42] British and French prestige in the Middle East fell to an all-time low. Many Arabs were grateful for American opposition to the Suez aggression. In such circumstances one might have anticipated new U.S. initiatives to capitalize upon this strong position in the Middle East to prevent further Soviet encroachments.

But instead of new policies, the United States government reverted to the familiar theme of "defending the Middle East." The form in which this was expressed was the Eisenhower doctrine, which stated that

> ... the United States is prepared to use armed forces to assist any nation or group of such nations requesting assistance against armed aggression from any country controlled by international communism. . . .

The rationale lying behind the Eisenhower doctrine was somewhat more complex than the terms of the doctrine indicate. American officials realized that the Suez crisis had seriously undermined the ability of the British and French to play a role in stabilizing the Middle East. By asserting the Eisenhower doctrine, they were letting it be known that the United States would still respect the principles of the Tripartite Declaration. The United States therefore declared itself the major peacekeeper in the Middle East,

[41]In Hughes, op. cit., p. 213, Eisenhower is quoted as saying, "Are they going to *dare* us—dare *us* to defend the Tripartite Declaration?"

[42]Eisenhower, op. cit., pp. 185-186. Cutting off private aid to Israel, which amounted to about $100 million yearly, was contemplated if Israel refused to withdraw.

not only against "international communism," but against other sources of instability as well. But to many Arabs, who felt that the United States was incapable of distinguishing between Communism and Arab nationalism, the Eisenhower doctrine seemed to be the perfect justification for future American involvement in inter-Arab conflicts. Nasser, not without some justification, felt that the doctrine was aimed against him and he reacted with predictable hostility.[43]

Once again, American policy as expressed in the Eisenhower doctrine was less a response to domestic pressures than a reflection of the limited imaginations of top policymakers. Formulas derived from U.S. experiences in Turkey and Iran were still influencing policies toward the Arab world a decade later. The major sources of limitations on policymakers at this time were of their own creation and were a psychological nature. American officials accepted uncritically a large number of value-laden terms to describe the Middle East, and when all of these were strung together, the policies they led to were nearly predictable. For example, phrases such as "power vacuum," "traditional Soviet interests in the Middle East," "outflanking NATO," and "the strategic crossroads of three continents" promoted an image of the importance of the Middle East and of the threat to U.S. interests there that inevitably led to thoughts of military responses and alliances to deal with the political problems of the area. Were it not for the fact that this approach to the region practically destroyed any basis for dealing with many of the Arab states, the Eisenhower doctrine would have been harmless enough. As it was, its effects were relatively limited and short-lived. Even the landings in Lebanon in July, 1958, were more the last act in a worn-out approach to the Middle East than a reaffirmation of a cherished policy.[44]

The theme of anti-Communism in the Eisenhower doctrine dominated public and private thinking on the Middle East during 1957 and 1958. American concern over Communism and Soviet domination in the Middle East had grown since the early 1950s. Under this influence, U.S. policymakers viewed events in Jordan and Syria in 1957 with great anxiety.

In Jordan, a pro-Nasser regime had come to power in October, 1956, in an election that was closer to being democratic than any previous one. The United States seems to have viewed the outcome as a reflection of Nasser's subversive, and perhaps even worse, pro-Communist influence.

[43]See the "Exchange of Letters between President John F. Kennedy and President Gamal Abd an-Nasir," *Middle Eastern Affairs* (November, 1962), Vol. 13, p. 275; also Eisenhower, *op. cit.*, pp. 115-116, on the decision after Suez to try to build up King Saud as a counterweight to Nasser.

[44]Malcolm Kerr, "Coming to Terms with Nasser: Attempts and Failures," *International Affairs*, Vol. 43, No. 1 (January, 1967), p. 74.

Accordingly, the United States gave support to King Hussein the following spring so that he might stand up to this threat to his authority. The Sixth Fleet made a few menacing maneuvers, the King re-established control, and the crisis subsided.

But in Syria events seemed much more serious, especially after a pro-Soviet officer was named Chief of Staff. While the story of U.S. efforts to prevent what was feared to be an impending Communist takeover has yet to be fully revealed, it is clear that there arose deep concern in Washington about the whole Middle East "going Communist."[45] The Turkish government became particularly insistent that something be done to remove the regime in Damascus, and for a time the Iraqis seemed willing to take the lead in any such operation.[46] The United States, while not being the primary instigator of these military pressures on Syria, seemed prepared to give help if it should be needed "following Syrian aggression."

The Syrian crisis subsided, however, as the Arab countries, led by Saudi Arabia, backed down from any challenge to Syria and instead began to warn against U.S. aggression. Then, in a dramatic move to solve internal problems of anarchy and of a growing Communist challenge, the Syrians turned to Egypt with a plea for immediate union between the two countries. The United States was saved from the onus of doing to the Syrian Communists what the Egyptians were equally happy to do.

But fear that Syria had almost "gone over to the Communists" haunted policymakers who dealt with the Middle East. The result of this anxiety was that when a new crisis arose in the region, as it was bound to do, the hand of the Communists was once again perceived. This time, however, the threat appeared in Lebanon.

Civil war had begun in Lebanon in the spring of 1958, partly as a result of pro-Western President Camille Chamoun's desire to extend his term of office, in violation of the constitution.[47] Syria seems to have given some aid to the rebels, and Chamoun was extremely anxious to obtain U.S. support, including the dispatch of troops if necessary. The United States was sympathetic to his request, but did not act immediately. By early July it seemed that the crisis was subsiding.

Then, on July 14, 1958, the pro-Western regime in Iraq was overthrown in a military coup. Once again the specter of Communist aggression in the

[45]Eisenhower, *op. cit.,* pp. 196-198.

[46]Patrick Seale, *The Struggle for Syria: A Study of Post-War Politics* (London: Oxford University Press, 1965), pp. 296-302, gives a detailed account of this episode.

[47]Robert Murphy, *Diplomat among Warriors* (Garden City: Doubleday & Co., 1964), pp. 404-405, gives some of the background to this crisis and describes his own important role as President Eisenhower's envoy in resolving the dispute.

Middle East arose in the minds of some Americans. In an atmosphere of immense confusion U.S. troops were ordered to land in Lebanon to provide security for Chamoun's government.[48]

The landing of American troops was intended to reduce the possibility that the Iraqi revolution would set off a shock wave of unrest throughout the Arab world that might endanger the regime in Jordan. Overthrow of the Jordan government could prompt Israel to seize the West Bank of the Jordan River, which could trigger a full-scale Arab-Israeli war. A show of American and British force, it was hoped, would prevent this sequence of dangerous events.

With unusually good luck, this unique example of a U.S. military venture in the Middle East was quite successful. Virtually no hostilities occurred, a measure of calm was rapidly brought to the country, and U.S. efforts to mediate the conflict in Lebanon produced a successor to Chamoun who was acceptable to the United States and Nasser, as well as to the Lebanese.

By October, 1958, U.S. troops were withdrawn from Lebanon, and a turbulent era in American relations with the Middle East came to a close. In retrospect, it seemed to some observers that American troops were less important in solving the crisis than were the mediating skills of the President's envoy, Robert Murphy. This was perhaps a hint that diplomacy might be at least as effective as military action in dealing with many problems in the Middle East.

A major obstacle to the success of American policy efforts in the first decade of active involvement in the Middle East was misjudgment by officials of the region's political forces. For example, policymakers overestimated both the vulnerability of the Arab countries to Communist or Nasserist "subversion" and the military threat from the Soviet Union in regions other than the Northern Tier. They underestimated the insolubility of the Arab-Israeli dispute and the opposition of Arab nationalism to both Western influence and Soviet Communism; and they overvalued regional military alliances. Had it not been for these misunderstandings of regional political forces, the United States might have made fewer efforts to enlist Arab countries in defense agreements and would have felt less compelled to intervene openly or clandestinely in inter-Arab and internal Arab

---

[48]A barely disguised account of what went on in the State Department in response to the Iraqi coup is given in B. M. Sapin, *The Making of United States Foreign Policy* (New York: Praeger, 1966), pp. 389-391, in an essay by Charlton Ogburn. See also C. W. Thayer, *Diplomat* (New York: Harper, 1959), Chap. 1-3. It was reported in the *Los Angeles Times*, November 8, 1968, p. 6, that the National Security Council opposed sending troops to Lebanon, but Eisenhower overruled their objections.

problems. Positive neutralism might have been accepted, and the Aswan Dam agreement might have been carried through. But the Arab-Israeli conflict and inter-Arab tensions would no doubt have remained. It would have been difficult to satisfy Egypt's request for arms, primarily for reasons of American domestic politics, as long as those arms might be used against Israel. This was clearly the point where American efforts to court Nasser were most likely to break down. The Soviet Union eventually recognized this vulnerable point in American policy.

New Policies toward the Arab World, 1959-1967

The decade from 1959 to 1969 encompassed the greatest successes and most dramatic failures of American policy in the Middle East. Once again the critical measures of success or failure lay in U.S. relations with Nasser and in the degree of conflict between Israel and her Arab neighbors. Other regional interests of the United States were also changing during the decade, partly in response to developments in the Arab-Israeli area. For example, the very close relations between the United States and the Northern Tier countries deteriorated somewhat, because of active Soviet diplomacy and because the Soviet Union had become a regional power of considerable importance. The Cyprus dispute between Greece and Turkey further worsened American-Turkish relations.

These developments were generally accepted in Washington with a degree of calm that would have been unlikely in the previous decade. This was due primarily to the fact that perceptions of U.S. interests in the Middle East were changing and policymakers were becoming more sophisticated in understanding the forces of Arab nationalism, positive neutrality, and anticolonialism.

The changing evaluation of U.S. interests was related to technological developments that reduced the importance of certain "vital interests" to U.S. global strategy. As ICBMs evolved in the late 1950s, forward bases and missile sites in the Middle East seemed less important to the global military posture of the United States. Oil came to be seen more as an economic problem than a vital resource. The U.S. could tap other sources of oil, though at substantially higher production costs, and the oil market seemed to favor the buyer. The Middle Eastern countries, on the contrary, had to sell their oil to Western Europe, for no alternative market existed. In the 1960s the Soviet Union did not seem capable of consuming the oil of the Middle East, although it might be able to cast doubt on the continuing flow of oil to Western Europe on favorable terms. The prospect that the Soviet Union might become an oil-importing country by the 1970s somewhat altered this picture by the late 1960s. But the threatening image of the Soviet hand on the oil tap of the Middle East had begun to fade. Likewise, the Suez Canal, although considered a convenience, appeared not quite as "vital" to world commerce as before, particularly after the Arab-Israeli war of June, 1967. Clearly, the U.S. objective in the Middle East of keeping the Soviet Union out had failed by 1958, but the consequence were less catastrophic than had been feared.

United States objectives in the Middle East after 1958 reflected these changes. The dominant concern was to avoid a direct United States–Soviet Union confrontation in the Middle East that could lead to a nuclear war between the superpowers. Since a renewal of conflict between Arabs and Israelis could increase the likelihood of this possibility, containment of the Arab-Israeli dispute became a second objective of U.S. policymakers. To reach these objectives, the United States tried to encourage the Arab states, in particular the U.A.R., to concentrate on internal economic development. Thus, a third "interest" of the United States became the promotion of "development" in the entire region. If these objectives could govern policy, other interests or concerns, such as oil, Israel's security, the Suez Canal, overflight rights. American investments, and use of military facilities, would be safeguarded.

This redefinition of U.S. interests was made possible in part by the realization that the crises of 1957 and 1958 had led neither to a Communist-dominated nor to a Nasser-dominated Middle East. After 1958 the Iraqis were bitterly hostile to Nasser, and as Iraq moved closer to the Soviets, Nasser became shrilly anti-Communist. The Syrian-Egyptian union proved not to be the prelude to a massive, Nasser-oriented, united Arab world but, rather, a source of persistent tension in inter-Arab relations. When the union dissolved in 1961, many felt that Arab unity was a harmless fiction. Finally, following the Israeli withdrawal from Sinai in 1957, relative calm came to the Israeli-Egyptian border, and some Americans were convinced that time would accomplish what no deliberate policy could possibly achieve.

Essential to the success of the revised American approach to the Middle East was the decision to take new initiatives toward Nasser and to allow him to practice positive neutralism so long as he was willing to keep the Arab-Israeli dispute "on ice." As an incentive for Nasser to cooperate, the United States began a large-scale program of food aid, consisting of PL 480 shipments of wheat, in 1959. Although the aid was ostensibly given "without strings," both sides seemed to understand that moderation toward Israel was expected of Nasser.

From 1959 to 1963 this policy worked remarkably well, and the Middle East dropped from the headlines to a much welcomed obscurity. Talk of a *modus vivendi* with the Soviets in the Middle East was common, and for the first time essays on the Middle East showed a trace of optimism.[49] The reversal of these favorable developments and the events that finally led to the war of June, 1967, are most instructive in revealing the difficulties of following a coherent and effective policy toward the Middle East. The experience also illustrates the problems faced by Americans in carrying out sustained initiatives in the foreign policy generally, and shows how Congress and public opinion can undermine policies favored by only one part of the foreign affairs bureaucracy.[50] In addition, U.S. policy toward the Middle East in the 1960s reveals the inability of top-level decisionmakers to give sustained attention to noncrisis areas.

A "new look" in America's Middle East policy emerged in 1959 and 1960, and the Kennedy Administration was the beneficiary of renewed contacts with Nasser. This policy fitted remarkably well into the overall pattern of Kennedy's foreign policy, for it stressed both dialogue and development. Two Presidential advisers were particularly anxious to pursue these initiatives: Walt Rostow was a theoretician of economic development, and Robert Komer became an advocate of dialogue.

President Kennedy himself seems to have believed it possible to pursue new policies in the Middle East and perhaps even to move toward a partial settlement of the Arab-Israeli conflict. Aware of the potential influence of the American Jewish community against any policy it saw as favorable to the Arabs or hostile to Israel, Kennedy concluded after his election, according to a close adviser, that he could resist Zionist pressures because the Zionists had nowhere else to go but the Democratic Party. During his Presidential campaign, Kennedy had avoided the temptation to make strongly pro-Israeli speeches, despite his concern for the New York Jewish vote. Thus he felt that his hands were not tied in dealing with the Middle East.

In addition to continuing aid to the U.A.R. and increasing his contacts with Arab heads of state, Kennedy was also eager to eliminate or minimize some of the basic causes of the Arab-Israeli conflict. The Arab refugee problem seemed the best place to begin. A solution to this problem, it was thought, might reduce tensions throughout the Middle East.

[49]For example, see R. H. Nolte, "United States Policy and the Middle East," in G. G. Stevens (ed.), *The United States and the Middle East* (Englewood Cliffs, N. J.: Prentice-Hall, 1964).

[50]An exaggerated concern with the influence of domestic groups on foreign policy is found in G. F. Kennan, *op. cit.,* p. 185, where he wrote the following after a brief trip through the Middle East in 1944: "Our government is technically incapable of conceiving and promulgating a long-term consistent policy toward areas remote from its own territory. Our actions in the field of foreign affairs are the convulsive reactions of politicians to an internal political life dominated by vocal minorities."

As early as spring, 1961, the Kennedy Administration was exploring the idea of having a special United Nations representative look for new solutions to the Arab refugee problem. The President of the Carnegie Endowment for International Peace, Joseph E. Johnson, was asked to become the Special Representative of the United Nations Conciliation Commission for Palestine (UNCCP) in August, 1961. He was requested to submit a proposal for settling the Arab refugee problem in accordance with numerous U.N. resolutions. Johnson's interim report of November suggested that the chances for finding a solution to the refugee problem were sufficiently high to justify continuing the effort. From this second assignment, Johnson produced a plan in the fall of 1962 that recognized the right of Arab refugees to repatriation or compensation, while providing means to ensure that the number of Arabs who might actually return to Israel would be kept to a level acceptable to the Israeli government. This promising initiative failed, however, and the reasons are once again instructive.[51]

From the beginning, the Johnson mission seemed to have strong backing in the State Department. Support from other quarters, however, was less forthcoming. The American public showed little interest in a proposal to settle the refugee problem. President Kennedy himself, while apparently concerned with the issue, had only limited time and resources to devote to this complex problem.

The Israelis, who have consistently argued since the early 1950s that no settlement of the refugee problem could take place outside the framework of a full Arab-Israeli peace treaty, strongly opposed the Johnson plan. Israeli opposition raised the domestic political costs to the President of supporting the plan. The Egyptians were also skeptical of the proposal. As long as the plan seemed to have some chance of being accepted, efforts were made to reduce domestic opposition to the Johnson plan, and the United States made direct requests to the Israelis to temper the opposition of their American supporters. It became clear, however, that the Johnson initiative was something of a political liability for Kennedy.

The end of the Kennedy Administration's attempts to deal with the refugee problem came in the fall of 1962. As the Congressional elections approached, the President was obviously interested in getting as many Democrats as possible elected. Some of the large campaign contributors to the Democratic Party were Jews sympathetic to Israel, and Kennedy was reportedly told that some campaign contributions would be withheld from Democratic Congressional candidates unless the Johnson initiative

[51]J. E. Johnson, "Arab vs. Israeli: A Persistent Challenge to Americans," *The Middle East Journal*, Vol. 18, No. 1 (Winter, 1964), pp. 1-14.

was stopped.[52] In the absence of countervailing pressures, this threat may have been effective, and eventually the Johnson initiative lost Presidential backing.

The fate of the Johnson plan for Arab refugees illustrates only one facet of the interplay between domestic politics and foreign policy. Although U.S. foreign policy in the Middle East is not simply dictated by pro-Israeli pressure groups, certain policy initiatives can be strongly influenced by the combined efforts of mobilized Jewish opinion and the threat of withholding campaign contributions.

While pro-Israeli pressures need not necessarily constrain a determined President, they do mean that any policy initiative seen as hostile to Israel or favorable to the Arabs runs clear domestic political risks. If such efforts are to be made, means may be sought to deflect domestic pressures, either by adopting a United Nations formula or by pursuing the policy in private rather than in public. This requires concentration and sustained attention on the part of policymakers, and in the absence of compelling reasons to devote large resources to such initiatives it is more likely that policy will follow lines of less resistance.

The failure of the Johnson mission was not responsible, however, for the deterioration of U.S.-U.A.R. relations between 1964 and 1967, that may have made the outbreak of war in 1967 more likely than would otherwise have been the case. Rather, it was the Yemeni conflict and the attempts to the United States to use food aid for political purposes that led to the downward spiral in U.S.-U.A.R. relations.

As early as December, 1962, the United States had decided to recognize the Yemen republic, despite the hostility of Jordan and Saudi Arabia to this decision. Recognition was granted in the belief that the Yemeni republicans were effectively in control of most of the country and with the desire to prove that the United States did not always side with traditional forces in the Middle East.[53] With recognition, however, came involvement, and soon the United States was seeking for some means to mediate the dispute between Nasser and Saudi Arabia's King Faisal in the Yemen. Several near successes were achieved, but each time agreements broke down. Meanwhile, the United States was implying to Nasser that continued PL 480 aid was contingent upon his withdrawal from the Yemen. While this type of "string" seems to have been tacitly accepted by Nasser with regard to Israel, it was too much for him to allow the United States to dictate

[52]This interpretation is supported by reports of several well-placed informants.

[53]J. S. Badeau, who was largely responsible for the U.S. decision to recognize the Yemeni republican regime, gives a detailed account of this episode in *The American Approach to the Arab World* (New York: Harper, 1968), Chap. 7.

U.A.R. policy in the Arab world as well. Strains inevitably emerged in U.S.-U.A.R. relations.

By 1963-1964 several changes were apparent in United States policy toward the Middle East. First, there was growing disillusionment with the policy of trying to maintain close relations with Nasser. Congress was unhappy with the policy of giving aid to the U.A.R. while Egyptian troops were participating in the Yemeni conflict. Senator Hickenlooper of Iowa was particularly concerned with this issue.

A shift in policy paralleled the decline in U.S.-U.A.R. relations, namely a gradual increase in U.S.-Israeli military cooperation following the sale of Hawk missiles to Israel in 1963. With time, the supply of sophisticated U.S. weapons to Israel became a major element in U.S.-Israeli relations. For the United States, the provision of conventional arms to Israel became an important means of forestalling Israeli development of nuclear weapons. United States concern over Israel's nuclear potential grew out of a general opposition to nuclear proliferation and a fear of the consequences of such development in the Middle East.

Against this background of disillusionment with Nasser and closer cooperation with Israel, top U.S. policymakers simply lost interest in the Middle East. President Johnson was generally less concerned with trying to carry on a policy of dialogue with the Arab states than Kennedy had been, and as the intractable problems with Vietnam grew in 1964 and 1965, neither the President nor the Secretary of State had much time to consider the equally complex, but less urgent, issues of the Middle East. When the attention of the top-level policymakers is focused elsewhere, it is nearly impossible to carry out sustained initiatives in the Middle East. Policy almost necessarily becomes reactive, and only crises bring on new decisions.

Toward the end of 1964 U.S.-U.A.R. relations began to decline rapidly. Added to the Yemeni conflict, which was a persistent source of tension, was a series of unpleasant incidents that increased bad feelings on both sides. When the U.A.R. aided the Congo rebels in 1964 and the United States became involved in the Stanleyville rescue operation, U.S. and U.A.R. policies in the Congo clashed head on. In Cairo, African students burned down the United States Information Agency (USIA) library as Egyptian police stood quietly by.[54]

At this very time, the U.S. Congress had under review a request to extend PL 480 aid to Egypt, and Senators and Congressmen were predictably unenthusiastic about continuing aid to Nasser. Tension increased when the U.A.R. air force shot down an American oil company plane that had strayed into Egyptian air space. The U.S. Ambassador in Cairo, Lucius

[54]See Kerr, "Coming to Terms with Nasser," p. 79.

Battle, had been approached by the Egyptians about the possibility of increasing the food aid program before the end of the calendar year. Given the events of the preceding weeks, Battle refused to discuss the matter of the increase. In a typical bit of rhetoric, Nasser reacted to what he perceived as a U.S. threat to cut off aid by declaring at Port Said, on December 23, 1964:

> But if the Americans think that they are giving us a little aid to dominate and control our policy, I would like to tell them we are sorry. . . . The U.S. ambassador has told the deputy premier that he cannot at present talk about this matter [PL 480 aid] at all. Why? Because he does not like our conduct, that is, conduct here in Egypt. I would like him to know that whoever does not like our conduct can go drink up the sea. If the Mediterranean is not sufficient, there is the Red Sea too. We can give him that as well. What I want to say is that we cannot sell our independence for the sake of 30 or 40 or 50 million [Egyptian] pounds.[55]

To the anger of the Egyptians, the United States began to delay shipments of wheat that had already been promised.

When the PL 480 agreement expired in June, 1965, the State Department was able to secure further aid on a short-term, three-to-six-month basis, after intense pleading with Congress. Ambassador Battle continued to try to convince Nasser that the United States wished to cooperate with the U.A.R., but expected cooperation in return. Further aid would depend on an improved climate in U.S.-U.A.R. relations in order to overcome political problems in the United States. The few instances of Nasser's willingness to demonstrate good will, such as the cessation of aid to the Congo rebels and help in reconstituting the USIA library, generally went unnoticed in Washington. Nonetheless, Battle's personal relations with both Nasser and the influential editor of *Al Ahram,* Mohammed Hassanein Heykal, were quite good.

After a brief improvement, U.S.-U.A.R. relations rapidly deteriorated in late 1966 and early 1967.[56] United States aid to the U.A.R. was finally suspended in February, 1967, and in March Ambassador Battle left Cairo. His replacement did not arrive until late May. In the intervening months, one more unpleasant incident occurred in the Yemen, when two Americans were arrested on contrived charges. Secretary of State Rusk was extremely

[55]Radio Cairo, December 23, 1964.

[56]The same process could be observed in U.S. relations with Algeria, and once again food aid became a major irritant as the United States tried to link continued shipments of wheat to a less anti-American stance toward the Vietnam war. The Hickenlooper amendment also created difficulties in trying to maintain reasonably good relations.

annoyed, and diplomatic relations with the U.A.R. were nearly broken. In this atmosphere, the events leading to the Arab-Israeli war of June, 1967, took place.

U.S. Policy and the Six-Day War

Signs of renewed Arab-Israeli tensions had been recognized in Washington early in 1966. The Israeli attack on the Jordanian town of Samu in November, 1966, confirmed the growing danger to peace, as did the Israeli air battle with the Syrians in April, 1967. These two events momentarily alarmed Washington policymakers, but in early May there was little sense of impending war except in the highest levels of the State Department. Not until mid-May did the growing crisis in the Middle East demand serious attention throughout the government.[57]

With the announcement by President Nasser on May 22 that the Straits of Tiran would be closed to Israeli shipping and to strategic cargoes bound for the Israeli port of Eilat, a renewed war between Arabs and Israelis seemed imminent to many officials in Washington. What occurred in U.S. policymaking circles over the next three weeks is almost impossible to know with certainty, and many of the high-level participants in these confusing events provide quite different accounts of what decisions were made, the motivations of key actors, and the expectations that guided policy choices. Such confusion is not uncommon in the making of foreign policy, but in the Arabi-Israeli case the normal difficulties were componded by the fact that the locus of decisionmaking rapidly shifted from the "expert" level of the State Department to the senior levels of State, to the Pentagon, and to the President and his close advisers. Under-Secretary of State Eugene Rostow was one of the major figures responsible for Middle Eastern policy before the war of June 5, and McGeorge Bundy subsequently played an important role in coordinating American policy in the aftermath of the war. Neither of these men claimed to be an expert on the Middle East, but both enjoyed the confidence of the President and were sensitive to general problems of foreign policy and to such political constraints on policymakers as public opinion and Congressional attitudes.

[57]The following version of U.S. policy and the June, 1967, war is based primarily on interviews with American participants in the events described. In addition, some useful information has been drawn from published works, especially: Michel Bar-Zohar, *Histoire secrète de la guerre d'Israel* (Paris: Fayard, 1968); Walter Laqueur, *The Road to Jerusalem: The Origins of the Arab-Israeli Conflict* (New York: Macmillan, 1968): Theodore Draper, *Israel and World Politics* (New York: Viking, 1968); Maxime Rodinson, *Israel and the Arabs* (London: Penguin Books, 1968); and E. V. Rostow, *Law, Power and the Pursuit of Peace* (Lincoln: University of Nebraska Press, 1968), Chap. 5.

Several questions concerning United States policy before and immediately after the June war have been raised. Among the most intriguing are the following: Did U.S. policy seek to restrain both the Arabs and the Israelis from starting a war or was American policy really that of quietly urging Israel to reopen the Straits of Tiran by itself? Was the effort to put together a multilateral fleet a serious one, and were unilateral U.S. actions considered? How committed were U.S. policymakers to aiding Israel if it got into military trouble? How confident was the United States that a diplomatic solution to the crisis could be found? Finally, what impact did oil companies or American Zionists have on U.S. foreign policy in this crisis? Some of these questions can now be answered with confidence.

Following the closing of the Straits of Tiran, at least four distinct groups, each with its own policy preferences and concerns, influenced the actions of the United States government. Within the Department of State, the top-level decisionmakers and the desk officers of the Near Eastern Affairs Bureau followed divergent lines of thought and proposed quite different actions. At the top level, Eugene Rostow and Dean Rusk preferred some form of action that would both prevent war and keep Nasser from winning a diplomatic victory. It is fair to say that they were deeply concerned over the possibility that Nasser might emerge from the crisis as a revitalized force in the Middle East, and visions of a "Nasserite" takeover in the oil-rich Arab countries were not absent from their minds. The combined desire to deflate Nasser's prestige and to prevent war led to their activist orientation.

Some of the "Arabists" in the State Department, as well as Ambassadors to Arab countries, shared few of the beliefs of their superiors. They were pessimistic about the prospect of finding a peaceful solution to the crisis, and above all felt that the United States should not get involved in a potentially violent conflict in the Middle East. The historical analogy that dominated their thinking was the Suez crisis of 1956. Some feared that if the United States moved to open the Straits of Tiran, it might provoke a violent confrontation with Nasser, and the United States might be obliged to attack Egyptian air fields. Such military action on Israel's behalf looked all too much like the British-French-Israeli collusion that occurred in 1956. In the aftermath of that crisis, of course, British influence in the Middle East rapidly declined. A prolonged political crisis or a violent confrontation between the United States and the U.A.R. would severely damage American interests throughout the Arab world. If conflict was inevitable, it was thought, Israel should act alone, and preferably only against Egypt. Prompt Israeli action to reopen the Straits might serve to limit the war and prevent Jordan from being drawn in. Few doubted that Israel would easily defeat the Arab armies, and some felt that an Israeli victory, followed by U.S. pressure to bring about Israeli withdrawal, would allow the United States to emerge from the crisis in a very strong position. The combination of these images led them to believe that the United States should take no overt action in the crisis.

Reactions in the Pentagon to the crisis in the Middle East seemed to center on the image of a "second Vietnam." Because of the massive American involvement in Southeast Asia, the military was reluctant to use force in another part of the world. Secretary of Defense Robert McNamara was reported to have feared another "McNamara's war." In addition to this anti-interventionist sentiment, the military seemed convinced that Israel could easily win if fighting were to break out in the Middle East. With this assurance, the Pentagon was quick to demonstrate that American involvement, even in an effort to reopen the Straits, might require a large commitment of both air and land forces, which were not then available in the area. No use of American forces, whether unilateral or multilateral, seemed attractive to military planners.

President Johnson and his advisers in the White House were deeply aware of the need for Congressional approval for any commitment of U.S. forces. Conscious of the lessons of Vietnam and the aftermath of the Gulf of Tonkin resolution, and anticipating demands by Senator Fulbright and others that any U.S. action should receive prior clearance from Congress, the President was cautious in considering alternative policies. He did, however, express strong approval of having a multilateral fleet open the Straits.

Against this background of diverse images—a strengthened Nasser, the Suez crisis of 1956, Vietnam, and a reluctant Congress—policies were considered and decisions were made. Immediately after the Straits of Tiran were closed, the British had suggested that a multilateral naval force be assembled to reopen the Straits. American policymakers welcomed this initiative and began to sound out other nations concerning their participation in such a fleet.

After considerable debate at high levels in the government, alternative policies were seriously considered. The first was to go ahead with the multilateral fleet to open the Straits. The second was to allow the Israelis to act on their own.[58] Top Presidential advisers all advocated the first alternative, and the Pentagon was given primary responsibility for assembling the necessary forces.

The Israelis had been asked by the United States to refrain from action for 48 hours after the closing of the Straits. After further requests, the United States government thought it had two weeks before Israel would act on its own. During that time the United States was to try to induce action by the United Nations. If this failed, a group of maritime nations would be

[58]Bar-Zohar, *op. cit.,* p. 142. Also, Draper, *op. cit.,* pp. 89-90.

asked to join in declaring the Straits of Tiran international waters, which could then justify the use of a multilateral fleet to reopen the Straits.

The visit of Israeli Foreign Minister Abba Eban to the United States on May 26-27 to discuss the multilateral fleet added to the confusion surrounding the crisis. The United States had assumed that the closure of the Straits of Tiran was the major reason for the crisis, but by the time Eban arrived in Washington, the Israeli government professed that the real threat came from the concentration of Egyptian troops in Sinai. Through Eban, the Israelis tried to play up the threat of attack from the U.A.R., but U.S. officials, on the basis of intelligence reports, were skeptical of the Israeli evidence. The suspicion was widespread that the Israelis were providing inaccurate intelligence to support their claim of an impending Egyptian attack. A crisis of confidence between Israel and the United States and between Eban and his own government seems to have grown out of this argument over whether the issue at stake was the closure of the Straits or the mobilization in Sinai.[59]

Meanwhile, U.S. efforts to form a multilateral fleet and to secure a declaration of maritime powers were meeting with little success. The Pentagon remained skeptical of the usefulness of such a fleet, and seems to have done little to bring it into existence. In his meeting with Eban, President Johnson told the Foreign Minister that the United States was serious about reopening the Straits but that such action would take time and would require Congressional approval. Eban was thought by some to have left the meeting with a feeling of disappointment. President Johnson himself turned to his aides after Eban's departure and reportedly said: "I've failed. They'll go."

When Eban returned to Israel, however, he argued that the United States should be allowed to pursue its efforts to reopen the Straits. He stressed the determination of the United States to act, which was not believed by many of his colleagues, some of whom felt that the United States would prefer to have Israel deal with the problem itself.

As the crisis continued, the Israelis became increasingly skeptical of the willingness of the United States to act, and the head of Israeli Intelligence Services, Meir Amit, was sent on a secret mission to the United States to verify the impression that no initiatives would be forthcoming to reopen the Straits and that the United States would not be too upset if Israel acted

[59]Laqueur, *op. cit.*, p. 135. Abba Eban brought to Washington the text of conversations with Dulles in 1957, describing the understanding reached on terms for Israeli withdrawal from Sinai. The understanding acknowledged Israel's right under Article 51 of the United Nations Charter to use force to open the Straits if they were closed by force. The American copy of this document could not be located immediately, though its authenticity was verified.

on its own.[60] But rather than check with Secretary Rusk or Under-Secretary Rostow at the State Department, he conferred with people at the Pentagon, where he must have learned of the doubts that existed from Secretary McNamara on down about the multilateral fleet. It seems unlikely that he was told that Israel should strike on its own, but he no doubt was led to believe that the United States would take no immediate action to reopen the Straits or to convince Nasser to back down in the Sinai. Amit's subsequent report to the Israeli Cabinet, it has been asserted, strengthened the forces calling for war. In Washington, some top-level State Department officials suspected that the Pentagon was undercutting their policy, but in the prevailing chaos it was difficult to know what was happening in different parts of the bureaucracy.

After Amit's visit to Washington and his conversations at the Pentagon, war in the Middle East may have become inevitable. Nonetheless, the United States continued to try to prevent the outbreak of violence. Diplomatic efforts in Cairo were beginning to pay off, and an exchange of visits by U.S. and U.A.R. Vice-Presidents was arranged. Zakaria Mohieddin was to arrive in Washington on June 7, and the United States urged Israel to refrain from any action until after that date.[61] An understanding was reached that the United States would see that the continued closure of the Straits would bring no economic hardships to Israel, and Washington had good reason to believe that the Israelis would not undertake any armed action until June 8 or 9. Some even felt that the crisis had passed its peak and that a diplomatic settlement was not far off. The United States continued to explore the possibility of joint action with the British and Dutch to reopen the Straits, but no final action was ever taken. Instead, on June 5, the Israelis attacked with a precise and well-planned air strike against Egyptian air fields.

The reaction in Washington to the outbreak of fighting in the Middle East was mixed. Many top officials were both surprised and angry that Israel had begun the war. A few felt, however, that the United States was "off the hook" for the moment. In the first chaotic days of the war these feelings coalesced into a number of assumptions that were to guide U.S. policy in the aftermath of the war.

U.S. Policy after June, 1967

On June 5, the first day of the Arab-Israeli war, there was considerable anxiety among high-level policymakers over the outcome of the war.

[60]Laqueur, op. cit., p. 141.

[61]Bar-Zohar, op. cit., p. 183, describes U.S. policy as trying to restrain Israel, getting multilateral support to reopen the Straits, and attempting to work out some arrangements with the U.A.R.

McGeorge Bundy, who was later in the week appointed to serve as White House coordinator for the Middle East, is said to have felt that an Israeli defeat would be disastrous for the United States, for in such circumstances the United States would be obliged to consider intervention with military force, a particularly painful decision to contemplate in view of the danger of a Soviet-U.S. confrontation. When it became apparent that Israel had rapidly achieved victory, many in the United States government breathed a sigh of relief. The conclusion seems to have been reached that Israel must be kept strong in order to ensure that the United States would not be drawn into any future wars in the Middle East. This orientation was bolstered by the widespread feeling that Nasser had brought on the crisis by breaking his 1957 understanding on the Straits of Tiran. In his speech of June 19, President Johnson stated: "If any single act of folly was more responsible for this explosion than any other, I think it was the arbitrary and dangerous announced decision that the Straits of Tiran would be closed."

From this anxiety over U.S. involvement came the determination not to allow Israel to be forced to withdraw from newly occupied territories for anything short of a "real peace settlement." Although some officials familiar with the Middle East were skeptical that a "lasting peace" could be achieved, nearly all of the President's advisers felt that there should be no return to the "unstable *status quo ante*." This time, it was felt, Israel deserved real security from her military victory. A major influence in this decision was U.S. public opinion, which was overwhelmingly pro-Israeli.[62] The press, television, and radio in the United States conveyed the image of an incredibly clever David defeating a clumsy and irrational Goliath. The government's decision to support the Israeli position in the postwar period was made easier by the public consensus that Israel was not the aggressor in the war.

By reinterpreting its pledge to ensure the territorial integrity of all states in the Middle East,[63] the United States government was able to adopt the position that Israel could use the newly acquired territories to bargain for a real peace settlement. President Johnson's speech of June 19 and the U.N. Security Council resolution of November 22, 1967, contained the outline of the kind of political settlement favored by the U.S. government. The points included free navigation in international waterways, solution of the refugee problem, recognition of the right of all states to live in peace

---

[62]A top policymaker reported that in the midst of the crisis, one of the leading poll-takers in the U.S., Louis Harris, personally told him that U.S. public opinion had rarely been so unanimous as it was in support of Israel.

[63]U.S. support for territorial integrity, it was said, applied only to recognized frontiers, not to armistice lines, which the Armistice Agreements of 1949 had said could be changed by agreement as part of the transition to peace.

within secure and recognized boundaries, and withdrawal of Israeli forces from territories occupied during the war.

After intensive diplomatic efforts on behalf of the November resolution of the Security Council, the United States abstained from taking positions on substantive issues of a peace settlement. Mediation efforts were primarily entrusted to Ambassador Gunnar Jarring, while behind the scenes the State Department and the President's personal representatives maintained contact with all parties to the conflict. Representations were often made to the Israelis concerning the occupied territories and questions of procedure in negotiations, and slight modifications in the Israeli position were brought about. Basically, however, little happened to bring the Arabs and Israelis closer together during the 19 months of peacemaking efforts by the Johnson Administration. But while President Johnson's attempts to reach a settlement of the Arab-Israel dispute were unsuccessful, his Administration made several critical policy decisions that revealed the desire of the United States to keep Israel militarily strong.

After the June war, both Jordan and Israel approached the United States government with requests for arms. The Jordanians, to whom the United States had traditionally supplied arms, needed them both to protect themselves against Israeli reprisals and to bolster the regime against the possible threat from Palestinian commandos. Negotiations on arms for Jordan were extremely difficult, but when the Israeli government agreed that it preferred to see Jordan supplied by the West rather than by the Soviet Union, some arms were promised. The high degree to which American policy toward the Arabs was influenced by Israel is illustrated by this example.[64]

The Israeli request for 50 Phantom jets was linked to the French refusal to deliver 50 Mirage fighters to Israel and to the Soviet's rapid resupply of weapons to the Egyptians. During most of 1968, the Johnson Administration put off any announcement of a decision on this matter, despite great pressures to agree to the sale. Some Pentagon experts were convinced that Israel did not need the planes and feared that further U.S. supplies to Israel would only escalate the arms race in the Middle East. But in an election year, with both Presidential candidates calling for the sale of Phantoms to Israel, pressures became almost irresistible. When Senator Symington made passage of the foreign aid bill conditional upon the sale of Phantoms to

[64]Israeli Prime Minister Levi Eshkol was asked about U.S. arms to Jordan in *Davar*, January 24, 1969. He replied: "In fact, the Americans had no need to ask us whether they should give those tanks [to Jordan] or not . . . . they are not yet our satellite. Of course, they did not want us to cause an outcry and make protests. The President himself said: 'If Eshkol says we should not give tanks to Husayn, but instead should send him to graze in foreign pastures—to receive tanks from Abd an-Nasir or from Russia through Abd an-Nasir—then we shall not give tanks to the Jordanians . . . .' It was as if I had been given a veto right . . . ."

Israel, President Johnson, who had agreed in principle to sell Phantoms to Israel as early as Premier Eshkol's visit in January, 1968, finally announced the sale. With this decision, the Johnson Administration took a decisive step toward strengthening Israel's military capability. New diplomatic initiatives were left to President Nixon.[65]

The Nixon Administration found itself faced with the possibilities of doing nothing to resolve the Arab-Israeli conflict, of trying for a "full settlement," or of limiting itself to partial solutions of specific problems associated with the tensions in the Middle East. Both France and the Soviet Union were particularly insistent in pressing for greater involvement of the "four powers" in the search for peace in the Middle East. The Nixon Administration responded favorably to their initiatives, and a series of bilateral and multilateral discussions began with the aim of bringing the Arabs and the Israelis closer to some acceptable forms of peace settlement. In the ensuing months, little progress was made and few officials in Washington were optimistic that a full settlement could be reached. Meanwhile the level of violence continued to rise.

Finally, in the fall of 1969 the United States put forward specific proposals for the resolution of the conflict. The essential elements of a settlement were to be Israeli withdrawal and Arab commitments to peace. For several months these proposals formed the backdrop for intense diplomatic activity. Israel began deep bombing raids into the U.A.R. Soviet involvement in Egyptian defense grew dramatically with the provision of SAM II and SAM III missiles and Soviet combat pilots. In this atmosphere, pressures for the United States to supply Israel with massive military aid became very great. Instead, however, a U.S. peace initiative was launched in June 1970. To the surprise of many, it led to U.A.R. and Israeli acceptance of a cease-fire. During August, however, evidence had accumulated that each side, but especially the U.A.R., had used the cease-fire to strengthen its defenses. In September 1970, civil war erupted in Jordan and Egyptian President Nasser died. In the resulting confusion, the U.S. Government decided to provide Israel with large quantities of arms, to be covered by credits of $500 million. At the same time the United States was making efforts to find a way for regaining the initiative toward peace.

IV. The Nature of Constraints on U.S. Policy in the Middle East

On the basis of the evidence provided by past examples of U.S. policy-making in the Middle East, it is possible to speculate on the constraints

[65]On January 19, 1969, *Al Ahram* published part of the last major statement of U.S. policy sent by the Johnson Administration to the Soviet Union in response to earlier Soviet proposals.

that may be faced by American decisionmakers over the next few years. Constraints of two basic types should be distinguished. A policymaker may intellectually be capable of examining a wide range of possible policies, but he may conclude that either the nature of international politics or his own political system rules out certain possibilities. These are seen as constraints on policymaking. A second type of constraint, at times closely linked to the above, acts directly on individuals by limiting the range of policies they are willing to consider. An ideology, an operational code, a strong belief in lessons of the past, and constricted imaginations all serve as psychological constraints on policymakers.

The international system—the reality of Soviet power, the intractability of the Cyprus dispute, of the Arab-Israeli conflict, and of inter-Arab fighting—imposes the most severe limits on effective American policy in the Middle East. In many cases, for example, the failure of U.S. initiatives to deal with the Arab-Israeli dispute has been the result of Israeli, U.A.R., or Jordanian policies. The constraints on the parties to the conflict sharply limit the possibilities for the United States to find workable policies. But the American political process and beliefs of decisionmakers have also at times unnecessarily narrowed the margin of choice and led to policies that had little chance of succeeding or that had long-range consequences that might have been more clearly foreseen than was the case. These latter two sources of difficulty in the process of making foreign policy are often less recognized and more in need of analysis than the external constraints imposed by the international environment.

Forces that limit the ability of individuals to deal with problems of foreign policy are extremely difficult to analyze, let alone change. No individual, whether a detached analyst or an involved decisionmaker, can divest himself of many distorted or simplifying assumptions about the Middle East and about foreign policy in general. For example, the American temper of pragmatism and liberalism has at times led policymakers to seek total "solutions" to problems of the Middle East. Such solutions contain an element of large-scale engineering, based as they are on a belief that political problems can be approached by means of "economic development" or, more recently, "nuclear desalination." American policies in the Middle East tend at times to follow these rather simplistic lines.

A second effect of America's brand of pragmatism is that U.S. policymakers find it difficult to deal with revolutionary, anti-status-quo powers. In the contest between Arabs and Israelis, the latter almost invariably start with major advantages because they are "more like us." Similarly, the "moderate" Arab states will continue to have better relations with the United States than will the "radicals." Thus, the orientations of top policy-makers will strongly affect the choice of Middle East countries in which the United States becomes involved and the kinds of solutions to regional problems that policymakers will favor.

More interesting than the predispositions of American policymakers are the constraints on policy generated by the complex workings of the U.S. political system. Because authority for foreign affairs is dispersed in the U.S. government, problems of coordination and long-range planning almost inevitably arise. It has been particularly difficult to sustain a coherent policy in the Middle East because of the constant possibility that public opinion and organized pressures, often expressed through Congress, can undermine initiatives seen as too favorable to the Arabs in general and to the U.A.R. in particular.

Crises heighten the normal bureaucratic confusion in Washington. In the absence of firm and consistent Presidential leadership, a determined nation can influence agencies in the government to support positions that run contrary to declared American policy. The Israelis have proved to be particularly effective in enlisting the aid of influential men throughout the government, and their skill in advancing their own cause is recognized even by the State Department, where it is common to hear that the Israelis are much easier to deal with than are pro-Israeli American Jews.

The influence of the American Jewish community, especially individual Jewish leaders, has often been overrated. But no American politician can totally ignore the wishes of this articulate and powerful minority. While public opinion in general is only mildly pro-Israeli, a significant minority of the population is deeply committed to Israel's welfare. An impressive example of domestic Jewish influence on U.S. foreign policy was seen in 1947 and 1948, in the events that led to U.S. recognition of the state of Israel. No pro-Israeli effort since has approached the level of organization and skill in articulating interests as the Zionist movement of those years.

The way in which pressures are exerted in Israel's behalf has changed. Personal contacts with the President or Congressmen have become more important than the direct efforts of Jewish organizations. Jewish campaign contributors in both parties may have more influence than the heads of pro-Israeli organizations. Congress is the easiest target of American Jewish influence. The State Department and the Pentagon are generally most resistant. The White House falls in the middle, occasionally responding to pro-Israeli demands but also screening out many unwanted communications.

To see the influence relationship, or the activities of interest groups, as a one-way process would be misleading.[66] Rather, lobbying and counter-lobbying occur, and Jewish leaders are often called in and asked to transmit governmental positions to their own more militant constituents.

The net effect of the efforts of American Jewish groups has been to create a generally sympathetic feeling toward Israel in much of the American population and its leaders. Direct attempts to block policies, such as opposition to the Johnson proposal for Arab refugees, may succeed if other forces are pushing in that direction. But pro-Israeli groups rarely get everything they want. Their efforts have been indirectly important in U.S. policy by defining, through the mass media, the nature of problems in the Middle East, by portraying President Nasser as an arch villain, and by persuading Congressmen to support the Israeli side of the conflict.

Future developments within Israel and the United States may weaken the day-to-day influence of pro-Israeli American Jews. Some of the younger generation of American Jews, particularly among the "new left," seem to be less interested in Israel and Zionism than their parents. More importantly, the Israelis prefer to make their own representations to the United States government. But in any future crisis, where Israel's security or existence was at stake, the pressures that could be mounted by the American Jewish community for U.S. support of Israel would be great indeed. Most American policymakers have incorporated into their view of the Middle East the belief that the United States is strongly committed to the continued existence of Israel. How this commitment might be acted upon in specific circumstances is much less clear.

Compared to the influence of the American Jewish community, that of American oil companies is slight. Whatever their behavior on matters of domestic politics, the oil companies have usually been cautious in trying to determine American policy on the Arab-Israeli question.[67] Their opinions are generally heard and are often solicited, but virtually no intensive efforts to alter U.S. policies on the Middle East have come from the oil companies.

[66]A more accurate view of lobbying and influence relationships in general is found in R. A. Bauer, Ithiel de Sola Pool, and L. A. Dexter, *American Business and Public Policy: The Politics of Foreign Trade* (New York: Atherton Press, 1963), pp. 466-489. Communications are seen less as vectors than as "triggers," which release a "fixed potential" that has been built up by "traces of previous communications."

[67]American oil companies are sensitive to the dangers of displeasing American Jewish opinion by seeming to be anti-Israeli. An article by the Vice-President of Standard Oil of New Jersey in the company's publication, *The Lamp* (Spring, 1968), p. 19, noted: "In the past, economic realities have ultimately prevailed over political considerations, and there is reason to expect that they will in the future." The statement referred to probable Arab behavior toward the West, but was seen as being anti-Israeli by some Jewish groups. Over 200 credit cards were turned in by American Jews as a result.

President Johnson reportedly saw two oil company presidents after the June, 1967, war, but their influence on any of his decisions was not apparent.

While oil company representatives may have some influence on U.S. policy in Saudi Arabia, Kuwait, and the Persian Gulf, the fear of a domestic Jewish boycott of their products has kept them from publicly adopting a strongly pro-Arab position in the Arab-Israeli conflict. In addition, many oil company executives feel that regional instability, which might threaten their oil investments in the conservative Arab states, is as likely to result from the actions of the radical Arab regimes as of the Israelis. Consequently, whatever efforts they make tend to favor the "moderate" Arab regimes or Iran.

Considerations about Middle Eastern oil affect U.S. policy in the Middle East differently from the influence of oil companies themselves. It is widely understood that Middle Eastern oil is extremely important to Europe. In addition, the U.S. balance-of-payments problem is alleviated by an annual return of about $1 billion from American investments in Middle Eastern oil. Thus, both Europeans and Americans are uneasy over the possibility of oil pipelines being cut and oil being withheld by the Arabs for political reasons. These fears tend to moderate U.S. policies that might anger the Arab world, but in a crisis they usually amount to little more than a a cautionary note.

It is now generally believed that the oil countries of the Middle East find it economically necessary to sell their oil to the West; that the Soviets will not provide an alternative market in the near future; and that under most circumstances the West will continue to receive Middle East oil on tolerable terms. If Iraq refuses to sell oil, Iran or Libya will be only too glad to increase its output. Other sources of oil, such as the arctic regions, may also begin producing by the mid-1970s, which will gradually reduce the strategic importance of Middle Eastern oil to the West. Consequently, the degree to which Middle Eastern oil enters the calculations of policymakers is less than in the immediate postwar years. Growth of Soviet interest in Middle East oil and political instability in the oil-rich Arab countries could alter this picture significantly in the 1970s.

The combined impact of the constraints imposed on U.S. policymakers by the American political style, by the American political system, by the international environment, by American public opinion, by American Jewish groups, and by oil companies would seem to be overwhelming. But the pressures do not all flow in the same direction, nor are they constant and unchangeable. Realistically weighing these constraints, an American policymaker might conclude that at the very least he cannot adopt a policy that would seriously endanger Israel. Likewise, in considering policy alternatives in the Middle East, the United States government can be expected to consider the effect new initiatives will have on Israel's security and bargaining position. If a policy is likely to meet with strong Israeli opposition, this may be considered sufficient reason for deciding against it.

As part of the reaction to the war in Vietnam, new constraints on foreign policy seem to have developed. For example, it has become extremely difficult to advocate unilateral policies that might be opposed by Congress in the near future. Large amounts of aid will not be available to countries of the Middle East, nor will massive PL 480 food programs be resumed for the Egyptians and other unfriendly regimes in the next few years. Small-scale technical assistance may provide the basis for building new relations with some countries of the Middle East. But deep involvement in the region seems unlikely for at least the first half of the 1970s.

Commitment to Israel's continued existence now seems to be the least-challenged principle in America's Middle East policy. Other limits on U.S. policy are less well defined. Some stem from earlier involvement in the area and some result from the trauma of Vietnam. After all these constraints are realistically weighed, what range of possible policies can the United States seriously consider?

V. Possible U.S. Policies in the Middle East

In the 1970s American policymakers will be searching for new approaches toward the states and problems of the Middle East. The likely persistence of regional disputes—between Israel and the Arab states, among the Arabs themselves, between Turks and Greeks over Cyprus, between Iran and the Arab states bordering on the Gulf—increases the likelihood of outside powers' involvement in the region, either to exploit the disputes for their own purposes or to resolve or contain conflicts that threaten other interests. The broad outlines of the major choices open to the United States in its future relations with Middle Eastern countries are already apparent. Decisions on future policies will require assessments of U.S. objectives in each subregion of the Middle East and judgments about the most effective means for realizing those objectives.

Goals in foreign policy are rarely clear-cut or logically derived. Descriptions of goals may add little to the understanding of actual state behavior. Nonetheless, a distinction between two basic types of objectives for the United States in the Middle East seems useful for analytical purposes. The first would be to preserve stability, contain regional conflicts, and limit Soviet influence while avoiding situations that might lead to dangerous confrontations with the Soviet Union. This set of objectives would amount to a holding operation designed to limit the damage to American interests, both global and regional, that might result from serious conflicts in the Middle East. The second possible objective would be to solve or settle some of the outstanding political conflicts of the region. The intention here would be to remove the causes of conflicts, through full or partial settlements, rather than simply containing them. And instead of merely limiting Soviet influence, the United States might seek to produce conditions that would diminish Soviet standing in the region.

In pursuing either of these alternative goals, the United States could choose relatively active or passive means, depending on the priority accorded to the problems of the Middle East over those of other parts of the world. The passivity-activity dimension would also reflect assessments of the dangers involved in the political situation at any given time and the susceptibility of local problems to outside manipulation and intervention. Scarce resources and limited attention by top decisionmakers may also act as constraints on activist policies in the Middle East.

Future American policies in the Middle East, whether active or passive, may involve diplomatic, military, and economic efforts. Active policies will generally involve strong diplomatic and perhaps military initiatives, and less active ones will rely more on economic and trade relations.

The possibilities generated by combining the objectives, the active-passive continuum, and the military, economic, and diplomatic components of foreign policies are numerous, though only a portion of the logical possibilities may be pertinent in any particular context. The objectives and degree of American involvement are the most critical defining characteristics. Four major possibilities, each of whch may have a military, diplomatic and economic dimension, can be readily identified, as is shown in the table below.

Table 18

Possible U.S. Policies in the Middle East

Degree of U.S. Involvement	Objectives	
	Containment of Conflict	Resolution of Conflict
Passive	Hands-off policy; accept status quo	Partial solutions; incremental strategy
Active	Defense of status quo; alliances, aid, Sixth Fleet presence	Grand diplomacy; package settlements; great-power approaches

Containment

When the United States has pursued relatively passive strategies to contain or limit regional conflicts, the military component has taken the form of an offshore naval presence, a show of the flag, and small military-aid programs to friendly countries. The economic and diplomatic elements of such strategies have involved limited aid programs and modest initiatives to reduce tensions. United States policies have followed these lines in several parts of the Middle East, especially since 1958. The Persian-Arabian Gulf and North Africa are areas where such policies may be followed in the future. The American approach to inter-Arab conflicts has at times been of this "hands-off" variety as well.

In the 1950s more active defense of the status quo and efforts to limit regional conflicts characterized American Middle Eastern policies. Bases, military pacts, large-scale military aid, and the Lebanon landings of 1958 represent the military dimension of this type of policy. Other examples include the dispatch of a squadron of U.S. planes to Saudi Arabia in 1963 to reduce the likelihood of a Saudi-Egyptian military clash and the suggestion of using a multilateral fleet to reopen the Straits of Tiran in 1967.

Along with military efforts, economic measures have often been used to maintain or restore the *status quo ante* in the Middle East. In 1957 the threat of economic sanctions was instrumental in obtaining Israeli withdrawal from Egyptian territory. Diplomatic efforts were also a major part of the active defense of the existing political order, as evidenced by the Tripartite Declaration, the Eisenhower Doctrine, American opposition to the British-French-Israeli attack on Egypt in 1956, efforts to prevent war immediately before June, 1967, and attempts to bring about Israeli withdrawal from Sinai in 1957 through agreements on the Straits of Tiran.

Conflict Resolution

Policies designed to resolve or settle problems in the Middle East have included various mixtures of diplomatic, military, and economic efforts. Where the attempt was activist, the goal was comprehensive package settlements. More passive strategies have sought partial solutions to problems. The United States has frequently followed incrementalist strategies dealing with issues one at a time. Behind such efforts lay the hope that an outside stimulus could start a snowballing process that would reduce tensions.

A second American approach has been to try for full settlement of the major causes of instability in the Middle East. This orientation represents a more global attack on problems, on the theory that the United States should do more than resolve issues piecemeal. The interrelatedness of Middle East problems has made this approach seem necessary, but also vastly increases its chance of failure.

Efforts at partial solutions to problems have included the offer of military aid and proposals of defensive alliances. For example, in the early 1950s the United States considered offering arms to Egypt in the hope that Nasser would moderate his stance toward Israel and join in a regional defense pact. Ultimately, this policy was not implemented, and the Soviet Union became Egypt's main source of arms.

More common than military actions have been economic and diplomatic initiatives. The Eric Johnston plan for sharing the Jordan waters, the Aswan Dam offer, and proposals for large-scale nuclear desalting plants have been advanced as means toward partial settlement of divisive issues. In addition, substantial quantities of food aid were given to Middle Eastern countries, especially the U.A.R., in an effort to affect policies on Arab Israeli and inter-Arab issues. Diplomatic initiatives aimed at partial settlements have included Joseph Johnson's proposal on Arab refugees, Dulles' speech to the Council on Foreign Relations in 1955, U.S. activities that facilitated British withdrawal from its base at Suez in 1954, support of the UNEF units in Sinai after 1957, and recognition of the Yemeni republic in 1962. Future encouragement of the creation of a Palestinian entity on the West Bank of the Jordan River would fall into this category.

Active American efforts to deal with the major problems of the Middle East include the Truman doctrine of 1947, which was designed to reduce the Soviet threat to Greece and Turkey. Because this policy succeeded, policymakers gradually transformed it into a doctrine of containment of Soviet influence throughout the Middle East. The United States has demonstrated active opposition to Soviet pressures through military, economic, and diplomatic initiatives. More limited to the diplomatic sphere have been the efforts, particularly by the Nixon Administration, to reach a full settlement of the Arab-Israeli conflict by consultation with the great powers and the regional parties to the conflict.

No single American policy is likely to be effective for the great range of problems and conflicts affecting the area from Morocco to Iran. In order to survey the major possibilities for United States policy in the future, problems in each part of the Middle East must be identified. Those between Arabs and Israelis are probably the most difficult to deal with and will require the most attention. The Northern Tier countries are also important to the United States, but pose a different set of issues. Inter-Arab conflicts, the Persian-Arabian Gulf, and North Africa are likely to present fewer problems to the United States in coming years, but deserve some attention here nonetheless.

The Arab-Israeli Conflict

For two decades the Arab-Israeli dispute has continued at a high level of intensity, at times breaking into war. Outside powers have generally been unable to bring the major protagonists closer together, and the parties themselves have been unwilling to resolve the conflict. Consequently, the choices available to the United States in dealing with this clash of Israeli and Arab nationalisms have never been attractive.

In the aftermath of the June, 1967 war, the United States government consciously decided that there should be no return to the unstable armistice arrangements of previous years. Instead, Israeli occupation of Arab territory was to serve as a form of pressure to bring the Arabs to make peace with Israel. The United States, especially under the Johnson Administration, abstained from taking public positions on substantive matters in the conflict, arguing that the Arabs and Israelis should reach agreement with one another through the U.N. intermediary, Gunnar Jarring. The United States did strive, however, through diplomacy, to secure adoption of the November 22, 1967, United Nations resolution calling for a full settlement. In addition, in October, 1968, the United States announced its decision to sell 50 Phantom jets to Israel. The rationale of these actions was to keep Israel strong so that U.S. involvement could be minimized, while allowing time to convince the Arabs to make peace with Israel. This general policy orientation can be considered one that tried to promote resolution of the conflict at low cost to the United States through diplomatic actions and military aid.

Limited Involvement: Stabilizing the *de facto* Situation

The Johnson Administration's policy of relative noninvolvement, based on the hope that time, regional forces, and modest pressures from outside powers might lead to a resolution of the Arab-Israeli conflict, did not reach its announced goals. Thus, the United States probably will not consider limited involvement in the near future as a step toward resolution of the Arab-Israeli conflict.

The United States may, however, adopt limited involvement as a low-cost means of promoting the stability of the status quo. This would probably require that the United States emphasize economic and military aspects of policy rather than diplomacy. The advantage of reduced involvement in the Arab-Israeli conflict would be to minimize the danger of being drawn into future conflicts. Military aid to Israel might be continued so that in case of a future conflict the undeclared U.S. commitment to Israel would not have to be put to the test.

The disadvantages of this policy to the United States would be most apparent in the Arab world. Unless the American government visibly applies pressure on Israel to withdraw from Arab territories, there may be little chance of improving U.S.-Arab relations. Stabilizing the *de facto* lines will be difficult because Arab irredentism and guerilla actions can be expected to continue. United States policymakers may decide that the surest way to guard against renewed war and U.S. involvement is to guarantee Israel's military superiority. To sweeten this bitter pill for the Arabs and to protect residual U.S. interests in Arab countries, the United States may find it prudent to give small amounts of economic aid to Jordan and perhaps other countries. In addition, encouragement of U.S. private sector activities might be expected.

In short, then, the United States may choose a policy of relative noninvolvement aimed at stabilizing the post-1967 Arab-Israeli situation. Israel would be kept strong, and perhaps aid and private investments would help to maintain U.S. interests in the Arab countries. Soviet influence in the Arab world may grow, but not dramatically. European countries may be encouraged, as in the past, to become more involved in the region as alternative arms suppliers or as sources of aid. Deep American involvement in the Arab world would be judged unlikely in the absence of a settlement; high levels of aid to Israel would be deemed unnecessary.

Adoption of a policy of limited involvement would be most likely if (1) an Arab-Israeli peace settlement seemed impossible, (2) Israel refused to withdraw from occupied territories, and (3) the potential U.S. influence in the area appeared limited. Israel's development of nuclear weapons would favor such a policy because it would assure Israeli security even if the Arab-Israeli conflict seemed insoluble. Disengagement and detachment would also seem attractive if Soviet influence in the region were to decline.

Some military aid to Israel could continue, and the Sixth Fleet might remain in the Mediterranean, but its purpose would be largely symbolic, given its modest capacity to project military power. In essence, this would be a low-cost, low-risk policy that would accept the erosion of U.S. interests and influence in the Arab countries. It would be based on evidence of Israeli ability to defend itself against any possible attack. Soviet non-involvement in the region makes this a more plausible policy than does an aggressive U.S.S.R. policy. Any credible Soviet military threat to Israel would rapidly undermine the key assumptions on which this policy would be based.

A second kind of low-involvement policy could result from a desire to minimize the negative impact of the continuation of the *de facto* situation on American interests in the Arab world. This policy could include a tacit acceptance of the territorial status quo, based on a feeling of U.S. inability to bring about Israeli withdrawal, accompanied by a public posture favoring the return of all occupied territories and east Jerusalem to the Arabs in return for contractual peace arrangements.[68] The aim of such a policy

[68]Arguments along these lines have been presented most persistently by John C. Campbell. See, for example, his article, "The Middle East," in Kermit Gordon (ed.), *Agenda for the Nation* (Washington, D.C.: Brookings Institution, 1968).

would be to dissociate the United States from Israel in the minds of Arab leaders, thereby increasing the chances for better relations with both moderate and radical Arab regimes. At the same time, it would be hoped that a public American posture opposing Israeli occupation of the West Bank and Sinai might set off political debates within Israel that would bring to the fore moderates who might seek to regain U.S. favor, thereby perhaps opening new prospects for a settlement.

The success of this policy in both the Arab states and Israel would depend heavily upon its credibility. Arabs would need to be convinced that the United States was really incapable of getting Israel to withdraw before they would give the United States any credit for opposing Israel. Likewise, Israelis would have to believe that the United States intended to back up its opposition to continued occupation of Arab territory before any agonizing reappraisal would take place. In other words, Arabs and Israelis would have to hold opposite beliefs about American capabilities and intentions requiring each to change its normal view of the matter. To both sides, the American position might appear rather hollow. To lend credibility, policymakers might have to supplement diplomatic acts with economic and perhaps military ones; for example, military aid and sales to Israel might be reduced or suspended and some economic aid given to Arab regimes.

The conditions which could lead to this policy of limited initiatives to improve relations with the Arab world, while at the same time retaining a minimal commitment to Israel for her survival, would include dissatisfaction with Israeli intransigence and overtures for better relations from the Arab states, especially the U.A.R. Concern over excessive Soviet influence in the region might also lead to a policy of political competition in the Arab world. The desirable though perhaps unlikely result of this policy would be a return to positive neutrality by some of the radical Arab states in return for U.S. diplomatic support on the issue of Israeli territorial withdrawal. The United States might also engage in modest aid programs and encourage private-sector activity in the region. The Soviets would probably still supply arms but would not thereby have exclusive influence over the Arabs. Israeli security would be ensured by European arms shipments to Israel, modest U.S. supplies, or Israeli manufacture of its own weapons. Little change would be expected in the tensions between Arabs and Israelis in the short run, but at least some American interests in the Arab world might be defended and Soviet influence checked. By the end of 1969 there was some evidence that the policy of the Nixon Administration was moving in this direction.

Partial Settlements and Agreements

The United States may consider using its influence over Israel and the Arab states to encourage partial settlements of outstanding disputes as a means of lessening tensions and reducing the chances for conflict. Earlier efforts of this sort dealt with refugees, navigation rights, and water; these topics might eventually be dealt with as isolated issues apart from a general settlement. Past initiatives were largely unsuccessful, however, and little has happened since the June, 1967, war to improve the chances for partial settlements.

The issues posed by the existence of Arab refugees, the closure of the Suez Canal, the prospects for nuclear desalination, and continued Israeli occupation of the West Bank seem to be the primary candidates for partial accommodations. American initiatives on the refugee problem could take the form of giving aid to improve the conditions of the refugees or to integrate them into normal economic activities in Jordan and elsewhere. In addition, the United States might also apply pressure on Israel to recognize the right of refugees from 1948 to choose repatriation or compensation, in exchange for some safeguards limiting the number that could actually return to Israel. Finally, the United States might offer the option of generous compensation and resettlement in Western countries to refugees. Whether or not these efforts could help to resolve the complex refugee problems would depend greatly on conditions at the time the policy was implemented. A strong Palestinian commando movement could probably prevent it from succeeding. Timing and the diplomatic preparations accompanying the effort would be of great importance.

The closure of the Suez Canal after June, 1967, was not seen as a major inconvenience to the United States directly, and the United States did not try to open it in the absence of a general settlement. It was widely believed after the June, 1967, war that the Soviet Union was more anxious than the United States to use the Canal and this led to a noticeable lack of enthusiasm in Washington for reopening the Canal. Nonetheless, Great Britain, the European countries, and India were all inconvenienced by the Canal's closure and wanted to have it reopened, although they had adapted remarkably well by using other trade routes. If the Europeans were to push for the opening of the Canal, and if the Soviets were about to force the issue as well, the United States might choose to use its limited influence on Israel to clear the Canal. The United States would certainly argue, however, that the Canal should be available to Israeli shipping in these conditions.

Washington policymakers have at times considered the possibility of a partial Jordanian-Israeli settlement. If the Israelis should ever decide that continued occupation of the populated areas of the West Bank were not in their interest and were willing to make an accommodation on the basis that the evacuated areas would not be remilitarized, the United States could probably help to secure the necessary assurance from Jordan. The regime in Jordan has been reluctant to pursue this course, however, in part because of the danger that the Egyptians or the Palestinian commandos could exert great pressure on any Arab leader who made peace with Israel. Since this hypothetical settlement would probably not include much of Jerusalem, it seems unlikely to appeal to the Jordanians.

As another partial settlement, creation of a Palestinian entity in the West Bank has also been suggested.[69] Following the June, 1967, war, some attention was paid to this possibility, but U.S. policymakers generally preferred that the West Bank be returned to Jordan. If its return were ruled out by the lack of a peace settlement, however, a case might be made for the United States to support creation of a Palestinian entity that would eventually determine its own future, either to be an independent state or to join with Jordan or Israel. Such an arrangement might also be coupled to a partial solution of the Arab refugee problem. A Palestinian entity that provided an outlet for Palestinian national aspirations might help to dissociate Palestinian irredentism from Egyptian military power. Whether the United States would promote this idea would be critically determined by relations with the Jordanian regime. Unless the Palestinians themselves showed interest in such a solution to the post-1967 Israeli occupation of the West Bank, the plan would stand very little chance of succeeding.

None of these partial solutions seems easily attainable, except those relating to water and agriculture, which are largely peripheral to the Arab-Israeli conflict. In many ways, partial settlements are as difficult to obtain as full settlements, and incrementalist strategies have not proved much more effective than full-scale efforts. Where full settlements are unsuccessful, efforts to achieve partial settlements do not necessarily provide a fall-back position.

Even in the absence of an overall Arab-Israeli settlement, it may be possible for the United States and the Soviet Union jointly to work out partial agreements that would lower the risk on both sides of being drawn into future conflicts. Despite the incompatibility of many of their interests, the great powers may both wish to lower tensions in the Middle East to help client regimes survive and to avoid the outbreak of costly wars. The two areas where U.S.-Soviet agreements may be sought are those of arms control and of understanding regarding military intervention and nonintervention.

The states of the Middle East have received huge quantities of modern

[69]See, for example, the article in *The Times* (London), May 17, 1968, unsigned but generally attributed to Cecil Hourani.

weapons in the past decade, and a complex series of arms races has developed.[70] Since the June, 1967, war, the United States and the Soviet Union have been the primary arms suppliers, with Britain and France playing less important roles. Following the cease-fire, the Soviet Union rapidly resupplied its Arab clients, making up most of their losses while attempting to upgrade the quality of their equipment and to improve the training of their troops. The United States responded to these developments, as well as to domestic pressures, by announcing in October, 1968, the agreement to sell 50 Phantom jets to Israel. The United States has been eager to reach understandings with the Soviet Union on reducing or at least containing the level of arms sent into the region, but the Soviet Union has refused to talk about arms limitations until Israel has withdrawn from Arab territory.

Although it would seem unrealistic to expect the Soviet Union to renounce its major trump of providing arms to the Arabs—especially in the absence of a settlement favorable to its clients—the United States may still be able to reach an agreement with the Soviet Union on the amounts and sophistication of weapons to be provided to client states. In return for U.S. assurances of trying to prevent Israeli development of nuclear weapons, the Soviet Union might accept limitations on the types of weapons it would supply to its clients. While tacit agreements of this sort may be possible, depending on the global nature of U.S.-Soviet relations, they would probably be more likely if a settlement were reached that included Israeli withdrawal from Arab territories occupied in the 1967 war.

A second area of possible U.S.-Soviet cooperation is less dependent upon a full settlement for success. In the course of discussions, the two parties might be able to agree, at least informally, on rules to govern intervention in future conflicts between Israel and the Arab states. The terms could specify, for example, that both states agree as they did in June, 1967, to remain uninvolved militarily, at least as long as vital population centers of their clients are not threatened. Alternately, the Soviets might be made to recognize that United States intervention—to the limited degree that this would be possible in a rapid war—would be a consequence of an imminent Arab defeat of Israel, while the United States might acknowledge that excessive Israeli advances into Syria or the U.A.R. could lead to some Soviet response.

In crisis situations there would be a high premium for both powers on signaling to one another the limited goals sought by intervention and the

---

[70]Two studies have examined the arms races in considerable detail. See J. C. Hurewitz, *Middle East Politics: The Military Dimension* (New York: Praeger, 1968); and Nadav Safran, *From War to War: The Arab-Israeli Confrontation, 1948-1967* (New York: Pegasus, 1968).

desirability of avoiding direct confrontation. Joint U.S.-Soviet efforts to bring about a cease-fire might conceivably be backed up by threats of coordinated U.S.-Soviet intervention to put an end to the fighting and to separate the combatants. While both of these latter types of agreements seem more to the advantage of the U.S.S.R. than to that of the United States, this asymmetry is based on the assumption that Israel will be the likely victor in a future Arab-Israeli war. If that were not obviously the case, the United States might be interested in urging the Soviet Union to restrain its clients. In any case, talks with the Soviet Union may improve each side's understanding of the consequences of a renewal of war in the Middle East. By lowering the chances of accidents and misinterpretations, tacit understandings could reduce tensions.

Policies for a Full Settlement

American policies toward the Arab-Israeli conflict since 1946 have fluctuated between attempting to stabilize the *status quo* and pushing, with varying degres of involvement, for a full resolution of the issues of refugees, navigation rights, territorial boundaries, and belligerency. Peace between Arabs and Israelis was seen as the desired outcome of the latter approach, whereas the former hoped to reach the seemingly more realistic goal of stability and containment of conflict. The search for a full settlement has been considered illusory by some policymakers, and in the absence of a major crisis or a fear of deterioration of the *de facto* situation the United States has generally been content to pursue the less ambitious goals.

The Arab-Israeli war of June, 1967, however, represented a sufficiently dramatic shift from the *status quo* that one could hope for more than a return to the armistice agreements of the 1950s and early 1960s. The 1967 war itself was cited as evidence of the fragility of those arrangements, and U.S. policymakers feared that a return to the *status quo ante* might reproduce the conditions that had made war inevitable and that had raised the specter of a U.S.-Soviet confrontation. In the wake of their astonishing victory in the June war, Israeli officials were reportedly waiting for the telephone call from Cairo or Amman that would signal an Arab desire to make peace. Some American policymakers apparently believed that these expectations were reasonable. In any case, few recommended that Israel should be required to withdraw from Arab territory as in 1957.

In the aftermath of the June, 1967, war, the issues dividing Arabs and Israelis were numerous. From the American standpoint, the prerequisite to any full settlement was a willingness on the part of the Arabs to make a contractual peace with Israel; this willingness would be balanced by Israeli withdrawal from occupied territories. The issue of Jerusalem's status and Jordan's rights in the city was particularly thorny, and there was talk of a unified city in which Jordan could play a substantial role. Other matters that the United States considered essential in any package settlement were solution of the refugee problem, demilitarization, and the opening of the Suez Canal and the Straits of Tiran to Israeli shipping. Other issues, such as the Arab primary and secondary boycott of Israel, the modality for reaching agreement, and the form of a peace settlement, were complicating but less difficult factors.

If the objective of obtaining a full Arab-Israeli settlement were adopted as a policy guideline by American decisionmakers, the means to this end would still need to be identified. Debate has generally centered on how aggressively the United States should become involved in the search for a settlement and whether that participation should be unilateral or multilateral.

Under the Johnson Administration, the policy of the United States was to hold out for a full settlement with the hope that forces at work in the region would lead to that result without much American involvement. Efforts to facilitate agreement included discreet, behind-the-scenes talks with all parties. Great-power or multilateral discussions were not viewed as promising ways to advance the search for peace.

A more active and consciously multilateral approach to the Arab-Israeli conflict was adopted by the Nixon Administration early in 1969.[71] In response to French and Soviet suggestions that the great powers play a more direct and coordinated role in bringing about a settlement along the lines of the United Nations Resolution of November 22, 1967, the Nixon Administration began high-priority, bilateral discussions with the British, the French, and the Soviets. In April they decided to hold four-power talks in New York. Simultaneously the United States and the Soviet Union increased the frequency of their own discussions of the Middle East in Washington.

The U.S. motive for holding these talks seemed to be a concern that the Arab-Israeli impasse would have a long-range, detrimental impact on American standing in the Middle East, particularly in the moderate Arab countries. The possibility of renewed war in the future seemed high, and few American officials could regard with equanimity the prospect of a fourth round of Arab-Israeli fighting. Publicly, President Nixon spoke of the Middle East as a "powder keg" and of the dangers of a great-power confrontation. Other officials spoke more realistically of a gradual deterioration of the American position in the region and the long-term dangers that the *de facto* situation might lead to.

[71]Some of the reasons behind the Nixon Administration initiatives can be found in the article by Charles Yost, "Israel and the Arabs: The Myths that Block Peace," *The Atlantic Monthly* Vol. 223, (January, 1969), pp. 80-85.

By engaging in the four-power talks, the United States hoped to serve as a catalyst to break the stalemate between the U.A.R. and Israel. The Jordanians, it was thought, could be brought to a reasonable settlement, and the Syrians could be ignored so long as they refused to accept the Security Council resolution of November, 1967. Since the U.A.R. would be asked to make concessions as part of a settlement, American officials felt that the Soviet Union should be required to extract those concessions. This would necessitate considerable willingness on the part of the Soviets to cooperate, and judgments differed on the real Soviet interest in a full settlement of the Arab-Israeli conflict. Initial progress was made in getting Soviet acceptance of some U.S. positions on the need for a package settlement. By late 1969, however, there were signs that the U.S. strategy was encountering difficulties.

While the United States was trying to use the Soviet Union to extract concessions from the U.A.R., the Soviets were pressing the United States to persuade Israel to withdraw from Arab lands. Each major power pleaded its inability to influence its client unless decisive policy changes were made on the other side. Initially, the great powers did not strive to impose a settlement on the Arabs and the Israelis, for they recognized that it might be impossible to get Israelis or Egyptians to accept such a settlement unless it was to their advantage. In the talks, the two major powers seemed to be trying to negotiate by proxy for their clients, drawing them into the discussions through frequent consultation, and hoping that eventually substantive issues would be raised and compromise positions would emerge. The United States appeared to believe that at some point Arabs and Israelis should begin discussions, perhaps through an intermediary such as Ambassador Jarring, to work out the details of a settlement. The Soviets, of course, were less insistent upon this point.

Multilateral efforts to reach a full settlement of the Arab-Israeli conflict run the risk of failure on several counts. First, the great powers themselves could fail to agree and the talks might then be broken off. Second, they might agree on principles, but disagree over means of implementation, producing terms so abstract that they could be ignored. Third, the great powers might be in full accord and still find themselves unable to persuade the Arabs or the Israelis to move from their intransigent positions.

If such large-scale multilateral efforts break down, the way this happens will influence the alternatives then available to the American government. For example, if disagreement between the Soviet Union and the United States leads to an impasse, the United States might decide that it is futile to work for partial understanding with the Soviets over arms control or nonintervention. Alternatively, if client intransigence results in breakdowns in multilateral diplomatic efforts, the great powers might continue to work together to clarify areas of mutual interest. If both powers consider the

American clients responsible for the impasse, policy alternatives may differ from those to be considered if the opposite were true. For example, Israeli intransigence in the face of reasonable concessions from the U.A.R. might present a set of conditions that could lead the United States to dissociate itself from Israeli goals.

Whether multilateral approaches to a full settlement of the Arab-Israeli dispute fail or succeed, pursuit of this type of policy requires sustained attention from the high-level policymakers. The difficulties of following such a policy are apparent from past efforts. The costs of this approach are the greatest, but the benefits of its success are the most obvious. Other policies available to the U.S. government if a multilateral, full settlement is not reached would include the pursuit of great power talks leading to partial understandings. The United States might also reduce its involvement in the Arab-Israeli dispute to a minimal commitment to Israeli security. The United States might also choose to dissociate its policy from Israeli objectives, and try to improve relations with the Arab states. None of these choices would be likely to lead to a full settlement, but any one might help to stabilize the *status quo* or prevent a serious decline in U.S. influence in the moderate Arab states.

Inter-Arab Conflicts

Related to the Arab-Israeli dispute, but hardly identical with it, are the tensions that divide the Arab states themselves. Inter-Arab relations are more complex than simple dichotomies of "moderates" *vs.* "radicals" or "conservatives" *vs.* "progressives" would suggest. At most, the "moderate" and "radical" labels apply to foreign policy stances, identifying the Soviet Union as the major arms supplier of the "radicals" and the United States or European countries as suppliers of the "moderates."

Before 1958 the West was heavily involved in inter-Arab disputes, especially those between Iraq, Egypt, and Syria. Since then American involvement has been episodic and primarily in Saudi Arabian-Egyptian conflicts. From 1962 to 1967 the Yemen became a divisive issue in Saudi-Egyptian relations, and the United States found itself attempting to mediate. United States efforts consisted mainly of diplomacy and food aid to Egypt, but also had a modest military dimension, as evidenced by the dispatch of a squadron of American jet aircraft to Saudi Arabia in 1963 as a deterrent against Egyptian attacks on Saudi territory.

By the late 1960s most American officials believed that the United States should not commit itself on most inter-Arab issues. Despite the intensity of many of the conflicts in the Arab world, with the exception of the Yemen, military force has rarely been used by Arab states against their Arab enemies. As long as this remains true, the United States is not likely to be drawn more deeply into inter-Arab conflicts. Consequently, the preferred policy for the United States is likely to remain one of minimal involvement.

One area where a hands-off policy in inter-Arab affairs might seem least attractive to the United States is Jordan. If, for example, Jordan were willing to make a separate settlement with Israel, the regime in Amman would no doubt be attacked diplomatically by the U.A.R. and would certainly be threatened by militant Palestinian commandos. In such circumstances, the United States might send massive aid, including military assistance, to Jordan. Alternatively, the regime in Jordan might collapse from internal pressures or as a result of Israeli reprisal raids. In the subsequent chaos Iraq, Syria, Saudi Arabia, and Israel might all try to take some Jordanian territory. If the United States hoped to keep Jordan a viable state, some form of intervention, at least on the diplomatic level, might be required.

The dangers to other moderate or conservative Arab states such as Lebanon, Kuwait, and Saudi Arabia seem less likely to bring on American involvement in inter-Arab disputes. The landing of U.S. troops, such as in Lebanon in 1958, seems unlikely in the 1970s. For example, the coup in Libya in September, 1969, brought no immediate American response. Unless circumstances change dramatically, American involvement in inter-Arab disputes will most likely be limited to small quantities of economic aid and occasional diplomatic support for one side or the other.

North Africa

The states of North Africa, or the Maghrib, are Arab in character, but possess their own distinctive problems and are marginal to most Arab-Israeli and inter-Arab quarrels. Morocco has been the least involved in issues of the Middle East, while both Algeria and Tunisia have had brief, episodic, and generally unsatisfying dealings with their eastern Arab brethren.

American policy has sought to avoid a dramatic polarization of the Maghrib that would place Algeria against the pro-Western regimes of Morocco and Tunisia. The United States has enjoyed good relations with Morocco and Tunisia, but has had rather poor ones with Algeria. Algeria has received large quantities of arms from the Soviet Union, has adopted strongly anti-American positions on international issues, and has been defiantly proud of its independence from Western influence. The United States did, however, provide Algeria with large quantities of food aid in the early 1960s, and since the June, 1967, war, when diplomatic relations were broken, the United States has officially encouraged U.S. private business in Algeria. The agreement in 1969 for very large purchases of Algerian natural gas by a U.S. company shows the possibilities for close commercial links between countries that have only minimal diplomatic ties.

Despite superficial appearances, North Africa seems unlikely to be the focus of many international crises in the future. Maghribi cooperation may be tenuous at best, but progress has been made since 1968 in lessening tensions between Morocco and Algeria. Despite its radicalism and military superiority, Algeria is not an irredentist power and is unlikely to threaten any of its neighbors seriously. Consequently, it would seem that the United States could adopt a relaxed attitude toward the region, offering modest technical aid to all three countries, encouraging private American commercial activities, and occasionally reassuring Morocco that it is not isolated and friendless. European states, which are strongly interested in Libyan and Algerian oil and gas, might be encouraged to cultivate good relations with the states of North Africa. In any case, the United States should be able to maintain good relations, at a low level of involvement, with all three countries in the Maghrib.

The Northern Tier

Next to the Arab-Israeli problem, the United States has devoted most attention in the Middle East to its relations with the countries of the Northern Tier, especially Turkey and Iran. It was in those two countries that the United States faced the realities of the threat of post-World War II Soviet expansion, in reaction to which the doctrine of containment emerged. In the 1950s it seemed that Turkey and Iran had been able to create viable regimes in the face of Soviet power, and relations between the United States and both countries were close. In return for generous U.S. military and economic aid the United States obtained bases, intelligence facilities, and overflight rights from Turkey. In 1959 the United States formalized its commitment to the independence of each of these countries in bilateral security agreements.

In the Northern Tier, both successful and unsuccessful American policies have been closely tied to the behavior of the Soviet Union. As the Soviets began to shift from hostility toward coexistence with Ankara and Teheran, American relations with both allies were affected. Iran, after having been a target of vehement Soviet attacks, came to enjoy tolerable relations with its powerful northern neighbor. After American economic aid was reduced in the late 1960s, Iran sought to improve relations with Moscow. In 1967 they agreed upon a sale of arms.

During the 1960s the United States remained more deeply involved in Turkey than in Iran, with a large U.S. military presence, partly because of Turkey's membership in NATO. Tensions in U.S.-Turkish relations arose over the scale of American involvement in Turkey and the Cyprus dispute. President Johnson's warning to Turkey in 1965 not to attack Cyprus under threat of withholding the U.S. commitment in case of Soviet aggression greatly strained American-Turkish relations. The persistence of the Cyprus dispute between Greece and Turkey has gradually weakened U.S. influence in Ankara.

The movement toward positive neutrality by Turkey and Iran has been accepted with surprising calm by U.S. policymakers. The issue of the scale of military aid to Turkey as a price for continuing U.S. base and overflight rights is, however, likely to remain a source of friction between the two nations.

Regarding both Turkey and Iran, U.S. policy will probably evolve toward accepting a greater freedom of maneuver on the part of both allies. Their relative strategic importance to the United States is considerably less than it was in the 1950s, and American interests in the Northern Tier have declined since the early 1960s. Amicable relations and modest U.S. aid to both countries seem possible for the 1970s. So long as Soviet policy is one of cooperation and détente, neither Iran nor Turkey will demand closer ties to the United States. If Soviet policy becomes more aggressive, however, or if Soviet influence in the Arab states grows dramatically, both countries may again turn to the West for help. If at that point the United States wishes to become more involved with substantial new initiatives, the residual sources of tension in both U.S.-Turkish and U.S.-Iranian relations will probably not impede closer ties. Resolution of the Cyprus dispute would, however, help American-Turkish relations. With Iran, the United States will probably seek an understanding on future developments in the region of the Persian, or Arabian, Gulf.

The Gulf

In the late 1960s American policymakers began to think about one area of the Middle East where there had been little previous involvement, namely, the Persian-Arabian Gulf. As was true in other parts of the Middle East, American concern grew as the British, who had been the custodians of the area, announced their intention of withdrawing military forces from the area by 1971.

A number of local conflicts exist in the Gulf area, most notably those between Iraq and Iran over the Shatt al-Arab, between Iraq and Kuwait, and between Iran and Arab states over Bahrein. Each of these poses some threat to countries traditionally friendly to the United States. In addition, private U.S. investment in the region's oil is large, and therefore the United States has an obvious interest in stability.

As elsewhere in the Middle East, American policy will be affected by Soviet actions. Barring large-scale Soviet intervention, the United States is likely to remain aloof from the Gulf area, relying on Iranian-Saudi Arabian cooperation to maintain stability. Toward this end, the United States may try to use its good offices to resolve the dispute over Bahrein.

In order to keep from becoming deeply involved in the Gulf area, the United States may also encourage the British to retain a modest naval presence even after 1971. At the same time, the United States might make it clear to the Soviet Union that U.S. military noninvolvement in the region would depend upon the U.S.S.R. remaining absent as well. If this policy succeeds, the Gulf will not be a region of major concern to American policymakers. Given the indigenous elements of instability, however, unforeseen developments could lead to greater U.S. involvement, perhaps in the form of a naval fleet operating from an island naval and air base in the Indian Ocean. In the late 1960s, however, most American policymakers hoped to avoid precisely this type of military involvement in an area where the United States has had no compelling national interests or history of past activity. Detachment was seen to be the preferred posture for the future.

VI. Future Problems in Middle East Policymaking

The concept of national interest has served as a common if often misleading means for explaining the actions of governments in international affairs. The concept has been particularly deceptive as applied to the Middle East, since distinctions between derived and intrinsic and nonvital interests have rarely been clarified. Much of what has concerned outside powers in the Middle East has been of a derivative nature. For Britain, a European nation with deep involvement in South Asia, the Middle East has been important as an avenue of transit. For the United States, the concern with European security after World War II increased the importance of Middle Eastern oil. The creation of the state of Israel in 1948 and the persistent commitment of an influential segment of the American public to Israel's welfare has added Israeli security to the list of U.S. interests in the area.

As the Soviet Union expanded its influence and presence in the Middle East, it became a high-priority American interest to limit this expansion while avoiding a direct confrontation with the Soviet Union. In fact, concern for avoiding armed clashes with a major power over the Middle East may eventually dominate most other interests. In this case, "vital interest" can be defined literally as that which is essential to the nation's survival, and avoidance of strategic nuclear warfare certainly fits this requirement. Other interests may then be seen as concerns of varying degrees of importance. What the United States will be willing to do in their defense is likely to be conditioned by the U.S.-U.S.S.R. relationship.

Most American policymakers dealing with the Middle East have come to view interests in less absolute terms than in the 1940s and 1950s. Even oil is viewed less as a vital resource than as an economic problem, primarily of European concern. Transit rights, overflight privileges, and the Suez Canal are all perceived as conveniences of secondary importance. The growth of Soviet influence in the region does worry policymakers, but few believe that the Soviet Union will find it easy to establish hegemony throughout the Middle East. Israeli security continues to be of deep concern to many Americans, but repeated demonstrations that Israel can defend itself have relieved policymakers of considering the U.S. response if a new Middle East war were to result in Israeli defeat. The simplistic assumption most often encountered is that the United States would intervene to prevent the destruction of the state of Israel, but it is not hard to imagine circumstances in which U.S. determination and capabilities to intervene would be greatly in doubt.

The strategic importance of the Middle East to the United States has changed during the 1950s and 1960s. With the development of ICBMs and Polaris submarines, the need for American bases on the perimeter of the Soviet Union has declined. Intelligence-gathering facilities in the region are still of high value, but alternative locations could be found. Fears are often expressed that the Soviets will penetrate the Middle East and thereby outflank NATO, but this danger is still slight. Certainly the Soviet Mediterranean fleet does not yet pose a threat against Europe, and the prospects for large-scale, secure Soviet bases at Marsa al-Kabir, Alexandria, or Latakia have not seemed good in the late 1960s.

If a relatively flexible notion of interests is used by American policymakers in thinking about the problems of the Middle East, some misleading assumptions about the imperatives of policy may be eliminated. Constraints on individual policymakers may be lifted so that a wide range of possibilities can be explored. If domestic or bureaucratic constraints later emerge to limit policy choices, at least the resulting decisions will not have been made in ignorance of other options.

To widen the range of possibilities for consideration in the future, American policymakers should be aware of the dangers of using false or misleading analogies. A policy that has worked in one part of the world may not be relevant in another part. Likewise, a policy that has been tried and failed may be appropriate and succeed at another time. The temptation to simplify the complexities of world politics by evoking lessons from the past is very great, but decisionmakers should be skeptical of images of Munich, Hitler, the Marshall Plan and, more recently, Vietnam when thinking about the Middle East.

When suggesting choices, policymakers tend to err on the side of seeing constraints as more rigidly fixed than they in fact are. By imposing a veto over their own recommendations, middle-level officials may deprive their superiors of seeing relevant policy recommendations. The difficulty for policy specialists, of course, is avoiding irrelevance. At some point in the decisionmaking process, top officials will make judgment of political feasibility, but often these assessments are based on partially inaccurate images of constraints. Most domestic constraints, such as public opinion and Congressional attitudes, are not permanent. Costs may be incurred in trying to alter them, but counterlobbying and firm Presidential support seem capable of changing some constraints.

A persistent difficulty for policymakers who have dealt with the Middle East has been the search for technical or economic solutions to political problems. Americans are often fascinated by grandiose, technically sophisticated projects that promise to bring development and stability to poor countries. The frequent talk of nuclear desalination in the Middle East has largely ignored the cogent arguments against such an undertaking, both on economic and security grounds.

The Vietnam war has convinced policymakers that multilateral approaches to international conflicts are nearly always preferable to unilateral action. This may be a reasonable assumption in many circumstances, but it could be misleading as a new dogma in U.S. foreign policy. Also, multilateral approaches need not always include the four "great powers," the United States, Britain, France, and the Soviet Union. For some purposes, West Germany and Japan may be more important nations with which to discuss policy initiatives.

The United Nations provides a means of avoiding unilateral U.S. action, but there are clear limits on how much it can accomplish in the Middle East, particularly considering the Israelis' deep distrust of that body. Nonetheless, the United Nations may serve as a convenient forum for the actions of interested parties, and may permit the United States government to shield itself from domestic criticism. Multilateral efforts, however, will require more time and generally produce less decisive policies than unilateral actions.

Policymakers are left with the dilemma of finding means to exercise influence in the Middle East without becoming so deeply involved that "boomerang effects" occur. Some nonlinear relationship seems to exist between influence and involvement, whereby small degrees of involvement often produce a strong basis for influence, while heavy involvement undermines the capacity to use one's power. Since no metric has been devised to measure these intangible qualities, the politician is left with his own judgment in finding some balance between involvement and influence.

Given the intractability of many of the problems of the Middle East, American policymakers will undoubtedly continue to find it difficult to pursue successfully their numerous and conflicting objectives in the Middle East. The question of how best to use America's limited influence without becoming more involved than is desired has no easy answers. A better understanding of past policy difficulties can, however, enhance prospects for marginally improving American policies in the Middle East in the 1970s.

CHAPTER 15

Soviet Policy in the Middle East*

Part I: Policy from 1955 to 1969

Arnold L. Horelick

I. Introduction

After a decade and a half of strenuous efforts to gain friends and influence policies in the third world, including the commitment of more than $6 billion in economic-aid offers to some 40 developing countries and $5 billion in military assistance to a large fraction of them,[1] the U.S.S.R.'s record is extremely uneven. Some of the most lavishly supported efforts have boomeranged disastrously, as in Indonesia; others, in scattered parts of Africa, South Asia, and more recently in Latin America, have turned out rather well, at least according to the modest standards by which the Western powers have learned to judge the political effectiveness of aid programs. In only one part of the third world, however, have Soviet political, military, and economic assistance programs achieved success on anything approaching a regional scale.

It is in the Arab-populated area stretching from the eastern end of North Africa eastward to the Fertile Crescent and in a pocket at the western tip of the Arabian peninsula that Soviet presence and influence have grown most conspicuously. States in which the Soviet Union is the most influential extraregional power, the U.A.R. Syria, Iraq, Yemen, the People's Republic of Southern Yemen, and perhaps Algeria and the Sudan, contain some 70 percent of the people of the Arab Middle East and produce around 55 percent of the gross regional product.[2] In no countries outside of

*This is a joint report consisting of two studies of Soviet policy in the Middle East — the first, by Arnold L. Horelick, a retrospective analysis and the second, by Abraham S. Becker, an examination of future Soviet options. Each author assumes full responsibility for his own paper while gratefully acknowledging the contribution of his collaborator in long discussions of the issues, in advice and assistance, as well as in detailed critiques of drafts of their respective papers.

[1]U.S. Department of State, Director of Intelligence and Research, *Communist Governments and Developing Nations: Aid and Trade in 1967*, Research Memorandum, RSE-120, August 14, 1968, pp. 2-6; *idem, Communist Governments and Developing Nations: Aid and Trade in 1968*, RSE-65, September 5, 1969, pp. 2-4.

[2]But less than 10% of its oil. The great-power orientation of the new Libyan regime was still unclear at the end of 1969.

Eastern Europe are Soviet foreign policy positions more faithfully supported than in what Moscow calls the "progressive" Arab states. Of the half-dozen or so ideologically favored developing countries (the composition changes from time to time) said by the Soviet Union to be following the "noncapitalist path of development" under the leadership of "revolutionary democratic" regimes, three are in the Middle East: the U.A.R., Algeria, and Syria. Five other Arab states, Iraq, Yemen, Southern Yemen, the Sudan, and Libya, are presently governed by regimes classified as "progressive" by Moscow.

By the end of 1967 the Soviet Union and its East European allies had already poured into the Middle East military equipment and related assistance valued at more than $3 billion, the lion's share of which went to the U.A.R. ($1.5 billion). This compares with a total of $5.5 billion in Communist military aid extensions to all non-Communist states from 1954 through 1967. During 1967 the U.A.R. passed Indonesia ($1.34 billion) as the largest single recipient of such military assistance. Syria, which received some $460 million in extensions of military aid between 1956 and 1967, is doubtless the per-capita leader.[3]

The concentration of Soviet economic credits and grant extensions to Middle Eastern countries has been somewhat less lopsided but still disproportionately high, accounting for approximately one-third of all such Soviet extensions to underdeveloped countries between 1954 and 1968. Only India, with a population more than 15 times that of Egypt, surpasses the U.A.R. in total Soviet credits and grants extended ($1.6 billion as against $1 billion).[4]

Finally, it is to the waters that wash the shores of the Middle East's littoral states that the Soviet Union has dispatched the only permanent military presence it maintains outside the U.S.S.R., Eastern Europe, and their immediately adjacent waters.[5]

Few observers of the post-World-War-II scene could have foreseen the pace and scope of the U.S.S.R's penetration of the Arab Middle East. Indeed, to Stalin and his associates this must have seemed a most improbably susceptible and only marginally interesting target area. The Soviet Union's present visibility in the area has distorted many retrospective appraisals of the role played by the Arab East in Soviet foreign policy both

[3]U.S. Department of State, *Communist Governments and Developing Nations: Aid and Trade in 1967,* p. 6.

[4]U.S. Department of State, *Communist Governments and Developing Nations: Aid and Trade in 1968,* p. 3. If East European extensions are added, the gap between India and the U.A.R. is narrowed to $0.3 billion ($1.9 and $1.6 billion respectively).

[5]Of course, by regarding the Mediterranean as an extension of the Black Sea (since 1968), the Soviet Union in effect makes adjacent waters of the eastern Mediterranean.

before and after 1955. There is a strong tendency in many contemporary accounts to overstate the importance attached to the area by Soviet leaders in the past and to exaggerate the purposefulness of the Soviet policies and behavior that led to the U.S.S.R.'s present extensive involvement. Dazzled by Moscow's high silhouette in the Arab world today, many observers have underestimated the extent to which the evolution of Soviet policy there has been derivative, ensuing from the pursuit of more highly valued extra-regional objectives, and reactive, improvised in response to opportunities that presented themselves as a consequence of events over which the Soviet Union had little control, or as the unintended consequences of actions undertaken for other purposes.[6]

Failure to appreciate the fortuitous as well as the deliberate elements in the evolution of Soviet policy and to distinguish the instrumental uses of the region from its intrinsic value to the U.S.S.R. may produce a somewhat distorted perspective on Soviet Middle Eastern policy, particularly regarding Soviet options and policy choices in an uncertain future.

In the first part of this study are examined the interplay of factors and events that led the Soviet leaders after Stalin's death to make the Middle East the prime focus of their extra-European foreign policy. This analysis of the factors in Soviet Middle Eastern policy and the path by which it arrived at its present position provides the foundation for Part II of this discussion, in which are delineated alternative future Soviet policies, the conditions under which they might be adopted, and their implications for future political and economic development in the Middle East. The purpose, after charting the course of Soviet policy in the 1950s and 1960s, is to explore the impact that a range of plausible Middle East and related contingencies seems likely to have on the direction of Soviet policy in the 1970s.

II. Basic Factors in Soviet Policy

This analysis of Soviet Middle Eastern policy in the years since its activation in the mid-1950s hinges on the shifting relationship between two sets of factors. The first set comprises the larger global impulses and objec-

[6]An extreme example of the tendency to overrate Soviet purposefulness and control is the elementary error of logic committed by those who inferred from what they perceived as the large gains won by the U.S.S.R. as a result of their clients' defeat in the Six-Day War, that the Soviets had deliberately instigated the war with precisely that outcome in mind (Sir John Clubb, *New York Times*, October 29, 1967); or that Soviet policy was at least accidentally super-Machiavellian, since, "given the expectation of an Israeli victory, it would be rationally appropriate, from the Soviet viewpoint, to recommend a war-instigating policy [in order to] register substantial . . . gain at American expense" (George Heitmann, "Soviet Policy and the Middle East Crisis," *Survey* [October, 1968], p. 143).

tives that prompted the Soviet Union to establish and then extend a bridge-head in the region, as well as the extraregional constraints that have set limits to Soviet policy. These factors include, above all, aspects of the global U.S.-Soviet relationship pertinent to the Middle East. A second group embraces those factors that bear on the U.S.S.R.'s relationship to states in the area proper and to the explosive intraregional conflicts that have made the Middle East the cockpit of the postwar world.

In the rapidly changing political and military circumstances of the past decade and a half, the relative weights assigned to these two sets of global and regional factors in Soviet policy deliberations have fluctuated widely. The present Soviet policy posture in the Middle East is the culmination of a series of largely *ad hoc* responses and initiatives taken by a succession of Soviet leaders in a remarkably fluid policy environment in which basic regional objectives as well as strategies and tactics (not to mention ideological dicta) underwent frequent revision and emendation. At virtually every stage after 1955 the net effect of these essentially opportunistic Soviet adaptations to rapidly changing circumstances was to raise Moscow's stakes in the area and to expand the range of operative regional objectives that Soviet leaders could choose to pursue.

The fact that the overall thrust of Soviet Middle Eastern policy has been so overwhelmingly in the direction of deeper involvement in the affairs of the region does not mean that the basic considerations bearing on Soviet policy have always pointed in the same direction. Tension between factors pointing in different directions has been chronic, and at certain critical junctures sharp conflict between spokesmen for competing interests may be presumed to have occurred. The Six-Day War was probably such a critical juncture, although the policy adjustment that was ultimately made in response to it only raised the U.S.S.R.'s Middle East profile still higher.

In no phase of Soviet Middle Eastern policy since the mid-1950s has any extraregional factor weighed more heavily than the Soviet Union's relations with the United States. However, the aspect of Soviet-American relations that has been most salient and the weight accorded it relative to cross-cutting regional considerations have varied greatly over time. Initially, it was the strategic military aspect that was the most compelling factor in Soviet policy. The U.S.S.R. leap-frogged into the Arab Middle East in 1955 when Egypt offered it an opportunity, simply by buying Soviet weapons, to disrupt the British-sponsored, American-backed plan to link the so-called Northern Tier states in a military alliance along the southern periphery of the U.S.S.R. With manned aircraft of intermediate range still providing the principal means for conducting strategic nuclear war, any Western effort to include in an anti-Soviet military pact new territories from which nuclear weapons could be launched against the Soviet Union was bound to be regarded as a threat to the most vital Soviet security interests. By 1958, however, the Suez war and Iraq's withdrawal from the Baghdad Pact had created a new Middle Eastern political climate that virtually eliminated the danger that any group of Arab states could be organized into a Western nuclear *place d'armes* against the U.S.S.R. Moreover, advancing military technology, notably the perfection of inflight refueling techniques, the introduction of true intercontinental bombers, and the development of long-range ballistic missiles, drastically reduced SAC's requirement for forward strategic air bases, which had in any case become extremely vulnerable to Soviet-based nuclear weapons. Thus, within a few years after the U.S.S.R. established itself as a power to be reckoned with in the Middle East, the strategic defensive impulse that had powered its breakthrough into the region was largely dissipated. By the 1960s the U.S.-Soviet strategic military relationship had only marginal significance as a global factor that Soviet Middle Eastern policy was designed to affect; as Soviet policy began to fix on objectives in the Middle East itself, the U.S.-Soviet strategic balance became crucial as the principal source of constraint on Soviet behavior that might impinge on U.S. interests in the region.

Coincident with the narrowing of the gap between American and Soviet strategic nuclear forces in the mid-1960s, the balance of local U.S. and Soviet theater forces assumed growing importance. During the decade after the initial Soviet penetration of the Arab Middle East, the U.S.S.R. had no permanent military presence in the region: none was required to achieve the Soviet Union's initial limited objectives. Beginning around 1964, as part of a broader effort to strengthen the "blue water" capabilities of the Soviet Navy, the U.S.S.R. began to deploy a small naval force in the Mediterranean, apparently designed to keep tabs on the U.S. seaborne nuclear deterrent force stationed there. In the second half of the decade the Soviet Mediterranean Squadron grew into a permanent fixture, its military function still largely oriented to a strategic defense role; however, the Arab-Israeli war of June, 1967, imparted to it a regional political-military significance that was out of proportion to its modest capacities to perform military operations of any large local consequence. By the end of the decade the Soviet Mediterranean Squadron was firmly established as an instrument of Soviet Middle Eastern policy and was emerging as a potential agent for Soviet policy in outlying areas accessible through the strategic waterways of the Middle East.

What had begun as a limited Soviet "spoiling" operation against the hapless Baghdad Pact was broadened in the years after the Suez war into a far-reaching effort, first to root out U.S. influence from "progressive" Arab states (a category that tended to be synonymous with recipients of large supplies of Soviet weapons), and then to diminish U.S. influence in the area as a whole. Partly in pursuit of these ends and partly because circumstances drew it in, the Soviet Union became increasingly involved in the internal affairs of the Arab world. In the late 1950s and early 1960s internal Arab affairs took on an independent significance for Soviet policy that they lacked at the start.

To increase its own influence in the Arab world and to promote the cold war against the United States, the U.S.S.R. cultivated patron-client relationships with several radical nationalist Arab states, above all with Egypt. The Soviet Union nourished this relationship not only by providing clients with arms and economic assistance, but also by aligning itself more and more openly on their side in the two polarizing conflicts that threatened peace and stability in the region: (1) the inter-Arab struggle, initially within the ranks of the anti-Western states of Egypt, Syria, and Iraq, but later chiefly between the radical Arab states and the Western-oriented conservative or traditional states, including the oil-rich Gulf states; and (2) the Arab-Israeli conflict, which, on the Arab side, had greatest salience for Egypt and Syria, the U.S.S.R.'s chief clients, and Jordan, an American protégé.

Of the two conflicts, the inter-Arab struggle between radicals and conservatives had the highest potential payoff for the U.S.S.R. in the 1960s, since success for Soviet clients could be expected to produce basic foreign policy reorientations in the pro-American traditionalist Arab states that succumbed to radical nationalism. But it was the second conflict that proved to be the more explosive of the two and the more prolific generator of Arab demands for Soviet military assistance and political support. After the June, 1967, war Soviet Middle East policy became tied closely to achievement of Soviet clients' minimal demands in the conflict with Israel, since the political survival of those Arab regimes seemed to depend on their satisfaction. Although the Arab-Israeli conflict was intrinsically marginal to Soviet interests, the U.S.S.R. found itself under great pressure to deliver on promises to secure withdrawal of Israeli forces from occupied Arab territories. Without direct Soviet participation, renewal of the general fighting against Israel promised only another, perhaps fatal, defeat for Soviet clients and humiliation for the Soviet Union. Since the U.S.S.R. was reluctant to incur the risk of confronting the United States that its own military intervention would entail, and was unable to compel Israel to accept the "political solution" that the United States opposed, Moscow adopted a two-track strategy in the Middle East at the close of the decade. The Soviet Union actively sought Washington's collaboration in working out and imposing on Israel a political solution that would satisfy its clients' minimal demands while simultaneously, but within limits imposed by its temporary need to enlist U.S. collaboration, Moscow continued to encourage the Arabs to expel the United States from the region. In a sense, the wheel had come full circle, and the U.S.-Soviet relationship once again, but under radically altered circumstances, dominated Soviet Middle East policy deliberations.

III. The Evolution of Soviet Middle Eastern Policy

The Czarist Heritage and Early Soviet Policy

The Arab world was never a high-priority region for Soviet foreign policy before the 1950s. Soviet Middle Eastern policy had always been fixed on the contiguous non-Arab states of Turkey and Iran. In this preoccupation, the Bolsheviks were in accord with the traditions of Czarist foreign policy. Despite easy generalizations about the continuity of recent Soviet Middle Eastern policy and traditional Russian policies toward that region, the "Eastern question" that preoccupied the Czars and their ministers in the eighteenth and nineteenth centuries was radically different from the Middle Eastern question that absorbs the attention of their Communist successors. For Czarist Russia, the Eastern question revolved around the fate of Constantinople and the Turkish Straits and the disposition of the Balkan territories of the crumbling Ottoman Empire. The Sultan's vast Arab domains aroused Russian interest intermittently, but only in response to opportunities for exploiting them to threaten Constantinople from the rear (e.g., the episode of Catherine's extension of military assistance to Egypt). Imperial Russia's primary objective in seeking to control the Turkish Straits was not so much to challenge the West's naval monopoly in the Mediterranean as to prevent or limit the passage of Western men-of-war from the Mediterranean into the Black Sea.

Farther to the east, Russia's expansion into the Caucasus during the nineteenth century brought it into contact with Persia (Iran), over which the Czars sought for almost two centuries to establish hegemony, only to be blocked by England, with which Russia was ultimately obliged to share spheres of influence.

Early in the twentieth century, the October Revolution sharply, if only temporarily, reversed the thrust of Russia's traditional Middle Eastern policy, but did not alter its geographical foci. Renouncing Czarist territorial and commercial claims against Russia's southern neighbors, the young Soviet Republic moved quickly to cultivate good state-to-state relations with Turkey and Persia, if not actually to convert them into allies then at least to neutralize them and to prevent them from falling into the camp of their principal opponents, the British.

The same anti-British impulse led Moscow simultaneously to sound the call for a general uprising throughout the Arab world, now divided by a variety of dependency devices between England and France. But the call had little practical effect. The Soviet Union gained some sympathy for itself among Arab nationalists when it renounced all secret treaties to which Czarist Russia had been a party and divulged the provisions of the Sykes-Picot Treaty of 1916, whereby Britain and France had agreed to divide the Arab portions of the Ottoman Empire between themselves. The Soviet government moved quickly to recognize the newly created king-doms of Nejd and Hejaz (later Saudi Arabia) in 1926 and of Yemen in 1928. But the Soviet Union's only direct state-to-state contacts with the Arab world were restricted to those independent enclaves; elsewhere, in the British- and French-dominated states and dependencies, it was excluded. There the Soviet Union could exert influence only through the small illegal Communist parties that were formed in the 1920s in the more advanced parts of the region. This influence was neligible, however, for the Arab Communist parties, composed largely of minoritarian members and operat-ing on the basis of Comintern directives that were framed primarily with China in mind,[7] remained narrowly sectarian in outlook and failed to establish vital relationships with the rising forces of Arab nationalism. During the mid-1930s period of "Popular Fronts," when the Comintern encouraged broad Communist collaboration with nonproletarian parties and movements, the search for allies against British and French imperialism had already led many Arab nationalists to look toward Nazi Germany, precisely the power against which the "Popular Front" was aimed. Arab nationalist flirtation with the Soviet Union's World War II enemies deepened still further Moscow's built-in mistrust of Arab bourgeois nationalist move-ments, confirming Soviet suspicions of their readiness to sell out to the highest imperialist bidder.[8]

Ironically, it was Hitler, during the Nazi-Soviet Pact interval, who tried to induce Stalin to direct his imperial aspirations toward the south, where they could be satisfied at Britain's expense, rather than toward the Balkans, on which Germany had designs. Far from demonstrating the U.S.S.R.'s unrequited passion for southward expansion, as most accounts have it, the captured German documents in which the 1940 Nazi-Soviet discussions are recorded show clearly that the initiative for the U.S.S.R.'s proposed south-ward expansion "in the direction of the Indian Ocean" came entirely from the German side and that Hitler and Ribbentrop failed to induce the Russians to reciprocate German enthusiasm for the proferred Berlin award. The more eloquently Hitler proclaimed Germany's understanding for

[7]And which proved by 1927 to have been disastrously inappropriate even there.
[8]For the standard treatment of this period, see Walter Z. Laqueur, *The Soviet Union and The Middle East* (New York: Praeger, 1959), pp. 7-134.

Russia's "natural tendency" to expand in southerly directions, the more doggedly did Molotov return to the contiguous-area questions that really concerned Moscow, the Balkans, the Turkish Straits, and Finland.[9] Moreover, Moscow's counterproposal in Hitler's paper exercise to divide the British Empire also redefined Hitler's proposed sphere of influence for the Soviet Union as "the area south of Batum and Baku in the general direction of the Persian Gulf."[10] This more modest—and also somewhat more precise and realistic—formulation placed the center of the Soviet Union's Middle Eastern territorial aspirations in eastern Turkey and northern Iran, the traditional objects of Russian policy, and appeared at most to include only Iraq among the Arab lands.

Thus, during the entire interwar period, Soviet foreign policy in the Middle East continued to be focused on relations with contiguous non-Arab states. Blocked by a Western *cordon sanitaire*, the Soviet Union moreover lacked effective access to the Arab world, and its surrogates, the local Communist parties, sectarian in outlook as were their Russian Comintern mentors, proved unable to establish themselves as vital political forces in the region.

Did this prolonged Soviet quiescence in the Arab world signify low interest or merely lack of opportunity? In foreign policy matters, interest and opportunity are too interdependent to permit a definitive answer. Without interest, opportunity will neither be perceived nor seized; interest too long denied opportunity for advancement will eventually fade. This much can be said, however. Neither ideological preconceptions, cultural affinity, historical inertia, nor strategic calculations impelled the Soviet Union to search for opportunities to penetrate the Arab Middle East. At the same time, the Soviet Union's lack of physical access to the Arab world and the weakness of the Communist movement there acted as barriers to the stimulation of strong interest in Arab affairs in the Politburo.

The First Cold War Decade

The Soviet Union's early postwar bid to the Western allies for a little place in the Middle East scene was no more consequential than Hitler's invitation

[9]Raymond J. Sontag and James S. Beddie (eds.), *Nazi-Soviet Relations, 1939-1941* (New York: Didier, 1948), pp. 217-259. When Hitler's proposition was first put to Molotov by Ribbentrop, the Soviet Foreign Minister coolly inquired which sea the Reich Foreign Minister had in mind (p. 221). The same preoccupation with what was close to the Soviet Union had been revealed earlier when Molotov, responding to an initiative by the Italian Ambassador in Moscow, said that the U.S.S.R. would recognize Italy's hegemony in the Mediterranean, provided that Italy recognized the Soviet Union's in the Black Sea (p. 161).
[10]*Ibid.*, p. 258.

to Stalin to carve out a huge sphere of influence extending to the Indian Ocean. But the Soviet Union's demand for a trusteeship over the Italian colony of Tripolitania was not so much an indication of a particular Soviet regional interest as a specific instance of a general Soviet effort to secure the largest possible share of the spoils of war, including all the trappings of its newly won great-power status. As Molotov put it at the Paris Conference of Foreign Ministers in the spring of 1946, the Soviet Union's new stature in the world entitled it to act as trustee over "some satisfactory territory." British opposition frustrated this Soviet bid as well as related Soviet proposals to take over from Italy control of the Red Sea port of Massawa in Eritrea and the Dodecanese Islands in the Mediterranean.[11]

Far more ominous was the revival of Russian ambitions to control the Turkish Straits and to dominate northern Iran. Although these long-standing imperial goals were now pursued more forcefully than at any time since the Czars, the effort not only failed to achieve its objectives but also proved highly counterproductive. To defend their independence and territorial integrity, Turkey and Iran were virtually driven into alliance with the United States, which by 1947 had succeeded Great Britain as the foreign protector of Turkey and Iran (as well as of Greece, which was threatened by Communist armed insurrection). With U.S. and British backing, the Turks bluntly rejected all Soviet demands for territorial cessions and joint control of the Straits, and the U.S.S.R. ultimately withdrew them after Stalin's death in 1953.[12] In Iran, the Shah's troops, ignoring Soviet protests, deposed the puppet regimes in Persian Azerbaijan and Kurdistan left behind by the departing Russian force in 1946, and the Iranian parliament refused to ratify the charter for a joint Soviet-Iranian oil company, the creation of which had earlier been agreed to by the Iranian government under Soviet duress. In time the Soviet Union resumed toward Turkey and Iran the neutralization policies of the pre-World-War-II period. But not before the threat to Soviet security interests that Moscow began to perceive in the alignment of these neighboring Muslim countries with the West had led the Soviet Union to seek instruments for countering it among the Arab states on the far side of the Northern Tier.

This threat was not to materialize fully until 1955. Until it did, Soviet policy toward the Arab world remained largely one of inaction. Formally, Soviet access to the area had been improved by the British-sponsored

[11]See David Dallin, *Soviet Foreign Policy after Stalin* (Philadelphia: Lippincott, 1961), pp. 105-107.

[12]Stalin's successors acknowledged to the Turks that postwar Soviet territorial demands had been unjust. This was the only explicit confession of a Soviet foreign policy misdeed during Stalin's rule, apart from Khrushchev's apology to Tito for Beria's alleged incitement of the 1948 Soviet-Yugoslav split.

wartime establishment of diplomatic relations with a number of Arab states (Egypt, 1943; Syria, Lebanon, and Iraq, 1944), but in practice the Soviet Union played no substantial role in Arab affairs during most of the first postwar decade. There was one brief but fateful exception to this general rule of low Soviet political profile in the area: the Soviet Union's active support for the partition of Palestine and the creation of the state of Israel, 1947-1948.

Moscow's sudden departure from Bolshevism's traditional hostility to Zionism in 1947-1948 was no shortsighted blunder soon corrected by the Soviet leaders, nor was it a Machiavellian ploy that worked out with brilliant success. In voting for partition, recognizing Israel, and facilitating the shipment of arms from Eastern Europe to defend the new state, the Soviet Union was not provoking the anger of tens of millions of Arabs merely to gain the good will of 600,000 Palestinian Jews; but neither were the Soviet leaders so clairvoyant as to forsee the incredible chain of events that would eventually make Soviet clients of Israel's bitterest enemies. The U.S.S.R.'s Palestine policy in 1947-1948 was governed by the same objective that had guided it since the creation of the Mandate system: the quickest possible expulsion of the British, whom early Bolsheviks regarded as the wily and powerful leaders of the international anti-Soviet camp (a role not unlike that attributed to it during the nineteenth century by the Czar's ministers).

As early as 1920 the Soviet-controlled Baku Conference of Eastern Peoples protested the imminent acquisition of the Palestine Mandate by Great Britain (which was then firmly committed to the creation of a Jewish national home in Palestine), preferring that it be granted instead to the Muslim Turks, who strongly opposed Jewish colonization of the Holy Land. In the 1920s and 1930s Arab nationalism appeared to be the only plausible anti-imperialist force in Palestine; that it sometimes manifested itself in pogroms was regrettable but unavoidable, given provocation by the Zionists, who were, objectively at least, the handmaidens of British imperialism, to be condemmed by Arab fellaheen and Jewish workers alike.[13]

By 1947, however, the situation had changed radically. The militant, disciplined, and highly organized Jews of Palestine, whose numbers had increased considerably, had proved to be the only effective anti-British force in the country. With Britain about to withdraw, partition seemed the best alternative to ward off a U.N.-sponsored trusteeship plan that would doubtless have been administered by Western military forces. In these

---

[13]Communists in both the U.S.S.R. and Palestine hailed the Mufti-led Arab uprisings of 1929 and 1936 as "basically progressive," despite their violently anti-Jewish character. (See Judd L. Teller, *The Kremlin, the Jews, and the Middle East* [New York: Yoseloff, 1957], pp. 145-162.)

circumstances, Andrei Gromyko rose before the U.N. General Assembly on May 13, 1947, and without so much as mentioning the word "Zionism," reversed the Soviet Union's long-standing and unqualified opposition to Zionism's political goal. He announced the U.S.S.R.'s support for "the right of the Jewish people" to realize their striving "for the creation of their own state" in Palestine, a country in which they, as well as the Arabs, had "historical roots."[14]

Soviet willingness to incur Arab wrath in 1947-1948 shows how little impressed Moscow then was with the anti-imperialist potential of Arab nationalism. As for Arab Communist parties, their prospects seemed so poor anyway that the new blow dealt them by the Soviet position on Israel could make little difference. The Jews of Palestine, their Zionist creed now conveniently ignored, had forced out the British imperialists; the invading Arab armies, if not repulsed, could only cause their return, or the intrusion of a new imperialist policing agency. Objectively, it was now the Arab invaders who served imperialist purposes.

Opening to the Arab World

The collaboration of leading Arab nationalists with Nazi Germany in the 1930s and 1940s perhaps gave the Soviet Union special reason for distrusting them, but in the early postwar years Moscow evinced no great enthusiasm for any of the non-Communist Afro-Asian national liberation movements, and was particularly critical of those that achieved statehood by peaceful means. In Stalin's view, the prewar correlation of forces had genuinely changed only in those parts of the world where the vacuum left by retreating Axis armies had been filled by the Soviet Union itself or by Communist-led regimes responsive to Soviet discipline. The emerging nations to which Western imperialist powers had voluntarily granted independence had merely exchanged overt colonial status for a slightly camouflaged version of the same thing.

The Stalinist "imperialist lackey" model of the new nations was one of the "leftist" conceptions employed in the early postwar years to mobilize the "socialist camp" against imperialism in a dichotomized world that precluded middle positions and third forces. By the early 1950s, however, that model had already outlived its usefulness. The determination of developing nations such as India and Burma to maintain independent, neutralist, and passionately anti-imperialist (therefore potentially anti-Western) foreign policies could no longer be ignored, even if it could not yet be satisfactorily explained. By failing to establish positive political relationships with such neutralists, the Soviet Union was not only foreclos-

[14]*Pravda,* May 16, 1947.

ing foreign policy options for itself but also leaving the West free to deal with the new nations as it pleased.

In the last years of Stalin's life the Soviet Union had already begun cautiously to explore the grounds for collaboration with neutralists (particularly with the Indians during U.N. maneuverings to end the Korean war); Stalin's death in 1953 accelerated the process of change in the U.S.S.R.'s basic orientation vis-à-vis the developing countries. New policies did not emerge full-blown, however, and the doctrinal revisions necessary to legitimate such new policies were not introduced until almost three years after the dictator's death. Stalin had bequeathed no clear mandate for radical change, and the new "collective leadership" lacked sufficient authority to make far-reaching policy or doctrinal innovations quickly or explicitly. Moreover, the most experienced Soviet leader in international affairs, Foreign Minister Vyacheslav Molotov, was extremely reluctant to abandon the familiar rigidity of "two-camp" politics for the uncertain rewards of flirting with anti-Communist neutrals.

For these reasons and perhaps also because of their ignorance of the Afro-Asian world, the members of Khrushchev's rising faction initially concentrated their energies on atmospherics, on efforts to change attitudes toward the Soviet Union in nations that made up what came to be known in 1956 as the "Zone of Peace." Foreign travel by the Khrushchev-Bulganin duo was the principal means for improving the atmosphere. In the course of these leaders' unprecedented visits to India, Burma, and Afghanistan in 1955, the Soviet Union first entered, on a modest scale, the field of foreign economic assistance to non-Communist nations.

While the top Soviet leaders concentrated on building new options for Soviet policy among Asian neutralist nations, the Western powers had been inadvertently laying the groundwork for a dramatic Soviet breakthrough in the Arab Middle East. Soviet policy in that region had again become quiescent after the flurry of activity connected with the partition of Palestine. The U.S.S.R. had been unsuccessful in its attempt to join in the four-power guarantees of existing Arab-Israel armistice lines and thereby secure Western recognition of Soviet great-power status in the Middle East. But the British, French, and Americans, having excluded the Soviet Union diplomatically by their Tripartite Declaration of May, 1950, now overplayed their hand in claiming a Soviet threat to the region, and in the end produced such deep anti-Western hostility in some Arab states as to move them to invite into the area the very Soviet pressure the West sought so vigorously to exclude.

As leader of the Arab League and unwilling host country for the huge British military base at Suez, Egypt took the lead in Arab opposition to the West, rejecting the Tripartite Declaration as an implied demand that the Arabs recognize Israel and denouncing Western regional defense plans as schemes to perpetuate British military bases. The Soviet Union naturally welcomed Egypt's defiance of the West and applauded in 1951 when Cairo unilaterally renounced the 1936 Anglo-Egyptian Treaty and rejected U.S. and British invitations to participate in a Middle East Defense Organization (MEDO). As when the U.S.S.R. had supported the Zionist founders of Israel, Soviet approval of Egypt's policies had nothing to do with the country's social system or the ideology of its leaders. Indeed, in 1952 when the Free Officers deposed Farouk and formed a new government in Cairo, Moscow was suspicious of what was objectively bound to be a more "progressive" Egyptian regime, fearing that the new Naguib-Nasser government might agree to a compromise with London that would permit the British to maintain a military presence at the Canal. As late as October, 1954, when Egypt signed a new treaty with England, it may have appeared to Moscow that Nasser, despite his rhetoric about independence and Arab nationalism, was going to be a less effective anti-imperialist force than Farouk's ministers had been.[15]

Within a half-year, however, the situation was dramatically altered by the Baghdad Pact, a product of Washington's desire to forge a Middle East defense system oriented on the Northern Tier states (which were presumed, unlike Egypt, to be genuinely concerned over the Soviet threat) and London's search for a new formula to preserve its strategic foothold in Iraq before the expiration of the British-Iraqi Treaty of Alliance in 1957. The price paid by the West for the dubious advantage of bringing a single Arab state, Iraq, into its alliance system proved exorbitant. Formation of the Baghdad Pact created a community of interests between Egypt and the Soviet Union where none had existed before and set the stage for the U.S.S.R.'s dramatic breakthrough into the Arab Middle East. To the Soviets, the Baghdad Pact appeared a particularly ominous exercise in the classical tactics of "capitalist encirclement." By linking NATO and SEATO (Southeast Asia Treaty Organization) through a network of overlapping memberships, the United States and Great Britain were closing the hostile imperialist ring around the Soviet Union. Buffer states along the southern frontiers of the U.S.S.R. were being incorporated into Western-led anti-Soviet military alliances that would make available new bases from which nuclear-weapon-carrying bombers could be launched against the

[15]While the new treaty required the evacuation of British bases in the Suez Canal Zone in 20 months, it also provided that the bases would again be available for British use in case of an attack by a foreign power on any Arab country *or Turkey*, a stipulation that in light of Turkey's adherence to NATO had a clearly anti-Soviet connotation.

U.S.S.R.[16] Moreover, the Baghdad Pact was "open-ended," and the Western powers clearly intended to reinforce the new anti-Soviet barrier in the south by extending it to include at least other Arab states in the Fertile Crescent.

Moscow's predictable ire had presumably been discounted by the signatory governments, but the Baghdad Pact's searing impact on the Arab world had not been so clearly foreseen. It polarized the states of the region between Cairo and Baghdad, catapulted Nasser into world prominence as leader of anti-Western Arab nationalism, and raised Nasserism to a political force of pan-Arab dimensions.

Infuriated by what he regarded as Iraq's betrayal of the Arab cause and its challenge to Cairo's ambitions to lead the Arabs in world politics, Nasser now shared with the Soviet Union a set of common objectives: to prevent other Arab states from joining the Baghdad Pact; to undermine Iraq's position at potential leader of a pro-Western group of Arab states; and to eliminate remaining Western military footholds in the Arab world.

The precise sequence of events that led to the unprecedented Soviet-Egyptian arms deal of 1955 (Czechoslovakia served as proxy for the U.S.S.R.) remains unclear and is a subject of some controversy.[17] Whether the initiative came technically from Cairo or from Moscow, and precisely when, is not crucial, however, for a broad understanding of Soviet policy.[18] The shipment of Soviet bloc arms to Egypt admirably served to advance common Soviet and Egyptian interests. The West's monopolistic control of the arms market for the Middle East had given it tremendous leverage over the Arabs. Cairo had always deeply resented the arms limitations imposed by the Western powers; after Iraq joined the Baghdad Pact, thus ensuring preferential treatment for itself, the Western arms monopoly became intolerable to Nasser. Arms from the Soviet bloc, in unprecedented volume, not only provided him with a means to circumvent Western limitations on arms deliveries without having to align himself, as Iraq had done, with the West; it also provided Egypt with what must have seemed excellent prospects for overcoming Israeli military superiority, again demonstrated in February, 1955, by a large Israeli raid on Egyptian positions in the Gaza Strip.

For the Soviets, on the other hand, the effect of their arms deliveries to

[16]In a series of interlocking treaties beginning in February, 1955, Turkey, Iraq, Iran, and Pakistan were linked to Great Britain in a defense pact with which the United States "associated" itself.

[17]The most recent and carefully documented account is in Uri Ra'anan, *The USSR Arms the Third World: Case Studies in Soviet Foreign Policy* (Cambridge, Mass.: The M.I.T. Press, 1969), pp. 13-172.

[18]The question of timing is more critical for an appreciation of Egyptian calculations and particularly for assessing the role played by the February, 1955, Israeli raid on Gaza.

Egypt on the Arab-Israeli regional military balance was a marginal consideration, perhaps even slightly embarrassing; Communist spokesmen carefully avoided connecting the arms deal with the Arab-Israeli conflict, representing it exclusively as "a commercial arrangement" intended to strengthen Egypt's independence of the West. Privately, Moscow no doubt considered the possibility of sabotaging the Baghdad Pact more than enough reason for making the arms deal. The Soviet leaders doubtless hoped that Egypts' rejection of alliance with the West would prove contagious. If "reactionary" Arab monarchs should fall in the process, so much the better, but at this stage it was Nasser's anti-Westernism rather than the internal character of his regime that Moscow wished other Arab states to emulate. Soviet observers perceived no "socialist" tendencies in the pre-1956 Nasser regime. At best the revolution Nasser claimed to be leading could qualify in Soviet eyes as "antifeudal" (agrarian reformist); it was expected that Egypt would rely on private capital for its industrialization and would follow an essentially capitalist path of development.[19]

Khrushchev and his colleagues could hardly have expected that provision of Soviet bloc arms to Egypt would make of Nasser an ally or even a steady client. They could not yet have had much confidence in Nasser's reliability; the West was still actively courting him, particularly with the Aswan High Dam offer. Nor was Soviet strategic power great enough to lend effective support to a distant ally who might come under armed attack, and who could not readily be disciplined to avert military confrontations. Indeed, the Soviet Union, just beginning to emerge from its period of greatest vulnerability to American strategic power, was only then acquiring a small initial intercontinental bomber capability. Locally, the Soviet Union had no military presence at all, lacking both reliable access to the region and instruments for projecting its military power.

It would be a mistake to infer from the prominent role that the Soviet Mediterranean Squadron came to play in the U.S.S.R.'s Middle Eastern policy a decade later that the 1955 "breakthrough" reflected revived Soviet aspirations in the Mediterranean. On the contrary, only the year before, Soviet naval policy had turned decidedly anti-high-seas, from which it did not change until the next decade. Precisely when the U.S.S.R. was activating its Middle Eastern policy, Khrushchev dismissed Navy Minister Admiral Kuznetsov, a long-time proponent of a large blue-water Soviet

---

[19]A recent Soviet analysis of stages in the development of Egypt's revolution states quite bluntly that the Nasser regime radicalized first its foreign and then its domestic policies only because it was "impelled" to do so by the West's hostility to Egypt's independent foreign policy, particularly by creation of "the clearly anti-Egyptian Baghdad Pact" (G. Mirsky, "Novaia Revoliutsiia v OAR," *Mirovaia Ekonomika i Mezhdunarodnye Otnosheniia*, No. 1 [January, 1969], pp. 38-48).

fleet (including aircraft carriers and overseas naval bases), and announced his intention to scrap virtually the entire Soviet cruiser force, downgrade surface ships, and concentrate naval investment on submarines.[20] Achievement of the Soviet Union's limited "spoiling" objective in the Middle East did not require an actual Soviet military presence in the area; moreover, given the great disparity between U.S. and Soviet forces globally as well as regionally, a Soviet effort to establish a Middle East military foothold in the 1950s would probably have been rejected as "adventurist" as well as unnecessary.

Suez and Its Aftermath

The year that followed Nasser's announcement of the arms deal in September, 1955, was crucial for the evolution of Soviet policy. It transformed the politics of the Middle East in ways that neither the Russians nor the Egyptians could have foreseen, opening broad new fields of action in the region for both. Expanded economic, cultural, and diplomatic relations between Egypt and the Communist world developed quickly after the summer of 1955. Egypt recognized Communist China and the Soviet Union moved more openly in the United Nations to support the Arab side in the Arab-Israeli conflict. Disturbed by mounting expressions of Cairo-Moscow international solidarity, as well as by Nasser's campaign to subvert the Baghdad Pact, the United States in July, 1956, withdrew its tentative offer to finance the Aswan High Dam. Nasser retaliated by nationalizing the Suez Company and the 1956 Suez crisis was launched.

The Soviet leaders displayed for the first time during that period what have since emerged as recurrent traits of Soviet Middle East crisis behavior. Moscow's decision to provide arms to Nasser had deeply exacerbated Egypt's relations with the West and had helped to escalate the Arab-Israeli conflict as well. The first of these developments suited Moscow's interests, and the second was compatible with them, provided actual hostilities that might wipe out the center of Arab anti-Westernism could be averted. Once the catalytic effects of the arms deal began to make themselves felt, however, Moscow's control over events, including the behavior of its new friend, proved to be limited.

Bulganin was probably telling the truth when he wrote to Anthony Eden and Guy Mollet that "we learned about the nationalization of the Canal only from the radio."[21] But if Moscow was not consulted or even informed

[20]See Robert W. Herrick, *Soviet Naval Strategy* (Annapolis: U.S. Naval Institute, 1968), pp. 67-91.

[21]Quoted in Laqueur, *The Soviet Union and the Middle East*, p. 237. Similarly, in May-June, 1967, Soviet officials privately insisted that Moscow had neither been consulted nor informed in advance about Nasser's decision to close the Straits of Tiran to Israel.

in advance about the Suez nationalization, the Soviet leaders nonetheless enthusiastically endorsed the Egyptian President's precipitous act of defiance and opposed all efforts to defuse the crisis by creating an international regime for the management of the Canal. The Soviet Union egged Nasser on, warned the British and French against using force to impose their will, and failed to take any initiative to avert a military conflict even when war clouds gathered ominously over the Mediterranean in mid-October.

The parallels with May-June, 1967, are striking; but the differences in Soviet behavior after the outbreak of war are also instructive. When it became clear in 1956 that the United States would insist upon British, French, and Israeli withdrawal, the Soviet leaders warned Israel that its very existence was threatened by participation in the attack on Egypt and even issued vague hints of a Soviet rocket attack against Britain and France.[22] While these Soviet threats—Moscow's first tentative exercise in ballistic blackmail—evidently did not play a decisive role in the decision of the Western powers to liquidate the enterprise, they did gain for the Soviet Union politically valuable credit in the Arab world for achieving that outcome. These threats, though essentially empty, probably seemed reinforced by bold Soviet words during the 1957 and 1958 "crises" in Syria and Iraq and may also have aroused mistaken expectations in some Arab quarters about Soviet willingness to use force on behalf of Middle Eastern clients. These expectations were destined to be disappointed more than a decade later when the United States adopted a posture toward the Arab-Israeli war of June, 1967, that was strikingly different from its 1956 position.

Instead of toppling Nasser and wiping out Russia's newly acquired foothold, the ill-fated Anglo-French-Israeli adventure at Suez enhanced still further the rising prestige of the Egyptian President and his Soviet supporters. It succeeded only in turning the retraction of British power and influence from the eastern Mediterranean into a head-long rout. Britain's expulsion, completed two years later by the overthrow of the Hashemites and Nuri al-Said in Baghdad, left the Soviet Union face to face in the Middle East with the United States, which moved quickly to replace Great Britain as guardian of Western interests in the area. The Eisenhower doctrine, a unilateral U.S. statement promulgated in January, 1957, virtually superseded the Tripartite Declaration of 1950.

The Suez war also increased the salience of the Arab-Israeli conflict, both in the local politics of the region and in Soviet Middle Eastern policy.

[22]"What kind of position would Britain be in if she had been attacked by stronger powers with all kinds of modern offensive weapons at their disposal? . . . If rocket weapons were used against Britain and France, you would doubtless call that a barbarous act" (Bulganin to Eden, *Pravda,* November 6, 1956).

The Soviet attitude toward Israel had begun to sour long before the Suez war for reasons that had nothing to do with the Arab-Israeli conflict. Sick with suspicion of anything foreign that might possibly enjoy a modicum of sympathy in the U.S.S.R., Stalin found intolerable Soviet Jewry's warm response to the creation of Israel, symbolized by the moving reception accorded in Moscow to Golda Meir, Israel's first Ambassador to the Soviet Union. The domestic impact of the rebirth of the Jewish state, both in the Soviet Union and in Eastern Europe, contributed to the outbreak in 1948 of attacks upon "rootless cosmopolitans," suppression of institutionalized expressions of Jewish ethnic consciousness, severance of Soviet Jewry's ties with Jews abroad, and, finally, press attacks on Israel as a "bourgeois," Zionist state and "an agency of Western imperialism." A month before Stalin's death, the Soviet Union severed diplomatic relations with Israel after a bomb was exploded in the garden of the Soviet Embassy in Tel Aviv, presumably as a protest against the anti-Israeli and anti-Semitic character of charges leveled against Soviet Jewish physicians in the so-called "Doctors' Plot."

Ironically, Soviet policy with respect to the Arab-Israeli conflict first became unfriendly in Israeli eyes only after Stalin's successors restored diplomatic relations with Israel. Even in Stalin's declining years, when Soviet hostility to Israel was most pronounced, Moscow did not move beyond the official position of neutrality that it professed to hold after 1949. It was only in 1954 that the Soviet Union began to vote occasionally on the Arab side at the United Nations, instead of abstaining, as had been Moscow's custom in the early 1950s. The first Soviet Security Council veto in Egypt's favor was cast in 1954 against a New Zealand resolution calling for freedom of navigation in the Suez Canal.

Still, when the arms deal was concluded with Egypt in 1955, Moscow denied that it had anything to do with the Arab-Israeli conflict. The Soviet Union counseled Israel to remain aloof from the mounting struggle between Egypt and the West and to look forward to a period when, with imperialist powers driven out of the Middle East, the Arab-Israeli quarrel could easily be patched up. The U.S.S.R. refused to acknowledge that the arms imbalance created by Soviet weapons shipments to Egypt raised Arab hopes of destroying Israel. Instead the Soviet Union declared, as in its Foreign Ministry statement of April, 1956, that imperialism alone profited from the Arab-Israeli conflict and that the U.S.S.R. was prepared, with other United Nations member states, to help the Middle East attain peace on the basis of securing the legitimate rights of all concerned.

After Suez, the Soviet leaders no longer had to pretend that their military support of Egypt and of other Arab states which they began to supply was unrelated to the Arab-Israeli dispute. On the contrary, that festering conflict became the centerpiece of Soviet policy, which increasingly linked it with the broader struggle between "imperialism" (headed by the United States, which used Israel as its tool) and the "Arab national liberation movement" (headed by the Soviet-supported "progressive" Arab regimes). The Soviet Union did not, however, go so far as to endorse the radical Arab position that held that the Arab-Israeli dispute was an anti-imperialist colonial conflict that could be resolved only by liquidation of the imperialist base.

During the two years that were bracketed by the Suez war of 1956 and the Baghdad coup of 1958, the limited objectives that had originally brought the Soviet Union into the Arab Middle East were essentially realized. Not only was the West's attempt to incorporate the Arab states of the eastern Mediterranean into an anti-Soviet military alliance paralyzed, but the original Baghdad Pact system was itself crippled by the defection of Iraq. Britain's humiliating expulsion from the region was the realization of a long-standing Soviet objective, only partially offset by the emergence of the United States as the West's new champion in the Arab Middle East. America was incomparably stronger than Great Britain, but the U.S. military presence (almost entirely offshore) was far less extensive than Britain's had been, and its political sphere of influence outside the Arabian peninsula was limited to the three smallest states of the region.

With the disintegration of the Baghdad Pact system, the Soviet Union ceased to regard its position in the Arab Middle East exclusively in instrumental terms as contributing to the realization of essentially extra-regional strategic goals; Moscow began to concern itself more directly with political objectives in the Middle East *per se*. For several years the Soviet leaders had evidently been prepared to trade their new position of special advantage as arms supplier to Egypt and Syria for Western agreement to desist from efforts to organize an anti-Soviet bloc in the Middle East.[23] After the 1958 Iraqi coup the Soviet leaders no longer

[23]Khrushchev reportedly told Eden in London in April, 1956, that the Soviet Union was ready to abstain from arms shipments to the Middle East if the West would act similarly, i.e., curtail deliveries to Iraq and Iran, thus destroying the Baghdad Pact (see Dallin, *Soviet Foreign Policy*, p. 403). After the Suez war, the Soviet Union proposed to the Western powers (February 12, 1957) to replace the 1950 Tripartite Declaration, which excluded the U.S.S.R., with a four-power joint proclamation of principles, including an agreement "not to deliver arms to countries of the Middle East." The Soviet Union in return would be the beneficiary of a ban on great-power military alignments with the Middle Eastern states, the liquidation of all foreign bases, and the withdrawal of foreign troops. The Soviet draft referred to "the Near and Middle East," which in Soviet terminology includes Turkey, Pakistan, and Iran, as well as the Arab lands and Israel. (See text in S. Merlin, ed., *The Big Powers and the Present Crisis in the Middle East* [Rutherford: Farleigh Dickinson University Press, 1968] pp. 181-187).

advanced such proposals, evidently believing they now had more to gain from supplying arms to the radical Arab states than from curtailing U.S. military ties with the Northern Tier states, ties which were weakening in any case. By the end of the 1950s it was already clear that the imminent advent of intercontinental missiles would greatly reduce the strategic significance of the Middle East in the overall U.S.-Soviet military balance. Moscow now turned its attention for the first time to the political and social character of the Arab regimes that were recipients of Soviet military and economic assistance.

Soviet Involvement in Arab Politics: The Dilemma of Choice

Around the end of 1958 Khrushchev evidently came to believe that Egypt's heavy dependence on the Soviet Union for arms and economic aid could be translated into Soviet political leverage over Egypt's internal development. This leverage was to be applied particularly to persuade Nasser to cease his persecution of Egyptian Communists and to enlist their collaboration in the "progressive" remolding of Egyptian society.

Moscow's concern over Nasser's attitude toward native Communists, the central question of classical Soviet policy toward bourgeois nationalist regimes, was more than an expression of the ideological preferences of Soviet leaders regarding the evolution of Egypt's social and political system. Nasser's persecution of Egyptian Communists had for several years been a source of embarrassment to the U.S.S.R. in the international Communist movement, where confidence in Moscow's leadership had been gravely shaken by the exposure of Stalin's crimes and the 1956 upheavals in Eastern Europe. More immediately important, however, Khrushchev probably hoped that an alliance of Nasser and the Egyptian Communists would cement Soviet-Egyptian bonds and reduce the danger that Nasser might later decide to loosen his ties with the U.S.S.R. and maneuver between the two superpowers for maximum gains. Evidently this is precisely what Nasser did have in mind, as became painfully clear to the Soviet Union by 1959.

Moreover, since Nasser's influence was making itself felt politically throughout the Arab world, the role he permitted Communists to play in Egypt might well become the model for radical nationalist regimes elsewhere. Moscow's anxiety about Nasser's hostility toward Arab Communists became especially acute after the merger of Egypt and Syria early in 1958. Communist influence had grown rapidly in Syria after the overthrow of the Shishakli military dictatorship in 1954. As political power gravitated toward the new Ba'athist Party in Damascus, Syria's foreign policy became stridently anti-Western and decidedly pro-Soviet. However, unlike Egypt, in Syria a reciprocal relationship clearly seemed to exist between the accumulation of Soviet military equipment, which began to enter the country in large quantities late in 1956, and the growth of Communist influence in the political system. It was to aid the Ba'athist regime that the Soviet Union assumed for the first time the role of Syria's great-power protector. In the fall of 1957 Khrushchev threatened military intervention in the event that Turkey went ahead with an alleged U.S.-sponsored invasion of Syria designed to overthrow the country's "progressive" regime. Rhetorically at least, the Soviet government extended itself further for Damascus in 1957 than it had for Cairo a year before.

Thus, when the Syrian Ba'athist leaders and their army supporters persuaded Nasser to agree to a merger of the two countries (instead of the looser federal union that had been expected), Nasser's attitude toward the Arab Communists became critical for Soviet interests not only in Egypt, but also in Syria, where the prospects for Communism had seemed incomparably brighter.

The Soviet Union, which had no choice in any case, accepted with seeming good grace the submergence of the Syrian polity into the U.A.R. The Soviet leaders were obliged as well to accept, but not without bitter recrimination, the prompt extension of Nasser's anti-Communism to Syria. Concern that political power was slipping out of their hands, perhaps into those of the Communists, is reportedly what moved the Syrian Ba'athists to press for complete unity with Cairo;[24] Nasser alleged a year later that a Communist coup in Syria had been narrowly averted by the merger.[25] In any case, the union with Egypt dealt Syrian Communism a heavy blow.

By 1958 the "free-ride" phase of the Soviet Union's entry into the Arab Middle East was clearly over. Having acquired multiple interests in the region, the U.S.S.R. had to face the problem of choosing among possibilities, none of which was optimal. Support of Nasser evidently meant, as the union with Syria demonstrated, abandonment of local Communists to his tender mercies. Pressure against him to modify his anti-Communist posture risked pushing the most prestigious Arab nationalist leader back into the hands of the West, with which he was in any case inclined to flirt for bargaining purposes.

After the July, 1958, coup brought to power in Baghdad a pro-Soviet regime that soon became bitterly anti-Nasserist, it seemed that Moscow was going to have to choose between these two traditional rivals for Arab hegemony. Qasim's overthrow of the Hashemite kingdom in Iraq destroyed at one blow the rationale of the Baghdad Pact and wiped out British influence overnight. True, Iraq had less than a quarter of Egypt's popula-

[24]See Laqueur, *The Soviet Union and the Middle East*, pp. 259-261.
[25]*New York Times*, April 17, 1959, cited in Dallin, *Soviet Foreign Policy*, p. 472.

tion, but it was close to the Soviet Union, rich in oil resources, and strategically located at the head of the Persian Gulf. Moreover, the Qasim regime at once adopted a permissive attitude toward Iraqi Communists, who quickly developed into the single most important political force in the country, collaborating with Qasim to suppress the Iraqi Ba'ath Party.

By contrast, Nasser's repression of Communists both in Egypt and in Syria embarrassed the Russians and fueled thinly veiled Chinese Communist attacks on Moscow for collaborating with regimes that murdered Communists (the Syrian Communist Party leader, Khalid Bekdash, forced into exile by Syria's merger with Egypt, popped up in Peking, where he was lionized by the Chinese Communist leaders). From the CPSU's highest tribunal, the Twenty-First Party Congress (January, 1959), Khrushchev publicly attacked wrong "opinions" in the U.A.R. about Arab Communists. In March he openly opposed Nasser's bid to incorporate Iraq into the U.A.R., pointedly stating that there was no reason why countries that broke the fetters of colonialism had to "join some union of states, submit to one government, or follow the guidance of a single leader."[26]

But while Moscow criticized Nasser and showered favors on the new Baghdad regime, it was careful not to permit state-to-state relations with the U.A.R. to deteriorate. Tension over Nasser's domestic anti-Communism had not prevented the U.S.S.R. from cooperating fully with Egypt during the crisis precipitated by the Iraqi revolution and Lebanese civil war in the summer of 1958, when they perceived a U.S. threat to their larger common interests in the region. Nasser reportedly persuaded Khrushchev that American and British landings in Lebanon and Jordan and Turkish troop movements near the Iraqi border were aimed not just at restoring the monarchy in Baghdad but at crippling the Arab revolution in the United Arab Republic as well. Khrushchev thereupon offered to stage large-scale military maneuvers on the Soviet borders with Turkey and Iran. He warned Nasser that the move was no more than a bluff: he had no intention of precipitating a military conflict with the United States. But Khrushchev had perceived a far greater threat to Soviet interests in the Middle East than Nasser's persecution of Egyptian and Syrian Communists, and acted at Nasser's behest to ward off that threat.[27]

Moreover, even during the years of open Soviet-Egyptian polemicizing over the local Communist issue, Moscow made available substantial financial and technical assistance for Egyptian economic development. Early in 1958 the Soviet Union extended a 700-million-ruble ($770-

[26]*Pravda,* March 17, 1959, cited in Dallin, *op. cit.,* p. 478.

[27]An account of this episode, derived from an article by Mohammed Hassanein Heykal in *Al Ahram* of January 22, 1965, is contained in Nadav Safran, *From War to War* (New York: Pegasus, 1969), pp. 115-118.

million U.S. dollars) credit to Cairo to finance Egyptian industrialization and later that year agreed to assist in building the first stage of the Aswan High Dam, for which it extended another 400-million-ruble ($440-million) credit. In 1960 another 400 million was allocated for construction of the second stage and a related hydroelectric power station. These were all long-term credits, reportedly repayable at low (2.5%) interest rates over 12 years after completion of the projects.[28]

Events soon proved the wisdom of Soviet restraint in dealing with Nasser during the tense years of 1959-1961. Syria, after splitting from the U.A.R. in 1961, was taken over by a regime no less assiduous than Nasser's in repressing Communists and a good deal less "progressive" in its economic and social policies. By then, Moscow's enthusiasm for the Qasim regime in Baghdad had also cooled. Qasim's suspicion of Iraq's Communists had been aroused by the bloody Kirkuk insurrection attempt launched by the militant leftist wing of the Iraq Communist Party in 1959; in 1960 his regime began to suppress the pro-Muscovite faction as well. Moreover, in 1961 Qasim launched a large-scale military campaign against the Kurds, long the objects of special Soviet solicitude. Finally, the Free Officers' coup of February, 1963, brought in a new regime that was disposed to cooperate with the U.A.R., thus reducing pressures on Moscow to choose between Cairo and Baghdad. The new Iraqi leaders celebrated their advent to power with a bloodbath whose principal victims, after Qasim himself, were the Iraqi Communists.

Meanwhile, the Soviet view of Nasser improved considerably, not only because the alternatives turned sour, but also because Nasser had proved himself to be the most durable of the anti-imperialist Arab nationalist leaders and the only one invested with pan-Arab charisma. The pro-Nasserist Yemen revolution in 1962, supported by Egypt with Soviet-equipped troops, must have demonstrated again to the Soviet leaders that Nasser was the most vital political force in the Arab world. Strategically located at the crossroads of the Middle East and Africa, the U.A.R. was also attractive as a conduit for the shipment of Soviet weapons to politically sensitive areas where the U.S.S.R. wished to avoid direct involvement. Some of the Soviet arms delivered to Egypt in the early 1960s eventually found their way to the Congo, as well as to the Yemen. Moreover, Egypt's internal course after 1961 assumed a progressively more leftist course, with whole-sale nationalization and expropriation creating a large public sector in the economy.

[28]It was on the strength of these credit extensions that *Pravda,* on May 1, 1961, warned Egyptian critics of the Soviet Union not to "cut down the tree whose shade they are enjoying." (Cited in Abraham Ben-Tzur, "Soviet-Egyptian Relations," *New Outlook* [May, 1964], p. 31).

It still remained to work out a *modus vivendi* between Nasser and the Egyptian Communists. Nasser stubbornly refused to conform to Moscow's progressively relaxed formulas for favored third-world political leaderships. In 1960 the "national democratic state" was introduced into Soviet and world Communist doctrine as a suitable transitional form for developing countries, in which Communists and nationalists would collaborate to complete the anti-imperialist and antifeudal revolution. This collaboration would take place under bourgeois nationalist leadership, but the Communists would preserve their separate identity, uphold a distinctive radical program of social and economic transformation, and eventually assume leadership in the next, socialist, phase of the revolution. The problem was that even the most "progressive" third-world leaders, like Nkrumah, Touré, and Ben Bella, not to speak of Nasser, would not tolerate rival political organizations, particularly not such highly disciplined and organized ones as Communist parties.

The Soviets began in the early 1960s to seek some new way of reaching an accommodation with the Nasser-type phenomenon of a one-party, anti-imperialist, pro-Soviet regime that conducted radical social and economic reforms with a vaguely socialist orientation, but that would not permit a Communist Party to exist. In Khrushchev's last years, despite opposition from the Chinese and other "dogmatists" in the international movement, the Soviet Union began urging what were termed "revolutionary democratic" regimes to permit Communists to work within their one-party framework. Khrushchev reportedly worked out such an arrangement with Ben Bella during a visit to Algeria in the spring of 1964 after the National Liberation Front (FLN) Congress. A similar arrangement whereby Communists would be released from detention centers and permitted to work for the regime as individuals but not as a party, was evidently also worked out with Nasser. By the time Khrushchev arrived in Egypt in May, 1964, to celebrate completion of the first stage of the Aswan High Dam, Egyptian Communists had already been released from camps in the Western desert and many were working, as individuals, in the Arab Socialist Union and in the Egyptian press. In 1965 the Egyptian Communist Party quietly dissolved itself, presumably in fulfillment of the agreement between Khrushchev and Nasser. Khrushchev personally rewarded Nasser for liberating the Communists and presiding over the liquidation of their party by making him a "Hero of the Soviet Union."[29]

[29]The Presidium of the U.S.S.R. Supreme Soviet, which alone is authorized to make "Hero of the Soviet Union" awards, was obliged to back up Khrushchev's initiative but withheld from Nasser (while bestowing it on Ben Bella) the title "comrade."

End of the Khrushchev Era

Khrushchev's demonstrative enthusiasm for Ben Bella and Nasser was at least partly self-serving. By creating the impression that the Soviet Union was making great "gains for socialism" in the Arab world, he doubtless hoped to restore some of the international prestige he had lost after the Cuban missile crisis as well as to take the play away from his Chinese Communist rivals, who were increasing their activity in the third world. In support of Khrushchevs' effort, a genuinely revisionist doctrine had been elaborated by Soviet academicians to show that an economically under-developed state without a substantial industrial proletariat or a vanguard Communist party to act as its surrogate could nevertheless embark on the path to scientific socialism.[30] The historic mission of the weakly developed industrial proletariat could be carried out by nonproletarian strata oriented on the working class whom the "logic of the struggle" would (somehow) lead first to oppose capitalism and later to adopt socialism. These "revolutionary democratic" regimes would be assisted by the Soviet Union, which would perform by proxy the functions that, according to classical Marxist-Leninist doctrine, can be carried out only by the vanguard party of the indigenous proletariat.

The great danger of betting heavily on the "socialist" future of the "revolutionary democrats" was that so much depended on the subjective factor. Without a disciplined Communist Party to run the political system, neither the loyalty nor the longevity of friendly "revolutionary democrats" could be counted on. The policy, moreover, was bound to be resented by

[30]See particularly the following articles on the third world in the journal *Mirovaia Ekonomika i Mezhdunarodnye Otnosheniia*: G. Mirskii, "Tvorcheskii marksizm i problemy natsional'no-osvoboditel'nykh revoliutsii" ("Creative Marxism and the Problems of National-Liberation Revolutions"), No. 2 (February, 1963), pp. 63-68; R. Avakov and L. Stepanov, "Sotsial'nye problemy natsional'no-osvoboditel'noi revoliutsii" ("The Social Problems of National-Liberation Revolution"), No. 5 (May, 1963), pp. 46-54; Iu. Ostrovitanov, "Sotsialisticheskie doktriny razvivaiush-chikhsia stran: formy,i sotsial'noe soderzhanie" ("The Socialist Doctrines of Devel-oping Countries: Forms and Social Content"), No. 6 (June, 1964), pp. 82-91; V. Tiagunenko, "Aktual'nye voprosy nekapitalisticheskogo puti razvitiia" ("Current Problems of the Non-Socialist Road of Development"), No. 10 (October, 1964), pp. 13-25 and No. 11 (November, 1964), pp. 15-28; and A. Arzumanian, "Itogi mirovogo razvitiia za 100 let i aktual'nye problemy mezhdunarodnogo revoliut-sionno-osvoboditel'nogo dvizheniia" ("The Last 100 Years of World Development and Current Problems of the International Revolutionary-Liberation Movement"), No. 12 (December, 1964), pp. 74-97. And from the journal *International Affairs* (Moscow), see K. Brutents, "Integral Part of the World Revolutionary Process," No. 2 (February, 1964), pp. 30-37; and K. Ivanov, "The National-Liberation Move-ment and the Non-Capitalist Path of Development," No. 9 (September, 1964), pp. 34-43.

Communists in the third world to whom it conveyed the paradoxical message that they could count on strong Soviet support only so long as the countries in which they operated were governed by "bourgeois" leaderships that were hostile to or at least kept their distance from the U.S.S.R. The more "progressive" and pro-Soviet a developing country became, the more likely was the U.S.S.R. to embrace its leaders (usually anti-Communist military officers of petit-bourgeois origin) as "revolutionary democrats" and to acquiesce in their liquidation of local Communist parties.

The men who succeeded Khrushchev did not share his high personal stake in the "revolutionary democrats" of the Arab world. With their emphasis on restoring order in the world Communist movement and their renewed commitment to the primacy of the professional party man at home, they initially adopted a more cautious attitude toward radical non-Communist regimes in the third world, particularly emphasizing a more businesslike approach to economic assistance. The new leadership's retreat from Khrushchevian optimism about prospects in the developing countries was spurred by a series of setbacks early in its rule. Within a year after Khrushchev's "resignation," a procession of his one-time favorites in the third world followed him into retirement, all ousted by military coups or countercoups: Ben Bella of Algeria, Nkrumah of Ghana, and Sukarno of Indonesia. These dramatic demonstrations of the fragility of "progressive" regimes in Asia and Africa were quickly reflected in Soviet doctrinal literature, where expectations of "socialist" victories in the third world were scaled down; there were sober appraisals of weakness in the political, economic, and social foundations of "revolutionary democratic" regimes and warnings that many setbacks would have to be endured before the "noncapitalist path of development" to socialism could be successfully negotiated.

On the policy level, diplomatic attention and new foreign aid began to shift toward a select few strategically critical "nonprogressive" developing countries, most of which were "reactionary" even by Western standards, and some of which were allied to the United States. In the Middle East, the most dramatic changes came with respect to Turkey and Iran. At the end of 1964 Turkey's growing irritation with the Johnson Administration's Cyprus policy made Ankara increasingly attentive to Soviet bids for *rapprochement*, which had been spurred by the removal of U.S. Jupiter missiles from Turkey the year before.[31] Receptivity to Soviet blandishments

---

[31]The American substitution of Polaris submarines in the Mediterranean for land-based strategic missiles along the Soviet Union's Northern Tier also stimulated the Soviet requirement for a seaborne strategic defense force in the Mediterranean. See below, p. 595.

also grew in Iran, where Teheran's doubts about the worth of the CENTO alliance were deepened by what was perceived as American indifference to a growing Egyptian threat in the Persian Gulf area. Moscow made it clear that it did not regard the formal ties of Turkey and Iran to the United States as barriers to major improvements in relations and in 1965 announced that it was extending credits of $330 million to Iran and $210 million to Turkey. The Soviet Union also agreed to purchase Iranian natural gas to be piped into the U.S.S.R. In that year, too, a series of high-level state visits was initiated between the Soviet Union and its two southern neighbors, ultimately bringing Premier Kosygin to Ankara and Teheran and President Demirel and the Shah to Moscow. The Soviet-Iranian *rapprochement* was capped in 1967 when the Shah agreed to buy an estimated $110 million worth of Soviet military equipment.

The more prudent style of the new Soviet leaders and their deepening involvement with the nonradical states of the third world evidently gave rise to concern among "revolutionary democrats" that Soviet interest in their regimes might be slackening. Uncertainty about the intentions of the new Soviet leaders must in some measure have influenced Nasser's decision to make his first visit in seven years to the Soviet capital in August, 1965, to meet with Khrushchev's successors. There, Party First Secretary Brezhnev publicly reassured Nasser, whom he welcomed "not only as President of the U.A.R., but also as President of the Arab Socialist Union," that the Soviet Union's friendship with Egypt was not "a coincidence or the fruit of the efforts of a single person."[32]

The tide, however, seemed to have turned against "progressive forces" in the Arab Middle East. King Faisal's proposal for a traditionalist-dominated Islamic Pact threatened to subordinate Nasser, whose large army in the Yemen was being fought to a standstill by inferior, Saudi-supported royalist forces. During Nasser's visit to Moscow, both he and his Soviet hosts repeatedly attacked U.S.-inspired efforts to "roll back" left-oriented regimes everywhere in the third world. Nasser warned that the danger of imperialist "plots against the people" in the Middle East would grow unless countered by "our joint action." Brezhnev, citing U.S. intervention in Vietnam as the measure of American willingness to go to "the furthest limit of impudence," also emphasized "the vital importance of the cohesion of all progressive, revolutionary and democratic forces." There was a small but highly significant difference in the Egyptian and Soviet formulations: Nasser stressed joint action with the Soviet Union; Brezhnev emphasized unity of leftist forces in the third world.

[32]Radio Moscow in Arabic, August 27, 1965.

The U.S.S.R. and the Six-Day War

Against this background of waning "progressive" fortunes in the third world, a new Syrian coup in February, 1966, brought to power the left wing of the Ba'ath Party, which loudly proclaimed friendship for the Soviet Union and commitment to radical social, political, and economic reform. Still smarting from the uninterrupted series of setbacks suffered by the "progressive" camp, the Soviet leaders were happy to reciprocate the embrace of the radical Ba'athists of Syria, whose advent to power offered Moscow a fresh opportunity to add a second pillar to the U.S.S.R.'s Arab Middle East structure.

Soviet-Syrian relations had gradually improved in the mid-sixties, particularly after the Syrian nationalization measures of 1965, but the closeness of 1956-1957 had never been restored. The Ba'athists who came to power in the 1963 coup preferred to keep their distance from both the Soviet Union and China; at home, they looked upon the Syrian Communists as rivals rather than allies. The left Ba'athists differed from their predecessors on both counts. Not only did they openly parade their friendship for the Soviet Union, they also brought a member of the Syrian Communist Party into the government and permitted Bekdash to return to the country from his long exile in Eastern Europe.

However, the left Ba'athist coup, led mainly by minority Alawite military officers, did not suddenly impart stability to Syrian politics. Perhaps if the Soviet leaders had been less sensitive to the real or imagined dangers of "roll-back" in the third world and less vulnerable to charges of abandoning friends under fire, they might have been more cautious about committing themselves to a regime with such uncertain prospects. But in the circumstances prevailing in the spring of 1966, Moscow decided to grasp the hand held out by the Atassi-Zuayyin leadership as if welcoming back an old friend. Military assistance was sharply accelerated. And with much fanfare, the Soviet Union announced it was extending a $133-million credit to finance construction of the Euphrates Dam. Most striking, however, was Moscow's effusive political support of the new Damascus regime in the face of sharply rising tension along the Syrian-Israeli border.

The domestic weakness of the new Syrian regime led it to curry popular favor in the usual manner, by demonstrating extravagant bellicosity toward the Zionist "gangster state." Heating up the Arab-Israel conflict and making Syria appear as the spearhead of the Arab cause, the new Syrian radical leaders also pressed their struggle against the conservative regimes of Jordan and Saudi Arabia, charging them with complicity in an imperialist-Zionist plot to overthrow the revolutionary regime in Damascus. There was a marked increase in the shelling of Israeli settlements from Syrian border positions and in terrorist attacks by Syrian-based *al-Fatah* infiltrators; no effort was made to conceal the regime's collaboration with the Palestinian raiders, and Damascus declared that it would do nothing to interfere with Fedayeen operating from Syrian territory. Inevitably, pressures began to mount in Israel for retaliatory action against Syria.

The Soviet leadership's conduct during the year of mounting tension along the Israeli-Syrian border that preceded the June, 1967, war has been variously interpreted. Some observers have concluded that the U.S.S.R. deliberately encouraged the rise in tension, willingly accepting its war-provoking potential; others have inferred from the same behavior not so much (mis)calculated deliberation as gross irresponsibility reflecting radical underestimation of the Arab-Israeli conflict's volatility. The pattern of Soviet behavior suggests that there is some truth to both of these perceptions.

If the Soviets were concerned during the year-long buildup of tension that the conduct of the Syrian leaders might be too provocative, there is no evidence that they attempted to dampen it. Certainly they made no public efforts to restrain Damascus; and in the light of Moscow's overt position, private efforts, even if undertaken, would probably have lacked persuasiveness. Publicly, the Soviet Union gave the radical Syrian regime unambiguous political and diplomatic support against Israel, both within the United Nations and outside it. As early as the spring of 1966, the Soviet Union began to depict the new left Ba'athist rulers in Damascus as the intended victims of an imperialist plot to overthrow them; Israel was the tool of that plot. On May 27, 1966, the Soviet Union asserted its own national interest in the security of the Damascus regime, stating that the U.S.S.R. "cannot and will not remain indifferent to attempts to violate peace in a region located in direct proximity to the borders of the Soviet Union."[33]

Moscow's private response to Israeli diplomatic efforts to get the U.S.S.R. to restrain Syria was not much different from the Soviet Union's public line. The Israelis were told they exaggerated the terrorist issue. (Publicly, Soviet spokesmen went so far as to assert that the terrorists were merely figments of Israeli imagination.[34]) In any case, the Syrian government could in no way be held responsible for such terrorist activities. Finally, Israel was warned against permitting itself to be used as a tool of imperialists and oil monopolists, who were determined to overthrow the new leftist regime in Damascus.

From the Soviet point of view, these blatantly propagandistic arguments

[33]*Pravda,* May 27, 1966.

[34]Referring to the Fedayeen operating from Syria, *Sovetskaia Rossiia,* May 21, 1966, declared: "These groups are clearly mythical."

had some basis in political reality. Surrounded on almost every side by unfriendly neighbors, the Damascus regime was highly unstable and may well have seemed after Greece the most likely next target of the imperialist "roll-back" campaign. Already embarrassed by its inactivity in the face of the escalating U.S. military effort against North Vietnam, Moscow may have feared that any effort to restrain its new Middle Eastern protégé would suggest the U.S.S.R.'s impotence in still another area, much closer to home. The Soviet Union doubtless appreciated that Syria was deliberately exploiting the Israeli issue to rally internal political support and to disarm other Arab opponents. Moreover, the linkage of the United States and other Western powers with Israel and the conservative Arab states in an anti-Syrian plot served larger Soviet anti-American purposes in the region. There was some risk in raising tensions with Israel, but the Syrian leaders presumably believed, and may have so persuaded Moscow, that it was riskier not to. In the year before the June war, therefore, Soviet policy approached the question of Syrian-Israeli border tension with two partly complementary, partly contradictory sets of objectives in view:

1. To exploit the tension in order to help shore up the unstable Syrian regime; to unite "progressive" Arab forces (particularly Egypt and Syria) around this issue; and to discredit the Western powers and the conservative Arab states for their hostility to the leading anti-Israel force in the region;

2. To deter large-scale Israeli retaliation that might endanger the survival of the Damascus regime.

The tension between these objectives is self-evident; their complementarity, as it turned out, was illusory, resting as it did on the assumption that, together with Soviet arms and political support, radical Arab unity, which was to be promoted by exploiting Israeli-Syrian tension, would deter Israel from responding militarily. In addition, Moscow may have counted on Washington to exercise a degree of restraint on Israel that the U.S.S.R. would not bring to bear on Syria.

Growing Soviet willingness to exploit openly the Arab-Israeli conflict became particularly evident in the year before the June war. Prior to that time, the Soviet Union had resisted Egyptian pressure to join wholeheartedly in endorsing the Arab position. Publicly, Moscow continued to regard the Arab-Israeli dispute as a national conflict to be resolved through peaceful coexistence, once Israel separated itself from the imperialist camp. By implication this seemed to mean preservation of the Jewish state within 1949 boundaries. In November, 1965, the two wings of the Israeli Communist Party—one "Jewish" (Maki), the other "Arab" (Rakah)—journeyed to Moscow to argue their respective cases. The judgment at that late date was that the conflict was still an interstate one.

Six months later the verdict was reversed. Under the impact of the left Ba'athist coup in Damascus and the threat of the Saudi campaign for Islamic union, the Soviet Union may have concluded that a more explicit anti-Israel stand was needed to consolidate the radical Arab grouping. At the Twenty-Third Soviet Party Congress in April the Soviets clearly chose in favor of the pro-Arab wing of the Israeli Communist Party. Statements of support for the "just rights of the Palestinian Arabs," a vague formulation that could be interpreted as raising doubts about the finality of the 1949 *de facto* arrangements, began to appear regularly in joint Soviet-Arab communiqués in 1966.

There is no clear evidence on how far the U.S.S.R. was prepared to back Arab irredentism. Moscow was almost certainly not prepared to endorse calls to throw Israel into the sea; allegedly, Ahmad Shukairy, head of the militant Palestine Liberation Organization before the Six-Day War, was refused admittance to the Soviet Union on a number of occasions. A Soviet-backed Arab military atempt to liquidate Israel as a state would have posed high risks for the U.S.S.R. whether it succeeded or not. Failure would have placed the entire Soviet-radical Arab patron-client relationship in question, and success would have raised the specter of American military intervention and of a possible U.S.-Soviet confrontation. It has been argued, however, that Moscow and Cairo reached some kind of common understanding during the years immediately preceding the June war on a "solution" of the Palestine problem through truncation of the area of the state of Israel and dilution of its Jewish majority through infusion of the bulk of the Arab refugees. Israel would cease to be a Zionist state but would become a Jewish-Arab state with an area, if not necessarily enclosed within the same borders, equivalent to that provided for by the 1947 partition. Given the demographic facts of life in the Middle East, there would be reasonable prospects for its eventual transformation into an Arab-Jewish state, an innocuous companion piece to Lebanon.[35]

Considering the utility of the Arab-Israeli conflict to the Soviet Union in the decade after 1955, one may wonder whether Moscow would have looked forward to this or any "solution" of the problem. On the other hand, the achievement of a "solution" seemed far enough removed in time to allow perhaps for an irreversible consolidation of the Soviet position in the interim. There may well have been considerable pressure on Brezhnev and Kosygin at least to state a private position on the desired outcome; as

[35]Moshe Sneh, "The Soviet-Egyptian 'Solution' to the 'Israel Problem,'" *International Problems* (Tel Aviv), VII:1-2 (May, 1969), 24-25. Sneh, chairman of the Central Committee of the Maki, cites Gomulka, Meir Wilner, head of the Arab- and Moscow-oriented Rakah wing, and Heykal, but does not provide direct documentary evidence for his position.

such the indicated scheme is plausible. In any case, by the spring of 1967 the U.S.S.R. had no public commitment to maintain the 1949 armistice arrangements. The Soviet and radical Arab public positions on the Arab-Israeli dispute were drawing together, a process which was intensified by the Six-Day War.

By the spring of 1966 promotion of radical Arab unity, particularly between the U.A.R. and Syria, had become a major Soviet objective, both to cement the pro-Soviet orientation of the two states and also to discourage Israeli retaliation against Damascus. During his May, 1966, visit to Cairo, Soviet Premier Kosygin urged Nasser to improve the U.A.R.'s relations with Syria, with whose governments the U.A.R. had been quarreling since the 1961 split. The Moscow-inspired Cairo-Damascus *rapprochement* culminated in a new U.A.R.-Syrian defense pact signed in November, 1966.

It has been suggested, notably in British Foreign Office circles, that Moscow encouraged closer U.A.R.-Syrian ties in the expectation that Nasser would prove able to cool the anti-Israel ardor of his more militant associates, as he had done so skillfully at the time of the 1964 Arab summit conference. It is true that Nasser had held to a consistently sober posture toward Israel ever since 1956, repeatedly warning against a premature Arab military challenge. But such an interpretation, which is unsupported by anything that Soviet spokesmen are known to have said publicly or privately to Western or Israeli sources, implies that the U.S.S.R.'s position in Damascus was so tenuous that Moscow was unwilling to risk it by directly pressuring the Syrians to moderate their provocative behavior, and that Moscow was obliged to resort instead to such convoluted means of influencing Syrian behavior as to leave the situation at least twice removed from Soviet control. If the Soviet Union's intention in promoting a Cairo-Damascus axis was to dampen Syria's anti-Israel ardor, it was based on a serious miscalculation: the signing of the Egyptian-Syrian Defense Pact, together with Moscow's strongly supportive declaratory policy, served only to embolden the Syrians. When the Israelis chose in November, 1966, to retaliate against the Jordanian village of Samu for a terrorist raid evidently staged through Jordan but launched from Syria, Damascus probably concluded that Soviet and Egyptian protection had successfully deterred Israel from retaliating directly against Syria. Incidents along the Israeli-Syrian border grew in intensity and led finally to the April 7, 1967, battle, the largest Arab-Israeli clash since the Suez war, in which Israel shot down six Syrian MIG-21s while suffering no losses of its own.

Perhaps the April 7 clash caused the Soviet leaders to pause and to recalculate the dangers of continuing to support the policy of the past year, but by April 21, when the U.S.S.R. addressed its strongest warning note yet to Israel,[36] Moscow had evidently decided that the political costs of acting as the restrainer of Syria outweighed the risks of continuing Syrian bellicosity. Within weeks the wisdom of this Soviet choice was put to the test by the explosive combination of two events: a new internal political crisis in Syria and a fresh wave of Syrian-based terrorist activity against Israel. The new domestic crisis, touched off early in May by the religious community's protests against publication of an antireligious article in a Syrian army magazine,[37] forced the unsteady Ba'athist regime on the defensive. To discredit and disarm internal opponents, Damascus attempted to link the new domestic disturbances to a massive, coordinated imperialist plot, spearheaded by Israel but including Saudi Arabia and Jordan, to bring down the government. The Soviet press joined in publicizing the Syrian version of the plot, initially concentrating its fire on the alleged role of the monarchical Arab states.

In raising alarms about the imminent threat of an Israeli invasion, the Syrian leaders evidently calculated that they had nothing to lose and everything to gain. To the extent that Damascus relied on the Egyptians to deter Israel, it was essential to make the threatened attack appear so substantial that Nasser could not dismiss it. On several previous occasions the Egyptian President had insisted that the U.A.R.'s defense treaty obligations to Syria did not cover "border incidents, regardless of their scope or origin," but only the contingency of full-scale war.[38] In a public speech after the war, Nasser explicitly attributed to "our Syrian brothers" the first reports that Israel had mobilized large forces (18 brigades) along the Syrian frontier.[39] But at the same time, Nasser stated that the U.A.R. independently confirmed that Israel was mobilizing "no less than 13 brigades" on the Syrian border.[40]

We do not know precisely what role Soviet warnings played in Nasser's decision to act in mid-May. Some Western accounts have stated that reports of Israeli troop concentrations on the Syrian border originally came to

[36]Moscow charged that politically "impatient" circles in the Israeli government were turning Israel into a puppet of foreign forces, "thus endangering the essential interests of their state." Israel's policies toward its Arab neighbors for the past few years, the Soviet statement warned, were "risk-laden" and "pregnant with dangers" (*Pravda*, April 21, 1967).

[37]See the excellent account in C. Ernest Dawn, "The Egyptian Remilitarization of Sinai, May 1969," *Contemporary History*, III: 3 (1968), 201-224.

[38]See, for example, Nasser's remarkably candid account in an August, 1965, speech before Egyptian students in Moscow, of previous Syrian attempts to embroil the U.A.R. in war with Israel over incidents along the Syrian-Israeli border. Radio Cairo, August 30, 1965.

[39]July 23, 1967, speech.
[40]*Ibid.*

Nasser from Soviet sources. Such reports had been publicized several times before by Soviet sources, as in October, 1966, at the United Nations by Nikolai Fedorenko and in February and April, 1967, in the Soviet press. During the May, 1967, crisis, the Soviet press made no allusions to an alleged Israeli troop buildup until May 16, two days after Nasser had begun the remilitarization of Sinai. The Soviet intelligence contribution that was publicly acknowledged by Nasser on two separate occasions had to do not with "hard" verifiable information pertaining to Israeli troop deployments, but with "strategic intelligence" concerning alleged Israeli military plans and intentions. Thus, Nasser said, "our friends in the Soviet Union" warned the visiting U.A.R. parliamentary delegation (which left the U.S.S.R. on May 14) that "there was a premeditated [Israeli] plan" to invade Syria and that the invasion was about to take place.[41] Reviewing the events leading up to the war in his June 19 speech at the United Nations, Soviet Premier Kosygin spoke of information that the Soviet government "and I believe others too" began receiving about an Israeli plan to make a swift strike against Syria at the end of May.[42]

Only one Egyptian source has alluded to Soviet intelligence reports concerning Israeli troop deployments. At the trial of Shams Badran after the war, the former U.A.R. Defense Minister is reported to have testified that U.A.R. Chief of Staff Muhammed Fawzi went personally to Syria to investigate reports of Israeli troop concentrations and reported back that the Soviets "must be having hallucinations."[43] Nasser proceeded nevertheless with his demonstrative movement of Egyptian military forces into the Sinai desert. If he did so knowing reports of Israeli troop concentrations to be false, he may still have been influenced in one of two ways by Soviet warnings:

1. He may have believed the Soviet report that an Israeli attack on Syria was in the offing. Presumably he knew that Israel could mount a substantial attack quickly without massive advance mobilization.

2. He may have interpreted the Soviet warning as an expression of Soviet backing for a move that he wished to make to serve his own broader purposes, particularly to revive his declining prestige in the Arab world.[44]

Whether or not Moscow specifically recommended Nasser's initial move, the conspicuous dispatch of Egyptian infantry and armor into the Sinai beginning May 14 met with prompt Soviet approval as an appropriate tactical measure and a healthy symbol of radical Arab solidarity. Soviet behavior during the preceding weeks had clearly been designed to encourage Nasser to make some kind of deterrent move that would draw Israeli

[41]June 9 and July 23, 1967, speeches.
[42]*Pravda*, June 20, 1967.
[43]*Al Ahram,* February 25, 1968.
[44]See particularly the explanation offered by Safran, *From War to War,* p. 285.

pressure from Syria, preventing possible Israeli military action which, even if limited in scope, might have disastrous political consequences for the Syrian regime and embarrass its Soviet patron. With Egyptian forces poised on Israel's border, it would be harder for Nasser not to come to the assistance of the Syrians. The Israelis would know this too, and would therefore be deterred from striking. During the first few days after Egyptian forces began moving across the Canal into the desert, both Nasser and the Soviet leaders may have looked forward to sharing the credit for a relatively cheap political victory over Israel and the Western sponsors of the "plot" against Syria.

Soviet sources have repeatedly insisted to Western observers that the Soviet government was neither consulted nor informed in advance about Nasser's next moves: his May 18 demand for the removal of UNEF forces from Egyptian territory and his announcement four days later that the Gulf of Aqaba would be closed to Israeli shipping and to strategic cargoes destined for Eilat. These Soviet disclaimers may well be true, but they do not absolve the U.S.S.R. of a heavy share of responsibility for the violent explosion to which these Egyptian actions led. Certainly what happened between May 14 and June 5 was not the implementation of some kind of jointly prepared Soviet-Egyptian blueprint or scenario. Indeed, Nasser himself could not have known in advance what his next move would be since each move was highly contingent on the behavior of actors over whom neither he nor the Soviet leaders had a great deal of control. For example, Nasser's demand that UNEF forces be totally withdrawn came only after the U.N. Secretary-General had refused to receive U.A.R. Chief of Staff General Fawzi's request to General Rihkye to remove UNEF forces stationed along the Egypt–Israeli border and to redeploy them in the Gaza Strip. Nevertheless, the Soviet Union gave full political support to Nasser's May 18 demand for total withdrawal of UNEF forces from the Gaza area and the Sinai Peninsula on the grounds that "their presence in this situation would give Israel advantages for staging a military provocation against Arab countries."[45] There is no evidence that the Soviet Union made any effort in the United Nations to work out a face-saving arrangement that would have kept a U.N. presence in the area, at least at Sharm-el-Sheik. The Soviet government did stop short of publicly endorsing Nasser's closure of the Straits of Tiran to Israel, perhaps because Moscow did not wish to adopt a position from which it might have to back down if the blockade were lifted by negotiations or by Western naval force.

It is hard to judge from Soviet behavior during the acute crisis period initiated by Nasser's May 22 blockade announcement whether Moscow

[45]Soviet government statement on the situation in the Middle East, *Pravda*, May 24, 1967.

underestimated the probability of war, miscalculated the likely military consequences, or simply found itself powerless to affect the course of events. The alternatives are not mutually exclusive, and perhaps all of these factors operated to produce the generally obstructionist posture that the Soviet Union assumed toward the war-prevention initiatives of other powers. At the first Security Council meeting on May 24 Soviet Ambassador Fedorenko chided the Western powers for "dramatizing" the situation, complaining that there was not "sufficient ground for such a hasty convening of the Security Council."[46] As late as May 29, Fedorenko still balked at discussing anything except Egypt's complaint against Israel.[47] Moreover, President de Gaulle's proposal for concerted four-power action, endorsed by U.S. Ambassador Arthur Goldberg in the Security Council on May 24, was also rejected by the U.S.S.R. With Soviet cooperation, a big power compromise might well have been worked out, which, at the very minimum, could have greatly increased the political cost to Israel of striking the first blow. But the Soviet leaders were apparently unwilling to open up any distance between themselves and their Arab clients or to deprive themselves of the political payoffs they evidently expected to garner from an Arab political victory over Israel in the face of U.S. opposition.

Moreover, the Soviets permitted Nasser to circulate, without correction, an interpretation of Soviet promises of support that went far beyond anything that Moscow had theretofore asserted or subsequently stated it was prepared to endorse at the time. In a widely publicized speech delivered at the height of the crisis, Nasser said that his War Minister, Badran, had returned from his May 25-29 visit to the Soviet Union with a message from Kosygin that Russia would "stand with us in the battle" and "would not allow foreign intervention that would prevent a return to the state of affairs before 1956."[48] At a minimum, this suggested that the Soviet Union endorsed Nasser's blockade of the Straits of Tiran and that it "would not allow" U.S. or multilateral Western maritime intervention to reopen it. If the Soviet position was so understood in Egypt and Syria, such an understanding could only abet Arab belligerency. Even if Nasser knew better privately, the Arab world would expect him in the absence of contradictory evidence from authoritative Soviet sources to behave as if his expressed understanding of the Soviet position were correct. Nasser had said many times that Arab military action against Israel had to await propitious international circumstances because powerful foreign forces stood behind Israel. If the Soviet Union was prepared to prevent external intervention

[46]Arthur Lall, *The UN and the Middle East Crisis* (New York: Columbia University Press, 1968), p. 29.

[47]*Ibid.*, p. 38.

[48]*New York Times,* May 30, 1967.

in support of Israel, how could Nasser fail to press Israel to the limit?

Can obstructive Soviet behavior at the United Nations be squared with the Soviet government's urgent notes to President Nasser and Premier Eshkol, delivered personally by the respective Soviet Ambassadors during the early hours of May 27, requesting that neither side should be the first to fire? In urging restraint on both sides, the Soviet Union was acting in concert with the United States, at American request. President Johnson, responding to a false alarm about an imminent U.A.R. attack on Israel transmitted to Washington by visiting Israeli Foreign Minister Abba Eban on May 25, had urged Premier Kosygin to join him in a concerted action to restrain the two parties. But the Soviet Union had every reason to support the American President's effort to avert military hostilities in the region so long as the new status quo created by Nasser's moves during the preceding week remained frozen, pending a "nonmilitary" solution of some unspecified type at some indeterminate time. The moderately worded Soviet note presented to Eshkol by Soviet Ambassador Chuvakhin said it was necessary to resolve the conflict by "nonmilitary means," but advanced no concrete suggestions for satisfying Israeli grievances. Given the Egyptian *faits accomplis* of May 18 and May 22, the Soviet Union's admonition to both Nasser and Eshkol not to open hostilities objectively favored the Arab cause.[49]

President Johnson's urgent request that Moscow use its influence in Cairo to restrain Nasser may have been taken as evidence both by the Egyptians and Russians that Washington was unwilling to "unleash Israel," much less to assist it militarily, and would rely instead on negotiations and political compromise to resolve the crisis. (And compromise would by definition constitute an improvement for the Soviet-supported side as compared with the *status quo ante*.) Nasser appears genuinely to have believed that Israel fighting alone could not defeat the combined Arab forces, and Soviet verbal behavior, both public and private, strongly indicates a belief that Israel would not dare to launch a general attack in the face of American opposition.[50] Moscow's attention in any case was bound to be fixed on Washington, for it was only as a consequence of American military action that the necessity to contemplate Soviet intervention could become acute.

During the last days before the outbreak of fighting, the top Soviet leaders behaved as if they believed the immediate crisis was past. The last

[49]By contrast, Israel was asked by President Johnson to refrain from military action in order to give Washington time to explore the possibilities for organizing a multilateral naval force to open the Straits of Tiran by force, if necessary.

[50]Only since the end of 1968 have the Soviets shown signs of understanding that the political relationship between Israel and the United States is not so simple as their propagandists and diplomats routinely depicted it.

week of May had been filled with the exchange of urgent messages with Washington, Cairo, and Tel Aviv. High-ranking delegations from the "progressive" Arab states, including U.A.R. Minister of War Badran and President Atassi of Syria, had been received in the Kremlin. A decision had been taken to reinforce the small Soviet naval squadron in the Mediterranean, and on May 31 the first of ten Soviet warships from the Black Sea Fleet passed through the Turkish Straits. But on that very same day, as if to underline private assurances, freely dispensed by Soviet diplomats in the West, that there would be no war in the Middle East, Party General Secretary Brezhnev and Premier Kosygin as well as Defense Minister Grechko departed on a ceremonial visit to the Soviet Fleet in Murmansk and Archangel that was to keep them out of the capital until the very eve of the war. The number-three man, Podgorny, titular President of the U.S.S.R., had departed earlier on a state visit to Afghanistan, from which he returned in leisurely fashion only on June 3, after lingering en route for two days in Soviet Central Asia.

If the outbreak of war took the Soviet leaders by surprise, its outcome doubtless shocked them even more. Their apparent equanimity in the face of mounting Arab-Israeli tensions may have reflected not only belief that Israel would not act alone, but also miscalculations of the regional military balance. It is doubtful that their estimates were so far removed from reality that they expected the U.A.R. and Syria to drive the Israelis into the sea—they might have behaved more prudently if they had believed that, if only out of concern that such a contingency might provoke U.S. intervention. It does seem clear, however, that they did not believe that Israel could crush all her opponents almost simultaneously, in a matter of days. The Soviet leaders may have assumed that the mobilized Arab forces arrayed against Israel were at least strong enough to buy time for the Soviet Union, working with the other great powers through the United Nations, to stop the war well short of a conclusive outcome. Even a limited Arab defeat may have been seen as netting a political gain for the Soviet Union as the (more or less) successful diplomatic champion of the Arab side.

To sum up this reconstruction of Soviet miscalculations that contributed to the outbreak of the June, 1967, Middle East war: Soviet decisionmakers seriously underestimated the volatility of the festering Arab-Israeli conflict. They displayed a poor understanding of the built-in escalatory pressures operating on the leaderships of both sides. Just as Moscow failed to appreciate before the May crisis how provocative Syrian-based terrorist activities were to Israel, the Soviet leaders overestimated the Israeli government's willingness or ability to tolerate indefinitely the blockade of Eilat and the Egyptian mobilization in Sinai. This may have reflected the Soviet leaders' underestimation of Israel's capacity for independent action. Moscow's strategy of promoting radical Arab unity on a militantly anti-Israel basis revealed a startling ignorance of the powerful association in the Arab national consciousness between unity and revenge against Israel. Finally, the Soviets evidently miscalculated the regional military balance, assuming considerably greater military capacities for their clients than they were to demonstrate.

Reconstruction after the June War

Once Israel struck, the Soviet Union quickly made it clear by immediate resort to the "hot line" that its overarching interest was to avoid a military confrontation with the United States. For the Soviet Union's Arab clients, this meant there could be no Soviet intervention to prevent a calamitous rout at the hands of the Israelis.[51] In Moscow, tension with the U.A.R. must have arisen when Nasser charged that U.S. aircraft had participated in the initial Israeli air strikes against the Egyptian air force. Knowing from its observation of the U.S. Sixth Fleet that the charge was false, Moscow doubtless saw this as a desperate Egyptian effort to embroil the Soviet Union in the conflict. To some in Moscow, Nasser must then have seemed not only incompetent but perhaps even perfidious.

Faced with one of the great debacles of its foreign policy, the Soviet Union might conceivably have chosen after June to disengage itself from the radical Arab cause, gradually if not all at once. Perhaps such an alternative was considered in Moscow in the aftermath of the June war; there is some evidence of division in the leadership at that time.[52] But the immediate Soviet reaction was to keep options open on the Arab side while foreclosing them with Israel by breaking off diplomatic relations with Tel Aviv. Even before the Israeli advance into Syria was terminated, massive air deliveries of Soviet replacement weapons for the U.A.R. and Syria began pouring into the Middle East. These weapons could not

---

[51]Only during the final day of fighting on the Syrian front, when it was uncertain how far Israeli forces would advance before accepting the cease-fire, did the Soviet Union reportedly issue private warnings to the United States that it might intervene on behalf of Damascus if Israel did not stop. (See the account in Michel Bar-Zohar, *Histoire secrète de la guerre d'Israel* [Paris: Fayard, 1968] pp. 304-313.) In fact, the U.S.S.R. did not go beyond severing diplomatic relations with Israel. It is doubtful whether the U.S.S.R. could have intervened quickly enough and in sufficient force to have affected the outcome in any case. Among bad outcomes for Moscow, a futile intervention against Israel was second only to a military confrontation with the United States.

[52]The First Secretary of the Moscow City Party Committee, V. Yegorychev, was purged, reportedly for criticizing the Politburo's handling of the Middle East crisis. The substance of Yegorychev's criticism, if indeed he did criticize, is not known.

possibly have been uncrated, assembled, and assimilated by shattered Arab forces in time to affect the outcome of the war. They began to arrive before the Soviets could have had any confidence that either Nasser or the Syrian left Ba'athist leaders would survive politically. The deliveries may thus have been intended not only to shore up the positions of faltering client leaders, but also to demonstrate to their possible successors that the U.S.S.R. was still willing to place its arsenal at the disposal of the Arab cause. Within weeks, however, it was clear that the Soviet leaders had decided to clear the rubble and rebuild their damaged positions in the Middle East on the same foundations as before. More than anything else, it was probably Nasser's skillful political salvage operation at home and the leftward shift of his new post-June government that persuaded Moscow to keep its bets on the Egyptian President.

After agreeing suddenly on June 6 to call for a cease-fire without requiring Israeli withdrawal, the Soviets, once the fighting had stopped, gave full support at the United Nations to the hard-line Arab position, except that unlike the Arabs, Soviet spokesmen, including Premier Kosygin, explicitly acknowledged Israel's right to exist as a state. Diplomatically Moscow sought to maximize political pressure on Israel to withdraw from occupied Arab territories and to isolate the United States as the sole great-power supporter of Israel. The Soviet Union demanded that Israel be labeled an aggressor and be compelled to withdraw and pay damages under threat of U.N. sanction. Rejecting the U.S. "package" approach to a Middle East peace, the U.S.S.R. aligned itself with the defeated Arab states in insisting on complete Israeli withdrawal as a precondition to any discussion of a settlement.

In fact, however, the Soviet Union had no independent position on a Middle East settlement, except perhaps with regard to reopening the Suez Canal, whose closure seriously burdened the large Soviet assistance program to embattled North Vietnam. This was demonstrated in July 1967, when Soviet Foreign Minister Gromyko reportedly reached agreement in private negotiations with U.S. Ambassador Goldberg on a package-type formula for settlement, only to back off when several Arab delegations, notably the Algerians, informed the Russians that they would vote against it in the General Assembly.[53]

By November, 1967, the Soviets had moved some distance from the extreme hard-line Arab position, quietly ignoring Syrian objections and coordinating diplomatic positions almost exclusively with the U.A.R. Cairo and Moscow agreed to go along with the British-authored Security Council resolution of November 22, which was sufficiently vague in substance to

[53]Lall, *The UN,* pp. 210-213.

gain four-power assent and to escape outright rejection by any of the principals save the diehard Syrians. In practice it accomplished little more than to provide Ambassador Gunnar Jarring with authority to explore the modalities of a settlement with the contending sides. But in the process of arriving at the November resolution the Soviet Union made clear to its Arab friends not only that it was unprepared to use its own forces to secure an Israeli withdrawal, but that it would not support an attempted Arab "military solution," at least not until chances for regaining the occupied Arab lands by political means were exhausted.

The leading role of the Soviet Union in the U.N. debates on the Middle East and Premier Kosygin's meeting with President Johnson at Glassboro, New Jersey, reflected in diplomatic terms how firmly established the Soviet Union had now become, despite the humiliating defeat of its clients, as one of the two big powers in the Middle East. After what appeared to be a near-fatal setback to the Soviet position in the region, the role and presence of the U.S.S.R. in the Middle East continued to grow at the end of the 1960s in several dimensions at once.

Political and Military Influence

The scope of Soviet policy in the Middle East was greatly enlarged after the June war. Soviet military influence (advisers, technicians, ground crews, and reportedly even pilots) replaced that of the U.A.R. in the Yemen after Nasser was obliged to withdraw Egyptian forces. With the creation of the People's Republic of Southern Yemen in November, 1967, and leftist coups in the Sudan and Libya in 1969, the ranks of the "progressive" Arab states were greatly augmented, creating a still broader field for the growth of Soviet influence. However, while the Soviet Union's support was warmly welcomed in the new radical states, patron-client ties were not yet firmly established as the 1960s came to a close. The new rulers of Libya preferred to purchase French rather than Soviet weapons, and together with the Sudanese appeared to be aligning themselves directly with U.A.R. foreign policy, evidently avoiding intimate policy consultations with the Russians. In Southern Yemen the Chinese Communists outflanked the Soviet Union on the left and appeared to have won patronage of the most radical political forces in that new republic. Even among the older "progressive" states, Soviet influence, while great, did not seem to give the U.S.S.R. a high degree of control over client's policies. Moscow continued to extend aid to the Syrian regime, but modulated its praise for the Damascus rulers (to whom Soviet diplomats privately referred with contempt) after the June war. The Syrians sought to gain leverage by making periodic gestures in the direction of Peking, which doubtless deepened still further Soviet uneasiness about Syrian reliability. Although the new Iraqi Ba'athist leaders received additional weapons and a growing share of Soviet economic aid after the July, 1968, Baghdad coup, they continued to embarrass their Soviet sponsors by feuding publicly with the Syrian Ba'athists and indulging in wild excesses, including public executions, against political enemies at home.[54] Only with the U.A.R., which emerged from the June war more than ever the pivotal state for Moscow in the Middle East, did the U.S.S.R. appear to have an intimate political relationship, but clearly not one in which Nasser was a mere satellite. Thus, while the number of left-leaning "progressive" Arab states grew substantially after the war and the radical Arabs' overall dependence on the Soviet Union for arms and political support increased even more, the U.S.S.R. did not succeed in achieving a high degree of political control in any client state.

Communications

Soviet lines of communication throughout the area generally and from the Middle East into East Africa have been spreading rapidly in the past several years. Commercial air service from the Soviet Union and eastern Europe to the Arab world and East Africa has been substantially expanded. Maritime communication has also grown, and Soviet vessels have made increasingly frequent appearances at Red Sea and Persian Gulf ports. However, expansion has been severely constrained by the closure of the Suez Canal, which makes the Persian Gulf less accessible to the Soviet Union's Mediterranean Squadron than to its Pacific Fleet.

Economic Penetration

In wake of the June war the Soviet Union has entered a small opening wedge into Arab oil resources. In addition to assisting Syria in the development of its small oil fields, the U.S.S.R. has acquired a contract from Iraq to explore new oil fields and is to be paid for its services in crude oil, a practice that is becoming common in Soviet technical deals with nationalized oil companies.[55]

Arms Shipments

Since the June war, the Soviet Union has delivered arms to some ten states in the region, six of which (U.A.R., Syria, Iraq, Algeria, Yemen, Southern Yemen) have military establishments that are essentially Soviet-equipped

[54]However, Soviet relations with Baghdad noticeably warmed after the Iraqi government agreed in March, 1970, to recognize the autonomy of the Kurds within the Iraqi state, a settlement long favored by the U.S.S.R.

[55]See Chap. 15, Part II, pp. 626-628, for further discussion of Soviet interests in Persian Gulf oil.

and dependent almost exclusively upon the Soviet Union for spare parts and replacements. The June war made dependence on the Soviet Union for arms more critical than ever for the U.A.R. and Syria and only slightly less so for Iraq, which became a "front-line" state of sorts by deploying forces against Israel in Jordan and which also faced a mounting threat of armed conflict with its neighbor Iran.

On-the-Ground Presence

The physical Soviet presence on the ground in the Arab Middle East has grown very substantially. The most striking increase has been in Soviet military advisers and technicians attached to the U.A.R. and Syrian armed forces, estimated around the end of 1969 at 3000 for the U.A.R. and more than 1000 in Syria. Soviet officers were reported to be not only with U.A.R. training units in the rear but also with operational units along the Suez front. Elements of the Soviet Mediterranean Squadron were present a good deal of the time in Egyptian and Syrian ports, and there were occasional visits by Soviet bomber squadrons to Arab military air fields. In addition, Egyptian air fields and Soviet-supplied TU-16 (Badger) aircraft were reportedly being used by the U.S.S.R. for Soviet-manned reconnaissance flights over the U.S. Sixth Fleet.

In the spring of 1970 there was a dramatic increase in the Soviet on-site military presence in Egypt. Apparently implementing an agreement reached with Nasser during his unannounced visit to Moscow in January, the Soviet Union began to emplace highly advanced SAM-3 surface-to-air missiles at key points in the Nile Delta.[56] By midyear some 22 such sites were already in place, reportedly built and operated by Soviet crews.[57] In mid-April, Israel charged that Soviet pilots were flying "combat sorties" in the Nile Delta region; Washington reports confirmed that Soviet pilots had taken to the air in Egyptian MIG-21s, evidently to protect the new SAM-3 installations. At midyear, there had still been no reports of Israeli-Soviet air combat, but there was widespread concern that such a confrontation might occur if Soviet SAM-3s and pilots were to appear in the battle-torn Suez Canal sector as well.[58]

Naval Presence

Perhaps the most portentous manifestation of the enhanced presence of

[56]*New York Times,* March 19 and March 30, 1970.
[57]"Red Star over the Nile," *Newsweek,* June 1, 1970, pp. 38-43.
[58]There was one precedent for this new direct involvement of Soviet pilots in a Middle East arena of military conflict. Soviet pilots reportedly flew briefly for the republican side in the Yemen civil war after the withdrawal of U.A.R. forces in 1967, but this activity was terminated when one Soviet pilot was shot down and his identity determined.

the U.S.S.R. in the Middle East is the Soviet Mediterranean Squadron, which has grown substantially in size and capabilities since the June war. The stationing of a small Soviet naval force in the Mediterranean on a more or less permanent basis appears to date from around 1964. Gradual increases occurred in each of the next two years, and Soviet naval elements began regular visits to U.A.R. ports in 1966. As noted earlier, the initial impetus for the creation of the Squadron seems to have come from a requirement to cover the U.S. seaborne nuclear deterrent force in the Mediterranean, particularly the Polaris submarine force. The Soviet Mediterranean Squadron still appears to be configured primarily for anticarrier attack force and antisubmarine warfare missions. A desire to improve the Soviet Union's capability to project military power into remote areas was probably also a factor in the decision to deploy the Mediterranean Squadron. In any case this factor grew in significance as Soviet interests in the area came under military threat and opportunities grew for the Soviet Union to exercise its naval force in the Mediterranean. There was a substantial increase in the size of the Soviet force just before and after the June, 1967, war and steady moderate growth in the next two years to a level of between 40 and 60 vessels of various types, the numbers fluctuating with the season. The most important new addition to the squadron after the June war was the *Moskva,* a helicopter carrier, the first such vessel in the Soviet navy.

Protection of friendly Arab states became an avowed mission of the Soviet Mediterranean Squadron after the June war, but the squadron's capability to perform this mission is still poor. Despite the reactivation of Soviet marine infantry (estimated at a total of 6000 to 12,000 men servicing all four Soviet fleets), the Soviet Union's amphibious capability in the Mediterranean, as elsewhere, is weak. The missile-launching craft that provide the bulk of the firing power of the squadron are optimized for antiship activities rather than the ground-support mission. The squadron's organic air defenses are considered to be poor, and there are no Soviet bases from which ground-based air cover could be provided. Unless the air-cover deficiency can be corrected, perhaps through the use of Egyptian or Syrian airfields, the war-fighting capability of the Soviet Mediterranean Squadron against an opponent with a moderately sophisticated air force is dubious.

South of the Mediterranean, the utility of the squadron depends on the fate of the Suez Canal. Soviet-improved port facilities for the squadron are available in the Red Sea area. Elements of the Soviet navy also made their first appearance in the Persian Gulf after the June war, but had to be brought all the way around from Pacific and Baltic Sea bases. Without freedom to transit the Suez Canal, Soviet naval forces are incapable of mounting an impressive threat in the Red Sea, the Persian Gulf, or the Indian Ocean, and lack even a readily usable show-the-flag capability.

But even with its modest present capabilities, the Soviet Mediterranean Squadron has already had a significant psycho-political effect in the region and has created some new military options for the U.S.S.R.

1. The West's naval monopoly in the Mediterranean has been broken. For the first time in its history, Russia has established a permanent naval presence there, giving it the advantage of visibility in both southern Europe and the Muslim littoral states.

2. By some unknown degree, the Soviet Mediterranean Squadron has degraded the strategic offensive capabilities of the U.S. Sixth Fleet and of Polaris submarines stationed in the Mediterranean. Apart from the kill capabilities of the Soviet Mediterranean Squadron, Soviet intelligence and reconnaissance capabilities against U.S. Mediterranean naval forces have clearly improved.

3. Some measure of deterrent support for the Soviet Union's Arab clients is probably provided by the presence of Soviet ships from the squadron in Arab ports. Israel's avoidance of retaliation against U.A.R. naval targets after the sinking of the destroyer *Eilat* by a Soviet-built Styx missile in October, 1967, may have been due to the presence of Soviet naval vessels in Egyptian ports.

4. Although the principle constraint on the use of the Sixth Fleet in the Middle East is the dearth of Arab states that would welcome it, the presence of the Soviet Mediterranean Squadron has probably also contributed in some measure to U.S. perceptions of reduced freedom of military action in the region. There now can be no *certainty* that U.S. Mediterranean-based military operations will be unopposed locally by the U.S.S.R.

5. The Soviet Union now has a capability to make at least small unopposed amphibious landings from waterways of the Middle East. This creates the possibility for future Soviet *faits accomplis* in remote unprotected areas where even small-scale operations might have large political consequences.

6. The Soviet Mediterranean Squadron also provides the Soviet Union with a possible force for use on request to help maintain internally threatened Arab clients.

7. Creation of the Soviet Squadron provides the basis for a possible future extension of Soviet naval operations into the Red Sea, the Persian Gulf, and the Indian Ocean, but this depends heavily on reopening of the Suez Canal.

IV. New Opportunities, New Dangers

In view of the enlarged Soviet role and presence in the Middle East since the June, 1967, war, the range of Soviet objectives that may now seem operationally relevant to Soviet policymakers has probably expanded.

Opportunities for Soviet policy have become more varied and far-reaching, and better instruments than ever before are now available for policy implementation. Within the Middle East the Soviet leaders have gained positions from which the following broad objectives might plausibly be pursued.

1. Further restriction of American influence in the Arab world and of American access to its resources and people; eventually, expulsion of the United States and achievement of unchallenged Soviet predominance at the crossroads of the European, Asian, and African continents.

2. Replacement of British influence as Britain liquidates its military presence east of Suez; at a minimum, frustration of any U.S. effort to fill the void.

3. Radicalization of politics in the currently moderate and traditionalist parts of the Arab world through support and encouragement of the undermining activities of the radical Arab states or of local insurgent movements.

4. Increased access to Arab oil, as well as attainment of some capacity to influence the terms on which the West receives Arab oil.

5. Establishment of the first substantial Soviet sphere of influence in a noncontiguous area.

6. Eventually, Communization of the region or parts of it and creation of a third-world showplace for Soviet-style socialist modernization.

The expanded Soviet role and presence in the Middle East also opens broader perspectives for the Soviet Union with respect to related extra-regional objectives.

1. While "turning NATO's southern flank" in the traditional military sense implies a level of war so high as to make such a maneuver extraneous even if technically feasible, the Soviet military presence in the Mediterranean, particularly if it were augmented and provided with air cover, could be exploited politically in peacetime to strengthen neutralist trends in the Mediterranean NATO states. The psycho-political effect of a growing Soviet force would be especially great if the American Mediterranean presence were simultaneously being reduced.

2. Creation of a base for future Soviet operations in East Africa (particularly through Egypt and the Sudan).

3. Establishment of a maritime communications base for a deepened Soviet strategic relationship with India, which may have become a long-term Soviet security objective in the light of deteriorating Sino-Soviet relations.

If opportunities to extend Soviet objectives in the Middle East have grown in the aftermath of the June, 1967, war, so too have the dangers confronting Soviet policy in the region. The dangers are chronic and stem from the profound political instability, economic backwardness, and social discohesiveness of the client regimes that provide the U.S.S.R. with its political base in the Middle East. These fundamental flaws and deficiencies were all exacerbated by the traumatic shock of the Six-Day War, which also revealed that in the absence of fundamental change in the Arab social order, even lavish supplies of advanced Soviet armament could not make Arab armies perform like modern military forces.

That Soviet influence increased on balance in client states after the debacle of the June war is not a tribute to the diplomatic skill and persuasive powers of the Soviet leaders. It is a mark of the further weakening of their protégés, which only deepened their dependency on the patron. From Moscow's point of view, this weakness may appear so profound that it debases the political value of the dependency relationship that arises from it. A political base is built so that it can be used to achieve some political end. But the Soviet Union's extensive political base in the Middle East is so insecure that shoring it up has become the major Soviet policy preoccupation in the region. Preserving that base has increasingly required Moscow to make as its own, causes that seem essential to its clients' survival but that are themselves of little or no intrinsic value to the U.S.S.R. Currently such a cause is "liquidation of the traces of the Israeli aggression," above all the withdrawal or eviction of Israeli military forces from Arab territories occupied during the June war. Pursuit of that cause by the necessary means could entail costs and risks that the Soviet Union is unwilling to assume on its clients' behalf; failure to achieve that objective, however, could bring down those shaky clients upon whom the entire Soviet Middle Eastern position has been built.

Soviet policymakers are thus exposed in the Middle East to a set of risks and dangers that are a function of their clients' weakness.

1. Client regimes may be toppled for any one of a variety of reasons which the Soviet Union cannot control or can control only at great cost and risk: if the clients seek a "military solution" and are again defeated by Israel; if they agree to a "political solution" that unleashes violent domestic reaction; if they make neither full-scale war nor peace and their "attrition" campaign fails to dislodge the Israelis; or if, preoccupied with the struggle against Israel, they fail to make minimal economic, social, and political gains at home.[59]

2. The Soviet Union faces the risk of military confrontation with the United States if it participates directly in an Arab war against Israel, but it faces humiliation for itself and perhaps fatal defeat for its clients if they

[59]Traditionally pro-Western governments in the "front-line" Arab states of Jordan and Lebanon are probably rendered even more unstable than Soviet client regimes by the unresolved Arab-Israel conflict, but there is no "pro-Western" state in the region that plays as central a role in U.S. policy as the U.A.R. does in the Soviet Union's.

should launch a new war without active Soviet support.

3. The danger of betrayal has always haunted Soviet relations with bourgeois nationalist allies. To the extent that Arab clients of the U.S.S.R. perceive the United States as the only power capable of dislodging Israel—even if they are convinced of Washington's disinclination to do so—this danger will persist in Soviet eyes.

4. A real settlement of the Arab-Israeli dispute, on the other hand, or limited agreements that drastically reduced its salience, including arms control agreement, or even habituation to a new status quo, would reduce critical Arab dependence on the Soviet Union for weapons and for political support in the Arab-Israel dispute. Dependence based on the need for foreign economic and technical assistance could readily be transferred to a Western donor.

5. Finally, even if all of these dangers can be averted and Soviet clients preserved, the question will still remain whether the costs and risks of maintaining and increasing Soviet influence in the Arab world will be justified by the benefits received. Maintenance and extension of the Soviet position is almost certain to grow in economic cost. The present clients of the U.S.S.R. are all economically weak and have few resources needed by the U.S.S.R. Those that have some oil resources desperately need the revenue they can earn from selling it for development purposes. Their political instability makes the risk component of any Soviet investment in their future high and in that sense raises the cost of such an investment. Finally, increased Soviet political and economic investment in a growing number of "progressive" Arab states will almost certainly generate demands for a beefed-up and costly Soviet military presence in the region.

V. The Transformed Basis of Soviet Policy

Events of the past few years, particularly those connected with the Six-Day War, have transformed the basic factors determining Soviet Middle Eastern policy, elevating some in importance at the expense of others, and bringing into play some entirely new ones.

Soviet Middle Eastern policy emerged from the June war linked more tightly than ever to the Arab-Israeli conflict. In the eyes of the U.S.S.R.'s Arab clients, Israel's stunning victory submerged all other regional issues, including some dearer to the hearts of the Soviet leaders. Moreover, the results of the war changed the nature of the Arab-Israeli issue for the Arab client states and therefore, indirectly, for the U.S.S.R. as well. No longer did hostility toward Israel simply mean preparing for the ultimate onslaught to satisfy Arab honor and to "recover the rights" of dispossessed Palestinian brothers. The Soviet Union had no interest in resolving that conflict, only in capitalizing on it by presenting itself to the Arabs as the source of weapons that had to be accumulated for the ultimate day of reckoning, which Moscow probably hoped would be postponed indefinitely. After June, however, Arab client grievances assumed an even more fundamental and much less readily postponable character: now the immediate issue was restoration of their territorial integrity, an objective so basic that the very life of the defeated Arab regimes seemed to depend on its early achievement. Since the entire Soviet position in the Middle East was based on the U.S.S.R.'s relationship to those regimes, particularly to Nasser's, "liquidation of the traces of the Israeli aggression," an objective not intrinsically vital to the U.S.S.R., became its central policy preoccupation, to which other more highly valued Soviet goals in the region had at least temporarily to be subordinated. Thus the Soviet Union acquiesced in the decision of its clients at Khartoum in August, 1967, to suspend subversive activities against the Western-linked moderate and conservative Arab monarchies in the interest of bringing maximum Arab pressure against Israel to withdraw. This also required the Soviet Union to welcome the raising of the Arab oil embargo against the West, since the subsidies that the oil-rich states agreed to provide to the defeated Arab governments were to come from oil revenues. The alternative was for the U.S.S.R. to assume the huge burden itself.

Since the Soviet Union was unwilling to risk confronting the United States by intervening militarily to force Israeli withdrawal (Moscow probably lacked the necessary local military capabilities in any case) and was clearly unable to compel Israel to accept a "political solution" which the United States opposed, the urgent need to secure Israeli withdrawal led the Soviet Union at the end of 1968 to seek U.S. collaboration in working out and imposing on Israel a settlement that would satisfy minimal Arab demands. While the tactic was designed to preserve the political base upon which Moscow rested its hopes for ultimately expelling the United States from the region, temporarily at least, Moscow sought to act in concert with Washington. Soviet-U.S. discussions of the modalities of a settlement were conducted in both a two-power and a four-power context throughout 1969. Although no striking progress was recorded, neither party seemed inclined to break off the talks. Their termination without a successful outcome would signal collapse of the Soviet-preferred "political-solution" approach and would put Moscow on the spot with its restive Arab clients.

Meanwhile, larger extraregional considerations have also argued against Soviet actions in the Middle East that might substantially raise U.S.-Soviet tensions. This was true despite the U.S.S.R.'s striking progress in closing the strategic nuclear power gap that had separated it from the United States since 1945. Theoretically, the imminent approach of strategic parity between the two superpowers might be expected to reduce the risk that local conflicts in which they might become involved would escalate to general war. Moreover, Soviet remote-area conventional military capabilities were still growing at the end of the 1960s, while the United States was evidently entering a phase of retrenchment in its overseas military and political activities. Nevertheless, as the new decade opened, the Soviet Union for a variety of reasons seemed determined to explore the groundwork for a détente in its central strategic relationship with the United States and Western Europe, and gave strong evidence of wanting to avoid direct confrontation with America in the Middle East and elsewhere.

A major reason for the U.S.S.R.'s apparent turn toward détente was the escalating Sino-Soviet conflict, which erupted in 1969 into open border fighting, involving the employment of artillery and armor, with casualties that reportedly ran into the hundreds. Tension along the 4500-mile Sino-Soviet border was already tying down substantial Soviet forces, and the possibility that more military resources might be required if a border agreement with Peking could not be negotiated also served to constrain Soviet behavior in areas of potential conflict with the United States.

China's emergence, at the end of the 1960s, from the "Cultural Revolution" that had brought its foreign policy activities to a standstill increased the danger that the U.S.S.R. might soon be confronted in the Middle East by a rival willing to outbid Moscow for the favor of Arab extremists. The prospect was that growing Chinese pressure on Soviet policy from the left would probably encourage Arab militants to push Moscow for actions likely to raise tensions with the United States. While China's limited resources and access to the region would hardly permit it to compete with the U.S.S.R. as the major conventional arms supplier for radical Arab states, the potential for mischievous Chinese influence was great with respect to the problem of nuclear proliferation in the Middle East. Israeli acquisition of a nuclear capability as an "ultimate deterrent," either to buttress its conventional military superiority or to compensate for its erosion, would almost certainly generate Arab demands for a countervailing or superior Arab-controlled nuclear capability; this the U.S.S.R. would be extremely reluctant to grant. Precisely what response the Soviet Union would make in such a contingency might depend critically on whether China was willing and able to satisfy Arab requests for nuclear weapons if the U.S.S.R. refused outright transfer.

Finally, a new complication for Soviet Middle East policy was developing in connection with the post-June war growth of the Arab-Palestinian movement, toward which Moscow had still not clearly defined its position at the end of the decade. On the one hand, the Soviet Union was reluctant to remain aloof from a radical nationalist movement that was attracting widespread sympathy among the masses throughout the Arab world and that was being courted by the Chinese Communists. But the Fedayeen also posed a potential threat to present Soviet client regimes, for which they would be poor substitutes from the Soviet point of view. Above all, there was the danger that Fedayeen extremism, particularly if its adherents gained state power somewhere in the Arab world, might trigger off the large-scale Middle Eastern military conflict that the U.S.S.R. wanted to avoid. Finally, the Soviet leaders, whatever their private positions on the ultimate solution of the "Palestine question," were still reluctant to associate themselves openly with forces dedicated to liquidating Israel as a state.

Buffeted by these cross-pressures, the Soviet Union during the two and a half years after the June war assumed an appropriately ambiguous posture toward the resurgent Palestinian movement that was evidently designed to keep open as many options as possible. Moscow gave general expressions of support to what it termed the Palestinians' "just struggle against Israeli aggression," explicitly recognizing as legitimate those military activities conducted by the Fedayeen in "occupied areas," but was reluctant to define exactly where it placed the dividing line between Israel proper and "occupied areas."

Part II: Future Policy Alternatives

Abraham S. Becker

VI. Introduction

Given the history of Soviet relations with the Middle East and especially the nature of the ties developing since the Six-Day War, what is future policy toward the area likely to be? An attempt simply to project current trends risks accelerated depreciation, as events overtake publication lead time. Instead, it seems preferable to distinguish significant points along the spectrum of policy options and to inquire into the conditions under which the alternative policies might become feasible and, from Moscow's point of view, desirable. The goal of such an approach is not to predict future Soviet policy but to outline the complex web of options under various policy environments in the Middle East—to provide not a detailed map but only a sketch of the terrain, with deeper exploration of only a few salient features of the landscape.

The set of policy choices is in theory a continuous spectrum and therefore provides an embarrassment of riches. One method of circumventing that difficulty is to define alternative policies as *directions* of movement from a zero point of present policy along an axis that may be called "involvement in Middle East affairs." Thus, two basic Soviet options are distinguished—lesser and greater involvement.

"Involvement" is characterized by six policy elements: (1) Soviet support of Arab positions with respect to the Arab-Israeli conflict and its settlement; (2) the scope and nature of the U.S.S.R.'s political relations with the Arab states of the Middle East; (3) the intensity of the Soviet effort to displace Western (especially U.S.) influence and presence in the Middle East; (4) the nature and extent of Soviet military force deployment in the region; (5) the level and type of economic aid extended by the U.S.S.R. and other Communist states to Middle Eastern states; and (6) the level and type of military aid.[1]

Policy change takes place in a multifaceted environment. Among the conditions making alternatives desirable or feasible, ten are considered

---

[1]It is evident that the policy elements are not fully coordinate. Extension of aid is conditioned by the other elements, and it may be questioned whether element (1) is not instrumental, i.e., dependent on (2) and (3) or perhaps even (4). But this should not be a significant barrier to the discussion below.

605

here: (1) internal economic and political developments in the Soviet Union; (2) the state of Soviet-East European relations; (3) the state of the Sino-Soviet controversy; (4) Soviet military capabilities for remote-area warfare; (5) the state of the global relationship between the United States and the U.S.S.R.; (6) U.S. Middle Eastern policy; (7) the state of the Arab-Israeli conflict; (8) internal developments in the Middle Eastern states; (9) extent of nuclear proliferation in the region; and (10) the availability and quality of extra-Middle Eastern targets of opportunity for Soviet penetration. It will be readily apparent that both the policy elements and the conditions are closely related to the factors whose role in past Soviet policy was described in Part I of this report.

In developing the analysis, perhaps the most difficult conceptual problem is that the functional relation between conditions and policy elements cannot be defined precisely. Instead an attempt is made to describe the shape of the curve, at least in certain intervals, and to clarify the relation between necessary and sufficient conditions by roughly ordering them. Failing that, it is possible at least to suggest certain "critical clusters" of condition elements relative to specific policy packages.

So far only two policy orientations have been defined—greater and lesser involvement. These are refined by subdividing them at points where policy or conditions appear significantly altered. Increased involvement is divided according to the *degree of control* exercised by the Soviet Union over the policy and behavior of its client states. From Moscow's point of view this may be stated simply as the degree of confidence it can have that its clients will act in accordance with Soviet wishes. It would be futile to attempt to define a graduated scale of control. Since degrees of control are relevant only to greater involvement, this analysis categorizes current relations between the U.S.S.R. and all its Mideast clients (except the U.A.R.), which evidently still retain considerable policy latitude, as "low [Soviet] control." This is in contrast with "high [Soviet] control," as yet nowhere realized, under which a client's policy and its implementation are more or less subject to Soviet approval and guidance. It is difficult to characterize Moscow's hold on Cairo: "high control" is an exaggeration, but the relationship may already have passed beyond "low control." More will be said about this later, but it is important to emphasize that this discussion deals only with large, discrete changes; there is no attempt to depict the transition from one to the other state of control.

It seems less useful to subdivide lesser involvement by a corresponding change in a policy element. On the other hand, there is a significant distinction between lesser involvement brought on by developments exogenous to the Middle East and the same policy engendered by regionally endogenous factors. Conceivable examples of the former would be protracted Sino-Soviet war or severe resource constraints in the Soviet Union; an example of an endogenous development would be a political upheaval in the U.A.R.

Part II analyzes the alternatives of lesser and greater involvement in terms of first the policy elements and then the conditions appropriate to them. The discussion also examines the major regional implications of the policy alternatives under specified conditions—implications for (1) the outcome of the Arab-Israeli conflict; (2) the regional arms balance, excluding the forces of the major powers; (3) inter-Arab relations; and (4) prospects for regional economic development. The geographical focus of Part II, like Part I, is on Israel and the core of the Arab world— roughly, Egypt and the Fertile Crescent—but brief consideration is also given to Soviet activities in other areas of the Middle East, particularly the Persian Gulf.

VII. Lesser Soviet Involvement

In June, 1970, when Soviet and Israeli air forces appear to be on the brink of clashing over the Suez Canal, it may seem misplaced to devote any attention to the possibility of diminishing Soviet involvement in the Middle East. The likelihood is clearly for movement in the opposite direction. Nevertheless, it may be instructive to examine the relations of policy and conditions of lesser involvement, if only to make explicit what environmental shocks would be required to bring about such a policy change.

Lesser involvement means, first and foremost, diminished cultivation of client relationships and attenuation of commitments to clients, especially the explicit or implicit readiness to intervene in regional armed conflict. It also means that the size and obtrusiveness of Soviet forces deployed on and immediately adjacent to Arab shores would be reduced. The Mediterranean Squadron could be oriented more or less exclusively toward an anti-NATO role or, a more drastic alternative, Soviet forces in the Mediterranean could be reduced to a small offshore presence with missions confined to showing the flag. New foreign aid commitments, both military and economic, might be substantially curtailed and drawings on prior commitments stretched out. Foreign aid extensions could be expected to be even more highly selective than they are now, both in recipients and in content, and the terms on which aid is extended would harden correspondingly.[2] Increasing reluctance to intervene in regional quarrels, withdrawal of forward force

---

[2]Lesser involvement does not preclude the cultivation of state-to-state relationship on a neutral plane—with conservative states or even erstwhile radicals—in which mutually beneficial commercial ties may be the aim rather than the frankly political objectives that were paramount before the change.

deployments, and reduction of military and economic aid would signify decreased Soviet will or capacity to prevent outcomes of the Arab-Israeli conflict previously regarded as inimical to the interests of the radical Arab states. Moscow's control over the character and outcome of the conflict would be degraded.

If such policy changes did occur, their great historical significance would be in reversing an era beginning in the middle 1950s, which saw the introduction and consolidation of Soviet power in a region from which it had long been excluded. The Eisenhower Administration had hoped to use American power to "roll back" Soviet forces from then advanced positions in Central-Eastern Europe. Perhaps the hypothesized reversal of Soviet progress in the Middle East, occurring without direct intervention of American forces, could be dubbed "fallback."

To define "fallback" is one thing; to suggest a plausible set of enabling or impelling conditions is quite another matter. Soviet stakes in the Middle East are now far too high for it to countenance disengagement, unilateral or multilateral, except under extraordinary conditions (some of which will be mentioned below). Fear that restraint in the exercise of Soviet power and influence in the region would afford the United States an opportunity to supplant the U.S.S.R. in a strategic area is a potent deterrent to Moscow's disengagement. The need to protect positions in the U.A.R., Syria, Iraq, Sudan, and Southern Yemen is underscored by the success of counter-revolution in a number of former client states. To abandon positions now held would be to discredit further the already tarnished reputation of the U.S.S.R. in the world Communist movement, whose cohesion is strained by nationalism and Sino-Soviet hot- and cold-war rivalry.

Against these enormous losses, to what balancing gains could the Soviet Union look forward? Reduced economic drain and a lessened danger of superpower confrontation. The economic burden of Soviet involvement is irksome but, at least for the present, tolerable. The U.S.S.R. does indeed wish to avoid playing confrontation politics in the Middle East, but it would have to be convinced that the risks of involvement were very high before it would contemplate paying the price entailed by disengagement. Since the end of 1968, Moscow has been seeking to avoid such a predicament by attempting to enlist Washington's support in imposing the "political solution" to the Arab-Israeli conflict. Indeed, one successful outcome of the Soviet-American discussions could help assure the U.S.S.R. that the impasse can be circumvented. If, as many now hope, the bilateral negotiations result in a minimal agreement by the superpowers that they will not be dragged into a possible fourth round of the Arab-Israeli conflict, the Soviet Union's incentive to disengage now would diminish sharply, at least on this score. To both sides it probably appears that the fact of a Soviet-

American dialogue taking place in itself tends to reduce the danger of confrontation.

It is conceivable that the U.S.S.R. would be agreeable to defining spheres of influence, provided its clients were minimally satisfied. A delineation based on the status quo after June, 1967, would clearly not meet that requirement. One based on a return to the status quo before the May-June, 1967, crisis—that is, without resolving the Arab-Israeli conflict—*would* appeal to the Soviet side. True, the "political solution" would ease the pressure on Jordan and Lebanon as much as, if not more than, on the U.A.R. and Syria, but it would constitute a victory for Cairo and Moscow that would consolidate the radical Arab camp, allowing the fundamental regional conflicts full play to chip away at the U.S. sphere, particularly in the Persian Gulf, an area of considerable potential interest to the U.S.S.R. Thus, the alternative of return to the *status quo ante* should lead to greater not lesser involvement. Something in between is conceivable in principle and has been the U.S. goal in entering big-power negotiations. Yet even an intermediate arrangement is likely to assume the character of one or the other extreme: either it threatens the basis for a Soviet position in the client states,[3] in which case it is still necessary to ascertain how the U.S.S.R. was brought to accept such an unfavorable resolution, or its logic suggests greater Soviet involvement in Middle Eastern affairs. As the United States is discovering, détente in the Middle East is extraordinarily elusive, even as a concept. Lesser Soviet involvement is unlikely to be achieved through negotiation. Of course, disengagement triggered by other factors could be formalized or even cushioned by negotiation.

It seems clear that a substantial diminution in Soviet Middle Eastern involvement could only come about as a consequence of one or more major setbacks, originating either in the Middle East or in the internal Soviet and Communist world scene. These two contingencies are discussed below, but no attempt can be made to specify how either could come to pass or the probability of their occurrence. Nonetheless, it may be useful to set out the general features of an environment in which Soviet disengagement is at all conceivable.

Reorientation of Radical Arabs

As a convenient shorthand, lowered involvement via developments endogenous to the Middle East is denoted "erosion [of the Soviet position]." Erosion is postulated as the consequence of transformation of the political

---

[3]Arms control is the most important example here. See, in this connection, Geoffrey Kemp, *Arms and Security: The Egypt-Israel Case* (London: Institute for Strategic Studies, October, 1968), pp. 22-25.

character and basic big-power orientation of the radical Arab states,[4] which occurs as the result of internal upheavals, unimpeded by the Soviet Union, or of growing non-Soviet (U.S., British, French, Chinese) influence over radical Arab forces, weaning them from their dependence on the U.S.S.R. The two may be combined: the success of the foreign power's effort may be conditional upon or assured by the coming to power of a new, Western-oriented or pro-Chinese leadership, which event the Soviet Union is unable to forestall or negate, perhaps in part because its local force is inadequate for successful intervention.

These appear to be sufficient conditions for erosion; among the necessary conditions perhaps it should be postulated that no other regional political forces—neither the present conservative Arab states nor the Palestinian movement—appear as feasible and attractive substitute loci of Soviet activity. Concern here is with the direction of change, so the effects under consideration could occur from the "defection" of one radical Arab element or of a number of them in concert. Of course, the significance of the shift could hardly be insensitive to the identity and number of the defectors. A disaster in the U.A.R. would give the greatest wrench to the Soviet policy wheel; the impact of corresponding changes in, say, the Sudan or Southern Yemen would be substantially smaller.

Whether erosion results from internal client-state tensions or from a direct attempt by a foreign power to weaken the Soviet tie, the process would be related to the focal concern of the region, the Arab-Israeli conflict. Several possibilities are conceivable, although of varying plausibility.

A declared and apparent U.S. policy to maintain Israeli local military superiority, embodying effective military aid and an offshore military presence sufficient to deter the Soviet Union from active intervention on behalf of the radical Arab states[5] might in time convince the Arabs that the U.S.S.R. could not deliver on its promises to help them realize their claims on Israel. The resulting frustrations could mount to the boiling point and either induce a switch in Arab foreign policy orientation to, say, France or China, or spill over in revulsion against any external entanglement, in an elevation of national particularism over Pan-Arabism.

American policy since the June war, although not unreservedly pro-Israel, has nevertheless complicated U.S. relations with the conservative Arab states. Continuation of that policy or shifting to an outright pro-Israel

---

[4]Or of the Palestinian movement, should any part of it come under significant Moscow influence.

[5]Subsumed here is deterrence of Soviet retaliation for Israeli reprisals in response to the gamut of Arab official and unofficial armed attacks.

line might be expected to complicate these relations further. Yet inability of the U.S.S.R. to deter the United States from adopting that line by capitalizing on the opportunity to undermine U.S. influence in the conservative states is a necessary condition of erosion in this case. If that paradox were to occur, it would be attributable to some combination of the conservatives' conflict with Arab radicals, dependence on Western distribution channels for the marketing of Middle East oil (see below, however, pp. 626-628), and diminished U.S. concern about Soviet-radical Arab penetration of the conservative states. Since the combination is viewed as improbable in many U.S. government circles, the unqualified pro-Israel policy is unlikely to prove attractive.

Washington might actively attempt to woo the Arab radicals and might view that effort as requiring a simultaneous loosening of ties to Israel. Or, a variant of this notion, the United States might seek to exert pressure on Israel for suitable concessions, when presented with the opportunity to weaken the Soviet position by a decision of the radical Arabs to turn to the United States as the sole force capable of securing even partial satisfaction of Arab demands.

Could the American gambit succeed? Washington will not supplant Moscow as supplier of sophisticated arms on a lavish scale, and might not necessarily win Cairo's favor by pressuring Israel to return the Sinai. The effort would risk strengthening the Soviet hand; it would appear to demonstrate the fruitfulness of the Soviet campaign to isolate the United States unless the latter went along with the "political solution" and could increase pressure on the United States for additional concessions at Israel's expense. There is probably a limit to how far any American Administration is prepared to go in bargaining away Israel's winnings, and that limit is likely to be short of present Arab demands.

Perhaps more important, concessions could not be extracted from Israel without great difficulty, particularly if Israel saw itself being abandoned by the United States. In the process, the Soviet Union, with its unequivocal political support of the radical Arab cause and its large-scale economic assistance and military aid, might have little difficulty maintaining its patron-client ties intact.

The intent and effect of an active French Mediterranean policy is difficult to appraise. So far the major demarche of the Franco-Libyan arms deal seems only to have complicated the American effort to contain the escalation of the regional arms race. It is still unclear whether Paris is not in effect acting in unwitting partnership with Moscow or Cairo.

Erosion of the Soviet position could also be activated by a loss of saliency of the Arab-Israeli conflict to the radical Arab states. This might occur in the wake of a separate Israeli-Jordanian settlement or some kind of Palestinian entity arrangement. In either case, de-escalation of the conflict would require "solution" of the refugee question. The prospects of settlement appear bleak. King Hussein seems to have lost most of his room for maneuver as the Fedayeen have assumed a dominant position on the East Bank. Within Israel there is great interest in a West Bank Palestinian entity, but the concept is still unacceptable to the Fedayeen, as far as can be judged.

A turn to Peking by one of the U.S.S.R.'s radical Arab clients seems relatively unlikely now. There are few ways in which China can supplant the Soviet Union as a pro-Arab force in the world arena. The major possible exception is in nuclear weaponry. If, in the face of a revealed Israel nuclear capability, the U.S.S.R. hesitated to provide its clients with matching force, the radical Arab states would very likely turn to Peking. Alternatively, the Arabs might not wait for Israel to attain a nuclear capability before demanding one for themselves. Should their hopes of reversing the outcome of June, 1967, appear to be doomed because there was little or no prospect of overcoming Israel's conventional military superiority, they might demand nuclear weapons in order to force the Israelis to withdraw. Soviet reluctance to accede to these demands could also induce the Arabs to turn to the Chinese. Assuming an offer from Peking were feasible or forthcoming, Chinese nuclear weapons in Arab hands would pose a severe dilemma for Soviet policy. The Soviets might withdraw, but more likely they would attempt to forestall the act. The most probable outcome is greater involvement (see below, p. 624), although failure to forestall might induce them to disengage.

Erosion of the Soviet position in the Middle East need not signify diminished superpower competition elsewhere around the globe. Hostility and competition could be undiminished or could even increase eleswhere. If the demonstrated inadequacy of the U.S.S.R.'s third-area military capabilities helped to persuade the Soviet Union to reduce its regional commitment, a rapid and extensive buildup of just such globally mobile, remote-area, war-fighting forces could be regarded as necessary to prevent erosion (or allow penetration) elsewhere. Moscow's inclination to cut its losses in the Middle East could be strengthened by the perception of opportunities elsewhere that appeared to promise gainful employment of the instruments of Soviet third-world policy (see below, however, p. 614). On the other hand, erosion need not be incompatible with general U.S.-U.S.S.R. détente. It is not inevitable that Middle East erosion alone would impel the U.S.S.R. in that direction, but erosion in the area could reinforce other forces pushing for détente—for example, considerations of strategic balance.[6]

Crisis in the Communist Camp

The alternative path to lesser involvement would be through radical change in the internal environment of the Soviet Union, in its relations with its closest allies in Eastern Europe, or in its conflict with China.

The contingencies at issue are something on the order of: (1) a major, prolonged decline of the Soviet rate of growth, in which the claims of consumption, investment, and strategic deterrence constitute more or less inexorable resource constraints on a forward third-world policy; (2) a severe Soviet succession crisis, tending to limit the availability of either leadership or energy for external involvement; (3) widening breaches in Soviet-East European relationships with an effect similar to that of (2), or tending to drive home the sobering realization of the fragility of even the most cherished ties; and (4) outbreak of large-scale conventional war with China. In general, a sufficient condition for lesser involvement in this case would be a set of events within the Communist world whose effect would divert the Soviet Union from its interests in the Middle East and toward greater inwardness.

If the sufficient conditions appear improbable, the necessary conditions are amorphous. Short of assuming an internal crisis so severe as to render Soviet policy totally insensitive to developments in third areas, a generalized necessary condition may be defined as the absence of easy opportunities for maintaining Moscow's influence and involvement in the Middle East. That is, the state of Soviet remote-area warfare capabilities, the Arab-Israeli conflict, internal developments in Middle East states, and U.S. Middle East policy are such that the Soviet Union cannot work out an equilibrium position at the levels of political, economic, and military

[6]The combination of Middle East erosion and global Soviet-American détente could sharply attenuate the potentially radicalizing effect of the Sino-Soviet conflict on Soviet policy. Soviet fear of being "outflanked on the left" has lent a force to the Chinese hostility considerably beyond the actual material capacity of the Communist Chinese Peoples' Republic (CPR) to outbid the U.S.S.R. in third-world areas. Erosion of Soviet influence in the Middle East of course would add considerable weight to the Chinese ideological attack, and U.S.-U.S.S.R. détente would offer incontrovertible proof of the "collusion of the imperialists with the modern revisionists." But détente would not have been achieved if the danger of being "outflanked" had not already been submerged (by the threat of large-scale Sino-Soviet war) or discounted (perhaps because of its diminishing real significance, perhaps because of the greater importance attached to accommodation with the U.S. on general strategic grounds). Either way, there are higher-priority objectives at issue here for the Soviet Union, and it must be assumed that the outcome is unaffected by events on this front.

support of the radical Arab states which it is capable of sustaining under the conditions of its internal crisis. Or, if equilibrium can be attained, it is at a level of influence and involvement below that characteristic of the present policy. The more drastic the exogenously generated Soviet disengagement, the greater is the range of contingencies in regional developments with which Soviet policy would be compatible.

If such a sharp crisis were to occur in the Communist world, it would undoubtedly be accompanied by a general turning down of the burners of U.S.-U.S.S.R. global competition as the Soviet leadership husbanded its scarce resources for the highest-priority objective of securing the home front.[7] Or, if the issue concerned a crisis other than Sino-Soviet war, would Moscow resort to foreign adventure, which in a time-honored school of thought is supposed to provide the unifying force where none can be mustered internally? And if the Middle East looked uninviting for that purpose, perhaps somewhere else. But whatever disadvantages the Middle East possesses—local instability, danger of great-power confrontation, the high cost of staying in the game—are shared by other regions. The latter are also geographically more remote from the home base and thus may be more costly to reach and affect. The Soviet Union's prospects for soothing a Moscow headache by flexing its still embryonic African or Latin American leg muscles seem poor. The diversion is obviously irrelevant in the case of Sino-Soviet war.

VIII. Greater Soviet Involvement

Policy

The distinguishing features of greater Soviet involvement are in the spheres of force deployment, relations with radical Arab clients,[8] and anti-U.S. activities. With elements of the Soviet air force already deployed in the U.A.R., in addition to a sizeable contingent of field advisers, the U.S.S.R.'s military involvement in the Middle East is already high. Having proceeded this far, Moscow may be brought, willingly or otherwise, to a direct clash with Israel. Soviet pilots are now flying covering air patrol over the Nile, complementing the line of Soviet-manned SA-3 missiles. That line could be moved to the Suez Canal, an action which Israel has asserted it will attempt to frustrate. Even if military confrontation with Israel is avoided, increased involvement is likely to mean a general strengthening and deepening of the Soviet military presence in the region. The Soviet Mediterranean

[7]It could be argued that intensification of the cold war would contribute to the internal crises that are the proximate causes of the postulated change in Soviet Middle East policy. The consequences would still be the same.

[8]On the possibility of conservative Arab clients, see below, pp. 624-625.

Squadron could be expanded and furnished with air cover, either based in radical Arab countries or in a fleet-air arm. Even ground troops might be stationed in the region, especially in the contingency of "high control" (which will be discussed below).

Relationships with clients would become more closely knit, and under appropriate conditions might be formalized in explicit Soviet commitments to military intervention, including nuclear guarantees. With respect to Arab nonallies or nonclients, the Soviet attitude could be expected to conform to the perception of the opportunities presented and hence could range from indifference to determined interventionism. Whether with the one group or the other, Soviet relations with the Arab world would have as a basic aim the eradication of the vestiges of Anglo-American presence and influence in the region.

There are, however, several aspects of such a Soviet policy orientation that may be sensitive to large differences in degree of control exercised by the U.S.S.R. over its clients' policy and behavior. As indicated earlier, it seems advisable not to attempt an operational definition of control and a precise specification of its level for different policy sets. "Low control" is seen to characterize present U.S.S.R. relations with all its Middle Eastern client states except the U.A.R.; "high control" would characterize a situation where policy initiatives are not undertaken by Arab leaders without Soviet approval and where Moscow can count on acceptance of Soviet initiatives by local leadership.

For all its presumed appeal from a Soviet viewpoint, high control may be expensive to achieve and maintain. As will be noted later, it may require drastic contingencies in most client states to induce the U.S.S.R. to undertake the burden, even if local conditions thrust the opportunity forward. Nonetheless, the distinction is an important one. With low control, Soviet policy is constrained by the vagaries of regional politics; high control offers a range of options that require less concern about local sensibilities. Manifestly, the lower the degree of Soviet control, the more wholeheartedly the U.S.S.R. must identify itself with its clients' position in the Arab-Israeli conflict, given the importance attached to the problem in the scale of Arab values and granted that the Soviet Union wishes to retain and expand its base of support in the region. High control would reduce the necessity for undeviating verbal adherence to the Arab cause, because it would reduce the freedom of the client to punish the patron for breach of loyalty. With high control the way might be open for Soviet enforcement of a compromise settlement—should that prove desirable to the U.S.S.R. on other grounds—that the Arabs would have considered unacceptable under conditions of low control.

These are not necessary outcomes of high control, only possible ones.

To require that a client abjure some of his most highly cherished political values could require a Stalinist terror apparatus that proved impossible to maintain in the mother country. Without it even puppets would have to reckon with popular sentiment. Not all public *sancta* remain unaffected by the passage of time, and to that extent the problem of enforcing high control could be reduced. Nevertheless, the Soviet Union might still find it to its interest to adhere to a position that its clients would have espoused under low control, if for no other reason than to avoid unfavorable impact on other clients still enjoying relations of low control.

Aid policies under greater involvement would likely be highly differentiated. Military assistance to clients under low control might have to be generous in order to maintain their allegiance, or in order to strengthen military factions arrayed against others in a struggle for internal power. Each of these factors would become less relevant if and as the U.S.S.R. achieved high control; hence, the rate of growth, if not the level of military support for the client's forces might shrink accordingly. On the other hand, there are still other reasons for a continued high or even augmented level of military shipments to the radical states—related to promotion of the Arab-Israeli conflict or the usefulness of such states as proxy spearheads into contiguous areas (East Africa, the Persian Gulf), reasons that may not be sensitive to the degree of control the Soviet Union exercises. Presumably even a decreased level of military aid is possible under high control in a trade-off with increased Soviet force deployments. The rate of substitution of local for Soviet forces would tend to be high, in view of both the doubtful reliability of local forces and the multiple-mission character of Soviet forces.

The flow of economic aid to client states would likely continue at a high level in either contingency: under conditions of low control, at least as "insurance" if not as a conscious instrument for directing societal development in desired channels; under high control, by a "showcase" motivation, the necessity to demonstrate progress in an area where, the first stages of the social revolution having been completed, the "contradictions" of bourgeois or prebourgeois social organization are being surmounted. The criteria by which aid is dispensed—for what purposes, in what forms, and under what conditions—might differ, tending to be locally determined under low control and Soviet-determined under high control. Tangible economic assistance to nonclient states in the region need not be ruled out. Indeed, under high control, Moscow might feel obliged to proffer large amounts of aid on favorable terms to the conservative states to sweeten the sour taste left by the creation of actual or quasi-Soviet satellites in the Middle East.

Conditions

In contrast to the relatively few strands connecting policy elements and conditions of lesser involvement, the corresponding relations for greater involvement are multiple and complex. It is easier to designate necessary than sufficient conditions; indeed, on the latter score only possible "critical clusters" can be suggested. Necessary conditions here are the converse of the contingencies earlier described as possible triggers to lesser involvement: maintenance of regional tension under one or both of the basic area conflicts; availability of Soviet resources and energies for external initiatives; relative stabilization of internal Soviet élite power relationships; a *modus vivendi* with the East European Communist states[9]; and no large-scale war with China. The sufficient conditions are interconnections of the state of the Arab-Israeli conflict; Middle East internal political developments; U.S.-Middle East policy; and the U.S.-U.S.S.R. global politico-military relationship.

Inability to secure a satisfactory post-June war settlement has led the radical Arab states to greater dependence on Soviet aid, including the use of Soviet pilots and other military personnel to defend the airspace over the Nile. If current efforts are insufficient to expel the Israelis from the Sinai, the U.A.R. will presumably make greater demands on the U.S.S.R. Similarly, heightened conflict on the Jordan River may impel Amman— whether ruled by Hashemites or by *Fedayeen*—to turn to Moscow for the arms Washington is reluctant to furnish. The Soviet response to these demands can be expected to depend partly on the evolution of the U.S. position in the conflict.

Limited American assistance and undefined commitments to Israel after June, 1967, have helped to maintain the latter's superiority in conventional weaponry and, until early 1970, deter open Soviet intervention. Fear of confrontation with the U.S. may have abated somewhat in Moscow, enough to encourage assumption of a direct role in Egyptian air defense. Further significant expansion of the U.S.S.R's direct military role, assuming no resumption of Israeli air attacks in the Nile Valley, would depend on the absence of signals from Washington that the latter intended to take suitable counteractions. If the "post-Vietnam syndrome" came to dominate American policy in the Middle East, the way would clear for whatever level of Soviet involvement could emerge from interaction of Soviet-Arab interests and bargaining positions (see also below, p. 621). It seems fair to say that the Arab position would necessarily be weak and that the

[9]Whether the arrangement with the East Europeans is established on Soviet terms or on those of the erstwhile satellite seems less important than the absence of open conflict. A similar requirement is placed on Sino-Soviet relations.

imbalance would be accentuated if the U.S. withdrew its military forces from the Eastern Mediterranean.[10] Since U.S. disengagement from the Mediterranean is unlikely to be followed by engagement in the Persian Gulf, the lure to greater Soviet involvement there as well would be obvious.

As long as the Arabs retained hope of regaining the lost territories without direct Soviet military intervention, their relations with the Soviet Union were plainly those of low control. Because Soviet military involvement in Egypt has become direct and sizeable in recent months, it may be argued that the degree of control Moscow exercises in Cairo has also increased. The level of Soviet control is probably a function both of the client's need and of the perceived danger of confrontation with the United States. With each succeeding step, the increase of the Soviet military presence enhances the chances of American military response. Thus, should the U.A.R. feel it requires further Soviet intervention—air defense in the Canal Zone or support of a Sinai invasion—the U.S.S.R. would confront a high-risk, high-cost set of futures. At this point, if it wanted to stay in the game, Moscow would be more likely to demand a higher level of control.

These brief considerations of the role of the Arab-Israeli conflict in Soviet policy indicate that U.S. policy in the Middle East is as critical a variable, if not more so, with greater than with lesser involvement. Let us now examine the U.S.-Arab dimension of the U.S.-Middle East policies just outlined. Two hypothetical postures, not necessarily mutually exclusive, seem worth considering: (1) U.S. attempts to wean away the radical Arab states (see the parallel under lesser involvement); (2) U.S. maintenance or reinforcement of a strong commitment to the conservative Arab states.

It was suggested earlier that as long as the Arab-Israeli conflict remains at fever pitch, U.S. efforts to drive a wedge or exploit existing tensions between the radical Arabs and the U.S.S.R. are likely to be of doubtful promise. But if the effort were undertaken and did appear to stand some chance of success, it seems axiomatic that the U.S.S.R. would resist. In the case of the U.A.R., Soviet resistance could be expected to be strenuous indeed. To repeat, success of the U.S. maneuver in the U.A.R. would mean a severe defeat for Soviet policy, with repercussions at home and abroad that could be painful to the U.S.S.R. The Soviets might thus

---

[10]The Sixth Fleet has not been conspicuous by its presence in the eastern Mediterranean; by "withdrawal" is meant something akin to a declaration of intent that events in that theater are not considered to impinge on U.S. "vital interests."

increase their involvement in an effort to outbid the United States. Such an effort could be conducted while Soviet control remained at the present level, but should there be an acute danger of erosion of its position in the U.A.R., the U.S.S.R. would be tempted to "pre-empt" by seeking high control. To succeed, Moscow would have to be able to count on a strong local base of support for its intervention. The risk of failure would be high; paradoxically, so too might be the costs of success in alarming other existing or potential clients. The dilemma for Soviet policy would be acute.

Suppose now that the Arab-Israeli conflict entered a phase of subdued tension, perhaps as a consequence of the realization that neither diplomacy nor warfare could remove the Israelis from occupied territories, possibly in the aftermath of a costly and unsuccessful effort to dislodge them by force. The situation described implies an American policy that directly or indirectly holds the U.S.S.R. at bay, and, as indicated, this could threaten erosion of the Soviet position. However, in the ensuing crisis besetting the radical Arab forces, it is not inconceivable that the balance would settle in favor of even more militantly pro-Soviet forces. Either outcome suggests additional channels for the institution of higher levels of Soviet control over their clients.

High or higher Soviet control over radical Arab forces without U.S. disengagement would be likely to lead to a flareup of the conflict between radical and conservative Arabs, temporarily deactivated by the struggle to undo the Six-Day War. It is, of course, U.S. policy to cultivate good relations with the conservative states, although historically this has not helped the American standing in the radical Arab states and has tended to raise the temperature of the internecine conflict. To some extent, the dependence of the radical Arab states on Soviet material and political support is positively related to the degree of inter-Arab acrimony. If so, should the prospects of high control improve as the controversy intensifies? The converse, that the controversy would become more intense if the radical Arab regimes came under high or higher control, seems plausible, as indicated. However, the transition from low to high control is probably less a function of the state of the inter-Arab conflict (through magnification of radical Arab dependence on the Soviet Union) than a consequence of internal transformations in the radical Arab states. As in the past, such transformations may be seen partly as responses to critical challenges, of which the Arab-Israeli conflict is one of the most important.

On first reflection, prolongation of the current crisis stage of the Arab-Israeli conflict appears calculated to put a damper on inter-Arab strife—witness the post-1967 inter-Arab truce (an uneasy one, to be sure),

formalized by the Khartoum agreement in August of that year.[11] Nevertheless, the imminence of a fourth round could evoke demands for increased
conservative support, as at Rabat in December, 1969, or could portend
further radicalization of the radicals and the creation of new Soviet clients
(i.e., Jordan), as noted earlier. Either contingency is capable of independently stirring up the smoldering embers of radical-conservative hostility.
A somewhat similar set of conclusions could be drawn from the assumption
of a low-intensity equilibrium in the Arab-Israeli conflict.

An attempt to trace the path of Soviet policy must view these conflicts
jointly and in interaction with American policy in the Middle East. Part I of
this chapter stresses that both conflicts have a similar function with respect to
Soviet policy: they provide the opportunity and some of the instruments for
Soviet penetration of the region. At polar extremes, it seems obvious that
(1) peaceful solution of these conflicts must undermine the *raison d'être*
of the Soviet presence in the Middle East, and (2) withdrawal of U.S.
presence in the region grants the Soviet Union, if not virtual *carte blanche*,
at least freedom from a critical constraint.

But the extremes are highly unlikely. More probable contingencies the
Soviet Union would have to face would be varying combinations of the U.S.
policies followed in the past. It is outside the scope of this study to suggest
detailed U.S. policy alternatives, but a general formulation of the Soviet
reaction can be drawn as follows. U.S. policy that challenges the radical
Arab states—in either or both of the two central conflicts of the Arab
world—provides opportunities for Soviet involvement; U.S. policy that
simultaneously or independently threatens superpower military conflict
raises the risks of such involvement. The escalation of risk for the U.S.S.R.
is partly connected with the unpredictability of its clients' behavior, and to
that extent the risks can be reduced by attaining a higher degree of control.
Nevertheless, there are residual risks, not amenable to manipulation by
changes in control, that are a function of the determination of the United
States to respect commitments and protect perceived interests. That
determination is undermined by the incompatibility of the various U.S.
commitments and interests. Unfortunately for the United States, the Arab-
Israeli conflict is close to being a zero-sum game, at least as viewed by the
chief participants. In pursuing a course of action simultaneously aiming at

[11]It has been observed that Saudi Arabia's King Faisal would probably be among
the last to welcome a settlement of the "Palestine problem" for fear that it would
free Nasserite energies and resources for renewed attention to the Arabian Peninsula.
See, for example, J. Gaspard, "Feisal's Arabian Alternative," *The New Middle
East* (March, 1969), pp. 16-17. On the other hand, the Arab-Israeli conflict sends
distinct shock waves to Saudi Arabia, presumably making it more difficult for
Faisal to carry on business as usual with the oil companies.

ensuring Israel's survival, securing friendly relations with conservative Arab states, and preventing the solidification of a permanent Soviet presence allied with radical Arab idology, the United States cannot be said to have been more than partly successful.

Determination to respect one's commitments and protect one's interests imply a military force in readiness and a will to use that force. The Sixth Fleet, which is virtually coterminous with the U.S. military presence in the Middle East, has an avowed commitment only to NATO and the United States.[12] In contrast to the Soviet Mediterranean Squadron, which has a proclaimed, although deliberately vague, mission to protect the Arab states, the U.S. Sixth Fleet has no public commitment to either Israel or the conservative Arab states. That the U.S.S.R. believes nevertheless in the existence of such an American commitment, at least in a showdown, is probably true and a crucial component of the Sixth Fleet's deterrent power in limited war situations.

The shadowy nature of the Sixth Fleet's limited war mission presents something of a dilemma to the United States: to concretize a commitment is to risk the displeasure of at least some of the Arab states and the necessity of choosing in a crisis between humiliating withdrawal and possibly dangerous confrontation with the Soviet Union.[13] On the other hand, to refuse to make the commitment explicit may induce the protagonists to draw improper conclusions and take steps that could embroil the United States more deeply in the conflict. To escape that dilemma, it is of course in the U.S. interest that the solidity of its imprecise commitments not be put to the test. This requires delicate maneuvering between timidity and bluster in reaction to Soviet and Soviet-client challenges and, given the strong "no-more-Vietnams" current in American thinking, suggests that the scales are more likely to tip in the direction of timidity. If the Soviets suspect that this is true, and if they have the stomach for the job of getting the answer, all the U.S. muscle in the Mediterranean, Red Sea, or Persian Gulf will not deter greater Soviet involvement. In this sense, the political effects of American withdrawal could be manifested without the departure of a single supply ship from the waters of the region.

Clearly, a major factor in turning the Soviet Union toward greater involvement in Middle East affairs is the global U.S.-U.S.S.R. relationship. The less confident the Soviet Union feels about its strategic position, the more highly attuned it is to Washington signals, the less enthusiasm it will display for increased Middle East involvement—or, the more likely it will

[12]The U.S. commitment to Iran is through CENTO and is only against the U.S.S.R. Moreover, it requires Congressional authorization to be implemented.

[13]For a comparable Soviet dilemma, see p. 624.

be to seek high control if greater involvement is desired on other grounds. It goes without saying that a general weakening of the U.S. global position would open the doors wide to Soviet initiative in the Middle East, even with low control. In general, it is Soviet calculations of American (worldwide) reactions to a particular line of action that is the direct link between the global struggle and developments in the Middle East.

One aspect of the global struggle deserves additional comment here —the relation between the strategic and third-area components of the superpower military balance. When the Soviet Union began to take an active part in the underdeveloped world's affairs, it did so without any third-area military force to speak of and under the handicap of strategic inferiority vis-à-vis the United States. Since the Soviet Union was relying on native anticolonialism as the primary means of expelling the West, it neither needed nor wanted to employ force in these areas,[14] especially as long as the former colonial force appeared to be in general retreat. It is true that the left wing of the Communist movement led by China continually demanded of the Soviet Union a more intensive effort to further the national liberation movement and derided Moscow's fears of escalation of local war into general war. The Soviet response to this challenge, only partly self-serving, was the claim that the growing strategic military force of the U.S.S.R. would increasingly serve to guarantee the uninterrupted development of national liberation movements by deterring the colonialists from intervening to promote counterrevolution.

Incipient revolutions were stifled (Congo, 1961) and counterrevolution did take place (Ghana, 1964; Indonesia, 1965), but not through imperialist intervention, and they could not be prevented by narrowing the U.S.-Soviet strategic gap. Even if Western intervention had been a factor, a nuclear response would have been out of the question. Massive retaliation was no more rational a response to third-area conflict for the Soviet Union than it was for the United States. Strategic power, it became clear, was relatively impotent in third areas except possibly to deter direct, overt superpower intervention by posing the threat of escalating local to general war. Yet, since Soviet involvement in these areas had been increasing, the Soviet stake was rising, and by the same token, so were the costs of any setbacks.

The military lessons of this dilemma were becoming apparent in the middle 1960s at the same time that an embryo Soviet fleet appeared in the Mediterranean.[15] Though considerably expanded in the three years before

[14]See the discussion in Part 1, pp. 564-565, of the struggle over the Baghdad Pact.

[15]The Soviet Squadron's primary missions related to NATO and the general-war capability of the Sixth Fleet (see above, pp. 555, 595), but third-area considerations were also involved.

the Six-Day War, the Soviet Squadron was in no position to shore up Arab positions as they crumbled before the Israeli onslaught in June, 1967. It was not configured to perform the operations that would have been useful to the Arab combatants. In particular, it lacked organic air cover, and after the destruction of the Arab air forces, Israeli airpower constituted a significant threat to the Mediterranean Squadron. To a considerable extent, then, the June war experience reinforced the earlier lesson, that more powerful third-area force were needed to defend growing Soviet interests in such areas.

But in an age of nuclear parity, the value of a superpower's third-area forces is greatest in situations where the other superpower's interests and commitments are not jeopardized. Had the Soviet Mediterranan Squadron been structured to intervene successfully against Israel in June, 1967, it is still questionable whether Moscow would have directed it to do so, fearing to provoke U.S. counterintervention. Soviet reluctance would have been the more marked, the greater the inferiority it perceived between its own and American regional forces. It is clear that weak Soviet third-area forces require a disproportionate strategic imbalance in their favor, or an evident deterioration in American determination to check Soviet expansion, to assure impunity for Soviet intervention against U.S. clients or protégés. Where the superpowers perceive rough parity in their strategic relation, at least the absence of unmistakable first-strike capability, the fear of escalation may be sufficient to deter either side from risking confrontation. For this reason, the U.S.S.R. may have much to gain by strengthening the Soviet Mediterranean foil to the Sixth Fleet, keeping the latter at arm's length to provide Moscow with greater freedom of maneuver in dealing with local conflict not involving American clients. Such additions to the Soviet "blue-water" force would be the more valuable if the Suez Canal were reopened, given the Soviet footholds in the Yemen, Southern Yemen, and Somalia, and for use in regions where the U.S. presence is only shadowy. If, at the same time, Washington's resolve in the Middle East were throught to be weakening, a strong Soviet force in the region might also deter effective American response to threats against its clients and protégés. Hence there are incentives for the U.S.S.R. to move rapidly to build up both types of capabilities—strategic and third-area limited war—and to some extent these capabilities are mutually reinforcing.

Still another element in Soviet calculations, though undoubtedly less critical, is the controversy with Communist China. Until the outbreak of armed clashes on the Sino-Soviet frontiers in 1969, there was a tendency in the West to dismiss the importance of Chinese pressure as a factor in

Soviet decisionmaking.[16] On the other hand, many observers were inclined to view Soviet interest in big-power talks on the Middle East as attributable to the desire to avoid entanglements there at a time when the U.S.S.R. faced a potential conflict on the Manchurian or Central Asian borders.

These conclusions are not necessarily inconsistent. In another form they reflect the dilemma of priorities that is an inevitable constraint on the activist policy of a power with worldwide interests but severely limited resources. With respect to Soviet policy toward China, this dilemma, as noted earlier, has an additional Middle East dimension—nuclear proliferation. Under the constant goad of Chinese charges of collaboration with imperialism and betrayal of the cause of national liberation struggles, the Soviet Union is possibly somewhat more inclined to the promotion of radical Arab causes than it would be without Chinese pressure. As long as the material manifestations of this conflict are limited in the Middle East to economic assistance or even to provision of conventional military equipment, the U.S.S.R. can have high confidence of being able to outbid the Chinese and can be content with low control. However, should the radical Arab states turn to the Chinese for nuclear weapons and receive them, in response to an Israeli nuclear capability or simply as a shortcut to overcoming Israeli conventional military superiority, the Soviet Union must intervene or withdraw. Nuclear weapons in Arab hands under conditions of low control would confront the U.S.S.R. with the nightmare alternatives of either cutting its ties to the radical Arab states before superpower confrontation materialized or sticking with its client and facing the prospect that general nuclear war could be triggered by the actions of forces whose motives have nothing to do with basic Soviet national interests.

Increased Soviet involvement could also be brought about by exploiting targets of opportunity in the region, from the Atlantic to the Persian Gulf. A frequently mentioned example is Jordan. Moscow has made clear for some time that if King Hussein turned to it for planes and tanks, he would be welcomed. The history of the Soviet Union's relations with the U.A.R. shows that radical orientation in internal policy is not a prerequisite for becoming a Soviet client. There is, to be sure, a clear preference in the Soviet doctrinal literature for states that have progressed beyond the stage of "bourgeois national" to the stage of "national democratic" revolution in the general "national liberation struggle." But through painful experience

---

[16]Before the Six-Day War, East European diplomats in Tel Aviv were convinced of the contrary, and the leadership of the Communist Party of Israel (Maki) believes that an attempt to pre-empt the Chinese accounted in considerable part for the warmth of the Soviet embrace of the left-wing Ba'ath leadership after the Syrian revolution in February, 1966. More recently, in Southern Yemen Moscow has been reacting to a Peking effort to win over the radical leadership.

the Soviet Union seems to have become less confident of the irreversibility of that progression and uncertain about the dynamics of transition to the third stage, the "socialist revolution." It is doubtful that the U.S.S.R. is interested in rapid conversion of national democratic to socialist regimes in the near future.

More to the immediate point, there is little in the doctrinal literature to suggest that the internal social structure of a developing country is more important than its position on international problems of concern to the U.S.S.R. Because Soviet leaders cannot help viewing the world through Marxist-Leninist spectacles, one may suppose that they are more likely to feel comfortable with the radicals than with the conservatives. The fear of "betrayal," which has deep historical roots in the Soviet political consciousness and has been reinforced in the contemporary period, may be presumed to similarly incline Soviet policy toward hedging its bets and plunging in a small number of cases where the risks seem low. With a conservative client, the risks may be viewed as low, and the commitment can be more readily kept limited. In any case, the temptation to exploit an opportunity to extend the anti-NATO front, no matter in what guise it appears, will be great. The probability that conservative Arabs will become Soviet clients appears to depend much less on the patron's than on the potential clients' willingness.

It has been a Western fear that the Hashemite regime in Jordan might not survive the near-term stresses of prolonged Arab-Israeli conflict. Hence a potential Soviet client could appear in the form of a Palestinian state whose creation would not diminish the saliency of the Arab-Israeli conflict. There are two possibilities to be considered under this heading: (1) a Palestinian state erected on the West Bank alone or joined with the East Bank; (2) Transjordan transformed into a Palestinian state with the West Bank still held by Israel. The first case, a Palestinian state on both banks of the Jordan with irredentist ambitions toward the rest of what used to be Mandated Palestine, is unlikely: it presupposes a settlement imposed on Israel over its violent opposition, a contingency that in turn presupposes a radical change in U.S. policy. The second is a variant on the status quo that might well lead to greater Soviet involvement, depending on the nature of the regime displacing the Hashemites.

The politics of the Palestinian movement are murky, but an orientation to the Soviet Union by some Fedayeen organizations is not inconceivable. On the Soviet side, signs of interest in closer relations with the Fedayeen multiplied in the latter part of 1969 and early 1970, after several years of more or less open hostility. Moscow is probably operating with various motives: fear of large-scale war triggered by Fedayeen attacks on Israel, concern about Chinese attempts to gain a foothold in the movement, and desire to expand Soviet influence to a significant new force in the region.

The Soviet approach to the Fedayeen has had to be cautious, given the evident inconsistency of full support of the Fedayeen with the line of political solution based on the November, 1967, Security Council resolution. That resolution calls for a settlement to which the State of Israel is clearly a party, but the Fedayeen demand that state's liquidation. How the Soviet Union will reconcile this contradiction remains to be seen. In the meantime, a token of Moscow's earnest good will has been deposited in the form of a new Fedayeen organization, *al-Ansar,* set up in early 1970 by the Arab Communist parties.

Although there is a long history of conflict between the Soviet Union (or Imperial Russia) and Turkey and Iran, the most significant feature of their recent relations is *rapprochement.* The transformation of the cold-war relation has proceeded sufficiently far that U.S. bases in Turkey are probably unusable except for direct and unambiguous NATO-related functions, which limits the scope of possible U.S. interventions in the Middle East. It is conceivable that U.S.-Turkish relations may cool much further if Moscow plays its cards deftly. Nonetheless, there is little likelihood that Turkey will become a Soviet client or, for that matter, Iran, despite its purchase of military equipment from the U.S.S.R. But the West has become increasingly concerned about possible Soviet penetration of the Persian Gulf. Iraq and Southern Yemen are counted among Moscow's radical-state clients; the Republic of Yemen is attempting to balance off East against West. In 1969 two attempted coups against the Saudi monarchy were reported, as were scattered actions by a "national liberation front" operating in Dhofar against the Sultan of Muscat and Oman.

The key to Soviet intentions in the Persian Gulf would seem to be the nature of Soviet interest in Middle Eastern oil. If all that were involved were Soviet domestic requirements, there is no question that U.S.S.R. reserves are more than adequate for the foreseeable future. However, other considerations must enter the calculation, notably Soviet commitments to other Communist states and the significance of petroleum exports as earners of scarce foreign exchange. In 1968, the Soviet Union exported 86 million tons of crude, refined, and synthetic oil, 28 percent of total crude production. Almost half of aggregate exports went to Eastern Europe (including Yugoslavia) and Cuba; most of the rest was dispatched to non-Communist Europe and Japan.* Eastern Europe produced on its own less than 20 million tons of crude and imported only small amounts from non-Soviet sources. At the beginning of 1969 the Soviet Minister of the Petroleum

*TsSU SSSR, *Narodnoe khoziaistvo SSSR v 1968 g.* (Moscow: Statistika, 1969), pp. 191, 657; Ministerstvo vneshnei torgovli SSSR, *Vneshniaia torgovlia Soiuza SSR za 1968 god* (Moscow: IMO, 1969) pp. 67-68.

Industry declared that because of growing domestic requirements, exports would probably not increase very much in the future. Imports of Soviet crude oil by Eastern Europe were exempted from the ceiling; these were expected to continue to increase rapidly, leaving considerably reduced quotas for the rest of the world.[17] The gross production target for 1975 released as part of the same announcement, 460 million tons, is lower than a 1967-announced goal for 1975 and implies a 10 percent cut in the 1980 target as well.[18]

In the middle of January, 1970, the CPSU Central Committee and Council of Ministers announced a number of measures to support development of a major oil production area in the Tiumen district of western Siberia. Whereas 1969 output in this "third Baku" was 21 million tons, and the 1970 plan called for "over 30" million tons, the 1975 target was set at 100-120 and that for 1980 at 230-260 million tons.[19] It is noteworthy that the announcement contained no reference to revised total national goals for 1975 and 1980. In view of Soviet expectations for a leveling off or even decline in production in the "second Baku," the Ural-Volga region, which in 1970 is scheduled to provide three-fifths of aggregate output,[20] it is possible that the five- and ten-year overall programs have not been markedly intensified.

Thus, burgeoning requirements within the U.S.S.R. and in Eastern Europe will be straining available Soviet production supplies. Presumably, more could be produced but at considerably increased cost. The Soviet decision to limit expansion of exports of Soviet output may also be affected by the realization that the opportunity cost of a ton of exported crude oil, replaced by an equivalent amount of solid fuel, is perhaps six times as high as the production cost of crude. Of course, rapid expansion of natural gas would lower the opportunity cost of oil exports considerably.[21] In this situation, Middle East oil—overflowing in abundance, cheap to produce— can hardly fail to arouse acquisitive speculations. Once, such speculations

[17]See, however, p. 628, n. 23. Western observers have tended to believe that exports to hard-currency markets would have priority over shipments to Eastern Europe, given the Soviet balance-of-payments problems and the rising costs of fuel exploration and transportation. See, for example, Stanislaw Wasowski, "The Fuel Situation in Eastern Europe." *Soviet Studies,* Vol. 21, No. 1 (July, 1969), pp. 44-46.

[18]Radio Free Europe, "Soviet Oil Trading in 1967; Outlook for Exports Grown Dim," January 13, 1969; *New York Times,* January 11, 1969, p. 39; "Russian Reserves Are Inadequate," *Petroleum Press Service,* April, 1969.

[19]*Pravda,* January 15, 1970.

[20]Interview with the Minister of the Petroleum Industry, V. D. Shashin, in *Ekonomicheskaia gazeta,* No. 4 (January, 1970), p. 6.

[21]Robert W. Campbell, *The Economics of Soviet Oil and Gas* (Baltimore: Johns Hopkins Press, 1968), pp. 237-238.

would have had to be dismissed out of hand, when the Soviet Union had neither the logistical apparatus to bring the oil to market nor the access to marketing channels to dispose of it. The latter is far less of a problem now with the growth of the oil independents; the former is being rapidly developed in a fleet of tankers and a network of pipelines.

In brief, whether for its own and Eastern European needs or for the sake of earnings in hard-currency markets, it is conceivable that the Soviet Union would have a serious economic interest in importing Middle Eastern oil. On a limited scale, it is doing so already—from Algeria in the west to Iran in the east. Of course, it is the political motives behind possible Soviet interest that have agitated Western observers. In particular, concern has been voiced that the Soviet Union would attempt to deny oil supplies to the West or permit access only under restrictive conditions.[22] The concern seems ill-founded at present: any Soviet attempt to establish and exploit a monopoly position might boomerang, spurring a feverish search for alternative sources of supply and undermining the Soviet political posture regionally and globally. Most likely Moscow's interest in Persian Gulf oil will remain "commercial" rather than "colonial."[23]

The Persian Gulf fuses this commercial interest with strategic interests in an area of long-time historical concern to Russia, Czarist or Communist. Britain's decision to withdraw from east of Suez must have quickened Soviet anticipation. In the meantime, access to the Gulf is seriously hampered by the continued closure of the Suez Canal; the several visits of Soviet naval units to the Gulf had to draw on either the Pacific or the Baltic fleets. As the U.S.S.R. is cultivating both Iran and Iraq, it is in the potentially awkward position of having to decide how to support their rival claims—for example, over the Shatt al-Arab passage to the Gulf. Iraq may still have ambitions in the direction of Kuwait. Iran could come into conflict with the Trucial States and Saudi Arabia or with the radical nationalist movements in the area, whose spearhead might be a current Soviet protégé, Southern Yemen. In general, Soviet interests in the Persian Gulf, directly or by proxy, are potentially a significant challenge to Iran, which would like to regard itself as the protector and stabilizer of the Gulf. The reopening of the Suez Canal might hasten the approach of an actual conflict of interest.

[22]For a while it was thought possible that the Soviet Union also wished to use control over Middle East oil supplies as a weapon of political control over East Europe. Apparently, however, the U.S.S.R. has been urging its Communist allies to go out into the Middle Eastern market on their own, allegedly because of the eastward movement of Russia's center of oil production (*New York Times*, November 24, 1969, p. 6).

[23]Robert E. Hunter, *The Soviet Dilemma in the Middle East, Part II: Oil and the Persian Gulf* (London: Institute for Strategic Studies, October, 1969), pp. 2-12.

In the Maghrib, the Soviet Union has had close relations with Algeria. Relations with Morocco, Tunisia, and—until the overthrow of the monarchy—Libya have been distinctly cooler. Indeed, Morocco and Libya were sufficiently fearful of their Soviet-client neighbor's ambitions that they tended to look to the West (the United States and Britain, respectively) as sources for substantial augmentation of their defense capacity. Libya has now joined the ranks of the radical states but for the moment appears more likely to become a satellite of the U.A.R. than a client of the U.S.S.R. Moroccan fears of the U.S.S.R. have abated to the point of purchasing Soviet arms. On the other hand, France is seeking a more active role in the Maghrib, and Algeria has begun to adopt a somewhat less clearly pro-Soviet stance. Here the scope for Soviet initiative may depend largely on the interaction between Algerian ambitions and societal change in Morocco and Tunisia.

A more exotic development impelling the Soviet Union to greater involvement would be a Middle East replay of the Castro gambit—unsolicited declaration by a radical Arab state of its full conversion to Marxism-Leninism and a demand for immediate incorporation in the socialist camp. It is not clear that such a unilateral—and, from the Soviet point of view, probably unwelcome—declaration would necessarily lead to high control. The experience with Castro points to the contrary: acceptance into the socialist camp deepened the Soviet commitment without cutting significantly into the autonomy Castro enjoyed by virtue of his distance from Moscow. On the other hand, perhaps the relative proximity to the U.S.S.R. of a Middle East state might be a factor in the other direction. In any case, the impact on the conservative Arab states could be expected to be unfavorable and possibly severe. Soviet exploitation of new targets of opportunity would be hindered by the stigma of neo-imperialism.

In general, the significance of increasing the number of Soviet clients is not self-evident. Does it *ipso facto* increase Soviet capacity to influence Middle East events? Moscow can now boast a sizeable number of clients in the region, but the relation between the U.S.S.R. and its most reliable client, the U.A.R., is difficult to characterize. Who controls whom is not always clear. Nasser claimed that debtors are stronger than creditors, and privately, the Russians themselves have complained, not always disingenuously, of the cantankerousness of the Egyptians and Syrians. That the U.S.S.R. is one of the major factors in the Middle East was made possible in the 1950s by the confluence of changed Soviet perspectives on the Arab national movement after 1953 and the interests of radical nationalist élites in a few Arab states, notably the U.A.R. The societal processes in the Arab world that helped bring about confluence—generally lumped under the headings of modernization and Westernization—are still very much at work, witness the Libyan coup of September, 1969. The addition of new clients could be less a sign of Moscow's enhanced ability to guide Middle East developments than of its historical good fortune.

No doubt, the weight of Soviet power on the several radical Arab states creates great leverage in Middle East affairs for the radical camp. On the other hand, the increased strain imposed by adding new but unstable and demanding clients could offset gains in unity of purpose and strengthening of the centripetal forces of Arab politics. The acquisition of new clients might also have repercussions elsewhere in the region. So too would an attempt to intensify control over any of them. Heightened control of policy direction in one capital might be counterbalanced by restiveness in another, induced by the very intensification of control. The Soviets are probably far from having achieved a psychological aura of invincibility, where stepping up control over one client leads to diminishing resistance among neighboring (actual or potential) clients. If the effort to tighten control were successful at all, Moscow might have to pay a price, perhaps an increasing one, for extension or intensification of the patron-client relationship. Even if the U.S.S.R. should wish to play a larger role in the internal politics of the Middle East and its contiguous regions, experience has shown that the third world provides slippery ground on which to maneuver. The Soviet doctrinal literature testifies to Moscow's realization of this truth.

IX. Implications of the Alternative Policies

As indicated earlier, only the implications of alternative Soviet policies for the Middle East are dealt with here; no attempt is made to trace the ramifications of these policies for Soviet-American relations or for developments in other spheres of world politics.

Local Military Balance

Soviet involvement in the Middle East began with military aid to Egypt and Syria. Arms supply remained a major instrument of Soviet policy, and today the combination of Soviet weapons and Soviet personnel is a critical factor whether there is regional war or peace. Thus, it is appropriate to begin this discussion with the impact of alternative Soviet policies on the Arab-Israel military balance. Evidently, a Soviet reduction of its involvement in the region would be an unfavorable portent for Arab hopes of attaining military superiority over the Israelis, even if the latter were handicapped by severe restrictions on supply from the United States. It seems unlikely that an alternative source of conventional arms could be found that could remotely match, in quantity and quality, the enormous flow of

Soviet military aid to the U.A.R., Syria, and Iraq—to mention only the states directly involved in the Arab-Israeli conflict.[24]

To this generalization there is the surprising exception presented by the large Franco-Libyan arms deal in January, 1970, whose ultimate consignee may be the U.A.R. A similar transaction with Iraq has long been rumored and may yet be consummated. The French embargo on shipment of arms to Middle East combatants has been elastic enough to overlook Iraqi forces in Jordan and the evident ties between Libya and the U.A.R., but so far the customers, actual or potential, of the renowned Mirages have been those capable of paying hard cash or providing oil exploration privileges. In these respects the U.A.R. and Syria appear less favorable prospects for France. In general, it is difficult to believe that France is prepared to embark on a policy of supplying Israel's direct and immediate enemies in accordance with their expressed requirements.

The other conceivable supplanter of the U.S.S.R. is Communist China, but the latter can be ruled out of the running for now. China's conventional arsenal is too backward and its own needs too pressing to provide a significant margin for export. However, China cannot be easily dismissed as a possible source of nuclear arms assistance. Under circumstances suggested earlier, the radical Arab states might seek Chinese nuclear support. It is by no means clear that Peking would welcome such a request; that would depend not only on the size of its nuclear stocks but also on its estimate of the attendant risks in relations with the Soviet Union and the United States. Should the request be granted, the military advantage garnered by the Arabs [25] is unlikely to be more than fleeting. The probability of an Israeli pre-emptive response is very high, and few combinations are more likely to guarantee the immunity of Israeli pre-emption from international pressure than Chinese nuclear involvement with Soviet disengagement. The outcome of this scenario could be disastrous for the Arabs. Of course, if the pre-emptive attack were less than fully successful, the disaster could encompass Israel as well.

The set of outcomes with respect to the military balance is more complex if the U.S.S.R. involves itself more deeply in Middle Eastern affairs. Assuming that full-scale war is somehow averted, the immediate result is likely to be an intensification of the Middle Eastern arms race, especially if the U.S.S.R. exercises only limited control over the actions of its clients. Under low control and greater involvement, the prospects of Moscow and Washington reaching agreement to reduce the flow of arms to the region appear even dimmer than at present. The chances might

[24]Moreover, that aid has been made available on extremely favorable terms, amounting in many cases to outright grants.

[25]On the assumption that they possess the means of delivery as well as the weapons.

become brighter if the Soviet Union achieved high control, but the significance of such an agreement diminishes rapidly in proportion to the increase in Soviet military presence on Arab soil.

Without an arms control agreement, only continuing and substantial outside (presumably American) assistance could prevent reversal of the military balance to Israel's disfavor. Despite the clear intention of the Israelis to seek maximum feasible self-sufficiency in arms, a significant weakening of the U.S. commitment in a period of growing Soviet involvement would degrade the Israeli military posture. It would do so even if not accompanied by an embargo on sales of arms to Israel, simply by undermining deterrence of direct Soviet intervention through attenuation of the likelihood that the United States would come to Israel's aid *in extremis*. The result could be at least a joint U.S.S.R.-Arab capacity to deny Israel military victory in a future round and possibly assurance of Arab military preponderance.

In this eventuality, Israel's development and announcement of a nuclear capability might not enhance its offensive power. The Soviet Union would be likely to respond by at least unfurling a nuclear umbrella over its clients, if not by actually deploying nuclear weapons on Arab territory.[26] Conceivably, Israeli nuclear weapons could be used effectively against an attempt to recapture the Sinai but probably at high political and military cost. More likely, the role of Israeli nuclear forces would be confined to one of ultimate deterrence. Even this conclusion depends on the assumption that Arabs or Russians would be restrained by appreciation of the onus accompanying the first post-World-War-II use of nuclear weapons (and against a small state), or by the threat of the obliteration of several Arab urban centers. It is hardly conceivable that Israel could threaten the Soviet heartland, and under conditions of high control that fact could weigh heavily in the Soviet decision whether to allow a massive conventional attack on Israel. The minimum deterrent value of an Israeli nuclear capability would be considerably enhanced only if the U.S. commitment, even though weakened, retained a refusal to tolerate a Soviet or Soviet-sponsored *first strike, nuclear* attack on Israel.

Outcomes of the Arab-Israeli Conflict

The probability that the Arab-Israeli conflict could be settled to the relative satisfaction of one or the other party depends similarly on the path of Soviet policy. Reduced Soviet involvement increases the likelihood of a settlement favoring Israel, whether through a freezing of the status quo with a reduced probability of the outbreak of full-scale war, or through arrangements

[26]Ratification of the Nuclear Non-Proliferation Treaty gives the Soviet response a quasi-legal basis, as the superpowers have committed themselves informally to protect signatories from nuclear blackmail.

involving some Israeli withdrawal from territories occupied in June, 1967, but under conditions conforming more or less to Israel's requirements. The latter outcome would be the more likely, since the withdrawal of both the implicit threat of Soviet intervention and active Soviet support of the radical Arab states, especially if accompanied by a more active U.S. policy, would tend to fracture the still fragile structure of Arab unity. Settlement on Israeli terms would be likely to intensify the process, to convert a process of fracturing to one of fragmentation.[27]

Conversely, enhanced Soviet involvement—which, under conditions of low control, has been presumed to require virtual identification of the U.S.S.R. with the radical Arab position—would reduce the likelihood of an Israeli-preferred resolution of the Arab-Israeli conflict. Maintenance of a credible U.S. commitment to Israel would be a major factor in extending the status quo; the weakening of that commitment could presage a political-military outcome relatively unfavorable to Israel—even, as suggested earlier, with an Israeli nuclear force in being. Almost by definition, low control means Soviet inability to enforce a settlement on its clients; high control would raise the possibility but remove the necessity of such enforcement.

If Soviet involvement increased in the face of a strong or strengthened U.S. commitment to Israel that proved incompatible with the maintenance of friendly American ties with conservative states, the U.S.S.R. and its radical clients would establish a more or less cohesive front. This coalition would be likely to last as long as the conflict with Israel remained at the center of Middle Eastern concerns. Settlement of the conflict on terms unfavorable to Israel would disclose fissures in the front that would eventually revive traditional inter-Arab conflict. It is conventional wisdom that, in general, the less salient the Arab-Israeli and the U.S.-Soviet conflicts as foci of Middle Eastern concerns, the more likely are inter-Arab disputes to recur along traditional axes; the more salient the conflicts, the more probable is the formation of at least temporary alliances of erstwhile foes. But the converse can also be true: as the failure of the Rabat summit conference in December, 1969, showed, the frustration of Arab hopes for the "political solution" of the Arab-Israeli conflict was met by conservative reluctance to shoulder additional financial or military burdens. Whether one or the other outcome in fact ensues probably depends on political and social developments within particular conservative states.

Economic Development

It would exceed the limits of this part to attempt to predict the course of economic development under the impact of alternative Soviet policies. But

[27]See Mohammed Hassanein Heykal's editorials on U.S. policy in *Al Ahram*, June 13 and 20, 1969.

some very general considerations do merit brief mention. The development problem as viewed in the literature is a complex of efforts to raise domestic savings and levels of capital imports, on the one hand, and, on the other, to remold the society so as to create an environment favorable to the promotion of economic development. Although it is undoubtedly a considerable oversimplification, perhaps the "pure" savings-investment problem can be treated separately from what has come to be called the problem of modernization. It is generally accepted now that the latter is crucial, the former of far less importance.

In principle, the radical Arab states could raise the share of aggregate resources devoted to investment and, to a lesser extent, increase the rate of growth of the capital stock equally well under various degrees of Soviet involvement in the Middle East. High levels of Soviet military and economic aid could ease the burden of diverting resources to military preparedness and directly or indirectly augment the domestic investment potential. Students of Egyptian development using conventional notions of development requirements are inclined to view current trade patterns as distorted by political considerations and the burden of the U.A.R. rearmament effort, resulting in a heavy trade dependence on the U.S.S.R.[28] Presumably, then, even the reduction of Soviet aid as Soviet involvement diminished might well be compensated through reorientation of the direction of Egyptian trade. The Syrian situation differs in some respects but probably not radically. On the other hand, should the U.S.S.R. seek and achieve high control under increased involvement, it could be expected to push for the kind of intensive development effort that is one of its major sales pitches in advertising the relevance of the Soviet model to the problems of the less-developed countries.

But this immediately raises the question of the utilization of investment and of the social-psychological order within which development is to take place. Modernization is thought of as a process institutionalizing goal-directed change, an engine of societal change fueled by the motivation of catching up with more advanced societies. In the latter respect, of course, the Soviet Union is the world's outstanding example of the transforming power of the slogan "catching up with and surpassing the advanced capitalist states." Should the U.S.S.R. seek and achieve a sufficiently high level of control over the radical Arab states to propel the societies in question from "national democracy" to the socialist revolution, it might succeed thereby in penetrating to the roots of the political-social problems that have barred these states from realizing anything but a fraction of their potential. This is not to say that the socioeconomic history of these states has been

[28]For example, see B. Hansen, *Economic Development in Egypt* (RM-5961-FF, The Rand Corporation, October, 1969), pp. 88-89.

static in a period of Soviet encouragement (and to some extent even tute-lage) but also low control. Some progress would be maintained even if the present situation continued, although the effects of the Middle East conflict on development prospects are difficult to evaluate.[29] On the other hand, partial or complete Soviet withdrawal from the region (and "settlement" of the Arab-Israeli conflict) could be expected to strengthen the centrifugal forces within the erstwhile client states. Whether other stimuli to moderniza-tion could be sustituted is anybody's guess.

These remarks focus on the radical Arab states. The modernization movement in the conservative states is also affected by Soviet involvement, particularly as it strengthens the competitive lure of the radical social policy of Soviet clients. Intensification of the conservative-radical conflict may be expected to heighten these effects, although Soviet satellization of one or another of the radical states could have an impact to the contrary, inducing a swing to the right in the conservative states. A weakening of Soviet involve-ment in the Middle East would then imply a corresponding weakening of the pressure on the conservative states. But here, perhaps, it would be wise to desist from spinning out still further the already thin strands of specula-tive deduction.

X. Prospects

Part II of this chapter has attempted to analyze the forms, conditions, and implications of alternative Soviet policies in the Middle East. Almost from the outset it was made clear that little confidence is placed in the likelihood of lesser Soviet involvement. That assessment is probably widely shared but it may be worth spelling out. If the arguments of this study are correct, there is significant asymmetry in the policy alternatives. Movement toward greater involvement can be continuous, induced by a variety of regional and extra-regional developments and manifesting itself to different degrees in various policy dimensions. With lesser Soviet involvement, it is more difficult to frame a plausible scenario of continuous movement; decreased involvement seems to require relatively severe shocks which must generate large, discrete changes in policy. At present, occurrence of either of the two classes of shocks described seems improbable.

Neither the economic and political difficulties experienced by the Soviet Union nor its troubled relations with Warsaw Pact allies should be taken lightly, but there is nothing in the current scene to suggest that these prob-lems will become so unmanageable in the near and middle term as to force diminishing involvement in the Middle East. Perhaps they might make the

[29]See Charles Cooper's introduction to Charles Cooper and Sidney Alexander (eds.), *Economic Development and Population Growth in the Middle East* (New York: American Elsevier, in press).

Soviet Union more prudent and less eager to expand its involvement, but it seems farfetched to suggest that they could lead to a substantial disengagement. On the other hand, large-scale conventional war with China could produce a serious constraint on Soviet expansion in the Middle East, but the chances of Sino-Soviet war seem to have diminished with the continuation of talks between the two sides.

There is evidence of friction between the Soviet Union and its radical Arab clients, even of considerable resentment generated by the mushrooming presence of the Soviet military in the U.A.R. However, the latter development presumably also signifies solidification of Moscow's position in Cairo. The U.S.S.R. has moved far to support radical Arab objectives, perhaps because it has come to believe them more consonant with Soviet interests in the region. The dependence of the clients on the patron is greater than ever; perhaps so too are clients' hopes of realizing their political-military goals. Erosion of the Soviet position through internal transformations in the Arab states seems remote.

The future would seem to promise only greater Soviet involvement. Indeed, the process has already moved the region to the brink of renewal of full-scale war. But three years after the Six-Day War, which has turned out to have an open-ended aftermath, the danger is now of active Soviet participation. Should the fourth round of the Arab-Israeli conflict break out, it would probably mark the further consolidation of Soviet power in the Middle East. That may be the result even if major warfare is avoided.

Except in the U.A.R., the likelihood of a Soviet attempt to achieve high control over its clients appears doubtful: the external psychological effect would seem undesirable from Moscow's point of view and the drain on Soviet resources possibly higher than it could contemplate with equanimity. In the U.A.R. the Soviet Union may be seeking higher control in order to minimize the risk of either confrontation with the United States or the necessity to withdraw from the region, and this seems a more likely approach to high control than a deliberate effort to impose it. Nevertheless, increasing Soviet involvement without sufficient control could generate tensions that might be resolved at the extremes of the spectrum, either less involvement or high-control greater involvement.

Author Index

Page numbers set in italics designate those pages on which the complete literature citation is given.

Numbers in parentheses designate the footnote numbers where information is given.

638

Subject Index

Entries followed by *n* indicate that information is given in a footnote.

640

Arab commandos (*see* Palestinian resistance movement)
Arab Higher Committee (1930's), 54, 62
Arab-Israeli conflict
ad hoc settlement, Israel's rejection of, 187–190
Algeria's response to, 11, 12, 183
alternative outcomes, probability assessed, 152–154, 632, 633
antiguerrilla activities, Israeli options, 145–147
Arab attitudes, through Israeli eyes, 111, 117–119, 132, 275
Arab policymaking deficiencies
domestic political constraints, 109
inter-Arab divisions, 60–63
military and diplomatic weaknesses, listed, 54, 55, 98, 123
unclear objectives, 56–60
arms-race aspect of, 85–91, 148, 539, 540, 630–632
artillery exchanges since 1969, 96, 97
Britain's historic involvement in, 273, 274, 430–432
cease-fire agreement (1970), 526
compared with Cyprus conflict, 324
de-escalation prospects assessed, 140
"destruction-of-Israel" concept, attempts to define, 57–59, 304n, 313, 318
and Egypt's domestic politics, 112, 113
Fedayeen raids, as substitute for Arab state action, 98, 99
imposed settlement, by great powers, 153, 186–190
and Israeli-occupied territories, Arab non-recognition of, 267, 268
and Israel's internal politics, 16–19, 177–194
Jewish perception of Arab hostility, 111, 117–119, 172, 175, 275, 313, 314
and Jordanian policies, 20, 21, 63–65, 99, 137–140, 256–258, 538, 539, 545
and Lebanon's ethnic dilemma, 20, 21, 99, 260, 261
military balance, assessed, 91–95, 101–107, 628–630

military options, future Israeli, 122–127, 149, 150
military strategy
Arab, 98, 99
Israeli, 97, 98, 105
and North African Arab States, 11, 12, 21, 401–405
and nuclear weapons acquisition, risks evaluated, 129–131, 150, 189, 190, 517, 603, 612, 624, 631, 632
Palestine civil war phase (1947–1949), 275–277
partial settlements, prospects for, 538–541
peace negotiations
Big Four initiative, French emphasis on, 472, 476–478, 481–483, 487, 526, 542, 589
future Soviet policies, considered, 632, 633
future U.S. policies, considered, 538–544
Israel's attitude toward, 132–140, 181, 186–194
multilateral efforts, prospects for success, 543, 544
Soviet-U.S. attempts, 100–105 *passim*
U.S. initiatives, 503–505, 513, 525, 526
theoretical settlement, outlines, 318
and refugee issue, 11, 131, 132, 151, 152, 267–324
"solution" of, by Egypt and Soviet Union, 584, 585
Soviet benefits, in Israeli view, 120, 121
Soviet involvement in, 72, 558, 559, 563, 564, 568–572 *passim*, 581–592, 601, 602, 632, 633
status quo ante, as Arab-Soviet goal after defeats, 59, 60, 148, 609
and Syria's response, 239–242, 581–586
and Tunisia's response, 11, 12, 399
and United Nations
Arab interpretations of Assembly resolutions, 58, 59
peacekeeping force, and current stalemate, 104, 482, 483
Security Council resolution (November 1967), 136, 137, 148, 183,

641

643

[Eshkol, Levi—continued]
and May-June crisis (1967), 178–181, 183, 590
on occupied territories, attitude toward, 136, 181
on U.S.-Israel relations, 525n
Europe (see Eastern Europe; Western Europe)
European Economic Community (EEC)
Middle Eastern applicants, 448
and North African Arab states, 404, 405
Evian Agreements for Franco-Algerian Cooperation (1962), 411, 468, 469

Faisal (King)
and Khartoum formulas, 67, 620n
resistanct to Egypt's influence, 49, 51, 52
Faisal (Prince), 43, 247
Farouk (King), 35, 503, 566
al-Fatah
Algerian influence on, 404
appeal to conservative peasants, 253, 260, 263
Israeli view of, 125
and Jordanian sovereignty, 256–258
mentioned, 22, 23n, 304, 306, 313
origins, 62, 98, 99
Syrian attitude toward, 239, 582
total strength, estimated, 64n
Fatemi, Hussein, 365
Fawzi, Muhammed, 587, 588
Fedayeen (see Palestine resistance movement)
Fedorenko, Nikolai, 587, 589
Fertile Crescent
internal political constraints, 225, 261–263
See also Iraq; Jordan; Lebanon, Syria
Forrestal, James, 497, 498, 499
France
and Algeria, relations, 12, 406, 407, 410–413, 466, 467, 469
Algerian immigration to, 405
and Arab nationalism, ambivalent attitude toward, 464–467
and Baghdad Pact, hostility toward, 466

and Big Four talks, emphasis on, 473, 476, 477, 481–487 passim
challenge to British hegemony in Middle East, 427, 463
and Christians in Middle East, protection of, 462, 463
cultural and religious interests in Middle East, 449, 450, 483–485
economic interests in Middle East, 447, 448, 485, 486
and Egypt, relations, 463, 467–473 passim
Entreprise de Recherches et d'Activités Pétroliéres (ERAP), 476, 485, 486
Gaullist policies
on independent defensive stature, 94
toward Middle East, 13, 14, 27, 446, 452, 468–479, 486, 487
toward Third World nations, 472, 473
historic involvement in Middle East, 461–465
and Iran, relations, 471, 486
and Iraq, relations, 466, 469, 475, 476
and Israel, relations
arms embargo (post-1967), 13, 14, 87, 93, 101, 148, 474–487 passim 525
cooperative missile development, 94
early friendship/arms agreements, 175, 465–472 passim
gunboats incident (1969), 481, 482
trade relations, 486
warming trend, 147, 148
Jeanneney Commission report (1963), 469–471
and Jordan, relations, 469, 471
and Lebanon, relations, 464–467, 471, 472, 478, 485, 487
and Libya, arms sale to, 482, 483, 611, 631
Mandatory policies of, 228, 247, 248, 464, 465
and Morocco, relations, 405, 410, 467
military interests in Middle East, 448, 449
naval status of, 4
and North African Arab states, 6, 12, 14, 101, 407, 408, 463, 464
oil policy, 464, 472, 485

650

651

654

658

660

661

662

Muslim Brotherhood, 249
National Bloc, 229, 230
National Command Council, veto
    power of, 233
Nationalist Party, 35, 229, 230, 248
National Revolution Council, 235
National Social Party, 35
under Ottoman administration, 226
Palestinian refugees in, 284, 285n, 287,
    295, 301
Parti Populaire Syrian (PPS), 229, 263
People's Party, 248, 249
Shaab Party, 229, 230, 232n
and Six-Day War (1967), performance
    during, 239, 261
social bases of politics, 227, 228
Socialist Party, Ba'ath merger (1953),
    229, 230, 232
and Soviet Union
    military aid, 554, 574, 581, 596
    relations (pre-June 1967), 83, 90,
        236, 240, 241, 574, 581–586, 624n
    relations (since June 1967), 594
Sunni majority, dominance of, 226, 228
trade pattern, 240
and Turkey, relations, 241
urban social structure, 226, 227
and U.S. relations, 240, 510

al-Talhouni, Bahjat, 461
Teheran Declaration (1943), 358
Transjordan (see Jordan)
Tripartite Declaration (1950), 74, 173,
    467, 502, 506, 508, 565, 566, 570,
    572n
Tripolitania, Soviet demand for trustee-
    ship over, 562
Trucial States
    British protection of, 437, 438
    federation, 438
Truman, Harry, decision to recognize
    Israel, 496–500
Truman Doctrine, 495, 501n
Tunisia
    and Arab-Israeli conflict, 11, 12, 399
    and Arab League, 399, 404
    and Egypt, relations, 398, 399, 403
    and European Economic Community,
        408
    and France, relations, 398, 399, 408,
        466, 467

as potential leader of Arab world, as-
    sessed, 414
and Six-Day War, 400, 401
and U.S., relations, 409
See also North African Arab states
Turkey
    and Baghdad Pact, 119n
    and Soviet Union, relations, 72, 73,
        559, 579, 580, 624
    and Syria, relations, 241
    and U.S., relations
        anti-Americanism and, 80
        bilateral alliance, 71, 73, 79, 500,
            546, 547
        and Cyprus dispute, 547, 579
        missiles and U-2 flights, 75

Ulbricht, Walter, 459
United Arab Republic (see Egypt)
United Kingdom (see Britain)
United Nations
    Arab diplomatic failures, cited, 54, 55
    Arab mistrust of, 271
    Conciliation Commission for Palestine,
        (UNCCP), 270, 278, 279, 306, 307
    Economic Survey Mission (Clapp Mis-
        sion), 282, 283, 287, 288, 294
    Emergency Force (UNEF), Egypt's
        policy toward, 60, 588
    expenditures on Palestinian refugees,
        288, 289, 303
    France's participation, 474–477, 487
    Hammarskjöld plan for refugee inte-
        gration, 291–294, 303, 321
    and Iran, Soviet expansion into, 493
    Israeli mistrust of, 271
    Israel's obligations, in Arab eyes, 58,
        59, 307, 312
    Italy's arms control proposals, 456
    and North African Arab States' inde-
        pendence, 396
    Palestine trusteeship plan (1948), U.S.-
        sponsored, 499, 500
    partition plan (1947), 274, 277, 499
    peacekeeping force, and current Arab-
        Israeli conflict, 104, 482, 483
    and refugee repatriation
        Assembly Resolution 194 (1948),
            278, 281, 303, 307
        Security Council Resolution 242
            (1967), 312

663

Selected Rand Books

Baum, Warren C. *The French Economy and the State*. Princeton University Press, Princeton, New Jersey, 1958.

Becker, Abraham S. *Soviet National Income 1958-1964*. University of California Press, Berkeley and Los Angeles, California, 1969.

Brodie, Bernard. *Strategy in the Missile Age*. Princeton University Press, Princeton, New Jersey, 1959.

Dorfman, Robert, Paul A. Samuelson, and Robert M. Solow. *Linear Programming and Economic Analysis*. McGraw-Hill Book Company, Inc., New York, 1958.

Goure, Leon. *The Siege of Leningrad*. Stanford University Press, Stanford, California, 1962.

Gurtov, Melvin. *Southeast Asia Tomorrow: Problems and Prospects for U.S. Policy*. Johns Hopkins Press, Baltimore, Maryland, 1970.

Halpern, Manfred. *The Politics of Social Change in the Middle East and North Africa*. Princeton University Press, Princeton, New Jersey, 1963.

Hirshleifer, Jack, James C. DeHaven, and Jerome W. Milliman. *Water Supply: Economics, Technology, and Policy*. The University of Chicago, Chicago, Illinois, 1960.

Horelick, Arnold L., and Myron Rush. *Strategic Power and Soviet Foreign Policy*. University of Chicago Press, Chicago, Illinois, 1966.

Hosmer, Stephen T. *Viet Cong Repression and Its Implications for the Future*. D. C. Heath & Company, Lexington, Massachusetts, 1970.

Hsieh, Alice Langley. *Communist China's Strategy in the Nuclear Era*. Prentice-Hall, Inc., Englewood Cliffs, New Jersey, 1962. (Also available in paperback.)

Johnson, John J. (Ed.). *The Role of the Military in Underdeveloped Countries*. Princeton University Press, Princeton, New Jersey, 1962.

Johnstone, William C. *Burma's Foreign Policy: A Study in Neutralism*. Harvard University Press, Cambridge, Massachusetts, 1963.

Kecskemeti, Paul. *Strategic Surrender: The Politics of Victory and Defeat*. Stanford University Press, Stanford, California, 1958. (Also available in paperback.)

Kecskemeti, Paul. *The Unexpected Revolution*. Stanford University Press, Stanford, California, 1961.

Lubell, Harold. *Middle East Oil Crises and Western Europe's Energy Supplies,* Johns Hopkins Press, Baltimore, Maryland, 1963.

McKean, Roland N. *Efficiency in Government through Systems Analysis: With Emphasis on Water Resource Development.* John Wiley and Sons, Inc., New York, 1958.

Melnik, Constantin, and Nathan Leites. *The House Without Windows: France Selects A President.* Row, Peterson and Company, Evanston Illinois, 1958.

Nelson, Richard R., Merton J. Peck, Edward D. Kalachek. *Technology, Economic Growth and Public Policy.* The Brookings Institution, Washington, D.C., 1967.

Pincus, John A. *Economic Aid and International Cost Sharing.* Johns Hopkins Press, Baltimore, Maryland, 1965.

Rush, Myron. *Political Succession in the USSR.* Columbia University Press, New York, 1965.

Rush, Myron. *The Rise of Khrushchev.* Public Affairs Press, Washington, D.C., 1958.

Selin, Ivan. *Detection Theory.* Princeton University Press, Princeton, New Jersey, 1965.

Speier, Hans, and W. Phillips Davison (Eds.). *West German Leadership and Foreign Policy.* Row, Peterson and Company, Evanston, Illinois, 1957.

Trager, Frank N. (Ed.). *Marxism in Southeast Asia: A Study of Four Countries.* Stanford University Press, Stanford, California, 1959.

Wolf, Charles, Jr. *Foreign Aid: Theory and Practice in Southern Asia,* Princeton University Press, Princeton, New Jersey, 1960.

Wolfe, Thomas W. *Soviet Power and Europe, 1945-1970,* Johns Hopkins Press, Baltimore, Maryland, 1970.